CATHOLIC RECORD SOCIETY

PUBLICATIONS

(RECORDS SERIES) VOLUME 70

ISBN 0 902832 09 3

Printed in Great Britain
by Hobbs the Printers of Southampton

THE ENGLISH JESUITS
1650-1829

A Biographical Dictionary

By

GEOFFREY HOLT, S.J.

CATHOLIC RECORD SOCIETY
1984

INTRODUCTION

In the last volumes of his *Records of the English Province of the Society of Jesus* (1877-83) Brother Henry Foley included short biographical sketches of the members of the province from the first English Jesuits to the time of writing and also of the members of the Scottish and Irish Jesuit missions which were not part of the English province. As more sources, particularly in Rome, have become available since Foley's time it is now possible to compile more detailed biographies and this has been the object of this volume. The list of biographies (some 1560 of them) includes those who entered the Society of Jesus between January 1st, 1650 and the Catholic Emancipation Act of April 1829. More research needs to be done on the period before 1650, and after 1829 information is readily available in more easily consulted sources.

The following are entered in this dictionary:

(1) Jesuits of the English province (not the Scottish or Irish missions), or who worked in the English province or the missions attached to the English province, or who were English or Welsh in origin, or who joined the English province having entered the Society in another province.

(2) Those who left the Society after completing the noviceship or who died in the noviceship (but not those who left the noviceship unless there is some possibility of their having completed it) and those who were due to finish their noviceship in the September of 1773 when the Brief of Suppression of the Society was promulgated in Flanders.

(3) Foreigners who worked in England and Wales or in the houses of the province on the Continent after 1650.

(4) Those who are recorded as having died at unknown dates (because of the possibility that they entered the English province after 1650).

(5) Those who are stated in some records to have been members of the English province but are not found in the annual catalogues of the province under the name recorded.

(6) Those received into the Society of Jesus *in articulo mortis.*

(7) Henry Foley refers occasionally to the 'Catalogue of Deceased in the Louvain University Library' and enters as possible members of the English province those in the Catalogue with likely sounding names or who died in places on the Continent where there were English Jesuit houses. He has been followed in this.

The catalogues of the province are an important source of information but they have not survived for every year. When a Jesuit was stationed on the Continent they usually provide detail about his residence and work; should he, however, be in England, Wales or in the missions of the province in Maryland or Pennsylvania they give very little information for obvious security reasons. It is only from 1767 that they mention places of residence in England and Wales. During the period of the suppression of the Society from 1773 they do not, of course, exist and other records provide less information than usual. After 1803 they have survived, but for a few years only before 1829; fortunately information from other sources for that period can fill the gaps.

1

It seems likely that the catalogues were usually compiled towards the end of the calendar year and that the information they contain is true for the end of one year until the autumn of the next. They were probably prepared on the Continent and so, because of communication difficulties, may not be always up-to-date and may be mistaken in detail. Such errors and errors made by copyists seem sometimes to be repeated from year to year. For some reason the form of catalogue that has survived for the years between 1727 and 1730 give less detail than usual.

Before the suppression of the Society in 1773 the houses of the English province on the Continent were:

(1) Watten near Saint-Omer. This was the noviceship till 1765. Apart from the novices there would also be in the house the Rector and Master of Novices, a few priests engaged in administration, perhaps a few retired or sick priests and some laybrothers. The noviceship lasted two years but some of the laybrothers continued to work in the house after completing their noviceship. From 1752 till 1765 there was also at Watten a preparatory school for St Omers College. Watten was lost to the Jesuits at the suppression of the Society in 1773.

(2) Liège. This was the house of studies (three years of philosophy and four of theology towards the end of which they were ordained priests) for young Jesuits (known as scholastics) after finishing their noviceship. Some went to St Omers College to teach for a few years between philosophy and theology. In the house there would be in addition to the scholastics, a Rector, priests engaged in lecturing and administration and laybrothers. In 1773 this became the Liège Academy – a school and a seminary for the training of priests both conducted by the ex-Jesuits. In 1794 it migrated to Stonyhurst.

(3) At Ghent was the tertianship where the young priests spent up to a year after ordination. Apart from them there were in the house a Rector, one or two priests concerned with administration, perhaps some retired or sick priests and some laybrothers. The novices were also here from 1765 until the suppression when the house was seized by the government of the Austrian Netherlands.

(4) St Omers College in the town of Saint-Omer but normally called by its anglicised name. It was a boarding school founded in 1593 for boys from England and Wales though some came from Scotland and Ireland, from elsewhere in Europe, from Maryland and Pennsylvania and the West Indies. When the College was seized by the French government in 1762 the school migrated to Bruges and thence in 1773 to Liège. In the eighteenth century the English Jesuits had preparatory schools for St Omers College and later for the College at Bruges; they were at Boulogne (1742-52), Watten (1752-65) and at Bruges itself (1765-73). The staff at St Omers and Bruges was made up of a Rector/Headmaster, priests engaged in administration and teaching, some younger not yet ordained Jesuits who spent some few years teaching and some laybrothers.

(5) Bruges College and preparatory school see no. 4 above.

In England and Wales the Jesuit missionaries were based in nominal Colleges (the more important areas) or Residences (the others) consisting of counties or groups of counties. During the period before the suppression of the Society they were as follows:

The College of St Ignatius – the counties of Middlesex, Surrey, Kent, Berkshire and Hertfordshire.

The College of the Holy Apostles – the counties of Suffolk, Norfolk, Cambridge and Essex.

The College of St Aloysius – the counties of Lancashire, Cheshire, Westmorland and, until 1660, Staffordshire.

The College of the Immaculate Conception – the counties of Derbyshire, Leicestershire, Nottinghamshire and Rutland.

The College of St Francis Xavier – the whole of North (until c.1666) and South Wales and the counties of Monmouthshire, Herefordshire, Gloucestershire and Somersetshire.

The Residence of St Michael – Yorkshire.

The Residence of St John the Evangelist – the counties of Durham, Cumberland and Northumberland.

The Residence of St Dominic (it became the College of St Hugh in 1676) – Lincolnshire.

The Residence of St George – Worcestershire and Warwickshire.

The Residence of St Mary – the counties of Oxfordshire, Buckinghamshire, Bedfordshire and Northamptonshire.

The Residence (after 1675 College) of St Thomas of Canterbury – the counties of Hampshire, Wiltshire, Sussex and Dorset.

The Residence of St Stanislaus – Cornwall and Devonshire.

The Residence of St Chad – Staffordshire; set up in 1660, it became a College c.1671.

The Residence of St Winefrid – North Wales; set up c.1666.

Some English Jesuits worked as missionaries in Maryland and Pennsylvania, for a few years in New York and occasionally in Virginia and New Jersey and the West Indies. Others were stationed in the English Colleges at Rome and Valladolid, as confessors at Rome, Loretto and convents in Flanders. Some were involved in financial business in Rome, Paris, Antwerp, Brussels or Madrid as money was invested in these places because, owing to the penal laws, it was less safe in England. A few priests sometimes travelled on the Continent as chaplains to the English families who supported them or as tutors to the sons of such families. Some were military chaplains. Early in the eighteenth century a few were engaged in the Episcopal seminary at Liège at the request of the prince bishop.

Some points to be noted in regard to the period before the suppression of the Society in 1773
(1) When it is said that a Jesuit died in England it may in fact be England or Wales. Place of burial has been given when known.

(2) Some *aliases* may only have been used when at school at St Omers College. If an *alias* is the name by which a man was usually known it has been used in this dictionary with a cross-reference.

(3) Entries in accounts have been useful in establishing the residence of a Jesuit in England and Wales but as some account books are not paged or foliated an exact reference cannot always be given. Evidence from financial papers may not be up-to-date as there may have been delay in making up the accounts.

(4) The provincial and his assistant, or socius, travelled on business in Flanders and in England and Wales so a fixed residence cannot normally be given for them.

(5) There was a period in the 1740s when the young Jesuits were sent to study theology at other Colleges of the Society in France or Germany owing to financial difficulties experienced by the College at Liège. This could happen at any time to the individual student.

(6) It has not proved practicable to distinguish between the Old and New Styles in the Calendar. Up to 1752 in England the Old Style was in use but on the Continent the New. The year has been taken to begin on January 1st.

(7) Many of the laybrothers joined the province from places in Flanders. The laybrothers were not often stationed in England and Wales before the suppression of the Society.

(8) Priests at various times acted as military chaplains on the Continent or in England or Ireland. They are entered in the index under the heading 'military chaplains'.

(9) In the text places are mentioned only briefly; the counties in which they are situated are given in the index.

(10) Almost all English Jesuits made their noviceship at Watten, their studies at Liège, their tertianship at Ghent and some taught before ordination at St Omers College. In the index no references to their stay in these houses for those purposes are entered.

(11) A number of Jesuit priests, mostly from French provinces apparently, arrived at Liège after the expulsion of the Society from France in 1762. Described in the province catalogues as exiles, it is presumed that they lectured to the students or performed other duties in the house and their names have therefore been entered in the dictionary.

Some points to be noted in regard to the period after 1773

(1) The Catholic Emancipation Act became law in April 1829. It was foreseen that a clause in the Act (which was not in fact enforced) would forbid, or make it very difficult for, a religious order to receive novices. Accordingly about a dozen likely candidates were admitted to the Society in March 1829 though they were not to begin their noviceship until later. Eleven of these entered the noviceship eventually, two of them leaving as novices. The other nine have been entered in the dictionary.

(2) A number who entered the Society before Catholic Emancipation are not to be found in Foley's list because they were still living when he wrote. They have all been included in the dictionary.

(3) From 1803 surviving members of the suppressed Society were readmitted if they wished. An article on this subject is in *Archivum Historicum Societatis Jesu* vol. XLII.

(4) After the suppression the Jesuits did not return to Scotland until 1859 and from then on Scotland was part of the English province.

(5) At the Restoration of the Society the English Jesuits were stationed at Stonyhurst, at Hodder Place nearby or on missions throughout England and Wales. The restored province developed from these beginnings.

(6) St Mary's Hall, Stonyhurst, was the house of studies for philosophy from 1830 till 1926 and for theology from 1830 till 1848 when St Beuno's College was opened as the theologate and remained so until 1926.

(7) Hodder Place, Stonyhurst, was the noviceship and tertianship from 1803 till 1854. A preparatory school also was opened there in 1807.

(8) Beaumont Lodge was the noviceship from 1854 till 1861 when a house at Roehampton was acquired for that purpose. Beaumont Lodge then became a boarding school – Beaumont College.

(9) Because of lack of facilities and other difficulties in England early in the nineteenth century the young Jesuits were often sent abroad for their noviceship and studies.

(10) In the nineteenth century the English province cared at various times for missions in Bengal, Jamaica, British Honduras, British Guiana and Barbados and a College in Malta. Some of the Jesuits in this dictionary worked in these missions. The mission in Southern Africa was entrusted to the English province towards the end of the century.

I wish to thank the following who have kindly been of assistance to me in various ways in the preparation of this dictionary – the Archivist of St Mary's Priory, Fernham, Oxfordshire; the Reverend F. Edwards, S.J.; Mr. J. H. Hopkins, Librarian of the Society of Antiquaries of London; the Reverend T. McCoog, S.J.; Professor H. Mattingly of New York University; Miss E. Poyser, Archivist of the Archdiocese of Westminster; Lt.-Colonel L. de C. F. Robertson, O.B.E., K.S.G.; the Reverend F. J. Turner, S.J., Librarian at Stonyhurst College; Sister Mildred Murray-Sinclair, O.S.B. of St Scholastica's Abbey, Teignmouth; Mr. M. Walsh and Mr. S. Poole of the Heythrop College Library; Mr. J. A. Williams. Special gratitude is due to the Reverend W. Vincent Smith for the trouble he took in providing me with copies of papers, the results of his own researches. I wish to thank also Mr. A. F. Allison and Mr. P. R. Harris of the Editorial Committee of the Catholic Record Society.

London 1978-1981

LIST OF ABBREVIATIONS

b.	born
br.	brother
bu.	buried
c.	circa
d.	died
e.	educated
E.C.	English College
f.	folio
ff.	following or folios
n.	number
nov.	noviceship
O.P.	Dominican Order
O.S.B.	Benedictine Order
p.	page
phil.	philosophy
readm.	readmitted
s.	son
S.C.	Scots College
S.J.	Society of Jesus
tert.	tertianship
theol.	theology

MANUSCRIPT SOURCES

Note. The manuscript sources consulted are each given a code number which is placed before it in the lists that follow. This number is used throughout the text to indicate that a manuscript is being used as a source of information. The numbers in order are to be found in one or other of the three groups of manuscripts – in the English Jesuit Province Archives, at Stonyhurst or in Other Sources. If a number is not in its place in one group it is to be found in the correct order in one of the other two. (It should be noted, however, that no manuscript is numbered 143, 144, 145, 146, 147, 148, 149).

English Jesuit Province Archives
  (1) William Strickland's Letters, 1786-1811
  (2) Catalogus Dimissorum
  (3) Restoration, Paccanarists, Stonyhurst papers, 1763-1829
  (4) Maryland Letters, 1772-1835
  (5) Notes on Thomas Falkner
  (6) Letters of Marmaduke Stone, Nicholas Sewall, James Connell, 1776-c.1833
  (7) Letters of Charles Plowden, 1764-1821
  (8) Bishop Milner's Letters, volumes I and II, 1790-1803, 1803-26
  (9) Liège Procurators' Correspondence, 1682-1739
 (10) Letters of Bishops and Cardinals, 1753-1853
 (11) Foreign Correspondence, 1776-1859
 (12) Notes and Fragments, 1585-1790, by John Thorpe
 (13) English Province Correspondence, 1746-1854
 (14) Correspondence relating to St Omers and North Wales, 1666-1781
 (15) Letters of non-Jesuits, 1766-1857
 (16) Colleges in Belgium papers, 1729-1876
 (17) Bruges Colleges Destroyed, by C. Plowden, 1807
 (18) Notes on the Re-establishment of the English Province S.J., by C. Brooke, c.1844
 (19) Re-establishment of the English Province S.J. 1773-1829, by T. Glover
 (20) Transcripts of letters from John Thorpe to Henry, 8th, Lord Arundell, 1773-1791
 (21) Historical Collections, I and II, by C. Brooke
 (22) Plowden and Strickland Letters (transcripts), 1779-1791
 (23) College of St Aloysius accounts, 1700-1849
 (24) College of St Aloysius accounts, 1710-1884
 (25) College of St Aloysius accounts, 1770-1813
 (26) College of St Aloysius papers, Bedford Leigh to Formby
 (27) College of St Aloysius papers, Gillmoss to Portico/Prescot
 (28) College of St Aloysius papers, Rixton to Wigan
 (29) College of St Aloysius, West Leigh Tithes papers, 1656-1933
 (30) College of St Aloysius papers, St Wilfrid's Preston
 (31) Residence of St Mary papers, 1729-1876

(32) Old College of St Francis Xavier papers I, 1743-1847
(33) Old College of St Francis Xavier papers II, 1779-1855
(34) Old College of St Francis Xavier papers III, 1746-1854
(35) Residence of St John District accounts, 1749-95
(36) Residence of St John papers, 1717-1858
(37) Residence of St George papers, 1635-95
(38) Residence of St George papers, 1666-1849
(39) Residence of St George papers, 1640-1902
(40) Residence of St George District accounts, 1695-1760
(41) College of the Holy Apostles – Galloway Letters, 1762-80
(42) College of the Holy Apostles papers, 1775-1840
(43) College of the Holy Apostles District accounts, 1667-1844
(44) College of St Thomas of Canterbury papers, 1613-1839
(45) College of St Ignatius papers, 1750-1874
(46) College of St Ignatius (Farm Street) papers, 1802-65
(47) Residence of St Stanislaus papers, 1655-1845
(48) Residence of St Michael papers, 1813-60
(49) Scottish mission papers
(50) College of St Hugh papers, 1723-1869
(51) Varia, 1706-1815
(52) India papers, 1802-1911
(53) Miscellaneous papers, 1771-1820
(54) Letters, etc., 1773-1804
(55) Letters, etc., 1805-18
(56) J. Thorpe – Miscellaneous Letters 1754-92
(57) J. Thorpe – Letters to C. Plowden, I and II, 1781-6, 1787-92
(58) Thornton – Constable Correspondence (transcripts), 1721-8
(59) Correspondence of Thomas Le Pointe, 1791-1818
(60) Notes on Coldham
(61) Miscellaneous Correspondence, 1819-20 (PD/1)
(62) English province, S.J. transcripts (14/2/16)
(63) Spinkhill papers
(64) English province accounts, 1729-65
(65) Province accounts, 1752-69
(66) Province accounts, 1738-42
(67) Province accounts, 1766-1808
(68) Province accounts, 1751-93
(69) Province accounts (annuities), 1766-1800
(70) Province accounts with individuals, 1728-65
(71) Province accounts (annuities), 1754-68
(72) Province accounts, 1786-1817
(73) Province accounts (annuities), 1788-1800
(74) Province accounts, 1730-38
(75) Province accounts, 1800-13
(76) Province accounts, 1769-94
(77) Accounts of the London procurator of Bruges College, 1763-74
(78) T. Lawson's London accounts, 1791-1807

(79) Lancashire District Memoranda, 1725-47
(80) Lancashire accounts, 1766-79, 1790-91
(81) Lancashire accounts, 1730-32
(82) Lancashire accounts, 1730-34
(83) Lancashire accounts, 1733-40
(84) Lancashire accounts, 1732-9
(85) Lancashire accounts, 1733-51
(86) Lancashire obligations and donations, 1725-64
(87) Lancashire accounts, 1798-1823
(88) Account of expenses for Mr. Dennet, 1787-89
(89) Fr Postlewhite's List of Missions
(90) Obits and Catalogues, 1726-1848
(91) Province Note and Address book
(92) Miscellaneous Maryland papers (BN3/1/1,4)
(93) Missionary Oaths taken at Liège Academy and Stonyhurst, 1785-1820
(94) Papers of John Dunn
(95) Transcripts by John Morris from Archives du Royaume, Brussels, Jésuites Prov. Flandro-Belgique – St Omers College accounts, 1692-1708, and from the Louvain University Library
(96) Kirk Biographies, I, II, III
(97) Miscellaneous Liège papers (U1/5)
(98) Miscellaneous Stonyhurst papers (U1/13)
(99) Windleshaw burials (UR/2)
(100) Williamson's tenement, St Helens papers (UR/1)
(101) Miscellaneous St Helens papers (UR/3)
(102) Miscellaneous Residence of St George papers (PF/3)
(103) Metcalf trust papers, 1791 (SW/8)
(104) Eccleston papers (6/4/1/4)
(105) Gillmoss papers (SR/9)
(106) Miscellaneous papers of C. Plowden (SM/3,4,5)
(107) Miscellaneous province financial papers, 1776-1826 (AE/6)
(108) Catalogi Varii (14/1/1)
(109) Province statistics (14/1/1)
(110) Miscellaneous papers (XX/1,2)
(111) Extracts from Louvain archives (14/2/1/2)
(112) Welsh Jesuits during the persecution by T. P. Ellis
(113) Catalogi provinciae Angliae
(114) English province obituary
(115) Province register
(116) Syllabus Admissorum
(117) Miscellaneous Obit lists (14/2/1/1,3,4,5)
(118) Notes on Oliver's *Collections*
(119) Lancashire accounts, 1752-69
(194) Return of papists in the diocese of London, 1780 (partial transcript U1/6)
(195) Manuscript of Foley's *Records*
(196) Miscellaneous Biographical papers (59/42)

(197) Notes on Foley's Collectanea volumes
(202) Corrections to Foley's Collectanea volumes by Fr Godfrey Anstruther, O.P.

Stonyhurst Archives

(120) D.I.15 – Letter book of the London procurator of St Omers College, 1732-5 and 1745-7
(121) Transcripts of some Weld letters
(122) A.II.21 – Mss-Varia
(123) A.IV.13 – Transcripts from Archives du Royaume, Brussels. Archives Jésuitiques, Province Gallo-Belgique, Carton 31
(124) B.V.4 – Letters on the Jesuits
(125) C.I.1 – Wills
(126) C.I.2 – Wills
(127) C.II.4A – Fundatio Bavarica Collegii Anglo-Leodicensis
(128) C.II.4C – Liège Affairs; Letters of Fr Nicolas and Fr Barrow
(129) C.III.13 – Giffard Letters
(130) C.IV.1 – Bruges, Liège, Stonyhurst Letters etc., 1808-20
(131) C.IV.2 – Bruges, Liège, Stonyhurst Letters etc., 1821-59
(132) C.IV.15 – Fr Reeve's Letters, 1779-1826
(133) C.IV.16 – Paccanarists and S.J. Affairs, 1800-41
(134) Minister's Journal
(135) Stonyhurst Anglia A5
(136) Stonyhurst Anglia A6
(137) Stonyhurst Anglia A7
(138) Stonyhurst Collectanea M
(139) Stonyhurst Collectanea N1
(140) Stonyhurst Collectanea N2
(141) Stonyhurst Collectanea P2
(142) Transcripts of extracts from Dr. Oliver's Notebook

Other Sources

(150) Rome, S.J. Archives. Epist. Gen. (Original letters 1750-1853 are in English Jesuit province archives)
(151) Cambridge Record Office. Sawston letters
(152) Lancashire Record Office. West papers I and II
(153) Ushaw College Library Mss. vol. I. Sabran letters
(154) Oxford, Bodleian Library. Rawlinson Mss. D 1283
(155) Ushaw College Library Mss. I,II,III
(156) Ushaw College Library. Eyre papers
(157) Leeds Diocesan Archives. Bishop William Gibson's Faculty book
(158) Transcript of Bishop Francis Petre's Confirmations, 1752-8
(159) Northumberland Record Office. Constable Mss. Notes on, by the Rev. W. Vincent Smith
(160) Hull University Archives Department. Constable of Everingham Mss. Notes on, by the Rev. W. Vincent Smith

(161) Northumberland Record Office. Account book of John Hebden, c.1702-16
(162) Notes by the Rev. W. Vincent Smith on the Haggerston chaplains based on the Constable of Everingham Mss.
(163) Archives of the Diocese of Hexham and Newcastle. The Treasurers' Account Books, 1741-1826
(164) House of Lords Mss. Return of papists for the Diocese of Durham, 1767
(165) Long Horsley parish registers
(166) Westminster. Archives of the Archdiocese. Bishop Douglass's Diary I and II
(167) Ushaw College Library. Visitations and Confirmations of the Vicars Apostolic of the Northern District, 1768...
(168) Cambridge University Library. Ms. L1.1.19. Letter Book of Fr John Warner, 1679-86
(169) Westminster. Archives of the Archdiocese. Papers 155/2,3,6,7,8,9,11,18
(170) Brussels. Archives du Royaume. Archives Jésuitiques, province Gallo-Belgique, n.26 – St Omers College accounts c.1686-c.1709
(171) Brussels. Archives du Royaume. Archives Jésuitiques, province Gallo-Belgique, n.31
(172) St James, Spanish Place, London. Registrum Baptizatorum...in Capella Hispaniarum, Londini, 1732-61
(173) Our Lady of the Assumption and St Gregory, Warwick Street, London. Registrum Baptismale Capellae Catholicae Regis Bavariae, Londini, 1748-70
(174)-
(178) Gent. Rijksarchief. Jesuiten, nos. 76,84,85,86,87
(179) Westminster. Archives of the Archdiocese. AWAZ.12,13
(180) Westminster. Archives of the Archdiocese. AWAZ.14
(181) Westminster. Archives of the Archdiocese. AWAD.15
(182) Westminster. Archives of the Archdiocese. AWAD.28
(183) Westminster. Archives of the Archdiocese. Epistolae Variorum 3
(184) Westminster. Archives of the Archdiocese. Epistolae Variorum 4
(185) Westminster. Archives of the Archdiocese. Epistolae Variorum 5
(186) Westminster. Archives of the Archdiocese. Z.69
(187) Westminster. Archives of the Archdiocese. vol. 38
(188) Westminster. Archives of the Archdiocese. vol. 40
(189) Old Brotherhood Mss. Books 3 and 4
(190) Oxford, Bodleian Library. Rawlinson Mss. D.21
(191) Ushaw College Library. St Omers papers, LL.3/3,4
(192) Valladolid. English College Library. Correspondence between E.C. Valladolid and St Omers College
(193) Rome. S.J. Archives. Anglia Mss.
(198) St Mary's Priory, Fernham. Annals of Princethorpe I
(199) St Mary's Priory, Fernham. Accounts I
(200) St Mary's Priory, Fernham. Accounts II
(201) Westminster. Archives of the Archdiocese. Paris Seminary Collections, C.16

(203) House of Lords Mss. List of papists in the several counties, 1680, Northumberland
(204) Westminster. Archives of the Archdiocese. vol. 41

PRINTED SOURCES

(Arranged in the alphabetical order of the abbreviations used)

	Indicated by
Transactions of Architectural and Archaeological Society of Durham and Northumberland	AADN
Archivum Historiae Pontificiae (1978)	AHP
Archivum Historicum Societatis Jesu (1932...)	AHSJ
Charlton Anne, E. M. *Burghwallis and the Anne Family* (n.d.)	Ann
Anstruther, G. *The Seminary Priests* (1968-77)	Ans
Proceedings of the Society of Antiquaries of Newcastle-upon-Tyne	ANT
Williams, J. A. *Bath and Rome* (1963)	BAT
Beales, A. C. F. *Education under Penalty* (1963)	Bea
Berkeley, J. *Lulworth and the Welds* (1971)	Ber
Birt, H. N. *Obit Book of the English Benedictines from 1600 to 1912* (1913)	Bir
Tanner, M. *Brevis Relatio Felicis Agonis...* (1683)	BR
Burton, E. H. *The Life and Times of Bishop Challoner, 1691-1781* (1909)	Bur
Buscot, W. *The History of Cotton College* (1940)	Bus
The Camden Society volumes	Cam
Cansick, F. T. *A Collection of Epitaphs...in...St Pancras, Middlesex.* 2 vols (1869, 1872)	Can
Catalogus Defunctorum Societatis Jesu, 1814-1970 (1972)	CDSJ
Catalogus S.J. in Gallia, 1814-27 (1892)	CG
Challoner, R. *Memoirs of Missionary Priests* (1924)	Cha
Chadwick, H. *St Omers to Stonyhurst* (1962)	Chad
The Chetham Society volumes	Che
Catalogi S.J. in Imperio Rossiaco, 1803, 1805, 1807, 1809, 1811, 1817, 1819	CIR
Coleridge, H. J. *St Mary's Convent...York* (1887)	Col
Costello, M. G. *St Richard's, Slindon* (n.d.)	Cos
Catalogus Provinciae Campaniae, S.J., 1766	CPC
Croft, W. and Gillow, J. *Historical Account of Lisbon College* (1902)	Cro
Catholic Record Society (Records Series)	CRS
Catholic Record Society (Monograph Series)	CRS.Mon
Catholic Record Society (Occasional Publication Series)	CRS.OP
Catholic Registers of the City of Worcester (1887)	CRW
Calendar of State Papers	CSP
Transactions of the Cumberland and Westmorland Antiquarian and Archaeological Society	CWAA
Davey, E. C. *Notable Catholics who Lived and Died at Bath between 1678 and 1823*	Dav

Knox, T. F. *The First and Second Diaries of the English College, Douay* (1878)   DD

The Dictionary of National Biography   DNB

Proceedings of the Dorset Natural History and Archaeological Society   DNHA

Dodd, C. (*vere* Tootell, H). *The Church History of England . . .* (1737-42)   Dod

Estcourt, E and Payne, J. O. *The English Catholic Nonjurors of 1715* (1885)   E and P.

Essex Recusant (1959. . .)   ER

Florus Anglo-Bavaricus (1685)   FAB

Foley, H. *Records of the English Province of the Society of Jesus* (1877-83)   Fo

Clermont, Lord. *A History of the Family of Fortescue* (1880)   For

Foster, J. *Alumni Oxonienses* (1891)   Fos

Cokayne, G. E. *The Complete Peerage of England, Scotland and Ireland, Great Britain and the United Kingdom*   GEC

Gibson, T. E. *Lydiate Hall and its Associations* (1876)   Gib.1

Gibson, T. E. (ed) *A Cavalier's Notebook* (1880)   Gib.2

Gillow, J. *Bibliographical Dictionary of the English Catholics* (1885-1902)   Gil

Gillow, J. (ed) *The Haydock Papers* (1888)   Gil.HP

Hamy, A. *Les Jésuites Anglais expulsés de Boulogne en 1752* (1904)   Ham

Hay, M. *The Enigma of James II* (1938)   Hay

Humphreys, A. L. *East Hendred, a Berkshire Parish* (1923)   Hen

Historical Manuscripts Commission Reports   HMC

Hughes, T. *The History of the Society of Jesus in North America* – Text and Documents vols (1908-17)   Hu

Hudleston, John. *A Brief Account of Particulars occurring at the happy death of . . . Charles II . . .* (1688)   Hudl

Hunter, T. *The Life of Catherine Burton* (ed. H.J.C. 1876)   Hun

The Journal of Imperial and Commonwealth History   JICH

Kirk, J. *Biographies of English Catholics in the Eighteenth Century* (ed. Pollen, J. H. and Burton, E. 1909)   Ki

Kent Recusant History (1979. . .)   KR

Lancashire and Cheshire Record Society volumes   L and C

Letters and Notices (1862. . .)   L and N

Leite, S. *Historia da Companhia de Jesus no Brasil* (1938-50)   Lei

Leys, M. D. R. *Catholics in England, 1559-1829* (1961)   Ley

Ward, T. G. and Warren, L. *The Manor Mission of Low Furness* (1979)   LF

Transactions of the London and Middlesex Archaeological Society   LMAS

London Recusant (1971. . .)   LR

Melville, A. M. *John Carroll of Baltimore* (1955)   Mel

Miller, J. *Popery and Politics in England, 1660-1688* (1973)   Mil

The Month (1864...)	Mon
Norfolk Archaeology	NA
Tyrer, F. (ed) *The Great Diurnal of Nicholas Blundell* (1968-72)	NB
Northern Catholic History (1975...)	NCH
Necrology English Province S.J., 1561-1937 (1938)	Nec
Smith, S. *History of the New Hall Community of the Canonesses Regular of the Holy Sepulchre* (1899)	NewH
Nolan, P. *The Irish Dames of Ypres* (1908)	Nol
North West Catholic History (1969...)	NWCH
O'Keefe, M. C. *Four Martyrs of South Wales and the Marches* (1970)	O'Ke
Oliver, G. *Collections Illustrating the History of the Catholic Religion in the Counties of Cornwall, Devon, Dorset, Somerset, Wilts and Gloucester* (1857)	Ol
Oliver, G. *Collections towards Illustrating the Biography of the Scotch, English and Irish Members S.J.* (1838)	Ol.2
Anon. *Chronicle of the First Monastery for O.S.B. Nuns founded at Brussels, 1597* (1898)	OSBB
Annals of the English Benedictines of Ghent (1894)	OSBG
Payne, J. O. *Records of the English Catholics of 1715* (1889)	Pa
Payne, J. O. *Old English Catholic Missions* (1900)	Pa.2
Philip, M. *A Jesuit at the English Court* (1922)	Phi
Recusant History (1951...) Volumes 1-3 were entitled *Biographical Studies*	RH
Records of the Scots Colleges (1906)	RSC
Staffordshire Catholic History (1961...)	SCH
Gerard, J. *Stonyhurst College Centenary Record* (1894)	SCR
The Stonyhurst Magazine (1881...)	SM
Sommervogel, C. *Bibliothèque de la Compagnie de Jésus.* 8 vols and supplements (1890-1911)	Som
Stonyhurst Lists 1794-1886 (1886)	Stol
Surtees Society volumes	Sur
Sutcliffe, E. F. *Bibliography of the English Province of the Society of Jesus, 1773-1953* (1957)	Sut
Tyldesley, T. *The Tyldesley Diary* (ed. Gillow, J. and Hewitson, A. 1873)	Tyl
Victoria County History	VCH
Venn, John and J.A. *Alumni Cantabrigienses* (1924-7)	Venn
Ward, B. *Dawn of the Catholic Revival, 1781-1803* (1909)	WAR
Blundell, M. (ed). *Cavalier; Letters of William Blundell to his friends* (1933)	WB
Weldon, B. *Chronological Notes containing the Rise, Growth and Present State of the English Congregation of the Order of St Benedict* (1881)	Wel
Trenqualeon, M. de. *West Grinstead et Les Caryll*	WGC
Whatmore, L. E. *Recusancy in Kent; Studies and Documents* (1973)	Wha

Wood, A. *Athenae Oxonienses* (ed. Bliss, P. 1813-20)	Woo
Worcestershire Recusant (1963...)	WR
Yorkshire Archaeological Society volumes	YA

ACTON, Thomas ?*alias* Edwards. Priest.
 b.1640, Worcestershire. S.J. December 20th, 1662, Watten. Watten
(nov) 1663-4. Liège (phil) 1667. St Omers College 1669, 1672. Liège
(theol) 1674-5. Ordained priest April 13th, 1675. Ghent (tert) 1676.
College of the Holy Apostles 1678-9 (Bury St Edmunds). College of St
Thomas 1680. College of St Aloysius 1681-3. Residence of St John
1684-6. College of the Holy Apostles 1687-93, 1696 (Norwich 1687-8).
College of St Francis Xavier 1697. Liège 1699, 1701. In England 1703.
College of St Thomas 1704-5. College of St Chad 1706. College of St
Thomas 1708. College of St Ignatius 1709. College of St Thomas
1710-14. St Omers College 1715-21. d. March or May 21st, 1721, St
Omers College. (Fo.7; 113; 114; 43, f.9; CRS.63; NA.37/165; For
writings see Som; Nec).

ADAMS, James *alias* Hacon and Spencer. Priest.
 b. November 3rd, 1737, East Anglia, s. of William and Anne or
Sarah (Spencer). e. St Omers College 1746 – 55. S.C. Douay 1755-6.
S.J. September 7th, 1756. Watten (nov) 1756-8. St Omers College 1761.
Bruges College 1763-4. Liège (theol) 1767. Ordained priest c.1767.
Ghent (tert) 1767-8. College of St Aloysius 1768 (Southworth, Croft,
Leigh). College of St Chad 1769-74-? (Aston). London 1798, 1800.
Dublin 1802. d. December 6th, 1802, Dublin. (Fo.7; CRS.12/85;
CRS.69; 113; 114; SCH.3/5; Gil.1/6; 13 ff.95, 99; 21; 41 n.115; 49; 54
ff.5v, 16v; 29 f.324; 65; 68 pp. 78, 133; 25; 80; 137 ff. 86-7; DNB;
RSC.89; 111; 119 ff.40, 42. For writings see Sut. Som.).

ADDIS, Bernard. Priest.
 b. February 28th, 1791, London. s. of Henry and Mildred (Gosling)
of Norwich. e. Sedgley Park 1797-1801; Stonyhurst 1801-7 and 1811-4.
S.J. October 7th, 1814. Hodder (nov) 1814-6. Stonyhurst (phil) 1816-9.
Clongowes, Ireland (theol) 1819-22. Ordained priest June 1st, 1822.
Rotherwas 1822. Worcester 1822-3. Exeter 1823. Lincoln 1823-5.
Boston 1825-8. Portico 1828-9. Stonyhurst 1829-46. Mount St Mary's
College 1846-7. Stonyhurst 1847-9. St Beuno's College 1849-52. Mount
St Mary's 1852-9. Richmond, Yorks, 1860-3. Skipton 1864-73.
Roehampton 1873-9. d. October 6th, 1879, Roehampton. bu. Manresa
cemetery, Roehampton. (Fo.7; 115; SCH.3/22; LR.6/39; 6 f.229; 116;
Stol; 142; 202).

ADDISON, Thomas or John ?*alias* Alison or Alanson, William. Priest.
 b. 1634, Yorkshire. E.C. Valladolid 1660-7. Ordained priest c.1661.
S.J. July 1st, 1668. Watten (nov) 1669. Residence of St Michael 1672-85
(York prison c.1678). d. March 21st or 23rd, 1685 ?York. (Fo.7;
CRS.30, 168; 113; 114; Nec; Ans.3/1; 168 f.2).

ALBIN, Robert or Richard. Priest.
 b.1630, Lancashire. e. St Omers College 1647 (or earlier)-51.
S.J.1651. Watten (nov) 1651-3. Liège (phil) 1653-6. Liège (theol)
1656-60. Ordained Priest March 27th, 1660. Ghent (tert) 1661. Liège
1663-7. d. December 8th, 1667, Tongres near Liège. (Fo.7; CRS.69;
113; 114; FAB.68; ER.4/82).

ALDRED, Robert *alias* Turner. Priest.
  b. June 9th, 1673, Norfolk or London. s. of Thomas and Elizabeth.
  e. St Omers College ?-1695. S.C. Douay 1695-7. S.J. September 7th,
  1697. Watten (nov) 1697. Liège (theol) 1699-1703. Ordained priest
  1703. Ghent (tert) 1704. St Omers College 1704-6. College of St
  Aloysius 1707-28 (Little Crosby). d. February 23rd, 1728, Little
  Crosby. bu. Harkirke cemetery. (Fo.7; RSC.63; 113; Nec; 23 ff. 62v,
  142; 79 p.5; NB.3/234; 91; Che.N.S.12; CRS.69).
ALEXIS, John Baptist. Priest.
  Exile from Flandro-Belgic province S.J. Liège 1763-4 (113).
ALISON or ALANSON see Bruerton, John.
ALISON or ALANSON, William ?see Addison, Thomas or John.
ALLAIN, Francis Cosmas Damian. Priest.
  Exile from France. Market Rasen 1794-6. York, Bar convent
  1796-1800. Returned to France. d.1811, France. (CRS.4/377;
  CRS.22/197, 200-01; Col.255; 50 ff.30v, 210).
ALLAN, William *alias* Lancaster. Priest.
  b. February 10th, 1732 or 1733, Yorkshire. e. St Omers College
  c.1743-50. S.J. September 7th, 1750. Liège (phil) 1752-3. Liège (theol)
  1756-c.60. Ordained priest c.1757. Liège 1761. Rome 1763-72. Ghent
  1772-3. Carleton, 1773-81. ?Hales Place, Canterbury 1786, 1787.
  Isleworth 1790-1810. ?Turnham Green 1810-14. d. January 26th, 1814,
  Isleworth or Turnham Green. bu. Hammersmith churchyard. (Fo.7;
  CRS.12/123; CRS.13/301, 312-4; CRS.32/168-9; CRS.69; 13 ff.254,
  270, 333; 16 ff.21v, 35v; 44 f.45; 54 f.178v; 69; 155/2 nn.121, 127; 180 Z
  14; 182; 111; 114; LR.1/33, 3/56, 62, 119)
ALLEN, Francis. Laybrother.
  b. April 20th, 1644, Shropshire. ?e. St Omers College 1662-8; St G.
  Douay c.1675. S.J. October 9th, 1678. Watten (nov) 1679. Ghent
  1680-2. Residence of St Winifred 1683-4. Residence of St George
  (?Evelinch) 1685. College of St Hugh 1686. ?College of St Ignatius
  1687. In England 1688, St Omers College 1689. Watten 1690. St Omers
  College 1691-6. Liège 1697-1712. d. March 23rd, 1712, Liège. (Fo.7;
  CRS.69; WR.20/49; 113; 114).
ALLOWAY, John or James. Priest.
  b. April 3rd, 1743, Oxfordshire. s. of William and Catherine of
  Henley. e. St Omers College ?-1755. E.C. Rome 1755-66. S.J. October
  9th, 1766, Rome. Ordained priest c.1768. To English province 1769.
  Liège 1769. Antwerp 1769-73. Hooton 1776-1805. Pylewell 1805-7. Re-
  entered S.J. before 1808. Portico 1807-8. d. March 15th, 1808, Portico.
  bu. Windleshaw. (Fo.7; CRS.12/100; CRS.14/296; CRS.40/213;
  CRS.69; Ki.2; NWCH.1971/62; AHSJ.42/307; Nec; 113; 13 ff.328,
  356, 375; 21 v.2; 55 ff.27v, 126v; 67; 25 f.35; 80; 90 f.122; 167/31; 109;
  114).
ANDERSON see Dormer, William (2).
ANDERSON, – .
  Mentioned as being a Jesuit in 1691 but not found in the catalogues

under this name. (Fo.7).

ANDERSON, John *alias* Simpson. Scholastic.

From Richmond, Yorkshire. ?s. of George and Anne. e. St Omers College 1732-c.40. S.J. September 9th, 1740-1743 or 1744. Watten (nov) 1740, 1741. Liège (phil) 1742. (CRS.69; 113; 150 III(2) 27/7/43; 140 n.45).

ANDERSON, Trinian. ?Scholastic.

b.1721. From Yorkshire. e. St Omers College ?-1741. S.J. October 4th, 1741. Watten (nov) 1742. In England 1743 (nov). No evidence found that he completed the novitiate. (Fo.7; CRS.69; 113; 140 n.45).

ANDERSON, William *alias* Sheffield. Priest.

b. June 12th, 1689, Lincolnshire. e. St Omers College before 1721. S.J. September 7th, 1721. Watten (nov) 1723. Liège (phil) 1724-6. Liège (theol) 1726-9. Ordained priest c.1729. Ghent (tert) 1730. Kingerby 1730-64. Rector of College of St Hugh 1756-64. d. August 23rd, 1764, Kingerby. (Fo.7; CRS.22/197; CRS.69; CRS.Mon.2/389; Gil.4/73; YA 77/221; HMC.10th Report, App.4/183, 187; Nec; 113; 114; 91; 21 v.2; 50 ff.16, 77, 187; 64 p.172; 156 App.1).

ANDERTON, Francis. Priest.

b.1665. s. of Sir Francis, Bt. and Elizabeth (Somerset) of Lostock, Lancashire. E.C. Rome 1684-5. S.J. June 21st, 1685. Watten (nov) 1685-6. Liège (phil) 1687, 1689. Rome (theol) 1692-3. Ordained priest c.1694. Liège 1696-7, 1699-1701. Travelling 1701. In England 1703. College of St Ignatius 1704-8. Residence of St Michael 1709-10. Residence of St John 1711-23 (Haggerston Castle and Gateshead 1711-23). d. August 22nd or 23rd, 1723, Newcastle upon Tyne. (Fo.7; 113; Gib.1/52-3, 65; CRS.40/103; 159; 162; Nec).

ANDERTON, Sir James Bt. *alias* Somerset. Scholastic.

b.1678 or 1684. s. of Sir Charles Bt. and Margaret (Ireland) of Lostock, Lancashire. e. St Omers College 1695 or earlier – ? S.J. September 7th, 1704. Watten (nov) 1705-6. 4th Bt. 1705. Liège (phil) 1708-10. d. not ordained, October 5th, 1710, St Omers College. (Fo.7; CRS.69; 113; 193, Anglia 35 f.278; Gib.1/55, 64 ff.; Nec; 114).

ANDERTON, Stephen.

S.J.1662. Watten (nov) 1662, 1663. Not found again in the records under this name; no evidence to show that he completed the noviceship. (113).

ANDERTON, William. Priest.

b. April 24th, 1754, Lancashire, s. of William. e. Bruges College 1769-73. Liège Academy 1781, 1783, 1787, 1792. Ordained priest March 11th, 1780. S.J. August 7th, 1806. Hereford 1799 or earlier – 1823. d. September 28th, 1823, Hereford. bu. Hereford Cathedral churchyard. (Fo.7; CRS.69; LR.6/51; Chad.367; CRS.12/156; CRS.13/202; 113; 114; 3 f.37; 1 f.152v; 6 f.230; 10 f.245; 13 ff.273, 373; 33 ff.61v, 63, 83, 87, 112, 117; 34 ff.108v, 209, 211, 216; 56 f.307; 25; ff.32, 45; 80; 93; 118; Nec).

ANDREWS, Francis *alias* or *vere* Evans. Priest.

b.1659, Monmouthshire. e. ?St Gregory's, Douai c.1672; St Omers
College ?-1679. S.J. September 7th, 1679. Watten (nov) 1679-81. Liège
(phil) 1681-4. Liège (theol) 1684-8. Ordained priest c.1688. College of
St Francis Xavier 1689-93, 1696-7, 1699-1701, 1703-6, 1708-16, 1718,
1720, 1724-7 (The Priory, Monmouth ?-1727). d. March 28th, 1727,
Monmouth. (Fo.7; CRS.69; 91; Nec).

ANGIER, Thomas (1). Priest.

b. February 19th, 1730, Norwich. Uncle of the next. e. St Omers
College c.1746-52. S.J. September 7th, 1752. Watten (nov) 1752-4.
Liège (phil) 1755-7. St Omers College 1757-8. Liège (theol) 1758.
Ordained priest 1760. Travelling 1759-61. Ghent (tert) 1762. Watten
1763. Bruges College 1764-73 (Rector 1773). Norwich 1774-88. d. June
12th, 1788, Norwich (Fo.7; CRS.69; 113; 114; Nec; SCH.12/19, 23;
NA.37/159; 7 f.87; 16 f.100; 17 p.3; 21 v.2; 41 nn.34, 116, 124, 131; 151
ff.144, 146; 76; HMC 10th Report App.4/190; 121; 175; 176; 126; Ber.
pp.133 ff.).

ANGIER, Thomas (2). Priest.

b. December 10th, 1754, Norwich. s. of Samuel. Nephew of Thomas
Angier (l). e. Bruges College 1765-72. S.J. September 7th, 1772. Liège
Academy 1774-90. Ordained priest March 8th, 1780. Readm. S.J.
December 1803. Oxburgh Hall 1790-5. Bury St Edmunds 1795-1826.
New Hall 1826-37. d. January 18th, 1837, New Hall. bu. New Hall
convent cemetery. (Fo.7; 113; 114; 115; 116; CRS.7/204-5, 213;
CRS.69; ER.5/98; Nec; 3 ff.37, 51; 6 f.122v; 13 ff.219v, 287; 15 ff.12,
284v; 21 v.2; 42 ff.190, 197v, 205v; 51 f.208; 90 f.54; 93 p.7; 133 f.46;
97; 121).

ANSELM see Rogers, Philip.

ARCHBOLD, Richard. Priest.

b.1713, Ireland. s. of Robert and Mary. e. St Omers College
c.1725-31. S.J. October 18th, 1731-1754 or 1755. Liège (phil) 1733-5.
Liège (theol) 1736-9. Ordained priest c.1739. Maryland 1740-9. College
of Ignatius 1750. Belhouse 1751-3. Spinkhill 1753. (Fo.7; CRS.69; 113;
91; 111; 150 III (2) 7/2/39; 64 pp.354, 472, 520; 65; 68 p.31; 92; 51
f.311v).

ARCHER, John *alias* Groves. Priest.

b.1627 or 1628, ?Monmouthshire. s. of John and Mary. e. Ghent.
E.C. Rome 1647-50. S.J. June 15th, 1650. Watten (nov) 1650-2. Liège
(phil) 1652-3. Liège (theol) 1653-7. Ordained priest March 31st, 1657.
Ghent (tert) 1657-8. College of St Francis Xavier 1658-67, 1669-74
(Rector 1670-4). d. February 4th, 1674 in England. (Fo.7; 113; 114;
CRS.40/40; CRS.55/504; Nec).

ARCHER, Richard.

d. in England, date and place unknown. (Fo.7; 114).

ARDENSON, James. Priest.

d. September 4th, 1694 but not in English province catalogues under
this name. (Fo.7).

ARMSTRONG, Daniel *alias* or *vere* Mumford or Montford, Joseph. Priest.

b.1643. ?From Scarrington, Nottinghamshire. E.C. Valladolid
1660-7. Ordained priest c.1667. In England 1667-75. S.J. August 14th,
1675. Liège (nov) 1675-6. E.C. Valladolid 1677-84. Residence of St
Michael 1685. College of St Ignatius 1686. d. July 8th, 1686 in England,
(Fo.7; CRS.30/xxxii, xxxiii, 169, 175; Ans.3/6; 113; 114; Nec).

ARNOULT, Michael. Laybrother.
b.1643, Flanders. S.J. November 23rd, 1664. Watten (nov) 1664-6.
Watten 1667, 1669. St Omers College 1672. Watten 1673-5. d. April
27th, 1675, Watten. (Fo.7; 113; 114; Nec).

ARTHUR see Mannock, Francis.

ARUNDELL, Hon. Charles. ?Scholastic.
b.1668 or 1669, Worcestershire. s. of Thomas, 4th Lord Arundell
and Margaret (Lucy, *née* Spencer). e. St Omers College ?-1689. S.J.
September 7th, 1689. Watten (nov) 1689. College of St Ignatius 1691.
d. before 1693. No evidence that he completed the novitiate. (Fo.7;
CRS.69; 113; Nec.).

ASHBY see Turner, Anthony; Middlehurst, James.

ASHBY, John see Turner, Edward.

ASHTON see Powell, Francis.

ASHTON, John. Priest.
b. May 3rd, 1742, Ireland. e. St Omers College ?-1759. S.J.
September 7th, 1759. Watten (nov) 1761. Liège (theol) 1763-4.
Ordained priest c.1765. Ghent (tert) 1766. Maryland 1767-1815. d.
January 3rd or February 4th, 1815, Portobacco, Maryland. (Fo.7; 113;
CRS.69; 114; Hu.Text 2/696; 65; 68 p.77; Nec.).

ASHTON, Thomas *alias* Du Puy. Priest.
b.1662 or 1665, London or Lancashire. S.J.1684. Watten (nov) 1685.
Liège (phil) 1686. Liège (theol) 1687. Ordained priest 1689. Watten
(tert) 1689, 1690. St Omers College 1691-3, 1696-7. Watten 1699-1701.
St Omers College 1703-6. d. October 8th, 1707, Watten. (Fo.7; 113;
114; 170 ff.58v, 143v, 144, 254v; 140 n.45; Nec.).

ASPINALL or ASPINWALL, Edward *alias* or *vere* Pinnington. Priest.
b.1678, Lancashire. e. St Omers College 1693 or earlier – 96. S.J.
February 23rd, 1697-1707. Watten (nov) 1697. Liège (phil) 1699-1700.
Liège (theol) 1701-5. Ordained priest c.1705. Ghent (tert) 1706.
Residence of St George 1706-7 (Spetchley). (Fo.7; Ki.7; CRS.69;
RH.1/47, 243; WR.30/11; 12 f.78; 40 ff.26, 30; DNB.).

ASPINALL, Henry *alias* or *vere* Brent. Priest.
b. March 25th, 1715, Lancashire. e. St Omers College 1729-34. S.J.
September 7th, 1734. Watten (nov) 1734. Liège (phil) 1735, 1737, 1738.
St Omers College 1739-40, 1742-5. La Flèche (theol) 1747-8. Ordained
priest c.1747. Liège 1749-50, 1752-3, 1755-6, 1758, 1761. Watten
1763-5. Durham 1766-72. Wardour 1772-5. Irnham 1775-84. d.
January 9th, 1784, Irnham. bu. Irnham parish churchyard. (Fo.7;
CRS.69; CRS.Mon.1/148n, 159; CRS.12/39; 113; 114; NCH.4/13;
SCH.12/19; 13 ff.35, 96; 21 v.2; 44 ff.277-8; 50 f.31v; 65; 76; 68 p.334;
Chad. 330; 164; 01.246; 140 n.45; 117; Nec. For writings see Som. s.v.

Brent, Henry).

ASPINALL, Joseph *alias* or *vere* Brent. Priest.

    b. September 16th, 1726. From Lancashire. e. St Omers College c.1738-45. S.J. September 16th, 1745. Watten (nov) 1746. Liège (phil) 1747-9. Liège (theol) 1750. Ordained priest c.1752. Watten 1752-3. Ghent 1754-8. Watten School 1761. d. July 13th, 1763, Ghent. (Fo.7; CRS.69; 113; 114; Nec.).

ASPINALL, Thomas *alias* or *vere* Brent. Priest.

    b. September or October, 1719. From Lancashire. e. St Omers College 1735-40. S.J. September 7th, 1740. Watten (nov) 1740, 1741. Liège (phil) 1743. Cologne (theol) 1744, 1746. Trèves (theol) 1747. Ordained priest c.1747. Ghent (tert) 1748. St Omers College 1749. Watten 1750. Hampreston and Stapehill 1751-4. College of St Aloysius 1754-8 (Crosby 1755-59). St Omers College 1761-2. In England 1763. Watten 1764. Brough 1765-9. Moseley 1769-73. Bruges College 1773. Liège Academy 1773. d. October 25th or 26th, 1773, Liège. (Fo.7; CRS.69; SCH.3/6; HMC. 10th Report App. 4/184; Pa2.26; Chad.314; E and P.325; Gil.4/172; Nec; 113; 44 ff.262-3; 51 ff.304, 307; 64 pp.318, 518, 527; 65; 76; 68 p.101; 86; 90 f.176v; 111; 119 ff.6, 7, 9, 10, 17; CRS.0. P.1/162; 121).

ASTLEY see Phillips, Vincent.

ASTON or ASHTON, Herbert *alias* Barrett.

    S.J. c.1682. Not in English province catalogues under these names. (Fo.7).

ASTON, William. Priest.

    b. April 22nd, 1735, London. s. of Edward and Anne (Bayley). ?br. of Lord Aston. e. St Omers College c.1747-51. S.J. September 7th, 1751. Watten (nov) 1752. Liège (phil) 1753-6. St Omers College 1756-62. Bruges College 1762. Liège (theol) 1762-5. Ordained priest 1765. Bruges School 1767-73 (Superior 1767-73). Ghent 1774. Liège Academy 1774-6, 1797-8. Canon of S. Jean de Liège. d. March 15th, 1800, Liège. (Fo.7; CRS.69; Gil.1/83; Chad.363; CWAA.79/133; Ki.7; CRS.19/220; 113; 114; 7 f.107; 15 f.16v; 16 ff.9, 12v; 34 n.206; 51 f.67; 53 f.9; 77; 69;90 f.54; 94 f.230; 175; 176; 177; 178; 121; Nec. For writings see Som.).

ATKINS, Francis. Priest or Scholastic.

    b. October 26th, 1733, Bombay, of British parentage. s. of Francis. e. Greenwich Academy 1741-8. A convert 1749. S.J. 1752 in Brazil province. Exiled to Portugal 1759 and imprisoned till 1777. d.1778, Lisbon. (Fo.7; Lei.7/268, 8/66).

ATKINSON, James or John. Priest.

    b. November 12th, 1687. From Lancashire or Worcestershire. s. of George and Lucy (Withy). E.C. Rome 1703-8. S.J. February 24th, 1708, Rome. Ordained priest before 1723. Rome 1723-5. Loretto 1725-43. Livorno 1743. Rome 1744, 1746-50, 1752-8, 1761. d. March 23rd or 24th, 1763, Rome. (Fo.7; CRS.40/133; Nec; 113; 9 n.163; 91; 111).

ATWOOD, Peter. Priest.

b. October 18th, 1682, Worcestershire (?Claines). s. of George and Winefrid (Petre). e. St Omers College ?-1703. S.J. September 7th, 1703. Watten (nov) 1704, 1705. Liège (phil) 1706. St Omers College 1708. Liège (theol) 1709-12. Ordained priest c.1711. Maryland 1712-6, 1720, 1724-8, 1730, 1733-4 (Superior in Maryland 1734). d. December 25th, 1734, Newtown, Maryland. (Fo.7; CRS.69; Hu.Text 2/685; Nec; E. and P.85, 355; 113; 114; 91).

AUBEIL, Francis or Marcus or Martin d'. Priest.

S.J. in France. College of St Ignatius 1676, 1680-7 (French chapel, London) (Fo.7; 11).

AUCKLAND see Oakley, Francis.

AUDLEY, James *alias* Tuchet or Touchet. Scholastic.

b. March 25th, 1666, London. ?s. of James, 5th Earl of Castlehaven and Anne (Bard). e. St Omers College ?-1694. S.J. April 10th, 1694-1703. Liège (phil) 1696-7. Liège (theol) 1699-1703. Left 1704, not ordained. (CRS.69; 113; 150 III, (1) 2/2/04, (2) 25/11/02).

AVVARO, George. Priest.

b. January 29th, 1810, Italy. S.J. December 1st, 1825, Turin province. To English province c.1850. Jamaica 1852-3. British Honduras 1853-73 (Superior 1853-72). (Fo.7; 113).

AYROLI, John Baptist *alias* Lucas and Justiniani. Priest.

b.1652, Genoa. S.J. 1670, Milan province. Liège (theol) 1682. Ordained priest c.1682. Residence of St George 1684, 1685. College of the Holy Apostles 1686, 1687, 1689, 1691-3, 1696. Residence of St George 1697, 1699-01, College of St Ignatius 1703-6, 1708, 1710. St Germain 1711-2, 1714-5. To Italy 1715. (Fo.7; CRS.62 passim; Chad.256; 113).

BABTHORPE, Albert. Priest.

b.1646, Mechlin. s. of Sir Ralph and—(Hamilton) of Babthorpe, Yorkshire. e. St Omers College c.1658-64. S.J. December 31st, 1664. Liège (phil) 1667, 1669. Liège (theol) 1672-4. Ordained priest 1674. Ghent (tert) 1674. Watten 1675-80. College of St Aloysius 1680-1720 (Scarisbrick c.1698. Croxteth 1701, 1704. ?New House 1704-14. Croxteth 1715. Rector 1705-11 and 1713-8). d. April 13th, 1720, Croxteth. (Fo.7 and p.1405; CRS.69; NB.1/53, 2/62, 286; Gil.2/309, 5/60; CRS.8/320; Nec; 113; 114; 23 f.35; 27 f.200; 89; 168 f.75).

BABTHORPE, Richard. Priest.

b.1618, Yorkshire. s. of Sir William and Grace (Tyrwhitt) of Babthorpe, Yorkshire. e. St Omers College c.1631-41. E.C. Rome 1641-8. Ordained priest April 15th, 1645. To England 1648. S.J. November 16th 1651. Watten (nov) 1651. Residence of St Mary 1653-65. Ghent 1667. Residence of St George 1669, 1672-6, 1678-81. d.1681, Stafford. (Fo.7; CRS.69; Ans.2/10; CRS.8/320; CRS.40/24;

CRS.55/470; Nec: 113; 114).

BADNAM or BODNAM see Lazenby, John.

BAILLIEU or BAILLEUL, James. Laybrother.
   b. August 15th, 1650 or 1651, Artois. ?br of John. S.J. July 24th,
   1690. Watten (nov) 1691, 1692. Watten 1693, 1696-7, 1699-01, 1703. d.
   February 7th or 8th, 1703 or 1704, Watten. (Fo.7; Nec; 113; 114).

BAILLIEU, John. Laybrother.
   b. November 11th, 1648, Artois. ?br. of James. S.J. January 28th,
   1682. Ghent 1683. Liège 1684-7. Paris 1689-90. Antwerp 1691-2.
   Watten 1693. Liège 1696, 1697, 1699, 1701, 1703-6, 1708-15. d. May
   13th, 1715, Liège. (Fo.7; Nec; 113; 114).

BAINES see Mico, Edward; Norris or Norrice, Andrew; Preston, William;
   Sanders, Francis; Turner, Anthony.

BAKER see Jones, William.

BAKER, Bernard. Priest.
   b. August 15th or 16th, 1698, Co. Meath, Ireland. e. St Omers
   College ?-1721. S.J. September 7th, 1721. Watten (nov) 1723. Liège
   (phil) 1724-6. St Omers College 1727-30. Liège (theol) 1733-5. Ordained
   priest c.1734. Liège 1736-9. College of St Ignatius 1739-41, 1744,
   1746-72 or 73 (London. Rector 1761-3). d. July 27th, 1772 or February
   1773, London. (Fo.7; CRS.19/220-364 passim; 13 f.96A; CRS.69;
   HMC.10th Report, App. 4/183, 186, 192; Nec; 66; LR.3/5, 8; 125;
   126; 91; 191; 111; 113; 114; 117).

BAKER, Charles or David see Lewis, David.

BAKER, John. Priest.
   b. March 30th, 1644, Madrid. e. St Omers College c.1666-70. S.J.
   September 7th, 1670. Watten (nov) 1672. Liège (phil) 1672-5. Liège
   (theol) 1676, 1678. Ordained priest April 9th, 1678. Ghent (tert) 1679.
   College of St Thomas 1679-86. In England 1688. Rome 1689-93.
   Loretto 1696. Rome 1697, 1699-01, 1703-6. Ghent 1708-9. Watten
   1710-19. d. August 29th, 1719, Watten. (Fo.7; CRS.69; Chad.191;
   Nec; 113; 114; 139 n.6).

BALDI, Angelus Dominic. Priest.
   b. Florence. S.J. Milan province. Liège (theol) 1682, 1683. Ordained
   priest April 17th, 1683. Ghent (tert) 1684. College of St Ignatius 1685-7
   (London). To Milan 1687. (Fo.7; 113; 150 II (3) 3/8/86, 30/8/87).

BANISTER see Selby, William.

BARKER see Eyre, William (2).

BARKER, John. Priest.
   b.1640, Essex. S.J. May 2nd, 1662. Liège (phil) 1663-5. Liège (theol)
   1667, 1669. Ordained priest April 5th, 1670. College of the Holy
   Apostles 1672-6, 1678-85. College of St Hugh 1686, 1687. College of
   the Holy Apostles 1689-93, 1696-1700 (Rector 1696-1700). Spetchley
   1700-02. College of the Holy Apostles 1703. d. June 10th, 1705 in
   England (?College of the Holy Apostles). (Fo.7; Nec; 113; 114; 40
   f.10).

BARNES see Hammerton, Peter.

BARNEWALL, Patrick. Priest.
b. October 10th, 1709, Bremore, Co. Dublin. S.J. November 9th
1726, Portuguese province. To English province c.1752. Preston
1752-61. Ingatestone 1761-2. d. February 1st, 1762 Ingatestone or
Preston. (Fo.7; ER.5/95; CRS.6/340; Nec; 113; 114; 21 v.2; 30 f.7a; 64
p.399; 68 p.124; 119 f.1; 158; 156 App.1).
BARON, John. Priest.
b. September 2nd, 1807, Blackburn. s. of John. e. Sedgley Park
1816-21; Stonyhurst 1821-7. S.J. September 21st, 1827. Hodder (nov)
1828. St Mary's Hall (phil) 1830. London school 1831-5. Stonyhurst
1835-40. St Mary's Hall (theol) 1840-3. Ordained priest September
19th, 1841. Hodder 1843-6. Croft 1846-7. Hodder 1847-8. Mount St
Mary's College 1848-54 (Rector). Wakefield 1854-70. Roehampton
1870. Mark Cross 1871-4. Wardour 1874-6. Holywell 1876-8. d. July
11th 1878, Holywell. bu.Pantasaph. (Fo.7; SCH.3/22; LR.3/65-6;
CRS.13/400; Nec; Stol; 113; 115).
BARRARD or BARRET, Richard *alias* Rigby. Priest.
b. August 15th, 1661, Lancashire. e. St Omers College ?-1679. S.J.
September 7th, 1690. Watten (nov) 1691, 1692. Liège (phil) 1693. Liège
(theol) 1696, 1697. Ordained priest 1698. Ghent (tert) 1699. St Omers
College 1701. College of St Thomas 1703 (Soberton). College of St
Ignatius 1703-6, 1708. College of St Thomas 1710-14. Residence of St
Stanislaus 1715-6. College of the Immaculate Conception 1718.
Residence of St Winefrid 1720, 1724-25 (nr Welshpool c.1727). In
England 1726-8, 1730. Watten 1733-8. d. January 29th, 1740, Watten.
(Fo.7; Nec; 44 f.167; 91; 113).
BARROW, Andrew. Priest.
b. January 27th, 1804, Manchester. e. Stonyhurst 1815-21. S.J.
November 2nd, 1821, Rome. Ferrara (phil) 1823. Rome (phil) 1824.
Stonyhurst 1825-32. St Mary's Hall 1832-5. Ordained priest December
20th, 1834. Stonyhurst 1835-6. Preston 1836-8. Hodder (tert) 1838-9.
Preston 1839-42 (Superior 1839-41). Stonyhurst 1842-5 (Rector).
Broughton Hall 1845-65 (Rector of College of St Michael 1860-5). d.
October 20th, 1865, Broughton Hall. (Fo.7; Nec; Stol; 113; 114; 115).
BARROW, Edward *alias* Davis. Priest.
b.1660, Westby in the Fylde, Lancashire. ?s. of John. Great-uncle of
Joseph and Richard. e. St Omers College ?-1683. S.J. September 7th,
1683. Watten (nov) 1684, 1685. Liège (phil) 1685-7. Liège (theol) 1689.
Ordained priest c.1690. Watten (tert) 1690. College of St Aloysius 1691,
1693, 1696-7, ?1700, 1701, 1703-6, 1708, 1710-11, 1714-7 (Westby 1701,
1715-7). Kelvedon 1718-20 or 21. d. August 1721, Kelvedon, Westby or
London. (Fo.7; ER.9/109; CRS.6/207n; CRS.15/3; Gil.HP.232-5;
Gil.1/145; Nec; 113; 23 f.35v; 43 ff.37v, 39, 40v; 114).
BARROW, Joseph. Priest.
b. September 27th, 1740, Westby in the Fylde. s. of Edward and
Anne (Hull). br. of Richard. gr. nephew of Edward. e. St Omers
College c.1751-8. S.J. September 7th, 1758. Liège (phil) 1761. Liège

(theol) 1763, 1764. Ordained priest 1765. Bruges College 1767, 1768.
Exeter 1768. Arlington 1769, 1772-3-? Tusmore ?-1781. Little Crosby
1783, 1784. Cowley Hill 1785, 1786, 1788, 1790-3. St Helens 1793-1813.
d. January 5th, 1813, St Helens. bu. St Helens chapel. (Fo.7; CRS.69;
CRS.6/208; CRS.23/138; 01.239; Nec; HMC.10th Report,
App.4/183; 113; 13 f.401; 15 f.62; 16 f.12; 65; 21 v.2; 23 f.270v; 44 f.45;
54 ff.156v, 161v; 68 pp.129, 133, 375; 80; 89; 155, II, n.129; 167 pp.22,
30; 101; 111; 117; 98; 114; 119 f.23).

BARROW, Richard. Priest.
    b. October 21st, 1738, Lancashire. s. of Edward and Anne (Hull). br.
of Joseph. gr. nephew of Edward. e. St Omers College c.1750-5. S.J.
September 7th, 1755. Watten (nov) 1756, 1757. Liège (phil) 1757, 1758.
St Omers College c.1760. Liège (theol) 1761. Ordained priest c.1763.
Ghent (tert) 1763-4. Residence of St Michael 1764. Pontfract 1767-86.
Blackrod and Wigan 1787-99. d. October 17th, 1799, Wigan. (Fo.7;
CRS.69; HMC.10th Report, App.4/183; CRS.6/208; CRS.1/138;
Nec; 113; 15 f.62v; 21 v.2; 54 ff.156, 156v.161; 65; 25 ff.102, 105, 113,
118, 145, 150, 158, 163; 80; 155, II, n.127; 167 p.38; 114; 117).

BARROW, Thomas. Priest.
    b. September 17th, 1747, Eccleston nr. Prescot. s. of Thomas and
May (Crookhall). e. St Omers and Bruges Colleges 1758-64. S.J.
September 7th, 1764. Liège (phil) 1767. Liège (theol) 1768-73. Ordained
priest c.1772. Liège Academy 1774-8, 1783, 1785-92, 1794. Stonyhurst
1795-6. Rotterdam and Liège 1796-8. Stonyhurst 1798, 1800-02. Liège
1802-14. d. June 12th, 1814, Liège. (Fo.7; CRS.69; SM.34/120 ff,
35/190 ff, 237 ff; HMC.10th Report App.4/192; Chad.375; DNB;
CRS.12/123; CRS.17/96, 141, 185; Nec; 113; 3 f.51; 4 f.113v; 166 I
p.70; 1 f.111seq; 13 ff.109v, 118, 158, 168, 186, 197, 276, 311v, 347v; 56
ff.258, 261v, 273v, 290v; 77; 25 ff.23, 29, 46; 80; 90 ff.145v, 146v; 93
ff.1, 3, 8v, 11, 20, 45; 157; 130; 131; 128; 137 f.86; 97; 104; 114; 119 ff.
18, 19).

BARRUEL, Augustine, de Priest.
    b. October 2nd, 1741, Villeneuve-de-Berg, Ardèche, France. S.J.
October 15th, 1756, Toulouse province. In England (London)
1792-1802. Returned to France 1802. Readm. S.J. October 14th, 1815.
d. October 5th, 1820, Paris. (CG.; CDSJ; CRS.12/146; 166 II p.39;
AHSJ.20/151. For writings see Som.).

BARRUM see Coniers or Conyers, Thomas (1) and (2).

BARTELOT or BERTLOE, Mark. Laybrother.
    b.c.1642, Artois. S.J. September 7th, 1669. Watten 1672, 16 75,
1678-80. Liège 1681, 1683-6, 1689-93, 1696, 1697, 1699-1701. d. June
29th, 1701, Liège. (Fo.7; 113; 114; Nec.).

BARTHOLOMEW, John see Ruga, Bartholomew.

BARTLET, Basil. Scholastic.
    b.1700. s. of Rowland and Anne (Tasburgh) of Hill End,
Worcestershire. br. of Felix. E. C. Douay ?-1720. S.J. ?-1737. In
England 1733-5. Left not ordained. (WR.20/50; Pa.75; Ki.12;

CRS.28/58, 80; 113; 38 ff. 12, 15, 19-24, 26, 28-9; 91).

BARTLET, Felix. Priest.

b. March 19th, 1708, Hanley Castle, Worcestershire. s. of Rowland and Anne (Tasburgh) of Hill End Worcestershire. br. of Basil. e. St Omers College c.1720-6. S.J. September 7th.1726. Watten (nov) 1727. Liège (phil) 1728, 1730. Liège (theol) 1732, 1733, 1734. Ordained priest 1734. Ghent (tert) 1734-5. College of St Thomas 1735-8 (?West Grinstead 1736). Residence of St Mary 1739-42. Residence of St George 1743-74 (Hanley Castle 1753, 1765, 1767-74). Worcester ?-1777. d. May 14th, 1777, Worcester. (Fo.7; CRS.69; WR.20/51-2, 72; E. and P.294; Nec; 113; 21 v.2; 38 f.197; 74; 91; 125; 117).

BARTON see Harvey, John and Thomas; Pelcom of Pelcon, Peter.

BASSET see Challoner, William.

BASSIN see Fisher, Honoratus.

BATEMAN, James. Priest.

b. October 9th, 1805, Lancaster. e. Stonyhurst 1820-? S.J. September 7th, 1826. Montrouge (nov) 1826. Hodder (nov) 1827. Stonyhurst (phil) 1828. Stonyhurst 1830-3. Stonyhurst (theol) 1833-7. Ordained priest September 24th, 1836. Wigan 1837-8. Chipping 1838-40. Irnham 1840-4. Hodder (tert) 1844. Worcester 1844-6. Chipping 1846-58. Preston 1858-61 (Rector 1858-61). St Beuno's College 1861-5. Blackpool 1865-74. Bournemouth 1874-7. New Hall 1877-9. d. June 17th, 1879, New Hall. bu.New Hall. (Fo.7; Stol; CG; CRS.17/96; CRS.36/4; Nec; 113; 115; 114. For writings see Sut.Som.).

BAVART or BOUVART, John Baptist. Laybrother.

b.1681 or 1682, Saint-Omer. S.J. July 30th, 1706. Watten 1708, 1710. Liège 1711-12, 1714-6, 1718. Watten 1723-4. d. August 6th, 1724, Watten. (Fo.7; 113; 114).

BAXTER see Case, William.

BAXTER, Roger. Priest.

b.1793, Walton-le-Dale, near Preston. e. Stonyhurst 1806-? S.J. September 7th, 1810-26. Hodder (nov) 1810. Stonyhurst (theol) 1815. Ordained priest c.1817. U.S.A. 1817-25. Montrouge (tert) 1825. Enfield 1825-6. (Fo.7; Hu.Docs.I/527; CRS.36/271; Stol; CG; Gil.1/157-8; 150 (1750-1853) ff.182, 204v; 6 f.253; 2; 21 v.2; 34 f.173v; DNB; 94 ff.196-7, 198-9, 202-3, 204-5, 210-11, 214-5, 220-21, 222-3, 225-6. For writings see Sut.Som.)

BAYNHAM, John *alias* Knight. Priest.

b. December 1st, 1720, Worcestershire. e. St Omers College c.1735-40. S.J. September 7th, 1740. Watten (nov) 1742. Liège (phil) 1743. Paderborn (theol) 1744. Büren (theol) 1746. Ordained priest c.1746. Ghent 1747. Watten 1748. College of St Chad 1749-51 (?Moseley or Bromley). Residence of St George 1751-96 (Grafton and Purshall Hall c.1755-96). d.February 24th, 1796, Purshall Hall. (Fo.7; CRS.69; WR.8/28, 15/2 ff, 23 ff; HMC.10th Report App.4/183; Nec; 113; 114; 117; 38 ff.31v, 73v, 124).

BEADNALL or BREADNALL, James. Priest.

b. April 8th, 1718, Northumberland. e. St Omers College c.1735-9.
S.J. September 7th, 1739. Watten (nov) 1739, 1740. Liège (phil) 1741.
Büren (phil) 1743. Büren (theol) 1744, 1746. Ordained priest c.1746. St
Omers College 1747. Maryland 1749-72. d. April 9th, 1772, Newtown.
(Fo.7; CRS.69; Hu.Text II/693; Nec; 113; 114; 91; 92).

BEAUGRAND, Cornelius. Laybrother.

b.1634, Ypres. S.J. November 23rd, 1664. Watten 1667, 1669,
1672-6, 1678. College of St Ignatius 1679-81, 1684-7, 1689-93,
(imprisoned 1694), 1696. Ghent 1697, 1699-1701, 1703-14. d. February
12th, 1716, Ghent. (Fo.7; 113; Chad.191, 239; 168 ff.2, 36, 76; 170
f.23; 95 p.801; Nec; 114).

BEAUMONT see Poyntz, John.

BEAUMONT, Francis *alias* or *vere* Williams. Priest.

b. October 18th, 1682, Monmouthshire. e. St Omers College
c.1698-1702. S.J. September 7th, 1702. Watten (nov) 1703. Liège (phil)
1704-6. St Omers College 1708. Liège (theol) 1710, 1711. Ordained
priest 1711. Maryland 1712-19. Ince Blundell 1722-38. d. May 13th,
1738, Ince Blundell. bu. Harkirke cemetery. (Fo.7; CRS.62/281;
CRS.69; CRS.13/186; NB.3/85; Gib.1/290; CRS.25/113;
Che.N.S.12/85; Nec; Hu.Text II/686; 91; 113).

BEAUMONT, Henry. Scholastic.

e. Stonyhurst 1801-? S.J. 1807-c.19. Stonyhurst 1810, 1815, 1816. It
is not clear that he ever took his first religious vows and he does not
seem to have been ordained. (116; 113; 7 f.381; Stol).

BEAUMONT, John. Priest.

b. June 14th, 1787, Stone Easton, Somerset. s. of John and Margaret
(Tatlock). e. Stonyhurst 1800-? S.J. September 7th, 1807. Hodder
(nov) 1807. Stonyhurst (phil) 1809. Stonyhurst (theol) 1812. Ordained
priest December 18th, 1812. Alnwick 1812-31. St Mary's Hall (tert)
1831. Stockeld Park 1832. South-hill 1832-57. Clitheroe 1857. d.
December 20th, 1857, Clitheroe. bu. Stonyhurst. (Fo.7; Stol; Pa.2/10;
01.240; CRS.4/435; Nec; 113; 114; 115; 6 f.206; 7 f.177; 36 ff.4a, 83; 93
pp.78, 79; 116).

BEAUMONT, Joseph. Priest.

b. June 14th, 1702, Somerset. s. of Joseph and Hannah (Harding) of
Stone Easton. br. of William. e. St Omers College 1714 or earlier -15 or
later. S.J. September 7th, 1723. Watten (nov) 1724. Liège (phil)
1725-27. Liège (theol) 1728, 1730. Ordained priest c.1730. Ghent 1733.
College of St Aloysius 1735-73 (Eccleston 1733, 1738; Cowley Hill near
Prescot 1742-73). d. February 13th, 1773, Cowley Hill. bu.Windleshaw
cemetery. (Fo.7; CRS.69; HMC.10th Report, App.4/183, 192, 194;
CRS.17/22; CRS.23/138; Nec; 113; 13 ff.23v, 26, 45v, 68, 71v, 73v,
81v; 21 v.2; 23 ff.84, 89v, 152; 24 f.347v; 26 f.59; 34 f.130; 64 pp.151,
238; 66; 91; 51 f.311; 156 App.I; 111; 99).

BEAUMONT, William (1). Priest.

b. January 29th, 1697, Stone Easton, Somerset. s. of Joseph and
Hannah (Harding) of Stone Easton. br. of Joseph. S.J. September 7th,

1718. Watten (nov) 1720. Liège (phil) 1723. Liège (theol) 1724-27. Ordained priest c.1727. In England 1728. Residence of St Stanislaus 1733-8, 1740-1, 1744, 1748-58 (Bonham 1728-54-?). Sobertcn 1760-3. Lulworth 1764. d. October 15th, 1764, Stone Easton. (Fo.7; CRS.Mon.1/172, 245; CRS.6/365; CRS.13/181, 187; HMC.10th Report, App.4/192; 01.240; Nec; 113; 44 ff.87, 167; 89; 91; 111; 114).

BEAUMONT, William (2) ?or James. ?Scholastic.
   b. October 8th, 1750. S.J. September 7th, 1771. Ghent (nov) 1772, 1773. ?Liège Academy 1776. d. ?Liège, 1778. (113; 90 f.54; AHSJ.42/292).

BEAUMONT, William (3). Scholastic.
   e. Stonyhurst 1807-? S.J. September 7th, 1813-21. Hodder (nov) 1815. Stonyhurst (phil) 1816, 1817. Stonyhurst 1818, 1820-21. Left, not ordained, 1821. (113; 116; Stol; 2).

BECKETT see Fairfax, Thomas.

BEDELY, Francis. Scholastic or Laybrother.
   d. Liège, date unknown. (Fo.7; 114; Nec).

BEDINGFELD, Anthony. Priest.
   b. October 10th, 1697, Suffolk. s. of Francis and Dorothy (Bedingfeld) of Redlingfield Hall, Suffolk and Bures Hall, Norfolk. e. E. C. Douay ?-1714; St Omers College 1714. S.J. December 31st, 1714. Watten (nov) 1715. Liège (phil) 1716-8. Liège (theol) 1720, 1723. Ordained priest c.1723. Ghent (tert) 1724. Liège 1725, 1726. Travelling 1727, 1728, 1730. Ghent and Brussels 1732. College of St Thomas of Canterbury 1733-4 (West Grinstead). College of the Holy Apostles 1735-8, 1740 (Redlingfield Hall. Flixton). Socius to the Provincial 1740-1. Liverpool 1741-3, 1745-7. Travelling 1748. Ghent 1749. Antwerp 1750-1. d. June 2nd, 1752, Liège. (Fo.7; CRS.7/241; CRS.9/183-4; CRS.13/176, 181; CRS.69; CRS.62/101, 148, 161; Nec; 113; 150 III(2) 20/1/32, 3/6/41; 26 f.178; 64 p.88; 74; 85; 91; 156 App.1; 109; E and P.254; 114).

BEDINGFELD, Matthew *alias* or *vere* Mildmay *alias* Winter. Priest.
   b.c.1640, Oxfordshire. ?s. of Matthew Bedingfeld of Amersden, Oxfordshire and Brussels. e. St Omers College 1658-64. S.J. September 9th, 1664. Liège (phil) 1667, 1669. Ordained priest c.1672. St Omers College 1672. College of the Holy Apostles 1672. College of St Thomas of Canterbury 1673. Ghent (tert) 1674, 1675. College of St Aloysius 1676. Residence of St Stanislaus 1678-87, 1689-93, 1696-7, 1699 (?Treludro in Cornwall c.1678 at Humphrey Borlase's house). College of St Thomas of Canterbury 1700-01. Residence of St Stanislaus 1703-12. d. March 5th, 1713, Residence of St Stanislaus. (Fo.5/965 ff,7; CRS.7/432-3; CRS.47/66, 219; CRS.69; Nec; GEC. s.v. Borlase and vol.1 App; 113; 114).

BEESTON, Francis. Priest.
   b. June 15th, 1751. e. Bruges College 1765-71. S.J. September 7th, 1771. Ghent (nov) 1772, 1773. ?To England 1773. Liège Academy 1776, 1781, 1783, 1786. Ordained priest but date not found. U.S.A. 1786 till

his death. d. December 9th, 1806 or 1809 or 1810, U.S.A. (Fo.7;
CRS.12/107; CRS.69; AHSJ 42/308; Hu.Text II/700; Mel.101; Nec;
113; 3 ff.37, 51; 4 f.16; 22 f.115; 54 f.163v; 53 f.51; 76; 72; 90 f.54; 114).

BEESTON, Henry. Priest.

b. June 19th, 1797, near Lanherne, Cornwall. e. Stonyhurst 1811-16.
S.J. September 7th, 1816. Hodder (nov) 1816. Stonyhurst (phil)
1818-21. Rome (theol) 1821-4. Ordained priest July 11th, 1824.
Stonyhurst 1824-32. Portico and Prescot 1832-6. Socius to the
Provincial 1839. Portico 1840-1. New Hall 1841-3. Leigh 1843.
Worcester 1843-6. d. December 12th, 1846, Worcester. bu. Worcester
churchyard. (Fo.7; 01.240; Stol; Nec; NewH.175; 113; 115;114; 116)

BEESTON, James *vere* Bourgeois. Priest.

b. January 5th, 1738, French Flanders. S.J. September 7th, 1760.
Watten (nov) 1760, 1761. Liège (phil) 1763, 1764. Liège (theol) 1767.
Ordained priest c.1767. Bruges College 1768, 1769, 1771-3. ?To
England 1773. Cherry Orchard 1779. Courtfield 1779, 1781, 1784,
1785. Broughton 1786. Worcester 1792-6, 1798. Canford 1799-1801. d.
May 19th, 1801, Canford. (Fo.7; CRS.12/78; CRS.43/124, 137;
WR.20/70; CRW.38 ff; 01.241; Nec; 113; 3 f.30; 1 f.126; 13 f.269; 16
f.97v; 33 ff.5, 19; 44 f.173; 54 ff.168v, 252; Pa.2 24; 114; 117).

BEESTON, Robert ?*alias* Hill. Priest.

b. October 5th, 1659, Lincolnshire. e. St Omers College c.1673-80.
S.J. September 7th, 1680. Watten (nov) 1681. Liège (phil) 1682, 1683,
1684. Liège (theol) 1685-7. Ordained priest c.1688. Ghent (tert) 1689.
Liège 1690-3. St Omers College 1693-4. Watten 1694-7. St Omers
College 1697-1700. College of St Aloysius 1701. Residence of St George
1703-5 (Worcester?). Watten 1706-11 (Rector 1709-11). Ghent 1712-4
(Rector). Rome 1714-5. Watten 1715-21 (Rector). Provincial 1721-4.
Watten 1724-30 (Rector). d. August 9th, 1732, St Omers College.
(Fo.7; Gil.1/171; CRS.69; CRS.62/214 ff; WR.20/71; Chad.228; Nec;
113; 150 III(1) 4/6/08, 13/2/12; 150 III (2) 19/10/20, 5/4/21, 20/5/24,
4/1/21 (soli); 9 n.258; 193, Anglia.35/307; 140 n.45; 114; 91; 40 p.14.
For writings see Som.).

BELL, George. Laybrother.

b. January 1st, 1670 or 1671, London. S.J. October 9th, 1697.
Watten (nov) 1699. Liège 1700, 1701, 1703-6, 1708, 1709. Watten
1710-13, 1714-6, 1718, 1720. Paris 1723-4. Liège 1725-30; Antwerp
1732-5. Ghent 1735-8, 1740-1, 1743-4, 1746-50. d. August 11th, 1751,
Ghent. (Fo.7; Nec; CRS.62/59; 113; 114; 91; 109).

BENNETT, James. Scholastic.

b.1744. S.J. 1761-65 or later. Liège (phil) 1763, 1764. Nothing
further found. (Fo.7; 113).

BENNETT, John *alias* or *vere* Gosling. Priest.

b. March 17th, 1692, London. S.J. September 7th, 1710. Watten
(nov) 1711. Liège (phil) 1712, 1714. Liège (theol) 1715, 1716, 1718.
Ordained priest c.1719. Ghent (tert) 1720. Maryland 1723-7. Ghent
1728. In England 1730. College of St Aloysius 1733-8, 1740, 1743-4,

1746-50 (Lytham 1728-41. Highfield near Wigan 1741-51). d. April
2nd, 1751, Highfield. bu. Wigan. (Fo.7; CRS.16/424; CRS.15/4;
Hu.Text 2/687; CRS.25/116; Gil.HP.236; Nec; 113; 24 f.347; 85; 86;
91; 156 App.1).

BERBEOL or BERBEOTT, John. Laybrother.
b.1651, France. S.J. June 20th, 1676. Watten (nov) 1676. Maryland
1677, 1679-83. d. November 7th, 1684, Watten or in Maryland, 1684.
(Fo.7; Nec; Hu.Text II/686; 113; 114; 193 Anglia 34/396).

BERCHE, Charles. Laybrother.
b. March 9th, 1732, Belgium. S.J. May 28th, 1755-59. Watten (nov)
1755. Watten 1756-8. (91; 113).

BERESFORD, William *alias* or *vere* Clod. Priest.
b. February 4th, 1670, Lincolnshire. e. St Omers College ?-1692. S.J.
September 7th, 1692. Watten (nov) 1693. Liège (phil) 1696. Ordained
priest 1697. To England 1698. Liège (theol) 1699. Rheims (theol)
1700-1. Liège (theol) 1702, 1703. Ghent (tert) 1704. College of St
Ignatius 1705. College of St Hugh 1706, 1708, 1710-12, 1714-6, 1718,
1720, 1724. d. March 12th, 1726, in the College of St Hugh. (Fo.7;
CRS.69; Nec; 150 III(1) 4/11 1702; 123 IIIB f.356; 113).

BERINGTON, John *alias* Harper. Priest.
b. March 19th, 1673, Herefordshire. e. St Omers College ?-1691. S.J.
September 7th, 1691. Watten (nov) 1692, 1693. Liège (phil) 1696. Liège
(theol) 1697, 1699. Ordained priest c.1699. Ghent (tert) 1700-01.
Maynes Hall. Little Singleton 1701-21. Westby 1721-41. Lytham
1741-3. d. August 28th, 1743, ?Lytham. bu. Lytham parish church.
(Fo.7; CRS.69; CRS.13/187; CRS.15/4; CRS.16/424, 565, 580-1;
Gil.HP.236; Nec; 23 ff.35, 133; 24 f.5v; 85; 91; 156 App.1; 113; 114).

BERLEUR, Everard. Laybrother.
b. September 9th or December 25th, 1724, Liège or Saint-Omer. S.J.
1750-56. Watten (nov) 1750. St Omers College 1752-5. Liège 1756.
(113; 91; 7 f.65; 111).

BERMINGHAM, Nicholas *alias* Darcy. Priest.
b. November 26th, 1721, Co. Galway, Ireland. S.J. September 28th,
1740, Irish Mission at Bordeaux. May have worked briefly in England
from 1746. To Ireland before 1752. (Fo.7 and 5).

BERMINGHAM, William *alias* Nugent. Priest.
b. April, 1694 or 1692, in France. e. St Omers College ?-1710. S.J.
September 7th, 1711-24 and September 7th, 1729-37. Watten (nov)
1712, 1713. Liège (phil) 1714, 1715, 1716. Liège (theol) 1718. La Flèche
(theol) 1720. Ordained priest c.1721. Ghent 1723, 1724. Watten (nov)
1730. College of the Immaculate Conception 1733. Residence of St
George 1734. College of the Immaculate Conception 1735, 1736, 1737.
(Fo.7; CRS.69; 113; 91; 74; 40 pp.86, 88; 150 III (2) 15/4/24, 5/8/24,
20/11/37).

BERODE, James. Laybrother.
b. September 3rd, 1679, Saint-Omer. S.J. August 14th, 1711. Watten
(nov) 1711. Liège 1712-16, 1718, 1720. Ghent 1723. d. January 17th,

1724, Watten. (Fo.7; 113; Nec; 114).

BERRY, William *alias* or *vere* Corker *alias* Hutchinson. Priest.

    b.1627 or 1629, Lincolnshire. S.J. 1655-1670 or 1671. Watten (nov) 1656. Liège (phil) 1657, 1658, 1659. Liège (theol) 1660, 1661, 1663. Ordained priest 1663. Ghent (tert) 1664-5. St Omers College 1667. Residence of St Michael 1669. Ghent 1670. (Fo.7; Chad.184; 113).

BERTIE, Jerome. Priest.

    b. March 22nd, 1673, Lincolnshire. s. of Jerome and Elizabeth (Cape) of Lown. e. St Omers College ?-1693. S.J. September 7th, 1693. Liège (phil) 1696, 1697. Liège (theol) 1699-1701, 1703. Ordained priest c.1703. Ghent (tert) 1704. Ghent 1705-39. d. February 28th, 1739. (Fo.7; CRS.69; E and P.166; Nec; 113; 114; 91).

BEVAN, John. Priest.

    b. January or June, 1702, St Germain, France. e. St Omers College 1713 or earlier-1718. E.C. Valladolid 1718-24. Ordained priest c.1724. S.J. September 7th, 1724. Watten (nov) 1725. Liège (theol) 1726, 1727. Paris 1728. d. May 4th, 1728, St Germain. (Fo.7; CRS.69; CRS.62 index; Ans.4/32; CRS.30/183; 113; Nec.).

BEVERIDE see Eberson, Thomas.

BIL, James or Peter de. Laybrother.

    b. May 19th, 1707, Flanders. S.J. September 7th, 1732-43. Watten (nov) 1734. St Omers College 1735, 1736, 1737. Antwerp 1737, 1739, 1740, 1741. Ghent 1742, 1743. (Fo.7; 113; 109; 150 III (2) 2/3/43, 27/7/43).

BILLINGE see Laurenson, Richard.

BILLINGE, Charles. Priest.

    b. December 16th, 1735. Nephew of Richard and George. e. St Omers College 1751-3. S.J. September 7th, 1753-67. Watten (nov) 1754, 1755. Liège (phil) 1756, 1757, 1758. St Omers College 1761. Ordained priest c.1762. Watten school 1763, 1764. Bodney 1765. Moseley ?-1767. (Fo.7; CRS.69; CRS.6/219; 01.328; SCH.14/393; 64 p.268; 65; 77; 41 nn. 18, 22, 23; 91; WR.39/40 – 1).

BILLINGE, George. Laybrother.

    b. July 7th, 1678, Lancashire. ?s. of John and Margaret (Bradshaw) of Billinge. br. of Richard and uncle of Charles. S.J. September 7th, 1729. Paris 1733-37. Watten 1737-9. d. January 26th, 1739, Watten. (Fo.7; CRS.6/219; Nec; 91; 113; 114).

BILLINGE, Richard *alias* Bradshaw. Priest.

    b.1674 or 1676, Lancashire. ?s. of John and Margaret (Bradshaw) of Billinge. br. of George. Uncle of Charles. e. St Omers College 1688-98. S.J. September 7th, 1698. Watten (nov) 1699, 1700. Liège (phil) 1701, 1703. Liège (theol) 1704, 1705, 1706. Ordained priest 1706. Watten 1708, 1709. College of St Aloysius 1710-24. (Rector c.1718-24). In England 1726-28, 1730. (Croxteth ?-1720. Brinn 1720-33). d. January 1733, Brinn. (Fo.7; CRS.69; CRS.6/219; CRS.25/114; CRS.13/180; NB.2/266, 316; NB.3/6, 46; Nec; 113; 23 f.147; 28 f.191; 91; 169/3; 26 ff.67, 69).

BILLINGTON, John.
    d. Liège, date unknown. (Fo.7).
BIRCH see Pendrill, William.
BIRD, John. Priest.
    b. September 14th, 1783, Betchworth, Surrey. s. of Christopher and Anne (Webb). e. Stonyhurst 1795-1803. S.J. September 26th, 1803. Hodder (nov) 1803, 1804, 1805. Stonyhurst 1805-9. Stonyhurst (theol) 1809-13. Ordained priest December 16th, 1808. Preston 1813-34 (Superior 1832-4). Socius to the Provincial 1834. Provincial 1834-41. Preston 1841-2 (Rector). Pontefract 1842-8. Portico 1848-9. Preston 1849-50. Worcester 1850-3. d. June 8th, 1853, Worcester. bu. Worcester church yard. (Fo.7; Stol; Nec; 113; 115; 116; 93 p.71; 94 ff.19-20, 24, 154-5, 164-5, 200-1, 205-6, 332-4).
BIRKBECK, Edward *alias* Pole or Poole. Priest.
    b. December 24th, 1667, Westmorland. s. of Thomas and Margaret (Catterick) of Hornby Hall, Brougham, Westmorland. br. of Gervase. e. St Omers College ?-1690. S.J. September 7th, 1690. Watten (nov) 1691, 1692. Liège (phil) 1693. Liège (theol) 1696, 1697. Ordained priest 1699. Ghent (tert) 1699, 1700. St Omers College 1701, 1703, 1704, 1705. College of St Ignatius 1706. College of St Aloysius 1708. College of St Hugh 1709, 1710. College of the Holy Apostles 1711. Ghent 1712-16, 1718, 1720. d. January 9th, 1722, Ghent. (Fo.7; CRS.69; CRS.14/166; Nec; 113; 114).
BIRKBECK, Gervase *alias* Pole or Poole and Catterick. Priest.
    b.1671, 1674 or 1675, Westmorland. s. of Thomas and Margaret (Catterick) of Hornby Hall, Brougham, Westmorland. br. of Edward. e. St Omers College 1694-8. S.J. September 7th, 1698-c.1701 Watten (nov) 1699, 1700. Residence of St John (still a novice) 1701. No evidence that he completed the noviceship. (Fo.7; CRS.69; CRS.14/165-6; Ans.3/16).
BIRKETT, Joseph. Laybrother.
    b. March 1694 or 1696. S.J. September 7th, 1753 or 1754. Watten 1757, 1758, 1761, 1763, 1764. Ghent 1767-9. d. December 25th, 1770, Ghent. (Fo.7; 111; 113; 114; 91; Nec).
BLACKBURN, John. ?Scholastic.
    b.1658. s. of Richard of Stockenbridge or Okenbridge, Lancashire. e. St Omers College ?-1680. S.J. September 7th, 1680-?81. Watten (nov) 1680, 1681. No evidence that he completed the noviceship. (Fo.7; CRS.69; CRS.6/192n; 113).
BLACKISTON, Francis *alias* Smith. Priest.
    b.1635, Lincolnshire. e. ? E.C. Douay 1650; St Omers College 1656 or earlier -57. S.J. September 7th, 1657 or 1658. Watten (nov) 1658. Liège (phil) 1659, 1660, 1661. Liège (theol) 1663, 1664, 1667. Ordained priest April 9th, 1667. Ghent 1669. Residence of St Mary 1672, 1673. College of St Thomas of Canterbury 1674, 1675, 1676. College of St Hugh 1678. Nottingham prison 1679, 1680. College of St Aloysius 1683-93, 1696, 1697, 1699-1701. d. May 19th, 1701, in England. (Fo.7;

DD.82; Nec; CRS.69; 193 Anglia 34/369; 113; 114).

BLACKISTON, John see Blackiston, William.

BLACKISTON, William or John *alias* Travagan. Priest.

b. October 8th, 1698, Northumberland. e. St Omers College ?-1718.
E.C. Valladolid 1718-23. Ordained priest c.1723. S.J. October 31st,
1723. Watten (nov) 1724. Liège (theol) 1725, 1726. E.C. Valladolid
1726-33. Watten 1734-7. St Omers College 1738, 1739. Boulogne 1740,
1741. Boulogne School 1742-52 (Superior). St Omers Junior School
1753 (Superior). Watten School 1754, 1755 (Superior). Watten 1756-61
(Rector). St Omers College 1761, 1762. Ghent 1763, 1764 (Rector).
Bruges College 1764, 1767. d. January 26th, 1768, Bruges. (Fo.7;
CRS.69; CRS.30/xxxv, 184; Chad.271 ff; CRS.29/163; Ham.14, 21,
55; 113; 150 III(2)9/11/37, 3/6/41; 9 nn.249, 251; 91; 14 f.243; 16 f.12;
51 ff.67, 311; 121).

BLAIR, James. Priest.

b. January 15th, 1693, London. ?s. of Sir Adam Blair. e. St Omers
College ?-1713. S.J. September 7th, 1713. Watten (nov) 1714. Liège
(phil) 1714-18. Liège (theol) 1720. Ordained priest c.1722. St Omers
College 1723, 1724. Liège 1725. St Omers College 1726. Liège 1727,
1728, 1730, 1734. Watten 1735. Antwerp 1736-42. Residence of St
Stanislaus 1743. Crondon Park 1744. Residence of St Stanislaus 1746,
1747 (Exeter 1746). St Omers College 1748, 1749. Liège 1750, 1752-9. d.
May 28th or 29th, 1759, Liège. (Fo.7; CRS.69; CRS.6/328; 01. 242;
ER.4/119, 9/103; Nec; 113; 43 f.71; 91; 109; 114).

BLAKE , James *alias* Cross. Priest.

b.1649, London or Hampshire. E.C. Seville 1669-75. Ordained priest
1673. S.J. July 1st, 1675. Liège (nov) 1676. E.C. Madrid 1677-83. Liège
1684. College of St Ignatius 1685-7, 1689-93, 1696 (Rector 1696-1701),
1697, 1699-1701. Provincial 1701-4. College of St Ignatius 1705, 1706,
1708-16, 1718, 1720. Bromley, Essex 1720-8. d. January 29th, 1728,
Bromley. (Fo.7; Ans.3/18; ER.4/117, 9/103, 19/38; Pa.23; Gil.1/231;
CRS.29/101, 368; Che.64/453; Nec; 113; 150 II(3) 3/3/96, III(1)
20/5/01 and 29/11/10; 91; 168 f.90; 114; E and P.86; Ki.27; DNB. For
writings see Som.).

BLOUNT see Cotton, Alexander and George.

BLUETT see Risdon, Thomas.

BLUNDELL see Pemberton, John.

BLUNDELL, Francis. Priest.

b. August 13th, 1717, Lancashire. s. of Richard and Elizabeth
(Tickle) of Ince Blundell. e. St Omers College ?-1738. S.J. September
7th, 1738. Watten (nov) 1740. Liège (phil) 1740-1. Antwerp (phil) 1741.
Louvain (theol) 1743, 1744, 1745. Ordained priest c.1745. Ghent (tert)
1746. ?Brough 1746. Watten 1747-8. College of St Aloysius 1748, 1749.
Formby 1749-79. d. February 1st or 4th, 1779, Formby. bu. Formby.
(Fo.7; CRS.69; HMC.10th Report App.4/183; Gil.4/171; Gil.HP.215;
Nec; 113; 26 ff.280, 284v; 25 ff.5, 37; 80; 85; 158; 156 App.1; 155 III
185c; 109; 119 ff.3, 10, 17, 6, 9, 13, 15, 18, 21, 25, 31, 35, 42; 202. For

writings see Som.).
BLUNDELL, Joseph *alias* Selby. Priest.
　b. May 2nd, 1686, Lancashire. s. of William and Mary (Eyre) of
Crosby. e. St Omers College 1700-03. S.J. September 7th, 1703.
Watten (nov) 1704, 1705. Liège (phil) 1706, 1708. Liège (theol) 1709-12.
Ordained priest 1712. Ghent (tert) 1712-13. Stockeld 1713. Residence
of St Michael 1714, 1715, 1716. ?Selby c.1719. College of the
Immaculate Conception 1720-56 (Spinkhill 1721-56). Watten 1756-9. d.
July 27th, 1759, Watten. (Fo.7; Fo.5 pp.497, 734; CRS.69; NB.1/344,
II/55, 78; HMC 10th Report App.4/183-4; Nec; 113; 63 ff.54, 56v, 74v,
148; 91; 114).
BLUNDELL, Nicholas. Priest.
　b.1640, Crosby Hall, Lancashire. s. of William and Anne
(Haggerston) of Crosby. br. of Thomas. e. St Omers College c.1656-62.
S.J. September 7th, 1662. Liège (phil) 1664, 1665, 1667. Liège (theol)
1669. Ordained priest c.1670. Military chaplain, Flanders 1670. St
Omers College 1672-6. College of St Ignatius 1678. St Omers College
1679-80. d. December 20th, 1680, St Omers College. (Fo.7; CRS.69;
Gil.1/245; WB.134, 224; Nec; Mon.Jan.1879/64; 113; 114. For
writings see Som.).
BLUNDELL, Thomas. Priest.
　b. April 25th, 1648, Lancashire. s. of William and Anne
(Haggerston) of Crosby. br. of Nicholas. e. St Omers College 1660-?
S.J. September 7th, 1667. Liège (phil) 1669. St Omers College 1672-5.
Liège (theol) 1676, 1678. Ordained priest April 9th, 1678. Liège 1680-2.
Ghent (tert) 1683. Liège 1684-6, 1689. Watten 1690. St Omers College
1691. Liège 1692. Doctor of the University of Munster, Westphalia.
Lytham 1692-1702. d. May 27th, 1702, Lytham. bu. Harkirke. (Fo.7;
CRS.69; Gil.1/247; WB.227, 292; CRS.16/423; Che.N.S.12/81;
Mon.Jan.1879/64; Nec; 113; 150 II (3)1/4/84; 114. For writings see
Som.).
BLYDE, Benjamin. Laybrother.
　b. February, 1727, Yorkshire. S.J. January 24th, 1754. Watten (nov)
1754, 1755. Ghent 1756-8, 1761, 1764, 1767-9. Antwerp 1771-3. d. June
3rd, 1783, Antwerp. (Fo.7; Nec; 113; 77; 109; 91; AHSJ.42/295).
BLYDE, Ignatius. Priest.
　b. March 25th, 1720, ?Yorkshire. ?s. of Ignatius and Anne of
Peniston. e. St Omers College c.1754-6. S.J. September 7th, 1756.
Liège (phil and nov) 1757, 1758. Liège (theol) 1761. Ordained priest
c.1762. Residence of St George 1762. Ghent 1763. Doncaster 1764.
Ghent 1764, 1767-9. Liège 1771-3, 1776, 1781, 1783. d. September 1st
or 17th, 1788, Liège. (Fo.7; CRS.69; CRS.12/30; 113; 3 f.37; 64 p.421;
65; 90 f.54; 91; 114; 117).
BLYDE, John. Laybrother.
　b. April 3rd, 1715, Yorkshire. S.J. September 7th, 1760. Watten
(nov) 1761. Bruges College 1763, 1764. Watten 1767. Bruges College
1768, 1769, 1771-3. Antwerp 1774. d. May 10th or 12th, 1787,

Derbyshire. (Fo.7; AHSJ.42/295; Nec; CRS.12/28; 113; 15 f.12; 16 f.98; 91).

BLYDE, Joseph. Laybrother.
b. March 29th, 1725, Yorkshire. S.J. May 11th or 28th, 1755. Watten (nov) 1755. St Omers College 1756-8, 1761. Bruges College 1763, 1764, 1767, 1768, 1769, 1771-3. Wardour Castle 1773-92. d. November 3rd, 1792, Wardour. (Fo.7; CRS.Mon.1/180; CRS.12/40; 113; 111; 16 ff.12v, 98; Nec).

BOARMAN, Charles. ?Scholastic.
b. February 25th, 1751, Maryland. br. of John and Sylvester.
e. Bruges College c.1762-8. S.J. September 7th, 1770-? Ghent (nov) 1771, 1772. Liège (phil) 1773. To Maryland 1773. No evidence has come to light that he was ever ordained. (Fo.7; AHSJ.42/292; Hu.Text II 703; 113; CRS.69; 51 f.304. For writings see Som.).

BOARMAN, John. Priest.
b. January 27th, 1743, Maryland. br. of Charles and Sylvester. e. St Omers College 1752-62. S.J. September 7th, 1762. Watten (nov) 1763, 1764. Liège (theol) 1767, 1768. Ordained priest 1769. Sheffield 1769. (?Boulsterstone). Liège 1771-3. Maryland 1773. d.1797, Newtown, Maryland. (Fo.7; CRS.69; Hu.Text II 699; 113; 7 f.11; 51 f.304; 53 f.3; 65; 68 pp.375-6; 117).

BOARMAN, Sylvester. Priest.
b. November 7th, 1746, Maryland. br. of Charles and John. e. Bruges College c.1764-5. S.J. September 7th, 1765. Liège (phil) 1767, 1768, 1769. Liège (theol) 1771, 1772, 1773. Ghent 1773. Ordained priest 1772. Maryland 1774-his death. d.1811 or 1812, Newport. (Fo.7; CRS.69; AHSJ.42/293n; Hu.Text II 699; CRS.12/115; 113; 117; 16 ff. 22, 36; 4 f.63v).

BODENHAM, John *alias* Stanley. Priest.
b.1689, 1690 or January 8th, 1691, Herefordshire. s. of John and Mary (Trinder) of Rotherwas, Hereforshire. e. St Omers College ?-1707, S.C. Douay (phil) 1707-9. S.J. July 29th, 1709. Watten (nov) 1710, 1711. Liège (theol) 1712, 1713, 1714. Ordained priest c.1714. Ghent (tert) 1715. College of St Ignatius 1718. College of St Francis Xavier 1720. Burton Park 1721. College of St Francis Xavier 1724-40 (Rector 1724-34. At Courtfield 1724-40. Rector again 1739-40). Watten (Rector) 1740-1. College of St Francis Xavier 1742-50 (Courtfield. Rector 1746-50). College of St Aloysius 1750 (Rector. At Croxteth). d. October 29th, 1750, Croxteth. bu. Sefton. (Fo.7; CRS.69; RH.13/116; HMC.10th Report App.4/184-5, 198; Nec; Gil.5/61; CRS.22/307, 312; RSC.66; 113; 150 III (2) 25/7/39, 16/7/40; 85; 89; 91; 114; 156 App.1).

BODNAM see Lazenby, John.

BOELMANS, Lambert. Priest.
b.1649, Maastricht. S.J. September 9th, 1672. Watten (nov) 1673. Liège (phil) 1674. Liège (theol) 1674-8. Ordained priest April 9th, 1678. Watten 1679. College of St Ignatius 1680-3. Ghent 1684. Residence of

St Mary 1685. College of St Ignatius 1686. College of St Thomas of
Canterbury 1687, 1689. d.April 15th, 1690, London. (Fo.7; Nec; 113;
114; 140 n.45; 168 f.78).

BOERGUINION or BOURGIGNON, Giles. Laybrother novice.
S.J. September 7th, 1672. Watten (nov) 1672. d. September 10th,
1673, Watten. (Fo.7; Nec; 113; 114; 193, Anglia 34/794).

BOIS, de see Kingsley, Thomas.

BOLNEY, Richard. Scholastic.
b.1660, Hampshire. S.J. September 7th, 1678. Watten (nov) 1679.
Liège (phil) 1680-2. St Omers College 1683. Liège (theol) 1684. d. June
29th, 1685, Liège. (Fo.7; Nec; 113; 114).

BOLTON, John. Priest.
b. October 22nd, 1742. S.J. September 7th, 1761. Liège (phil) 1763,
1764. Bruges College 1766. Liège (theol) 1767-9. Ordained priest
c.1769. Ghent 1770. Maryland 1771-1809. d.September 9th, 1809,
Newtown, Maryland. (Fo.7; CRS.12/107; Hu.Text II 698; Nec; 113;
114; 4 ff.63v, 112v; 68 p.195; 77; 7 f.165v; 6 f.275).

BOONE, Edward. Priest.
b.1734, Maryland. s. of John. br. of John. e. St Omers College
c.1749-56. S.J. September 7th, 1756. Watten (nov) 1757, 1758. Liège
(theol) 1761, 1763, 1764. Ordained priest c.1764. Ghent 1764. Danby
1764-85. d. August 22nd, 1785, Danby. (Fo.7; CRS.69; Pa 2/28;
CRS.12/26; CRS.13/230, 237, 241, 249; Nec; 113; 65; 90 f.175; 155 II
n.127; 167 p.38; 117).

BOONE, John. Priest.
b.1735, Maryland. s. of John. br. of Edward. e. St Omers College
1749-56. S.J. September 7th, 1756. Watten (nov) 1757, 1758. Liège
(theol) 1761. Ordained priest c.1762. Stonyhurst 1763, 1764. Maryland
1765-70. Bruges College 1771. Ghent 1772, 1773. Burton Park 1774,
1775. Walton Hall ?1775-? Maryland 1784-95. d. April 27th, 1795,
Maryland. (Fo.7; CRS.69; RH.13/118; CRS.12/53; CRS.22/309,
318-9; Hu.Text II 686; 113; 4 f.20; 7 f.149v; 21 v.2; 76; 68 p.197; 80; 90
f.181; 155 II n.127; 92; 119 ff.18, 21, 23; 117).

?BOONE, Joseph. ?Priest.
b. Maryland. ?s. of Henry. ?cousin of Edward and John. ?S.J. Liège
1776. ?Priest. d. March 19th, 1779, Liège. (Fo.7 s.v.Boone, John; 90
f.54. Hu.Docs.I 661 n.51, 721 n.5, Hu.Text II 701).

BOOTH see Helsam, Richard.

BOOTH, Charles *alias* Brown. Priest.
b. September 8th, 1707, St Germain. br. or uncle of Ralph. e. St
Omers College c.1715-24. S.J. September 7th, 1724. Watten (nov)
1725, 1726. Liège (phil) 1727, 1728. Liège (theol) 1730. Ordained priest
c.1731. Ghent (tert) 1733. Residence of St John 1734-41. Loretto
1742-4, 1746. Weston 1747. Residence of St Mary 1748-50, 1752-4
(Tusmore 1752). In France and travelling 1755-8. Loretto 1761. E.C.
Rome 1762-6 (Rector). Antwerp 1767-9. Bruges School 1771. Liège
1772. Burton Park 1772-3. ?Wardour 1775. Wardour 1779-83.

Bonham 1783-5. Wardour 1785-97. d. March 11th, 1797, Wardour. bu.
Wardour chapel. (Fo.7; CRS.69; Ki.30; RH.13/117-8;
CRS.Mon.1/162-3, 174, 212; WR.20/62; HMC.10th Report,
App.4/184; CRS.12/57; CRS.22/308, 318; Nec; 113; 150 III (2)
9/12/41, 17/3/42; 13 f.198; 15 ff.10v, 11; 44 ff.119, 121-2, 235v, 305v;
47 f.187; 76; 91; 114; 20 f.98).

BOOTH, Ralph *alias* Sims. Priest.
     b. April 21st, 1721, St Germain. br. or nephew of Charles. e. St
Omers College ?-1737. S.J. September 7th, 1737. Watten (nov) 1738.
Liège (phil) 1739-41. Pont-à-Mousson (theol) 1743, 1744. Liège 1746.
Ordained priest c.1747. Ghent (tert) 1747-8. St Omers College 1748.
Watten 1749. College of St Francis Xavier 1750. Paris 1752. Watten
1753, 1754. College of St Ignatius 1754-8, 1763, 1764 (St Stephen's
Canterbury 1758). Bruges 1765. Liège 1767-9, 1771-3, 1776. d.
November 19th, 1780, Liège. (Fo.7; CRS.69; Ki.31; 188 n.117;
CRS.12/20; Nec; 113; 65; 68 p.253; 90 f.54; 114; 117; 91).

BOUCHEL(L) or BOUSHEL (L), Benedict or Louis. Scholastic.
     b. December 14th, 1737. From Belgium. S.J. September 7th, 1755.
Watten (nov) 1756. Liège (phil) 1757, 1758. Liège (theol) 1761. Left
1763, not ordained. (113; 91).

BOUCHER or BOUCHIER, Richard. Priest.
     b. August or October 17th, 1696, London. br. of William. S.J.
September 7th, 1713. Watten (nov) 1714. Liège (phil) 1715, 1716, 1718.
St Omers College 1720, 1723, 1724. Liège (theol) 1725-27. Ordained
priest c.1727. St Omers College 1728, 1730. Ghent 1731. Residence of
St Stanislaus 1731, 1733-40, 1742-44, 1746-58 (Superior 1733-58. At
Arlington 1730, 1751, 1758 and probably 1730-60). d. December 18th,
1760, Arlington. bu. Arlington parish churchyard. (Fo.7; HMC.10th
Report App.4/188; 01.244; Nec; 47 f.44; 64 pp.227, 267; 74; 91; 113; 51
f.311; 114).

BOUCHER or BOUCHIER, William *alias* Rozier. Priest.
     b. July 14th, 1682, Worcestershire. br. of Richard. e. St Omers
College c.1695-1700. Watten (nov) 1701. Liège (phil) 1703, 1704, 1705.
Liège (theol) 1706, 1708. Ordained priest c.1709. St Omers College
1710. Ghent (tert) 1711. Liège 1712-6, 1718, 1720, 1723. St Omers
College 1724. Residence of St George 1725 (Hill End 1725, 1727). St
Omers College 1728. Residence of St Michael ?-1731. Aston 1731-5.
Residence of St Stanislaus 1736. Lulworth 1737-57. (Rector of the
College of St Thomas c.1750-c.56) d. September 28th, 1757,
?Lulworth. (Fo.7; CRS.69; CRS.Mon.1/164; SCH.3/6; CRS.13/188;
WR.20/50; CRS.6/365; HMC.10th Report App.1/184; 01.245; Nec;
113; 44 ff.216v, 250-2, 255-6, 258-62, 266v; 64 pp.94, 258; 66; 91; 121).

BOUILLION, Arnold. Laybrother.
     b.1680 or 1683, Liège. S.J. December 31st, 1711. Watten (nov) 1712,
1713. St Omers College 1714-6, 1718, 1720, 1723-8, 1730, 1733-8. d.
June 1st, 1740, St Omers College. (Fo.7; CRS.62; Nec; 113; 91; 114).

BOULOGNE or BOULONGNE, Peter. Priest.

b. November 2nd, 1801, Bouchoir, Somme, France. S.J. September 11th, 1824 in France. Bengal mission 1844-6. d. September 20th, 1856, French Guyana. (113; CDSJ).

BOULT or BOLT, Henry *alias* McIntosh. Priest.

b. March 25th, 1670, Warwickshire. S.J. September 10th, 1691, Paris. Liège (theol) 1699, 1700. Ordained priest c.1699. Ghent (tert) 1701. Watten 1703-6. Loretto 1707-11. Residence of St George 1712-34 (Spetchley 1725-34 and probably from 1712. Superior c.1723-34). Liège 1734-7 (Rector). Provincial 1737-40. Liège 1740-3 (Rector). d. February 9th, 1743, Liège. (Fo.7; RH.1/47; WR.20/71, 30/12; Nec; 113; 114; 150 III (1) 1/5/06, III (2) 5/6/34, 22/6/37; 9 n.284; 74; 91).

BOURDEAUX, Nicholas or Joseph. Laybrother.

b.1677, Liège. S.J. October 22nd, 1707. Watten (nov) 1708. Maryland 1710-18. d. July, 1718, Maryland. (Fo.7; Nec; Hu.Text II 685; 113).

BOURGEOIS see Beeston, James.

BOURGIGNON see Boerguinion, Giles.

BOURNIER, John. Laybrother.

b. September 29th, 1759, Salines, Jura, France. S.J. September 7th, 1806. Hodder (nov) 1806-8. Hodder 1809. Stonyhurst 1809-12. Hodder 1809-38. d. January 10th, 1838, Hodder. bu. Stonyhurst. (Fo.7; Nec; CDSJ; 113; 114; 115).

BOUVART see Bavart.

BOYLE, Richard. Priest.

b. July 5th, 1806, London. e. Stonyhurst 1818-? S.J. September 3rd, 1825-46. Montrouge (nov) 1825, 1826. Dôle (phil) 1827. Aix (phil) 1828. Stonyhurst (theol) 1829-33. Ordained priest September 21st, 1833. Hereford 1833-41. Portico 1841. Broughton 1841-5. Hodder (tert) 1845. Enfield 1846. (113; WR.34/27; 117; CG. For writings see Sut.Som.).

BRACEY, Edmund. Priest.

b. April 5th, 1709, ?Beoley, Worcestershire. s. of Edmund. e. St Omers College c.1724-30. S.J. September 7th, 1730. Liège (phil) 1733, 1734. Liège (theol) 1735, 1736, 1737, 1738. Ordained priest April 5th, 1738. Ghent (tert?) 1738-9. Residence of St George 1739-40, 1742-4, 1746-50, 1752-8, 1763-4 (Superior 1748-53. At Beoley 1743, 1748, 1751, 1752; probably from 1739-64). Beoley 1767-9, 1771-3, 1776 (probably 1764-82). d. July 28th, 1782, ?Beoley. (Fo.7; Ki.33; E and P.294; HMC.10th Report App.4/183, 184-5, 197-8; SCH.12/19; WR.5/14, 7/2; 21 v.2; CRS.12/22; 113; 114; 64 p.352; 74; 91; 117).

BRADSHAW see Billinge, Richard.

BRADY, Joseph. Laybrother.

b. April 14th, 1802, Castlebury, Louth, Ireland. S.J. December 27th, 1827. Hodder (nov) 1827-9. St Mary's Hall 1830-43. Bengal mission 1843-7. Madura mission (French) 1847-75. d. March 6th, 1875, Negapatam, Madura mission. (Fo.7; CDSJ; 113; 115; 116. For writings see Som.).

BRAND see Pracid, Jeremiah.

BRAY or BRACEY, James *alias* Yeatman. Scholastic.
  b.1665, Scotland. e. St Omers College ?-1685. S.J. September 7th,
  1685. Watten (nov) 1685, 1686. d. March 12th, 1686, Watten. (Fo.7;
  CRS.69; Nec; 113; 114).

BRAYLSFORD see Newton, William (I).

BREADNALL see Beadnall.

BREBION, Francis. Laybrother.
  b. May 17th, 1629, Boulogne-sur-Mer. br. of John and Philip. S.J.
  August 10th, 1656. Watten (nov) 1656-58. St Omers College 1659-61,
  1663-5, 1669, 1672-6, 1678-81. Liège 1682-7. St Omers College 1689-94.
  d. February 9th, 1694, St Omers College. (Fo.7; Nec; 113; 114).

BREBION, John. Laybrother.
  b.1625, Boulogne-sur-Mer. br. of Francis and Philip. S.J. April
  12th, 1659. Watten (nov) 1659, 1660. Rome 1661, 1663-65, 1667, 1676,
  1678. d. probably in Rome, date not recorded. (Fo.7; 113).

BREBION, Philip. Laybrother.
  b. December 30th, 1630, Boulogne-sur-Mer. br. of Francis and
  John. S.J. September 2nd, 1653. Watten (nov) 1653-5. Liège 1656-8.
  Ghent 1659-61, 1663. Paris 1664, 1667. Antwerp 1672-9. Liège 1680-2.
  Socius to the provincial 1683. Liège 1684-5. Ghent 1686-7. In England
  1688. Ghent 1689. St Omers College 1689. Ghent 1690. St Omers
  College 1691-2. Watten 1693. Paris 1696-7, 1699-1701. Liège 1703. d.
  July 31st, 1703, Liège. (Fo.7; Nec; 113; 114; 170 f.144; 108).

BRECHTEL, George. Laybrother.
  b. in Switzerland. S.J. (date not recorded). E.C. Rome 1751-8. d.
  February 10th, 1763, Rome or Monte Porzio. (Fo.7; Nec; 113; 114; 12
  ff.188v ff.).

BREDA, Joseph (?van Breda). Laybrother.
  b. March 2nd, 1726, ?Eindhoven, Holland. S.J. November 7th,
  1754. Watten 1757. St Omers College 1758, 1761. Bruges College 1764,
  1767-9, 1771-3. Liège Academy 1774, 1776, 1781, 1783. d. after 1801,
  date and place not recorded. (Fo.7; AHSJ.42/296; 113; 3 ff.41, 55; 15
  f.12; 16 ff.12v, 98; 90 f.54).

BRENNAN or BRENAN, Thomas. Priest.
  b. December 12th, 1708 or January 2nd, 1709, Dublin. S.J. January
  2nd, 1726, Rome. To English province c.1765. Barlborough 1767-9,
  1771-3 (Rector of the College of the Immaculate Conception 1769-71).
  d. October 3rd, 1776, Derbyshire. (Fo.7; 113; 117; 63 ff.266, 268v;
  SCH.12/18).

BRENT see Aspinall, Henry, Joseph and Thomas; van Parys, John; Pracid,
  Jeremiah.

BRETT, Robert. Priest.
  b.1636, Somerset. s. of Sir Robert of Whitestaunton. S.J. September
  7th, 1657. Watten (nov) 1658. Liège (phil) 1659, 1660. Ghent 1661.
  Liège (theol) 1663, 1664, 1665, 1667. Ordained priest c.1667. Residence
  of St Stanislaus 1669, 1672, 1673. St Omers College 1674-6, 1678. d.

November 3rd, 1678, St Omers College. (Fo.7; Nec; 113;
VCH.Somerset, IV 233; 114).

BRETT, Thomas.
b.1648, London. S.J. 1667. No further information found. (Fo.7).

BREWER, John. Priest.
b. December 29th, 1732, Fishwick, near Preston. s. of John. br. of
Thomas. e. St Omers College 1746-52. S.J. September 7th, 1752.
Watten (nov) 1754. Liège (theol) 1756-8, 1761. Ordained priest c.1761.
Ghent 1763. Wardour 1764. Odstock 1764-5. Shepton Mallet 1765-97.
d. September 1st or 2nd, 1797, Shepton Mallet. bu. St Joseph's,
Bristol. (Fo.7; Nec; CRS.69; CRS.Mon.1/157, 165; Ki.33; HMC.10th
Report App.4/189; CRS.16/575; 01.246; 113; 114; 117; 34 ff.135-6,
138; 44 f.270; 65; 125; 119 f.14).

BREWER, Thomas. Priest.
b. June 19th, 1743. s. of John of Fishwick. br. of John. e. St Omers
College c. 1755-61. S.J. September 7th, 1761. Liège (phil) 1763, 1764.
Bruges School 1767-9. Ordained priest c.1771. Bruges College 1771.
Ghent 1772. Lydiate and Fazackerley 1772-80. Bristol 1780-7. d. April
16th or 18th, 1787, Bristol. (Fo.7; CRS.69; Ki.34; Gib.1/291;
CRS.3/81; CRS.12/28; CRS.16/375; 01.247; Nec; 32 f.115; 113; 21
v.2; 23 f.245; 27 f.216v; 32 n.57v; 76; 25 ff.22, 30, 37, 46, 61; 80; 94
ff.233-4; 155 III 185c; 105; 125; 119 f.23; 114).

BREWSTER, William or Francis. Priest.
b. October 10th, 1700, London. e. St Omers College c.1720. S.J.
September 7th, 1724. Watten (nov) 1725, 1726. Liège (phil) 1727, 1728.
Lyons (phil) 1728. Lyons (theol) 1730. Ordained priest c.1730. In
England 1733. Residence of St George 1734-9 (?Grafton). College of St
Ignatius 1740. Residence of St George 1741. College of St Ignatius
1743-7 (?Hales Place). Norwich c.1747-58. d. October 31st, 1758,
Norwich. (Fo.7; CRS.69; NA.37/158; HMC.10th Report App.4/184;
Nec; 113; 70 f.75; 13 f.37v; 43 ff.71v, 74v; 64 p.394; 40 pp.90, 92, 96;
91; 114).

BRIAN or BRIANT see Crane, William; O'Brien, John and Peter.

BRIDGE, John Brice. Priest.
b. November 2nd, 1793, Liverpool. e. Stonyhurst 1810-4. S.J.
September 7th, 1814. Hodder (nov) 1814-6. Stonyhurst (phil and theol)
1816-9. Ordained priest July, 1819, Dublin. Norwich 1819-22. New
Hall 1822-37. St Mary's Hall 1837-41 (supplied at Chipping 1840).
Stonyhurst 1841-2. Allerton Park (Stourton) 1842-60 (Rector of
College of St Michael 1849-60). d. February 20th, 1860, Allerton. bu.
Allerton. (Fo.7; NA.37/159; ER.5/97; 115; CRS.36/4; New H. 174;
Nec; 94 f.324. For writings see Som.).

BRIGHAM, Charles. Scholastic.
b. March 6th, 1802, Manchester. e. Stonyhurst 1814-? S.J.
September 7th, 1820. Hodder (nov) 1820. Rome (nov) 1821. Ferrara
(phil) 1822-4. Stonyhurst 1824. Paris (theol) 1825. Fribourg and Dôle
(theol) 1826-7. Stonyhurst 1827. Left not ordained, 1828. (2; 115; Stol).

BRIGHAM, Henry. Priest.

b. June 23rd, 1796, Manchester. e. Stonyhurst 1808-13. S.J. September 7th, 1813. Hodder (nov) 1813-5. Stonyhurst (phil) 1815-7. Stonyhurst 1817-8. Clongowes (theol) 1818-22. Ordained priest June 1st, 1822, Maynooth. Stonyhurst 1822-7. Hereford 1827-33. Hodder (tert) 1833-4. Preston 1834-6. Bury St Edmunds 1836-45. (Superior of College of Holy Apostles 1842-5). Stonyhurst 1845-7. Pontefract 1847-9. Oxford 1849-55. Teignmouth 1855-7. Ugbrooke 1857-60. Clitheroe 1860-5. Beaumont College 1865-81. d. May 26th, 1881, Beaumont. bu. Beaumont. (Fo.7; 01.248; 42 f.247; Stol; Nec; 115; 116).

BRINKHURST see Meara, George and William.

BROCKHOLES, Charles. Priest.

b.1684, Lancashire. s. of John and Anne (Barcroft) of Claughton. e. St Omers College 1700-05. S.J. September 7th, 1705. Watten (nov) 1706. Liège (phil) 1708, 1710. Liège (theol) 1711-3. Ordained priest c.1713. Maryland 1714-6-? St Omers College 1719, 1720, 1723. Ghent 1724. College of St Aloysius 1725. Croston 1728. Blackrod and Wigan c.1729-59. d. February 20th, 1759, Wigan. bu. Wigan. (Fo.7; CRS.62; CRS.69; HMC.10th Report App.4/184, 189; Hu.Text II 686; CRS.20/270; CRS.25/113; Nec; 113; 114; 21 v.2; 24 ff.6, 347v; 28 ff.195, 204, 271; 84; 85; 86; 91; 156 App.1; 158; 119 ff.3, 5, 8, 10, 12, 14, 16).

BROMFIELD, Laurence. Laybrother.

d. St Omers College, date not recorded. (Fo.7; Nec; 114).

BROOKE, Charles. Priest.

b. August 8th, 1777, Exeter. s. of James and Sarah (Hoare). e. Liège Academy 1788-92. Liège (phil) 1792-4. Stonyhurst (theol) 1794-8. Stonyhurst 1798-1822. Ordained priest June 12th, 1802, Maynooth. S.J. September 26th, 1803. Enfield 1822-6 (supplied from 1817). Provinicial 1826-32. Socius to the provincial 1832-4. St Mary's Hall 1834-8 (Rector). Stonyhurst 1838-42. Ireland 1842-3. Rector of College of St Aloysius 1842-4. Stonyhurst 1844-5. Exeter 1845-52. d. October 6th, 1852, Exeter. bu. St Nicholas' chapel, Exeter. (Fo.7; Chad.392; CRS.36/218; 01.249; 115; 113; 150 March 1829; 6 f.23; 11 ff.263v, 280v, 292v; DNB; 15 f.277; 24 f.73; 90 f.145v, 146v; 93 p.35. For writings see Sut.Som.).

BROOKE, Ignatius (1). Priest.

b.1671, Maryland. s. of Thomas. br. of Matthew and Robert. ?uncle of Ignatius (2) and Leonard. e. ?St Omers College ?-1692. E.C. Valladolid 1692-9. Ordained priest March 7th, 1696. S.J. July 24th, 1699. Watten (nov) 1699, 1700. E.C. Valladolid 1701-8. Watten 1710, 1711. College of the Immaculate Conception 1711-6, 1718. Residence of St Mary 1720. College of the Immaculate Conception 1723-c.35 (Rector 1728-35. At Boulsterstone near Sheffield serving Stannington c.1724-c.1733). College of St Thomas of Canterbury 1735-c.41 (Stapehill 1735. Canford 1738. ?Ladyholt 1741). Residence of St Mary

1743-7 (Superior 1743-c.47). Watten 1749. St Omers College 1750-1. d.
March 10th, 1751, St Omers College. (Fo.7; CRS.69; Ans.3/26;
CRS.44/12; Bur.1/48; CRS.25/112; CRS.30/xxxiv, 178; CRS.32/309;
Nec; 91; 113; 150 III (2) 1/5/28; 44 f.249; 156 xxx; 123 B f.360; 126).

BROOKE, Ignatius (2). Priest.
b. April 21st, 1751, Maryland. ? s. of Leonard. ?br. of Leonard.
?nephew of Ignatius (1), Matthew and Robert. S.J. September 7th,
1770. Ghent (nov) 1771, 1772. Liège 1773. Maryland 1773. Ordained
priest. d. after 1815, Maryland. (Fo.7; AHSJ.42/293, 309; Hu.Text
2/701; 113; 51 f.307).

BROOKE, Leonard. Priest.
b. January 14th, 1750, Maryland. ? s. of Leonard. ?br. of Ignatius
(2). ?nephew of Ignatius (1), Matthew and Robert. e. Bruges College
1763-9. S.J. September 7th, 1769. Ghent (nov) 1771. Liège (phil) 1772.
Liège (theol) 1773. Ordained priest. Slindon 1787-93. Lulworth
1793-1813. d. July 7th, 1813, Lulworth. bu. Lulworth. (Fo.7; CRS.69;
CRS.6/307; CRS.7/356, 361-3, 381; AHSJ.42/308; 01.251; 113; 13
ff.247, 292, 375v; 21 v.2; 51 ff.165, 307v; 53 f.51; 72).

BROOKE, Matthew. Priest.
b.1672, Maryland. s. of Thomas. br. of Ignatius (1) and Robert.
?uncle of Ignatius (2) and Leonard. e. ?St Omers College ?-1692. E.C.
Valladolid 1692-9. Ordained priest March 2nd, 1697. S.J. July 30th,
1699. Watten (nov) 1699. Liège 1701. Maryland 1703. d. Portobacco,
Maryland, 1705. (Fo.7; CRS.30/178; Ans.3/26; CRS.29/160; Hu.Text
II 75, 684; 113).

BROOKE, Richard. Scholastic.
b.1639, Hampshire. e. St Omers College 1651 or earlier—56. S.J.
September 7th, 1656. Watten (nov) 1656, 1657. Liège (phil) 1658, 1659,
1660. Liège (theol) 1661, 1663. Left 1663, not ordained. (Fo.7; CRS.69;
113; 150 II (2) Sept.1662).

BROOKE, Robert. Priest.
b. October 24th, 1663, Maryland. s. of Thomas. br. of Ignatius (1)
and Matthew. ?uncle of Ignatius (2) and Leonard. e. St Omers College
?-c.1683, S.J. September 7th, 1684. Watten (nov) 1684, 1685. Liège
(phil) 1686, 1687. Liège (theol) 1689, 1691-3. Ordained priest c.1692.
Military chaplain at Bruges 1694. Kelvedon c.1695. Maryland 1696-7,
1699-1701, 1703-6, 1708-14. (Superior 1708-12). d. April or July 18th,
1714, Newtown, Maryland. (Fo.7; CRS.69; Nec; Hu.Text II 683; 113;
114; 43 f.24).

BROOKE or BROOKES, Thomas. Priest.
b. July 6th, 1678 or 1679, Sussex or Rutland. s. of Thomas. e. St
Omers College ?-1692 or 1694. E.C. Valladolid 1692 or 1694-1701.
Ordained priest c.1700. S.J. June 10th, 1701. Watten (nov) 1703. Liège
1704. College of St Chad 1705. College of St Francis Xavier 1706.
College of St Chad 1708-12. College of St Francis Xavier 1712-6, 1718,
1720. Residence of St Mary 1724-37 (Tusmore c.1727). Giffords Hall
1738. Liège 1738-39. College of the Holy Apostles 1740. College of St

Thomas of Canterbury 1741, 1743-4, 1746-7. Residence of St George
1749, 1750. Tusmore and Waterperry 1750. Wootton 1750. Odstock
1752. College of the Holy Apostles 1753-4. College of St Thomas of
Canterbury 1755. College of St Ignatius 1756-8. d. March 6th, 1761,
Ghent. (Fo.7; CRS.69; CRS.30/179; CRS.Mon.1/164; Ans.3/27;
CRS.7/391, 399; 113; 114; 91; 44 f.263; 43 ff.61v, 63v; 64 pp.255, 256,
384; HMC.10th Report App.4/184; 111; CRS.13/181; 51 f.311).

BROOS, James. Laybrother.
    b.1633, Flanders. S.J. October 24th, 1655. Watten (nov) 1656, 1657,
    1658-60. Ghent 1661. Liège 1663-5, 1667, 1669. Watten 1672-6,
    1678-84. d. October 1st, 1684, Watten. (Fo.7; 113; 114).

BROWN, Andrew. Laybrother.
    b.1673, Norfolk. S.J. July 30th, 1697. Watten (nov) 1697. St Omers
    College 1699. Watten 1700-01. St Omers College 1703. d. April 26th,
    1703, St Omers College. (Fo.7; 113; 114).

BROWN or BROWNE, Edward. Priest.
    b. December 3rd, 1743, Antigua. e. Arras Jesuit College. S.J. July
    15th, 1767. phil and one year's theol studied before entry. Ghent (nov)
    1767. Liège (nov and theol) 1768, 1769. Ordained priest ?1770. d.
    December 7th, 1770, Liège. (Fo.7; 113; 114; 91; New H. 65-6).

BROWN or BROWNE, George *alias* Pippard. Priest.
    b. April 7th, 1670, Lancashire. S.J. October 7th, 1688. Watten (nov)
    1689. Liège (phil) 1691, 1692, 1693. Liège (theol) 1696. Ordained priest
    1696. St Omers College 1698. Travelling 1699, 1700, 1701. Residence of
    St John 1701, 1703-4 (Gateshead ?1701). Residence of St George 1705.
    Residence of St John 1706, 1708-16, 1720, 1723-c.30 (Gateshead or
    Haggerston ?-1714, 1724, 1725. Croxdale 1725-6. Gateshead 1727).
    Travelling 1734 (perhaps from 1727). d. May 4th, 1735, Pontoise.
    (Fo.7; CRS.8/242, 400; CRS.35/200; 113; 114; 36 f.264; 89; 91; 161
    f.146; 162. For writings see Som.).

BROWN, Ignatius. ?Priest.
    b. ?Waterford, Ireland. e. St Omers College ?-1679. S.J. 1679. Milan
    (nov) 1679. Genoa 1682-4. ?Ordained priest. ?To Irish mission. d.
    ?between 1698 and 1714 in Spain. (Fo.7; Fo.7 Irish list p.58; 168 f.79v;
    113; CRS.69).

BROWN, Joseph. Scholastic.
    b. June 13th, 1807, Bindon, Dorset. e. Stonyhurst 1822-? S.J.
    September 7th, 1828. Hodder (nov) 1828. St Mary's Hall (phil) 1830.
    Left 1831, not ordained. (115; 113; Stol).

BROWN, Levinius. Priest.
    b. September 9th, 1671, Norfolk. s. of Richard and Mary. e. St
    Omers College ?-1691. E.C. Rome 1691-8. Ordained priest June 16th,
    1696. S.J. October 23rd, 1698. Watten (nov) 1699. Liège 1700. College
    of St Thomas of Canterbury 1701, 1703-6, 1708-16, 1718, 1720 (Rector
    1715-c.20. At Ladyholt c.1701, 1706, 1707). E.C. Rome 1723-9
    (Rector). Watten 1730-3 (Rector 1731-3). Provincial 1733-7. Liège
    1737-40 (Rector). St Omers College 1740-1, 1743-4, 1746-58, 1761-4. d.

November 7th, 1764, St Omers College. (Fo.7; CRS.69; Ki.36;
Ans.3/27; CRS.44/112; Chad.270, 304; Gil.1/322; CRS.40/12; Nec;
91; 113; 150 III (2) July 1722, 30/6/29; 9 nn.166, 169, 297; 44 ff.150,
162; 170 f.5v; 123 IIIB f.360; 111; 114; 125. For writings see Som.).

BROWN, Thomas. Laybrother.
b. January 15th, 1745, place not recorded. S.J. August 30th, 1764.
Not a member of the English province. E.C. Rome 1772. Nothing
further on record. (Fo.7 pp.95, 954).

BROWN see Booth, Charles; Busby, George and John; Le Maitre, Charles;
Musson, Samuel.

BROWNBILL, Francis. Priest.
b. November 5th, 1793, Gillmoss, Lancashire. s. of George and
Margaret (Spenser). br. of James (2) and Thomas. e. Stonyhurst
1807-13. S.J. September 7th, 1813. Hodder (nov) 1813-5. Stonyhurst
(phil and theol) 1815-9. Ordained priest December 1819, Dublin.
Stonyhurst 1820-6. London 1826. Stonyhurst 1826-32. Hodder (tert)
1832. Stockeld Park 1832-8. (Superior, Residence of St Michael
1835-8). Worcester 1838-42. (Superior, Residence of St George
1839-42). Stonyhurst 1842-7. St Mary's Hall 1847-8. New Hall 1848-63.
London 1863. Exeter 1863. Hodder 1864-8 (Superior). Lincoln 1868-9.
Skipton 1869-72. Accrington 1872-3. Stonyhurst 1873-5. d. May 13th,
1875, Stonyhurst. bu. Stonyhurst. (Fo.7; Stol; Nec; CRS.6/183; 115).

BROWNBILL, James (1). Scholastic.
From Lancashire ? e. St Omers College c.1736-40. S.J. 1740. Watten
(nov) 1740, 1741. Liège (phil ?) 1743. Left 1748, not ordained. (Fo.7;
CRS.69; 113; 150 III (2)27/7/43, 27/4/43).

BROWNBILL, James (2). Priest.
b. July 31st, 1798, Gillmoss, Lancashire. s. of George and Margaret
(Spenser). br. of Francis and Thomas. e. Stonyhurst 1808-15. S.J.
September 7th, 1815. Hodder (nov) 1815-17. Stonyhurst (including phil
and theol) 1819-30. Ordained priest July 30th, 1829, Stonyhurst.
Ugbrooke 1830-5. Hodder (tert) 1835. St Mary's Hall 1835. Stonyhurst
1836-9 (Rector). Worcester 1840. Leigh 1840. London 1841-54
(Superior 1841-54). Bury St Edmunds 1855-65. London 1867-9.
Bournemouth 1869-71. Bury St Edmunds 1871-3. New Hall 1873-80. d.
January 14th, 1880, New Hall. bu. New Hall. (Fo.7; 115; CRS.6/183;
Nec).

BROWNBILL, Thomas. Priest.
b. December 25th, 1788, Gillmoss, Lancashire. s. of George and
Margaret (Spenser). br. of Francis and James (2). e. Stonyhurst 1802-6.
S.J. September 7th, 1806. Hodder (nov) 1806-8. Stonyhurst (phil and
theol) 1808-11. Hodder 1811-3. Ordained priest September 4th, 1813,
Stonyhurst. Hodder (supplied at Clitheroe) 1814-17. Stockeld Park
1817-27. Hodder 1827-42 (Superior). St Mary's Hall 1842-4 (Rector). d.
November 18th, 1844, St Mary's Hall. bu. Stonyhurst. (Fo.7; Stol;
CRS.6/183; 6/226v; 7/169; 115; 93 p.78).

BRUERTON, John *alias* Alison or Alanson. Priest.

b.1633, Shropshire. e. St Omers College 1647 or earlier-51. S.J.
September 7th, 1651. Watten (nov) 1651, 1652. Liège (phil) 1653, 1654,
1655. Liège (theol) 1656-59. Ordained priest, March 27th, 1660. St
Omers College 1660. Ghent (tert) 1661. Residence of St Dominic
1662-4, 1667. Residence of St Mary 1672-3, 1675. St Omers College
1675-6. Residence of St Mary 1678-83. College of St Ignatius 1683. d.
February 10th, 1684, in England. (Fo.7; CRS.69; 113; 114).

BRUNCHARD see White or Whyte, Henry.

BRUNE or BRUNET, Joseph. Laybrother.
b. April 8th, 1688 (possibly April 19th, 1674), Flanders. S.J. July 1st,
1708-17. Watten (nov) 1709, 1710, 1711, 1712. Ghent 1713, 1714.
Watten 1715, 1716. (113; 150 III (1) 22/6/15, 31/10/16, 27/2/17; 123 II
f.145).

BRUNEAU, Joseph. Priest.
b. October 28th, 1704. S.J. September 1721, Paris province. To
English province June 21st, 1768. Liège 1768-9, 1771-4. d. February
26th, 1774 ?Liège Academy. (91; 113; 117; 51 f.307).

BRUNETTI, Joseph. Priest.
b. July 25th, 1671, London. e. St Omers College ?-1689. S.J.
September 7th, 1689. Watten (nov) 1689, 1691. Liège (phil) 1692, 1693.
Liège (theol) 1696, 1697. Ordained priest 1698. Ghent (tert) 1699.
Residence of St George 1699, 1700, 1701, 1703 (Evelinch 1703 ?).
College of St Thomas of Canterbury 1704-6, 1708-10. Residence of St
George 1711-4. d. January 17th, 1716, Rotterdam. (Fo.7; 114; 113;
CRS.69; WR.20/71; Nec; 40 pp.8, 188).

BRUNING, Anthony (1) *alias* Hyde. Priest.
b.1636, Hampshire. s. of Anthony and Mary (Hyde) of Wymering.
?br. of Francis (1). e. St Omers College 1652-8. S.J. June 20th, 1660.
Watten (nov) 1660. Liège (phil) 1661, 1663-4. Liège (theol) 1664, 1665,
1667, 1669. Ordained priest March 31st, 1668. College of St Thomas of
Canterbury 1672. College of St Ignatius 1673-5. Liège 1676, 1678-80,
1682. Residence of St George 1683. Residence of St Michael 1684, 1685
(Superior). Liège 1686-7, 1689. Ghent 1691. College of St Thomas of
Canterbury 1691-3 (Slindon). College of St Ignatius 1696. College of
the Holy Apostles 1696-7, 1699-1701, 1703. College of St Ignatius 1704.
d. January 19th, 1704, London. (Fo.7; CRS.69; CRS.7/354; Nec; 113;
44 ff.134, 147v; 114; 43 ff.23v, 24, 24v, 25v, 26v, 27v).

BRUNING, Anthony (2). Priest.
b. December 7th, 1716, Hampshire. s. of George and Mary (Bryon)
of East Meon and Froxfield. Half-br. of Francis (2) and George. e. St
Omers College c.1726-33. S.J. September 7th, 1733. Watten (nov)
1734. Liège (phil) 1735-7. Liège (theol) 1738-41. Ordained priest
c.1741. Liège 1743-4, 1746. College of St Ignatius 1747. Travelling
1748. Liège 1749-50, 1752-8, 1761, 1763-4, 1767-9, 1771-5. d. August
8th, 1776, Liège Academy. (Fo.7; CRS.69; Gil.1/330; HMC.10th
Report App.4/184; DNB; Nec; 113; CRS.17/242, 244; 114; 150 III (2)
20/6/44; 74; 111. For writings see Som.).

BRUNING, Francis (1) *alias* Hyde and Grimsditch. Priest.
b.1648, Berkshire. ?s. of Anthony and Mary (Hyde). ?br. of
Anthony (1). e. St Omers College 1668 or earlier-70. S.J. September
7th, 1670. Liège (phil) 1672-5. Liège (theol) 1676, 1678. Ordained priest
October 9th, 1678. Ghent (tert) 1679. Hoogstraet 1680. College of the
Holy Apostles 1681-3. Residence of St Michael 1683-5 (Superior).
Residence of St John 1686-7, 1689-93, 1696-7, 1699-1701, 1703-14
(Superior 1708-11). d. November 23rd, 1714, in England. (Fo.7;
CRS.69; Nec; 113; 114; 168 f.86v; 43 ff.12, 14, 15).
BRUNING, Francis (2). Scholastic.
b.1732. s. of George and Anne (May) of East Meon and Froxfield,
Hampshire. br. of George. Half-br. of Anthony (2). e. St Omers
College c.1744-50. S.J. September 7th, 1750. Watten (nov) 1750. Liège
(phil) 1752. d. March 10th, 1753, Liège, not ordained. (Fo.7; CRS.69;
113; 114).
BRUNING, George. Priest.
b. September 19th, 1738, Hampshire. s. of George and Anne (May)
of East Meon and Froxfield. br. of Francis (2). Half-br. of Anthony
(2). e. St Omers College 1748-56. S.J. September 7th, 1756. Watten
(nov) 1757-8. Liège (theol) 1761, 1763-4. Ordained priest c.1763.
Britwell 1765, 1767-69, 1771. Southend 1772-80. Burton Park 1781-2.
Rotherwas 1783. ?Durham 1784. East Hendred c.1787-c.1796. ?Milton
c.1796-8. Isleworth 1798-1802. d. June 3rd or 5th, 1802, Isleworth. bu.
East Hendred. (Fo.7; CRS.69; RH.13/118; Gil.1/330; CRS.7/389;
CRS.13/292, 301; CRS.22/309, 319-20; DNB; 113; 13 ff.111, 135,
139v, 149, 155, 172, 176v, 201, 205, 207v, 221, 232; 44 ff.121-2, 164,
169, 182, 270, 277, 279; 114; Hen.241, 278; 35 f.232; LR.1/134;
War.II/181-2. For writings see Sut.Som.).
BRYON, Francis *alias* Plowden. Priest.
b. July 22nd or 23rd, 1725, Sussex. s. of Michael and Mary
(Tourner). e. St Omers College c.1739-42. S.J. September 7th, 1742-61.
Watten (nov) 1743. Liège (phil) 1744, 1746. Büren (theol) 1748, 1749.
Ordained priest c.1749. Ghent (tert) 1750. Rudge 1752. Residence of St
Michael 1752-4. London 1754. Haggerston 1754-5. Broughton 1755. St
Omers College 1755. Ghent 1755. Spinkhill 1756. Burton Park 1757.
Weston 1757. Ghent 1757, 1758. Culcheth 1758-9. (Fo.7; CRS.69;
LR.3/5; WR.20/62; HMC.10th Report App.4/184, 198; CRS.19/219;
113; 90 f.187; 91; 21 v.2; 64 pp.68, 265, 316, 420, 541, 545, 557; 65; 68
p.35; 35 f.50v; 109; 117; 119 f.8).
BUCK, John *alias* Parker. Priest.
b. February 11th, 1715, London. e. St Omers College c.1730-4. E.C.
Valladolid 1734-6. S.J. May 23rd 1736. Watten (nov) 1736, 1737. Liège
(phil) 1738. Liège (theol) 1739, 1740, 1741. Ordained priest c.1741.
Ghent (tert) 1743. Plowden Hall 1744-56. Alnwick 1756-70. d. January
13th, 1770, Alnwick. bu. Alnwick parish church. (Fo.7; CRS.69;
CRS.30/189; RH.10/165 ff; NCH.1/20; HMC.10th Report
App.4/193; Pa. 6; CRS.14/361; Nec; 114; 91; 113; 21 v.2; 36 ff.51, 206,

261; 64 p.515; 164; 169/3 and 7; 109; 35 ff.91, 105, 107, 200, 219).

BULLER, John. Priest.

b. February 25th, 1746. From Lancashire. s. of John and Elizabeth. e. St Omers and Bruges Colleges 1759-63. E.C. Valladolid 1763-8. S.J. December 9th, 1768. Ghent (nov) 1769. Liège (theol) 1771. Ordained priest c.1771. Ghent 1772. Little Crosby 1772-80. Ince (also Lydiate and Formby) c.1780-1811. d. December 14th, 1811, Ince. (Fo.7; CRS.30 xlvi, 190, 194-5; CRS.69; AHSJ.42/308; Gib.1/291; 114; 113; 3 f.3; 23 f.245; 27 f.216v; 76; 77; 25 ff.14, 16, 20, 23, 30, 35, 46, 53, 62, 72, 76, 80, 85, 90, 95; 80; 155 II 129; 155 III 185c; 167 pp.22, 30).

BULMER see Richardson, William.

BURCHARD see Parker, Thomas.

BURDETT see Hussey, Louis; Maire, Edward.

BURKE, Charles *alias* Lucas. Priest.

b. September 22nd or 23rd, 1713, London. s. of William. e. St Omers College c.1727-33. S.J. September 9th, 1733. Watten (nov) 1733, 1734. Liège (phil) 1735, 1737-8. St Omers College 1738-41, 1743-4. La Flèche (theol) 1744, 1746-7. Ordained priest c.1747. Liège 1749-54. Thorndon and Ingatestone c.1754-87. d. May 19th, 1787, Thorndon. bu. St Nicholas' church, Ingrave. (Fo.7; CRS.69; ER.2/30, 4/37-8, 5/74, 6/23, 9/104, 110; HMC.10th Report App.4/190, 196; Nec; 113; 114; 41 nn.48, 81, 107; 67; 140 n.45; 111; 51 f.311v; 43 ff.121, 157, 315-22; 3 ff.96,98; 194).

BURKE, William. Priest.

b. September 5th, 1711, Ireland. S.J. April 12th, 1731. Liège (phil) 1733, 1734. Liège (theol) 1735-9. Ordained priest c.1739. Ghent (tert) 1740, 1741. In England 1741. Watten 1741. In France 1744. d. March 27th, 1746, in England. (Fo.7; Nec; 113; 150 III (2) 27/10/42; 140 n.45).

BURLEY, William. Laybrother.

b. Maryland. S.J. c.1684 in Maryland. Maryland (nov) 1685, 1686-7, 1689-93, 1696-7, 1699-1701, 1703-9, 1724-6. d. date and place unrecorded. (Fo.7; Hu. Text II/682; 91; 113).

BURNELL, Francis. Priest.

b.c.1656, Lincolnshire. S.J. September 7th, 1676. Watten (nov) 1676, 1678. Liège (phil) 1679, 1680. Liège (theol) 1684, 1685. Ordained priest March 17th, 1685. Ghent (tert) 1685. College of St Francis Xavier 1686-7. In prison 1689. d.c.1689-90, ?in prison. (Fo.7; Nec; 150 II (3) 24/12/89, 11/3/90, 8/4/90; 113).

BURNETT, Thomas. Priest.

b.1659 or 1661, Yorkshire. e. St Omers College ?-1681. S.J. September 7th, 1681. Watten (nov) 1681. Liège (phil) 1683-5. Liège (theol) 1686-7, 1689. Ordained priest 1689. Watten (tert) 1690. St Omers College 1691. Residence of St Michael 1692-3. Broughton Hall c.1694-1727. (Superior of Residence of St Michael 1722-24 and 1725-27). d. January 9th, 1727, Broughton Hall. (Fo.7; Nec; CRS.69; WR.16/13; CRS.32/251; 91; 113; 150 III (2) 5/9/22).

BURTON, Christopher. Priest.
  b. July 8th, 1671 or 1672, Suffolk. s. of Thomas and Mary (Suttler) of Beyton near Bury St Edmunds. e. St Omers College ?-1693. S.J. September 7th, 1693. Liège (phil) 1696, 1697. St Omers College 1699, 1700-1. Liége (theol) 1703-5. Ordained priest c.1703. Ghent (tert) 1706. College of the Holy Apostles 1708. Formby c.1709-c.12. Ince Blundell c.1712-c.19. College of St Aloysius 1720, 1724. College of St Thomas of Canterbury 1725. Lytham c.1727-c.28.'St Omers College 1730. Liège 1733-4. Rome 1735-7. St Omers College 1738-40. Watten 1741, 1743. d. July 23rd, 1744, Watten. (Fo.7; CRS.69; E and P.257, 340; 113; 150 III (2) 5/6/34, 19/11/35; 89; NB. 1/206, 2/79; CRS.16/424; 91).

BURTON, Thomas.
  s. of Henry. m. Mary Suttler. Father of Christopher. After d. of his wife was received in S.J. on his deathbed, c.1696. (Fo.7; Nec; E and P.257).

BUSBY, George *alias* Brown. Priest.
  b. September 1st, 1638, Brussels. s. of John and Joan (Collyer). ?uncle of John. e. St Omers College 1653 or earlier-56. S.J. September 7th, 1656. Watten (nov) 1657. Liège (phil) 1658, 1659, 1660. Liège (theol) 1661. St Omers College 1663. Liège (theol) 1664, 1665. Ordained priest April 9th, 1667. Ghent (tert) 1667. Residence of St Dominic 1669. College of the Immaculate Conception 1672-6, 1679-80 (West Hallam, Derbyshire c.1678). In prison 1681-5 (condemned to death but reprieved). Kelvedon 1685. Watten 1686, 1687. Liège 1689-94. d. January 20th, 1695, St Omers College. (Fo.7; CRS.69; CRS.48/477-8; ER.5/95; Gil.1/349; Nec; 113; 114; 150 II (3) 21/4/91, III (2) 21/4/91; 168 f.2; 135 f.229; 43 f.18).

BUSBY, John *alias* Brown. Priest.
  b.1679, Oxfordshire. s. of Charles. ?nephew of George. e. St Omers College 1693-9. S.J. September 7th, 1699. Watten (nov) 1699-1701. Liège (phil) 1703, 1704. Liège (theol) 1705-6, 1708. Ordained priest 1708. Ghent (tert) 1709. St Omers College 1710-13. College of St Aloysius 1714-6 (Scholes c.1716). College of St Ignatius 1718, 1720. Brinn c.1720-c.32. York c.1732-c.33. Bristol c.1733-?43. (Rector of the College of St Francis Xavier 1734-39). d. July 20th, 1743, in England (?Bristol). (Fo.7; CRS.69; Gil.5/60; CRS.3/181; Nec; 91; 114; 113; 150 III (2) 29/11/38; 23 f.54; 26 f.76; 64 p.278; 74).

BUSBY, Thomas *alias* Roberts. Priest.
  b. December 1st, 1656, Buckinghamshire. ?br. of William. e. St Omers College ?-1675. S.J. September 7th, 1675. Watten (nov) 1676. Liège (phil) 1678, 1679. Liège (theol) 1680-3. Ordained priest December 18th, 1683. St Omers College 1684, 1685. Watten 1686. College of St Aloysius 1687. Residence of St George 1689-93. College of the Immaculate Conception 1696-7, 1699-1701, 1703-6, 1708-16, 1718, 1720, 1723-5, 1733-41, 1743-4, 1746-7 (Rector 1696-1706, 1711-4, 1736-8. At Holbeck Hall and Spinkhill c.1700. At Leicester c.1724. Spinkhill c.1743). Watten 1748. Liège 1749-50. d. April 25th, 1750,

Liège. (Fo.7; CRS.69; CRS.62/266; Fo.5/488; 113; 114; YA.77/29, 194, 201; 150III(1)11/1/10; 91).

BUSBY, William. Priest.

b.1646, Buckinghamshire. ?br. of Thomas. S.J. September 7th, 1667. Liège (nov and phil) 1669. Liège (theol) 1672-5. Ordained priest April 13th, 1675. Ghent (tert) 1676. St Omers College 1676-83. Paris 1684. Residence of St George 1685-92 (Superior c.1687-c.89 and 1692. At Worcester c.1688). d. April 6th, 1692, in England (?Worcester). (Fo.7; Nec; 113; 37 f.167).

BUSSON, James. Scholastic.

?From Paris. S.J. September 7th, 1811. Hodder (nov) 1811. Stonyhurst 1815-18, 1820-1. Left 1821, not ordained. (113; 7 f.314; 116; 2).

BUTLER, Hon. John *alias* Thompson. Priest. Baron Caher.

b. August 8th, 1727, ?Ireland. s. of Thomas, 6th Baron Caher and Frances (Butler). br. of Thomas (2). e. St Omers College c.1740-5. S.J. September 7th, 1745. Watten (nov) 1746. Liège (phil) 1748, 1749. St Omers College 1750-1. Liège (theol) 1752-4. Ordained priest June 16th, 1753. Ghent (tert) 1755. Warkworth and Tusmore 1756. Residence of St Michael 1756-8 (?York). Stapehill 1758-?60. Hereford c.1760-86. Nominated to bishopric of Limerick, 1778, but declined. Baron Caher for a fortnight 1786. d. June 20th, 1786, Hereford. (Fo.7; Fo.5/896-8; CRS.69; Nec; 10 f.40; 21 v.2; 33 f.22; 44 ff.268, 269; 51 f.149v; 64 pp.316, 514; 65; 114).

BUTLER, Thomas (1). Scholastic.

b. March 18th, 1683, Clonmel, Ireland. S.J. October 28th, 1700. Does not appear in the English province catalogues until—Liège (theol) 1711. d. January 24th, 1712, Liège. (Fo.7; Nec; 113; 114; 150 III (1) 20/6/1711).

BUTLER, Hon. Thomas (2) *alias* Thompson. Priest.

b. November 20th, 1718, Lancashire. s. of Thomas, 6th Baron Caher and Frances (Butler). br. of John. e. St Omers College c.1733-9. S.J. September 7th, 1739. Watten (nov) 1740. Liège (phil) 1741. Büren (theol) 1743, 1744. Paderborn (theol) 1746. Ordained priest c.1746. Ghent (tert) 1747. Rotherwas 1748-58 or later. Eyne 1767 or earlier-78. d. May 4th, 1778, Eyne. (Fo.7; CRS.69; HMC.10th Report App.4/190; 113; 21 v.2; 33 ff.2, 41, 72, 131; 34 ff.57, 59, 99; 51 ff.124v, 128; 64 p.434; 111; 117; 125).

BYERLEY, Charles. Priest.

b. May 2nd, 1718, Leicestershire. ?s. of John and Elizabeth (Berkeley) of Belgrave, Leicestershire. e. St Omers College c.1732-8. S.J. September 7th, 1738. Watten (nov) 1738, 1739. Liège (phil) 1740, 1741. Liège (theol) 1743. Ordained priest c.1744. Ghent (tert) 1744. Watten 1746-96 (an invalid). d.1796, Watten. (Fo.7; CRS.69; AHSJ.42/291; Chad 333; Nec; 111; 113).

BYERS see Moseley, Michael.

CADRON, Francis. Laybrother.

b. May 25th, 1728, Ghent. S.J. January 24th, 1754. Watten (nov) 1754, 1755. St Omers College 1756, 1757. Ghent 1758, 1761. Bruges College 1763, 1764. Liège 1767-9, 1771-3, 1776. d. April 10th, 1778, Liège. (Fo.7; 113; 114; 53 f.41; 90 f.54; 111).

CAELS, Francis. Laybrother.

b.1650, 1651 or 1652, Flanders. S.J. June or July 1676 or 1677. Watten (nov) 1678, 1679, 1680. Ghent 1681. Watten 1682. St Omers College 1683, 1684. Ghent 1685-7, 1689. Antwerp 1690. Watten 1691-3. Ghent 1696, 1697, 1699. Watten 1700-01, 1703-4. Ghent 1705. Watten 1706-11. d. August 23rd, 1711, Watten. (Fo.7; Nec; 108; 113; 114).

CALDWELL, John *alias* Fenwick. Priest.

b.1628, Durham. e. St Omers College 1654 or earlier-56. S.J. September 28th, 1656. Liège (phil) 1657, 1658, 1659. Liège (theol) 1660-4. Ordained priest 1664. Ghent (tert) 1665. St Omers College 1665-72. Watten 1672, 1673. College of St Ignatius 1674-9. Executed at Tyburn, June 20th, 1679. bu. St Giles-in-the-Fields churchyard. Beatified. (Fo.7; CRS.69; CRS.47 and 48; FAB. pp.99, 141, 151 ff., 168-70; BR. pp.54-6; DNB; 113; 114; 135 ff.193-4; Nec. For writings see Som.).

CALVERT, George. Scholastic.

b. December 15th, 1672, Maryland. S.J. January 28th, 1690. Watten (nov) 1690, 1691. Liège (phil) 1692, 1693. Left 1695, not ordained. (Fo.7; Hu.Text II 703; Hu.Docs. I 57-8; 113; 150 II (3) 27/7/94).

CANDISH see Taylor, Ralph.

CANNELL, James. Priest.

b.1649, Isle of Man. s. of —Cannell and Anne (Hesketh). e. St Omers College ?-1671. S.J. September 7th, 1671. Watten (nov) 1672. Liège (phil) 1673, 1674, 1675. St Omers College 1676, 1678. Ordained priest c.1678. Watten 1679. St Omers College 1680, 1681. College of St Hugh 1682. College of St Thomas of Canterbury 1683-5. College of St Aloysius 1686-7, 1689-93, 1696-7, 1699-1701, 1703-06, 1708-16, 1718, 1720 (Wigan c.1687, c.1701). d. March 27th, 1722, in England (?Wigan). (Fo.7; CRS.69; WB.158-9; Bea.250; Nec; 113; 114; 23 f.35v).

CAREY see Cary.

CARLETON see Caryll, Charles.

CARLOS, William or Charles *alias* Dorrington. Priest.

b.1631, Brewood, Staffordshire. s. of William. E.C. Rome 1655-6. S.J. May 5th, 1656, Messina. Ordained priest c.1667. Ghent (tert) 1667. College of the Holy Apostles 1669, 1672-6, 1678 (Kelvedon c.1676-9). d. January 26th, 1679, ?Kelvedon. (Fo.7; CRS.40/54; CRS.55/548; ER.5/35, 95, 9/108; Nec; 113; 114; 43 ff.9-12).

CARNE, Francis. Priest.

b. June 22nd or 24th, 1686, Somerset. S.J. September 7th, 1704. Watten (nov) 1705, 1706. Liège (phil) 1708, 1709. Liège (theol) 1710-3. Ordained priest c.1713. Residence of St John 1714. d. October 13th or

15th, 1715, in England. (Fo.7; Nec; 113; 114).

CARPENTER, Hermenegild. Priest.

b. February 1702 or 1703, Lille. e. St Omers College ?-1721. S.J.
September 7th, 1721. Watten (nov) 1723. Liège (phil) 1724-6. Liège
(theol) 1727. Ordained priest c.1729. Ghent (tert) 1730. College of St
Aloysius 1733-41, 1743-4, 1746, 1748 (Liverpool 1730-5 or later, Brinn
1740-8). College of St Ignatius 1749-54. St Croix, West Indies 1755.
College of St Ignatius 1755-c.64. Bonham 1766-7. Stapehill 1767-9.
Bury St Edmunds 1770. d. April 12th, 1770, Bury St Edmunds. (Fo.7;
CRS.69; 113; Nec; LR.1/76, 3/5.HMC.10th Report App.4/191;
CRS.43/126; CRS.4/257; 21 v.2; CRS.9/183; CRS.19/219; 90 f.186;
CRS.Mon.1/245; 01.259; 114; 91; 24 ff.6, 347v; 64 p.148; 156 App.1;
85; 26 ff.67, 69; 125).

CARPENTER, Mark.

d. St Omers College January 27th, 1683. Not found under this name.
(Fo.7)

CARPENTIER, Peter. Laybrother.

b.1639, Saint-Omer. S.J. August 14th, 1657. Watten (nov) 1658,
1659, 1660-3. Liège 1664-5, 1667, 1669. Rome 1672-5. Liège 1676,
1678-9. Socius to the provincial 1680. d. June 20th or 28th, 1681,
Ghent. (Fo.7; 113; 114; Nec).

CARR, James. Priest.

b. June 4th, 1795, Preston. s. of John and Hannah (Clayton). e.
Stonyhurst 1807-13. S.J. September 7th, 1813-27 and 29. Hodder (nov)
1813-5. Stonyhurst (phil) 1815-7. Stonyhurst (theol) 1817-8. Clongowes
(theol) 1818. Ordained priest September 4th, 1820. Stonyhurst 1821-2.
Norwich 1822-6. Worcester 1826-7. Stonyhurst 1827. Alton Abbey,
Staffordshire 1828. Stonyhurst 1829. (114; 115; 116; NA.37/159-60; 2;
Gil.1/402; CRS.16/579; Stol; WR.20/70; CRW.58. For writings see
Gil.1/403-4).

CARRINGTON see Smith, John.

CARROLL, Anthony. Priest.

b. September 16th, 1722, Ireland. s. of Daniel. e. St Omers College
1734-44. S.J. September 7th, 1744. Watten (nov) 1744. Liège (phil)
1746. St Omers College 1747-50. Liège (theol) 1752-4. Ordained priest
1754. Rheims (theol) 1755. Paris 1756, 1757. St Omers College 1757,
1758. Liverpool 1759. Norwich 1760, 1761. Lincoln 1761-4. Worcester
1764-6. Hooton 1766-8. Residence of St Stanislaus 1768 (?Exeter).
Bruges College 1768, 1769. Exeter 1769, 1772-3 (Superior of the
Residence of St Stanislaus 1771-3 ?). America 1774-5. Liverpool 1775.
?Shepton Mallet. ?Worcester. d.September 7th, 1794, London. bu. St
Giles-in-the-Fields. (Fo.7; CRS.69; WR.20/70; NA.37/165;
HMC.10th Report App.4/183; Gil.1/407; CRS.9/187-8; CRS.12/44;
DNB; Mel.38; Nec; Hu.Text II 699; 113; 7 f.9; 21 v.2; 24 f.41v; 64
pp.180, 188; 65; 68 pp.30, 132; CRS.0 P.1/179; 77; 70 f.103; 80; 86;
117; 119 ff.6, 39; 5 f.51. For writings see Sut.Som.).

CARROLL, James. Priest.

b. August 5th, 1717, Ireland. s. of Michael and Joanna (Brown). e. St Omers College 1732-9. S.C. Douay 1739. S.J. September 7th, 1741. Watten (nov) 1741. Munster (theol) 1744, 1746. Ordained priest c.1747. Ghent (tert) 1747-8. Maryland 1749-50, 1753-6. d. November 12th or 15th, 1756, Newtown, Maryland. (Fo.7; CRS.69; RSC.81; Hu.Text II 693; Nec; 113; 114; 92).

CARROLL, John. Archbishop.

b. January 8th, 1735, Upper Marlborough, Maryland. s. of Daniel and Eleanor (Darnall). e. St Omers College 1748-53. S.J. September 7th, 1753. Watten (nov) 1753-5. Liège (phil) 1756-9. Liège (theol) 1761. Ordained priest 1761. Liège 1762-4. Bruges College 1767-9. Travelling 1771-3. Bruges College 1773. Wardour 1773. Maryland 1774-1815. Bishop of Baltimore 1789. Archbishop 1808. d. December 3rd, 1815, Baltimore. (Fo.7; CRS.69; Mel.*passim;* CRS.Mon.1/148, 159; Ki.41; CRS.12/130; Nec; 94 ff.22-3, 194-5; Hu.Text II 699; 113; 4 *passim;* 7 ff.4v, 80v; 16 ff.77, 97v, 100; 114. For writings see Som.).

CARTER, Richard. Laybrother.

b. June 15th, 1634, near Warrington. ?br. of William. S.J. December 25th, 1662. Watten (nov) 1662, 1663. St Omers College 1664-5, 1667, 1669, 1672-3. Liège 1674-6, 1678-87, 1689-93, 1696-7, 1699-1701, 1703-6, 1709. d. April 27th, 1709, Liège. (Fo.7; Nec; 113; 114; 123 II 66).

CARTER, William. Laybrother.

b.1638, Lancashire. ?br. of Richard. S.J. February 4th or 5th, 1666. Watten 1669. Liège 1672. St Omers College 1673-6, 1678-87. d. September 22nd, 1687, St Omers College. (Fo.7; Nec; 113; 114).

CARTERET, Edward *alias* Fairfax. Priest.

b. June 26th, 1689, 1690 or 1691, London. s. of Sir Charles and Lady Mary (Fairfax). br. of George and Philip. S.J. September 7th, 1709. Watten (nov) 1710, 1711. Liège (phil) 1712-4. Liège (theol) 1715-18. Ordained priest c.1719. Ghent 1720, 1723. Watten 1724. St Omers College 1725-7. Stonyhurst c.1727-30. Stapehill 1730-4. Residence of St Michael 1735-39. Residence of St John 1740. College of the Holy Apostles 1741. College of St Hugh 1743-4 (Maidenwell 1743). Thurnham 1745-51. Brinn 1751-2. Wigan 1752. d. June 15th, 1753, Wigan. bu. Wigan church. (Fo.7; RH.2/69, 4/74; HMC. 10th Report App.4/184; Gil.4/327; CRS.20/183; CRS.25/117; 113; 91; 24 f.347v; 44 f.118; 64 pp.86, 225; 74; 86; 156 App.I; 119 ff.1, 3; 114).

CARTERET, George. Scholastic.

s. of Sir Charles and Lady Mary (Fairfax). br. of Edward and Philip. e. St Omers College 1713 or earlier -14. S.J.1714. Watten (nov) 1714, 1715. Liège (phil) 1716. Left c.1717, not ordained. (CRS.69; 113; CRS.62, index).

CARTERET, Philip. Priest.

b. May 19th or 20th, 1694, London. s. of Sir Charles and Lady Mary (Fairfax). br. of Edward and George. S.J. September 7th, 1709. Watten (nov) 1710, 1711. Liège (phil) 1712-4. St Omers College 1715-8.

La Flèche (theol) 1720. Ordained priest c.1721. Liège 1723-8, 1730, 1733. West Grinstead 1735. Slindon 1737. Socius to the provincial 1737-40. College of St Thomas of Canterbury 1740-1. Oxburgh 1742-7. Ghent 1747-51(Rector). Provincial 1751-56. d. March 28th, 1756, London. (Fo.7; CRS.62, index; CRS.7/167ff,396; LR.3/8; RH.4/74; HMC. 10th Report App.4/185, 188, 189; Nec; 91; 113; 150 III (2) 25/1/38, 19/8/42, 28/10/46; 10 f.18; 13 f.25; 44 f.196; 64 pp.89, 390; 74; 137 nn.97, 99; 111; 51 f.311; 114. For writings see Som).

CARY see Wolfall, John.

CARY, Benedict. ?Scholastic.

S.J.1667 a novice at Watten and probably also on an earlier occasion. No evidence found to show that he completed the noviceship. (Fo.7; 113)

CARY or CAREY, Charles *alias* Staveley. Scholastic.

b.1665, Devonshire. e. St Omers College ?-1682. S.J. September 7th, 1682. Watten (nov) 1683. Liège (phil) 1684, 1685. d. May 24th, 1686, Liège. (Fo.7; 113; CRS.69; 114; Nec).

CARY, Francis. Laybrother.

d. April 7th, 1685, Rome. Not found in the surviving English province catalogues under this name. (Fo.7).

CARYLL, Charles *alias* Charlton or Carleton. Priest

b. October 10th, 1685, Sussex. s. of Philip and Mary (Tufton) of Shipley. Cousin of Richard. e. St Omers College 1698-c.1702. S.J. September 7th, 1704. Watten (nov) 1705, 1706. Liège (phil) 1708, 1709. Liège (theol) 1710-3. Ordained priest c.1713. College of St Thomas of Canterbury 1714-6. Residence of St Stanislaus 1720. Gerard's Bromley c.1723-40. Stapehill c.1740-45. d. June 12th, 1745, Stapehill. bu. Hampreston church. (Fo.7: CRS.69; 113; CRS.43/126; 114; SCH.3/7; 91; 01.260; WGC. II App., pp 184, 218; Nec).

CARYLL, Richard *alias* Kelly, Paul. Priest.

b. April 2nd, 1962, Sussex. s. of John, 2nd Baron Caryll and Elizabeth (Harrington). Cousin of Charles. e. St Omers College ?-1711. S.J. September 7th, 1711. Watten (nov) 1712, 1713. Liège (phil) 1714, 1715. Liège (theol) 1716, 1718, 1720. Ordained priest c.1720. Lulworth 1722-3. Ladyholt 1723-4. Bonham 1724-7. Cheeseburn Grange 1727-c.37. College of St Thomas of Canterbury c.1737-51 (Stapehill c.1739-41. Stapehill 1745-51) d. February 18th, 1751, Stapehill. bu. Hampreston church. (Fo.7; CRS.69; Gil.1/421; CRS.43/119, 126; CRS. Mon.1/172; CRS.6/365; CRS.25/115; E and P 264; CRS.44/12; ANT.1918/69; 01.260; WGC. II App. and 184; Nec; 113; 114; 91; 44 f.87; 36 f.263).

CASE, James. Priest.

b. May 11th, 1691, Lancashire. ?br of William. S.J. September 7th, 1712. Watten (nov) 1713, 1714. Liège (phil) 1715, 1716. Liège (theol) 1718, 1720. Ordained priest c.1721. Ghent 1723. Maryland 1723-31 d. February 15th, 1731, St Inigoes, Maryland. (Fo.7; Hu. Text II 688; Bur.II/124; 91; 113; 114; Nec).

CASE, William *alias* Baxter. Priest.
    b. September 9th, 1689 or 1690, Lancashire. ?br of James. S.J.
September 7th, 1711. Watten (nov) 1712, 1713. Liège (phil) 1714, 1715.
Liège (theol) 1716, 1718, 1720. Ordained priest c.1720. Worcester
c.1723-47. (Superior of the Residence of St George 1736-40 and
1741-7). d. June or July 2nd, 1747, Worcester. (Fo.7; CRW.7; 113;
WR.20/68; Nec; 38 f.103; 39 f.204; 66; 74; 91; 102; 114).

CASSIDY see Stafford, Bernard.

CATANACH, James. Priest.
    b. May 31st, 1796, Alnwick. S.J. September 1st, 1822. Montrouge
(nov), 1823. St Acheul 1824-5. London school 1825-30. St Mary's Hall
(theol) 1830-3. Ordained priest September 21st, 1833, Stonyhurst.
Wigan 1833-7. d. April 10th, 1837, Wigan. bu. St John's Chapel.
(Fo.7; CG; LR.3/64; Nec; CDSJ; 113; 115;114).

CATESBY, Richard see Pleasington, Joseph.

CATTAWAY, Henry. Priest.
    b. September 26th, 1675, Suffolk. e. St Omers College ?-1693. S.J.
September 7th, 1693. Liège (phil) 1696, 1697. Pont-à-Mousson (theol)
1699, 1701. Ordained priest c.1701. Maryland 1703-5. College of St
Thomas of Canterbury 1706, 1708. College of St Chad 1708-11. College
of the Immaculate Conception 1712-6. d. March 13th, 1718, in England
or at Watten. (Fo.7; CRS.69; Hu. Text II 684; NB.1/27, 29, 94; 113;
150 III(I) 19/11/1701; Nec; 114).

CATTERICK see Birkbeck, Gervase.

CATWELL see Pelcom or Pelcon, or Percom, Peter.

CELOSSE see Selosse, Anthony (1).

CERF, John de. Laybrother.
    b. June 1st, 1697, Liège. S.J. June 20th, 1723. Watten (nov) 1724.
Liège 1725. Watten 1726. Liège 1727-8, 1730, 1733-41, 1743-4, 1746-50,
1752-8, 1761, 1763-4, 1767-9. d. May 5th, 1771, Liège. (Fo.7; Nec; 113;
114; 91).

CHADWICK, Francis. Priest.
    b. September 14th, 1801, Preston. s. of Francis and Margaret
(Whitehead). e. Stonyhurst 1808-18. S. J. September 7th, 1818.
Hodder (nov) 1818-20. Stonyhurst (phil and theol) 1820-30. St Mary's
Hall 1830-33. Ordained priest November 13th, 1830, Stonyhurst.
Stonyhurst 1833-4. Calcutta 1834-8. Stonyhurst 1838-9. Calcutta
1839-42. Worcester 1842. Stockeld 1842. Stonyhurst 1843. Holywell
1844-6. London 1851. Abbotsford 1852. London 1853-4. Oxford
1854-7. d. March 5th, 1857, Oxford. bu. Old St Clement's church yard,
Oxford (Fo.7; Stol; Nec; 113; 115; 6 f.257; 31 ff.87, 114; 52 f.23).

CHALLONER, Henry *alias* Ormes, Christopher. Priest.
    b.1639, Garstang. s. of William and Alice (Ormes). e. St Omers
College 1657 or earlier -59. E.C. Rome 1659-60. S.J. May 2nd, 1660, in
Rome. Ghent (tert) 1671. Liège 1672. d. April 28th, 1673, Liège. (Fo.7;
CRS.6/113n; CRS.40/62; CRS.55/574-5; Nec; 113; 150 II (2) 16/9/70,
20/9/70; 193 Anglia 34 f.353; 114).

CHALLONER, William *alias* Basset. Priest.
>?From Lancashire. E.C. Valladolid 1652. Ordained priest April 1st, 1656, Valladolid. S.J. May 2nd, 1659 in Spain but for English province. Villagarcia (nov) 1659. E.C. Valladolid 1660-5. d. May, 1665, Valladolid. (Fo.7; CRS.30/xxx, xxxi, 165; Ans.2/50; CRS.6/113n; Nec; 150 II (1) -/2/58).

CHAMBERLAIN see Pearce, James.

CHAMBERLAIN, James. Priest.
>b. September 20th, 1739. ?s. of Thomas and Mary (Johnson). ?br. of John. e. St Omers College 1753-c.57. S.J. September 7th, 1759. Watten (nov) 1761. Liège (theol) 1763, 1764. Ordained priest c.1765. Watten 1767-9. Ghent (tert) 1771. Maryland 1772, 1773. d. March 1st, 1779, Guiana. (Fo.7; CRS.69; Nec; Hu. Text II 698; 113; Chad.333; 114; 65; 117).

CHAMBERLAIN, John. Priest.
>b. August 3rd, 1727, Lancashire. s. of Thomas and Mary (Johnson). ?br. of James. E.C. Rome 1742-52. Ordained priest December 8th, 1751, Rome. S.J. November 3rd, 1752. Watten (nov) 1754. Watten School (Superior) 1757-8, 1761, 1763-4. Hammersmith 1767-9. York (Bar Convent) 1770-96. d. January 17th, 1796, York. bu. Holy Trinity churchyard. (Fo.7; CRS.4/377; CRS.40/199; CRS.Mon.2/388; Ans.4/61; LR.1/32; Pa.2/80; Chad.330; Nec; 113; 13 f.127; 22 ff.74, 88; 54 f.308v; 65; 76 f.78v; 25 f.21; 72; 80; 117; 114; 155 II 127; 167 pp.26, 38).

CHAMPION, John. Priest.
>b. January 17th, 1695, Cornwall. S.J. September 7th, 1713. Watten (nov) 1714. Liège (phil) 1715, 1716, 1718. Liège (theol) 1720, 1723. Ordained priest c.1723. St Omers College 1724-5. Ghent 1725. Residence of St Michael 1725-8 (Brough 1727, 1728). College of the Holy Apostles 1730-76 (Sawston 1733-76. Rector 1741-58). d. July 21st, 1776, Sawston. bu. Sawston. (Fo.7; 113; HMC. 10th Report App.4/185, 197; 90 f.34; Ki.43; ER.9/105; 150 III (2) 27/5/41; 41 n.54; 43 f.50v; 151 ff.9, 12, 15, 18, 19, 23, 25, 31, 33, 34, 40, 75, 122, 187, 193, 197-8, 237; 91; 64 p.244; 74; Gil.4/171; CRS.25/111; 126; 51 f.311).

CHAPELLE, Henry. Scholastic.
>b. January 5th, 1749, London. e. Bruges College c.1764-71. S.J. September 7th, 1771. Ghent (nov) 1771, 1772, 1773. (Fo.7; CRS.69; ?CRS.25/135; 113).

CHAPELLE, John Baptist. Priest.
>b. July 27th, 1733, Ward in Picardy. S.J. 1750 in France. Ordained priest ?1762. To the English province 1768. Aix-la-Chapelle 1771. Liège 1772-3. Ghent 1773. (Fo.7; AHSJ.42/291; 113; 16 ff.21v, 35v).

CHAPMAN, James *alias* St Leger. Priest.
>b. February 16th, 1694, London. S.J. September 7th, 1711-24. Watten (nov) 1711, 1712. Liège (phil) 1713, 1714, 1715. Liège (theol) 1716, 1718, 1720. Ordained priest c.1720. College of St Thomas of

Canterbury 1723. Ghent 1724. (113; CRS.62 index; 150 III (2) 16/2/15, 29/1/24,25/4/24,4/5/24).

CHAPMAN, John *alias* or *vere* St Leger. Priest.
b. September 16th, 1670, Kent. e. St Omers College ?-1692. S.J. September 7th, 1692. Watten (nov) 1693. Liège (phil) 1696. Liège (theol) 1697. St Omers College 1699-1701. Liège (theol) 1703-5. Ordained priest c.1702. Ghent (tert) 1706. Residence of St Mary 1708-16, 1720, 1724-8 (Superior 1711-27. Salden 1727. Windsor 1728). York (Bar Convent) 1728-9. d. December 22nd, 1729, York. (Fo.7; CRS.69; 113; CRS.Mon.2/388; 91; CRS.4/376; CRS.25/114; Nec).

CHARLTON see Caryll, Charles.

CHARNOCK, John *alias* Spencer. Priest.
b. June 21st, 1744, Wigan. e. St Omers and Bruges Colleges 1757-63. S.J. September 7th, 1763. Watten (nov) 1763, 1764. Liège (phil) 1765. Liège (theol) 1767. Bruges College 1768-9, 1771-3. To England 1774. Liège Academy 1774-94. Ordained priest at Liège Academy. Stonyhurst 1794-1804. d. March 1st, 1804, Stonyhurst. bu. Stonyhurst. (Fo.7; CRS.69; CRS.12/89; SCR.95, 103; 113; 3 ff.37, 51; 6 ff.22v, 39, 51; 13 f.158; 16 ff.78, 98; 76; 77; 25 f.24; 90 ff.54, 145v, 146v; 7 f.109; 53 f.51; 51 f.308v; 97).

CHATEAU, Benedict du. Laybrother.
b. April 6th, 1706 or 1716, Artois. S.J. August 14th, 1739. Watten (nov) 1740, 1741, 1743-4, 1746-9. St Omers College 1750. Boulogne School 1753. Watten School 1754-8, 1761-2. Ghent 1762-5. Watten School 1765-7. Bruges College 1768-9. Ghent 1770-3. d. December 1786, Saint-Omer. (Fo.7; AHSJ.42/295; 113; 117; 16 ff.22, 31; 67; 111).

CHERFOMONT or CERFOUMONT, Stanislaus. Priest.
b. July 14th, 1749. S.J. September 7th, 1771. Ghent (nov) 1772, 1773. Liège Academy 1776. Ordained priest at Liège. To America 1786. d. after 1794. (Fo.7; Hu. Docs.172 A2; Hu. Text II 700; AHSJ.42/292 ff; 113; 53 f.51; 11 f.50; 4 f.16; 90 f.54; 97).

CHETWIN or CHETWYND, Ralph *alias* Twisden, Bartholomew. Priest.
b.1641, Staffordshire. ?s. of Ralph and Dorothy (Twisden). e. St Omers College 1663 or earlier -65. S.J. September 7th, 1665. Liège (phil) 1667, 1669. Liège (theol) 1672, 1673. Ordained priest 1673. Ghent 1674. College of St Thomas of Canterbury 1675-6, 1678-83. College of St Ignatius 1684. College of St Thomas of Canterbury 1685-7. Horsham gaol 1688-9. College of St Thomas of Canterbury 1690-3, 1696-7. College of St Ignatius 1699-1701, 1703-5. Liège 1706-9. Ghent 1710. Watten 1711. College of St Ignatius 1712-4. Watten 1715-6, 1718. d. October 8th, 1719, Watten. (Fo.5/781-3; Fo.7; Nec; CRS.69; 113; 114; 123 IIIB f.369; 171).

CHILD see Curzon, Peter.

CHORLEY, Thomas. Priest.
b. June 13th, 1688, Lancashire. s. of Richard of Chorley Hall. ?e. St Omers College 1695-1701. S.J. September 7th, 1705. Watten (nov)

1706. Liège (phil) 1708-10. Liège (theol) 1711-4. Ordained priest c.1713. Liège 1715, 1716, 1718. d. October 28th, 1718, in England. (Fo.7; CRS.69 (s.v. Gillibrand); 113; 114; CRS.6/95; Nec).

CHRISTOPHER, William. Laybrother.

b. 1657, Monmouthshire. S.J. May 18th, 1687. Watten (nov) 1687. Residence of St Winefrid 1689 (in prison 1688-9). College of St Aloysius 1691. Residence of St Winefrid 1692-3. Antwerp 1695-6. Residence of St Winefrid 1699, 1700-01, 1703-5 (Holywell 1701-4). d. December 15th, 1705, in England. (Fo.7; NB.1/32; Nec; 113; 112 p.86; 193 Anglia 35/125; 109; 114).

CHURCH, Edward. Priest.

b. November 15th, 1728, Cornwall or London. e. St Omers College c.1742-8. S.J. September 7th, 1748. Watten (nov) 1749. Liège (phil) 1750, 1752. St Omers College 1753-8. Liège (theol) 1758, 1760-1. La Flèche (theol) 1761. Ordained priest c.1760. Liège 1763-6. Lulworth 1766-73. Salisbury 1774-5. Garswood 1777, 1783-4, 1790, 1793. ?Portico 1795. Rixton 1800-20. S.J.1803. d. January 22nd, 1820, Rixton. bu. St Joseph's chapel, Leigh. (Fo.7; CRS.69; CRS.6/365; CRS. Mon.1/168; Gil.4/106; CRS.12/145; 01.262; Nec; 91; 113; 7 f.11; 13 f.390v; 44 ff.229v, 315-7; 54 ff.49, 212; 65; 25 f.84; 87; 155/2/129; 167 pp.23, 29; 23 f.104; 80; 121; 20 f.98).

CHURCHILL, William. Scholastic.

b.1656, Belgium. e. St Omers College ?-1675. S.J. September 7th, 1675. Watten (nov) 1676. Liège (phil) 1677. Antwerp 1677-9. Liège (theol) 1680-2. Watten 1683. d. March 25th, 1684, Watten, not ordained. (Fo.7; CRS.69; Nec; 113; 114; 168 f.1; 109).

CLARE see Eden, James; Warner, John (2).

CLARKE, Henry. Priest.

b. April 3rd, 1669 or 1670, County Durham. e. St Omers College ?-1690. S.J. September 7th, 1690. Watten (nov) 1691, 1692. Liège (phil) 1693. Liège (theol) 1696, 1697. Ordained priest 1699. Ghent (tert) 1699. Residence of St George 1701, 1703-6 (Worcester 1700-?). College of St Ignatius 1708, 1709. Residence of St George 1710. College of St Ignatius 1710-29 (London c.1710, 1724-9. Arrested 1729). d. November 6th or 7th, 1729, London. (Fo.7; CRS.69; LR.2/21, 3/5; Nec; 113; 12 f.124; 40 pp.34, 188; 91).

CLARKE, James. Laybrother.

b.1641, Ireland. S.J. November 20th, 1671. Watten (nov) 1672. St Omers College 1675. He does not appear again in the existing English province catalogues. (Fo.7; 113).

CLARKE, John. Priest.

b. March 17th, 1662, Ireland. e. St Omers College ?-1681. S.J. September 7th, 1681. Watten (nov) 1681, 1682. Liège (phil) 1683-5. Liège (theol) 1686-9. Ordained priest 1689. Ghent (tert) 1690. Ghent 1691-2. Watten 1693. Ghent 1696. Liège 1697. Watten 1699-1701. Ghent 1703. Spain (military chaplain) 1703-4.Ghent 1705-6, 1708. Liège 1708. Watten 1709-14. Ghent 1715-21. d. May 1st, 1723, Ghent.

(Fo.7; CRS.69; DNB; Nec; 113; 114; 193 Anglia 35/295; 123 II ff.64, 82; 95 p.795).

CLARKE, Malachy. Priest.

b. June 25th, 1805, Dublin. br. of Thomas Tracy and cousin of Thomas. e. Stonyhurst 1815-22, 1824. S.J. September 18th, 1825-39. Chieri near Turin (nov) 1825-7. Dôle (phil) 1827-8. Aix (phil) 1828-9. Stonyhurst (theol) 1829-30. St Mary's Hall (theol) 1830-3. Ordained priest September 21st, 1833. Stonyhurst 1833-4. Wigan 1834-7. Broughton Hall 1837-8. Norwich 1839. (Fo.7; 2; 113; NA.37/165).

CLARKE, Thomas Tracy. Priest.

b. July 4th, 1802, Dublin. br. of Malachy and cousin of Thomas. e. Stonyhurst 1815-c.21. Maynooth (phil) 1821-3. S.J. September 7th, 1823. Montrouge (nov) 1823-5. Hodder 1825-9. St Mary's Hall (phil) and theol) 1830-6. Ordained priest September 24th, 1836, Stonyhurst. Norwich 1837-8. Preston 1838. Pontefract 1839. France (tert) 1840. Stonyhurst 1841-5. Hodder 1845-54 (Rector). Beaumont 1854-60 (Rector). London 1861-2. d. January 11th, 1862, London. bu. St Thomas' churchyard, Fulham. (Fo.7; Nec; 113; 114; 115; CG; For writings see Sut).

CLARKE, Thomas. Priest.

b. January 24th, 1804, Dublin. Cousin of Malachy and Thomas Tracy. e. Stonyhurst 1814-c.20. S.J. September 7th, 1823. Montrouge (nov) 1823-5. St Acheul (phil) 1825-6. Stonyhurst 1826-32. St Mary's Hall (theol) 1832-4. Ordained priest December 20th, 1834, Stonyhurst. Gillmoss 1834-41. Hodder (tert) 1841. Lydiate 1841-42. Mount St Mary's College 1842-3 (Rector). Preston 1843. Socius to the provincial 1843-4. Irnham 1844-5. Lincoln 1845-7. Market Rasen 1847-8. St Beuno's College 1848-50. Market Rasen c.1850-9. Tunbridge Wells 1859-67. Wardour 1867-70. Blackpool 1870. d. September 2nd, 1870, Blackpool. bu. St John's church, Poulton-le-Fylde. (Fo.7; Nec; CRS.22/198; Gil.5/61; 113; 114; 115).

CLARKE, William. Priest.

b.1669, London. S.J. September 7th, 1687. Watten (nov) 1687. Liège (phil) 1689-92. Ingolstadt (theol) 1693, 1696. Ordained priest c.1696. St Omers College 1697. College of St Francis Xavier 1699-1701, 1703-16, 1718, 1720, 1724-5, 1726-8, 1730, 1734 (Rector c.1707-15. At Hereford 1724, if not earlier – ?34). d. February 6th, 1734, Hereford. (Fo.7; 91; 113; 114; 150 III (1) 24/7/06, 8/6/15; Nec).

CLARKSON, Edmund. Laybrother.

b. March 23rd or 29th, 1668, Lancashire. S.J. November 20th, 1695. Watten (nov) 1696. Liège 1697, 1699-1701, 1703-4. Maryland 1705-14. St Omers College 1714-16, 1718, 1720, 1724-30, 1733-4. d. December 4th, 1734, St Omers College. (Fo.7; CRS.62/47; 91; 113; 114; Hu. Text II 685; Nec).

CLARKSON, George. Priest.

b. May 4th, 1738, Southhill, Lancashire. e. St Omers College 1751-8. S.J. September 7th, 1758. Liège (phil) 1761-2. Liège (theol) 1763-5.

Ordained priest c.1765. Ghent 1766. Canford 1766-9. Stapehill 1770.
?Bodney 1770. Leighland 1771-2. Slatedelf and Brindle 1772-91.
Southhill (whither the chapel was moved) 1791-1813. d. November 5th,
1813, Southhill. (Fo.7; CRS.69; CRS.43/123, 126; CRS.Mon.1/157;
RH.6/77; Nec; 113; 114; 13 f.430; 21v.2; 23 f.245; 28 f.47; 34 ff.40v,
50v; 41nn.91, 102; 44 ff.227v, 274, 276; CRS.4/434; 54 ff.223, 242; 65;
76; 68 pp.125, 129, 25 ff.45, 56, 64, 72, 75, 84, 90, 97, 104, 111, 152; 80;
AHSJ.42/308; 155/2/129, 3/185c; 167 pp.22, 30; 01.263; 119 ff.12, 17,
25).

CLARKSON, Joseph. Laybrother.
b.1734. S.J. September 7th, 1760. Watten (nov) 1761. Bruges
College 1763-4, 1767-9, 1771. No further information discovered.
(Fo.7; 113).

CLAYTON, George see Kingsley, Ignatius George.

CLEMPSON, Ignatius. Laybrother.
b. May 20th, 1693, Staffordshire. S.J. February 4th, 1713-20.
Watten (nov). 1714. Watten 1715-6. Maryland 1720. (Fo.7; 113;
CRS.62/59; Hu. Text II 686, 688; 150 III (2) 7/12/20).

CLIFFORD, Hon. Charles Walter. Priest.
b. April 26th, 1804, Ugbrooke, Devonshire. s. of Charles, 6th Lord
Clifford and Eleanor Mary (Arundell). e. Stonyhurst 1811-c.20. S.J.
November 1st, 1823. Rome (nov) 1823-5. Rome (phil and theol) 1825-9.
Stonyhurst 1829-30. St Mary's Hall (theol) 1830-35. Ordained priest
September 22nd, 1832, Stonyhurst. Preston 1835-8. Wardour 1838-40.
France (tert) 1840-1. Madura, India 1841-4. d. May 25th, 1844,
Trichinopoly. (Fo.7; 115; 114; Nec; 113; Stol. For writings see Som).

CLIFFORD, Walter. Priest.
b. March 13th, 1773, Tixhall, Staffordshire. s. of the Hon. Thomas
and Barbara (Aston). e. Sedgley Park 1783-6. Liège Academy 1785-94.
Stonyhurst 1794, 1800-01, 1803. Ordained priest May 30th, 1801. S.J.
November 2nd, 1803. Stonyhurst 1803-5. Palermo 1806. d. July 23rd,
1806, Palermo. (Fo.7; CRS.13/205; SCH.3/22; Chad.392; Ki.46;
Bus.108; 113; 116; 166 II p.66; 6 f.23; 51 f.211; 55 f.37v; 90 ff.144v,
146v; 93 pp.27, 47; Nec).

CLIFTON see Green, Thomas or Joseph.

CLIFTON, Francis (1). Priest.
b. April 2nd, 1702, Nottinghamshire. S.J. September 7th, 1719.
Watten (nov) 1720. Liège (phil) 1723, 1724. St Omers College 1724-7.
Ingolstadt (theol) 1728, 1730. Ordained priest c.1732. Liège 1733-6. St
Omers College 1737. Residence of St John 1738-41 (Newcastle 1741).
Liège 1741. Residence of St Stanislaus 1743-4. Stapehill 1745-6. College
of the Holy Apostles 1746-7. Swynnerton 1748—c.56. College of St
Hugh 1756 (?Lincoln). Appointed Rector of St Omers College 1757. d.
April 16th, 1757, Dunkirk. (Fo.7; Ki, 48; SCH.3/7; HMC.10th Report
App.4/187, 198; Nec; 113; 150 III (2) 3/6/41, 19/8/41; 9 n.242; 44
f.258; 64 p.264; 90 f.186; 114; 91).

CLIFTON, Francis (2) see Fanning, Dominic.

CLIFTON, James. Priest.
> b. ?April 3rd, 1698, Lancashire. s. of Cuthbert and Dorothy (Winckley). Nephew of William. br. of Thomas. S.J. September 7th, 1719. Watten (nov) 1720. Liège (phil) 1723, 1724. Liège (theol) 1725-7. Ordained priest c.1728. Ghent (tert) 1728. Little Crosby (serving Lydiate occasionally) 1728-50. d. September 27th, 1750, Little Crosby. bu. Harkirke cemetery. (Fo.7; NB.3/236n; HMC.10th Report App.4/185; Gib.1/289; CRS.6/194; Che.N.S.12; Nec; 113; 24 ff.6, 345, 347v, 348; 27 f.228; 84; 85; 91; 114; 156 App.1).

CLIFTON, Thomas. Priest.
> b. April 7th, 1700, Lancashire. s. of Cuthbert and Dorothy (Winckley). Nephew of William. br. of James. S.J. September 7th, 1718. Watten (nov) 1720. Liège (phil) 1723. St Omers College 1724-7. Liège (theol) 1728, 1730. Ordained priest 1730. Ghent 1731. Watten 1732. Residence of St John 1734-8, 1740-1, 1743-4, 1746-8 (Callaly, then Long Horsley 1741-8). Odstock 1748-9. Loretto 1749, 1750. E.C. Rome 1752-5. Ghent 1756-73 (Rector 1757-64). d. April 27th, 1777, Ghent or in Shropshire. (Fo.7; CRS.Mon.1/164; CRS.6/194; CRS.13/302; 133; 64 pp.375, 386; 12 f.133; 16 f.35; 44 f.261; 36 f.265; 91; 156 n.xi and App.1; 117).

CLIFTON, William. Priest.
> b. February 9th, 1678, Lancashire. s. of James and Anne (Brent or Bond). Uncle of James and Thomas. e. St Omers College 1697 or earlier -99. S.J. September 7th, 1699. Watten (nov) 1700. Liège (phil) 1701-4. Liège (theol) 1705, 1706, 1708. Ordained priest 1708. Ghent (tert) 1709. St Omers College 1710-6. Formby and New House c.1718-49. d. August 29th, 1749, New House, Ince Blundell. bu. Harkirke cemetery. (Fo.7; CRS.69; NB.3/19n; Gil.2/309; CRS.25/113; Che.N.S.12; Nec; 113; 23 f.117; 24 ff.5v, 345, 347v; 27 f.201v; 85; 91; 114; 156 App.1).

CLINTON see MacKenzie, Alexander.

CLOD see Beresford, William.

CLORIVIÈRE, Peter de *alias* Pigot and Rivers. Priest.
> b. June 29th, 1735, St Malo. S.J. August 14th, 1756 in France. Liège (theol) 1763-4. Ordained priest September 1763. In England 1766. Ghent 1767-9. Brussels 1770-4. In England c.1805. Readm. S.J. 1805. Returned to France in or before 1814. (Fo.7; 113; 150 (1750-1853) f.175v; 7 f.105v; 13 f.60v; 57 II ff.195v, 261; 68 p.75; CG; 108; OSBB.197; AHSJ.42/307; Nec).

CLOSETTE, John or Joseph. Priest.
> b. February, 1752, Flanders. e. Bruges College ?-1771. S.J. September 7th, 1771.Ghent (nov) 1772, 1773. Liège Academy (theol) 1773-4, 1776. Ordained priest 1776, Liège. Waterperry 1776-9. Callaly 1779-81. Wardour 1781. d. October 23rd, 1781, Ludwell near Wardour. bu. Tisbury Church. (Fo.7; CRS.69; AHSJ.42/292; CRS.42/137; CRS.7/320, 391, 401; Nec; CRS.Mon.1/161; 113; 90 f.167; 21v.2; 76; 114).

CLOUGH see Fourniers, Nicholas.

CLOUGH, Francis. Priest.

b. March 25th, 1810, near Liverpool. br. of James. e. Stonyhurst 1826-9. S.J. March 26th, 1829. Hodder (nov) 1831-3. St Mary's Hall (phil) 1834-6. Stonyhurst 1836-41. Louvain (theol) 1841-2. St Mary's Hall (theol) 1842-3. Ordained priest September 23rd, 1843, Liverpool. Lydiate 1843-7. Mount St Mary's College 1847-8 (Superior). Socius to the provincial 1848. Stonyhurst 1848-61 (Rector). Liverpool 1861-4 (Superior). Socius to the provincial 1864-7. Beaumont College 1867-71 (Rector). Liverpool 1871-8. St Beuno's College 1878-9. New Hall 1879-85. Beaumont and Roehampton 1886-8. St Mary's Hall 1888-91. d. June 22nd, 1891, St Mary's Hall. bu. Stonyhurst. (115; Stol; Nec).

CLOUGH, James. Priest.

b. January 11th, 1803, near Liverpool. br. of Francis. e. Stonyhurst 1824-7. S.J. September 21st, 1827. Hodder (nov) 1827-9. St Mary's Hall (phil) 1829-31. Stonyhurst 1831-2. St Mary's Hall (theol) 1832-5. Ordained priest April 4th, 1835, Oscott. Yarmouth 1835-41. Pylewell 1841-4. Hodder (tert) 1844-5. Croft 1845-7. Lydiate 1847-8. Hereford 1848. Wardour 1848. d. November 3rd, 1848, Wardour. bu. Wardour. (Fo.7; 115; CRS.14/298; Stol; Nec).

CLOUGH, Richard *alias* Fourniers. Priest.

b. November 28th, 1728, Shropshire. e. St Omers College c.1737-44. S.J. September 7th, 1744. Watten (nov) 1746. Liège (phil) 1747-8. St Omers College 1749-52. Liège (theol) 1753-6. Ordained priest c.1757. College of St Ignatius 1757. Residence of St Winifred 1758. Aldenham 1761, 1762. Oxburgh 1762-6. Worcester 1766-77. d. January 19th, 1777, Worcester. bu. St Oswald's, Worcester. (Fo.7; CRS.69; WR.20/69; Nec; CRW.72; 113; 21v.2; 41nn.16, 28; 64 pp.270, 442; 65; 117; 195 V ff.100v, 102).

CLOVEL see Gerard, Philip, Thomas (1) and Thomas (2).

COBB, George. Scholastic.

b. February 27th, 1808, London. br. of William. e. Stonyhurst 1819-26. S.J. September 7th, 1826. Montrouge (nov) 1826, 1827. d. June 6th, 1827, Paris. (Fo.7; Stol; Nec; 115).

COBB, William. Priest.

b. February 27th, 1804, London. br. of George. e. Stonyhurst 1818-24. S.J. September 7th, 1824. Montrouge (nov and phil) 1824-7. Stonyhurst 1827-34. St Mary's Hall (theol) 1834-8. Ordained priest September 23rd, 1837. Stonyhurst 1838-42. Norwich 1842-4. Mount St Mary's College 1844-6 (Superior). Provincial 1848-51. London 1851-5. Ulverston 1855-6. London 1856-8. Norwich 1858-61. Preston 1861-74 (Rector 1861-70). Blackpool 1874. Preston 1874. Accrington 1875-7. d. March 7th, 1877, Accrington. bu. Stonyhurst. (Fo.7; NA.37/162, 165-6; 115; Nec; Stol; CRS.20/12. For writings see Sut).

COLE, Joseph. Priest.

b. April 9th, 1727, Maryland. ?s. of Edward. ?br. of Robert. e. St Omers College c.1740-7. S.J. September 7th, 1747. Watten (nov) 1747-9. Liège (phil) 1750. St Omers College 1752-8. Liège (theol) 1761.

Ordained priest c.1762. d. December 10th, 1763, Rome. (Fo.7;
CRS.69; Hu. Text II 703; Nec; 113; 114; 191).

COLE, Robert. Priest.

   b. December 23rd, 1732, Maryland. s. of Edward. ?br of Joseph. e.
St Omers College c.1748-52. S.J. September 7th, 1752. Watten (nov)
1752-4. Liège (phil) 1755, 1756. Liège (theol) 1757, 1758. Ordained
priest c.1760. Ghent (tert) 1761. College of St Thomas of Canterbury
1762-7 (Marnhull 1765-7). Swynnerton 1767. College of the Holy
Apostles 1768 (Mr Wright's, Essex). Crondon Park 1769-1803 or 1805.
Re-entered S.J.1805 or later. Bury St Edmunds 1803 or 1805-12. d.
April 28th, 1812, Bury St Edmunds. bu. Bury St Edmunds chapel.
(Fo.7; AHSJ.42/307; CRS.69; Hu. Text II 703; SCH. 3/7, 17/41;
HMC. 10th Report App.4/194; CRS.6/329; ER.4/119-20, 5/94,
9/103, 105; 13 ff.290, 326; 41n.81; 44 ff.229, 273; 43 f.163; 64 p.387;
65; 114; Nec).

COLEMAN, Peter. ?Priest.

   d. 1685. Not found under this name in the records of the English
province. (Fo.7; 01.2/56)

COLGRAVE, Andrew. Priest.

   b. September 17th, 1717, in France. S.J. September 2nd, 1734 or
1733 in France. To English province 1754. College of St Ignatius 1756-8
(Linstead Lodge 1758). Residence of St George 1760. College of St
Ignatius 1763, 1764. Spetchley 1766-8. d. October 19th, 1768,
Spetchley. bu. Spetchley churchyard. (Fo.7; RH.1/48; WR.30/11;
CPC; 64 p.421; 65; 68 p.79; 111; Nec; 113; 114).

COLLINGWOOD, Charles. Priest.

   b.1664, Northumberland. s. of George and Agnes (Fleming) of
Eslington. br. of Robert and Thomas (2). Nephew of Thomas (1). S.J.
September 7th, 1688. Liège (theol) 1689-91, Ordained priest April 14th,
1691. St Omers College 1692, 1693. To England c.1695. Residence of St
Mary 1696-7, 1699-1701, 1703-16. (Sandford 1718). d. February 6th,
1719, ?Sandford. bu. Sandford-on-Thames parish church. (Fo.7;
HMC. 10th Report, App.4/185; Pa.101-2; E and P.202-3; CRS.7/389;
113; 114; 170 f.1v; Nec).

COLLINGWOOD, Robert. Priest.

   b.1657, Northumberland. s. of George and Agnes (Fleming) of
Eslington. br. of Charles and Thomas (2). Nephew of Thomas (1). e. St
Omers College ?-1677. S.J. September 7th, 1677. Liège (phil) 1679-81.
Liège (theol) 1682-6. Ordained priest 1686. Watten (tert) 1686. College
of St Chad 1687, 1689, 1691-2 (Boscobel 1691). Residence of St John
1693. College of St Chad 1694, 1696-7, 1699-1701, 1703-16, 1718, 1720,
1724-8, 1730, 1733-9 (Rector 1704-35. Blackladies 1694-c.1714.
Swynnerton 1714. Boscobel 1715-c.1727. Blackladies c.1727-c.34.
Boscobel c.1734-40). d. January 24th, 1740, ?Boscobel. bu. Blackladies
chapel. (Fo.7; CRS.69; E and P.209, 346; Nec; SCH. 3/7, 14/304; Pa.
101-2; Ki, 52; CRS.14/250; 113; 114; 91; 129).

COLLINGWOOD, Thomas (1) *alias* Errington. Priest.

b.1631 or 1632, Northumberland. s. of Cuthbert and Olive (Wyvill) of Daldon, Co. Durham and Eslington. Uncle of Charles, Robert and Thomas (2). e. St Omers College 1650 or earlier -52. S.J. September 7th, 1652. Watten (nov) 1652, 1653. Liège (phil) 1654-6. St Omers College 1657, 1658. Liège (theol) 1659, 1660. Ordained priest 1661. Ghent (tert) 1661. Residence of St Michael 1663, 1664, 1667, 1669, 1672-6, 1678-80 (Superior 1672-80. York 1679). d. November 1st, 1680, in England. (Fo.7; CRS.69; CRS.14/92n, 250; Nec; CRS.Mon.2/253n; 113; 114).

COLLINGWOOD, Thomas (2) *alias* Durham. Priest.

b.1651, Durham. s. of George and Agnes (Fleming) of Eslington. br. of Charles and Robert. Nephew of Thomas (1). S.J. September 7th, 1676. Watten (nov) 1678. Liège (phil) 1679, 1680. Liège (theol) 1681-4. Ordained priest March 17th, 1685. Ghent (tert) 1685. Residence of St John 1686-7, 1691-3, 1696-7, 1699-1701, 1703-16, 1720, 1724, (Biddleston 1701-25). d. July 5th, 1725, Biddleston. bu. Alwinton churchyard. (Fo.7; LR.1/117; AADN XI/423; CRS.14/250; NCH.10/12; Nec; 113; 36 f.260; 114; 123 II f.127).

COLLINS see Pordage, William

COLLINS, Francis. Scholastic or Laybrother.

d. November 12th, 1696, Liège. Not found in the catalogues of the English province under this name. (Fo.7).

COLLINS, Thomas. Scholastic or Laybrother.

d. June 20th, 1682, Augsburg. No further information found. (Fo.7; 114).

COLLINS, William (1). Priest.

b.1650, Kent. e. St Omers College 1662-5 or later. S.J. September 7th, 1669. Liège (phil) 1672, 1673. Liège (theol) 1674-8. Ordained priest c.1678. St Omers College 1679-82. College of St Ignatius 1683. College of St Thomas of Canterbury 1684-7, 1689-91. College of St Ignatius 1692-3. College of the Holy Apostles 1694, 1696-7, 1699-1701, 1703 (Fithelers 1697-8). Belhouse-?1704 d. July 21st, 1704, in England. (Fo.5 p.527 seq., 7; CRS.69; 113; 43 ff.21v, 26; 114; Nec; ER.4/120, 9/105).

COLLINS, William (2). Priest.

b. September 25th, 1683 or 1684, London. s. of Charles. e. St Omers College c.1701. S.J. September 7th, 1704. Watten (nov) 1705, 1706. Liège (phil) 1708, 1709. Liège (theol) 1710-13. Ordained priest c.1713. Soberton 1713. St Omers College 1713-4. College of St Ignatius 1715-6, 1718, 1720. Residence of St George 1721, 1724-8, 1730, 1733-41, 1743-4 (Grafton 1727, 1743). d. September 5th, 1745, Grafton. (Fo.7; 113; CRS.62; WR.20/71; 40 f.60; 44 f.167; 91; HMC. 10th Report, App.4/185; Nec; 114).

COLOSS or COLOOS or SELOSSE, Peter. Laybrother.

b. September 14th, 1721, near Watten. S.J. May 2nd, 1751. Watten (nov) 1752. Watten 1753-8, 1761, 1763-4. Bruges College 1767-69, 1771-3. Liège Academy 1773-6. d.September 12th, 1776, Liège Academy. (Fo.7; 91; 113; 90 f.34; 117; AHSJ.42/294; 16 f.12v; 51 f.307).

COMBERFORD or COMERFORD, Gerard. Priest.
b.1632, Ireland. S.J.1651. Watten (nov) 1652. Liège (theol) 1653-6.
Ordained priest 1657. Ghent (tert) 1657. Liège 1658, 1659. Residence of
St Mary 1660. Residence of St Dominic 1661, 1663. Residence of St
George 1664, 1665. College of the Holy Apostles 1667. No further
information found. (Fo.7; 113).

COMPTON, James. Priest.
b. May 10th, 1748. S.J. September 7th, 1765. Liège (phil) 1768, 1769.
Bruges College 1769, 1771. Liège (theol) 1772, 1773. Ordained priest
?1773. Entered O.S.B.1774. (Fo.7; 113; Bir.296; AHSJ 42/290-1; 7
f.19; 51 ff.304, 307).

CONDESTABLE see Tockets, Alexius.

CONIERS see Poulton, John.

CONIERS or CONYERS, Christopher. Priest.
b. March 11th, 1669, Kent. S.J. September 7th, 1688. Watten (nov)
1689, 1690. Liège (phil) 1691-3. Liège (theol) 1696. Ordained priest
1697. Ghent (tert) 1697. Watten 1697-8. College of Thomas of
Canterbury 1699-1701, 1703-9 (Soberton ?1701-7). Travelling 1710,
1711. College of St Ignatius 1712, 1713. College of the Immaculate
Conception 1714. Travelling 1715. College of St Thomas of Canterbury
1716. College of St Ignatius 1718, 1720, 1724-5 (Richmond, Surrey
1724 or earlier - 30). d. August 29th, 1730, Richmond. (Fo.7;
CRS.7/297; Nec; 91; 113; 150 II (3) 1/2/98; 44 ff.155, 162; 170 f.4v;
123 IIIB f.256).

CONIERS or CONYERS, George (1). Scholastic.
b.1636, London. e. St Omers College 1649 or earlier − 53. S.J.
September 7th, 1653. Watten (nov) 1654, 1655. Liège (phil) 1656. St
Omers College 1657. d. December 13th, 1657, at Liège or in England,
not yet ordained. (Fo.7; CRS.69; 113; 114; Nec).

CONIERS or CONYERS, George (2). Priest.
b. May 29th, 1644 or 1646, Kent. e. St Omer College 1664 or earlier
− 65. S.J. September 7th, 1665. Watten (nov) 1667. Liège (phil) 1669.
St Omers College 1672. Liège (theol) 1673-6. Ordained priest April 4th,
1676. Watten (tert) 1678. At Omers College 1679-87, 1689-90. St
Germain 1691, 1692. Watten 1693. College of St Ignatius 1696-7,
1699-1701, 1703, 1704-11. d. February 28th, 1711, in England. (Fo.7;
CRS.69; 113; 114; 150 II (3) 24/9/86).

CONIERS or CONYERS, John *alias* Minshall. Priest.
b.1675 or 1676, Kent. s. of James and Elizabeth. ?br. of Thomas (1)
and Leonard. E.C. Rome 1693-4. S.J.1694 in Rome. Rome 1696-7,
1699, 1701, 1703-13. Ordained priest c.1708. Macerata 1714. Loretto
1715-6. Fano 1723 (Rector). Still in Italy 1724. Date and place of death
not found. (Fo.7; CRS.40/113; 113).

CONIERS or CONYERS, Leonard. Priest.
b. August 6th, 1671, Kent. ?s. of James and Elizabeth. ?br. of
Thomas (1) and John. e. St Omers College ?-1690. S.J. September 7th,
1690. Watten (nov) 1691, 1692. Liège (phil) 1693. Liège (theol) 1696,

1697. Ghent 1698. Ordained priest 1699. St Omers College 1699. Ghent 1700. College of St Chad 1701. College of St Thomas of Canterbury 1703-16, 1720, 1724-8, 1730, 1733-41, 1745 (Wardour c.1701-7. Soberton 1715-45). d. July 15th, 1745, Soberton. (Fo.7; CRS.69; 113; CRS.44/11; CRS.Mon.1/151, 197, 243; 13 f.13; 44 ff.162, 167, 198; 91; Bur.1/148; 170 ff.4v, 5v, 245v; 123 IIIB f.357; 114; Nec).

CONIERS or CONYERS, Thomas (1) *alias* Barrum. Priest.

b. July 29th, 1664 or 1665, Kent. ?s. of James and Elizabeth. ?br. of Leonard and John. e. St Omers College ?-1685. S.J. September 7th, 1685. Watten (nov) 1686. Liège (phil) 1687-90. Liège (theol) 1691-3. Ordained priest c.1694. St Omers College 1696-7, 1699-1701, 1703-16, 1718, 1720. d. May 6th, 1721, St Omers College. (Fo.7; CRS.69; 113; 114; 150 III (2) 10/10/07; Nec; CRS.62 index).

CONIERS or CONYERS, Thomas (2) *alias* Barrum. Priest.

b. December 31st, 1715, Kent or London. s. of Symbert. e. St Omers College c.1727-34. S.J. September 7th, 1734. Watten (nov) 1734, 1735. Liège (phil) 1736-7, 1739. Liège (theol) 1740, 1741. Ordained priest c.1741. Residence of St Stanislaus 1743-4, 1746. Rotherwas 1747. Odstock 1748-50. Crosby 1751. Dunkenhalgh 1752-?54. Scotney 1754-8. Eccleston Hall 1758-79 or 80. d. April 20th, 1780, in Lancashire. bu. Windleshaw cemetery. (Fo.7; CRS.69; 113; 21 v.2; 23 ff.91, 93, 95, 187; 26 f.284v; 27 f.272; 28 ff.16, 17, 26, 47, 167; 34 f.57; 29 f.323; 64 pp.386, 536, 540; 65; 68 pp.253, 255; 74; 86; HMC.10th Report App.4/185; CRS.36/218; 30 f.32v; 119 ff.2, 5, 7v, 11, 15; 156 App.1; 155 III 185c; 114; Nec).

CONNELL, George. Priest.

b. June 11th, 1800, near Cork, Ireland. e. Stonyhurst 1812-18. S.J. May 10th, 1818. Hodder (nov) 1818-20. Rome (theol) 1820-2. Stonyhurst 1822-30. St Mary's Hall (theol) 1830-3. Ordained priest September 22nd, 1832, Stonyhurst. Stonyhurst 1833-6. Preston 1836-42. Hodder 1842-5 (Rector). Malta 1845-50 (Rector). Stonyhurst 1850-3. d. March 29th, 1853, Stonyhurst. bu. Stonyhurst. (Fo.7; 113; 115; 6 f.257; Stol; CRS.20/12).

CONNELL, Michael. Priest.

b. September 23rd, 1688, Ireland. S.J. September 7th, 1707. Watten (nov) 1708, 1709. Liège (phil) 1710-2. Liège (theol) 1713-5. Ordained priest c.1715. Ghent (tert) 1716. Ghent 1718. E.C. Valladolid 1718-24. College of St Ignatius 1725. d. 1726, in England. (Fo.7; CRS.30/182; 113; 90 ff.9, 24; Nec; 9 ff.73-4).

CONNOLLY, John. Priest.

b.1779, Ireland. ?e. Stonyhurst 1799-? S.J. September 7th, 1805-1806 and August 31st, 1807. Hodder (nov) 1807. Sicily (phil and theol). Stonyhurst 1810 (phil and theol). Ordained priest c.1810. Hodder 1811. Irnham 1812. Oxford 1812-18. d. September 5th, 1818, Oxford. bu. old St Clement's church, Oxford. (Fo.7; 113; 114; Nec; 62 n.351b; CRS.7/407-9; 21 v.2; 31 pp.52-5; 7 f.214; 6 f.204).

CONRAD, Peter. Priest.

b.c. 1622, Ireland. S.J. 1653 (already a priest). Watten (nov) 1653-5.
Liège 1656. College of St Aloysius 1657. To Ireland 1658. (Fo.7; 113).

CONSTABLE, Ignatius *alias* Place. Priest.

b. January 7th, 1666, Yorkshire or Norfolk. S.J. August 9th, 1709
(having studied phil and some theol in Rome). Watten (nov) 1710.
Liège (theol) 1711-14. Ordained priest c.1714. Ghent 1715. College of
the Holy Apostles 1716, 1718, 1720 (?Fithelers. ?Flixton). Residence of
St George c.1723-5 (Grafton c. 1725). d. August 21st, 1727, in England.
(Fo.7; 113; 114; 91; WR.20/71; 43 f.35v; Nec).

CONSTABLE, John *alias* Lacey. Priest.

b. November 10th, 1676 or 1678, Lincolnshire. br. of Joseph or
Marmaduke. e. St Omers College c.1689-95. S.J. September 7th, 1695.
Watten (nov) 1696. Liège (phil) 1697, 1699-1700. Liège (theol) 1701,
1703-4. Ordained priest c.1704. Ghent 1705. Liège 1706-11. Watten
1712-3. St Omers College 1714. Watten 1715, 1716, 1718, 1720. College
of St Chad 1723-43 (Rector 1735-?43. Swynnerton c.1723, 1727,
1734-43). d.April 7th, 1743, Swynnerton. bu. Swynnerton parish
church. (Fo.7; CRS.69; 113; DNB, 91; CRS.62 index; 114; SCH.3/7,
8/8-9; Ki.54-5; Nec. For writings see Gil.1/552-5. Som).

CONSTABLE, Joseph or Marmaduke. Priest.

b. 1672, 1673 or 1674, Lincolnshire. br. of John. e. St Omers College
?-1690. S.J. September 11th, 1690. Paris (nov) 1690, 1691. Liège (phil)
1692, 1693. Liège (theol) 1696-7, 1699. Ordained priest 1699. Ghent
(tert) 1699, 1700. Paris 1701. College of the Holy Apostles 1703-10.
College of St Thomas of Canterbury 1711. Clermont 1714, 1715. La
Flèche 1716, 1718. Travelling 1720. Residence of St Michael 1723,
1724. Residence of St George 1725 (Worcester 1725 -? Sherington near
Weobley ?-?1733). Kelvedon 1733. Socius to the provincial 1734-7. St
Omers College 1737-9 (Rector). College of the Holy Apostles 1740.
College of St Ignatius 1741. Residence of St Michael 1743-7 (York
1743-c.46). Watten 1748, 1749. d. January 28th, 1750, Watten. (Fo.7;
CRS.69; 113; CRS.62/14; WR.20/66; 150 III (1) 14/5/1718, III (2)
4/6/35, 10/8/37; 64 p.248; 91; 156 App.1; 170 f.245v; 123 III B, f.360;
114; Nec).

CONSTABLE, Michael. Priest.

b. May, 1648 or 1649, Yorkshire. S.J. September 7th, 1668. Watten
(nov) 1669. Liège (phil) 1672, 1673. St Omers College 1674-8. Liège
(theol) 1679-81. Ordained priest April 5th, 1681. St Omers College
1682. Ghent (tert) 1683. St Omers College 1684-93 (Rector 1688-93). St
Germain 1693, 1696-7, 1699-1701, 1703-7. d. July 21st, 1707, St
Germain. (Fo.7; 113; 114; Nec).

CONSTABLE, Robert (1). Priest.

b. February 15th, 1673 or 1674, Yorkshire. S.J. May 9th, 1711.
Watten (nov) 1712. Liège (phil) 1713. Liège (theol) 1714-6. Ordained
priest c.1716. Travelling 1720. Burton Park 1721. College of the Holy
Apostles 1721-5. Travelling 1725-8, 1730. Watten 1731, 1733. College
of St Ignatius 1734. Travelling 1735. Watten 1736-8. d. February 4th,

1739, Watten. (Fo.7; 113; 91; RH.13/116; 74; 43 ff.40, 41v, 44, 45; CRS.22/306, 312; 114; Nec).

CONSTABLE, Robert (2). Priest.

b. October 2nd, 1705, Thirsk. s. of John and Anne (Otterburn) of Thirsk. e. St Omers College ?-1722. E.C. Rome 1722-9. Ordained Priest September 8th, 1728, Rome. S.J. September 7th, 1729. Travelling 1730, 1733-4. Residence of St Mary 1735-7. Watten 1738-40. College of St Thomas of Canterbury 1740, 1741. Wardour 1743-59. Watten 1759-66 (Rector 1761-4). York 1767-70. d. February 5th, 1770, York. (Fo.7; 91; CRS.69; 113; CRS.Mon.1/156; CRS.Mon.2/278, 390; Ans 4/69; 21 v.2; 64 p.375; 65; 66; HMC. 10th Report App.4/184; Ki.56; CRS.40/169; 01.274; 111; 51 f.311; 114; Nec; 9 f.192).

CONWAY, John. Laybrother.

b.1625, Dunkirk. S.J. March 7th, 1651. Watten (nov) 1651, 1652. St Omers College 1653-61, 1663-5, 1667, 1669, 1672-3. Brussels 1674-84. Ghent 1685-7, 1689. d. November 11th, 1689, Ghent. (Fo.7; 113; 114; Nec; 109)

CONWAY, William (1) *alias* Parry. Priest.

b.1659, Flintshire. e. St Omers College c.1674-9. S.J. October 14th, 1679. Watten (nov) 1679, 1680. Liège (phil) 1683. Liège (theol) 1684-7. Ordained priest c.1688. d.February 25th, 1689, Ghent or in England. (Fo.7; CRS.69; 113; 114; 168 f.80; Chad.196; Nec).

CONWAY, William (2) *alias* Wright. Priest.

b. July 14th, 1683, Flintshire. e. St Omers College ?-1702. S.J. September 7th, 1702. Watten (nov) 1703. Liège (phil) 1704-6. Liège (theol) 1708-10. Ordained priest c.1710. Ghent (tert) 1710. College of St Francis Xavier 1711-13. Ghent 1714. Watten 1715-6. Ghent 1718, 1720, 1723-7. St Omers College 1728, 1730, 1733-41. d. September 13th, 1741, St Omers College. (Fo.7; CRS.69; 113; 91; CRS.62 index; 150 III (2) 26/6/1723; 114; Nec).

CONYERS see Coniers.

COOK, Anthony. Laybrother.

S.J.1681-3 or 4. Watten (nov) 1681, 1682. Liège 1683. (113).

COOK, James. Laybrother.

b.1652, 1653 or 1655, Yorkshire. S.J. June 20th, 1676. Watten (nov) 1676. St Omers College 1678, 1679. Liège 1683, 1684. Residence of St Winifred 1685, 1686. College of St Ignatius 1687. Rome 1689, 1691-3, 1696-7, 1699-1701, 1703-16, 1720, 1724-8, 1730, 1733-8. d.?1739, ?Rome. (Fo.7; 113; 91; Chad.228; 12 f.178v).

COOK see Heveningham, John.

COOPER, Thomas. Priest.

b. December 13th, 1812, Chorley. e. Stonyhurst 1824-31. S.J. March 26th, 1829. Hodder (nov) 1831-34. St Mary's Hall (phil) 1834-6. Stonyhurst 1836-42. St Mary's Hall (theol) 1842-4. Ordained priest September 28th, 1844, Stonyhurst. Stonyhurst 1844-5. Mount St Mary's College 1845-7. Stonyhurst 1847-68. Prescot 1868-73. Clitheroe 1873. d. April 14th, 1873, Wakefield. bu. Spinkhill churchyard. (Fo.7;

115; Stol; Nec).

COPE or COUPE, John. Laybrother.

b. March 13th, 1792, Whittle, Lancashire. S.J. September 20th, 1827. Hodder (nov) 1829-31. Hodder 1831-45. St Mary's Hall 1845-62. Roehampton 1862-80. d.December 3rd, 1880, Roehampton. bu. Roehampton S.J. cemetery. (Fo.7; 113; 115; Nec).

COPE or COUPE, Joseph. Priest.

b. June 8th, 1790, Hoghton near Blackburn. e. Stonyhurst 1801-7. S.J. September 7th, 1807-15 and July 1816. Hodder (nov) 1807-9. Stonyhurst (phil) 1809-15. South-hill 1816. Stonyhurst (theol) 1816-7. Ordained priest December 16th, 1817, Durham. Gillmoss 1818-34. d. December 20th, 1834, Gillmoss. bu. Gillmoss. (Fo.7; 113; 115; Gil.5/61; Nec; Stol).

COPLEY, William. Priest.

b. January 7th, 1668 or 1669, Surrey. ?s. of Roger and Anne. e. St Omers College ?-1686. S.J. September 7th, 1686. Watten (nov) 1686, 1687. Liège (phil) 1689, 1690. St Omers College 1691-3. Ordained priest c.1695. St Omers College 1695. Ghent (tert) 1695-6. To England c.1696. Gifford's Hall 1697-?9. Residence of St Winifred 1700. College of St Thomas of Canterbury 1701-2, 1704-5. College of St Ignatius 1706, 1708-13. Sutton Coldfield and/or Baddesley Clinton c.1714-27. d.November 29th, 1727, Sutton Coldfield or Baddesley Clinton. (Fo.7; CRS.69; 113; WR.20/58; 91; CRS.42/153; E and P.267; 43 ff.26-7; 40 f.46; 170 ff.2v, 16v, 129v, 245v; 123 III B f.356; Nec).

CORBE, Claud John. Priest.

b. January 24th, 1734, Brittany. S.J.1757, in France. Ordained priest c.1765, Limoges. To England 1791. Ashcombe and Deans Lease near Salisbury c.1801-6. Lulworth 1806. Courtfield 1806-15. Rotherwas 1815. Readm. S.J. d. June 22nd, 1815, Rotherwas. (Fo.7; 113; Nec; CRS.4/413, 417-8, 428; AHSJ.37/161, 42/307; 1 ff.150v, 260v; 6 f.133; 13 ff.296, 338, 365, 370, 399, 454v, 462; 59 ff.37-8, 40, 46; 01.278).

CORBIE or CORBY, Henry. Priest.

b. April 14th, 1700, Sussex. ?br of John. e. St Omers College ?-1722. S.J. September 7th, 1722. Watten (nov) 1724. Liège (phil) 1724-7. Liège (theol) 1728. St Omers College 1728, 1730. Ordained priest c.1730. ?Ghent (tert) 1731. Residence of St Michael 1731-41, 1743-5 (Brough c.1735-45). Watten 1745-56 (Rector). Provincial 1756-62. College of St Ignatius 1762-4 (Rector). Ghent 1764-5 (Rector). d. June 14th, 1765, Ghent. (Fo.7; CRS.69; 113; 114; LR.3/8; 21 v.2; 64 p.311; 74; 91; Gil.4/171; 120; 111; 126; 156 App1; Nec).

CORBIE or CORBY, John. Laybrother.

b. May 6th, 1691, Sussex. ?br of Henry. S.J. September 7th, 1714. Watten (nov) 1715, 1716. St Omers College 1718, 1720, 1723-8, 1730, 1733-41, 1743-4, 1746-7, 1749-51. d. May 15th, 1751, St Omers College. (Fo.7; 113; 114; 91; Nec).

CORBUSIER, Francis. Laybrother.

b. June 24th, 1713, Liège. ?br. of John. S.J. September 7th, 1743. Liège (nov) 1744. Liège 1746-50, 1752-5. St Omers College 1756-58, 1760-61. d. May 31st, 1761, St Omers College. (Fo.7; 113; 114; 121).

CORBUSIER, John *alias* Porter. Priest.

b. January 10th, 1707, Liège or Maastricht. ?br. of Francis. e. St Omers College ?-1726. S.J. September 7th, 1726. Watten (nov) 1727. Liège (phil) 1728, 1730. St Omers College 1733-6. Liège (theol) 1736-8. Ordained priest April 5th, 1738. Liège 1740-1, 1743. College of St Aloysius 1743-9 (Preston 1743. Hooton 1747, 1749). College of St Ignatius 1749. Hooton 1750, 1752-4. Gifford's Hall 1754. Crondon Park 1758. Weston 1758-9. Watten 1760, 1761. Liège 1763-4. d. September 8th, 1765, Scotney. (Fo.7; CRS.69; 113; 114; 91; WR.20/62; 150 III (2) 27/7/43; 24 f.347v; 64 pp.420-1, 524; 65; 74; HMC. 10th Report App.1/193; 140 n.45; 156 App.1; Nec).

CORBY see Corbie.

CORKER see Berry, William.

CORNEILLE or CORNEIL, Arnold. Laybrother.

b. April 11th, 1694, near Lille. S.J. March 3rd, 1714. Watten (nov) 1714, 1715. St Omers College 1715, 1716. Watten 1718, 1720. St Omers College 1724-8, 1730, 1733-4. d. June 24th, 1735, Lille. (Fo.7; 113; 91; CRS.62/59, 259n; Nec; 114).

CORNELISON, James. Priest.

b.1644 or 1646, Dunkirk. S.J. November 29th, 1664-74. Liège (phil) 1667, 1669. Liège (theol) 1672. Ordained priest c.1672. Watten 1672. Ghent (tert) 1673. (113; 150 II (2) 4/10/64, 21/9/71,20/5/73, 28/4/74, 1/9/74; 193 Anglia 34/382).

CORNWALLIS see Pracid, Jeremiah.

COTHAM, William (1). Priest.

b. December 31st, 1791, near St Helens. e. Stonyhurst 1802-9. S.J. September 7th, 1809. Hodder (nov) 1809-11. Stonyhurst (phil and theol) 1811-21. Ordained priest December 17th, 1818, Ushaw. Hodder 1821-2. Wigan 1822-3. Hereford 1823-5. Orrell Mount 1825-30. Stonyhurst 1830-7. Jamaica 1837-60 (Superior 1837-51). d. November 19th, 1860, Kingston, Jamaica. (Fo.7; 62 nn. 299, 300; 113; 115).

COTHAM, William (2). Priest.

b. August 30th, 1806, Liverpool. e. Stonyhurst 1819-26. S.J. September 7th, 1826. Montrouge (nov) 1826-7. Hodder (nov) 1827-8. Stonyhurst (phil) 1828-30. London school 1830-1. St Mary's Hall (theol) 1831-5. Ordained priest December 20th, 1834, Stonyhurst. Ugbrooke 1835-44. Hodder (tert) 1844-5. Ugbrooke 1845. Wigan 1845. Stonyhurst 1845-7. Wigan 1847-52. Portico and Prescot 1852-62. Liverpool 1862-5. St Helens 1865-73. Preston 1873-80. Prescot 1881-8. St Mary's Hall 1888-95. d. February 9th, 1895, St Mary's Hall. bu. Stonyhurst. (115; L.R.3/65; Nec).

COTTAM, William. Laybrother.

b. March 8th, 1713. S.J. September 7th, 1760. Watten (nov) 1761.

Watten 1763, 1764. d. February 8th, 1767, Watten. (Fo.7; 113; 91; 114; Nec).

COTTON see Tichborne, John (1).

COTTON, Alexander *alias* Blount. Scholastic.

b.1637, Somerset. s. of Edward and Mary (Brett). br. of George. e. St Omers College c.1649-55. E.C. Rome 1655-6. S.J. 1656 (Rome). Liége (theol) 1661. Left 1663, not yet ordained. (Fo.7; 150 II (2) 24/6/62, 7/10/62; CRS.69; CRS.40/55-6; CRS.55/551-2; 113).

COTTON, George *alias* Blount. Priest.

b.1636, London. s. of Edward and Mary (Brett). br. of Alexander. e. St Omers College c.1649-52. E.C. Rome 1652-3. S.J December 25th, 1653. Watten (nov) 1653-5. Rome 1655. Ordained priest before 1670. College of St Ignatius 1670-c.75. Bury St Edmunds c.1675-c.77. College of St Ignatius 1678. In France 1679, 1681-2. College of the Holy Apostles 1682. College of St Ignatius 1683. College of the Holy Apostles 1684-7. College of St Ignatius 1689-93, 1696. d. May 3rd or 23rd, 1697, London. (Fo.7; CRS.69; 113; CRS.40/51; CRS.55/537-8; 150 II (2) 1/9/70, 28/3/71; 43 ff.9, 10, 15, 17, 19; 114; Nec).

COTTON, John *alias* or *vere* Fletcher. Priest.

b. June 29th, 1724, Norfolk. e. St Omers College ?-1741. S.J. September 7th, 1741. Liège (phil) 1744. Trèves (theol) 1746, 1747. Cologne (theol) 1748, 1749. Ordained priest c.1749. ?College of St Francis Xavier 1749. St Omers College 1750. Bromley Hall 1751. Courtfield 1751-69 (probably continuously). d. July 24th, 1769, Courtfield. (Fo.7; 113; CRS.69; 91; ER.4/117, 10/39; 34 f.60; 64 pp.286, 503; 68 p.85; 126; 109; 111; 114; Nec).

COTTON, Richard *alias* Phillips. Priest.

b. November 5th, 1665, London. e. St Omers College?-1681. S.J. September 7th 1681. Watten (nov) 1682. Liège (phil) 1683-5. St Omers College 1686-90. Liège (theol) 1691-3. Ordained priest March 23rd, 1693. St Omers College 1696. Loretto 1697-9. Liège 1699-1701, 1703-6. College of the Holy Apostles 1709-20,1724-5, ?1726-8, 1730, 1733-9 (Rector 1714-c.19. Norwich 1713, 1725, 1727, 1740). d. April 17th, 1740, in England (?Norwich). (Fo.7; 113; 91; CRS.69; NA.37/158; 150 II (3) 23/11/97, 26/4/98; 55 f.128; CRS.7/55; 170 f.2v; 123 III B f.356. For writings see Som).

COUCHE, John. Priest.

b. April 14th, 1744, Tolfrey, Fowey, Cornwall. s. of William and Anne (Hoskins). br. of William and Peter. e. St Omers College ?-1762. S.J. November 8th, 1762. Watten (nov) 1763, 1764. Liège (theol) 1767-9. Ordained priest c.1770. Canford 1770-c.74. Lulworth c.1774-c.82. Soberton 1782-1813. Greenwich 1813. d. December 29th or 30th, 1813, Greenwich. (Fo.7; 114; Nec; CRS.69; 113; CRS.43/123, 127; Ans.4/17; AHSJ.38/472; 1 ff.65v, 73v, 90v, 103v, 132v, 258v; 13 ff.166v, 181, 182, 360, 438, 445v; 166 II p.146; 44 ff.50, 78, 235, 276; 76 f.77; 68 p.168; 69; 72; CRS.6/366; CRS.12/123; 01.277; 121; Ber.142; E and P.23).

COUCHE, Peter. ?Scholastic.

    b.1743. s. of William and Anne (Hoskins) of Tolfrey, Fowey. br. of John and William. e. St Omers College c.1755-61. S.J. September 7th, 1761. Liège (phil) 1763, 1764. Liège (theol) 1767. Left c.1767, ?not ordained. (Fo.7; 68 p.168; 113; CRS.69).

COUCHE, William. Scholastic.

    b. February 5th, 1732, Tolfrey, Fowey. s. of William and Anne Hoskins. br. of John and Peter. e. St Omers College 1743-9. S.J.1749. Watten (nov) 1750. Liège (phil) 1752. d. February 23rd, 1753, Liège, not yet ordained. (Fo.6/696 ff.; Fo.7; CRS.69; 113; 91; Gil.1/577; DNB; E and P.23; 114; Nec).

COUPE see Cope.

COXON, Thomas. Priest.

    b. March 20th, 1654, County Durham. S.J. September 7th, 1676. Watten (nov) 1676-8. Liège (phil) 1679, 1680. Liège (theol) 1681. St Omers College 1682-6. Liège (theol) 1687, 1689. Ordained priest 1687. Liège 1691-3. To England 1694. College of St Hugh 1696. Travelling 1699-1701. College of St Ignatius 1703-11, 1713-6, 1718, 1720, 1724-7 (London 1713-5, 1725, 1727). In England 1728, 1730. St Omers College 1733, 1734. d. May 6th or 7th, 1735, St Omers College. (Fo.7; 113; CRS.62; LR.3/8; 150 III (1) 14/9/09; DNB;58 p.69; 91; E and P.68; 170 f.1v; 140 n.45; Chad 251-8; 114; Nec. For writings see Som).

CRANE, William *alias* Brian. Priest.

    b.1650, Norfolk. s. of William and Frances (Bond) of Woodrising, Norfolk. e. St Omers College ?-1669. E.C. Rome 1669-76. Ordained priest March 24th, 1674. S.J. June 28th, 1676. Watten (nov) 1676. St Omers College 1678-9. France 1680-2. Residence of St George 1683. College of St Ignatius 1684-7, 1689-93, 1695. (Rector 1692-c.95). Residence of St George 1696. College of St Thomas of Canterbury 1697, 1699-1701, 1703-9 (Rector 1704-c.7). d. July 13th, 1709, in England. (Fo.7; CRS.69; 113; CRS.40/78-9; 114; Ans.3/42; 150 III (1) 11/3/1702; CRS.8/343; Nec).

CREW, George ?*alias* Ireland. Scholastic.

    b.1669, Lancashire. S.J.1687. Watten (nov) 1687. Liège (phil) 1689-92. Left 1693, not yet ordained. (113; 150 II (3) 12/1/1692, III (2) 21/4/1691).

CRIMMES see Williams, Francis.

CROFTS, John. Scholastic.

    b.1702, County Durham. e. St Omers College ?-1721. S.J.1721. Watten (nov) 1723. In England, ill, 1724. d.?1724 (Fo.7; 113; CRS.69).

CROFTS see Houseman, Christopher.

CROSBY, John *alias* Rowland. Priest.

    b.1637 or 1638, Worcestershire. e. St Omers College ?-1664. S.J. September 7th, 1664. Watten (nov) 1664. Liège (phil) 1667, 1669. Liège (theol) 1672, 1673. Ordained priest c.1672. Ghent (tert) 1674. Residence of St John 1676, 1678-87, 1689-93, 1696-7, 1699-1701, 1703-9 (Callaly c.1678). d. March 8th, 1709, in England. (Fo.7; CRS.69; 113;

CRS.8/344; 168 f.2; 140 n.45; Nec).

CROSS see Blake, James; Morris, James; Tristram, Joseph.

CROSS, Bernard. Priest.

b. April 8th, 1715, Teneriffe, Canary Islands. E.C. Valladolid 1736-7. S.J. May 8th, 1737. Watten (nov) 1737. Liège (phil) 1738-41. Wurzburg (theol) 1744. Ordained priest c.1744. Ghent (tert) 1746. London 1747-53. St Croix, West Indies 1753-5(Superior). Montserrat 1756-7. London 1758-75-?85 (Rector 1768-73). To Worcester 1785. d. April 22nd, 1785, Worcester. (Fo.7; CRS.30/189; 113; LR.1/76, 83, 2/41-2, 3/5-6; WR.20/70; 6 ff.268, 276; 51 f.149; HMC.10th Report App.4/183-4, 186-7, 189; CRS.38/170; 172; 173; Nec; 117).

CROSS, Thomas. Priest.

b. November 7th, 1739, Ince, Lancashire. Uncle of Tristram, Joseph. e. St Omers College c.1752-8. S.J. September 7th, 1758. Liège (phil) 1761. Liège (theol) 1763, 1764. Ordained priest c.1765. Rixton 1765. Richmond, Yorkshire 1765-6. Spinkhill or Holbeck 1766-1813. d. October 18th, 1813, Holbeck Hall. (Fo.7; CRS.69; 113; SCH.12/18, 20, 15/29; 6 f.268; 13 ff.300, 435; 21v.2; 48 f.35v; 63 f.297; 65; 68 p.372; 72; Ki.60; 119 f.31; Nec; 114).

CROSSLAND, Charles. Priest.

b. 1655, Yorkshire. s. of Sir John and Bridget (Fleming) of Helmsley. e. St Omers College ?-1677. S.J. September 7th, 1677. Watten (nov) 1678. Liège (phil) 1679-81. Liège (theol) 1682-5. Ordained priest c.1686. Watten (tert) 1686. College of St Thomas of Canterbury 1689-93, 1696-7, 1699-1701 (Wardour 1691-2, 1696). College of the Immaculate Conception 1703. Residence of St Mary 1704-5. College of St Thomas 1706, 1708. Residence of St Mary 1709. College of St Thomas 1710. Residence of St Michael 1711-6, 1718, 1720, 1724. d. March 30th, 1724, Yorkshire. (Fo.7; CRS.69; 113; 114; CRS.Mon.1/150; 44 f.147v; 150 II (2) 7/8/84; E and P.326; CRS.13/56; Nec).

CROSSLAND, Henry. ?Priest.

d. Watten, date unknown. (Fo.7).

CROUCHE, Ralph. Laybrother.

b.1620, Oxfordshire. S.J. April 18th, 1658 or 1659. Maryland (nov) 1659-61. To Europe 1661. Socius to the provincial 1663. Liège 1664-5, 1667, 1669, 1672-9. d. November 18th, 1679, Liège. (Fo.7; 113; 114; Hu. Text II 680).

CUERDON, Thomas. Priest.

b. June 25th, 1718, Lancashire. s. of William of Clayton-le-Dale. e. St Omers College 1733-7. S.J. September 7th, 1737. Watten (nov) 1738. Liège (phil) 1739-41. Wurzburg (theol) 1744. Molsheim (theol) 1746. Ordained priest c.1745. Ghent 1747-9. Watten 1749-50, 1752-8, 1761. Westby Hall 1761-92. Scholes 1792-3. d. March 31st, 1793, Scholes. (Fo.7; CRS.69; 113; CRS.15/4-5, 32; 68 p.332; 25 ff.30, 42, 48, 56, 63, 73, 81, 86, 95, 130; 80; E and P.132; 155 II 129; 155 III 185c; Ki.60; CRS.12/40; CRS.23/129; 167 pp.21, 30; Gil. HP.236; 119 ff.16, 19, 22,

25, 32, 35, 39; 114; Nec).

CUFFAUD, John *alias* Maynard. Priest.

b. August 28th, 1668, Hampshire. S.J.1688. Watten (nov) 1689, 1690. Liège (phil) 1691-3. Liège (theol) 1696. Ordained priest 1697. Ghent (tert) 1697. Residence of St Michael 1699-1701, 1703-5. Scarisbrick 1706-14. d. March 19th, 1716, Chester. (Fo.5/322; Fo.7/1405; 113; 114; Nec; NB.1/123, 134, 213, 2/97-8).

CULCHETH see Stanley, Henry (1).

CULCHETH, Charles *alias* Parker. Priest.

b. April 11th, 1631, Lancashire. s. of John and Jane (Hawarden) of Culcheth Hall. br. of William. e. St Omers College 1647 or earlier-1652. S.J. 1652. Watten (nov) 1653. Liège (phil) 1654-6. St Omers College 1657-61. Liège (theol) 1663, 1664. Ordained priest 1665. Ghent (tert) 1667. d.December 23rd, 1667, Ghent. (Fo.7; CRS.69; 113; 114; WB.92; Nec).

CULCHETH, James *alias* Parker. Scholastic.

b.1665, Lancashire. s. of Thomas and Anne (Bradshaigh) of Culcheth. br. of Thomas (1). e. St Omers College ?-1685. S.J.1685. Watten (nov) 1686. Liège (phil) 1687, 1689. Liège (theol) 1690-2. d. October 13th or 14th, 1692, Liège, not yet ordained. (Fo.7; CRS.69; 113; 114; Nec).

CULCHETH, Thomas (1) *alias* Parker. Priest.

b. July 25th, 1654, Lancashire. s. of Thomas and Anne (Bradshaigh) of Culcheth. br. of James. e. St Omers College 1669 or earlier - 1670 or later. S.J. September 7th, 1674. Watten (nov) 1674, 1675. Liège (phil) 1676. Liège (theol) 1679, 1680. St Omers College 1681-4. La Flèche (theol) 1685, 1686. Ordained priest c.1686. London, Savoy College 1687, 1688. Liège 1689-93, 1696-1701 (Rector 1698-1701), 1703-8. College of St Ignatius 1708-12 (arrested 1708). Provincial 1712-16. Liège 1716-20 (Rector). College of St Ignatius 1723-7 (Rector). Liège 1727-30 (Rector). d. February 10th, 1730, Liège. (Fo.7; CRS.69; 113; 114; 150 III (2) 12/7/27; 91; Chad.268; E and P.170; 193 Anglia 35/269, 306; 123 II f.157; CRS.62 index; Nec).

CULCHETH, Thomas (2) *alias* Lewis. Priest.

b. April 21st, 1741, Lancashire. s. of Thomas of Wappenbury, Warwickshire and Studley. e. St Omers College 1751-6. E.C. Valladolid 1756-63. S.J. June 28th, 1763. Watten (nov) 1764. Ordained priest c.1765. Brambridge 1767. Bruges College 1767. Residence of St Mary 1767. Wappenbury 1768-73, 1779. Wardour 1781-8. Chideock 1788-1807. Exeter 1807. Chideock 1807-9. Readm. S.J.1803. d. September 5th, 1809, Chideock. bu. Chideock. (Fo.7; CRS.69; 113; CRS. Mon.1/161-2; CRS.30/189; 114; CRS.42/137; SCH.12/16, 20; ER.5/97; WR.20/61; 6 f.92; 16 f.12; 21v.2; 38 ff.31v, 35 ff; 54 f.306; AHSJ.42/306; 51 f.165; 57 II f.74; 65; CRS.27/9, 14; 01.346; Nec; 44 ff.41v, 229v, 273).

CULCHETH, William *alias* Parker. Priest.

b.1637, Lancashire. s. of John and Jane (Hawarden) of Culcheth

Hall. br. of Charles. e. St Omers College 1652-8. S.J. September 14th, 1658. Watten (nov) 1659. Liège (phil) 1660, 1661. Liège (theol) 1663-5. Ordained priest 1667. Ghent (tert) 1667. Residence of St John 1669-70, 1672-7 (Superior c.1673-7). College of St Hugh 1678-84. d. March 23rd, 1684, Lincolnshire. (Fo.7; CRS.69; 113; 114; 168 f.1; Nec).

CURSON, Sir Peter *alias* Child. Priest.

b. July 31st, 1686 or 1687, Oxfordshire. s. of Sir John, 2nd Bart. and Penelope (Child) of Waterperry. e. St Omers College 1699-1701. S.J. September 7th, 1706. Watten (nov) 1708. Liège (phil) 1709-11. Paris (theol) 1713. Liège (theol) 1714. Ordained priest c.1715. Ghent (tert) 1715. Residence of St Mary 1720, 1724. College of St Thomas of Canterbury 1725-7, 1733-41, 1743, 1744, 1746-7, 1749-50, 1752-8, 1763-4 (Brambridge c.1724, 1727, 1737, 1741, 1743, 1752). 4th Bart.1750. d.February 25th, 1765, Winchester. bu. St James' cemetery, Winchester. (Fo.7; CRS.69; 113; 91; 114; 90. f.21; CRS.27/8; CRS.42/162; 44 ff.176, 195, 212; HMC. 10th Report, App.4/190; 111; Nec).

CURTIS, Maximilian see Short, Francis.

CUVELIER, Louis. Priest.

b. September 8th, 1804, Belgium. S.J. November 15th, 1825 in Belgium. Bengal mission 1844, 1845. d. August 22nd, 1845, at sea returning to Europe. (113; 52 f.23; CDSJ).

DAGBERT, William. Laybrother.

b. August 14th, 1704, near Calais. S.J. April 13th, 1725-27. Watten (nov) 1726, 1727. It is not clear that he completed the noviceship. (113; 91).

DALAS, Ignatius *alias* Stanford or Stamford. Priest.

b.1733, in France. S.J. August 22nd, 1761 in France. (phil before entering). To English province c.1763. Liège (theol) 1763, 1764. Ordained priest 1763, Cologne. Ypres (Irish O.S.B. convent) 1767-1807. d.October 6th, 1807, Ypres. bu. in convent chapel. (Fo.7; 113; Nec; Nol.311-3; Wel. App.51-2; AHSJ.42/291).

DALE, William. Scholastic.

b. November 14th, 1801, Colburn near Richmond, Yorkshire. e. Stonyhurst 1823-5. S.J. August 28th, 1825. Montrouge (nov) 1825-7. Stonyhurst (phil and theol) 1827-30. Left 1830, not yet ordained. (115; Stol).

DALY, Peter. Laybrother.

b. June 29th, 1797, Galway, Ireland. S.J. September 7th, 1818-32. Hodder (nov) 1818-20. Hodder 1820-7. Stonyhurst 1827-32. St Mary's Hall 1832. (115).

DANIEL, Francis. Priest.

b. February 8th, 1798, London. e. Stonyhurst 1810-16. S.J. September 7th, 1816. Hodder (nov) 1816-8. Stonyhurst (phil and theol)

1818-21. Rome (theol) 1821-4. Ordained priest July 11th, 1824, Rome.
London school 1824-5. Lincoln 1825-30. Soberton 1830. Courtfield
1830-3. Hodder (tert) 1833-4. Stonyhurst 1834-42 (Rector 1839-42).
Preston 1842-3. Stonyhurst 1843. Portico 1843. Pylewell 1844-5. Socius
to the provincial 1845. Holywell 1846-9. Socius to the provincial
1849-51. Preston 1851-5. Yarmouth 1855-65 (Rector of the College of
the Holy Apostles 1858-65). Broughton 1865-9 (Superior of the College
of St Michael). d. December 6th, 1869, Broughton. (Fo.7; 115;
LR.3/64; CRS.14/298; Stol).

DANIEL, John. Laybrother.
    b. Staffordshire. S.J. September 7th, 1687-91 or 92. Watten (nov)
1687. Liège 1689. St Omers College 1690. (113; 150 II (3) 30/6/91,
14/7/91).

DANIEL, Thomas *alias* West and Watson. Priest.
    b.1716, 1717 or 1720, Inverness. e. St Omers College 1749-51. S.J.
September 7th, 1751. Liège (phil) 1752-4. Liège (theol) 1756-8.
Ordained priest c.1757. Holywell ?1759, 1761. Swynnerton c.1761.
Watten 1763-5. Dalton in Furness c.1765-79. d. July 10th, 1779,
Sizergh. bu. Kendal parish church. (Fo.7; CRS.69; NWCH.1978
pp.14-33; 113; SCH.3/8; 14 f.92; 21v.2; Gil.2/15; CRS. OP.1/151; 155
III 185c; CRS.20/9-10; CRS.32/46, 56; 169/155/8, 9, 10; CWAA.79
pp.131-8; 65; 119 ff.32, 34, 39; 152; Nec; 114; DNB; For writings see
Sut; Som. (s.v. West).

DARCY see Bermingham, Nicholas; Eyre, Thomas

DARCY, John ?*vere* Forster. Laybrother.
    b.1628, Northampton. ?e. St Omers College 1649-c.52. S.J.1652-64.
Watten (nov) 1653. Watten 1654. Ghent 1655. Watten 1656. Liège
1657-60. Paris 1661, 1663. (Fo.7; ?CRS.69/105; 113).

DARELL see Tasburgh, Thomas.

DARELL, James. Priest.
    b. December 27th, 1707, Kent. s. of John and Olivia (Smith) of
Calehill. br. of John and Thomas. e. St Omers College c.1714-23. S.J.
September 7th, 1723. Watten (nov) 1724. Liège (phil) 1725-8. Liège
(theol) 1730. Ordained priest c.1731. St Omers College 1733. E.C.
Valladolid 1733-6. Ghent (tert) 1737. Residence of St Mary 1738.
College of St Ignatius 1739-41, 1744, 1746-50, 1752-8 (Calehill ?1741,
1751, 1758-75). d. May 18th, 1785, Liège. bu. church of the Canonesses
of the Holy Sepulchre, Liège. (Fo.7; CRS.69; 113; CRS.12/25; 117;
LR.3/55, 115; 91; CRS.17/173; CRS.30/ xxxviii, 187; Wha.58;
188 n.117; Nec).

DARELL, John. Priest.
    b. May 10th, 1705, Kent. s. of John and Olivia (Smith) of Calehill.
br. of James and Thomas. e. St Omers College c.1714-22. S.J.
September 7th, 1722. Watten (nov) 1723, 1724. Liège (phil) 1725-7.
Gratz (theol) 1728, 1730. Ordained priest c.1731. Broughton 1733-9.
Thorndon 1739-c.42. Callaly c.1742-52. St Omers College 1752-62
(Rector 1752-9). Bruges College 1762-66. Wealside 1767. d. March 7th,

1768, London. (Fo.7; CRS.62 index; CRS.69; 113; 91; 114;
RH.1/38; NCH.1/19; ER.5/36, 12/106, 114, 13/103; 150 III (2)
29/10/35; 21v.2; 43 f.71v; 64 p.237; 77; 74; 90 f.174; Chad.282, 318;
CRS.7/320; CRS.32/251; 156 App.I; 36 ff.136, 166; 121; 191 nn.9, 14;
Nec).

DARELL, Thomas. Scholastic.
    b. 1710 or 1711, Kent. s. of John and Olivia (Smith) of Calehill. br.
of James and John. e. St Omers College c.1725-8. S.J. September 7th,
1728. ?Watten (nov) 1730. Liège (phil) 1730, 1732. Liège (theol) 1733.
In England, ill 1734. d. November 22nd, 1734, in England, not
ordained. bu. Little Chart, Kent. (Fo.7; CRS.69; 113; 114; 91; 90 f.11;
74; LR.3/115; Wha. p.56; Nec).

DARELL, William. Priest.
    b.1651, Buckinghamshire. s. of Marmaduke of Fulmer,
Buckinghamshire. S.J. September 7th, 1671. Watten (nov) 1672. Liège
(phil) 1673-5. St Omers College 1676. Ordained priest c.1680. Watten
(tert) 1681, 1682. Liège 1683-6. College of St Ignatius 1687. In England
1688. Liège 1689-93. Paris 1695, 1696. St Omers College 1697. Liège
1699-1701, 1703-12 (Rector 1708-12). Paris 1712-6, 1720. St Omers
College 1720-1 (Rector). d. February 28th, 1721, St Omers College.
  (Fo.7; 113; 114; 150 III (2) 7/12/20, 15/3/21; Chad.256, 259, 275;
168 f.37v; 140 n.45; 184 n.96; Che.64/454; CRS.62 index; CRS.8/43-4,
346; Nec. For writings see Som; Gil.2/18-9).

DASSONVILLE, James. Laybrother.
    b. September 22nd, 1670, Dunkirk. S.J. February 1st, 1690. Liège
1691-3, 1696-7, 1699-1702. d. February 28th, 1702, Liège. (Fo.7; 113;
114; Nec).

DAVIDTS or DAVIDTZ, John. Laybrother.
    b. September 17th, 1708, Belgium or Germany. S.J. March 27th,
1733. Rome 1738-82. d. August 15th, 1782, Monte Porzio. (Fo.7; 113;
AHSJ.42/295).

DAVIS see Barrow, Edward; Fabri, James.

DAVIS, John *alias* Lamb. Scholastic.
    b.1679, Glamorgan. e.St Omers College ?-1699. S.J. September 7th,
1699. Watten (nov) 1699, 1700. Liège (phil) 1701, 1703-4. Liège (theol)
1705, 1706. d. October 14th, 1706, Liège, not ordained. (Fo.7; 113;
114; CRS.69).

DAVIS or DAVIES, Peter. Priest.
    b. August 27th or 29th, 1690 or 1692, London. e. St Omers College
?-1711. S.J. September 7th, 1711. Watten (nov) 1712, 1713. Liège (phil)
1714, 1715. Liège (theol) 1716, 1718, 1720. Ordained priest c.1720.
Maryland 1722-34. Burton Park 1735-7. Maryland 1738. Residence of
St Michael 1739-41, 1743-4, 1746-50, 1752-5 (Broughton 1739, 1741,
1743, 1748). Watten 1756-9. d. December 28th, 1759, Watten. (Fo.7;
113; CRS.69; 114; Hu. Text II 687; RH.13/116; 23 f.121; 64 p.354; 66;
74; 91; 156 App.I; YA.71/54, 316, 77/194; CRS.22/307; CRS.32/251;
92; 111; 51 f.311; Nec).

DAVIS, Thomas. Scholastic or Laybrother.
Date and place of death unknown(114).

DAYE, John. Scholastic or Laybrother.
Date and place of death unknown (114).

DEAN, Michael. Priest.
b. September 29th, 1695 or 1696, St Germain. e. St Omers College ?-1714. S.J. September 7th, 1714. Watten (nov) 1715. Liège (phil) 1716, 1718. Liège (theol) 1720, 1723. Ordained priest c.1724. Ghent (tert) 1724. Arras 1725. St Omers College 1726, 1727. Sherfield c.1727-36. College of the Holy Apostles 1736-7. College of the Immaculate Conception 1738-9. College of St Thomas of Canterbury 1740. College of St Ignatius 1743-4, 1746-50, 1752-4. Watten 1754-8. d.July 8th or 9th, 1760, Watten. (Fo.7; CRS.69; 113; 114; 91; CRS.43/5; 68 p.253; 74; CRS.62/110-11; Nec).

DEAN, Thomas *alias* Plowden. Priest.
b. February 2nd, 1693, Cadiz. s. of John and Frances (Plowden). E.C. Rome 1706-9. S.J. December 20th or 21st, 1709 in Rome. Liège (phil) 1712-14. Liège (theol) 1715, 1716, 1718. Ordained priest c.1719. d.September 17th, 1719, Ghent. (Fo.7; 113; 114; CRS.40/138; Ki.63; CRS.62/4; Nec).

DEAS, John. Laybrother.
b. October 31st, 1740, Maryland. S.J. September 7th, 1767. Ghent 1767, 1768. It is not clear that he completed the noviceship. (113; 7 f.11; Hu. Text II 703).

DELANEY, Henry. Scholastic.
b. May 29th, 1715, London. ?s. of Henry. ?e. St Omers College c.1727-32. S.J. September 7th, 1733. Watten (nov) 1734. Liège (phil) 1735-7. Liège (theol) 1738. Left 1738, not ordained. (91; CRS.69; 113; 150 III (2) 13/9/38, 8/11/38).

DEL POUE or POUVE, Philip. Laybrother.
b.1654, 1655 or 1656, Saint-Omer. S.J. November 12th, 1682. Watten (nov) 1682, 1683. Watten 1684-5. Liège 1686-7, 1689-93. Maryland 1695-9. Ghent 1700-01, 1703-11. St Omers College 1711-3. d. May 2nd, 1713, St Omers College. (Fo.7; 113; 114; Hu. Text II 683; 170 f.1v; 95 p.791).

DELVEAUX, Joseph. Laybrother.
b.1681, Namur. S.J. February 12th, 1701. Watten (nov) 1701. Maryland 1702-34. d.January 10th, 1734, Maryland. (Fo.7; 113; 114; 91; Hu. Text II 684).

DENNET, James. Priest.
b.June 11th, 1702, Lancashire. s. of James of Lydiate. e. St Omers College c.1714. S.J. September 7th, 1720. Liège (phil) 1723, 1724. Liège (theol) 1725-8. Ordained priest c.1728. In England 1730. Ghent 1731. College of the Holy Apostles 1731, 1733-4. Houghton Hall 1734. Travelling 1736-40. College of the Holy Apostles 1741, 1743-4, 1746-50, 1752-8 (Coldham 1751, 1752). Provincial 1762-6. Coldham 1766-87. Bury St Edmunds 1787-9. d. March 1st, 1789, Bury St

Edmunds. bu. St Mary's churchyard, Bury St Edmunds. (Fo.7; 113; 114; Nec; E and P.108; CRS.69; CRS.62/196; SCH.12/16, 19; 41 nn.31, 38, 44, 63, 130, 134; 54 ff.5, 99, 131; 42 f.160; 57 I/257, II/48; 60 f.6; 64 p.245; 88; 91; HMC. 10th Report App. 4/185-7; Gil.2/47-8. For writings see Som).

DENNIS or DIONYSIUS, Francis. Laybrother.
    b.1642, Saint-Omer. S.J. November 3rd, 1669. Liège 1672. St Omers College 1673. Madrid 1674, 1675. d. December 9th, 1675, Madrid. (Fo.7; 113; 114).

DE PAUWE, Giles. Scholastic.
    b.1732. S.J.1749. Watten (nov) 1750. Liège (phil) 1752, 1753. Left 1753, not ordained. (113; 91).

DE REUDDRE, Michael. Laybrother.
    b. June 7th, 1711, Saint-Omer. S.J. September 7th, 1738. Watten (nov) 1738, 1739. St Omers College 1740, 1742-4. His name has not been traced further. (Fo.7; 113; 91).

DE VISSCHER, John. Laybrother.
    S.J. December 24th, 1690. Watten (nov) 1691, 1692. d. July 11th, 1692, Watten. (Fo.7; 114; 91; 113).

DE VREESE, Cornelius. Laybrother.
    b. October 17th, 1710, Ghent. S.J. August 14th, 1739-47. Watten (nov) 1740, 1742, 1743. Liège 1744. Watten 1746. (91; 113).

DICCONSON or DICKINSON, Ignatius. Priest
    b. November 30th, 1663 or 1665, Lincolnshire. S.J. September 7th, 1685-1707. Watten (nov) 1685. Liège (phil) 1687, 1689-90. Liège (theol) 1691-3. Ordained priest March 21st, 1693. College of St Hugh 1696-7, 1699-1701, 1703-6. (Fo.7; 113).

DICCONSON or DICKINSON, Robert. Priest.
    b.1642, Lincolnshire. S.J. September 7th, 1663. Watten (nov) 1663, 1664. Liège (phil) 1667. Liège (theol) 1672. Ordained priest April 6th, 1672. Residence of St Stanislaus 1672, 1673. Ghent (tert) 1674. Residence of St Stanislaus 1675. Liège 1676, 1678-9. Watten 1680-2. Liège 1683-5. Ghent 1686-c.90 (Rector). St Omers College 1690. Liège 1691, 1692. d. February 14th, 1693, Liège. (Fo.7; 113; Nec; 150 II (2) 2/4/72; 140 n.45; 170 f.144).

DICCONSON or DICKINSON, Thomas *alias* or *vere* Roberts, Joseph. Priest.
    b.1651, Lincolnshire. S.J. September 7th, 1672. Watten (nov) 1673. Liège (phil) 1674-6. Liège (theol) 1678-81. Ordained priest April 5th, 1681. Residence of St John 1681-4 (Cartington c.1681). Ghent (tert) 1685. Residence of St John 1686-7, 1689-93. College of St Aloysius 1696-7, 1699-1705 (Rector 1704-5. Stonyhurst c.1701, 1703). d. May 2nd, 1705, in England (?at Stonyhurst). (Fo.7; 113; 150 III (1) 11/3/02; 114; 23 f.35; NB.1/44; Gil.4/326; 168 f.2).

DIDERICH or DIDERICK, John Baptist. Priest. Also known as Rich, Bernard.
    b. March 25th, 1726, Luxembourg. S.J. September 7th, 1745. To the

English province 1769. Pennsylvania or Maryland 1771-93. d. July 5th, 1793, Notley Hall, Maryland (Fo.7; 113; 117; 68 p.275; Hu. Docs.1/672-3, 720, Text 2/698; Mel.60, 140-1, 304n).

DIGGES, Francis. Priest.

b. February 4th, 1712, Maryland. s. of William. e. St Omers College c.1725-c.30. S.J. September 7th, 1733. Watten (nov) 1734. Liège (phil) 1735, 1736. Liège (theol) 1738-41. Ordained priest c.1741. Watten 1741. Kilvington 1743-? Berrington ?-1749-67. Holt 1767. Berrington 1767-76. Appears to have retired in 1776. d. November 25th or 28th, 1791, Berrington. bu. Holy Island. (Fo.7; CRS.69; 113; 114; NCH.5/15; 21v.2; 36 ff.136, 168, 185v, 260; 65; 68 pp.41, 93; Gil.5/5; CRS.12/21; CRS.19/303-4; 35 ff.48, 69v, 89v, 107, 139v, 140; 51 f.311; 117; Nec; 156 App.1).

DIGGES, John (1). Priest.

b. August 18th, 1712, Maryland. ?br. of Thomas. e. St Omers College 1728-c.30. S.J. September 7th, 1734. Watten (nov) 1734. Liège (phil) 1735-7. Liège (theol) 1738-40. Ordained priest c.1741. Maryland 1742-6. d.December 14th, 1746, Baltimore. (Fo.7; CRS.69; Hu. Text 2/692; 113; 114; 92; 140 n.45; 51 f.311; 91).

DIGGES, John (2). Scholastic.

b. October 23rd, 1746, Maryland. e. St Omers and Bruges Colleges 1760-c.66. S.J. September 7th, 1766. Liège (phil) 1768, 1769. To Maryland 1769. Nothing further appears to be recorded. (Fo.7; 113; CRS.69; 65; Hu. Text 2/703).

DIGGES, Thomas. Priest.

b. January 5th, 1711, Maryland. ?br. of John (1). e. St Omers College ?-1729. S.J. September 7th, 1729. Liège (phil) 1733, 1734. Liège (theol) 1734-7. Ordained priest c.1737. Liège 1738-40. Maryland 1741-1805 (Superior 1750-c.55). d. February 18th, 1805, Mellwood, Maryland. (Fo.7; CRS.69; 113; 114; Hu. Text 2/691-2; 92; 140 n.45; 92; 51 f.311v; 4 f.68; Nec; CRS.12/91).

DILLON see Neville, Charles.

DILWORTH, Thomas. Priest.

b. April 7th, 1796, near Preston. e. Stonyhurst 1810-14. S.J. September 7th, 1814. Hodder (nov) 1814-6. Stonyhurst (phil etc.) 1816-25. Rome (theol) 1825-8. Ordained priest April 5th, 1828, Rome. Stonyhurst 1828-30. Brough 1830-4. Hodder (tert) 1834. St Mary's Hall 1834-5. Spinkhill 1835-9. Wigan 1839-43. d. November 21st, 1843, Holywell. bu. Holywell. (Fo.7; 115; Pa.2/27; Gil.4/172; Stol; Nec).

DINSDALE, Joshua. Scholastic.

b. March 10th, 1703, Yorkshire. S.J. September 7th, 1725. Watten (nov) 1726, 1727. Liège (phil) 1728, 1730. Liège (theol) 1733, 1734. Left 1734, not ordained. (Fo.7; 113; 150 III (2) 8/1/35; 91).

DIONYSIUS see Dennis, Francis.

DOLEMAN, Thomas. Scholastic.

b.1669, Leicestershire. S.J. September 7th, 1684. Watten (nov) 1684, 1685. Liège (phil) 1686, 1687. Liège (theol) 1689, 1690. Left 1691, not ordained. (113; 150 II (3) 29/10/89, 2/9/90, 17/2/91).

DONAIN, Thomas. Laybrother.
   b. June 12th, 1651, Artois. S.J. March 24th, 1684 or 1685. Watten
(nov) 1685. St Omers College 1686-7, 1689. Watten 1690-1. Socius to
the provincial 1692-3, 1696. Antwerp 1696-1711. Socius to the
provincial 1712. Ghent 1713, 1714. d. September 10th, 1715, Ghent.
(Fo.7; 113; 108; 114; Nec; CRS.62/index).

DONERE or DONCRE, Anthony. Laybrother.
   b. February 2nd, 1695, Artois. S.J. August 14th, 1717. Watten (nov)
1718. Watten 1720. Liège 1723, 1724. Paris 1724-7. E.C. Rome 1728,
1730. d. February 2nd, 1732, Watten, (Fo.7; 113; 114; 91, Nec).

DONERE or DONCRE or DONKER or DONEKER, Nicaise. Laybrother.
   b. August 2nd, 1679, Artois. S.J. March 3rd, 1714. Watten (nov)
1714. Ghent 1715. Watten 1716, 1718. d. August 18th, 1719, Watten.
(Fo.7; 113; 114; CRS.62/59, 285n; Nec).

DONZÉ, Francis. Priest.
   S.J. in France July 23rd, 1761. Liège (theol) 1768. An exile from
France. Nothing further recorded. (113; CPC).

DORMER, see Smith, John; Huddleston, John.

DORMER, Lord Charles. Priest.
   b. January 13th, 1690, Peterley, Buckinghamshire. s. of Charles, 5th
Baron Dormer of Wyng and Catherine (Fettiplace). Half-br. of
Francis, John Baptist, Robert and William (1). S.J. September 7th,
1709. Watten (nov) 1710, 1711. Liège (phil) 1712-4. Liège (theol)
1715-6, 1718. Ordained priest c.1718. College of St Thomas of
Canterbury 1724, 1725, 1733-41, 1746-7 (Chichester. Catherington.
Woodmancote, 1741). 6th Baron 1728. Croxteth 1747-50. Poole Hall
1750, 1752. Puddington c.1753. Bromley Hall 1754-?1761. d. March,
7th, 1761, Peterley House. bu. Great Missenden. (Fo.7; 113; 114; 91;
Nec; 188 n.117; RH.1/139, 8/182; 24 f.343; 65; HMC. 10th Report
App.4/186, 193; Bur.1/148, 207; E and P.12; Gil.5/61; 156 App.1;
CRS.9/185-6; 188 n.117).

DORMER, Hon. Francis. Priest.
   b. September 14th, 1717, Hampshire. s. of Charles, 5th Baron
Dormer and Elizabeth (Biddulph). Half-br. of Charles. br. of John
Baptist, Robert and William (1). e. St Omers College c. 1725-34. S. J.
September 7th, 1734. Watten (nov) 1734, 1735. Liège (phil) 1736-8.
Liège (theol) 1740-2. Geist (theol) 1743. Ordained priest c.1743.
Coblenz 1744. St. Omers College 1746-8. Cherry Orchard 1748-70. d.
February 1st, 1770, Cherry Orchard. bu. St Maughan church,
Monmouthshire. (Fo.7; CRS.69; 113; 114; 91; 34 ff.11 ff; 64 p.280;
HMC. 10th Report App.4/186, 190; CRS.9/144; Nec; 41 n.84).

DORMER, Hon. John Baptist. Priest.
   b. January 2nd or 22nd, 1716, Hampshire. s. of Charles, 5th Lord
Dormer and Elizabeth (Biddulph). Half-br. of Charles. br. of Francis,
Robert and William (1). e. St Omers College c.1725-34. S.J. September
7th, 1734. Watten (nov) 1734, 1735. Liège (phil) 1736-8. Liège (theol)

1740-2. Ordained priest c.1741. d. June 26th, 1743, Liège. (Fo.7;
CRS.69; 113; 114; Nec; 91).

DORMER, Hon. Robert. Priest.

   b. February 26th, 1726, Buckinghamshire. s. of Charles, 5th Lord
Dormer and Elizabeth (Biddulph). Half-br. of Charles. br. of Francis,
John Baptist and William (1). e. St Omers College c.1737-43. S.J.
September 7th, 1743. Watten (nov) 1744. Liège (phil) 1746. Liège
(theol) 1747-8. Paderborn (theol) 1749. Liège (theol) 1750. Ordained
priest c.1751. St Omers College 1752, 1753. Odstock 1753. Stapehill?
Soberton 1763-71. Ghent 1771-2. Husbands Bosworth 1772. Beckford
1772-3-? Wappenbury ?1785-92. d. May 4th, 1792, Wappenbury or in
Herefordshire or Monmouthshire. (Fo.7; CRS.69; 113; WR.20/60, 61;
114; Nec; 117; CRS.12/37; CRS. Mon.1/165; 21v.2; 44 ff.167, 235; 64
pp.384, 516; 76; 68 pp.99, 196; 90 f.171; HMC. 10th Report
App.4/186, 194; 01.287).

DORMER, Hon. William (1). Priest.

   b. June 18th, 1696, Sussex or Hampshire. s. of Charles, 5th Lord
Dormer and Elizabeth (Biddulph). Half-br. of Charles. br. of Francis,
John Baptist and Robert. e. St Omers College 1713 or earlier — 1714.
S.J. September 7th, 1714. Watten (nov) 1714, 1715. Liège (phil) 1716,
1718. Liège (theol) 1720. Ordained priest 1723. In England 1723. Ghent
(tert) 1724. Residence of St Stanislaus 1725. In England 1726-8, 1730
(College of the Holy Apostles 1728). College of St Francis Xavier 1730,
1733-4, 1746-7 (Priory, Monmouth c.1728, 1730, 1742). College of St
Ignatius 1749-50, 1752-4. Bromley Hall 1754. College of St Thomas of
Canterbury 1755-8 (Stapehill 1757, 1758). d. June 27th, 1758,?
Stapehill. (Fo.7; CRS.69; 113; ER.4/117, 10/39; 114; 44 ff;217, 267;
43 ff.47-8; 64 p.375; 74; HMC. 10th Report App.4/184, 186; 91; CRS.62
index; Nec).

DORMER, William (2) *alias* Anderson. Priest.

   b. c.1710, London. S.J. September 7th, 1728-44. Ingolstadt (phil)
1730. Ingolstadt (theol) 1734, 1735, ?1736. Ordained priest c.1736.
Ghent (tert) 1737. St Omers College 1738. College of the Holy Apostles
1739. College of St Ignatius 1740. Kelvedon 1740. College of St Hugh
1742. (Fo.7; 113; 150 III (2) 18/7/34; 66; 91).

DORRINGTON see Carlos, William or Charles.

DOYLE, William. Priest.

   b.1716 or 1717, Dublin. S.J. 1734 or 1735, in France. Transferred to
English province c.1770. Cowley Hill ?1771-1785. d. January 15th,
1785, Cowley Hill. bu. Windleshaw cemetery. (Fo.7; 113; 117; 23 f.274;
51 f.110v; 155 2/129, 3/185c; 34 f.134v; CRS.12/25; 21v.2;
CRS.23/138; 167).

DOYNE, Joseph. Priest.

   b. November 11th, 1734, Maryland. e. St Omers College c.1755-8.
S.J. September 7th, 1758. Liège (phil) 1761. Liège (theol) 1763, 1764.
Ordained priest c.1764. Stonyhurst 1767-9, 1772-3. Rixton 1773-4.
Claughton 1775. Brinn 1775-81, 1783. Rixton 1783-4. Maryland

c.1785-1803. d. October 21st, 1803, St Thomas's Manor, Maryland.
(Fo.7; CRS.69; Hu. Text 2/700; 114; 113; 4 ff.20, 63v; 21v.2; 23 f.245;
26 f.94; 91; 80; 54 ff.16, 48; 68 p.129; 25 ff.37, 45, 59, 65, 85;
Gil.4/327; 155/2/129, 3/185c: CRS.12/89; 167 p.29).

DRAPER see Metcalfe, Joseph.

DRUMMOND see Trevanion or Travagnan, Charles.

DRURY, William. Laybrother.
> b. 1697 or 1698, Lincolnshire. S.J. September 7th, 1730. Watten
1733-8. Liège 1739-41. d. June 30th, 1741, Liège. (Fo.7; 113; 114; 91;
Nec).

DUCLOS, Anthony. Priest.
> French. College of St Ignatius 1763, 1764. Nothing further recorded.
(Fo.7; 113).

DUCROC or DUCRO, John Baptist. Laybrother.
> b.1702 or 1707, Artois. S.J. September 7th, 1732. Watten (nov)
1733, 1734. Liège 1735. St Omers College 1736-40. d. March 8th, 1740,
St Omers College. (Fo.7; 113; 114; 91).

DUDDLE or DUDDELL or DUDDIS, James. Laybrother.
> b.1653 or 1654, Lancashire. S.J. March or September 7th, 1683.
Watten (nov) 1684. St Omers College 1685-7, 1689. Watten 1690-2. St
Omers College 1693, 1696-7, 1699-1701, 1703-12. d. January 20th,
1712, St Omers College. (Fo.7; 113; 114; 170 f.7; Nec).

DUGUID see Leslie, Charles.

DUKE, Andrew. Scholastic or Laybrother.
> d. date and place unknown. (Fo.7; 114).

DUKE, Charles *alias* Harrington and Hayles.
> b.1649, Berkshire. s. of George. e. St Omers College c.1679-81. E.C.
Rome 1681-3. d. February 1st, 1683, Rome. S.J. before death. (Fo.7;
CRS.69; CRS.40/98; CRS.55/648).

DUNN, Joseph *vere* Earpe ?*alias* Hart. Priest.
> b. March 19th, 1746, Catterick, Yorkshire. e. St Omers and Bruges
Colleges 1758-64. S.J. September 9th, 1764. Liège (phil) 1767. Liège
(theol) 1768, 1769, 1771. Ordained priest 1771. Ghent (tert) 1772-3.
Bruges school 1773. Liège Academy 1774. Callaly 1774-5 or 6. Preston
1775 or 6-1827. d. November 19th, 1827, Preston. (Fo.7; CRS.69; 113;
6 ff.15, 87, 103, 119, 125, 129v, 158, 169v, 170, 189, 275v; 7 ff.134v,
145v, 395v; 8/2 ff.21, 36, 51, 63, 95, 129, 157, 170, 178, 186; 16 ff.78,
111; 21v.2; 30 ff.7a, 79; 152 n.62; 62 nn.14, 24, 135; 69; 94 *passim*;
142 p.4; 25 f.35; 80; Gil.2/143 ff; 155/2/129; CRS.7/320; 167 pp.21,
30; 177; 178. For writings see Gillow).

DUPUY see Ashton, Thomas.

DURAND or DURANT see Langworth, Basil.

DURHAM see Collingwood, Thomas (2); Smith, John (1).

DYNE, George. Laybrother.
> S.J.1706 in Maryland. Maryland 1708, 1710-11. d. January 11th,
1711, Maryland. (Fo.7; 113; 114; Hu. Text 2/685; Nec).

DYNE, John. Laybrother.

b. February 15th, 1656, Sussex. S.J. September 7th, 1681. Watten (nov) 1682. St Omers College 1683-7. Liège 1689-90. St Omers College 1691. Liège 1692-3, 1696. Maryland 1699-1701, 1703. d. April 11th, 1703, Maryland. (Fo.7; 113; 114; Hu. Text 2/683; Nec).

EARPE see Dunn, Joseph.
EAST, Henry. Laybrother.
> b.1649. S.J. March 18th, 1685. Watten (nov) 1685. d. May 2nd, 1686, Liège. (Fo.7; 113; 114; Nec).

EBERSON, Thomas *alias* Beveridge. Priest.
> b. March 12th, 1660, Leicestershire. e. St Omers College 1678 or earlier -79. S.J. September 27th, 1679. Ingolstadt 1682-5. Liège (theol) 1687. Ordained priest c.1689. Watten (tert) 1689. College of St Ignatius 1690-3, 1696. St Omers College 1697, 1699-1701, 1703-4. Liège 1705-6. Watten 1708. Socius to the provincial 1708-11. Watten 1712-5 (Rector). E.C. Rome 1715-23 (Rector). Liège 1724-8 (Rector 1724-7). Munich 1728, 1730. d. July 3rd or 30th, 1733, Liège. (Fo.7; CRS.69; 113; 9 nn.173, 278; 114; 12 f.131; 170 f.29; CRS.62 index; Nec).

EBORALL, James *alias* Eyre. Scholastic.
> b.1744. s. of Anne. e. St Omers and Bruges Colleges 1758-63. S.J. September 7th, 1763. Watten (nov) 1763, 1764. Left, not ordained, 1766. (91; CRS.69; 113).

ECCLESTON, Thomas (1). Priest.
> b.1643, Lancashire. s. of Thomas and Jane (Clifton) of Eccleston Hall, Lancashire. Uncle of Eccleston, Thomas (2). e. St Omers College?-1668. S.J. September 7th, 1668. Watten (nov) 1669. Liège (phil) 1672. Liège (theol) 1673-7. Ordained priest April 17th, 1677. College of St Aloysius 1679-87, 1689, 1691-4, 1696-7 (Southworth ?1677-?. Brindle c.1685-?1698). d. November 25th, 1698, ?Brindle, ?Southworth. (Fo.7; CRS.69; 113; 114; E and P.356; CRS.23/5; Chad.204; CRS.4/433; CRS.13/398; 101; Nec).

ECCLESTON, Thomas (2) *alias* Holland and Gorsuch. Priest.
> b.1659. s. of Henry and Eleanor (Blundell) of Eccleston Hall, Lancashire. Nephew of Eccleston, Thomas (1). e. St Omers College?-1677. E.C. Rome 1677-9. S.J. March 18th, 1697, in Rome. Liège (theol) 1699-1701, 1703. Ordained priest c.1703. College of St Ignatius 1704. Residence of St Michael 1705-14 (York ?-1710-14. Superior 1712-4). College of St Ignatius 1714-c.22 (Rector 1717-22). Ingatestone c.1724-9. Liège 1730-1. St Omers College 1731-43 (Rector 1731-7). d. December 30th, 1743, St Omers College (Fo.7; CRS.69; 113; 114; CRS. Mon.2/388; LR.3/6; ER.5/72, 12/110; 150 III (2) 20/1/31,5/6/34; 12 ff.102, 118; 91; Pa.149-51; DNB; E and P.117, 356; Gil.2/155-6; CRS.4/376; CRS.40/92-3; 101; Ki.68, 122; Nec. For writings see Som and Gillow).

ECCOP, Charles. Priest.

b. November 8th, 1697, St Germain. e. St Omers College 1714 or earlier-15. S.J. September 7th, 1715. Watten (nov) 1715, 1716. Liège (phil) 1718, 1720. Liege (theol) 1723, 1724. Ordained priest c.1724. Culcheth or Leigh c.1724, 1727-8, 1731-2, ?1733. College of St Ignatius 1734. d. January 15th, 1735, in England. (Fo.7; CRS.69; 113; 114; Nec; 91; CRS.13/371; CRS.25/114; CRS.62 index; 150 III (2) 18/1/21; 24 f.5v; 81).

EDEN, James *alias* Clare. Priest.

   b. September 12th, 1663, Co. Durham. s. of Nicholas. E.C. Lisbon 1683-6. Magdalen College, Oxford 1688. E.C. Rome 1689. Ordained priest March 25th, 1690. S.J. September 30th, 1692-6. Watten (nov) 1693. Ghent 1695-6. (113; Ans.3/54; Ki.68; Cro.195).

EDGE, Charles. Laybrother.

   b.1666 or 1667 or 1668, Denbighshire. S.J. January 12th, 1688 or 1689. Watten (nov) 1689. Liège 1690, 1691. Watten 1692-3, 1696-7, 1699-1700. St Omers College 1701, 1703-5. Liège 1705-11. Watten 1712-6, 1718. d. August 7th, 1718, Watten. (Fo.7; 113;114; 170 f.152v; Nec).

EDISFORD, Edward. Laybrother.

   b.1659, 1661 or 1664, Yorkshire. S.J. April 30th, 1700. Watten (nov) 1701. Liège 1703-16, 1718, 1720. Watten 1723-9. d. September 16th, 1729, Watten. (Fo.7; 113; 114; 91; Nec).

EDISFORD, John (1). Priest.

   b.1656, Yorkshire. Uncle of Edisford, John (2). e. St Omers College ?-1675. S.J. September 7th, 1675. Watten (nov) 1676. Liège (phil) 1679, 1680. Liège (theol) 1681-4. Ordained priest April 1st, 1684. Watten (tert) 1685. Residence of St John 1686-7. Carleton 1687-8. Residence of St John 1689-93. Residence of St Michael 1694-1719 (Superior c.1694-c.1703, 1715-19). Provincial 1719-20. d. August 13th, 1720, St Omers College. (Fo.7; 113; 114; CRS.69; Nec; CRS.62/73; 89; 123 III B f.287; 193/35 Anglia 127).

EDISFORD, John (2) *alias* Jackson. Priest.

   b. September 14th, 1700, Yorkshire. nephew of Edisford, John (1). e. St Omers College 1715-20. S.J. September 7th, 1720. Liège (phil) 1723, 1724. Liège (theol) 1725-8. Ordained priest c.1729. Liège 1730. Ghent (tert) 1733. Liège 1734-44, 1746-50. d. March 30th, 1750, Liège. (Fo.7; CRS.69; 114; 113; 91; CRS.62 index; Nec. For writings see Som).

EDISFORD, John (3) *vere* Swarbrick. Priest.

   b. February 1st, 1738, Lancashire. ?e. St Omers College ?-1759. S.J. September 7th, 1760. Watten (nov) 1761. Liège (phil) 1763, 1764. Liège (theol) 1767. Ordained priest c.1767. Bruges College 1768-70. Salisbury 1770-3. Exeter 1773, 1779, 1789. d. November 21st, 1789, Exeter. bu. St Olave's churchyard. (Fo.7; 113; 114; CRS.69; CRS.42/15; CRS. Mon.1/136, 149, 168; 44 ff.233, 235v; 47 f.17; 76; 68 p.109; 77; Gil.4/106; 01.291; 91; Nec).

EDWARDS see Acton, Thomas.

ELLERKER, John. Scholastic.

b. August 12th, 1732, Hart near Hartlepool, Co. Durham. br. of Thomas. e. St Omers College 1743-8. S.J. September 7th, 1748. Watten (nov) 1749. Liège (phil) 1750, 1752. Liège (theol) 1753, 1754. d. April 29th, 1756, Liège, not ordained. (Fo.7; CRS.69; 113; 114; 6 f.279; Nec).

ELLERKER, Thomas. Priest.

b. September 21st, 1738, Hart near Hartlepool, Co, Durham. br. of John. e. St Omers College c.1751-5. S.J. September 7th, 1755. Watten (nov) 1756, 1757. Liège (phil) 1758. Liège (theol) 1761. Ordained priest c.1762. Liège 1763-4, 1767-9, 1771-3. Liège Academy 1775, 1776, 1780-4, 1788, 1792, 1794. Stonyhurst 1794, 1795. d. May 1st, 1795, Stonyhurst. bu. Stonyhurst. (Fo.7; CRS.69; 113; 3 f.37; 114; 6 f.279; DNB; 13 f.146; 21v.1; 54 ff.37v, 60, 64v; 56 ff.331-2; 90 f.54; HMC. 10th Report App.4/186; Chad.369, 392; Gil.2/158; 157; 97; Nec. For writings see Som; Gil).

ELLIOT see Sheldon, Ralph.

ELLIOTT, Nathaniel *alias* Sheldon. Priest.

b. May 1st, 1705. From Gateacre Park, Shropshire. S.J. September 7th, 1723. Watten (nov) 1724. Liège (phil) 1725-7. St Omers College 1728, 1730, 1733. Liège (theol) 1734-7. Ordained priest c.1736. Weston 1738-40. Watten 1740-1. Residence of St George 1741-4, 1746. Socius to the provincial 1747-8. St Omers College 1748-52 (Rector). E.C. Rome 1752-62 (Rector 1756-62). St Omers College 1762. Bruges College 1762-6 (Rector). Provincial 1766-9. Holt 1769-74 -?80. d. October 10th, 1780, Holt. (Fo.7; 113; LR.3/9; 12 f.189; 13 f.101v; 41 nn.29, 37, 45, 57, 94, 51 f.67; 66; 68 p.42; 85; 91; HMC. 10th Report App.4/184; Gil.2/159; Ki.69; 111; Nec. For writings see Som; Sut).

ELLIS see Jump, Richard; Prince, Richard.

ELMES, Augustine. Laybrother.

b. February 2nd, 1646, Oxfordshire. S.J. November 10th, 1673. Watten (nov) 1673-5, 1676, 1678-9. Liège 1680-93, 1696-7, 1699-1701, 1703-5. d. November 14th, 1705, Liège. (Fo.7; 113; 114).

EMMOTT, John. Scholastic.

b. January 12th, 1733, London. ?s. of John and Monica. ?br. of Joseph. e. St Omers College ?-1752. S.J. September 7th, 1752. Watten (nov) 1752-4. Liège (phil) 1755. d. July 23rd, 1755, Liège, not ordained. (Fo.7; CRS.69; 113; 114; 91; 6 f.241; Nec).

EMMOTT, Joseph. Priest.

b. September 16th, 1734, London. s. of John and Monica. ?br. of John. e. St Omers College ?-1753. S.J. September 7th, 1753. Watten (nov) 1754. Liège (phil) 1756-8. Liège (theol) 1758-61. Ordained priest c.1761. St Omers College 1762. Bruges College 1762-4. Ghent 1765. College of St Ignatius 1766. Chiswick 1767-72. Croxteth, Gillmoss and Fazackerley 1772-1816. Readm. S.J.1803 or 1804. d.November 14th, 1816, Gillmoss. bu. St Anthony's, Liverpool. (Fo.7; CRS.69; 113; 114; LR.1/30, 3/5; 13 ff.299, 348, 409, 464; 21v.2; 27 ff.84, 85, 88, 115, 175;

65; 76; 25 f.20; 80; Chad. 293; Gil.5/61; 155/2/129, 3/185c; 167 pp.22, 30; 173; 105; 91; 6 f.241; Nec; AHSJ.42/306).

ENGLEBERT, Leonard. Priest? Laybrother? Scholastic?
  d. date and place unknown. (Fo.7; 114).

ENGLEFIELD or INGLEFIELD, John *alias* Stokes. Priest.
  b. 1676, Berkshire. ?s. of Anthony and Alice (Stokes) of White
  Knights, Berkshire. e. St Omers College 1692 or earlier-96. S.J.
  September 7th, 1696. Watten (nov) 1697. Liège (phil) 1699-1701. Liège
  (theol) 1703-6. Ordained priest c.1705. Ghent (tert) 1706. Residence of
  St Michael 1708-16, 1720, 1724-5 (Fountains Abbey). Marnhull.
  Clytha. d. February 6th, 1733, in England. (Long Horsley? and bu.
  there?). (Fo.7; CRS.69; 113; 114; Nec; CRS.56/171; 91; 165;
  CRS.13/179 n.6).

ENWRIGHT or ENRIGHT, John. Laybrother.
  b.1793, Castletown, Co. Limerick. S.J. November 12th, 1817.
  Hodder (nov) 1817-9. Stonyhurst 1820-1, 1825, 1828, 1835, 1840. St
  Mary's Hall 1841-2. d. December 15th, 1843, St Mary's Hall. bu.
  Stonyhurst. (Fo.7; 115; 113; Nec).

ERRINGTON see Collingwood, Thomas (1).

ETHERIDGE, James. Bishop.
  b. October 19th, 1808, Redmarley, Worcestershire. br. of John. e.
  Sedgley park 1817-20, Stonyhurst 1820-7. S.J. September 20th, 1827.
  Hodder (nov) 1827-9. St Mary's Hall (phil) 1830. Stonyhurst 1831-3. St
  Mary's Hall (theol) 1833-6. Ordained priest September 24th, 1836,
  Stonyhurst. Pontefract 1836-9. Norwich 1839-42. Mount St Mary's
  College 1842 (Rector). Hodder (tert) 1842. St Leonards-on-Sea 1843-4.
  Norwich 1844-51 (Rector of the College of the Holy Apostles 1846-51).
  St Beuno's College 1851-5 (Rector). Preston 1855-7 (Rector of the
  College of St Aloysius). British Guiana 1857 (Superior and Vicar
  General). Bishop of Torona and Vicar Apostolic of British Guiana
  1858-77. d. December 31st, 1877, at sea. bu. at sea. (Fo.7; 115;
  SCH.322; NA.37/165-6; Gil.2/182; Nec).

ETHERIDGE, John. Priest.
  b. November 11th, 1811, Redmarley, Worcestershire. br. of James.
  e. Stonyhurst 1820-7. S.J. September 20th, 1827. Hodder (nov)
  1827-29. St Mary's Hall (phil) 1830-1. Stonyhurst 1831-8. St Mary's
  Hall (theol) 1838-40. Louvain (theol) 1840-2. Ordained priest 1841.
  Stonyhurst 1842-5. St Mary's Hall 1845. St Helens 1845-7. St Mary's
  Hall 1847-8. St Beuno's College 1848-51 (Rector). Provincial 1851-3.
  Rome 1853-7. Liverpool 1857-82. d. December 21st, 1882, Liverpool.
  bu. St Swithin's churchyard, Gillmoss. (Fo.7; 115; 113; Nec).

EURE, William *alias* Every. Priest.
  b.1648, Lincolnshire. S.J. September 7th, 1669. Liège (phil) 1672. St
  Omers College 1673. Liège (theol) 1674-6. Ordained priest c.1678. In
  England 1678. College of St Hugh 1679-82. Liège (theol) 1683-4.
  Watten (tert) 1685. College of St Hugh 1686, 1687. York prison 1689.
  College of St Hugh 1690-3, 1696-7. d. March 3rd, 1698, in England

(?Lincoln). (Fo.7; 113; 114; Nec).

EVANS see Andrews, Francis; Fairchild, Thomas.

EVANS, Charles. Priest.

b.1640, Carnarvon. S.J. September 7th, 1661. Liège (phil) 1663-5. St Omers College 1667. Liège (theol) 1669, 1672. Ordained priest c.1672. Residence of St Winefrid 1672. Watten (tert) 1673. La Flèche, France 1674. College of St Aloysius 1676, 1678. France 1679. d. November 25th, 1680, Rome. (Fo.7; 113; 114; 168 f.77; 123 II f.107; Nec).

EVANS, Philip. Priest.

b.1645, ?near Abergavenny, Monmouthshire. s. of William and Winefrid (Morgan). e. St Omers College ?-1665. S.J. September 7th, 1665. Liège (phil) 1667, 1669. Liège (theol) 1672, 1673. Ordained priest 1674. Residence of St Stanislaus 1674. College of St Francis Xavier 1675-6, 1678 (Cardiff, Powis, Abergavenny, Skerr). In prison in Cardiff 1679. Martyred at Cardiff, July 22nd, 1679. Canonised. (Fo.7; CRS.69; DNB; 113; CRS.47/296ff; Chad.206; Gil.2/186; ? HMC. 11th Report App.II/230; FAB.178-181; BR.65-9; Cha.544; 12 p.78; Nec; 114; O'Ke.32 ff).

EVANS, Thomas *alias* Lewis, Francis. Scholastic.

b.1651,Hereford. e. St Omers College ?-1671. S.J. September 7th, 1671. Watten (nov) 1672. Liège (phil) 1673-5. Liège (theol) 1676-7. d. May 29th, 1677, Liège, not ordained. (Fo.7; CRS.69; 113; 114; 123 I/161; Nec).

EVERARD, William. Laybrother.

b.1632, Norfolk. S.J. 1657. Watten (nov) 1658, 1659, 1660, 1661. St Omers College 1663-7. d. September 28th, 1667, St Omers College. (Fo.7; 113; 114; Nec).

EVERY see Eure, William.

EWEN, James. Scholastic.

b. November 22nd, 1737. e. St Omers College c.1755-c.7. S.J. September 7th, 1757. Watten (nov) 1758. Liège (phil) 1761. St Omers College 1762. Left 1762, not ordained. (91; CRS.69; 113; Chad.313-5).

EXTON see Redford, Sebastian.

EYLES see Jackson, Ambrose; Isles, Ambrose.

EYRE see Eborall, James.

EYRE, Francis. Scholastic.

b.1669, Eastwell, Leicestershire. s. of Thomas and Mary (Bedingfeld). br. of Thomas and William (2). e. St Omers College ?-1687, S.J. 1687. Watten (nov) 1687. Liège (phil) 1689-91. Left 1693, not ordained. (Fo.7; CRS.69; 113; RH.9/5; 150 II (3) 21/6/92).

EYRE, Thomas *alias* Barker and Darcy. Priest.

b. December 22nd, 1669 or 1670, Eastwell, Leicestershire. s. of Thomas and Mary (Bedingfeld). br. of Francis and William (2). e. St Omers College ?-1687. S.J. September 7th, 1687. Watten (nov) 1687. Liège (phil) 1689-92. Liège (theol) 1693, 1696. Ordained priest April 21st, 1696. Liège 1697, 1699, 1700. Ghent (tert) 1701. Liège 1703-8. St Germain 1709-12. Socius to the provincial 1712-5. d. November 9th,

1715, London. (Fo.7; CRS.69; 113; 150 III(I) 30/1/1712, 27/8/1712, 17/9/1712; 114; DNB; Gil.2/197; Ki.72; CRS.62 index; RH.9/5, 30; Nec).

EYRE, Vincent. Scholastic.
    b.1674, Derbyshire. s. of Adam and Elizabeth (Burley) of Broadway. e. St Omers College 1693 or earlier - 98. S.J. September 7th, 1698. Watten (nov) 1699, 1700. Liège (phil) 1701-2. Left 1702, not ordained. (Fo.7; CRS.69; 113; 150 III(1) 2/2/1704; Gil.2/202).

EYRE, William (1) *alias* Alford. Priest.
    b.1638, Leicestershire. s. of Rowland and Ann (Smith) of Hassop. S.J. September 24th, 1658. Watten (nov) 1658, 1659. Liège (phil) 1660, 1661. Liège (theol) 1663-4, 1667. Ordained priest 1667. Ghent (tert) 1667. St Omers College 1669. Residence of St John 1672-4 (Eslingside). d. January 7th or 8th, 1675, in England. (Fo.7; 113; 114; RH.8/57, 9/5; Nec).

EYRE, William (2) *alias* Barker. Priest.
    b.1678, Leicestershire or Norfolk. s. of Thomas and Mary (Bedingfeld). br. of Francis and Thomas. e. St Omers College 1693 or earlier - 98. S.J. September 7th, 1698. Watten (nov) 1699, 1700. Liège (phil) 1701, 1703. Liège (theol) 1704-6. Ordained priest c.1707. Ghent (tert) 1708. St Omers College 1709-10. College of the Holy Apostles 1711-24. d. February 17th, 1724, in England. (Fo.7; CRS.69; 113; 114; Nec; 43 ff.34-5, 37, 38v, 39v, 40v).

EYSTON see Ingleby, Thomas.

EYSTON, George. Priest.
    b. July 23rd, 1667, 1670 or 1671, Berkshire. s. of George and Ann (Dormer) of East Hendred. e. St Omers College ?-1688. S.J. May 7th, 1688. Watten (nov) 1689, 1690. Liège (phil) 1691-3. Liège (theol) 1696, 1697. Watten 1697, 1699-1700. Ghent 1701, 1703-11. Ordained priest c.1710. Watten 1711-6, 1718, 1720, 1723-8, 1730, 1733-8, 1740-1. Ghent 1742, 1744. d. April 18th, 1745, Ghent. (Fo.7; CRS.69; 113; 114; 150 II(3) 31/8/1697, 21/6/98, III(1) 8/3/1710; 91; E and P.72; Nec).

EYSTON, Robert. Priest.
    b. March 13th, 1729, 1730 or 1732, Berkshire. e. St Omers College 1745-51. S.J. September 7th, 1751. Watten (nov) 1752. Liège (phil) 1752-5. Ordained priest April 17th, 1757. Ghent (tert) 1756-7. College of the Immaculate Conception 1757-8. Weston 1759. Crondon Park 1759-66. d. January 16th, 1766, Crondon Park. (Fo.7; CRS.69; 113; 114; 91; ER.4/ 119; 65; CRS.6/329; Nec).

FABRI, James *alias* Davis. ?Scholastic.
    b.1744. S.J. September 24th, 1760. To the English province 1768. Liège (theol) 1769. Does not appear to be mentioned again in the province records. (91; 113).

FABRI, John. ?Priest.

  b. July 3rd, 1734, Liège. S.J. September 7th, 1755. Watten (nov) 1756, 1757. Liège (theol) 1758. Ghent (tert) 1761. Left 1763. (91, 113).

FAIRBAIRN, Thomas. Scholastic.

  b. November 8th, 1799, Newcastle. e. Stonyhurst 1815-8. S.J. September 7th, 1818. Hodder (nov) 1818-20. Stonyhurst (phil) 1820-2. St Acheul (phil) 1822. Stonyhurst 1822-5. Fribourg (theol) 1825-7. Stonyhurst 1827. Left 1827, not yet ordained. (113; 115; Stol; 2).

FAIRCHILD, Thomas *alias* Evans. Priest.

  b. August 12th, 1715, London or Monmouthshire or Montgomeryshire. e. St Omers College c.1732-6. S.J. September 7th, 1736. Watten (nov) 1736, 1737. Liège (phil) 1738, 1740-1. St Omers College 1742-4, 1746. Strasbourg (theol) 1747-9. Ordained priest c.1750. Liège 1750, 1752-4. Rheims 1755. St Omers College 1756, 1757. York 1757/8-60 or 62. d. January 30th, 1764, York. (Fo.7; CRS.69; 113; 91; 114; CRS.4/376; 96 v.1; Nec; Col.154; 64 pp.316-7).

FAIRCLOUGH, John. Priest.

  b. May 4th, 1787, Wigan. s. of Robert and Jane (Booth). e. Stonyhurst 1802-6. S.J. September 7th, 1806. Hodder (nov) 1806-8. Stonyhurst 1808-27. Ordained priest June 5th, 1811, Durham. Stockeld Park 1827-8.South-hill 1828-31. St Mary's Hall 1831. South-hill 1831-2. d. November 16th, 1832, South-hill. bu. South-hill. (Fo.7; 115; 113; 114; Stol; 21v.2; CRS.4/435; Gil.2/218; 93 p.60; Nec).

FAIRCLOUGH, Joseph. Scholastic.

  e. Stonyhurst 1806-? S.J. September 7th, 1811. Hodder (nov) 1811-? Stonyhurst (phil) 1815. Left 1817, not ordained. (116; 113: 2; Stol).

FAIRCLOUGH, Matthew. Scholastic.

  e. Stonyhurst 1807-? S.J. September 7th, 1812. Stonyhurst (phil) 1815. Left 1816, not ordained. (116; 113; 2).

FAIRFAX see Carteret, Edward,

FAIRFAX, Joseph. Scholastic.

  b. April 17th, 1725, Yorkshire. S.J. September 7th, 1744. Liège (phil) 1746. No further mention of him has been found in the surviving records. (Fo.7; 113).

FAIRFAX, Thomas *alias* Beckett. Priest.

  b. October 24th, 1655 or 1656, Gilling, Yorkshire. ?s. of Nicholas and Isabella (Beckwith) of Gilling and Tanshelfe. e. St Omers College ?-1675. S.J. September 7th, 1675. Watten (nov) 1676. Liège (phil) 1678, 1679. Liège (theol) 1680-3. Ordained priest December 18th, 1683. Ghent (tert) 1684, 1685. Liège 1686. Oxford 1687, 1688, in prison 1689. Residence of St Mary 1690, 1691. Residence of St Michael 1692, 1693. Liège 1696. Residence of St Michael 1697. College of St Ignatius 1699-1701, 1703-9. Wardour 1710-13. College of St Ignatius 1714. ?Wardour 1715-6. d. March 2nd, 1716, ?at Wardour. (Fo.7; CRS.69; 113; 114; CRS. Mon.1/151-3; RH.3/96, 114n, 6/109; 21v.2; Gil.2/220-3; Ki, 76; 01.299; 123/2 f.174; 187 nn.53-55, 57, 64-5; DNB; Nec; CRS.62/35, 280, 305. For writings see Som).

FALKNER or FALCONER, Stephen. Priest.
b.1621 or 1622, Kent. e. St Omers College 1636 or earlier - 41. E.C.
Seville ?-1647. Ordained priest. S.J.1650. St Omers College 1652.
College of St Ignatius 1653. Residence of St John 1654-61, 1663-4.
College of the Immaculate Conception 1667. Ghent (military chaplain)
1669. d. December 1st, 1670, in England. (Fo.7; CRS.69; 113; 114;
Ans.2/100; 150 II(1) 10/6/50; Nec).

FALKNER or FALCONER, Thomas. Priest.
b. October 6th, 1707, Manchester. e. Manchester Grammar School.
S.J. May 15th, 1732 in Paraguay province. To English province c.1768.
Spetchley 1768-71. Winsley 1772-3-?. Gifford's Hall ?1776-8. Plowden
Hall c.1778-82-?84. d. January 30th, 1784, Plowden Hall. (Fo.7; 113;
114; Nec; RH.1/48, 10/165, 173n; WR.30/12; DNB; 65; Gil.2/224-6;
Ki.77; LR.6/79; SCH.12/19, 21; 5; 43 f.317. For writings see Som;
Sut.).

FANNING, Dominic alias Clifton, Francis. Priest.
b. November 6th, 1742, London. e. St Omers College 1755-62. S.J.
September 7th, 1762. Watten (nov) 1763, 1764. Bruges College 1767-9,
1771-2. Liège 1772-6, 1781, 1783-6, 1794. Ordained priest c.1773.
Holme Hall 1794-6. Salisbury 1796-9. New Hall 1799-1812. London
1812. d. May 23rd, 1812, London. bu. Old St Pancras churchyard.
(Fo.7; CRS.69; 113; Newh.74, 115, 121,123-5, 163; LR.7/21;
ER.5/97; 3 f.57; 1 ff.147v, 255v; 13 ff.204v, 278v, 341; 21v.2; 54 f.35;
51 f.306; 57/1 ff.148, 195v; 90 f.54; Chad 387; 166 I pp.48, 137;
CRS.17/95, 112, 135, 141; 01.265; CRS.4/273; 157; 114; Nec).

FARMER see Steynmeyer, Ferdinand.

FARRAR, James. Priest.
b. May 2nd, 1707, Lancashire. e. St Omers College ?-1725. S.J.
September 7th, 1725. Watten (nov) 1726, 1727. Liège (phil) 1727, 1728,
1730. Liège (theol) 1733, 1734. Ordained priest c.1734. Maryland
1734-46. Biddleston 1747-51. Gifford's Hall 1751-4. Hooton 1754-?63.
d. July 18th or 19th, 1763, Hooton. bu. Eastham church. (Fo.7;
CRS.69; 113; 114; 91; 90 f.20v; LR.1/117; 21v.2; 35 f.41; 64 pp.472,
524; 65; 86; 89; HMC. 10th Report App.4/186; 92; Hu. Text 2/690;
Nec).

FENTHAM, Henry alias Gifford and Key. ?Scholastic.
b. November 6th, 1736, Nottinghamshire. e. St Omers College
1753-6. E.C. Rome 1756-8. S.J. September 7th, 1758. Left 1761,
?not ordained. (Fo.7; 91; CRS.69; CRS.40/215).

FENWICK see Caldwell, John.

FEREIRA see Fidgett, John.

FERMOR See Turberville, John.

FERMOR, Henry alias Jermyn or Germin. Priest.
b.1637, Oxfordshire. ?s. of Henry and Ursula (Middleton) of
Tusmore. ?br. of Thomas. e. St Omers College 1650 or earlier -56. S.J.
September 7th, 1656. Watten (nov) 1657. Liège (phil) 1658-60. Liège
(theol) 1661-5. Ordained priest c.1665. Ghent (tert) 1667. Residence of

St Mary 1669. Ghent 1672. Residence of St Mary 1673. College of St
Thomas of Canterbury 1674, 1675. Residence of St Mary 1676.
Residence of St George 1678. Residence of St Mary 1679, 1680. d.
October 26th, 1680, in England. (Fo.7; CRS.69; 113; 114; Nec).

FERMOR, Thomas *alias* Jermyn. Priest.
    b. February 6th or 9th, 1649, Oxfordshire. ?s. of Henry and Ursula
(Middleton) of Tusmore. ?br. of Henry. e. St Omers College 1660-66 or
later. S.J. September 7th, 1667. Watten (nov) 1669. Liège (theol)
1672-5. Ordained Priest 1676. Ghent (tert) 1676. St Omers College
1678, 1679. College of St Francis Xavier 1680-3. College of St Ignatius
1684, 1685. College of the Immaculate Conception 1686,1687. In
England 1688. Ghent 1689, 1690. College of St Ignatius 1693.
Residence of St Mary 1693. College of the Holy Apostles 1696.
Residence of St Mary 1697. College of St Ignatius 1699-1701, 1703.
College of the Holy Apostles 1704, 1705. College of St Thomas of
Canterbury 1706. College of St Ignatius 1708-1710. d. May 28th, 1710,
in England. (Fo.7; CRS.69; 113; 114; Nec).

FERNANDEZ, Anthony. Priest.
    b. Portugal. S.J. ?in Portugal. To England 1662 with Queen
Catherine of Braganza. College of St Ignatius 1672, 1673. d. April
23rd, 1674, in England. (Fo.7; 113; 135 f.180; CRS.38/xi, xxxi; 114;
Nec).

FERNANDEZ, John. Laybrother.
    S.J. ?in Portugal. To England as companion to Fr A.Fernandez and
afterwards to Fr. A. Laurenzo. College of St Ignatius 1672-4, 1676,
1680-7, 1689. To Portugal 1689. (Fo.7; 113; CRS.38/xxxi).

FERRER see Ireland, Lawrence.

FETHERSTON, Thomas. Priest.
    b. April 24th, 1671, Lancashire or Cumberland. S.J. September
28th, 1690, Tournai. Liège (phil) 1693. Liège (theol) 1696. St Omers
College 1699-1701. Ordained priest 1702. Lulworth 1702. Liège (theol)
1703. Ghent (tert) 1704. College of St Chad 1705 (?Aston). College of
St Thomas of Canterbury 1706 (?Lulworth). College of St Chad 1708-9
(?Aston). College of St Thomas of Canterbury 1710-6, 1718, 1720-4
(Lulworth ?-1714-15-?24.Rector 1720-4). d. October 1st, 1724, Ghent.
(Fo.7; 113; 114; Nec; CRS.62/211, 236; Ber.106; CRS.6/365).

FIDGETT, John *alias* Fereira. Laybrother.
    b. August 10th, 1724, Colchester. S.J. October 9th, 1752, in Brazil.
Exiled from Brazil and imprisoned in Portugal 1759-77. (Fo.7/957;
Lei.7/269).

FINDENIER, Andrew. Laybrother.
    b. January 19th, 1729, Saint-Omer. S.J. December 31st, 1751.
Watten (nov) 1752, 1753. St Omers College 1754-8. d. March 29th,
1760, St Omers College. (Fo.7; 113; 91; 114; Nec).

FINES see Robson, Christopher.

FISHER, Honoratus *vere* Bassin. Priest.
    b. March 8th, 1741, France. S.J. September 20th, 1764. Phil. before

entering S.J. Liège (theol) 1767,1768. Ordained priest c.1768. Lille
1769, 1771. Working outside the English province 1772, 1773. Place
and date of d. not recorded. (Fo.7; AHSJ.42/291; 91; 113).

FISHER, Robert. Scholastic or laybrother.
     d. in England, date not recorded. (Fo.7;114).

FISHWICK, John. Priest.
     b. March 12th, 1804, Chorley, Lancashire. e. Stonyhurst 1814-21.
S.J. October 29th, 1821, in Rome. Rome (nov) 1821-3. Ferrara
(phil)1823. Rome (phil and theol) 1824-8. Stonyhurst 1828-32.
Ordained priest November 13th, 1830. Alnwick 1832-53. St Helens
1853-4. Norwich 1854-60. Stonyhurst 1860-2. St Beuno's College
1862-6. Rhyl 1866-7. d. March 6th, 1867, Rhyl. bu. Pantasaph. (Fo.7;
115; 113; NA.37/166; Nec).

FITZGERALD, Nicholas. Scholastic.
     b. September 29th, 1699, Alsace. S.J. September 7th, 1720. Liège
(phil) 1723, 1724. Liège (theol) 1725, 1726, 1727. Douay (theol) 1728.
Nothing further recorded. It is not clear that he was ordained priest.
(Fo.7; 113; 91; 150 III (2) 15/3/27, 8/5/28, 30/10/28 ,23/7/29).

FITZHERBERT, Robert. Scholastic.
     From Swynnerton, Staffordshire. s.of William and Elizabeth
(Owen). d.1708, St Omers College. Admitted S.J. *in articulo mortis.*
(Fo.7; CRS.69; Chad.245; Nec; 123 II f.68).

FITZWILLIAM or FITZWILLIAMS, John *alias* Villiers. Priest.
     b.1635, Lincolnshire. ?s. of William and Frances (Sullyard). e. St
Omers College 1648 or earlier – 54. S.J.1654. Watten (nov) 1655. Liège
(phil) 1656-8. Liège (theol) 1659-63. Ordained priest March 24th, 1663.
Maryland 1663-1665. d. October 30th, 1665, Maryland. (Fo.7; CRS.69;
113; 114; Nec; Hu. Text 2/680).

FLEETWOOD, Francis or John Walter *alias* Flichon and Flitun.
     b. March 9th, 1699, London. ?s. of William and Mary (Pigott) of
Colwich, Staffordshire. ?br. of John. e. St Omers College before 1722.
E.C.Valladolid 1722-3. Ordained priest c.1723. E.C.Douay 1724.
Twyford 1726-32. Painsley Hall 1732-5. S.J. June 20th, 1735. Watten
(nov) 1735, 1736. Liège 1737. Working outside the province 1738.
Residence of St John 1739. College of St Ignatius 1740, 1742-4, 1746
(Twickenham 1741). Swynnerton 1746. Travelling 1746-52. Residence
of St John 1752. Everingham c.1755-71. Liège 1771-4. d. July 10th,
1774, Liège. (Fo.7; CRS.69; Ans.4/103; 113; RH.14/176; LR.1/73;
54 f.308v; 150 III(2)9/11/37; 66; 160; Ki.87; CRS.7/257, 264;
CRS.30/184; 140 n.45; 188 n.6; Nec; CRS.27/2; Gil.2/296; 51 f.306v)

FLEETWOOD, John *alias* Flichon and Flitun. Priest.
     b. January 11th, 1703, London. ?s. of William and Mary (Pigott).
?br. of Francis (John Walter). e. St Omers College ?-1718. E.C.
Valladolid 1718-23. S.J. October 31st, 1723. Watten (nov) 1724. Liège
(theol) 1725-7. Ordained priest c.1728. Broughton 1728-? Maryland
1733. d. January 16th, 1734, Maryland. (Fo.7; CRS.69; 113; 114;
64 p.239; 74; 91; CRS.25/112; CRS.30/183; CRS.32/251; 92; Hu. Text

2/690; SCH. 3/9; Gil.2/296; Nec).

FLETCHER see Cotton, John; Pendrill, Richard.

FLETCHER, Thomas. Laybrother.
> b. June 20th, 1650, Lancashire. S.J. March 14th, 1686. Watten (nov) 1686. College of St Aloysius 1687. Watten 1689. St Omers College 1690-3. Watten 1696-1697. d. March 2nd, 1698, Watten. (Fo.7; 113; 114; Nec).

FLEURY, Charles *alias* Forrester. Priest.
> b. April 21st, 1739, in France. Nephew of Peter. S.J. September 13th, 1756, in France. To English province c.1764. Ghent 1767. Linstead Lodge 1767-9, 1772-5. Wardour 1775-1810. Irnham 1810-13. New Hall 1813-25. Readm. S.J.1803. d. May 2nd, 1825, New Hall. bu. New Hall cemetery. (Fo.7; 113; CRS. Mon.1/160, 244; 114; LR.3/61n; ER.5/97; 6 ff.117, 146v; 13 ff.102v, 288, 319, 352, 380, 415, 452; KR.1/18; 21v.2; 50 f.15v; 65; 94 f.324; CRS.17/94; 01.306; 133; 103; AHSJ. 42/305; NewH.164; 114; Nec).

FLEURY, Peter. Priest.
> b.c.1726. Uncle of Charles. S.J. in France. To England and Wardour during the French Revolution. d. December 6th, 1797, Wardour. bu. Wardour. (01.308).

FLICHON see Fleetwood, Francis (John Walter) and John.

FLITUN see Fleetwood, Francis (John Walter) and John.

FLOYD or LLOYD, Francis. Priest.
> b. November 17th, 1692, Wales. S.J. September 7th, 1710. Watten (nov) 1711, 1712. Liège (phil) 1713, 1714. Liège (theol) 1715-6, 1718. Ordained priest c.1719. Ghent (tert) 1720. Maryland 1723-9. d. November 13th, 1729, Maryland. (Fo.7; 113; 91; Nec; Hu. Text 2/687; 90 f.24v).

FONTAINE, Herman. Laybrother.
> b. January or February 2nd, 1688, Liège. S.J. August 9th, 1720. Watten (nov) 1724, 1725, 1726-8, 1730, 1731, 1733-41, 1744, 1746-50, 1752-4, 1756, 1758, 1761, 1764. d. October 6th, 1767, Watten. (Fo.7; 113; 114; 91; 140 n.45; Nec).

FONTAINE, John Baptist de la. Priest.
> b. May 30th, 1739, France. S.J. September 13th, 1757, in France. To English province c.1764. Ordained priest before 1767. Liège (theol) 1767. Ghent 1768. Thelton 1768-74. Bristol 1777-81. Liège Academy 1781, 1783. Montargis 1786-92. Bodney 1792, ?1795-6. Bury St Edmunds 1800. Kensington 1800, 1804, 1805, 1807. Readm. S.J. 1803. Haughley 1807. Pontefract 1809, 1810, 1812, 1815-6. Paris 1816, 1818-20. d. March 29th, 1821, Paris. (Fo.7; 113; 150; (1750-1853) f.178; 3 f.37; 1 ff.175v, 181, 187; 7 f.300v; 198 pp.434, 437, 443, 446-54, 461-2, 502; 199 p.120; 200; 13 f.364; 15 f.266; 21v.2; 41 nn.52, 95, 135, 136; 65; 76 f.114; 75p.54v; 78; CG; 166 II p.122; Pa.2/75; CRS.3/181-2; 20 f.184; 196; Nec. For writings see Som).

FORD see More, Henry or Francis.

FORREST, Philip. Laybrother.

b.1625, Artois. S.J.1651-9. Watten (nov) 1651, 1652, 1653-8. (Fo.7;113; 150 II (2) 2/8/59).

FORRESTER see Fleury, Charles.

FORSTER see Tatlock, Henry; ?Darcy, John.

FORSTER, Henry. Laybrother.
b. March 20th,1604, Suffolk. s.of Christopher and Elizabeth (Rookwood). Father of Joseph and Michael. e. St Omers College c.1615. S.J. (after death of wife) May 16th, 1653. Watten (nov) 1653, 1654, 1655-6. Ghent 1657-61, 1663-9, 1672-6, 1678-9. d. December 5th, 1679, Ghent. (Fo.7; CRS.69; 113; 114; Nec).

FORSTER, Joseph. Laybrother.
b.1631, Suffolk. s. of Henry and br. of Michael. e. St Omers College 1649-53. S.J. August 28th, 1653. Watten (nov) 1653-5. Ghent 1656, 1657. Brussels 1658-70. Paris 1672, 1673. Ghent 1674. Socius to the provincial 1675. St Omers College 1676. Socius to the provincial 1678, 1679. Antwerp 1679-86. d. April 13th, 1686, Antwerp. (Fo.7; CRS.69; 113; 114; 108; Nec).

FORSTER, Michael *alias* Gulick. Priest.
b.1642, Suffolk. s. of Henry. br of Joseph. e. St Omers College 1652-9. E.C. Rome 1659-60. S.J. June 15th, 1660. Watten (nov) 1660. Liège (phil) 1661, 1663. Liège (theol) 1664-5, 1667. Ordained priest c.1667. St Omers College 1669. Maryland 1669-84(Superior 1676-84). d. February 6th, 1684, Maryland. (Fo.7; CRS.69; 114; 113; CRS.40/63; Nec; Hu. Text 2/681).

FORSTER, Richard. Priest.
b. March 11th, 1672, Sutton, Lancashire. e. St Omers College ?-1692. S.J. September 7th, 1692. Watten (nov) 1693. Liège (phil) 1696. Liège (theol) 1697. Prague (theol) 1699-1701, Ordained priest 1701, Prague. Formby 1701-7 and New House. d. May 9th, 1707, New House. bu. Harkirke. (Fo.7; CRS.69; 113; 114; 23 f.35v; NB.1/38, 206; Gil.2/309; 170 f.245v; Che.N.S. 12; Gil.HP.249).

FORSTER, Thomas. Laybrother.
b. February 12th, 1689, Chester. S.J. February 4th or 10th, 1713-25. Ghent 1714-6. St Omers College 1718, 1720. Liege 1723, 1724. Ghent 1725. (113; 150 III (2) 6/10/25).

FORTESCUE, Sir Francis *alias* Stanley. Scholastic.
b.1662, Buckinghamshire. s. of Francis or John. e. St Omers College ?-1682. S.J. September 7th, 1682. Watten (nov) 1683. Liège (phil) 1684-7. Liège (theol) 1689-92. Residence of St Mary 1693. Left, not ordained, 1695. (Fo.7; CRS.69; 113; 150 II (3) 2/7/95; E and P.192; 31 f.4; For.254).

FOUR, John Baptist du.(1) Laybrother.
b. December 11th, 1700, Picardy. ?Uncle of the next. S.J. June 3rd, 1722. Watten (nov) 1723. St Omers College 1724-6. Watten 1727. Liège 1728, 1730, 1733-42, 1744. d. March 9th, 1746, Ghent. (Fo.7; 113; 114; 91; Nec).

FOUR, John Baptist du.(2) Laybrother.

b. May 29th, 1726, St Pol, Artois. ?Nephew of the last above. S.J.
July 15th, 1748. Watten (nov) 1748, 1749. St Omers College 1750,
1752-8, 1761. Bruges College 1763-4, 1767-9, 1771-3. d. 1792, Saint-
Omer. (Fo.7; 113; AHSJ.42/295; 16 f.12v;117).
FOURNIERS see Clough, Richard.
FOURNIERS, Nicholas *alias* or *vere* Clough. Priest.
b. June 17th, 1708, Montgomeryshire. e. St Omers College ?-1725.
S.J. September 7th, 1725. Watten (nov) 1725-7. Liège (phil) 1728, 1730.
Liège (theol) 1733. Ordained priest 1733. St Omers College 1734. Ghent
(tert) 1735. College of St Thomas of Canterbury 1736, 1737. Residence
of St Mary 1738. Scarisbrick 1738-72. Lydiate 1772-9. d. November
10th, 1779, Lydiate. (Fo.7/1406-7; CRS.69; 114; 113; Gib. 1/291; 117;
23 ff.192, 245; 24 f.347v; 27 f.216v; 25 ff.19, 25, 37, 46; 80; 91; HMC.
10th Report App.4/186, 189; 111; 51 f.311; 158; 156 App.1; 155
III/185c; Nec; CRS. OP.1/27).
FOXE, James *alias* Pole or Poole.(1) Priest.
b. March 25th, 1685, Yorkshire. ?e. St Omers College c.1702. S.J.
September 7th, 1707. Watten (nov) 1708, 1709. Liège (phil) 1710-12.
Liège (theol) 1713-5. Ordained priest c.1715. Ghent (tert) 1716. Flixton
1718. Residence of St Michael 1720, 1723-8-? (Richmond 1727-8).
Rome 1732. Boulsterstone 1734-9. Walton Hall 1741-c.53. College of
the Immaculate Conception 1755-8-? (Highfield, Derby 1759). d.
December 4th, 1760, in England. (Fo.7; CRS.69; 114; 91; 113; 43 f.38v;
74; HMC. 10th Report App.4/187; CRS.25/111; 111; YA.77/199, 215;
158; 156 App.1; Nec).
FOXE, James. (2) Priest.
b. July 17th, 1729, Shropshire. ? s. of Henry. e. St Omers College
c.1740-7. S.J. September 7th, 1747. Watten (nov) 1747. Liège (phil)
1749, 1750. Liège (theol) 1752-5. Ordained priest c.1755. Watten (tert)
1756, 1757. Soberton 1757. Bromley 1760-8. Aston 1769 (Rector of
College of St Chad 1767-69). Southworth 1769-95 (also served Dutton
and Leigh). d. March 29th, 1795, Southworth. bu. Windleshaw. (Fo.7;
CRS.69; 114; 113; SCH. 3/10, 17/20; 21v.2; 23 f.272; 26 f.201bv;
44 ff.167, 267; 64 p.257; 68 p.310; 25 ff.9, 24, 28, 40, 45, 52, 60, 63, 81,
86, 95, 102, 110, 111, 117, 135; 72; 80; HMC. 10th Report App.4/187;
111; 155 II/129, III/185c; Ki.88; CRS.13/399; 167 pp.23, 29; Nec).
FRAMBACH, James. Priest.
b. January 6th, 1723, Germany. S.J. October 19th, 1744. To the
English province c.1757. Pennsylvania 1758-95. d. August 26th, 1795,
in America. (Fo.7; 113; 197; Hu. Text 2/695; CRS.12/53; 92; Nec).
FRANKLAND, William. Scholastic.
b. March 22nd, 1700, York. e. St Omers College ?-1719. Watten
(nov) 1720. Liège (phil) 1723, 1724. Liège (theol) 1725-6. Cologne
(theol) 1727. Liège (theol) 1727. Left 1728, not ordained. (CRS.69; 113;
91; 150 III(2) 7/9/26, 29/5/28).
FREVILLE see Jenison, Michael, Ralph and Thomas (2).
FRYER, Edwin. Scholastic.

b. April 19th, 1811, York. e. Stonyhurst 1825-30. S.J. March 26th,
1829. Hodder (nov) 1830-2. St Mary's Hall (phil) 1833-5. London
School 1835-6. Left, not ordained, 1836. (115; LR.3/66; 2).

GADENNE, James. Laybrother
   b.1672, Lille. S.J. November 12th, 1699. Watten (nov) 1700, 1701,
1703. St Omers College 1704-6. E.C. Rome 1708-16, 1720, 1724-8,
1730, 1733-7, 1739-40. d.? between 1741 and 1743, ? Rome. (Fo.7; 113;
91; Nec).
GAGE see Petre, William; Plowden, Edmund.
GAGE, Charles *vere* Journo. Priest.
   b.1655 or 1656, Flanders. br. of Philip. e. St Omers College ?-1675.
S.J. September 7th, 1675-93. Watten (nov) 1676. Liège (phil) 1678,
1679. Liège (theol) 1680-3. Ordained priest 1683. Watten 1684-5. New
York 1686, 1687. Norwich 1688-93. (Fo.7; CRS.69; 113; NA.37/157;
150 II (3) 24/4/83, 8/11/92; 43 f.20; 168 f. 48v; Hu. Text 2/683).
GAGE, John (1) *alias* Lewis. Priest.
   b.1651, Sulfolk. ?s. of Sir Edward, Bart. and Elizabeth (Fielding) of
Hengrave Hall. e. St Omers College ?-1670. S.J. September 7th, 1670.
Liège (phil) 1672-5. Liège (theol) 1676,1678. Ordained priest April 1st,
1679. Ghent (tert) 1679. Bruges 1680. College of St Thomas of
Canterbury 1681, 1682. College of the Holy Apostles 1683-7, 1689,
1691-3, 1696-1701, 1703-29 (Rector 1725-7. Great Warningfield,
Sudbury 1727). d. January 12th, 1729, ? Great Warningfield. (Fo.7;
CRS.69; 113; 91; 168 f.89; 108; CRS.13/176; Nec; 43 ff. 16-49).
GAGE, John (2). Priest.
   b. August 7th, 1720, Stanningfield, Suffolk. s.of John and Elizabeth
(Rookwood) of Coldham. e.St Omers College c. 1729-40. S.J.
September 7th, 1740. Watten (nov) 1740, 1741. Strasbourg (theol)
1743, 1744. Ordained priest c.1744. Liège 1746, 1747. Ghent (tert)
1748. College of the Holy Apostles 1750-90 (Bury St Edmunds
1753-90). d. October 30th, 1790, Bury St Edmunds. bu. Stanningfield
church. (Fo.7; CRS.69; 114; 113; 91; Ki.93; SCH. 12/16, 19; LR.8/7;
13 ff.59v, 92v; 21 v 2.41 nn.6, 7, 13, 17, 30, 47, 79, 106; 42 ff.161v, 168,
209; HMC. 10th Report App.4/185-7; 188 n.97; 140 n.45; Nec).
GAGE, Philip *vere* Journo. Scholastic.
   b.1650, Flanders. br. of Charles. e. St Omers College 1668 or earlier
-69 or later. S.J. September 7th, 1673. Watten (nov) 1673, 1674. Liège
(phil) 1676. 1678. Liège (theol) 1679-82. Left, 1682, not ordained.
(Fo.7; CRS.69; 113; CRS.48/396n;150 II(3) 11/7/82; 168 f. 48v; CSP.
Dom.1682; p.618, 1683 Jan-June 37, 111-3, 116).
GAHAN, Matthew. Priest.
   b. February or September 7th, 1782, Dublin. S.J. September 7th,
1805, Irish province. Hodder (nov) 1805-7. Ordained priest July 16th,

1810, Palermo. Isle of Man 1824-37. d. February 22nd, Isle of Man.
(116; Fo.7, Irish section, 86).

GALLI, Anthony *alias* or *vere* Judoci. Priest.
From Italy. S.J.c. 1645, in France. To England with Mary of
Modena. College of St Ignatius 1674, 1676, 1680-7. In England 1688.
France 1689. St Germain 1691-3, 1696-7, 1699-1701, 1703. d.
September 3rd or 7th, 1703, Watten. (Fo.7; 113; 114; 150 II(2) 15/8/76;
123 IIIB f.250; 135 f.180; Nec).

GALLOWAY, Edward. Priest.
b. June 22nd, 1706, London. s. of Stephen and Elizabeth
(Turberville). e. St Omers College ?-1724. S.J. September 27th, 1724.
Watten (nov) 1725, 1726. Liège (phil) 1727, 1728. Liège (theol) 1730.
?London 1732-3. Liége (theol) 1734, 1735. Ordained priest 1735.
College of St Aloysius 1736-40. College of the Holy Apostles 1741,
1743-4. College of St Ignatius 1746-50, 1752-6. Travelling 1757. Paris
1758. Norwich c.1759-74 (Rector of the College of the Holy Apostles
1763-73). London 1774-9. d. June 23rd, 1779, London. bu. old St
Pancras churchyard. (Fo.7; CRS.69; 113; 114; NA.37/158-9;
SCH.12/16; LR.7/16; 150 III(2) 15/3/32, 10/1/33, 11/7/33; 13 ff.58,
98; 21v.2; 41 *passim*; 54 f.12; 151 ff.40, 41, 57; 91; HMC. 10th Report
App.4/184, 186, 193; E and P.176; Ki.94; Can: Nec).

GANTLET, Anthony. Priest.
d. in England, date not recorded. (Fo.7; 114; Nec).

GARBOT see Richardson, Robert.

GARDEN or GAIRDEN, James. Priest.
b.c.1718 S.J. Scottish misssion. d. May 7th, 1793, London. (Fo.7;
114; Nec; RSC. 77).

GARDINER, John. Priest.
b. July 29th, 1659, Lancashire. ?br. of William. S.J. September 7th,
1680. Liège (phil) 1683, 1684. Liège (theol) 1686. Ordained priest c.
1687. St Omers College 1687, 1689-90. Ghent 1691. College of the
Immaculate Conception 1691, 1693, 1696-7, 1699-1701, 1704-6,
1708-16, 1718, 1720, 1723-7. (Queeniborough 1714, 1715, 1727). d.
August 31st, 1727, Liège. (Fo.7; 91; 113; Nec; CRS.62 index).

GARDINER, Thomas. Scholastic.
b. November 25th, 1665, Maryland. e. St Omers College ?-1685. S.J.
1685. Watten (nov) 1685, 1686. Liège (phil) 1687, 1689-90. Liège (theol)
1691-3. Left 1694, not ordained. (Fo.7; 113; CRS.69; 150 III(2)
22/8/92, 5/12/93; Hu. Text 2/704).

GARDINER, William *alias* Taylor. Priest.
b.1651, Lancashire. ?br. of John. e. St Omers College 1662 or
earlier – 67. S.J. September 7th, 1673. Watten (nov) 1673. Liège (phil)
1674-6. Liège (theol) 1678-81. Ordained priest April 5th, 1681. College
of St Aloysius 1681-7, 1689-93. Kelvedon 1696. College of St Aloysius
1697, 1699-1701, 1703-6, 1708-16, 1718, 1720, 1723-5 (Dalton in
Furness. 1701, 1704, 1714; Pennington 1716; Dalton ?-1725). d. April
1st, 1725, Dalton in Furness (Fo.7; CRS.20/8-9; 113; ER.5/95, 9/108;

LF.18; 43 f.24; Pa.88; CRS.69 Nec).

GARNER, George. Laybrother.

b. April 5th, 1737, Lancashire. e. St Omers College 1749-c.53. S.J.July 1st, 1756-64. Watten (nov) 1756, 1757, 1758, 1761. Ghent 1764. (113; 91; CRS.69).

GAVAN or GAWEN, Henry ?*alias* Jones. Priest.

b.1668, London. ?s. of Thomas. e. St Omers College ?-1685. S.J. September 7th, 1685. Watten (nov) 1685,1686. Liège (phil) 1687, 1689. Liège (theol) 1690-2. Cologne (theol) 1693. Ordained priest c.1693. Residence of St George 1696. Liège 1699-1701. d. May 12th, 1701, Liège. (Fo.7; CRS.69; 113; Nec).

GAVAN or GAWEN, John. Priest.

b.1640, London. ?br. of Thomas. e. St Omers College ?-1660. S.J. September 7th, 1660. Watten (nov) 1661. Liège (phil) 1663-5. Rome (theol) 1667-70. Ordained priest c.1670. Ghent (tert) 1670-1. College of St Chad 1672-6, 1678-9 (Wolverhampton). Executed at Tyburn, June 20th, 1679. bu. St Giles-in-the-Fields churchyard. Beatified. (Fo.7; CRS.69; 114; 113; CRS.47/268; SCH.3/10; 150 II(2) 16/9/70,20/9/70; Gil.2/405; 193 Anglia, 34/363; 01.311; 135 ff.193-4; FAB. pp.119, 157, 170-2; BR. pp.57-61; Cha.527; Nec).

GAVAN or GAWEN, Thomas. Priest.

b.1646 or 1648, London. ?br. of John. S.J. September 7th, 1668. Watten (nov) 1669. Liège (phil) 1672. Liège (theol) 1673-6. Ordained priest c.1677. Maryland 1677-85. College of the Holy Apostles 1686-93 (Thelton 1686). College of St Thomas of Canterbury 1696-7, 1699-1701, 1703. College of St Francis Xavier 1704, 1705. College of St Ignatius 1706. College of St Hugh 1708-12 (Rector 1708-9). d. June 4th, 1712, in England. (Fo.7; 114; 113; Hu. Text 2/682; 150 III(1) 24/7/06; 43 ff.18, 20; Nec).

GAWEN see Hacon, Hubert.

GAZAIN or GAZIN see Robinson, John.

GEE, Henry de. Laybrother.

b. July, 7th, 1710, Liège. S.J. September 7th, 1740. Watten (nov) 1741. Maryland 1743-58. St Omers College 1761. Bruges College 1763-4. Ghent 1767-9. Bruges College 1771-2. d. April 2nd, 1772, Bruges College. (Fo.7; 113; 114; 111; Hu. Text 2/692; Nec).

GEISSLER, Luke. Priest.

b.1737, Germany. S.J.1755. To English province c.1768. Maryland or Pennsylvania 1769. Pennsylvania 1771. America 1772-86. d. August 11th, 1786, in America. (Fo.7; Hu. Text 2/697; 114; Nec; 113; 68 pp.78, 141; CRS.12/28).

GELIBOURN see Gillibrand, Thomas and William (1).

GENGIVAL or GINGIVAL, John. Laybrother.

b.1675, Liège. S.J. October 31st, 1702. Watten (nov) 1703, 1704, 1705-6, 1708. d. January 30th, 1708, Watten. (Fo.7; 113; 114; Nec).

GENIN, Gervais. Priest.

S.J. in France. To England with nuns from Liège in 1794. Holme

Hall, Yorkshire 1795. Dean House, Salisbury 1796-9. New Hall.
1799-1800. d. March 19th, 1800, New Hall. bu. New Hall. (Fo.7; 157;
CRS.17/91,129, 146; NewH.x, 101, 113, 162; Nec).

GEORGE see Joris, Henry John.

GEORGERIE, Charles. Priest.

    S.J. in Flandro – Belgic province. Liège 1763, 1764 as an exile but no
evidence found that he worked in the English province. (113; 114).

GERARD, John. ?Scholastic.

    s. of Richard and Judith (Stewart) of Ince. br. of William(1). d.
October 10th, 1696, St Omers College. No further record found. It is
possible that he was a boy in the school admitted S.J. on his deathbed.
(Fo.7; CRS.6/228; 95 p.827; Nec).

GÉRARD, Joseph. Priest.

    S.J. in France. d. November 28th, 1796, London. (CRS.12/60;
CPC).

GERARD, Philip *alias* Clovel and Smith, Joseph. Priest. 7th Lord Gerard of
Bromley.

    b. December 1st, 1665, Staffordshire. s. of Richard of Hilderstone,
Staffordshire. br. of William(2). e. St Omers College ?-1684. S.J.
September 7th, 1684. Watten (nov) 1684, 1685. Liège (phil) 1686, 1687.
Liège (theol) 1689-93. Ordained priest March 21st, 1693. College of St
Ignatius 1696. College of the Holy Apostles 1697. College of St Ignatius
1699. Ghent 1700-01. College of St Ignatius 1703. Residence of St Mary
1704, 1705. College of St Ignatius 1706. Residence of St Mary 1708,
1709. St Omers College 1710-16, 1718, 1720, 1723. Residence of St
Stanislaus 1725. In England 1726-8, 1730. 7th Lord Gerard of Bromley
1707. d. February 21st, 1733, in England. (Fo.7; CRS.69; 114; 113;
Gil.2/432; E and P.245, 345; Ki.95; CRS.62/1, 135; Nec).

GERARD, Thomas (1) *alias* Clovel. Priest.

    b.1640, Lancashire s. of Sir William, 3rd Bart. and Elizabeth
(Clifton) of Brinn. e. St Omers College 1654-60. E.C. Rome 1660-2.
S.J. March 25th, 1675, in Rome. Liège (theol) 1677-80. Ordained priest
c.1678. Residence of St Michael 1681 (near Tadcaster. Superior). d.
October 5th, 1682, in England. (Fo.7; 114; CRS.69; 113; CRS.40/63;
CRS.55/580; 150 II(2) 3/7/77; 168 f.2; Nec).

GERARD, Thomas (2) *alias* Clovel.

    b. July 23rd, 1667, Lancashire. s. of Richard and Isabella (Baldwin)
of Wigan. e. St Omers College ?-1686. S.J. September 7th, 1686.
Watten (nov) 1686, 1687. Liège (phil) 1689, 1690. Liège (theol) 1691-3,
1696. Ordained priest April 21st, 1696. College of St Aloysius 1697,
1699-1701, 1703-6, 1708, 1710-12 (Garswood c.1701-4-?). Watten 1713.
St Omers College 1714-15. d. December 14th, 1715, St Omers College.
(Fo.7; CRS.69; 114; 113; 23 f.35; NWCH.1969/130; E and P.148;
CRS.6/228-9; CRS.62 index; Nec).

GERARD, Thomas (3) *alias* Wright. Priest.

    b. October 14th, 1692 or 1693, Lancashire. s. of Thomas and Mary
(Wright) of Highfield. ?br. of William (3). e. St Omers College ?-1714.

S.J. September 7th, 1714. Watten (nov) 1715. Liège (phil) 1716, 1718.
Liège (theol) 1720, 1723. Ordained priest c.1724. Ghent (tert) 1724.
Maryland 1725-39. Ghent 1740. College of the Immaculate Conception
1741, 1743-1744, 1746-58 (Rector 1748-58. Belgrave 1744. Holt 1752).
d. April 15th, 1761, in England. (Fo.7; 114; CRS.69; 113; 91; Hu. Text
2/688; HMC. 10th Report App.4/187; 140 n.45; Nec; 51 f.311;
CRS.6/228; CRS.13/397; CRS.62/92).

GERARD, William (1). Scholastic.
    b.1656, Lancashire. s. of Richard and Judith (Stewart) of Ince. br. of
John. e. St Omers College ?-1675. S.J. September 7th, 1675. d.
September 24th, 1676, Liège, not ordained (Fo.7; CRS.69; 113; 114;
CRS.6/228; Nec).

GERARD, William (2) *alias* Clovel. Priest.
    b. August 4th, 1662, Staffordshire. s. of Richard of Hilderstone. br.
of Philip. e. St Omers College 1675-80. S.J. September 7th, 1683.
Watten (nov) 1684. Liège (phil) 1685. Liège (theol) 1686-7. Ordained
priest c.1688. Watten 1689-91. Ghent 1692. Watten 1693, 1696-7,
1699-1701, 1703-1706. d. March 2nd, 1706, Watten. (Fo.7; CRS.69;
114; 113; 140 n.45; Nec).

GERARD, William (3). Priest.
    b. November 6th, 1687, Lancashire. ?s. of Thomas and Mary
(Wright) of Highfield ?br. of Thomas (3). S.J. September 7th, 1707.
Watten (nov) 1708. Liège (phil) 1710-12. Liège (theol) 1713-5. Ordained
priest c.1716. Ghent (tert) 1716. Maryland 1719-31. d. April 16th, 1731,
Maryland. (Fo.7; 113; 114; Hu. Text 2/686; 91; CRS.6/228; Nec).

GERMIN see Jermyn.

GEX or GEZ, James. Laybrother.
    b. February 24th, 1689, 1690 or 1691, Saint-Omer. br. of Robert.
S.J. October 9th, 1715. Watten (nov) 1715, 1716. St Omers College
1720, 1723-7. Liège 1728, 1730. d. February 2nd, 1732, Liège. (Fo.7;
114; 113; 91; Nec).

GEX or GEZ, Robert. Laybrother.
    b. March or April 1st, 1701. br. of James. S.J. September 7th, 1724.
Watten (nov) 1725, 1726. Ghent 1726, 1727. Liège 1728. Watten 1730.
St Omers College 1733. Ghent 1734-7. Liège 1738-9. Watten 1739-41. St
Omers College 1743, 1745-7, 1749-50. d. January 14th, 1750, St Omers
College. (Fo.7; 114; 113; 150 III(2) 7/11/39; 91; Nec).

GIBSON, Francis. Priest.
    b.1668, 1669 or 1670, Warwickshire. ?s. of Sir Isaac and Katherine
(Waldegrave) of Combe. ?br. of Henry and Isaac. S.J. January 20th,
1687. Watten (nov) 1687. Liège (phil) 1689-91. Liège (theol) 1692, 1693.
Ordained priest c.1695. Residence of St George 1696-7, 1699-1701,
1703-6, 1708-13. College of St Hugh 1714-6, 1718. College of the Holy
Apostles 1718-23. College of St Ignatius 1724, 1725. Kiddington 1724
or 1725-?38. d. April 5th or 6th, 1738, Kiddington. (Fo.7; 91; 113;
CRS.7/396; CRS.17/458; Nec; 43 ff.39, 42).

GIBSON, Henry. Scholastic.

b. October 22nd, 1666 or 1667, Warwickshire. ?s. of Sir Isaac and Katherine (Waldegrave) of Combe. ?br. of Francis and Isaac. S.J. September 7th, 1687. Watten (nov) 1687. Liège (phil) 1689-92. Liège (theol) 1693. d. September 1st, 1694, Liège not ordained. (Fo.7; 114; 113; Nec).

GIBSON, Isaac. Priest.

b. January 15th, 1674, Warwickshire. s. of Sir Isaac and Katherine (Waldegrave) of Combe. ?br. of Francis and Henry. e. St Omers College ?-1693. S.J. September 7th, 1693 or 1695. Liège (phil) 1696, 1697. Prague (theol) 1699-1701. Ordained priest 1702. Ghent (tert) 1703. In England 1704, 1705. Residence of St Winefrid 1706. Residence of St George 1708-16, 1720, 1723-5. In England 1726-8, 1730 (Norton near Tewkesbury c.1730). Residence of St George 1734-8, d. November 10th, 1738, in England. (Fo.7; CRS.69; 114; 113; 91; Nec).

GIBSON, William. Scholastic.

b.1711, 1712 or 1713, Northumberland. s. of George and Mary (Bradshaigh) of Stonecroft. e. St Omers College ?-1731. S.J. September 7th, 1731. Liège (phil) 1733-5. St Omers College 1736-8, 1740-2. d. December 29th, 1742, Pont-à-Mousson, not ordained. (Fo.7; CRS.69; 114; 113; 91; Gil.2/443; E and P.206; 140 n.45; Nec).

GIFFARD or GIFFORD, John. Priest.

b. December 20th, 1683 or 1684, London. S.J. September 7th, 1705. Watten (nov) 1706. Liège (phil) 1708-10. Liège (theol) 1711-3. Ordained priest c.1713. St Omers College 1714-6, 1718, 1720. Residence of St Michael 1723-5. In England 1726-8, 1730. Residence of St Michael 1733-40 (Danby 1727-40). St Omers College 1741, 1743, 1746-7, 1749-50, 1752-6. d. August 21st, 1757, St Omers College. (Fo.7; 113; CRS.25/111; 91; 111; 150 III(2) 27/7/43; 89; CRS.13/229; Nec).

GIFFARD or GIFFORD see Wheble, James; Fentham, Henry; Hyde, Richard; Vavasour, William; Wright, Matthew.

GILDRIDGE or GILDREDGE see Kemp, Henry.

GILLIBRAND, Richard. Priest.

b. March 2nd, 1717, Chorley, Lancashire. s. of Thomas and Alice (Westby) of Chorley. br. of William (2). e. St Omers College c.1730-c.35. S.J. September 7th, 1735. Watten (nov) 1735-7. Liège (phil) 1738-40. Liège (theol) 1740-2. Trèves (theol) 1743. Ordained priest c.1744. Ghent (tert) 1744. St Omers College 1746. Residence of St George 1747. College of St Thomas of Canterbury 1749-51 (Odstock 1751). Crondon Park 1751. Maryland 1752-4. Haggerston 1755-8. Lincoln 1758-61. Arlington 1761. Rome 1763-4, 1767-9. Loretto 1769-73. d. March 23rd, 1774, Bath. bu. Bath Abbey. (Fo.7; CRS.69; 114; 113; 21v2; Hu. Text 2/694; 36 f.169; 50 f.138; 64 p.386; 65; HMC. 10th Report App.4/183; 35 f.51; 92; 109; ER.5/94; Bat.73; Nec; E and P.99).

GILLIBRAND, Thomas *alias* Gelibourn. Scholastic.

b. 1656, Lancashire. s. of John and Elizabeth (Chorley) of Chorley. br. of William (1). e. St Omers College ?-1676. S.J. September 7th,

1676. Watten (nov) 1676, 1678. d. October 7th, 1678, Liège, not
ordained. (Fo.7; CRS.69; 114; Nec; 113; E and P.99; 123 I f.96).

GILLIBRAND, William (1) *alias* Gelibourn. Priest.

b. October 1st, 1662, Lancashire. s. of John and Elizabeth (Chorley)
of Chorley. br. of Thomas. e. St Omers College ?-1682. S.J. September
7th, 1682. Watten (nov) 1682. Liège (phil) 1683-5. Liège (theol) 1686-9.
Ordained priest c.1690. St Omers College 1691-3. In England 1694-5. St
Omers College 1696. College of St Aloysius 1699-1701, 1703-6,
1708-16, 1718, 1720 (Chorley c.1701-8. Liverpool. Chorley c.1710). d.
April 1st, 1722, Lancashire. bu. Chorley. (Fo.7; CRS.69; 114; 113;
23 f.35; E and P.99, 110, 354; CRS.9/181; 170 f.2v; 123 IIIB; f.356;
NB. 1/159; Nec).

GILLIBRAND, William (2). Priest.

b. January 13th, 1716, Lancashire. s. of Thomas and Alice (Westby)
of Chorley. br. of Richard. e. St Omers College c.1730-c.33. S.J.
September 7th, 1735. Watten (nov) 1735-7. Liège (phil) 1738-40. Liège
(theol) 1741, 1742. Trèves (theol) 1743. Ordained priest c.1743. Ghent
(tert) 1744. In England 1746. Slatedelf and Brindle 1747-63.
Southworth 1763-4 and Leigh. Exeter 1764-8 (Superior of the
Residence of St Stanislaus 1765-c.68). North Ockendon Hall 1769.
Residence of St Mary 1771. Tusmore 1772, 1773 (Superior of Residence
of St Mary 1772-3). Chorley Hall ?-1779. d. March 22nd, 1779,
Chorley. (Fo.7; CRS. 69; 114; 113; SCH.12/17; ER.9/104, 113n;
21v.2; 24 f.347v; 26 f.201bv; 28 f.51; 41 n.48; 47 f.62v; 54 f.41v; 65; 85;
86; E and P.99; Gil.2/467; CRS.4/434; CRS.23/139; 01.313; 111; 156
App.1; 119 ff.4, 6, 8, 9, 10, 12, 13, 15, 16, 19, 20, 22, 23; Nec).

GILLIS, John.

d. July 8th, 1684, Louvain. Nothing further has been recorded; the
name may be an *alias* or he may not have been a member of the English
province. (Fo.7).

GINGIVAL see Gengival.

GITTINS, Joseph *alias* Williams. Priest.

b. October 11th, 1744, in Wales. e. St Omers College 1757-62. S.J.
September 7th, 1762. Watten (nov) 1763, 1764. Liège (theol) 1767-9.
Ordained priest 1769. Liège 1771. Ghent 1772. Wardour 1772.
Worcester 1772. Liverpool 1772-83. Worcester 1783-97. d. March 25th,
1797, Worcester. bu. St Oswald's church. (Fo.7; CRS.69; 113; 117;
CRS.Mon.1/148n, 159; WR.19/15, 20/70; CRW. pp.31 ff; 72; 80;
94 ff.233-4; 155 II 129; 155 III 185c; CRS.9/ 188; 3 f.28; 38 ff.197v,
201; 54 f.29; 57 I 41; 76 ff.48, 142; 68 p.196; 69; 25 f.15; Nec).

GLASSBROOK, William. Priest.

b. October 9th, 1799, Wigan. e. Stonyhurst 1813-9. S.J. September
7th, 1819-29. Hodder (nov) 1819-21. Stonyhurst (phil) 1821-3. Hodder
1824. Fribourg (theol) 1825-6. Dôle (theol) 1826-7. Ordained priest
December 31st, 1826, Sion. Stonyhurst 1827-9. (115; 21v.2; 113; 2).

GLOVER, Thomas. Priest.

b. March 5th, 1781, St Helens, Lancashire. e. Stonyhurst 1800-3.

S.J. September 26th, 1803. Hodder (nov) 1803-5. Stonyhurst (phil)
1805-6. Palermo (phil and theol) 1806-10. Ordained priest January
11th, 1807. Stonyhurst 1810-14. Edinburgh 1814-5. Stonyhust 1815-25.
Rome 1825-49. Walton Hall 1849. d. May 31st, 1849, Walton Hall. bu.
Sandal church. (Fo.7; 115; Stol; 1 f.234v; 11 ff.208v, 236; 15 f.257v;
19 p.190; 55 f.230; 93; 94 ff.308-9; Gil.2/497; 113; Nec. For writings see
Som).

GODDART, –

    ?admitted S.J. at the hour of death, 1679. (Fo.7; 168 f.79).

GONEUTTE, Cornelius. Laybrother.

    b. November 25th, 1666, Saint-Omer. S.J. September 8th, 1691-97.
Watten (nov) 1693, 1695. St Omers College 1696. (113; 150 II (3)
18/6/95, 12/5/96, 20/7/97).

GONEUTTE, James. Priest.

    b. September 17th, 1653, Artois. S.J. June 20th, 1688. Watten (nov)
1689 (already a priest ?), 1690-3, 1696. Ghent (tert) 1697. d. December
28th, 1698 on the journey to Maryland. (Fo.7; 114; 113; Nec; Hu.Text
2/683).

GOODEN, James. Priest.

    b. June or July, 1670, Derbyshire or Denbighshire. e. St Omers
College ?-1689. S.J. September 7th, 1689. Watten (nov) 1689-91. Liège
(phil) 1692, 1693. St Omers College 1695-8. Liège (theol) 1699-1701,
1703. Ordained priest 1702. Liège 1704-6, 1708-16, 1718, 1720-c.22
(Episcopal Seminary 1715-c.22). St Omers College 1722-27 (Rector
1722-5). Ghent 1728-30 (Rector). d. October 11th, 1730, St Omers
College. (Fo.7; CRS.69; 114; 113; 91; 150 III(2) 11/10/21; 9 n.70;
DNB; Chad.404; Gil.2/524; 170 f.30v; CRS.62 index; Nec. For
writings see Som).

GOODYEAR, Christopher. Laybrother.

    b. c.1650, Co. Durham. S.J. September 28th, 1672. Watten (nov)
1672, 1673, 1674-5. d. November 6th, 1675, Watten. (Fo.7; 114; 113;
Nec).

GOOLD, Anthony.

    b. October 16th, 1685, Ostend. s. of William and Agnes (Bauwen).
S.J. September 8th, 1704, in Mechlin. He may have entered S.J. in one
of the Belgian provinces as his name does not appear in the English
province records, or the name may be an *alias*. (Fo.7).

GORE, John. Priest.

    b. 1782, Ashton, Lancashire s. of Henry and Anne(Swarbrick). e.
Stonyhurst 1795-?1803. S.J. September 26th, 1803. Hodder (nov)
1803-5. Stonyhurst (phil and theol) 1807, 1810. Ordained priest March
14th, 1807, Wolverhampton. Served Dunkenhalgh 1807-15. Preston
1815-24. d.November 9th, 1824, Stonyhurst. bu. Stonyhurst. (Fo.7;
113; 6 f.237; 7 f.205v; 21v.2; 28 f.259;55 f.76; 90 ff.146-7; 93 pp.58, 59;
94 ff.5-8, 24, 60, 154-5, 164-5, 201-2, 204-5; Nec).

GORE see O'Neale, James.

GORSUCH see Eccleston, Thomas.

GOSLING see Bennett, John.

GOUGH, –

Admitted S.J. *in articulo mortis,* January 10th, 1727, St Omers
College. (Fo.7; 9 n.269).

GOWER, William. Scholastic.

b. June 26th, 1698, Staffordshire. ?s. of William and Helen or
Eleanor (Coyney) of Worcester. e. St Omers College 1714 or
earlier – 15. S.J. October 9th, 1715. Watten (nov) 1715, 1716. Liège
(phil) 1718, 1720. Left c.1720, not ordained. (CRS.69; 113; ?Pa.75; E
and P.247, 292; WR.22/33; CRS.62 index).

GOWER see Hornyold, Ralph.

GRADELL or GRADWELL see O'Neil, John.

GRANT, James. Priest.

b. November 19th, 1721, ? Edinburgh. ?s. of James and Mary
(Panton). S.J. September 25th, 1743, in France. Ordained priest May
27th, 1752, Rheims. To the English province 1757. St Omers College
1757-8. Liverpool 1758-67. Tusmore 1767-9. d. May 5th, 1769,
London. (Fo.7; 114; 113; 21v.2; 65; CPC; CRS.9/186; 109; 119 ff.2, 5,
10, 21, 26, 35; Nec; RSC.79).

GRASSI, John. Priest.

b. September 10th, 1775, Bergamo, Italy. S.J. November 11th or
21st, 1799, in Italy. Stonyhurst 1807-10. America 1810-c.15. d.
December 12th, 1849, Rome. (11 f.184v; 19 p.40; 55 ff.132, 146, 222v,
224; CDSJ; 93 p.75; 94 f.193; Mel.320. For writings see Som).

GRAVES see Smith, George.

GRAY, John. Priest.

b.1657 or 1658, London or Yorkshire. e. St Omers College ?-1677.
S.J. September 7th, 1677. Liège (phil) 1679-81. Liège (theol) 1682-5.
Ordained priest 1685. Watten (tert) 1686. Liège 1687, 1689-90. College
of St Thomas of Canterbury 1692-4 (?Brambridge 1691. Catherington
1692). Norwich 1695-6. Residence of St Michael 1697, 1699-1700 (York
1699). College of the Holy Apostles 1701, 1703. College of St Ignatius
1704. d. February 26th, 1705, in England. (Fo.7; CRS.69; 114; 113;
CRS. Mon.2/388; RH.1/139; NA.37/165; 43 f.24; CRS.9/108;
CRS.27/8; Nec).

GRAY see Jenison, Thomas.

GREATON, James or Joseph. Priest.

b. February 12th, 1679, London or Lancashire. e. St Omers College
?-1701. E.C. Valladolid 1701-7. Ordained priest c.1707. S.J. July 5th,
1708. Watten (nov) 1708. Liège (theol) 1710. St Omers College 1711.
Watten 1712-3. College of St Aloysius 1714. College of St Chad 1715-6,
1718, 1720. Maryland 1722-37. Pennsylvania 1738-47 (Superior
1740-7). Maryland 1747-9. Pennsylvania 1749. Maryland 1750, 1752. d.
August 19th, 1753, Maryland. (Fo.7; CRS.30/180; CRS.29/161, 344;
114; 91; Hu. Text 2/686; 113; Ans. 3/85; Nec).

GREEN see Jossaer, Bernard; Westby, Thomas.

GREEN, Edward *alias* or *vere* Wright or Green, Thomas. Priest.

b.1647, London. e. St Omers College 1665 or earlier – 68. S.J.
September 7th, 1668. Watten (nov) 1669. Liège (phil) 1672. Liège
(theol) 1673. St Omers College 1674. Liège (theol) 1676-9. Ordained
priest c.1678. College of St Aloysius 1680-2. College of St Hugh 1683.
France 1684. College of St Ignatius 1685-7 (Savoy College 1687).
College of St Thomas of Canterbury 1689-93, 1696-7, 1699. College of
St Ignatius 1700-01, 1703-4, 1706, 1708. Travelling 1709-11. College of
the Immaculate Conception 1712-3. College of St Thomas of
Canterbury 1714-6, 1718, 1720, 1723. Cheam c.1724-7. d. July 2nd,
1727, ? Cheam. (Fo.7; CRS.69; 91; 113; CRS.62 index; CRS.2/314;
123 II f.156; Nec).

GREEN, Francis. Priest.
b. March 1st, 1744 or 1748, Liverpool s. of Francis and Elizabeth
(Clifton). br. of Thomas. e. St Omers and Bruges Colleges ?-1764. S.J.
September 7th, 1764. Watten (nov) 1764. Liège (phil) 1767. Liège
(theol) 1768-71. Ordained priest 1772. Ghent 1772, 1773. d. January
14th, 1776, Tusmore. (Fo.7; CRS.69; 113; 16 ff.22, 36; 68 p.196;
6 f.235; 117; CRS.7/391).

GREEN, Stanislaus. Priest.
b. March 7th, 1662, London. e. St Omers College ?-1682. S.J.
September 7th, 1682. Watten (nov) 1682, 1683. Liège (phil) 1684-6. St
Omers College 1687. In England 1688. Liège (theol) 1689-92. Ordained
priest December 27th, 1691. St Omers College 1693, 1696-8. College of
St Aloysius 1699-1701, 1703-16, 1718 (Hooton c.1701, 1711). d.
November 9th, 1720, ? Hooton. (Fo.7; 113; CRS.69; 150 III(1)
28/6/10; NB.1/278; 23 f.35; 170 f.245v; 140 n.45; Nec).

GREEN, Thomas or Joseph *alias* Clifton. Scholastic.
b. August 6th, 1753, Liverpool. s. of Francis and Elizabeth (Clifton).
br. of Francis. e. Bruges College 1764-70. S.J. September 7th, 1770.
Ghent (nov) 1771, 1772. Liège (phil) 1773. Returned to England, not
ordained, 1774. (Fo.7; CRS.69; 113; AHSJ.42/192; Gil.3/39-40;
51 ff.304, 307).

GREEN, Thomas see Green, Edward.

GREEN, William. Scholastic or Laybrother.
d. Ghent, date unknown. No further information recorded. (Fo.7;
114).

GREGSON, Henry. Laybrother.
b.1640, Lancashire. S.J. June 20th, 1676 or 1677. St Omers College
(nov) 1678. Ghent 1679-82. Rome 1683-7, 1689-93. Liège 1696. d.
September 21st, 1696, Liège. (Fo.7; 114; 113; Nec).

GRENE, Christopher. Priest.
b. 1629, Kilkenny, Ireland. s. of George and Jane (Tempest). e. St
Omers College 1642-7. E.C. Rome 1647-54. Ordained priest September
7th, 1653. S.J. September 7th, 1658. Watten (nov) 1658, 1659. College
of the Holy Apostles 1660, 1661. Rome or Loretto 1663. Loretto 1669,
1673. Rome 1674-81. Loretto 1682-6. Rome 1686-97. d. November
11th, 1697, Rome. (Fo.7; 113; DNB; CRS.69; CRS.40/39; Ans.2/136;

Gil.3/48; 189 III 3 n.196; Nec; CRS.55/502; 9 ff.1-3; 135 ff.73v, 76v, 82v, 87v; 139 ff.295, 304. For writings see Som).

GREVILLE, – . Priest.

In Paris 1687. Maybe an error for Freville, Thomas *vere* Jenison (Fo.7)

GREY see Talbot, Gilbert.

GRIFFIN see Pigot or Pigott, Adam.

GRIFFIN, John. Scholastic.

b. September 15th, 1674, Warwickshire. ?br. of Nicholas. e. St Omers College ?-1691. S.J. September 7th, 1691. Watten (nov) 1692, 1693. d. October 18th, 1693, Liège, not yet ordained. (Fo.7; CRS.69; 113; 114; Nec).

GRIFFIN, Nicholas. Priest.

b. August 16th, 1672, Warwickshire. ?br. of John. e. St Omers College ?-1691. S.J. September 7th, 1691. Watten (nov) 1692, 1693. Liège (phil) 1696. Liège (theol) 1697, 1699-1700. Ordained priest 1700. Ghent (tert) 1701. Residence of St George 1703-20 (Superior 1715-20. Spetchley 1701-4, 1706, 1710-12). d. c.1720, place not recorded. (Fo.7; CRS.69; 113; RH.1/46; Nec; WR.14/26,30/10; 9 n.87; 40 pp.16ff, 188, 123 IIIB f.360).

GRIFFITH, George. Priest.

b. January 21st, 1668 or 1669, Flintshire. S.J. October 31st, 1688. Watten (nov) 1689, 1690. Liège (phil) 1691-3. Ordained priest c.1695. Ghent (tert) 1696. Residence of St Winefrid 1697-8, 1700-01, 1703-16, 1718 (Holywell 1701, 1718). d. August 2nd, 1718, Holywell. bu. Holywell parish church. (Fo.7; 114; 113; 112 p.89; E and P.347; CRS.3/107; Nec).

GRIMSDITCH see Bruning, Francis (1).

GRIVEL, Fidelis. Priest.

b. December 17th, 1769, in France. S.J. August 8th, 1803, in France. Stonyhurst 1817, 1828-30. Then France and America. d. June 26th, 1842, Georgetown, U.S.A. (Fo.7; 150 (1750-1853) f.191; 11 f.287; 55 f.303; CDSJ; CG. 110; 132 f.76; 134 17/10/28, 20/9/30).

GROU, John Nicholas. Priest.

b. November 24th, 1731, Calais. S.J. in France. Lulworth 1792-1803. d. December 13th, 1803, Lulworth. bu. Lulworth. (Fo.7; 114; Ber.195-6; CRS.6/367; CRS.12/89. For writings see Som).

GROVES see Archer, John.

GUILLICK see Wood, William.

GUILLIM see Tyrwhitt or Terrett, Henry.

GULICK, Nicholas. Priest.

b.1647 or 1648, Rouen. S.J. September 7th, 1668 or 1669-94. Liège (phil) 1672. Liège (theol) 1673. Ordained priest March 25th, 1674. Watten 1674, 1675. Maryland 1675-94. (Fo.7; 113; Hu. Text 2/681; 150 II (3) 4/12/88; 168 ff. 9, 80).

GULICK see Forster, Michael.

GWYNN see White, William.

HACON, Hubert *alias* Jermyn; Gawen, Hubert; Williams, Charles and
Hubert. Priest.
>b.1677, Norfolk. s. of James and ?Elizabeth. S.J. September 7th,
1698. Watten (nov) 1699, 1700. Liège (phil) 1701, 1703. Liège (theol)
1704-6. Ordained priest c.1707. Ghent (tert) 1708. St Omers College
1709. College of St Ignatius 1710-6, 1718, 1720, 1724-5 (Linstead
Lodge c.1724). In England 1726-8, 1730 (Ingatestone 1728-9). Sutton
Coldfield 1729-33. College of St Ignatius 1733-9 (Scotney 1733-?).
Wardour 1740-51. d. May 9th, 1751, Wardour. bu. Tisbury parish
church. (Fo.7; CRS.69; 114; 91; 113; CRS.Mon.1/155, 244; E and
P.196; ER.5/73, 9/106, 12/112; WR.20/58-9, 75 n.55; 21 v.2; 01.317;
43 f.47; Nec).

HACON see Adams, James.

HAGERTY or HEGARTY, John. Priest.
>b. October 29th, 1795, London. e. Stonyhurst 1812-5. S.J.
September 7th, 1815. Hodder (nov) 1815-7. Stonyhurst 1817-23.
Fribourg (theol) 1824-7. Ordained priest March 10th, 1827, Fribourg.
Wigan 1827-34. d. October 13th, 1834, Wigan. bu. Wigan chapel.
(Fo.7; 115; Stol; 116; Nec).

HAGGERSTON, Henry *alias* Howard. Priest.
>b.1658, Northumberland. s. of Sir Thomas, Bart. and Margaret
(Howard) of Haggerston. br. of John. e. St Omers College c.1671-8.
E.C. Douay 1678-9. S.J. October 17th, 1679. Watten (nov) 1679, 1680.
Liège (phil) 1681-3. Liège (theol) 1684-7. Ordained priest c.1688.
Residence of St John 1689-93, 1696-7, 1699-1701, 1703-11 (Haggerston
1691-1709). College of St Hugh 1712-3. Gateshead 1714. d. March
12th, 1714, ?Gateshead. (Fo.7; CRS.69; 114; 113; CRS.62/60; Chad.
195-6; Sur. 180/xi; 168 f. 79v; Nec).

HAGGERSTON, John. Priest.
>b. January 28th, 1661, Northumberland. s. of Sir Thomas, Bart.
and Margaret (Howard) of Haggerston. br. of Henry. e. St Omers
College ?-1680. S.J. September 7th, 1680. Watten (nov) 1681. Liège
(phil) 1682-4. Liège (theol) 1685-7. Ordained priest 1689. Watten (tert)
1689. St Omers College 1690. Residence of St John 1691-3, 1696-7,
1699-1701, 1703-16, 1720, 1723-4 (Haggerston 1691-1700. Cartington
1701. Widdrington Castle 1702. Haggerston 1704-8. Ellingham or
Long Horsley or Netherwitton 1709-?). d. February 6th, 1726, in
England. bu. Netherwitton (Fo.7; CRS.69; 114; 113; 36 f.260; E and
P.47; Sur. 180/xi; Nec).

HAGUEMAN or HAGHEMAN, Charles. Laybrother.
>b. May 10th, 1684, Bruges. S.J. October 9th, 1715. Watten (nov)
1715, 1716. Ghent 1718, 1720, 1723-8, 1730. Watten 1733. Ghent
1734-8, 1740-1, 1745-8. d. March 27th, 1748, Ghent. (Fo.7; 114; 113;
91; Nec).

HAINSTON, – . Laybrother.
>Liège 1678. No further information recorded under this name.
(Fo.7; 168 f.1).

HALES, Thomas ?*alias* Dawes. Laybrother.
b. December 21st 1659 or 1661, London or Sussex. S.J. March 11th, 1690. St Omers College (nov) 1690, 1691. Watten (nov) 1692. St Omers College 1693, 1696-7. Socius to the provincial 1699-1701. St Omers College 1703-9. d. January 24th, 1709, Arras. (Fo.7; 113, 114; Chad. 275; Nec).

HALL see Humberston, Edward and Henry.

HALL, Bernard see Lucas, John.

HALL, James. Scholastic.
b. March 11th, 1716, London. e. St Omers College ?-1734. S.J. September 7th, 1734. Watten (nov) 1734, 1735. Liège (phil) 1736-9. d. February 29th, 1740, Liège, not ordained. (Fo.7; CRS.69; 114; 113; 91; 125; 51 f.311v).

HALL, John. Priest.
b. 1664, London. S.J. September 9th, 1683. Watten (nov) 1683, 1684. Liège (phil) 1685-7. In England 1688. Liège (theol) 1689-92. Ordained priest April 14th, 1691. Maryland 1693-9. Watten 1700. Ghent 1701, 1703. d. July 9th, 1703, Ghent. (Fo.7; 114; 113; Hu. Text 2/683; Nec).

HALSALL, George. Priest.
b. September 17th, 1714 or 1715, Lancashire. s. of James and Anne (Bowker) of Aughton. ?e. St Omers College ?-1732. E.C. Rome 1732-9. Ordained priest July 20th, 1738, Rome. S.J. November 29th, 1739. Watten (nov) 1740. Liège 1741. In England 1742. Residence of St Winefrid 1743. Plowden Hall 1744. d. August 11th, 1744, Plowden Hall. (Fo.7; CRS.69; 114; 113; 91; Ans.4/126; 150 III(2) 3/6/41; 12 f.179; 14 ff.39, 46; E and P.110; Ki.109-10; CRS.40/188; 140 n.45; Nec).

HAMAIDE, Francis de la. Laybrother.
b. October 4th, 1677, Liège. S.J. March 11th, 1705-13. Watten (nov) 1705. Ghent 1706. Watten 1708, 1709. Liège 1710-13. (Fo.7; 113; 150 III(1) 1/4/1713).

HAMEL, Maurice du. Priest.
College of St Ignatius 1673 (preacher at the French embassy). (113)

HAMERTON see Hammerton.

HAMMERSLEY, Francis. Scholastic.
b. November 11th, 1744, Maryland. e. St Omers and Bruges Colleges 1760-66. S.J. September 7th, 1766. Ghent (nov) 1766, 1767. Liège (phil) 1768, 1769. Left c.1770, not ordained. (113; CRS.69).

HAMMERSLEY, Thomas. Laybrother.
b. February 13th, 1724, Staffordshire. S.J. September 7th, 1755. Watten (nov) 1756-8. Liège 1761, 1763-4, 1767-9, 1771-3. Gifford's Hall 1775-87. Coldham 1787-9-? d. December, 1804, ?Staffordshire. (Fo.7; AHSJ.42/294, 296; 1 f.225; 88; 54 ff.128v, 293; 51 f.307; 94 f.265; 111).

HAMMERTON or HAMERTON, Gervase. Priest.
b. 10th or 13th, March or April, 1668, Yorkshire. Nephew of Henry

(2) and Peter. S.J. 1686 or 1687. Watten (nov) 1687. Liège (phil)
1689-91. Liège (theol) 1692, 1693. Ordained priest c.1695. Ghent (tert)
1696. Southworth c.1697-1708. d. August, 1708, Southworth. bu.
Winwick. (Fo.7; 114; 113; E and P. 356; 23 f.35v; CRS.13/398).

HAMMERTON or HAMERTON, Henry (1).

Liège (phil) 1667. Nothing further found. The name may be an *alias*.
(113).

HAMMERTON or HAMERTON, Henry (2). Priest.

b. 1644, Yorkshire. s. of Philip and Dorothy (Young). br. of Peter.
Uncle of Gervase. e. St Omers College 1664 or earlier-65. S.J.
September 28th, 1669. Liège (phil) 1672, 1673. Liège (theol) 1674-8.
Ordained priest c.1678. St Omers College 1679, 1680. Residence of St
Michael 1681-7 (Superior 1682-4. Pontefract 1685, 1687-8). In York
prison 1689-93. Lincoln 1696. Norwich 1697-9. Ghent 1699-1701.
Watten 1703-6. Brussels 1707, 1708. In England 1709. College of St
Ignatius 1710. Residence of St George 1711. Residence of St Winefrid
1712, 1713. College of St Aloysius 1714. Kelvedon 1715, 1716. College
of St Ignatius 1716. d. February 24th, 1718, Ghent. (Fo.7; 114;
CRS.69; Nec; 113; ER.9/109; NA.37/165; 150 III(I) 12/11/07; 43
ff.23, 26, 27, 35; Gil.3/107; 193 Anglia, 35/126; 168 ff.77, 83v; 123 II
f.163, IIIB f.283; Bea.249).

HAMMERTON or HAMERTON, Peter *alias* Young and Barnes and
Peterson. Priest.

b. 1637 or 1638, near Pontefract, Yorkshire. s. of Philip and
Dorothy (Young). br. of Henry (2). Uncle of Gervase. e. St Omers
College 1655 or earlier-c.60. E.C. Rome 1660-1. S.J. July 10th, 1661.
Watten (nov) 1661. Liège (phil) 1663, 1664, 1665, Liège (theol) 1667,
1669. Ordained priest c.1669. College of St Hugh 1672-8, 1679-93,
1696 (Rector 1685-91. Lincoln 1687, 1688). College of St Ignatius 1697,
1699-1701, 1703. Provincial 1704-9. College of St Ignatius 1709-14. d.
November 29th, 1714, in England. (Fo.7; CRS.69; 114; 150 II(3)
18/8/85; 21 v.2; Ki.110; 123 IIIB f.265; CRS.40/63; 113; Nec; 43 ff.24,
26-7).

HAMMERTON or HAMERTON, William. Priest.

Ingolstadt 1682-4. Liège (theol) 1685, 1686. Ordained priest c.1686.
Residence of St John 1687. Nothing further recorded. (Fo.7; 113).

HANMER, John *alias* or *vere* Hunt. Priest.

b. December 24th, 1663 or 1664, Shropshire. e. St Omers College
c.1680. E.C. Douay (phil and theol). S.J. February 1st, 1691. Watten
(nov) 1691, 1692. Liège (theol) 1693. St Omers College 1694-6. Liège
(theol) 1696, 1697. Ordained priest 1697. Ghent (tert) 1699, 1700. St
Omers College 1701, 1703-5. College of the Holy Apostles 1706-14
(Kelvedon ?-1714). Newgate prison 1714. St Omers College 1715. d.
April 29th, 1716, St Omers College. (Fo.7; CRS.69; 114; 113; Nec;
CRS.62/111, 114, 119; CRS.63/85; RH.9/30; ER.5/35, 9/108-9;
Chad 251-2; 170 f.179; 43 ff.30, 34-5).

HANMER, Joseph. Scholastic.

e. St Omers College ?-1694. S.J. September 7th, 1694. Watten (nov) 1696. Liège (phil) 1697. Left 1697, not ordained. (CRS.69; 113; 150 II(3) 28/5/97, 8/6/97, 6/7/97).

HANNE, Charles. Priest.

b. March 11th or June 14th, 1711, Deviock, near Bodmin. ?s. of John and Dorothy (Tattershall). S.J. September 7th, 1731. Liège (phil) 1733-5. Liège (theol) 1736-8. Ordained priest 1739. St Omers College 1739-41, 1743-5. In England 1746. Residence of St George 1747, 1749-50, 1752-6 (Superior 1754-6. Worcester 1746, 1749). College of St Hugh 1756-8. Haggerston 1758-99, serving Berwick and Berrington at times. d. April 27th, 1799, Ellingham. bu. Holy Island. (Fo.7; 113; 117; RH.10/20; WR.20/68; CRW.15; 7 ff.128, 189v; 21 v.2; 163; 36 ff.185v, 260; 40 p.112; E and P.8, 23; Ki.86; Ol.319; 119 f.37; 156 VI; 114; 167 pp.19, 34).

HANSCOTTER, Charles. Laybrother.

b. January 29th, 1705, French Flanders. S.J. May 28th, 1743. Watten (nov) 1743, 1745, 1746, 1748-50, 1752-8, 1761, 1763, 1764. Bruges College 1767. d. January 23rd, 1768, Bruges. (Fo.7; 114; 113; 16 f.12v; Nec).

HAPPIET, Noel. Scholastic or Laybrother.

d. date and place unknown. (Fo.7; 114).

HARCOURT see Persall, John.

HARDESTY, John *alias* Tempest. Priest.

b. April 21st, 1681, Yorkshire. s. of William and Mary (Hargreaves *née* Tempest) of Norwood, Yorkshire. e. St Omers College 1695-9. S.J. September 7th, 1699. Watten (nov) 1700, 1701. Liège (phil) 1703, 1704. St Omers College 1705-9. Liège (theol) 1710-3. Ordained priest 1711. College of St Ignatius 1714. Liverpool c.1715-28-31 serving Lydiate 1727-8-31. Blandford 1732. Canford 1733-5. College of St Chad 1736-40, 1742-4, 1746-52 (?Aston 1738-41. Tixall 1741-52). d. May 1st, 1752, Daventry. (Fo.7; CRS.69; 114; 91; 113; SCH.3/11; 74; 89; 27 f.228; 90 f.186; NB.2/142n, 233, 3/157; HMC.10th Report App.4/187; Gib.1/287-9; Ki.111; CRS.7/263; CRS.9/182; Nec).

HARDING see Mansell, Thomas and William.

HARDING, Robert or John or Richard. Priest.

b. October 6th, 1701, Nottinghamshire. e. St Omers College ?-1722. S.J. September 7th, 1722. Watten (nov) 1723, 1724. Liège (phil) 1725-7. Liège (theol) 1728, 1730. Ordained priest c.1731. Maryland 1732-c.53. Pennsylvania c.1753-71. d. September 1st, 1772, Philadelphia. (Fo.7; CRS.69; 114; Hu. Text 2/689; 113; 64 p.230; 74; 91; 92; Nec).

HARPER see Berington, John.

HARRINGTON see Duke, Charles.

HARRIS see Hormasa, Raymond; Walmesley, Christopher.

HARRISON, Edmund. Priest.

b. March, 1727, 1728 or 1729, Lancashire. e. St Omers College c.1741-6. S.J. September 7th, 1746. Watten (nov) 1747. Liège (phil)

1749, 1750. Liège (theol) 1752-5. Ordained priest 1755. Ghent (tert) 1756, 1757. College of St Ignatius 1758. College of St Chad 1759. Biddleston 1759-61. Callaly 1761-2. College of St Aloysius 1763-4 (?Culcheth 1763). Loretto 1765, 1767-9. College of the Holy Apostles 1771. Bodney 1772, 1773. d. November 12th, 1801, Somers Town. (Fo.7; CRS.69; 114; 113; 21 v.2; 64 p.287; 65; 68 p.162; 86; CRS.12/82; 35 f.105; ?166 II p.87; 119 f.24; 111; Nec).

HARRISON, George. Laybrother.
    b. September 28th, 1645, Lincolnshire. S.J. December 2nd, 1688. Watten (nov) 1689, 1690. Ghent 1691. St Omers College 1692-3, 1696-7, 1699-1701, 1703-5. Ghent 1706, 1708-13. d. March 23rd, 1713, Ghent. (Fo.7; 114; 113; 170 f.34v; Nec).

HARRISON, Henry (1). Priest.
    b. 1652, Antwerp. S.J. September 7th, 1673. Watten (nov) 1673-5. Liège (phil) 1676, 1678. Liège (theol) 1679-82. Ordained priest 1682. Watten 1683. New York 1684-7, 1689. Ireland 1690. Watten 1691-2. Liège 1693-4. Loretto 1695-7. To Maryland 1697. d.1701, place not recorded; perhaps lost at sea before that date. (Fo.7; Hu. Text 2/682; 113; 150 II(3) 29/5/94, 16/4/95; 139 f.295; Nec).

HARRISON, Henry (2) *alias* or *vere* Hays or Hayes. Priest.
    b.1676, Lancashire. e. St Omers College 1694 or earlier-98. S.J. September 7th, 1698. Liège (phil) 1699-1701. Liège (theol) 1703, 1705-6. Ordained priest c.1704. St Omers College 1708. College of St Thomas of Canterbury 1709-11. Residence of St John 1712-5 (Eslington 1714, 1715. Ellingham 1715). St Omers College 1716, 1718. Residence of St Winefrid 1720. College of St Hugh 1722-7 (Rector 1724-7. Driby 1727). Watten 1729, 1730. Ghent 1730-4 (Rector 1731-4). Residence of St John 1734-8. d. October 15th, 1739, Scotney. (Fo.7; CRS.69; 113; 91; 114; CRS.62/60, 91, 146; 150 III(2) 12/4/21, 5/9/22, 24/2/31; 156 xi; 12 f.145; 36 f.265; 64 pp.51, 161; 156 xi; NCH.10/13; 123 II f.127; 109; Nec).

HARRISON, James *alias* Stockwood. Scholastic.
    b. June 10th, 1671 or 1673, Suffolk. e. St Omers College 1693 or earlier-95. S.J. September 7th, 1695. Watten (nov) 1696. Liège (phil) 1697, 1699. d. September 11th, 1699, Liège, not ordained. (Fo.7; CRS.69; 113; Nec; 43 ff.25 – 6).

HARRISON, John *alias* Wallis. Priest.
    b. July 4th, 1690, Valenciennes. S.J. September 7th, 1708. Watten (nov) 1709, 1710. Liège (phil) 1711-3. Liège (theol) 1714, 1716, 1718. Ordained priest 1718. Ghent (tert) 1720. London 1724. d. February 3rd, 1725, in England. (Fo.7; 114; 113; LR.3/5; Nec).

HART see Dunn, Joseph; Le Hunt, John.

HART, Alban. Scholastic.
    e. Stonyhurst 1817-20. S.J. September 7th, 1820. Hodder (nov) 1820. ?Rome (phil) 1824. Left 1826, not ordained. (113; 2; 6 f.257; Stol; Gil. 3/152).

HART, William *alias* Scrope or Scroop. Priest.

b. March 20th, 1640, London. e. St Omers College 1652-9. S.J.
1659. Watten (nov) 1660. Liège (phil) 1661, 1663-4. Liège (theol)
1664-6. Ordained priest 1667. d. October or November 15th, 1667,
Ypres. (Fo.7; CRS.69; 114; 113; Nec; 150 II(2) 12/6/66, 9/10/66;
FAB.64-5).

HARTLEY or HEARTLEY, John. Priest.

b. November 1st 1716, London. e. St Omers College ?-1733. E.C.
Valladolid 1733-9. Ordained priest at Valladolid or c.1741. S.J. June
13th, 1739. Watten (nov) 1739, 1740, 1739-44, 1746, 1748-50, 1752-8.
d. March 3rd, 1760, St Omers College. (Fo.7; CRS.69; 114; 113;
CRS.30/188; Ans.4/129; 140 n.45; Nec).

HARVEY see Mico, Edward.

HARVEY or HERVEY, George. Priest.

b. in the Low Countries. S.J. in the English province. Not found in
the province catalogues under this name. Date and place of death not
recorded (Fo.7).

HARVEY or HERVEY, John *alias* Barton. Priest.

b.1632, London or Yorkshire. ?br. of Thomas. e. St Omers College
1647 or earlier-51. S.J. September 7th, 1651. Watten (nov) 1651, 1652.
Liège (phil) 1653-5. Liège (theol) 1656-60. Ordained priest 1661. Ghent
(tert) 1661. College of St Ignatius 1663-5. Residence of St John 1667.
College of St Aloysius 1669. Residence of St George 1670, 1672-6,
1678-87, 1689-93, 1696-7, 1699-1705 (Grafton 1670, 1678, 1683.
Worcester 1703-?). d. August 14th, 1705, in England. (Fo.7; CRS.69;
113; WR.8/28, 16/16, 20/71; 39 ff.89v, 108v; 102; Nec; 37 f.152).

HARVEY, Thomas *alias* or *vere* Barton. Priest.

b.1632 or 1635, London or Yorkshire. ?br. of John. e. St Omers
College 1647 or earlier-53. S.J. September 7th, 1653. Watten (nov)
1653-5. Liège (phil) 1656-8. Liège (theol) 1659-61. Ordained priest
March 24th, 1662. College of St Aloysius 1663. Ghent (tert) 1664,
1665. College of St Aloysius 1667, 1669, 1672-6, 1678-80 (Poole Hall,
near Chester c.1678). College of St Ignatius 1681, 1682. New York
1683-93 (Superior 1685-c.90). Maryland 1696. d. 1696, Maryland.
(Fo.7; CRS.69; 113; 114; 168 ff.2, 44; Nec; Hu. Text 2/682).

HARVEY, William. Laybrother.

S.J. September 7th, 1816-22. Hodder (nov) 1817, 1818. Stonyhurst
1821. (116; 113; 2).

HASKEY see Reeve, Joseph and Richard and Thomas.

HATTERSKEY or HATHERSTY, Joseph. Priest.

b. October 15th, 1735 or 1736, Maryland or London. s. of Richard
and Elizabeth (Grogan). e. St Omers College ?-1749. E.C. Rome
1749-53. S.J. September 16th, 1753. Watten (nov) 1753-5. Liège (phil)
1756-8. Ordained priest c.1761. Ghent 1761. Biddleston 1761-2.
London 1762. Maryland and Pennsylvania 1762-71. d. May 8th, 1771,
Philadephia. (Fo.7; Hu. Text 2/695; CRS.69; 114; 91; 113;
CRS.40/205-6; LR.3/5; 21 v.2; 65; CRS.19/239; 35 f.105v; 92; 111;
Nec).

HAUBURN, William. Scholastic or Laybrother.
Date and place of death unknown. (Fo.7; 114).

HAUSSOULIER, Francis. Laybrother.
b. January 20th, 1730, in France. S.J. May 2nd, 1751. St Omers College (nov) 1752. Ghent 1753-8, 1761, 1763-4. Liège 1769, 1771-3. Liège Academy 1776, 1781, 1783. d. May 15th, 1785, Liège. (Fo.7; 117; 113; 3 ff.41, 51; 51 f.149; 90 f.54; AHSJ.42/294; 91).

HAVERLY, John. Scholastic or Laybrother.
Date and place of death unknown. (Fo.7; 114).

HAVERS, John. Scholastic.
S.J. April, 16th, 1663. Not found again in the surviving records under this name. May be the same as John Rivers *vere* Penketh.

HAVERS, Robert. Priest.
b. August 21st, 1813, Thelton Hall, Norfolk. ?s. of Thomas and Elizabeth (Cliffe). e. Stonyhurst 1822-9. S.J. March 26th, 1829. Hodder (nov) 1830-2. St Mary's Hall (phil) 1833-5. Stonyhurst 1835-7. St Mary's Hall (theol) 1837-41. Ordained priest September 19th, 1840, Stonyhurst. Stonyhurst 1840-3. Preston 1843-4. Yarmouth 1844. Preston 1844-50. Shepton Mallet 1850-5. Lulworth 1855-60. d. December 24th, 1860, Lulworth. bu. Lulworth. (Fo.7; 114; 115; 113; 01.324; Nec).

HAVERS, Thomas. Priest.
b. February 28th, 1668 or 1669, Thelton, Norfolk. S.J. September 7th, 1688. Watten (nov) 1689, 1690. Liège (phil) 1691-3. Liège (theol) 1696. Ordained priest April 21st, 1696. College of the Holy Apostles 1697, 1699. St Omers College 1700-01, 1703. Ghent 1704. Maryland 1705, 1706. College of St Ignatius 1708. Ghent 1709-12. Watten 1713-6, 1718, 1720, 1723-8, 1730, 1733-7. d. May 16th, 1737, Watten. (Fo.7; 114; 91; 113; Hu. Text 2/684; Nec; 43 ff.26, 30).

HAVET, Louis. Priest.
d. March 16th, 1703, Ghent. No further information discovered. He may have been a member of another province S.J. (Fo.7; 95 p.831).

HAWKER, John *alias* Thompson. Priest.
b. October 3rd, 1687, London. ?e. St Omers College 1698-1701. S.J. September 7th, 1704. Watten (nov) 1705, 1706. Liège (phil) 1708-10. Liège (theol) 1711-4. Ordained priest c.1713. St Omers College 1715. College of St Hugh 1715-6, 1718, 1720, 1724-5, ?1726, 1727-48 (Rector 1728-43. Lincoln 1727-34, 1738). York 1749-55. St Omers College 1755-8, 1761, 1763-4. d. June 14th, 1764, St Omers College. (Fo.7; CRS.69; 114; 91; 113; CRS.Mon.2/388; 150 III(2) 29/11/38; 21 v.2; HMC.10th Report App.4/187; Chad. 304; CRS.4/376; 111; 158; Nec; CRS.62/128, 270).

HAWKINS, Thomas *alias* Perkins. Priest.
b. December 21st, 1722, Slindon, Sussex. s. of Thomas and Jane (Saxby) of Slindon. e. St Omers College ?-1741. E.C. Rome 1741-7. Ordained priest February 12th, 1747, Rome. S.J. October 21st, 1747. Watten (nov) 1747, 1749. Brussels 1750. College of St Chad 1751-65

(The Rudge 1751 Swynnerton 1761-5. Rector 1758-64). Spinkhill 1766.
Liverpool 1766-7. Brambridge 1767-8. Oxburgh 1768-85. d. July 9th,
1785, Oxburgh. bu. Oxburgh church. (Fo.7; 117; CRS.69; 113;
Ans.4/134; SCH.3/11, 12/16, 12/20; 12 f.181; 13 ff.76v, 97A; 41
nn.25, 46, 65, 71, 100, 102, 125; 44 ff.229v, 232, 273, 275; 54 f.26v; 64
p.265; 65; 68 pp.107, 161, 201; 80; HMC. 10th Report App.4/187-8;
Ki.117; CRS.7/205, 227, 229, 243; CRS.12/26; CRS.27/9, 14-5;
CRS.40/198; 119 f.34; Nec).

HAYES, Joseph. Scholastic.
    S.J. September 7th, 1810-14. Hodder (nov) 1810-12. Left 1814, not
ordained (116; 2; 113).

HAYES or HAYS, Thomas. Priest.
    b. January 7th, 1746, Leigh, Lancashire. e. St Omers and Bruges
Colleges 1760-4. S.J. September 7th, 1765. Ghent (nov) 1765. Liège
(phil) 1767-9. Liège (theol) 1771-3. Ordained priest 1772. Ghent 1773.
Darnell Hall near Sheffield 1773-4. d. 1774 or 1776, Sheffield. (Fo.7;
113; CRS.69; 16 ff.22, 36; 155 II 121; CRS.8/352-3; 117; 90 f.33v).

HAYES or HAYS see Harrison, Henry.

HAYLES see Duke, Charles.

HAYMAN, Richard *alias* or *vere* Pearce or Pearse, John or Edward. Priest.
    b. July 11th, 1668, 1669 or 1670, Cornwall. S.J. September 7th,
1687. Watten (nov) 1687. Liège (phil) 1689-92. Liège (theol) 1693,
1696. Ordained priest April 21st, 1696. Residence of St Stanislaus
1697. College of St Thomas of Canterbury 1699-1701, 1703-5.
Residence of St Stanislaus 1706. College of St Thomas of Canterbury
1708-9. Residence of St Stanislaus 1710-6, 1720, 1723-5, 1727 (Superior
1711-14. Trevithick c.1727). In England 1728, 1730. Residence of St
Stanislaus 1733-7, 1739-43, 1745-6, 1748-55 (Trevithick c.1751). d.
April 30th, 1756, Fowey. (Fo.7; 114; 113; 89; 91; HMC. 10th Report
App.4/188; 01.324; 51 f.311).

HAYS see HAYES.

HAYWOOD, Francis. Laybrother.
    b.1628 or 1630, Ireland or London. S.J. July 30th or September 7th,
1651. Liège 1673, 1675-6, 1678-9. Watten 1680-5. Liège 1686-7,
1689-90. St Omers College 1691. Antwerp 1692-5. Ghent 1696-7,
1699-1701, 1703-5. d. March 15th, 1706, Ghent. (Fo.7; 114; 113; 108).

HEARN, George. Laybrother.
    b.1612, Northumberland. S.J. 1653. Watten (nov) 1653-5. He is not
traced further under this name. It is not clear that he completed the
noviceship (Fo.7; 113).

HEATH, Henry. Laybrother.
    b.1641 or 1645, Hampshire. S.J. September 7th, 1674. Watten (nov)
1674, 1675. Liège 1676, 1678-81. Watten 1682-3. Liège 1684-7. In
England 1688. Liège 1689-93, 1696. Ghent 1697, 1699-1701. d. January
18th, 1701, Ghent. (Fo.7; 114; 113).

HEATLEY, James. Priest.
    b. April 2nd, 1715, Lancashire. s. of Peter of Whittle-le-Woods. e.

St Omers College c.1732-5. S.J. September 7th, 1735. Watten (nov)
1735-7. Liège (phil) 1738-40. Liège (theol) 1741. Cologne (theol) 1742,
1743. Liège (theol) 1744. Ordained priest c.1744. Ghent (tert) 1745.
Boulogne School 1746-52. Watten School 1752-4. Ghent 1755.
Residence of St Michael 1756-8, 1763-4 (Broughton Hall 1757, 1758).
Broughton Hall 1767-9. Residence of St Michael 1771. Broughton Hall
1772-3-?82. d. May 11th, 1782, Broughton Hall. (Fo.7; CRS.69; 114;
65; 113; 85; 90 f.181; Pa.2.24; Gil.3/252; E. and P.129; 111; 117;
Ham.21; 158; 155 II 127; 167).

HEGERTY see Hagerty.

HELSAM, Richard *alias* or *vere* Booth. Scholastic.
    b. August 24th, 1698, London. S.J. September 7th, 1716. Watten
(nov) 1716, 1718. Liège (phil) 1720. d. April 21st, 1721, Brussels, not
ordained. (Fo.7; 114; 113).

HERBERT, William. Scholastic.
    b.1634, in Wales. e. St Omers College 1649 or earlier-54. S.J.1654.
Watten (nov) 1655. Liège (phil) 1656-60. St Omers College 1661. d.
August 4th, 1662, Watten, not ordained. (Fo.7; CRS.69; 114; 113).

HERBERT see Turner, John.

HERVEY see Harvey.

HESKETH, Richard. Scholastic
    b.1665, Lancashire. e. St Omers College ?-1685. S.J. 1685. Watten
(nov) 1685, 1686. Liège (phil) 1686-7, 1689-90. Left, not ordained,
1691. (Fo.7; 113; CRS.69; 150 II (3) 11/11/90, 17/2/91).

HESKETH, Thomas. Priest.
    b.1668 or 1669, Lancashire. e. St Omers College ?-1689. S.J.
September 7th, 1689. Watten (nov) 1689-91. Liège (phil) 1692, 1693. St
Omers College 1696, 1697. La Flèche (theol) 1699, 1700. Ordained
priest c.1701. La Flèche 1701, 1703-5. E.C. Rome 1708, 1709. St Omers
College 1711, 1712. d. August 2nd, 1712, Watten. (Fo.7; 113; 114;
CRS.69; 150 III(1) 14/1/08; CRS.7/94; Nec).

HESKETH, William. Scholastic.
    b. May 14th, 1717, Lancashire. s. of William and Mary (Brockholes)
of The Maynes, Little Singleton, Lancashire. e. St Omers College
1731-5. S.J. September 7th, 1735. Watten (nov) 1736, 1737. Liège
(phil) 1739, 1740. Liège (theol) 1741. d. December 30th, 1741, in
England, not ordained. (Fo.7; 91; CRS.69; 114; 113; 74; Gil.3/291; E
and P.133; Nec).

HEUSEUX, Giles. Laybrother.
    b. May 12th, 1715, Liège. ?br. of John. S.J. October 9th, 1741.
Watten (nov) 1742, 1743, 1744-5. Ghent 1746-8. d. February 27th,
1748, Ghent. (Fo.7; 114; 113; Nec).

HEUSEUX, John. Laybrother.
    b. November 26th, 1698, Liège. ?br. of Giles. S.J. September 7th,
1735. Watten (nov) 1736-8. Liège 1740-1, 1743-50, 1752-8, 1761,
1763-4, 1767-9, 1771. d. September 9th, 1771, Liège. (Fo.7; 114; 113;
Nec).

HEVENINGHAM, John *alias* Cook. Priest.
>b.1642, Staffordshire. e. St Omers College c.1660. S.J. September 7th, 1667. Watten (nov) 1669. Liège (theol) 1672, 1673. Ordained priest 1673. College of St Ignatius 1674-6, 1679-82. College of St Thomas of Canterbury 1683-6. College of St Ignatius 1687, 1689-90 (in prison c.1689). College of St Thomas of Canterbury ?1690, 1693 (?Wardour c.1690). College of St Francis Xavier 1696. College of St Hugh 1697, 1699-1701, 1703-6, 1708. d. August 19th, 1708, in England. (Fo.7; CRS.69; 113; Nec; CRS.Mon.1/150n).

HEWETT, John. Laybrother.
>b.1658, London. S.J. July 21st, 1680. Watten (nov) 1680. St Omers College 1681. Ghent 1682. Liège 1683, 1684. E.C. Rome 1685-7. d. October 30th, 1688, Rome. (Fo.7; 114; 113; 138 n. 94; Nec).

HEWETT, Richard. Laybrother.
>b.1636 or 1637, Lancashire. S.J. August 28th, 1664. Watten 1667, 1669. St Omers College 1672-83. Paris 1684-7. In England 1688. Watten 1689-93. d. April 9th, 1696, Watten. (Fo.7; 114; 113; 150 II(3) 7/8/84, 19/5/96; 168 f.65; Nec).

HICKS, Joseph. Laybrother.
>b. August 17th, 1718, Hampshire. S.J. September 7th, 1740. Watten (nov) 1740-2, 1743-4, 1746-9. Rome 1750-4. d. January 31st, 1755, Rome. (Fo.7; 114; 113; 12 f.188; Nec).

HICKSLEY, Thomas. Scholastic or Laybrother.
>d. Ghent, date not recorded. No further details found. (Fo.7; 114).

HIECQ, – . Priest.
>S.J. in Belgium. At Lulworth 1793. d. Lulworth. (Ber. 196; 7 f.155).

HIGGINSON, Thomas. Laybrother.
>b.1639, Warwickshire. S.J. September 9th, 1674. Watten (nov) 1674, 1675, 1676, 1678-9. Ghent 1680. d. July 1st, 1682, Liège. (Fo.7; 114; 113; Nec).

HILDESLEY, Francis. Priest.
>b.1655 or 1656, Oxfordshire. s. of Francis and Mary (Winchcombe) of Berkshire. e. St Omers College 1668-75. S.J. September 7th, 1675. Watten (nov) 1676. Liège (phil) 1678, 1679. Liège (theol) 1680-3. Ordained priest December 18th, 1683. Watten 1684. Residence of St Mary 1685-7, 1689, 1691-3, 1696-1716 (Superior 1696-1711). d. June 17th, 1719, in England. (Fo.7; CRS.69; 114; 113; 150 II(3) 1/9/85; E. and P.5; Nec).

HILDEYARD or HILDYARD or HILLIARD, Thomas. Priest.
>b. March 3rd, 1690, London. e. St Omers College 1702-7. S.J. September 7th, 1707. Watten (nov) 1708, 1709. Liège (phil) 1710-12. Liège (theol) 1712-5. Ordained priest c.1716. Ghent (tert) 1716. Liège 1718-20, 1723-6. College of St Francis Xavier 1727, ?1728, ?1730, 1733-8, 1740-6 (Rector 1742-6. Rotherwas 1727, 1743, ?1726-46). d. April 10th, 1746, Rotherwas. bu. Rotherwas. (Fo.7; CRS.69; 114; 113; DNB; 150 III(1) 10/12/12, 15/3/19, 27/7/43; 32 f.1; 91; Gil.3/304; Nec. For writings see Som).

HILDRETH, John. Priest.

b.1654 or 1657, Northumberland. e. St Omers College ?-1677. S.J. September 7th, 1677. Watten (nov) 1678. Liège (phil) 1679-81. St Omers College 1682-7. Liège (theol) 1689-92. Ordained priest March 25th, 1690. Evora, Portugal 1693, 1696. Ghent 1697. Loretto 1698-1701. St Omers College 1701. d. October 8th, 1702, ?Loretto. (Fo.7; CRS.69; 113; 150 II(3) 8/11/92, III(1) 26/7/98, 26/3/1701; Nec).

HILL see Beeston, Robert; Hutton, Robert; Lawson, Thomas (1); Stafford, Charles.

HILL, John. Priest.

b. September 24th or 26th, 1683, Montgomeryshire. ?s. of Richard and Elizabeth of Welshpool. S.J. September 7th, 1704. Watten (nov) 1705. Liège (phil) 1706, 1708. Liège (theol) 1709-12. Ordained priest 1712. Ghent (tert) 1712. ?Stapehill 1713. College of St Francis Xavier 1714-6, 1718, 1720, 1723-5. Pyle 1727. ?Powis c.1730. Holywell c.1733. College of St Ignatius 1734-8, 1740-4, 1746-51. d. April 25th, 1751, London. (Fo.7; 114; 113; 91; LR.3/5; 14 f.40; 112 p.93; CRS.3/107; CRS.7/171; 173; 125; 109; Nec).

HILLIARD see Hildeyard.

HILTON, Adam. Laybrother.

b. March 21st, 1658, Lancashire. S.J. June 19th, 1688. Watten (nov) 1689-91. Liège 1692-3, 1696-7, 1699-1701, 1703-5. St Omers College 1706, 1708-13. d. January 15th, 1714, St Omers College. (Fo.7; 114; 113; Nec; CRS.62/45).

HOBBS, John. Laybrother.

b. February 14th, 1653, Winchester. S.J. 1676 or 1677. Watten (nov) 1678. St Omers College 1679-87, 1689-94. d. March 7th, 1695, St Omers College. (Fo.7; 114; 113; 150 II(3) 22/4/95; 170 ff.lv, 7v).

HODGES see Massie or Masie, John.

HODGKINSON, Charles *alias* Siddle or Sydall, Charles or John. Priest.

b. June or July, 1700, Lancashire. s. of John and Alice. e. St Omers College ?-1722, E.C. Rome 1722-9. Ordained priest March 16th, 1726. S.J. October 27th, 1729. Watten (nov) 1730, 1731. Residence of St Michael 1733. Residence of St John 1734. Yarm 1735. Residence of St John 1736, 1737. Residence of St Michael 1738, 1740-4, 1746, 1748, 1750, 1752-8, 1764 (Yarm 1741. Brough 1745. Yarm 1753). Yarm 1767-9. d. April 23rd, 1770, Yarm. (Fo.7; CRS.69; 114; 91; 113; Ans.4/140; RH.8/163; 64 p.48; 74; 90. f.22; Gil.4/171; 156 App.1; 158; CRS.32/340; CRS.40/168; 111; Nec).

HODGSON, Charles. Priest.

b. November 20th, 1742, Little Plumpton, Lancashire. br. of James and John. ?e. St Omers College ?-1760. S.J. September 7th, 1760. Watten (nov) 1761. Liège (phil) 1763, 1764. Bruges College 1767-9. Liège (theol) 1771-3. Ordained priest 1771. Liège Academy 1776, 1779-83. d. October, 1808, Antwerp. (Fo.7; CRS.69; 117; 113; 51 ff.304, 307; 91; 3 f.37; 13 f.422; 69; 90 f.54; Gil.3/318. For writings see Som).

HODGSON, James. Scholastic.

b. May 2nd, 1744, Lancashire. br. of Charles and John. e. St Omers
and Bruges Colleges 1757-63. S.J. September 7th, 1763. Watten (nov)
1764. Liège (theol) 1767, 1768. Bruges College 1769. d. May, 19th,
1770, Lancashire, not ordained. (Fo.7; CRS.69; 114; 113; 91; 41 n.102;
65; Gil.3/319).

HODGSON, John. Priest.

b. November 1750 or 1751, Lancashire. br. of Charles and James. e.
Bruges College 1764-9. S.J. September 7th, 1769. Ghent (nov) 1771.
Liège (phil) 1772, 1773. Liège (theol) 1773, 1776. Ordained priest
c.1776. Dunkenhalgh 1779, 1783, 1784, 1790, 1802. d. April 27th,
1807, Dunkenhalgh. bu. Preston old parish church cemetery. (Fo.7;
CRS.69; 114; 113; AHSJ.42/293, 308; 91; CRS.36/218; 3 f.3; 13
f.251v; 51 f.307; 90 f.54; 53 f.51; 25 f.49; 155 II 129; 167 pp.21, 31; 80;
Nec; 6 f.267v; Gil.3/319).

HODGSON, Thomas. Priest.

b. November 2nd, 1682, Yorkshire. e. St Omers College ?-1703. S.J.
September 7th, 1703. Watten (nov) 1704. Liège (phil) 1705, 1706. Liège
(theol) 1708-11. Ordained priest 1711. Ghent (tert) 1711. Maryland
1712-6, 1720, 1723-5. d. December 14th or 18th, 1725 or 1726,
Bohemia, Maryland. (Fo.7; CRS.69; 114; 113; Hu. Text 2/685; Nec).

HOLCROFT or OLDCROFT, John. ?Priest.

e. St Omers College ?-1684. S.J. 1684. Liège (phil) 1686. Nothing
further recorded under this name but it may be an *alias* for Richardson,
John (1).

HOLDEN, Joseph. Priest.

b. March 9th, 1808, Blackburn. e. Stonyhurst 1824-9. S.J. March
25th, 1829. Hodder (nov) 1829-31. St Mary's Hall (phil) 1831-3.
Stonyhurst 1833-5. St Mary's Hall (theol) 1835-8. Ordained priest
September 23rd, 1837, Stonyhurst. Stonyhurst 1838-40. Pontefract
1840-2. New Hall 1842-7. Hodder 1847-8. Worcester 1848-54. St
Beuno's College 1854-6. Holywell 1856-8. London 1858-60.
Lymington 1860-5. Wardour 1865-7. Pontefract 1867-8. Portico
1868-9. Blackpool 1869-76. Stonyhurst 1876. Bournemouth 1877.
Yarmouth and Bury St Edmunds 1878-80. Holywell 1880. Bedford
Leigh 1881-9. Stonyhurst 1889-91. d. July 25th, 1891, St Mary's Hall.
bu. Stonyhurst (115; Stol; Nec).

HOLLAND see Eccleston, Thomas; Martindale, John.

HOLLAND, Alexander. Priest.

b.1623, Lancashire. E.C.Valladolid 1644-51. Ordained priest April
3rd, 1649. S.J. June 12th, 1651. Watten (nov) 1652. College of St
Aloysius 1653-61, 1663-70, 1672-6 (Rector 1666-c.70). d. May 27th,
1677, in England. (Fo.7; 113; 114; CRS.30/162; Ans.2/159; Nec).

HOLLAND, Richard or Joseph. Priest.

b.1676 or 1677, Lancashire. e. St Omers College 1693 or earlier-97.
S.J. September 7th, 1697. Watten (nov) 1697. Liège (phil) 1699-1701.
St Omers College 1703-6. Liège (theol) 1708-11. Ordained priest 1709.

Ghent (tert) 1712. St Omers College 1713. Travelling in France and Italy 1713-5. Belgium 1716. College of St Thomas of Canterbury 1718, 1720, 1724-5. Wardour 1726, 1727. College of St Thomas of Canterbury 1728-38 (Rector 1728-34. Wardour 1733, 1735). d. July 4th, 1740, Paris. (Fo.7; CRS.69; 113; CRS.62 index; CRS.Mon.1/153; 150 III(2) 29/6/09; 9 n.247; 21 v.2; 44 f.210v; 74; 91; 193. Anglia 35/350; 01.328; Nec).

HOLLAR, John. Priest.

b. April 17th, 1674, London. e. St Omers College 1693 or earlier-96. S.J. September 7th, 1696. Watten (nov) 1697. Liège (phil) 1699-1701. St Omers College 1701, 1703-6. Liége (theol) 1708. Ordained priest 1708. St Omers College 1709, 1710. La Flèche (theol) 1710, 1711. d. November 21st, 1712, near Là Fleche. (Fo.7; CRS.69; 114; 113; 150 III(1) 31/1/10; Nec).

HOLME see Howard, William.

HOLME, Edward *alias* Howard. Priest.

b. December 29th, 1740, Lancashire. ?s. of William of Eccleston, Lancashire. br. of Francis. Nephew of John. e. St Omers College c.1749-59. S.J. September 7th, 1759. Watten (nov) 1761. Liège (phil) 1761, 1762. Liège (theol) 1763-7. Ordained priest c.1767. Ghent 1767. Moseley 1767-9. ?Stapehill. Houghton 1771-81. Pontefract 1786, 1794, 1796, 1802-7. Readm. S.J. 1803 or 1804. d. December 5th, 1809, Pontefract. (Fo.7; CRS.69; 114; 113; SCH.3/1, 17/12, 19/10; 21 v.2; 48 f.394; 54 ff.285, 294, 308v, 338; 50 f.210v; 55 f.16; 65; 76; 68 pp.77, 125; 72; 80; Gil.4/122; CRS.12/107; 01.306, 328; 117; 119 ff.14, 20, 35; Nec; 155 2/127; 167; AHSJ. 42/300, 306).

HOLME, Francis *alias* Howard. Priest.

b. May 21st or 24th, 1724, Lancashire. ?s. of William of Eccleston, Lancashire. br. of Edward. Nephew of John. e. St Omers College c.1736-40. S.J. September 7th, 1740. Watten (nov) 1740, 1741. Liège (phil) 1743. St Omers College 1744, 1746-9. Liège (theol) 1752-4. Ordained priest 1752. Lulworth 1755-c.66. Richmond, Yorkshire 1767-93 or 94. Alnwick 1793 or 1794-1802. d. March 9th, 1802, Alnwick. bu. Alnwick parish church. (Fo.7; CRS.69; 114; 113; 6 f.166; 21 v.2; 35 ff.259-62; 44 ff.229v, 267-8, 269-70; 36 ff.4A, 260; 48 f.35v; 64 p.518; 65; 68 p.107; 72; 90 f.176v; HMC.10th Report App.4/191; 121; 126; 117; 155 2/127; 163; 167; CRS.4/377; CRS.6/365; CRS.13/242; CRS.OP.1/168; Nec).

HOLME, John *alias* Howard. Priest.

b. October 26th, 1718, Lancashire. Uncle of Edward and Francis. e. St Omers College c.1732-7. S.J. September 7th, 1737. Watten (nov) 1738. Liège (phil) 1740-2. St Omers College 1742, 1744, 1746-7. Ingolstadt (theol) 1748. Cologne (theol) 1749. Ordained priest c.1750. Liège 1750, 1752-8, 1761, 1763-4, 1767-73 (Rector 1767-73). Liège Academy 1773-83 (President). d. October 16th, 1783, Liège. bu. chapel of the convent of the Holy Sepulchre, Liège. (Fo.7; CRS.69; 114; 113; 54 f.55; Ki.130; CRS.12/23; CRS.17/87, 99, 242; 140 n.45; 7;

New H.69, 73; Chad. 362 ff; Nec).

HOLT, Gilbert. Priest.

b.1688 or 1689, Lancashire. e. St Omers College ?-1710. S.J.
September 7th, 1710. Watten (nov) 1711, 1712. Liège (phil) 1713, 1714.
Liège (theol) 1715, 1716. Ordained priest c.1718. College of St Ignatius
1720. Residence of St Mary 1724. d. May 22nd, 1725, in England.
(Fo.7; CRS.69; 114; 113; Nec).

HONORATO, Tomas. Laybrother.

b. December 31st, 1728. English. S.J. June 12th, 1749, in Brazil. No
further information found. (Lei.7/269).

HOOKER, David. Scholastic or Laybrother.

d. ?Florence, date unrecorded. (Fo.7; 114).

HOOPER, John. Scholastic.

?e. Stonyhurst 1812-? S.J. September 7th, 1816. Hodder (nov)
1816-8. Stonyhurst 1820, 1821. Left 1825, not ordained. (116; 113; 2;
Stol).

HOOPER, Thomas. Scholastic.

b. July 28th, 1801, Ilfracombe, Devon. e. Stonyhurst 1816-? S.J.
October 15th, 1822. Montrouge (nov) 1822-4. St Acheul (phil) 1824-6.
London school 1826. Stonyhurst 1827-30. St Mary's Hall (theol) 1830.
Left 1832, not ordained. (115; 2; CG).

HOPE, ?Edward *alias* Desperamus. Priest.

b. September 27th, 1737, on the island of Chios. s. of an English
father. S.J. November 6th, 1751. Thessalonica c.1770. Polotzk
1805-10-?. d. November 14th, 1812, ?Polotzk. (118; CIR.; 150
(1753-1850) p.167).

HORION, Charles. Laybrother.

b. December 31st, 1680, ?Mons. S.J. December 31st, 1702-11.
Watten (nov) 1703. Liège 1704-9. Watten 1710, 1711. (113; 150 III(1)
5/11/07, 7/1/08, 30/5/11; 193 Anglia 35/269, 273, 275, 280).

HORMASA, Raymond *alias* Harris. Priest.

b. September 4th, 1741, Bilbao, Spain. S.J. September 21st, 1756 in
Spain. To English province c.1767. ?Scarisbrick 1768. Liège 1770.
Ghent 1771. Walton Hall 1772, 1773. Liverpool 1773-83. Lydiate
(supplied) 1783. d. May 1st, 1789, Liverpool. (Fo.7; 114; 113; 3 f.28v;
57/1 f.34v; 76; 67; 68 p.195; 80; 90 f.186; 94 ff.74, 233-4, 241;
Gil.3/392; 155/2/127, 129, 3/185c; CRS.9/188; 117; Nec; Ley. 175.
For writings see Gillow).

HORNBY, Robert. Priest.

b.1646, Lancashire. e. St Omers College ?-1668. S.J. September 7th,
1668. Watten (nov) 1669. Liège (phil) 1672. Liège (theol) 1673-6.
Ordained priest c.1676. College of St Thomas of Canterbury 1678-87,
1689-95 (Rector 1692-5. Idsworth 1692). d. August 23rd, 1695, in
England. (Fo.7; CRS.69; 114; 113; CRS.44/12; RH.8/184; Ki.124;
CRS.9/108; 168 f.39v).

HORNE, William. Priest.

b. September 7th, 1736, Cronstadt. e. St Omers College c.1745-53.

S.J. September 7th, 1753. Watten (nov) 1753, 1754. Liège (phil)
1756-8. Liège (theol) 1761. Ordained priest c.1762. Bruges College
1763, 1764. Rixton 1766. Southworth and Croft 1767. Plowden Hall
1767. College of St Francis Xavier 1767. Sarnesfield 1768, 1769.
College of St Francis Xavier 1771. Sarnesfield 1772-86. Hereford 1786,
1788, 1790-2, 1795-6, 1799. d. November 13th, 1799, Rotherwas. bu.
Rotherwas. (Fo.7; CRS.69; 114; 113; 1 ff.8-9, 67; 21 v.2; 32 n.4; 33
nn.40, 74, 108-9; 34 f.67; 38 f.217v; 51 ff.146, 149, 153v; 65; 80;
HMC.10th Report App.4/188; 125; 109; 119 ff.30, 35, 37, 43;
WR.34/26; CRS.OP.1/67; Nec).

HORNYOLD, Ralph *alias* Gower. Priest.
    b. July 2nd, 1674, Worcestershire. s. of Thomas and Margaret
(Gower). e. St Omers College ?-1693. S.J. September 7th, 1693. Liège
(phil) 1696, 1697. Liège (theol) 1699-1701. Ordained priest 1702.
Lytham 1702-c.22. Stonyhurst c.1724-c.27. Brinn and Ashton, 1728,
1730-2, 1738-40 (Rector of the College of St Aloysius 1738-40). d.
October 13th, 1740, Ashton. (Fo.7; CRS.69; 114; 113; CRS.62 index;
12 f.100; 23 f.35; 24 f.5v; 81; 85; 89; 91; Gil.4/322; CRS.16/424;
CRS.25/114; 123 IIIB f.360; Nec; 26 ff.67, 69).

HOSKINS, Ralph. Priest.
    b. April 15th, 1729, Maryland. e. St Omers College 1747-9. S.J.
September 7th, 1749. Watten (nov) 1750. Liège (phil) 1752, 1753. St
Omers College 1754-8. Liège (theol) 1761, 1763-4. Ordained priest
c.1764. Ghent 1765. Waterperry 1766. Liverpool 1767-9. Brough
1769-94. d. April 15th, 1794, Brough. bu. Catterick parish church.
(Fo.7; CRS.69; 114; 113; Gil.3/408, 4/172; 6 f.165; 21 v.2; 65; 76 f.46;
80; 90 f.176v; CRS.7/321; CRS.9/187; 111; 117; 119 ff.37, 44; Nec;
155 2/187; 167 p.38. For writings see Som).

HOSKINS, Richard. Scholastic.
    b.1665 or 1667, Shropshire. e. St Omers College ?-1689. S.J. May
7th, 1689. Watten (nov) 1689, 1690. Liège (phil) 1691-3. d. May 11th,
1693, Liège, not ordained. (Fo.7; CRS.69; 113; Nec).

HOTHERSALL, Thomas *alias* Slater. Scholastic.
    b.c.1642, Grimsargh, Lancashire. s. of William and Anne (Slater).
?Uncle of William. e. St Omers College ?-1665. E.C. Rome 1665-c.68.
S.J. June 20th, 1668. Watten (nov) 1669. Ghent 1672. Liège (theol)
1673-5. Residence of St John 1676, 1678-80. Maryland 1681-93,
1696-8. d.1698, Maryland, not ordained. (Fo.7; CRS.69; 114; 113;
Hu.Text 2/682; CRS.40/72; CRS.55/608; Nec).

HOTHERSALL, William. Priest.
    b. July 19th, 1725, Grimsargh, Lancashire. ?Nephew of Thomas. e.
St Omers College ?-1742. S.J. September 7th, 1742 and September 7th,
1744, Watten (nov) 1743, 1744, 1746. Liège (phil) 1747. Heidelberg
(theol) 1748, 1749. Liège (theol) 1750. Ordained priest c.1751. Liège
1752-8, 1761, 1763-4. E.C. Rome 1766-73 (Rector). Rome 1773-7.
Liège Academy 1781. Lierre 1783-90. To England 1791. Thame Park
c.1794-9. Oxford 1799-1803. d. August 25th, 1803, Oxford. bu. St

Clement's chapel. (Fo.7; CRS.69; 114; 113; 3 ff.25, 37; 11 f.57v; 13 f.294; 56 f.330; 57/2 f.222v; 67; 69; Gil.3/411; Ki.128; CRS.7/391; 140 n.45; 118; Nec. For writings see Som.).

HOUGHTON, Henry *alias* More. Priest.

b. July 18th, 1710 or December 21st, 1710, Cheshire. e. St Omers College ?-1726. E.C. Valladolid 1726-33. S.J. June 28th, 1733. Watten (nov) 1734. Ordained priest c.1735. College of St Thomas of Canterbury 1735-7, 1739-40. West Grinstead 1741-50. d. July 9th, 1750, West Grinstead. (Fo.7; CRS.69; 113; 114; 91; CRS.30/185; Ans.4/144; Bur.1/148; WGC.2/333, 335, 345; Nec).

HOUGHTON, James. Laybrother.

b. September 13th, 1796, Warrington. S.J. September 7th, 1816. Hodder (nov) 1816-18. Stonyhurst 1818-76. d. February 27th, 1876, Stonyhurst. bu. Stonyhurst. (Fo.7; 113; 115; Nec).

HOUSEMAN, Christopher *alias* or *vere* Layton, Joseph and *alias* Crofts. Priest.

b. September 21st, 1726, Co. Durham. e. St. Omers College 1738-44. S.J. September 7th, 1744. Watten (nov) 1744, 1746. Liège (phil) 1747. Ingolstadt (theol) 1748. Cologne (theol) 1749. Liège (theol) 1750. Ordained priest c.1751. Ghent (tert) 1752. Watten 1753. College of the Holy Apostles 1753, 1754 (?Bury St Edmunds). Ghent 1755-8, 1761, 1763-4. Bruges School 1767-9. d. October 15th, 1769, Ghent (Fo.7; CRS.69; 111; 114; 113; 91; 16 f.12v; 64 p.520; 65; Nec).

HOWARD see Haggerston, Henry and John; Holme, Edward and Francis and John.

HOWARD, William ?*vere* Holme. Priest.

b. March 25th, 1687, Lancashire. e. St Omers College ?-1708. E.C. Valladolid 1708-13. Ordained priest 1713. S.J. November 12th, 1713. Watten (nov) 1714. Liège (theol) 1715-6, 1718, 1720. Danthorpe c.1723-c.35. Residence of St Michael 1736-9. Cliffe c.1739-53-?62. Watten 1763-4, 1767-9. d. August 6th, 1770, Watten. (Fo.7; CRS.69; 113; 114; CRS.30/181; Ans.3/106; 91; 156 App.1; 158; YA.77/213-4; CRS.32/268; Gil.4/122; Nec).

HOWE see Molyneux, Richard (2).

HOWE, Joseph *alias* Pendrill. Priest.

b. March 19th, 1711, Shropshire. ?br. of William. e. St Omers College c.1724-9. S.J. September 7th, 1729. Liège (phil) 1733. Liège (theol) 1734-7. Ordained priest c.1737. St Omers College 1739. Residence of St John 1740. Cheeseburn 1741. Pontop c.1745. Long Horsley 1747-92, serving Morpeth 1760-77. d. May 2nd, 1792, Long Horsley. bu. ?Long Horsley parish church. (Fo.7; CRS.69; 114; 113; NCH.8/12; 21 v.2; 36 ff.34, 136v, 165, 180, 268; 66; HMC. 10th Report App.4/188; 156 App.1; 35 ff.67 ff.84 ff.104 ff.127 ff.129v; 164; 167 pp.19, 34; 117; Nec).

HOWE, William *alias* Pendrill. Priest.

b. March 11th, 1701, Shropshire. ?br. of Joseph. e. St Omers College ?-1722. S.J. September 7th, 1722. Watten (nov) 1724. Liège (phil)

1725-7. Liège (theol) 1728, 1730. Ordained priest c.1731. ?Burton Park 1732. St Omers College 1732-7. E.C. Rome 1738-41, 1743-6. d. March 10th, 1746, Rome. (Fo.7; CRS.69; 91; 114; 113; RH.13/116; 150 III(2) 1/2/38; 12 f.178v; 43 f.54v; 64 p.88; 74; Nec).

HUBBARD, William. Laybrother.
b. September 18th, 1692, Staffordshire. S.J. August 14th, 1717-24. Watten (nov) 1718, 1720. Ghent 1723. (113; 150 III(2) 5/6/23, 22/4/24).

HUBERT, John Giles. Laybrother.
b. January 18th, 1734, Liège. S.J. May 14th, 1760. Watten (nov) 1761, 1763, 1764. Liège 1767-9. Nothing further recorded. (Fo.7; 113).

HUDDLESTON, John *alias* Shirley and Dormer. Priest.
b.1636, Clavering, Essex. s. of Sir Robert. e. St Omers College 1649 or earlier-55. E.C. Rome 1655-6. S.J. May 17th, 1656, Bologna. Ordained priest before 1669. To the English province 1670. Liège 1670, 1672. College of St Thomas of Canterbury 1673. College of St Ignatius 1674, 1675. College of St Hugh 1676-8 (Blyborough 1678). ?Montreuil 1679. Paris 1681, 1682. Liège 1683. College of St Hugh 1684, 1685. London (royal preacher) 1686, 1687. Liège 1689-91 (Rector). College of St Ignatius 1692-3, 1695. College of St Thomas of Canterbury 1696. College of St Ignatius 1697, 1699. d. January 16th, 1700, London. (Fo.7; CRS.69; 114; 113; 150 II(3) 2/7/95; Gil.3/460; Ki.66; CRS.40/54; 193. Anglia 34/353; 168 f.94v; 123 II f.154; Che.64/450; 154; CRS.55/547; DNB.s.v.Dormer; Nec. For writings see Som.).

HUGHES, John. Priest.
b. June 1st, 1754, London. e. Bruges School and College 1764-70. S.J. September 7th, 1770. Ghent (nov) 1771, 1772. Liège (phil) 1773. Liège Academy (theol) 1774-8. Ordained priest June 13th, 1778, Liège. Liège Academy 1778-94. Stonyhurst 1794-1808. Portico 1808-28. d. July 6th, 1828, Portico. bu. Portico chapel. (Fo.7; CRS.69; 113; 115; ER.9/106; 3 ff.37, 51; 6 ff.22v, 202v, 187, 208v, 243v, 246v, 262v; 7 ff.345v, 382v, 392v, 347v; 13 f.473v; 21 v.1 f.8, v.2; 55 ff.42, 178v; 90 f.54; 93 pp.37, 38, 41, 47; 94 ff.281-2; 51 f.307; 157; Nec).

HUMBERSTON, Edward *alias* Hall. Priest.
b. July 12th, 1635 or 1637, ?Hales Hall near Loddon, Norfolk. s. of Henry and Mary (Yaxley) of Chedgrave, Norfolk. br. of Henry. e. St Omers College 1653-9. E.C. Rome 1659-64. Ordained priest April 8th, 1663, Rome. S.J. April 18th, 1667. St Omers College 1669. Ghent 1671. St Omers College 1672-6, 1678-81. Socius to the provincial 1682. Liège 1683-6. London (Savoy School) 1687. Arrested 1688. St Omers College 1689-93. Liège 1696-7. St Omers College 1697, 1699-1701, 1703-6. d. October 23rd or 30th, 1707, Watten. (Fo.7; CRS.69; 114; 113; Ans.3/107; 150 II(3) 9/3/97; CRS.40/61; 123 II f.156; HMC. 14th Report App.4/211; CRS.55/570; Nec).

HUMBERSTON, Henry *alias* Hall. Priest.
b.1638, Norfolk. s. of Henry and Mary (Yaxley) of Chedgrave, Norfolk. br. of Edward. e. St Omers College 1653-8. S.J. September

14th, 1658. Watten (nov) 1658, 1659. Liège (phil) 1660, 1661. St Omers
College 1663-5. Liège (theol) 1667, 1669. Ordained priest April 4th,
1669. Ghent (military chaplain) 1672. College of St Ignatius 1673. Liège
1674-6. Residence of St Michael 1678. College of St Aloysius 1679-81
(Dunkenhalgh c.1678). Residence of St George 1683-7 (Superior).
Residence of St Mary 1687. Residence of St George 1689-96 (Superior
c.1693-c.95.?Worcester 1686, 1688, 1693). Provincial 1697-1701. St
Omers College 1701-5 (Rector). Liège 1705, 1706. Watten 1708. d.
December 13th, 1708, Watten. (Fo.7; 114; CRS.69; 113; WR.20/69;
150 II(3) 10/4/83, 8/2/98, III(1) 30/7/1701; 37 f.197; Gil.3/474;
Ki.132; 168 f.2; 170 f.152v; 136 f.282; Che.64/452; Nec. For writings
see Som.).

HUNT see Hanmer, John.

HUNTER, see Weldon or Welton, James and Thomas (or Fenwick) and
    William.

HUNTER, Francis. Laybrother.
    b. June 21st, 1627, Yorkshire. S.J. February 23rd, 1657. Watten
(nov) 1657, 1658. St Omers College 1659, 1660. Liège 1661, 1663-5,
1667, 1669-70, 1672-81. Socius to the provincial 1682. Liège 1683.
Socius to the provincial 1684-7, 1689. St Omers College 1691-2. Watten
1693. d. September 5th, 1693, Watten. (Fo.7; 113; 114; 150 II(2)
September 1670; Nec).

HUNTER, George. Priest.
    b. July 6th, 1713, Northumberland. br. of Thomas (2). ?Nephew of
Thomas (1). e. St Omers College c.1725-30. S.J. September 7th, 1730.
Liège (phil) 1733, 1734. In England 1735. St Omers College 1736-8,
1740-1. La Flèche (theol) 1743, 1744. Ordained priest c.1744. In
England 1746. Maryland 1747-56. In England 1756-9. Maryland
1760-9. In Canada and England 1769-70. Maryland 1771-9 (Superior
1756-63). d. August 1st, 1779, St Thomas's, Maryland. bu.
Portobacco. (Fo. 7; CRS.69; 114; 113; Hu.Text 2/692; 92; Ki.133; 140
n.45; Nec. For writings see Som.).

HUNTER, Thomas (1). Priest.
    b. June 6th, 1666, Northumberland. ?Uncle of George and Thomas
(2). e. St Omers College ?-1684. S.J. September 7th, 1684. Watten
(nov) 1684, 1685. Liège (phil) 1686, 1687. St Omers College 1689-93. La
Flèche (theol) 1696, 1697. Ordained priest c.1696. Antwerp 1699-1700.
Liège 1701, 1703-4. College of St Aloysius 1706-10 (Stonyhurst 1706-9).
College of the Holy Apostles 1711. College of St Ignatius 1712-4.
Rouen 1715. Montpelier 1716. College of St Ignatius 1718, 1720, 1724.
d. February 10th, 1725 ?Stonyhurst. (Fo.7; CRS.69; 114; 113; DNB;
150 III(1) 6/4/09; 89; NB.1/160; Chad.253-5; Gil.3/483; Ki.133; 185
n.103; 183 n.54; CRS.62 index; Nec. For writings see Som.).

HUNTER, Thomas (2) ?*alias* Weldon. Priest.
    b. June 7th, 1718, Northumberland. br. of George. ?Nephew of
Thomas (1). e. St Omers College c.1726-35. S.J. September 5th, 1735.
Watten (nov) 1736, 1737. Liège (phil) 1738, 1740. Liège (theol) 1741,

1742. Cologne (theol) 1743. Ordained priest c.1744. Ghent (tert) 1744.
St Omers College 1746-50, 1752-4. ?Richmond and Danby 1754. E.C.
Rome 1755-8. York 1763-6 (Superior of the Residence of St Michael
1763-6). Bruges College 1766-8. Hardwick 1768-71. Residence of St
Mary 1772. Ghent 1773. d. January 30th, 1773, Ghent. (Fo.7; CRS.69;
114; 113; CRS.Mon.2/388; 16 f.12; 21 v.2; 51 f.80; 65; 68 p.93; 96; 77;
CRS.4/376; Ki.133; 111; 119 f.27; Nec; CRS.13/229).

HUNTER, William. Priest.

b.1661, Yorkshire or Northumberland. S.J. September 27th, 1679.
Watten (tert) 1689. College of St Ignatius 1691. Maryland 1692-1723
(Superior 1696-1707). d. August 15th, 1723, Portobacco, Maryland.
(Fo.7; 114; 113; Hu.Text 2/683; Nec; 150 II(3) 20/12/95).

HUSSEY, Lewis *alias* Burdett. Scholastic.

b.1709 or 1711. s. of John and Mary (Burdett) of Marnhull, Dorset.
e. St Omers College c.1724-29. S.J. December 14th, 1729. Watten (nov)
1731. d. January 1st, 1733, Liège, not ordained. (Fo.7; CRS.69;
CRS.56/167; 114; 113; RH.2/58; 74; E and P.40; Nec; Gil.3/507).

HUTTON, Robert *alias* Hill. Priest.

b. September, 1628 or 1629. s. of John and Jane of Upton Warren,
Worcestershire. e. Ghent ?and St Omers College before 1648. E.C.
Rome 1648-53. Piacenza 1653-5. Ordained priest before 1656. S.J. May
27th, 1656. Watten (nov) 1656. St Omers College 1657. Residence of St
Dominic 1658. Watten 1659. St Omers College 1660-1, 1663-5. College
of St Ignatius 1667, 1669, 1672-3. College of St Aloysius 1674-6,
1678-87, 1689-92. d. September 14th, 1692 in England. (Fo.7; CRS.69;
114; 113; Ans.2/165; Gil.3/313; CRS.40/42; CRS.55/511; Nec).

HYDE see Bruning, Anthony and Francis.

HYDE, Richard. Priest.

b. August 29th, 1687, Berkshire. s. of Richard and Mary (Smith) of
Pangbourne. ?e. St Omers College c.1705. S.J. September 16th, 1706.
Watten (nov) 1708. Liège (phil) 1709-11. Liège (theol) 1712-4. Ordained
priest c.1715. Ghent (tert) 1715, 1716. St Omers College 1718, 1720-1,
1723-44 (Rector 1728-31 and 1742-4). d. February 27th, 1744,
Canterbury. (Fo.7; CRS.69; 114; 113; 150 III(2) 9/6/42; 9 nn.107, 167,
271; 91; Chad.261-5; 120; 170; 137 f.216; Nec).

IBBISON, John. Scholastic.

?e. Stonyhurst 1807-?12. S.J. September 7th, 1812. Hodder (nov)
1812-4. Stonyhurst (phil) 1815. Stonyhurst 1816. Stonyhurst (theol)
1817. Left 1818, not ordained. (116; 113; 2; Stol).

IBBOTSON, William. Priest.

b. December 4th, 1800, near Skipton, Yorkshire. e. Stonyhurst
1812-? S.J. September 7th, 1818. Hodder (nov) 1818-20. Stonyhurst
(phil) 1820-2. St Acheul (theol) 1822-4. Brig and Fribourg (theol)
1824-5. Ordained priest October 18th, 1825, Fribourg. Dorchester,

Oxon, 1825-6. Stonyhurst 1826. Pontefract 1826-9. Wigan 1829-33. St
Marys Hall 1833-4. d. March 3rd, 1834, St Mary's Hall. bu.
Stonyhurst. (Fo.7; 115; CRS.7/390; Stol; Nec).

IDLE, Timothy. Laybrother.
    b. September 30th, 1791, Marrick, near Richmond, Yorkshire. S.J.
September 7th, 1816. Hodder (nov) 1816-8. Stonyhurst or St Mary's
Hall 1818-55. d. March 4th, 1855, Stonyhurst. bu. Stonyhurst. (Fo.7;
115; 116; Nec).

IMBERT, John. Laybrother.
    b.1663 or 1666 or 1670, Nice. S.J. April 30th, 1700. Watten (nov)
1701. Ghent 1703-6, 1708-12. Liège 1713-6, 1718, 1720, 1723-4. d. April
24th, 1724, Liège. (Fo.7; 114; 113; Nec).

INGLEBY see Tidder, Edward.

INGLEBY, Peter. Priest.
    b. July 17th, 1691 or July 10th, 1692, Lincolnshire or Yorkshire. ?s
of Sir Charles and Alathea (Eyston). ?br. of Thomas. S.J. September
7th, 1712. Watten (nov) 1713, 1714. Liège (phil) 1715, 1716. Liège
(theol) 1718, 1720. Ordained priest c.1721. In England 1723. Residence
of St Mary 1724-5. In England 1726-8, 1730. Residence of St Mary
1733-41 (Sandford c.1727). d. June 2nd, 1741, in England. (Fo.7; 114;
113; 91; E and P.305-6; Nec).

INGLEBY, Thomas *alias* Eyston. Priest.
    b. June 10th, 1684, Yorkshire. s. of Sir Charles and Alathea
(Eyston). ?br. of Peter. e. St Omers College 1696-1703. S.J. September
7th, 1703. Watten (nov) 1705. Liège (phil) 1706, 1708. Liège (theol)
1709-12. Ordained priest 1712. Ghent (tert) 1713. College of St Thomas
of Canterbury 1716. College of St Aloysius 1718, 1720 (Billington).
Lulworth 1723-c.9. d. November 12th, 1729, Paris. (Fo.7; CRS.69;
114; 113; 91; 23 f. 122; 89; E and P.305-6; CRS.6/365; 01.334; Nec).

INGLEFIELD see Englefield.

IRELAND see Crew, George; Rockley, Francis; Thornton, James.

IRELAND, Laurence *alias* Ferrers. Priest.
    b.1634, Lydiate. s. of Edward and Margaret (Norris). e. St Omers
College c.1650. Married Anne Swarbrick who died December 28th,
1663. S.J. July 12th, 1664. Liège (phil) 1667. Liège (theol) 1669. Watten
1670. Ordained priest 1672. Holme-on-Spalding-Moor 1672. d. June
30th, 1673, in England, probably at York. (Fo.7; CRS.69; 114;
CRS.Mon. 2/99; CRS.4/272; Mon.Dec.1878/418; E and P.114; 113;
Nec; WB.134, 143-4, 313).

IRELAND, William *alias* Ironmonger. Priest.
    b.1636, Lincolnshire. ?s. of William and Eleanor or Barbara (Eure),
of Crofton Hall, Yorkshire. e. St Omers College c.1647-55. S.J.
September 7th, 1655. Watten (nov) 1656. Liège (phil) 1657-9. St Omers
College 1660-1, 1663-4. Liège (theol) 1664-7. Ordained priest 1667. St
Omers College 1669. Watten 1670, 1672. St Omers College 1672-7.
College of St Ignatius 1677-9. d. January 24th, 1679, Tyburn.
Beatified. (Fo.7; CRS.69; 114; 113; CRS.47/235; 150 II(2) Oct. 1664;

Gil.3/553; 135 ff.185, 187; 136 f.296; FAB.99, 141 ff; BR.16-26; DNB; Nec).

IRONMONGER see Ireland, William.

IRVINE, Charles. Priest.

b. October 13th, 1801, Dublin. e. Stonyhurst 1813-? S.J. November 2nd, 1821, Rome. Ferrara (phil) 1823-4. Rome (phil) 1824-6. Stonyhurst 1826-32. St. Mary's Hall (theol) 1833-6. Ordained priest September 19th, 1835, Stonyhurst. Stonyhurst 1836. St Helens 1836-42. Lydiate c.1842. To Calcutta 1842. d. June 3rd, 1843, at sea on the way to Singapore. (Fo.7; 115; Nec; Gib.1/293).

ISLES see Jackson, Ambrose.

ISLES or ILES or EYLES, Ambrose. Scholastic.

b. April 21st, 1742. e. St Omers and Bruges Colleges 1758-63. S.J. September 7th, 1763. Watten (nov) 1763, 1764. Liège (phil) 1765-7. Bruges College 1767-9. Left, not ordained, 1769. (CRS.69; 113; 48 f.26v, 92v, 94).

JACKSON see Edisford, John (2).

JACKSON, Ambrose *alias* or *vere* Eyles or Isles. Priest.

b. January 25th, 1685, Yorkshire. e. St Omers College c. 1699-c.1701. S.J. September 7th, 1704. Watten (nov) 1704. Liège (phil) 1706, 1708. Liège (theol) 1709-12. Ordained priest 1712. Dunkirk 1712, 1713. Residence of St Michael 1714-6, 1720, 1724-5. In England 1726. Residence of St Michael 1727-45 (Superior 1727-c.1645. Sutton, near Ferrybridge 1727-8, 1735, 1741). d. April 21st, 1746, Sutton. (Fo.7; CRS.69; 114; 113; 91; YA. 77/205; CRS.32/225; 109; CRS.25/112; Nec; 156 App.1).

JACKSON, John *alias* Johnson. Priest.

b. July 11th, 1698, London. e. St Omers College 1715 or earlier-19. S.J. September 7th, 1719. Watten (nov) 1720. Liège (phil) 1723, 1724. Liège (theol) 1725-7. Ordained priest c.1728. Ghent (tert) 1728. In England 1730. Residence of St Winifred 1733. College of St Ignatius 1734. College of St Hugh 1735-7. College of St. Aloysius 1738, 1739 (?Croston Hall). College of St Michael 1739. Residence of St Mary 1740-1, 1743-4, 1746-52 (Superior 1748-52. Kiddington 1750, 1752). Liège 1752 (Rector). d. June 19th, 1752, Liège or Spa. (Fo.7; CRS.69; 114; 113; 91; 64 p.466; 68 p.185; 85; HMC. 10th Report App.4/184, 189; CRS.17/459; Nec).

JACOBSON, William. Priest.

b. October 15th, 1692, Dunkirk. e. St Omer's College before 1713. S.J. September 7th, 1714. Watten (nov) 1715. Liège (phil) 1716, 1718. Louvain (theol) 1719-21. Ordained priest 1721. Ghent 1723. Watten 1723-8, 1730. Ghent 1731. ?Burton Park 1732. College of St Ignatius 1733. Watten 1734-7, 1739. Ghent 1740-2. Watten 1742-7. Ghent 1748-50, 1752-8. Watten 1763, 1764. d. June 11th, 1764, Watten. (Fo.7;

CRS.69; 114; 113; RH.13/116; 150 III(2) 6/2/23; 9 n.300; 64 pp.88, 162-3; 91; 140 n.45; 108; Nec; CRS.62 index).

JACOMIN see Jaquemin.

JAMAR, Henry. Laybrother.
b.1670, Liège. S.J. July 30th, 1697. Watten (nov) 1697, 1699. Maryland 1700-08. St Omers College 1709-11. Ghent 1711. ?Left 1711. (Fo.7; 113; 150 III(2) 31/7/1711, 18/10/1711; Hu.Text 2/684).

JAMESON see Sachmorter, Philip.

JAMESON, William. Scholastic.
b. March 11th, 1747, Lancashire. s. of William of Liverpool. e. St Omers and Bruges Colleges 1759-c.63. S.J. September 7th, 1765. Ghent (nov) 1765. Liège (phil) 1767-9. Bruges College 1769-73. To England at the suppression S.J., not ordained. (Fo.7; CRS.69; AHSJ.42/292; 113; 7 f.19; 16 f.98; 25 ff.2, 8; 80; 119 ff.36, 42).

JANION, George *alias* Selby. Priest.
b.1646, Lancashire. s. of George and Mary of Park Hall, Blackrod, Lancashire. br. of William. S.J. September 7th, 1668. Watten (nov) 1669. Liège (phil) 1672, 1673. Liège (theol) 1674-6. Ordained priest April 17th, 1677. Ghent (tert) 1678. Bruges 1679, 1680. College of St Hugh 1681. Residence of St John 1682-7, 1689-93, 1696-7. d. May 12th, 1698, in England. (Fo.7; 114; 113; CRS.6/231; 168 ff.75, 77v; Nec).

JANION, William. Priest.
b.1652, Lancashire. s. of George and Mary of Park Hall, Blackrod, Lancashire. br. of George. S.J. August 14th, 1672. Watten (nov) 1673. Liège (phil) 1674. Liège (theol) 1675-6, 1678. Ordained priest April 9th, 1678. Lierre 1678-81 (Military chaplain). Residence of St Michael 1681. College of St Aloysius 1682. College of St Ignatius 1683. Military chaplain 1684. College of St Ignatius 1685. Military chaplain 1685. d. December 15th, 1685, in England. (Fo.7; 114; 113; Chad.213; CRS.6/231; 168 f.62; Nec; 108).

JANSENS, James. Laybrother.
b. July 20th, 1699, Ghent. S.J. September 7th, 1726. Watten (nov) 1727, 1728. Ghent 1730, 1733-41, 1743-50, 1752-8, 1761, 1763-4, 1767-9. d. May 5th, 1771, Ghent. (Fo.7; 114; 113; 91; Nec).

JAQUEMIN or JACOMIN, Martin. Laybrother.
b. July 9th, 1702, Liège. S.J. September 7th, 1726. Watten (nov) 1727. St Omers College 1728. Liège 1730, 1733-7. Ghent 1737-41. Antwerp 1741-54. d. February 2nd, 1754, London. (Fo.7; 114; 113; 91; 108; Nec).

JEFFERY, Thomas *alias* Wakeman. Priest.
b. November 30th, 1703, London. e. St Omers College ?-1721. S.J. September 7th, 1721. Watten (nov) 1723. Liège (phil) 1724-6. Liège (theol) 1727, 1728. Ordained priest c. 1730. Ghent (tert) 1730. d. October 18th, 1730, Ghent. (Fo.7; CRS.69; 113; 91; Nec).

JEMMETT, Francis. Laybrother.
b. November, 1693 or 1695, Sussex. S.J. May 23rd, 1723. Watten (nov) 1723, 1724, 1725-8, 1730, 1733-5. Liège 1736-41. Ghent 1743-4,

1746-9. d. June 29th, 1749, Ghent. (Fo.7; 114; 113; 91; Nec).

JENISON, Augustine *alias* Sandford or Sanford. Priest.

b. April 20th, 1735, Durham. s. of John and Elizabeth (Sandford) of Walworth, Durham. br. of James and John. e. St Omers College 1751-5. S.J. September 7th, 1755. Watten (nov) 1756. Liège (phil) 1757, 1758. Pont-à-Mousson (theol) 1761. Ordained priest c.1762. Ellingham 1763-7. London 1767-8. Wardour 1768-72. d. December 1793 or early 1794, St Omers College. (Fo.7; CRS.69; 114; 113; Ki.137; CRS.Mon.1/157; LR.3/5; 21 v.2; 44 f.232; 36 f.185v; 57 1 f.207; CRS.12/44; CRS.19/307, 309; 01.335; 164; 121; RH.3/11; Nec).

JENISON, James. Priest.

b. May 14th, 1737, Walworth, Durham. s. of John and Elizabeth (Sandford). br. of Augustine and John. e. St Omers College 1746-55. S.J. September 7th, 1755. Watten (nov) 1756, 1757. Liège (phil) 1758. St Omers College 1761. Bruges College 1762-4. Ordained priest c.1765. Travelling 1766-9. Ghent 1770. Husbands Bosworth 1770. College of the Immaculate Conception 1771. Bath 1772, 1773, 1776, 1782, 1789-92. Lulworth c.1793-4. d. January 22nd, 1799, Bath. (Fo.7; CRS.69; 114; 113; CRS.65/73; CRS.66/7; CRS.Mon.1/158; 14 ff.123, 135, 148; 54 f.42v; 51 ff.72, 75v; 76; CRS.6/367; Ki.137-8; 01.335; 121; Ber.144 ff., 190; BAT.73; Nec. For writings see Sut.).

JENISON, John ?*alias* Thompson. Priest.

b. July 30th, 1729, Co. Durham. s. of John and Elizabeth (Sandford) of Walworth, Durham. br. of Augustine and James. e. St Omers College c.1740-45. S.J. September 7th, 1745. Watten (nov) 1746. Liège (phil) 1747, 1748. St Omers College 1749-55. Liège (theol) 1756, 1757. Ordained priest 1756. Ghent (tert) 1758. Wardour 1759-68. Preston 1768-75. Near Wigan 1776-? Liège 1784. d. December 27th, 1792, Liège. (Fo.7; CRS.69; 114; 113; CRS.Mon.1/156; HMC. 10th Report App.4/186, 189, 191; 155/185c; Ki.138; CRS.12/40; 01.335; RH.3/11; 6 ff.158, 275; 13 f.141v; 14 ff.95v, 123v, 125v, 148v; 21 v.2; 51 ff.73v, 75v; 30 f.7av; 56 ff.18v, 144v, 258; 57 1 f.167v; 64 p.375; 65; 68 p.135; Nec. For writings see Som. and Sut.).

JENISON, Michael *alias* Freville. Priest.

b. September 29th, 1655 or 1656, Co. Durham. s. of John and Catherine (Ironmonger) of Walworth. br. of Thomas (1) and William. e. St Omers College ?-1675. S.J. September 7th, 1675. Watten (nov) 1676. Liège (phil) 1678, 1679. Liège (theol) 1680-3. Ordained priest December 18th, 1683. St Omers College 1684, 1685. Watten (tert) 1686. College of St Thomas of Canterbury 1686-7, 1689-93 (Stapehill 1690). College of St Hugh 1696, 1697. College of St Thomas of Canterbury 1699-1701, 1703-16, 1718, 1720, 1723-5 (Stapehill 1706, 1707. Canford c.1724). In England 1726-8, 1730. Watten 1733-5. d. November 17th, 1735, Watten. (Fo.7; CRS.69; 114; 113; CRS.31/123; CRS.Mon.1/111n; 44 ff.140v, 147v, 157v, 162; 91; 01.336; RH.3/9-10; Nec).

JENISON, Ralph *alias* Freville. Priest.

b.1635 or 1638, Co. Durham. ?s. of John and Jane of Carlbury. ?br.
of Thomas (2). e. St Omers College 1651 or earlier-56. S.J. September
7th, 1656. Watten (nov) 1657. Liège (phil) 1658-60. St Omers College
1661, 1663-5. Liège (theol) 1667, 1669. Ordained priest April 20th,
1669. Residence of St John 1672-6, 1678-87, 1689-93, 1696-7,
1699-1701, 1703-16 (Superior 1678-c.85 and 1703-c.1708). d. March
19th, 1719, Harbour House, Durham. bu. Harbour House chapel.
(Fo.7; CRS.69; 113; RH.3/8; 36 f.261; Nec).

JENISON, Thomas (1) *alias* Gray. Priest.

b.1643, Northumberland. s. of John and Catherine (Ironmonger) of
Walworth, Durham. br. of Michael and William. e. St Omers College
1660 or earlier-63. S.J. November 24th, 1663. Watten (nov) 1664. Liège
(phil) 1667. Liège (theol) 1669, 1672. Ordained priest c.1672. Residence
of St George 1673. Ghent (tert) 1674. Residence of St Mary 1675.
College of St Hugh 1678. In prison, Newgate, 1678. d. September 20th,
1679, in Newgate. (Fo.7; CRS.69; 114; 113; CRS.47/132n, 286, 290;
RH.3/9-10; CRS.34/274; 138 n.94; FAB.187-8; BR.80-1; Nec. For
writings see Som.).

JENISON, Thomas (2) *alias* Freville. Priest.

b.1643, Co. Durham. ?s. of John and Jane of Carlbury. ?br. of
Ralph. e. St Omers College 1660 or earlier-63. E.C. Valladolid 1663-4.
S.J. June 1st, 1664, in Spain. Ordained priest 1674. Ghent (tert) 1676.
Ghent 1677 (Military chaplain). Brussels 1677-80. Loretto 1680-4. Paris
1685-9. St Omers College 1691-2. Socius to the provincial 1693.
Antwerp 1693. College of St Thomas of Canterbury 1696-7, 1699-1701.
d. April 2nd, 1701, London. (Fo.7; CRS.69; 113; 150 II(2) 12/1/75,
26/11/78, 16/11/80, II(3) 5/8/84, 13/5/85, 5/1/86; RH.3/8-9; 168
ff.19v, 26v, 63v, 76v; CRS.30/xxxi, 170; 108; Nec).

JENISON, Thomas (3). Scholastic.

b. September 15th, 1740, ?Durham. e. St Omers College c.1755-7.
S.J. September 7th, 1757. Watten (nov) 1757, 1758. Liège (phil) 1761.
Left, 1763, not ordained. (CRS.69; 113).

JENISON, William. Priest.

b.1653, Co. Durham. s. of John and Catherine (Ironmonger) of
Walworth, Co. Durham. br. of Michael and Thomas (1). e. St Omers
College ?-1675. S.J. December 7th, 1675. Watten (nov) 1676. Liège
(phil) 1678, 1679. Liège (theol) 1680, 1681. Ordained priest c.1681.
Ghent 1682. d. September 9th, 1683, in England. (Fo.7; CRS.69; 114;
113; RH.3/9-10; 140 n.45; Nec).

JENKINS, Augustine. Priest.

b. January 12th, 1747, Maryland. e. St Omers College 1761-6. S.J.
September 7th, 1766. Ghent (nov) 1767. Liège (phil) 1768, 1769. Liège
(theol) 1771-3. Ordained priest c.1773. To Maryland 1773. d. February
2nd, 1800, Maryland. (Fo.7; CRS.69; 114; 113; Hu.Text 2/700; 51
ff.304, 307; Ki.136; Nec).

JENKINS, George. Priest.

b. April 9th, 1799, London. Nephew of Peter. e. Stonyhurst 1810-6.

S.J. September 7th, 1816. Hodder (nov) 1816-8. Stonyhurst (phil)
1818-20. Rome (theol) 1820-4. Ordained priest July 11th, 1824.
Stonyhurst 1824-7. Rotherwas 1827-8. Boston 1828-9. London
1829-55. Bury St Edmunds 1855-61. d. February 20th, 1861, Bury St
Edmunds. bu. public cemetery, Bury St Edmunds. (Fo.7; 115;
LR.3/65; Nec. For writings see Som. and Sut.).

JENKINS, John. Laybrother.

    b. August 12th, 1669, Glamorgan. S.J. February 1701. Watten (nov)
1701, 1703. Liège 1704-6, 1708-16, 1718, 1720. d. May 12th, 1721,
Liège. (Fo.7; 114; 113; Nec).

JENKINS, Peter. Priest.

    b. September 21st, 1735, Sutton near Guildford, Surrey. Uncle of
George. e. E. C. Douay 1750-3, St Omers College 1753. S.J. September
7th, 1753. Watten (nov) 1753-5. Liège (phil) 1756-8. Liège (theol) 1761.
Ordained priest c.1762. Gilling ?1762, 1763-4, serving Helmsley.
London 1764-9. Hammersmith 1769. College of St Ignatius 1771.
London 1772, 1773. Waterperry 1780. Witham c.1782-4. Holt 1785-90.
Irnham 1791. Coldham 1802. Bury St Edmunds 1802-3, 1807-8, 1810,
1812, 1815-8. Readm. S.J. 1803. d. July 14th, 1818, Bury St Edmunds.
bu. Bury St Edmunds chapel. (Fo.7; CRS.69; 114; 113;
CRS.Mon.2/157; RH.6/41, 103; LR.1/33, 3/5; ER.3/43, 112; 4 f.36v;
6 f.122; 8 II n.77; 13 ff.137v, 141v, 275v, 287, 386; 45 n.27; 54 ff.93v,
135, 151; 76 f.78; CRS.7/391, 401; CRS.12/139; CRS.28/266, 291;
AHSJ.42/306; 173; 96 v.3; 103; Nec. For writings see Som. and Sut.).

JENNINGTON, Philip. Priest.

    d. February 8th, 1704, Ellwangen. He does not appear in the
province records under this name. (Fo.7; 95 p.83).

JERMYN see Fermor, Henry and Thomas; Hacon, Hubert.

JERNINGHAM, Francis (1). Priest.

    b. May 25th, 1688, Norfolk. s. of Sir Francis, 3rd Bart. and Anne
(Blount) of Costessey. ?Uncle of Francis (2). e. St Omers College
1701-7. S.J. September 26th, 1707. Watten (nov) 1708, 1709. Liège
(phil) 1710, 1711. Liège (theol) 1712, 1713. Ordained priest c.1714.
Ghent 1714. Costessey 1714-27. In England 1728, 1730. College of the
Holy Apostles 1733-5. College of St Ignatius 1735-8. d. November
30th, 1739, London. (Fo.7; CRS.69; 114; 113; 91; E and P.193; Ki.139;
CRS.22/278; 43 ff.38, 58v; Nec).

JERNINGHAM, Francis (2). Priest.

    b. July 4th, 1721, London. s. of Henry and Mary (L'Epine) of
London. ?Nephew of Francis (1). e. St Omers College 1734-8. S.J.
September 7th, 1738. Watten (nov) 1738, 1739. Liège (phil) 1740, 1741.
Paderborn (theol) 1743, 1744, 1746. Ordained priest c.1745. Rome
1747-52. d. June 12th, 1752, Rome. (Fo.7; CRS.69; 114; 113; 150 III(2)
14/9/43; 12 f.187; Nec).

JOHNSON see Jackson, John; Magee, David.

JOHNSON, Joseph (1). Priest.

    b. November 29th, 1737. S.J. September 7th, 1758. Liège (phil) 1761.

Liège (theol) 1763, 1764. Ordained priest c.1764. Kingerby 1764-80.
Wingerworth 1781, 1785, 1790, 1802-4, 1807, 1810, 1815. d. February
14th, 1817, Wingerworth. (Fo.7; 114; 113; SCH.12/19, 20, 26, 15/29;
50 ff.16v, 201; 64 p.188; 65; Gil.4/73; CRS.22/197, 200, 201; 96;
AHSJ.42/310; 107; 121; Nec).

JOHNSON, Joseph (2). Priest.
  b. April 28th, 1810, Liverpool. br. of William. e. Stonyhurst
1818-27. S.J. September 20th, 1827. Hodder (nov) 1827-9. St Mary's
Hall (phil) 1830-32. Stonyhurst 1832-6. St Mary's Hall (theol) 1837-40.
Ordained priest September 21st, 1839, Stonyhurst. Stonyhurst 1840-41.
Gillmoss 1841-4. Liverpool 1844-5. Hodder (tert) 1845-6. Liverpool
1846-53 (Rector 1851-3). Provincial 1853-60. Liverpool 1860 (Rector).
Stonyhurst 1861-8 (Rector). Preston 1868-73 (Rector of the College of
St Aloysius 1870-3). Socius to the provincial 1873-81. Wigan 1881-3.
Liverpool 1883-93. d. July 8th, 1893, Liverpool. bu. Lydiate. (113; 115;
Nec).

JOHNSON, Robert (1). Priest.
  b. July 2nd, 1745, Liverpool. Uncle of Robert (2) and great-uncle of
Robert (3). e. St Omers and Bruges Colleges 1758-64. S.J. September
7th, 1764. Ghent (nov) 1764. Liège (phil) 1766, 1767. Liège (theol)
1768-9, 1770-71. Ordained priest 1771. Bruges School 1772, 1773.
Liverpool 1773-4. Scarisbrick 1774-90. Lydiate 1790-1821 or 1822. St
Helens 1821 or 1822-23. Readm. S.J. 1814. d. November 20th, 1823, St
Helens. (Fo.7; 114; CRS.69; 113; ER.9/112; 1 f.53v; 6 ff.137, 206v; 13
ff.164, 256, 452; 15 ff.12v, 16v, 21; 25 ff.151, 170; 27 ff.206, 217; 54
f.53v; 30 f.4v; 77; 69; 94 ff.39-40, 43, 265, 268; Gib.1/292; 152 II 129;
CRS.9/187; 167 pp.22, 30; Gil.HP.211; AHSJ.42/309; Nec).

JOHNSON, Robert (2). Priest.
  b. June 13th, 1786, Liverpool. Nephew of Robert (1). e. Stonyhurst
1796-1803. S.J. September 26th, 1803. Hodder (nov) 1803-5.
Stonyhurst (phil) 1805-7. Stonyhurst (theol) 1808-12. Ordained priest
1809, Wolverhampton. Stonyhurst 1812. Gillmoss 1812-4. Richmond,
Yorkshire 1814-65 (Superior of the Residence of St Michael 1838-c.49).
d. January 12th, 1865, Richmond. bu. Richmond, Reeth Road convent
cemetery. (Fo.7; 115; 105; Nec).

JOHNSON, Robert (3). Priest.
  b. November 1st, 1803, Cobridge, Staffordshire. Great-nephew of
Robert (1). e. Stonyhurst 1813-21. S.J. November 2nd, 1821. Rome
(nov) 1821-3. Ferrara and Rome (phil) 1823-6. Hodder 1826-30. St
Mary's Hall (theol) 1830-4. Ordained priest July 12th, 1834,
Ampleforth. Brough 1834-41. Norwich 1841-2 (Rector of the Colleges
of the Holy Apostles and St Hugh). Calcutta 1842-7. New Hall 1847.
Wigan 1847. d. September 1st, 1847, South-hill. bu. South-hill. (Fo.7;
115; NA.37/165; 52 f.23v; Pa.2/27. New H.180; Nec).

JOHNSON, William. Priest.
  b. June 6th, 1812, Liverpool. br. of Joseph (2). e. Stonyhurst 1822-9.
S.J. March 25th, 1829. Hodder (nov) 1829-31. St Mary's Hall (phil)

1831-3. Stonyhurst 1833-42. Louvain (theol) 1842-3. Stonyhurst
1843-4. Ordained priest September 28th, 1844. Stonyhurst (theol)
1844-5. Preston 1845-9. Bristol 1849-63 (Rector of the College of St
George 1854-61). Exeter 1863-71. Wardour 1871. Preston 1872-3.
Oxford 1873-5. London 1875-7. Lulworth 1877-84. New Hall 1884-5.
Bournemouth 1885-92. d. February 6th, 1892, Bournemouth. bu.
Wimborne Road cemetery. (115; 113; Nec. For writings see Sut.).
JONES see Gavan, Henry.
JONES, Edward. Scholastic.
    b.1662, Herefordshire. ?br. of Thomas. S.J. September 27th, 1688.
Watten (nov) 1689, 1690. Liège (phil) 1691-3. Left c.1693, not
ordained. (Fo.7; 113; 150 II(3) 8/8/93).
JONES, Ignatius. Laybrother.
    b. February 2nd, 1685, Chester. S.J. October 7th, 1711-29. Watten
(nov) 1711-3. Liège 1713. St Omers College 1714-6, 1718, 1720. Ghent
1723-4. St Omers College 1725-8. (113; 91; 150 III(2) 3/11/25; CRS.62
index).
JONES, James.
    b. in Ireland. e. Stonyhurst 1805-?. Adm. S.J. *in articulo mortis*,
September 1809, in Liverpool. (Fo.7).
JONES, John (1). Priest.
    b. March 25th, 1683, Worcestershire or Gloucestershire. S.J.
September 7th, 1709. Watten (nov) 1710, 1711. Liège (phil) 1712-4.
Liège (theol) 1715-6, 1718. Ordained priest c.1718. College of St
Ignatius 1720. College of St Hugh 1724. Frickley c.1725-48. d. May
16th, 1748, Frickley. bu. Frickley. (Fo.7; 114; 113; 91; CRS.25/112;
CRS.32/248; Ann.21; YA.77/205; Nec; 156 App.1).
JONES, John (2) *alias* Scudamore. Priest.
    b. July 18th, 1721, Monmouthshire. e. St Omers College c. 1733-9.
S.J. September 7th, 1739. Watten (nov) 1739, 1740. Liège (phil) 1741.
St Omers College 1743-4, 1746-9. Liège (theol) 1750, 1752. Ordained
priest c. 1752. Ghent (tert) 1753, 1754. Liège 1755. College of St
Ignatius 1756-8. Travelling 1763, 1764. London 1768-9, 1771-3, 1784-6,
1789, 1791, 1803. d. May 31st, 1803, London. (Fo.7; CRS.69; 114; 113;
CRS.50/275; LR.1/74, 3/5, 7; 45 f.16 ff; 54 ff.42, 66, 71, 92, 151; 65;
77; HMC. 10th Report App.4/189; Gil.3/666; Ki.142; 173; 103. For
writings see Som. Sut.).
JONES, Thomas. Scholastic.
    b.1667, Herefordshire. ?br. of Edward. S.J. September 7th, 1688.
Watten (nov) 1689, 1690. Liège (phil) 1691-3. Left c.1693, not
ordained. (Fo.7; 113; 150 II(3) 8/8/93).
JONES, William (1) *alias* Baker. Scholastic novice.
    b. c.1652, Monmouthshire. e. St Omers College 1668 or earlier-70 or
later. S.J. September 7th, 1673. Watten (nov) 1673-5. d. August 22nd,
1675, in England. (Fo.7; CRS.69; 114; 113; Nec).
JONES, William (2). Laybrother.
    b. February 17th, 1724, Lancashire. S.J. September 7th, 1752.

Watten (nov) 1753, 1754. Rome 1755-8. d. February 28th, 1758, Rome. (Fo.7; 114; 113; Nec).

JORIS, Henry John *alias* George. Priest.

b. January 27th, 1733, London. s. of Henry and Joanna Catherine (Sientenoy). br. of Peter Andrew. e. Antwerp. S.J. September 3rd or 25th, 1752, Mechlin in Belgian province. To England 1794. Great Canford 1794-6. d. July 9th, 1796, Great Canford. bu. Great Canford. (Fo.7; 114; 166 I p.t; CRS.43/124; CRS.12/53; Nec).

JORIS, Peter Andrew. ?Priest.

b. November 30th, 1735, London. s. of Henry and Joanna Catherine (Sientenoy). br. of Henry John. S.J. September 8th, 1753, Mechlin in Belgian province. (Fo.7).

JOSSAER, Bernard *alias* Green. Priest.

b. March 23rd or July 4th, 1712, Dunkirk. br. of Michael. S.J. September 7th, 1731. Liège (phil) 1733-5. Liège (theol) 1736-8. Ordained priest c.1739. Ghent (tert) 1739. Liège 1740-41, 1743-4. Watten 1745-7. College of St Ignatius 1748-50, 1752-54 (Scotney 1754). Garswood c.1755-69. College of St Aloysius 1771. Garswood 1772, 1773. d. November 21st, 1775, Garswood. (Fo.7; 117; 113; 65; 140 n.45; CRS.0 P.1/68; 158; Nec).

JOSSAER, Michael. Priest.

b. April 8th or 16th, 1708 or 1709, Dunkirk. br. of Bernard. e. St Omers College ?-1727. S.J. September 7th, 1727. Liège (phil) 1729, 1730. Liège (theol) 1733-5. Ordained priest c.1736. St Omers College 1736, 1737. Watten 1737-8, 1740-41. Ghent 1743-4, 1746. Watten 1747-50, 1752-8. d. November 14th, 1759, Watten. (Fo.7; CRS.69; 114; 113; 91; 140 n.45; 111; Nec).

JOURNO see Gage, Charles and Philip.

JOY, Matthew. Priest.

b. June 3rd, 1742, ?Dorset or Wiltshire. e. St Omers College 1755-61. S.J. September 7th, 1761. Liège (phil) 1763, 1764. Liège (theol) 1767-9. Ordained priest c.1767. Bruges School 1771-3. ?Liège Academy 1774. Linstead 1775-8. Ellingham 1779-98. d. February 21st, 1798, Ellingham. bu. Ellingham. (Fo.7; CRS.69; 114; 113; 7 ff.128, 136v; 10 f.53; 21 v.2; 36 f.261; 54 f.36; 76 f.27; Pa.2/15; 163; 167 pp.19, 34; Wha.45; 16 f.111; Nec).

JUBERT, John Baptist. Laybrother.

b. October 3rd, 1706, Artois. S.J. May 23rd, 1727. Watten 1730, 1733-41. Liège 1742-3. Rome 1744-50. Liège 1752. St Omers College 1753. Antwerp 1754. Ghent 1755. Liège 1756-8, 1761, 1763-4, 1767. d. October 15th, 1768, Liège. (Fo.7; 114; 108; 113; 12 f.185v; Nec).

JUDICI see Galli, Anthony Mark.

JUMP, Richard *alias* Ellis. Priest.

b. February 28th, 1714, Cheshire. e. St Omers College 1728-c.36. S.J. September 7th, 1736. Watten (nov) 1736, 1737. Liège (phil) 1738-40. Liège (theol) 1742. Geist (theol) 1743. Ordained priest c.1743. Ghent 1745. St Omers College 1746-8. Maryland 1749-54. St Croix,

West Indies 1755. d. September 7th, 1755, St Croix. (Fo.7; CRS.69;
114; 113; LR.1/76; 92; Hu.Text 2/693; Nec).
JUSTINIANI see Ayroli, John Baptist.

KEENAN, Paul. Laybrother.
 b. June 29th, 1770, Derry, Ireland. S.J. October 7th, 1814. Hodder
(nov) 1814-6. Stonyhurst 1816-54 (probably). d. May 3rd, 1854,
Stonyhurst. bu. Stonyhurst. (Fo.7; 115; 113; 114; Nec).
KELLICK see Wood, William.
KELLY, John Joseph *alias* Stafford. Priest.
 b. December 2nd, 1743, in Ireland. s. of Barnet. e. St Omers College
1759-62. S.J. September 7th, 1762. Watten (nov) 1763, 1764. Liège
(theol) 1768. Ordained priest c.1769. Ghent (tert) 1769. Tusmore 1769,
1770. Ghent 1771. Croston 1771-3. Horton 1774. Beckford 1777.
(Fo.7; CRS.69; 113; 76 f.47; 91; 68 pp.150, 192-3, 195; 25 f.26; 80; 155
III 185c; ?Ki.216).
KELLY, Paul see Caryll, Richard.
KEMP, Henry *alias* Gildridge or Gildredge. Priest.
 b. February 2nd, 1672, Sussex. s. of Anthony and Mary (Gage) of
Slindon, Sussex. e. St Omers College ?-1690. E.C. Rome 1690-91. S.J.
July 1st, 1691. Watten (nov) 1692, 1693. Liège (phil) 1696. Liège (theol)
1697, 1699-1700. Ordained priest 1700. Ghent (tert) 1701. Residence of
St George 1702-6, 1708-14, 1720, 1723-5. In England 1726-8, 1730.
Residence of St George 1733-6 (Wootton Wawen 1705, 1717, 1724,
1727-c.37). d. November 28th, 1737, Watten or in England (?Wootton
Wawen). (Fo.7; CRS.69; 91; 113; WR.20/63-5, 21/40; 40 p.190; E and
P.263; CRS.2/338; CRS.7/354, 387; CRS.40/110; Nec).
KEMPER, Herman. Priest.
 b. July 22nd, 1745, Westphalia. Nephew of Wappeler, W. e. St
Omers and Bruges Colleges 1760-c.66. S.J. September 7th, 1766. Ghent
(nov) 1766, 1767. Liège (phil) 1768, 1769. Liège (theol) 1771-3. Bruges
College 1773. Ordained priest c.1774. Liège Academy 1776, 1781, 1783,
1787, 1788, 1789, 1792, 1794. Stonyhurst 1794-?99. Wigan 1799-1808.
New Hall 1808-11. Readm. S.J. 1803. d. April 8th, 1811, New Hall. bu.
New Hall cemetery. (Fo.7; CRS.69; 114; 113; ER.5/97; 3 f.37; 6 f.96;
13 ff.114, 146v, 158, 170, 344, 357, 378, 419; 16 ff.77v, 98; 21 v.2; 54
ff.276, 316; 55 f.180; 57 II ff.74, 264v; 25 ff.77, 85; 90 f.54; 93 p.23;
Chad.392; 94 ff.1-2; NewH.65-6, 164; 157; Che.72/101ff; Nec;
CRS.17/93; CRS.36/3, 16).
KENDRICK or KENDERICK see Peake, Robert.
KENNET, Charles. Priest.
 b. 1660 or 1662, Durham. s. of John and Troth (Tempest) of
Coxhoe, Co. Durham. e. St Omers College ?-1681. S.J. September 7th,
1681. Watten (nov) 1682. Liège (phil) 1683-5. Liège (theol) 1686-9.
Ordained priest 1689. Watten 1692. Liège 1693, 1695. Residence of St

Mary 1696. College of St Thomas 1697. Paris 1699-1701. College of St Ignatius 1704-6, 1708-16, 1718, 1720. Paris 1721, 1723-8. d. April 21st, 1728, Paris. (Fo.7; CRS.69; 114; 91; 113; LR.3/6; 150 II(3) 19/2/95, III(2) 15/10/21; E and P.51; 170 ff.1v; 138v; Nec; CRS.62/index; 12 ff.76, 78-81, 92, 94, 96-7, 99, 102-3, 105).

KERWICK, James. Laybrother.

    b.1796, Tipperary, Ireland. S.J. September 20th, 1827. Hodder (nov) 1827-9. St Mary's Hall 1830-2. Stonyhurst 1832-70. d. April 4th, 1870, Stonyhurst. bu. Stonyhurst. (Fo.7; 115; Nec).

KEY see Fentham, Henry.

KEYNES, Alexander *alias* Luttrell. Priest.

    b. February 13th, 1642, Somerset. s. of Alexander. e. St Omers College 1655 or earlier-1659. E.C. Rome 1659-66. Ordained priest April 4th, 1665, Rome. Brussels c.1666-c.69. S.J. November 11th, 1669. Residence of St Stanislaus 1672. Liège 1673-5. Residence of St Stanislaus 1676, 1678. Hoogstraet 1679. St Omers College 1680. Residence of St Stanislaus 1681-3 (Superior. Treludro, Cornwall c.1680). College of the Holy Apostles 1683-8 (Rector). St Omers College 1689. London 1690 (Rector of the College of St Ignatius). St Omers College 1691, 1692. Liège 1693. Ghent 1696. College of St Ignatius 1697. College of the Holy Apostles 1699-1701, 1703-6, 1708-9 (Norwich 1699). College of St Ignatius 1710-11. Ghent 1712-3. d. June 7th, 1713, Ghent. (Fo.7; CRS.69; 114; 113; Ans.3/122; NA.37/165; 150 II(3) 6/11/83, 20/1/88; 01.339; 140 n.45; 171; CRS.40/63; CRS.55/576; 123 I f.63; Nec; 43 ff.18, 23, 28, 30; 168 ff.79, 84).

KEYNES, Charles *alias* Newport. Priest.

    ?From Somerset. ?s. of Edward and Anne (Brett). ?e. St Omers College ?-1660 or 1663. E.C. Valladolid 1660 or 1663. S.J. March 5th, 1663, in Spain. Ordained priest c.1671. Watten (tert) 1672. Liège 1673. d. September 20th, 1673, Liège. (Fo.7; CRS.69; 114; 113; Nec; CRS.30/167; Gil.4/31).

KEYNES, Maximilian *alias* Luttrell and Newport. Priest.

    b. May 11th, 1652, London. e. St Omers College 1667 or earlier-70 or later. E.C. Seville 1671-3. S.J. September 7th, 1674. Watten (nov) 1674, 1675. Liège (phil) 1676, 1678. Liège (theol) 1679-82. Ordained priest 1683. Ghent 1683. St Omers College 1683, 1684. Residence of St John 1685. College of the Holy Apostles 1685-7. In England 1688. Ghent 1689, 1690. College of the Holy Apostles 1691-3. Liège 1696. Ghent 1697. College of the Holy Apostles 1699-1701, 1703-16, 1718 (Fithelers c.1699). Watten 1720. d. March 3rd, 1720, Watten. (Fo.7; CRS.69; 114; 113; ER.9/105; 150 II(3) 5/9/82, 6/11/83; Nec; CRS.30/167-8; 43 ff.17-20, 27, 30-31, 33).

KIDDER, Charles. Scholastic.

    b. March 1751. ?From Lincolnshire. e. St Omers and Bruges Colleges 1761-c.67. S.J. September 7th, 1769. Ghent (nov) 1771. d. April 9th, 1772, Liège. (Fo.7; CRS.69; 91; 113; Nec).

KILLICK see Wood, William.

KILLINGBECK see Pole or Poole, Michael (1).
KIMBER, Thomas. Priest.
     b. April 23rd, 1688, Oxfordshire. ?s. of John. ?e. St Omers College c.1701. S.J. September 7th, 1706. Watten (nov) 1708. Liège (phil) 1709-11. St Omers College 1712. Liège (theol) 1713-6. Ordained priest 1716. College of St Ignatius 1718, 1720, 1724-5. In England 1726, 1727. Residence of St Winefrid 1728-c.41 (Superior. Powis 1727, 1729, 1730, 1737-8). d. April 1st, 1742, Powis. (Fo.7; 113; 114; CRS.69; 23 f.63; 91; 26 f.176; HMC. 10th Report App.4/198; 169/155/3; 125; Nec).
KING, Ernest. Priest.
     b. c.1714. English. S.J. in Portugal. d. March 24th, 1762, ?Portugal. (Fo.7).
KING, James. Priest.
     b. February 28th, 1793, Blackmore Park, Worcestershire. e. Stonyhurst 1805-?. S.J. September 7th, 1811-33. Hodder (nov) 1811-3. Stonyhurst (phil) 1813-5. Stonyhurst (theol) 1815-8. Ordained priest September 19th, 1818, Oscott. Lincoln 1818-23. Irnham 1823-33. (115; 50 f.15v).
KINGDON, Abraham. Priest.
     b. September 8th, 1718, London. br. of John. e. St Omers College 1732-c.37. S.J. September 7th, 1737. Watten (nov) 1737, 1738. Liège (phil) 1739-41. Wurzburg (theol) 1743, 1744. Ordained priest c.1745. Ghent 1746, 1747. Watten 1749-50, 1752-8, 1761, 1763-4. Liège 1767-9, 1771-3. Liège Academy 1776, 1781. d. March 7th, 1782, Liège Academy. (Fo.7; CRS.69; 114; 113; 6 f.234v; 3 f.37; 90 f.54; Nec).
KINGDON, John. Priest.
     b. July 29th, 1716, Somerset. br. of Abraham. e. St Omers College 1732-c.35. S.J. September, 1735. Watten (nov) 1735, 1736. Liège (phil) 1738, 1739. Liège (theol) 1740, 1741. Munster (theol) 1743. Ordained priest 1743. Watten (tert) 1744, 1746. Waterperry 1746. Maryland 1747-58. Crondon Park 1758-9. Maryland 1759-61. d. July 7th, 1761, Portobacco, Maryland. (Fo.7; CRS.69; 114; 113; 91; ER.5/95; Hu.Text 2/693; 64 pp.209, 471; 92; 126; 140 n.45; Nec).
KINGSLEY, Ignatius George *alias* Clayton. Priest.
     b. May 25th, 1701, Cheshire. s. of George and Anne. br. of Owen and Thomas (2) ?and William. e. St Omers College 1714 or earlier-c.20. S.J. September 9th, 1720. Liège (phil) 1723, 1724. St Omers College 1725-8, 1730. Rome (theol) 1733, 1734. Ordained priest c.1735. Watten (tert) 1735. College of St Aloysius 1736-40. Weston 1740. Callaly, Haggerston, Cheeseburn Grange 1741-7. College of the Holy Apostles 1748-51 (Belhouse 1751). Rudge 1751. Soberton 1751-4. College of St Thomas of Canterbury 1755-8, 1763-4. Slindon c. 1765. Scotney c.1766. College of St Ignatius 1767. London 1768-9, 1771-3, 1787. d. September 5th or 6th, 1787, London; bu. Old St Pancras churchyard. (Fo.7; CRS.69; 114; 113; LR.3/5, 6, 7/18; WR.20/62; 43 f.81; 44 ff.167, 227v; 64 pp.265, 384, 472, 486; 40 p.99; 65; 85; 91; 156 App.1; CRS.7/320; CRS.12/28; 173; 125; CRS.62 index; NEC).

KINGSLEY, Owen Joseph or George. Priest.
    b. September 13th, 1697 or November 21st, 1699, Cheshire. s. of
George and Anne. br. of Ignatius George and Thomas (2) ?and
William. e. St Omers College 1713 or earlier-14 or later. S.J. September
7th, 1716. Watten (nov) 1716-8. S.C. Douay (phil) 1718. Tournai (nov)
1720. Liège (theol) 1723-5. Ordained priest c.1725. Ghent (tert) 1726.
Maryland 1726-8. In England 1728, 1730. College of the Immaculate
Conception 1733-6 (Belgrave c.1730). Watten 1737-8. d. January 24th,
1739, Watten. (Fo.7; CRS.69; 114; 113; Hu.Text 2/689; 91; RSC.71;
CRS.62/12, 152; Nec).
KINGSLEY, Thomas (1) *alias* de Bois. Priest.
    b.1650, Kent. s. of William of Canterbury. e. St Edmund's Hall and
Magdalen College, Oxford and St Omers College 1667-c.75. S.J.
November 7th, 1676. Watten (nov) 1676-8. Liège (phil) 1679, 1680.
Liège (theol) 1681-4. Ordained priest April 4th, 1684. Ghent (tert) 1685.
College of St Ignatius 1686, 1687. Linstead Lodge 1688. Newgate
prison 1689. College of St Ignatius 1690-3. d. October 15th, 1695 or
1696, London. (Fo.5 and 7; 114; 113; Bur.1/198; 193 Anglia 35/118;
Wha.49; Fos.2/855; Nec).
KINGSLEY, Thomas (2). Priest.
    b. December 21st, 1705, Cheshire. s. of George and Anne. br. of
Ignatius and Owen ?and William. S.J. September 9th, 1723. Watten
(nov) 1724. Liège (phil) 1725-7. Büren (theol) 1728. Cologne (theol)
1730. Ordained priest c.1732. Liège 1733-5. Watten 1736, 1737. College
of St Hugh 1738-9. Liège 1739-41, 1743. Rome 1744-5, 1746-7. Liège
1747-50. Residence of St George 1752. Bromley Hall 1752. College of St
Ignatius 1753-8, 1763-4, 1767-8. London 1769. College of St Ignatius
1771. London, Lord Widdrington's 1772, 1773. d. August 26th or 27th,
1781, London. (Fo.7; 114; 113; 91; LR.1/30; ER.4/117, 10/39; 150
III(2) 27/1/49; 12 f.185v; 64 p.474; 66; 74; CRS.7/354; CRS.9/20; 179;
126; Nec. For writings see Som.).
KINGSLEY, William. Priest.
    b. April 12th, 1696, London. ?s. of George and Anne. ?br. of
Ignatius, Owen and Thomas (2). S.J. September 7th, 1713. Watten
(nov) 1714. Liège (phil) 1715, 1716. Liège (theol) 1718, 1720. Ordained
priest c.1721. Liège 1723-8. Ellingham 1730-4, serving Alnwick and
Callaly. d. January 30th, 1734, Ellingham. (Fo.7; 114; 113; 36 f.36; 74;
91; 156 xi; Ki.249; CRS.7/319; Nec. For writings see Som).
KIRK, Thomas. Priest.
    b. March 14th, 1665 or 1666, Derbyshire or Nottinghamshire. e. St
Omers College ?-1689. S.J. September 7th, 1689. Watten (nov)
1689-91. Liège (phil) 1692, 1693. Liège (theol) 1696, 1697. Ordained
priest April 21st, 1696. St Omers College 1699, 1700. College of the
Immaculate Conception 1701, 1703-6, 1708-14. College of St Aloysius
1715-6, 1718. d. September 11th, 1718, in England. (Fo.7; CRS.69;
114;113; Tyl. pp.112, 172; 123 IIIB f.359; Nec).
KIRKHAM, Richard *alias* Latham. Priest.

b. July 31st, 1671, Lancashire. e. St Omers College ?-1691. S.J. September 7th, 1691. Watten (nov) 1692, 1693. Liège (phil) 1696. Liège (theol) 1697, 1699-1700. Ordained priest 1700. Ghent (tert) 1701. In England 1701-2. Maryland 1703-8. d.1708, at sea on the voyage to England. (Fo.7; CRS.69; 114; 113; Hu.Text 2/684; NB.1/33; 170 ff.5v, 245v; 123 IIIB f.357; Nec).

KITCHEN or KITCHIN see Smith, Edmund.

KNATCHBULL, Francis. Laybrother.

b.1641. S.J. November 26th, 1671. Watten (nov) 1672, 1673. St Omers College 1674. Maryland 1676. d. December 27th, 1676, Maryland. (Fo.7; 114; 113; Hu.Text 2/681).

KNATCHBULL, Robert. Priest.

b. September 2nd, 1716, Maryland. e. St Omers College c.1728-35. S.J. September 7th, 1735. Watten (nov) 1736, 1737. Liège (phil) 1738, 1739. Liège (theol) 1740, 1741. Ordained priest September 1742. Watten (tert) 1742. St Omers College 1744, 1746-7. Brough 1748-65. Ghent 1765-73 (Rector). Walton Hall c.1773-?. d. September 16th, 1782, Walton Hall. (Fo.7; CRS.69; 114; 113; 16 ff.20v, 35; 21 v.2; 24 f.348; 64 p.318; 65; 85; 90 ff.176, 176v; Pa.2/26; Gil.4/66, 171; 140 n.45; 91; Hu.Text 2/704; E and P.325; 155 2 127; CRS.13/247; Ki.146; Nec).

KNIGHT see Baynham, John; Meredith, Richard.

KNIGHT, George. Priest.

b. January 12th, 1733. s. of Henry and Elizabeth (Blake) of Cannington, Somerset. e. St Omers College 1752-4. S.J. September 7th, 1754. Watten (nov) 1755. Liège (phil) 1756-8. Ordained priest c.1761. College of St Hugh 1761-3 (?Irnham). Residence of St Stanislaus 1763, 1764. Dunkenhalgh 1766. Waterperry 1767. Maryland 1768, 1769. Waterperry 1770. College of St Francis Xavier 1771. Montgomeryshire 1772, 1773. Courtfield 1773, 1785-90. d. January 25th, 1790, Courtfield. bu. St Mary's, Monmouth. (Fo.7; CRS.69; 113; 114; Hu.Text 2/697; 33 ff.24, 27, 29; 34 f.63; 65; 64 pp.187-8; 68 pp.132, 372; CRS.4/411; CRS.9/141; 01.341; 96 v.1; 91; Nec).

KNIGHT, James. Priest.

b. July 20th, 1780, Cannington, Somerset. s. of James and Mary (Rowe). S.J. September 7th, 1816. Hodder (nov) 1816-8. Stonyhurst (phil) 1818-21. Stonyhurst (theol) 1821-3. Brig (theol) 1823-4. Ordained priest April 11th, 1824, Sion. Courtfield 1824-30. Soberton 1830-6. Tunbridge Wells 1838. Stockeld Park 1838-43. Chipping 1843-4. d. November 12th, 1844, Chipping. bu. Chipping chapel. (Fo.7; 115; CRS.44/11; CRS.4/425; CRS.36/5; Nec).

KNIGHT, Richard alias Thorold. Priest.

b. July 24th, 1720, Kingerby, Lincolnshire. s. of William and Lucy (Jennings) of Kingerby. e. St Omers College 1730-9. S.J. July 11th, 1739. Watten (nov) 1740, 1741. Liège (phil) 1742. Louvain (phil) 1743. Louvain (theol) 1745-6. Ordained priest c.1746. St Omers College 1747. Richmond, Yorkshire 1748-64, serving Danby 1755-8. Lincoln 1764-93

(Rector of the College of St Hugh c.1768-73). d. December 16th, 1793, Lincoln. (Fo.7; CRS.69; 114; 113; SCH.12/19; 21 v.2; 41 nn.31, 63; 54 ff.2, 14v, 39v, 50v, 54v; 50 ff.26v, 63, 143, 202; 65; 108; HMC. 10th Report App.4/183, 192; Gil.4/72; Ki.146; E and P.157; CRS.8/379; CRS.13/229; CRS.22/194; Nec).

KNOWLES, John. Laybrother.
> b. July 25th, 1696, Cheshire. S.J. September 7th, 1731. Watten (nov) 1733-7. Liège 1738. Maryland 1740-2. d. March 8th, 1742, Maryland. (Fo.7; 114; 91; 113; Hu.Text 2/692; 64 p.354; 92).

KORSACK, Norbert. Priest.
> b. June 6th, 1773, in Russia. S.J. 1787 or 1788 in Russia. To England 1807. Stonyhurst 1807-46. d. February 17th, 1846, Stonyhurst. bu. Stonyhurst. (Fo.7; 115; 150 (1750-1853) ff.57v, 80, 92, 98, 100, 126, 162; 1 ff.217, 253v; 55 ff.132, 146; 93 p.81; 94 ff.69-70; Nec).

LABAT see Le Batte.

LACEY see Constable, John; Prince, Richard.

LACEY, Edward. Laybrother.
> b. January 5th, 1677, Hampshire. S.J. May 7th, 1712. Watten (nov) 1713-6. d. March 18th, 1718, Ghent. (Fo.7; 114; 113; Nec).

LA COLOMBIERE, Claude de. Priest.
> b.1641, near Lyons. S.J.1659 in France. In England 1676-8 as preacher to the Duchess of York. Beatified. (Fo.7; 113; CRS.17/364; Phi. For writings see Som.).

LA CROIX, Stephen. Priest.
> b. September 26th, 1706. S.J. in France. Liège 1763, 1764, 1767-9, 1773. Returned to France 1773. It is not clear that he took part in the work of the English province. (Fo.7; 113; 51 f.307).

LALART, John Baptist *alias* Peters. Priest.
> b. September 7th, 1693, Arras. e. St Omers College before 1714. S.J. September 7th, 1715. Watten (nov) 1715, 1716. Liège (phil) 1718. Liège (theol) 1720. Ordained priest c.1723. Ghent 1723. College of St Ignatius 1724, 1725. In England 1726-8, 1730 (?Bristol c.1727). College of St Ignatius 1733-41 (London c.1727 then East Malling). d. September 25th, 1743, Boulogne. (Fo.7; CRS.69; 114; 113; CRS.62 index; 91; CRS.3/181; 01.342; Nec).

LAMB see Davis, John.

LAMBRECK or LAMBRECY, Anthony or Ignatius. Laybrother.
> b.1650, Artois. S.J. July 21st, 1680. Watten (nov) 1680. Maryland 1681-7, 1689-93, 1696. d.c.1700, ?Maryland. (Fo.7; 113; Hu.Text 2/682; Nec).

LANCASTER see Allan, William; Le Motte, James.

LANE see Mendoza, Christopher de.

LANE, Bonaventure. Priest.
> b. July 24th, 1684 or 1685 or 1689, Hampshire. e. St Omers College

c.1700-02. S.J. September 7th, 1706. Watten (nov) 1708. Liège (phil) 1709-11. Liège (theol) 1712. St Omers College 1713, 1714. Liège (theol) 1715, 1716. Ordained priest c.1717. Ghent 1718. College of St Thomas of Canterbury 1720. Residence of St George 1724. College of St Aloysius 1725. Scotney c.1727. Ladyholt ?-1730. Dunkenhalgh 1730-50. d. January 18th, 1750, Dunkenhalgh. (Fo.7; CRS.69; 114; 113; 91; 24 f.347v; 30 f.34; 64 p.86; 74; 81; 89; CRS.36/217-8; 156 App.1; Nec).

LANE, James. Priest.

b. November 11th, 1737, Worcestershire. e. St Omers College ?-1758. S.J. September 7th, 1758. Liège (phil) 1761. Bruges College 1763-7. Liège (theol) 1768, 1769. Ordained priest 1769. Ghent (tert) 1771, 1772. Britwell 1772, 1773. Courtfield 1773. Britwell 1776. Courtfield 1778, 1780, 1784, serving Hereford for a time. Norwich 1788-1821. d. April 5th, 1821, Norwich. bu. Bury St Edmunds chapel. (Fo.7; CRS.69; 114; 113; NA.37/159; 13 ff.175, 244, 255, 423, 460; 21 v.2; 33 ff.8, 19; 34 ff.61, 61v; 42 ff.11, 43; HMC.10th Report App.4/196; 94 ff.287-8, 291-2; 76 f.83v; CRS.7/389; 125; 117; Nec).

LANE, William. Priest.

b. January 30th, 1671 or 1672, Norfolk. ?e. St Omers College ?-1692. E.C. Valladolid 1692-9. Ordained priest September 22nd, 1696. S.J. July 24th, 1699. Watten (nov) 1699-1701. Liège 1701. College of St Thomas of Canterbury 1703-6, 1708-16, 1718, 1720, 1724-5. In England 1726-8, 1730. College of St Thomas of Canterbury 1733-50 (Rector 1738-50. Brambridge and Twyford c.1701, 1707. Padwell 1727, 1741. Stapehill c.1746-7. Twyford 1747. Padwell 1751. Slindon at some date). d. April 29th, 1752, Winchester. (Fo.7; CRS.69; 114; 91; 113; Ans.3/127; 44 ff.162, 259v; 89; HMC.10th Report App.4/189; Bur.1/148; CRS.7/354; CRS.27/1; CRS.30/178; Nec).

LANGDALE, Marmaduke. Priest.

b. October 28th, 1748, Manchester. s. of Philip. e. St Omers and Bruges Colleges 1760-65. S.J. September 7th, 1766. Ghent (nov) 1767. Liège (phil) 1768, 1769. Liège (theol) 1771. Bruges School 1772, 1773. Liège Academy 1776. Ordained priest July 24th, 1776, Cologne. Wigan and Blackrod 1777-86. d. November 3rd, 1786, Wigan. (Fo.7; CRS.69; 114; 113; 6 f.161; 22 ff.45-6; 21 v.2; 76; 77; 25 ff.41, 45, 51, 59, 64, 72, 75, 80, 86, 95; 94 ff.251-2; Ki.147; 155/2/129; 155/3/212c; 167 pp.23, 29; 16 f.78; Nec).

LANGFORD, Abraham see Meredith, Amos.

LANGFORD see Meredith, Edward.

LANGWORTH, Basil *alias* or *vere* Durand. Priest.

b.1632, Lincolnshire. e. St Omers College 1651 or earlier-52. E.C. Valladolid 1652-9. Ordained priest September 1657. S.J. October 17th, 1659. St Omers College 1660, 1661. Liège 1663. College of the Holy Apostles 1664-5, 1667, 1669. St Omers College 1672, 1673. Liège 1674, 1675. College of the Holy Apostles 1676, 1678. Watten 1679, 1680. College of the Holy Apostles 1681-3 (Rector c.1678-c.83). d. October

12th, 1683, St Omers College. (Fo.7; CRS.69; 114; 113; 150 II(2)
23/7/72, 26/3/78; 43 f.9; E and P.165; CRS.30/165; 168 f.79;
Ans.2/91; Nec).

LARDEUR or L'ARDEUR, Peter. Laybrother.
b. November 20th, 1654, Saint-Omer. S.J. February 1st, 1688.
Watten (nov) 1689. St Omers College 1690-93. Watten 1696-7,
1699-1701, 1703-6, 1708-12. d. January 5th, 1713, Watten. (Fo.7; 114;
113; Nec).

LATHAM see Kirkham, Richard.

LAUNEY or LAUNAY or L'AUNOY, Alan or Alembert. Priest.
S.J. in France. Liège 1773, 1781, 1783. d. April 23rd, 1789, Liège. (51
f.307; CRS.12/31; 3 ff.37, 51; Nec).

LAURENSON, James. Priest.
b. September 8th, 1781, Witham, Essex. s. of James and Martha
(Martin). Half-br. of John. e. Liège Academy 1791-4, Stonyhurst
1794-?99. Stonyhurst (phil and theol) 1799-1814. Ordained priest
December 16th, 1808, Wolverhampton. S.J. September 7th, 1814.
Hodder (nov) 1814-6. Ugbrooke 1816-31. Lincoln 1831-2. Wardour
1832-53. Worcester 1853-8. d. February 5th, 1858, Worcester. bu.
Worcester. (Fo.7; 115; 113; 6 f.282; 13 ff.484, 494; 15 ff.105v, 195v,
265v; 47 f.191v; 90 ff.145v, 146v; 93 pp.55,72; 94 ff.128-9; CRS.36/80;
01.344; NewH.150-51; Nec. For writings see Sut. and Som.).

LAURENSON, John. Priest.
b. January 6th, 1760, near Witham, Essex. s. of James and Martha
(Coleman). Half-br. of James. e. Bruges College c.1769-73, Liège
Academy 1773-9. Liège Academy (phil and theol) 1781, 1783, 1788,
1794. Ordained priest at Liège. Stonyhurst 1794-1803. S.J. July 16th,
1803. Hodder (nov) 1803-5. Clitheroe 1807. Brough 1807-30.
Stonyhurst 1830-2. Bury St Edmunds 1832-4. Left S.J. c.1817 and
readm. 1823. d. September 19th, 1834, Bury St Edmunds, bu. Catholic
churchyard Bury St Edmunds. (Fo.7; 115; 113; CRS.69; 3 ff.37, 51; 6
ff.23, 282; 7 f.164v; 11 ff.207-8, 233v; 21 v.2; 48 f.32v; 42 ff.218 ff.,
228 ff.; 53 f.51; 55 f.122; 57 II f.102; 90 ff.145v, 146v; Pa. 2/27;
CRS.13/208; Chad.391; Gil.4/150; 157; CRS.4/247; NewH.
pp.150-51; 116; Nec. For writings see Sut. and Som.).

LAURENSON, Richard *alias* **Billinge. Priest.**
b. February 15th, 1713, Lancashire. ?s. of John and Mary
(Bradshaw). e. St Omers College 1728-33. E.C. Valladolid 1733-9.
Ordained priest 1739. S.J. June 13th, 1739. Watten (nov) 1739. St
Omers College 1740. Ghent 1741. Residence of St Winefrid 1743-4,
1746-7 (Powis 1743). College of St Ignatius 1748-50. Residence of St
John 1752-61 (Hardwick 1749-61). Highfield 1761-2. Bodney 1762.
Coldham 1764. Crondon Park 1766-8. d. February 28th, 1769,
Crondon Park. bu. Stock, Essex. (Fo.7; CRS.69; 114; 113; Ans.4/33;
ER.4/119, 8/46, 9/104; 14 f.37v; 21 v.2; 35 ff.49, 103v; 41 nn.15, 43; 64
pp.57, 393; CRS.6/327; CRS.30/188-9; 36 ff.136v, 162; 68 f.38; Nec).

LAURENZO, Augustine. Priest.

S.J. in Portugal. To London as preacher to Queen Catherine of Braganza. College of St Ignatius 1676, 1682-7, 1689. To Portugal 1689. (Fo.7; 113; 150 II(2) October 77, II(3) 15/10/82, 31/5/87, 21/1/89; 193. Anglia 35/98).

LAURO, Lewis. Scholastic.
b. May 5th, 1704, in Spain. S.J. September 7th, 1726. Watten (nov) 1727. Liège (phil) 1728. d. May 29th, 1729, Liège, not ordained. (Fo.7; 113; 91; 114; Nec).

LAWSON, Henry *alias* Whitfield, Cuthbert. Priest.
b.1628, Northumberland. e. St Omers College 1653 or earlier-56. S.J. September 22nd, 1656. Liège (phil) 1658, 1659. Liège (theol) 1660, 1661. Ordained priest December 22nd, 1662. Residence of St Michael 1663. Ghent (tert) 1664, 1665. Residence of St Michael 1667, 1669, 1672-6, 1678. d.1679, in prison in York. (Fo.7; CRS.69; 114; 113; 89; Nec).

LAWSON, Thomas (1) ?*alias* Hill. Priest.
b. December 8th, 1666, Yorkshire. s. of Sir John, 1st Bart. and Catherine (Howard) of Brough. Great-uncle of Thomas Lawson (2). e. St Omers College ?-1684. S.J. September 7th, 1684. Watten (nov) 1684, 1685. Liège (phil) 1686, 1687. Liège (theol) 1689-93. Ordained priest March 23rd, 1693. E.C. Rome 1695-7, 1699-1701. Residence of St Michael 1701, 1703-6, 1708-15 (Superior 1714-5. ?Brough c.1701-15). St Germain 1715-7, 1720. Watten 1721-4 (Rector). Provincial 1724-5. Chaplain to the Duchess of Norfolk 1725-33. Watten 1734-40 (Rector). St Omers College 1740-1, 1743-4, 1746-50. d. December 18th, 1750, St Omers College. (Fo.7; CRS.69; 114; 113; CRS.62 index; 150 II(3) 15/1/95, III(2) 20/5/24, 7/11/33, 14/11/33; 12 ff.105, 131; 21 v.2; 90 f.184; 91; Chad.256; Gil.4/170; Ki.149; 193. Anglia 35/350; 170 f.245v; Nec. For writings see Som.).

LAWSON, Thomas (2). Priest.
b. March 20th, 1720. s. of Sir John, 3rd Bart. and Mary (Shelley) of Brough. Great-nephew of Thomas Lawson (1). e. St Omers College c.1732-6. S.J. September 7th, 1736. Watten (nov) 1736, 1737. Liège (phil) 1738-41. Liège (theol) 1742. Strasbourg (theol) 1742-4. Ordained priest c.1744. Liège 1746. Travelling 1748. St Omers College 1749, 1750. Watten 1752. Travelling 1753-6. St Omers College 1757-8, 1762. Bruges College 1762-72 (Rector 1766-9). Hammersmith 1772, 1773. London 1785, 1787, 1791, 1800, 1801, 1803. d. July 11th, 1807, London. bu. Old St Pancras churchyard. (Fo.7; CRS.69; 114; 113; LR.1/33, 3/7; 150 III(2) 18/3/41, 3/6/41, 1/9/42, 10/11/42; 13 ff.68v, 240, 312; 16 f.12; 45 n.27; 51 f.67; 56 f.325; 77; HMC.10th Report App.4/196; Chad.283 ff; Ki.149; CRS.24/78; CRS.25/63; 125; 133; 124; 121; 103; 119 f.25; Nec. For writings see Som.).

LAYTON, John see Leigh, Alexander; Leigh, John; Leigh, Philip.

LAYTON, Joseph. see Houseman, Christopher.

LAYTON, William. Scholastic or Laybrother.
d. place and date unknown. (Fo.7; 114).

LAZENBY, John *alias* Badnam or Bodnam. Priest.
b. May 25th, 1655, Oxfordshire. e. St Omers College ?-1675. S.J.
October or December 7th, 1675. Watten (nov) 1676. Liège (phil) 1678,
1679. St Omers College 1680. Liège (theol) 1681-4. Ordained priest
August 1st, 1683. Ghent (tert) 1685. College of St Hugh 1686, 1687. In
England 1688. Ghent 1689, 1690. College of St Hugh 1691-3. College of
St Ignatius 1696-7, 1699-1701, 1703-6, 1708-16, 1718, 1720, 1724
(?Standon 1706). d. August 25th, 1724, London. (Fo.7; CRS.69; 114;
113; 140 n.45; ER.11/38; Nec).

LEADBETTER, John. Priest.
b. September 7th, 1795, near Wigan. e. Stonyhurst 1811-4. S.J.
September 7th, 1814. Hodder (nov) 1814-6. Stonyhurst 1816-21. Rome
(theol) 1821. Modena (theol) 1821-3. Ordained priest June 1823,
Reggio. Grafton 1823-4. Worcester 1824. Pylewell 1824-6. Norwich
1826-32. Stonyhurst 1832-3. Enfield 1833-73. Blackpool 1873-6.
Stonyhurst 1876. d. May 20th, 1876, Stonyhurst. bu. Stonyhurst.
(Fo.7; 115; CRS.14/297, 304; CRS.36/218, 285 ff; NA.37/162; Nec).

LE BATTE or LABAT, David. Laybrother.
b.1669 or 1670, Navarre. S.J. 1710, in Maryland. Maryland (nov)
1710-4. Ghent 1715-6, 1718, 1720, 1723-8, 1730. d.1732, ?Ghent.
(Fo.7; 113; Hu.Text 2/685; 90 f.10v; Nec).

LE CHAPELAIN, Charles. Priest.
S.J. in France. Liège 1768, 1769. There is no evidence that he took
part in the work of the English province. (113).

LECKONBY, Richard. Priest.
b. June 7th, 1699. s. of Richard and Anne (Hesketh) or John and
Anne (Hoole) of Leckonby House, Great Eccleston, Lancashire. br. of
Thomas (1). ?Uncle of Thomas (2). e. St Omers College ?-1720. S.J.
September 7th, 1720. Liège (phil) 1723-5. Liège (theol) 1726-8.
Ordained priest c.1729. Croston 1730-71. d. May 8th, 1771, Croston.
(Fo.7; CRS.69; 114; 91; 113; 21 v.2; 24 f.345; 68 p.33; 82; 86;
HMC.10th Report App.4/186, 189; 156 App.1; 158; Tyl.156n; 111; 51
f.311; 119 f.3; CRS.O.P. 1/74; CRS.6/166; Nec).

LECKONBY, Thomas (1). Priest.
b. November 13th, 1707, Lancashire. s. of Richard and Anne
(Hesketh) or John and Anne (Hoole) of Great Eccleston, Lancashire.
br. of Richard. ?Uncle of Thomas (2). e. St Omers College ?-1721. S.J.
September 7th, 1721. Watten (nov) 1723. Liège (phil) 1724-6. Liège
(theol) 1727, 1728. Ordained priest c.1730. Ghent (tert) 1730. Maryland
1731, 1733-4. d. December 6th, 1734, Portobacco, Maryland. (Fo.7;
114; 91; 113; CRS.69; CRS.6/166; 92; Tyl.156n; Nec; Hu.Text 2/689).

LECKONBY, Thomas (2). Priest.
b. October 15th, 1717, Lancashire. s. of William and Anne
(Hothersall) of Leckonby House, Great Eccleston, Lancashire.
?Nephew of Richard and Thomas (1). e. St Omers College 1730-6. S.J.
September 7th, 1736. Watten (nov) 1736, 1737. Liège (phil) 1738-40.
Liège (theol) 1741. Munster (theol) 1743, 1744. Ordained priest c.1744.

Watten 1746. Swynnerton 1747. ?Callaly 1748. Pontop 1748-78. d.
February 14th, 1778, Pontop. bu. Lanchester. (Fo.7; CRS.69; 114;
113; RH.1/37; SCH.3/12; 21 v.2; 36 ff.137, 163, 183, 261; 64 p.536; 80;
85; E and P.132-3; 156 xviii, App.1; CRS.6/166; Ki.149; 35 ff.29 ff,
102v, 133v; Tyl.156n; 125; 118; 119 f.42; 164; Nec).

LE COMBE, John Baptist. Laybrother.
    b. April 9th, 1747, Belgium. S.J. May 23rd, 1771. Ghent (nov)
1771-3. Liège (nov) 1773. It is not clear that he completed his
noviceship. Returned to Flanders. (Fo.7; 113; AHSJ.42/295; 51 f.307).

LE COMTE or LE CONTE, Peter. Laybrother.
    b. April 24th, 1717, Saint-Omer. S.J. September 7th, 1740-50.
Watten (nov) 1741. St Omers College 1743. Liège 1744. St Omers
College 1746. Liège 1747-9. (Fo.7; 113).

LEDIOT see Lidiate.

LEE, John. Priest.
    b.1657, Kent. e. St Omers College ?-1678. S.J. September 7th, 1678.
Watten (nov) 1679. Liège (phil) 1680-2. Liège (theol) 1683-6. Ordained
priest 1686. Residence of St Winefrid 1687 (?Welshpool School).
    d.1687, in England. (Fo.7; CRS.69; 113; Nec).

LEFEVRE, George alias Robeck. Priest.
    b. Scotland. S.J. Scottish mission. College of St Ignatius 1670,
1672-6, 1696-7, 1699-1701, 1703. d. May 20th, 1703, London. (Fo.7;
113; RSC.49, 52).

LE FEVRE or LE FEBURE or LE FEBVRE, Nicholas. Laybrother.
    b. June 2nd, 1693, Tournai. S.J. August 9th, 1720. St Omers College
1723-8, 1730-1, 1733-44, 1746-58, 1761. Liège 1763-4, 1767-9, 1771-3.
d. November 17th, 1773, Liège. (Fo.7; 113; 91; Chad.275; 90 f.22v;
117; Nec).

LE FEVRE, Peter alias Van Dame, Louis. Laybrother.
    b. January 19th, 1642, Saint-Omer. S.J. September 7th, 1667.
Watten (nov) 1669. Brussels 1672-4. Ghent 1674-6, 1678-80. St Omers
College 1681-7, 1689-93, 1696-7, 1699-1701, 1703-6, 1708-12. d.
November 4th, 1712, St Omers College. (Fo.7; 113; 114; 108; Nec).

LE HUNT, John alias Thornton ?and Hart. Priest.
    b. June 2nd, 1675, Huntingdonshire. e. St Omers College ?-1693.
S.J. September 7th, 1693. Liège (phil) 1696-7. Ingolstadt 1699. Rome
1700. Liège (theol) 1701. Ordained priest 1703. Ghent (tert) 1703. In
England 1704. Residence of St John 1705-6. College of St Aloysius
1708-11 (New House 1708). Travelling 1711-19. Haggerston 1719-53.
Ellingham 1753-6. Durham 1756-9 (Superior of the Residence of St
John 1736-50). d. March 19th, 1759, Durham. bu. St Oswald's,
Durham. (Fo.7; CRS.69; 114; 113; 91; RH.14/176; NCH.4/13;
SM.35/415; 150 III(1) 22/3/04; 21 v.2; 35 ff.36, 46-7; 36 ff.136, 169,
172, 260, 271; 58; NB.1/193; HMC.10th Report App.4/193; 156
App.1; CRS.25/115; 109; 111; 159; 160; Nec).

LEIGH, Alexander alias Layton. Priest.
    b. March 29th, 1681, Lancashire. s. of Richard and Emerentia of

Ackhurst Hall, Orrell, Wigan. Nephew of John and Philip. e. St Omers
College 1696-1700. S.J. December 4th, 1700. Watten (nov) 1701. Liège
(phil) 1703-6. Liège (theol) 1708-11. Ordained priest 1710. Ghent (tert)
1712. Residence of St George 1714-6, 1719-20 (Rushock c.1719).
College of St Aloysius 1724-5. In England 1726-8, 1730. College of St
Aloysius 1733-4 (Preston 1727, 1728). Beoley c.1734-6. Ghent 1737.
Gifford's Hall 1737. St Omers College 1737. Slindon 1737-8. Ghent
1738. Watten 1739. Liège 1740-1. Newcastle 1741. College of St
Aloysius 1743-c.45 (Preston c.1745). College of St Ignatius 1746, 1747.
d. March 12th, 1748, in England. (Fo.7; CRS.69; 114; 113; WR.5/14,
20/71; 21 v.2; 64 pp.153, 253, 302; 40 f.58; 66; 74; 91; NWCH.1969/58;
156 App.1; CRS.6/220; CRS.25/113; 140 n.45; Nec).

LEIGH, John *alias* Layton. Priest.
     b.1639, Lancashire. s. of Alexander and Anne (Layton) of Orrell,
Wigan. br. of Philip. Uncle of Alexander. e. St Omers College 1655 or
earlier-60. S.J. September 7th, 1660. Watten (nov) 1660, 1661. Liège
(phil) 1663-5. St Omers College 1669. Liège (theol) 1672. Ordained
priest c.1671. St Omers College 1673. Ghent (tert) 1674. Residence of St
John 1675-6, 1678-9 (Witton near Morpeth c.1678 ?and Long Horsley).
St Omers College 1679-83. College of St Hugh 1684-7, 1689-96 (Rector
1692-6). Ghent 1696-1703 (Rector). d. December 1st, 1703, Mechlin.
(Fo.7; CRS.69; NWCH.1969/58; 114; 113; CRS.6/220; 168 ff.1, 24;
140 n.45; Nec).

LEIGH, Philip *alias* Layton and Metcalfe. Priest.
     b. February, 1650 or 1651, Lancashire. s. of Alexander and Anne
(Layton) of Orrell, Wigan. br. of John. Uncle of Alexander. e. St
Omers College 1667 or earlier-71. E.C. Rome 1671-8. Ordained priest
April 13th, 1675. S.J. June 20th, 1678. Watten (nov) 1679. Residence
of St John 1680-3. Rome 1684, 1685. Residence of St John 1686-9,
1691-1706, 1708 (Superior c.1691-c.1702. Gateshead c.1686, 1688,
1704). College of St Ignatius 1709, 1710. Residence of St Winefrid
1711-7 (Superior c.1714-?17. Powis c.1710. Holywell 1713, 1714). d.
January 1st, 1717, Holywell. (Fo.7; CRS.69; 114; 113; Ans.3/131;
NCH.3/13, 6/17; NWCH.1969/58; Gil.4/192; CRS.6/220; Ki.150;
CRS.3/107; CRS.35/199, 201; CRS.40/83-4; CRS.55/613; 169/3; 123
II f.170; Nec. For writings see Som.).

LEIGH, Roger. Priest.
     b. March 15th, 1708, Lancashire. s. of Roger and Alice (Catterick) of
Aspull, Lancashire. e. St Omers College 1726 or earlier-28. S.J.
September 7th, 1728. Liège (phil) 1730. Liège (theol) 1733-5. Ordained
priest 1735. College of St Aloysius 1736-8. College of the Holy Apostles
1739. College of St Aloysius 1739-42 (Liverpool ?-1741. Westby
1741-?). Gravelines 1744. Formby 1745. Watten 1746. College of St
Aloysius 1747-50, 1752-8, 1763-4, 1767 (Wigan. Rixton. Dutton. Brinn
1747-67). Culcheth, Dutton, Southworth, Leigh 1767-71-? Brinn 1776.
Wigan 1777. Croston 1778-9. d. January 29th, 1781, Wigan Lane.
(Fo.7; CRS.69; 114; 113; 23 ff,69, 141; 24 ff.36-7, 347; 66; 25 ff.35, 40;

80; 85; HMC.10th Report App.4/189; Gil.4/144; 158; 156 App.1; Ki.133, 150; CRS.9/185; CRS.13/372; CRS.15/4; Gil.HP.236; 119 ff.6, 8, 9, 12, 13, 15, 17, 19, 22, 26, 31, 36, 40, 42; CRS.O.P. 1/66; Nec).

LEITAN or LEITTEN, John. Laybrother.
    b. April 21st, 1701 or 1705, Munster, Westphalia. S.J. December 31st, 1730. Watten (nov) 1733, 1734, 1735-9. St Omers College 1740-1, 1743-4, 1746-50, 1752-8. d. January 12th, 1760, St Omers College. (Fo.7; 114; 91; 113; 51 f.311; Nec).

LE JEUNE, Joseph *alias* or *vere* Young. Laybrother.
    b.1679, 1680 or 1682, Saint-Omer. S.J. July 6th, 1709. Watten (nov) 1710, 1711, 1712, 1713. St Omers College 1714. Liège 1715-6, 1718, 1720, 1721, 1723-8, 1730, 1733-41. St Omers College 1743-4, 1746-7. d. January 31st, 1748, St Omers College. (Fo.7; 114; 113; 150 III(2) 18/1/21; 91; Nec).

LEM or LEMME, Nicholas. Laybrother.
    b.1657, Liège. S.J. November 20th, 1680. Watten (nov) 1681, 1682-7, 1689-93, 1696. Liège 1697. St Omers College 1699-1701, 1703-6, 1708-16, 1718, 1720. d. September 2nd, 1720, St Omers College. (Fo.7; 114; 113; Nec).

LE MAITRE, Charles *alias* Brown. Priest.
    b. June 22nd, 1672 or 1673, Tourcoign, Artois. S.J. November 20th, 1693. Liège (phil) 1696, 1697. Liège (theol) 1699-1702. Ordained priest 1702. Ghent (tert) 1703. In England 1704, 1705. College of St Thomas of Canterbury 1706, 1708-12. College of the Holy Apostles 1713-6, 1718, 1720, 1724-30 (Kelvedon 1719-31). St Omers College 1731. Worcester 1732-7. d. January 7th, 1737, Worcester. (Fo.7; 91; 113; 150 III(1) 4/2/02; ER.14/82-3; WR.20/67; 43 f.39; 64 p.39; 74; 170 f.245v; Pa.15).

LEMOS, Benedict de. Priest.
    S.J. in Portugal. To England as preacher to Queen Catherine of Braganza. College of St Ignatius 1676, 1680-88. To Portugal 1689. (Fo.7; 113; Hudl.35; 150 II(3) 20/9/87, 19/6/88).

LE MOTTE, James *alias* Lancaster. Priest.
    b. July 13th, 1712, Lancashire. s. of James and Mary (Robinson). E.C. Rome 1727-34. S.J. September 7th, 1734. Watten (nov) 1734, 1735. Ordained priest 1735 or 1736. St Omers College 1736. Liège 1736-8, 1740. Montserrat, West Indies 1740-2. Maryland 1744, 1746. Canada 1747. Maryland 1748. Montserrat 1749. Watten 1750, 1751. Loretto 1752-8. 1761, 1763-4. Husbands Bosworth 1764-7. Lanherne 1767. Leigh, Somerset 1768, 1769. Britwell 1771. Slatedelf 1771, 1772. d. September 17th, 1772, Slatedelf. (Fo.7; 114; 113; 90 f.22v; LR.1/83; 150 III(2) 28/12/43, 9/1/49; 21 v.2; 64 p.529; 65; 76 f.83; 68 pp.39, 41; 25 f.10; 70 f.82; 80; 85; HMC.10th Report App.4/189; CRS.4/434; Ki.147; CRS.40/179; 01.342; 140 n.45; Hu.Text 2/691; Nec).

LEONARD, Frederick or Ferdinand. Priest.
    b. September 28th, 1728, in Germany. S.J. October 23rd, 1747. To

the English province c.1760. Pennsylvania 1760, 1761. Maryland 1763, 1764. d. October 27th or 28th, 1764, Portobacco, Maryland. (Fo.7; 91; 113; 64 pp.67, 406; 68 pp.269, 272; 92; 121; Hu.Text 2/695; Nec).

LEOPARD or LEPPARD see Lewis, John.

LE POINTE, Thomas. Priest.
    b.1736 or 1738, Paris. S.J. in France. London 1798-1802, 1806, 1808-9, 1811-3, 1815-8. Readm. S.J. d. December 11th, 1818, in England. (Fo.7; 114; CDSJ; 7 f.411; 8 I f.178v, II nn.16, 17, 39, 101; 13 f.297v; 15 f.117; 55 f.303; 59 ff.3v, 6, 12v, 22v, 26v, 32v, 39v, 48v, 51Av, 52v, 59; 133).

LERIDAN, Philip. Laybrother.
    b.1683 or 1685, Artois. S.J. July 1st, 1708-28. Watten (nov) 1709. Maryland 1710-6, 1720, 1723-5. St Omers College 1726-8. (Fo.7; 91; 113; Hu.Text 2/685; 150 III(2) 25/8/25).

LESLIE or LESLEY, Alexander. Priest.
    b. November 7th, 1693, Aberdeenshire. s. of Alexander, Baron Leslie and Henrietta (Irvine) of Pitcaple. S.J. November 12th, 1712. To English province c.1737. Ingatestone 1738-42. E.C. Rome 1743-8. d. March 27th, 1758, Rome. (Fo.7; 113; ER.12/106, 112, 114; DNB; 150 III(2) 13/7/37; 12 f.185; 74; 197; Nec. For writings see Som.).

LESLIE or LESLEY, Charles ?*alias* Duguid. Priest.
    b.1745 or 1747. s. of Patrick Leslie Duguid, Baron of Balquhain and Amelia (Irvine). br. of James. S.J. in France. ?September 8th, 1764. ?Liège (phil) 1769. ?Hardwick, Northamptonshire 1788. ?Tusmore. ?Woodstock. Waterperry 1790-2. Oxford 1792-1806. ?Readm. S.J. d. December 28th, 1806, Oxford. bu. St Clement's chapel. (Fo.7; 114; SCH.15/28; WR.23/40; 1 f.185; 13 f.343; 21 v.2; 31 ff.18, 27, 31A, 39v, 44; 67; 50 f.30v; 30 f.85; 55 f.73v; 59 ff.11, 24; 69; 73 p.106; CRS.7/391-2, 398, 401-6; AHSJ.42/307; 109; Nec).

LESLIE, James. Priest.
    b.1741. s. of Patrick Leslie Duguid, Baron of Balquhain and Amelia (Irvine). br. of Charles. e. S.C. Paris. S.J. 1760 ?in France. To England c.1780. Kingerby 1780-2. Market Rasen 1782-93. Slindon 1793-7. Grafton 1797-1807. Oxford 1807-12. Stockeld Park 1812-6. ?Readm. S.J. d. August 25th, 1816, Stockeld Park. bu. Spofforth. (Fo.7; 114; CDSJ; SCH.15/28; WR.8/29, 9/14; 13 ff.309, 465; 21 v.2; 31 f.31A; 50 f.29; Gil.4/73; CRS.7/356, 363-4, 406-7; CRS.12/130; CRS.22/197; AHSJ.42/310; Nec).

LESTER or LISTER, Francis. Scholastic.
    b. November 2nd, 1704, in Wales. s. of Francis and Rachel (Taverner). E.C. Lisbon 1725-8. E.C. Rome 1728-9. S.J. September 7th, 1730. d. May 8th, 1732, Liège, not ordained. (Fo.7; 91; Cro.226; Nec).

LEUSON see Levison.

LEVESON see Levison.

LEVINGE, Richard. Priest.
    b.1687, in Wales. S.J. September 7th, 1705. Watten (nov) 1706.

Liège (phil) 1708-10. St Omers College 1711-5. Ordained priest c.1718.
E.C. Rome 1720-4. College of St Ignatius 1725. Isleworth 1726, 1727.
Holt c.1727-?. College of the Immaculate Conception 1733-45 (Rector
1738-45). d. December 5th, 1745, in England (?Holt). (Fo.7; 114; 113; 9
nn.120, 197, 211, 241, 277; 64 f.48; 91; CRS.62/index; Nec).

LEVISON or LEVESON or LEUSON, Edward. Priest.
    b.1642, Staffordshire. s. of John and Isabella (Langtree) of
Willenhall, Staffordshire. br. of Richard. e. St Omers College ?-1662.
E.C. Rome 1662-9. Ordained priest March 5th, 1667. S.J. November
13th, 1669. College of St Chad 1672-80. College of St Hugh 1681-3.
Residence of St Mary 1685-7. Oxford 1688. College of the Immaculate
Conception 1689. College of St Ignatius 1690. College of St Chad 1693.
Residence of St Mary 1696-7, 1699-1701, 1703-5. College of St Ignatius
1706. Belhouse 1708. Residence of St Mary 1708-10. College of St
Ignatius 1711-6, 1718, 1720. d. April 13th, 1720, London. (Fo.7; 114;
CRS.69; 113; CRS.40/66; Ans.3/132; ER.4/121; Ki.150; 123 II f.174;
Nec).

LEVISON or LEVESON or LEUSON, Richard. Priest.
    b.1649, Staffordshire. s. of John and Isabella (Langtree) of
Willenhall, Staffordshire. br. of Edward. e. St Omers College ?-1670.
S.J. September 7th, 1670. Liège (phil) 1672-5. Liège (theol) 1676, 1678.
Ordained priest April 1st, 1679. St Omers College 1679. College of St
Chad 1680. College of the Holy Apostles 1681, 1682. College of the
Immaculate Conception 1683-5 (Holt 1685). College of the Holy
Apostles 1686-7, 1689-93-1696 (Ingatestone ?1688-96). Residence of St
Winefrid 1697. Liège 1699-1700. College of St Ignatius 1701. Residence
of St Winefrid 1703-6. Residence of St George 1708-11. College of St
Chad 1712-4. d. September 14th, 1715, in England (?Staffordshire).
(Fo.7; CRS.69; 114; 113; ER.5/70, 9/106, 12/109; Gil.4/201; 170; 43
ff.21, 98-9, 103-4; Che.64/455; Nec. For writings see Som.).

LEWIS see Culcheth, Thomas; Gage, John; Louis, Peter; Saltmarsh,
Edward; Smith, Thomas (2).

LEWIS, David *alias* Baker, Charles or David. Priest.
    b.1671. s. of Richard and Mary of Monmouthshire. e. St Omers
College ?-1690. E.C. Rome 1690-1. S.J. February, 1691, in Rome.
Rome (nov) 1693. Rome (phil) 1696. Rome 1697, 1699-1701, 1703-6.
Ordained priest c.1705. Loretto 1706-14. Rome 1716, 1720, 1723-8,
1730, 1733-40. d.c.1741, ?in Rome. (Fo.7; CRS.69; 113; 91;
CRS.40/110; 123 II f.144; Nec).

LEWIS, Francis see Evans, Thomas.

LEWIS, James. Priest.
    b. January 7th or 13th, 1731, London. s. of John. e. St Omers
College c.1738-48. S.J. September 7th, 1748. Watten (nov) 1749. Liège
(phil) 1750, 1752. Liège (theol) 1753-5. Ordained priest June 13th,
1756. Watten (tert) 1756. Watten School 1757. St Omers College 1758,
1760, 1761. Watten 1761. Ferrybridge 1761-6. ?Brambridge 1766.
?Lindley 1767. ?Ghent 1767. Scotney 1767-9. Liège 1769-70. Winsley

1771. Scotland 1772, 1773. Waterperry 1775. d. September 27th, 1776, London. (Fo.7; CRS.69; 91; 113; LR.3/5; 34 f.62v; 65; 76 ff.19, 113; 68 p.43; Pa.2.26; CRS.7/391, 400; CRS.19/265; 44 ff.229v, 273; CRS.27/14; 121; Nec).

LEWIS, John *alias* Leopard or Leppard. Priest.
b. April 19th, 1721, Northamptonshire. e. St Omers College ?-1740. S.J. September 7th, 1740. Watten (nov) 1740, 1741. Liège (phil) 1743. Cologne (theol) 1744, 1746-7. Ordained priest c.1747. Ghent (tert) 1748. College of St Ignatius 1749-50. Maryland 1750-88 (Superior 1768-73). d. May 24th, 1788, Bohemia, Maryland. (Fo.7; CRS.69; 113; Hu.Text 2/694; 92; 111; Nec).

?LEWIS, John.
?Adm.S.J. *in articulo mortis*, 1679. (Fo.7; Nec; 168 ff.80v, 82v).

LEWIS, Theodore *alias* Shelley, Francis. Priest.
b.1633 or 1634, Hampshire. s. of William and Alice. e. St Omers College ?-1654. S.J. September 7th, 1654. Watten (nov) 1654, 1655. Liège (phil) 1656-8. Liège (theol) 1659-61. Ordained priest c.1663. Residence of St Thomas of Canterbury 1663. Ghent (tert) 1664, 1665. Residence of St Thomas of Canterbury 1667, 1669, 1672-3. College of the Immaculate Comception 1674-5. College of Thomas of Canterbury 1676, 1678-87, 1689-93, 1696-7, 1699-1701, 1703-7 (Rector 1679-91. Brambridge 1692, 1707). d. July 31st, 1707, in England (?Brambridge). (Fo.7; CRS.69; 114; 113; CRS.42/152; 150 II(3) 23/2/86, 14/5/92; 44 f.162; Ki.151; CRS.9/108; CRS.27/7-8; Nec).

LIDIATE or LYDIATE or LEDIOT, William. Priest.
b.1650, Lancashire. S.J. September 7th, 1673. Watten (nov) 1673. Liège (phil) 1674-6. Liège (theol) 1678-80. Ordained priest April 15th, 1681. College of St Aloysius 1681-7, 1689-91. d. October 30th, 1691, in England. (Fo.7; 114; 113;).

LIMA, Alexandre de. Scholastic.
b. April 21st, 1697, Louvain, of English parentage. S.J. August 14th, 1723, in Brazil. d. May 11th, 1727, Rio de Janeiro. (Lei.7/269).

LISTER see Lester.

LIVERS, Arnold. Priest.
b. May 11th, 1705, Maryland. S.J. September 7th, 1724. Watten (nov) 1724-6. Liège (phil) 1727, 1728. Liège (theol) 1730. Ordained priest c.1733. Ghent (tert) 1733. Maryland 1734-41, 1743-4. 1746-50, 1752-8, 1761, 1763-4. d. August 13th or 16th, 1767, Maryland. (Fo.7; 114; 91; 113; 92; Hu.Text 2/690; Nec).

LIVESAY, James. Laybrother.
b. October 9th, 1708, Lancashire. br. of John. S.J. September 7th, 1740. Watten (nov) 1740. St Omers College 1742-4, 1746-7. Boulogne School 1748. St Omers College 1749-50, 1752-8, 1761. Bruges College 1763-4. d. September 9th, 1766, Bruges. (Fo.7; 114; 91; 113; Nec).

LIVESAY, John. Laybrother.
b. June 24th, 1712, Lancashire. br. of James. S.J. September 7th, 1737. Watten (nov) 1738, 1740. St Omers College 1741-4, 1746-50,

1752-5. Watten 1756, 1757. St Omers College 1758, 1761. Bruges
College 1763-4. Bruges School 1767. Bruges College 1768. Bruges
School 1769, 1771-3. Lulworth 1774-81. d. October 9th, 1781,
Lulworth. (Fo.7; 117; 91; 113; AHSJ.42/294; 15 f.12; 16 f.12v; 111;
Nec).

LLOYD see Floyd.

LOCKHART or LOCKHARD, Thomas. Priest.
      b. May 30th, 1672, Herefordshire. e. St Omers College ?-1693. S.J.
October or November, 1693. Liège (phil) 1696-7. Liège (theol)
1699-1701. Ordained priest 1702. Ghent (tert) 1703. In England 1704,
1705. Residence of St George 1706, 1708-9. College of St Hugh 1710,
1711. College of St Thomas of Canterbury 1712-6, 1718, 1720. College
of St Ignatius 1724, 1725. Cheam c.1727. Crosby 1728-30. College of St
Aloysius 1737-41, 1743-4 (Brinn c.1740-44). d. March 2nd, 1744, in
England (?Brinn). (Fo.7; CRS.69; 114; 113; 150 III(1) 11/4/99; 89; 91;
CRS.2/314; CRS.25/114; 156 App.1; Nec).

LODGE or LUDD, Thomas. Priest.
      b. July 7th, 1726, Yorkshire. e. St Omers College c.1738-44. S.J.
September 7th, 1744. Watten (nov) 1744-6. Liège (phil) 1747. Germany
(theol) 1748. Molsheim (theol) 1749. Liège (theol) 1750. Ordained
priest c.1751. St Omers College 1752-6. Residence of St Stanislaus
1756-8. Lanherne 1758-64. d. January 6th, 1764, Lanherne. (Fo.7;
CRS.69; 114; 91; 113; 65; CRS.6/340; 01.347; Nec).

LOMAX, Charles. Priest.
      b. August 8th, 1810, Clayton Hall, Lancashire. s. of Richard
Grimshaw and Catherine (Greaves). br. of Walter and William. e.
Stonyhurst 1816-27. S.J. September 20th, 1827. Hodder (nov) 1827-9.
Stonyhurst (phil) 1829. St Mary's Hall (phil) 1830-1. London School
1831-3. St Mary's Hall (theol) 1833-7. Ordained priest September 24th,
1836, Stonyhurst. Boston 1837, 1838. Tunbridge Wells 1838-40.
Hodder 1840-1. Worcester 1841-2. Preston 1842. Lydiate 1842-3. St
Acheul (tert) 1843-4. Wigan 1844-6. Ugbrooke 1846-56. Teignmouth
1856-60. d. October 28th, 1860, Stonyhurst. bu. Stonyhurst. (Fo.7;
115; 113; Gil.4/322; Nec).

LOMAX, Laurence. Scholastic.
      b.1669 or 1671, Cambridgeshire. S.J. September 7th, 1687. Watten
(nov) 1687. Liège (phil) 1689-91. Liège (theol) 1691, 1693. Left 1696,
not ordained. (Fo.7; 113).

LOMAX, Walter. Priest.
      b. July 6th, 1808, Clayton Hall, Lancashire. s. of Richard Grimshaw
and Catherine (Greaves). br. of Charles and William. e. Stonyhurst
1816-27. S.J. September 20th, 1827. Hodder (nov) 1827-9. Stonyhurst
(phil) 1829-30. St Mary's Hall (phil) 1830-1. St Mary's Hall (theol)
1831-4. Ordained priest December 20th, 1834, Stonyhurst. Stonyhurst
1834-42. Worcester 1842-4. Norwich 1844-51. Richmond 1851-5.
Mount St Mary's College and Chesterfield 1855-6. Wakefield 1856-9.
Worcester 1861-5. Pontefract 1865-6. Wakefield 1866-7. Blackpool

1867-8. Rhyl 1868-70. Ruthin 1870-2. St Beuno's College and Denbigh 1872-3. Galashiels and Selkirk 1873. Clitheroe 1873-4. Everingham 1874-80. Wakefield 1880-3. Stonyhurst 1883-6. d. March 9th, 1886, Stonyhurst. bu. Stonyhurst. (Fo.7; 115; Gil.4/322; NA.37/166; Nec).

LOMAX, William. Priest.

b. April 26th, 1804, Clayton Hall, Lancashire. s. of Richard Grimshaw and Catherine (Greaves). br. of Charles and Walter. e. Stonyhurst 1811-22. S.J. October 15th, 1822. Montrouge (nov) 1822-4. Stonyhurst 1824-5. London School 1825-6. Stonyhurst 1826. Dôle (phil) 1827. Aix (phil) 1828. Stonyhurst (theol) 1829. St Mary's Hall (theol) 1830-3. Ordained priest September 21st, 1833, Stonyhurst. Preston 1833-9. Hodder (tert) 1839-40. Preston 1840-3. Stonyhurst 1843. Wardour 1843-5. St Mary's Hall 1845. Richmond 1845. Stockeld Park 1846-9. Pontefract 1849-56. d. May 8th, 1856, Pontefract. bu. Pontefract. (Fo.7; 115; 113; CRS.36/232; Gil.4/322; Nec for writings see Sut.).

LOMPARET, Maurice. Priest.

d. date unknown on journey to the Indies. (Fo.7; 114).

LOUIS or LEWIS, Peter. Laybrother.

b.1669 or 1671 or 1672, Saint-Omer. S.J. June 28th, 1703. Watten (nov) 1703, 1704. St Omers College 1705-6, 1708-16, 1718, 1720, 1723-8, 1730, 1733-4. d. May 24th, 1735, St Omers College. (Fo.7; 114; 113; 91; Nec).

LOVAT, Charles. Priest.

b. September 6th, 1799, Preston. e. Sedgley Park 1809-13, Stonyhurst 1813-7. S.J. September 7th, 1817-36. Hodder (nov) 1817-19. Stonyhurst (phil) 1819-21. Rome (theol) 1821-5. Ordained priest July 11th, 1824. Hereford 1825-7. Stonyhurst 1827-32. St Mary's Hall 1832-6. (115; SCH.3/23; 2).

LOVE or LOWE see Mendoza, Christopher de.

LOVELL, George. Priest.

b.1650, Oxfordshire. e. St Omers College 1664 or earlier-69. S.J. September 7th, 1669. Liège (phil) 1672, 1673. Liège (theol) 1674-8. Ordained priest April 9th, 1678. Liège 1679-81. Ghent 1682. College of St Aloysius 1683. In France 1684. College of St Aloysius 1685-7. In England 1688. In France 1689. Paris 1691-3. College of St Aloysius 1696-7. Paris 1698. College of St Aloysius 1699, 1700. Liège 1701. College of St Aloysius 1703-6, 1708-9 (Dunkenhalgh or Stonyhurst c.1701, 1708). In England 1710. College of St Ignatius 1711. College of the Holy Apostles 1712, 1713-4. College of St Ignatius 1715-6, 1718. New House 1719. d. December 12th, 1720, New House. bu. Harkirke cemetery, Little Crosby. (Fo.7; CRS.69; 114; 113; 23 f.35; NB.1/25, 191, 2/273, 3/29; Che.12; CRS.8/196, 198, 384; Nec).

LOWER, William. Priest.

b. December 26th, 1704, London. e. St Omers College ?-1722. S.J. September 7th, 1722. Watten (nov) 1723, 1724. Liège (phil) 1725-7. Liège (theol) 1728, 1730. Ordained priest c.1731. Liège 1733-42. E.C.

Rome 1743. d. October 4th, 1743, Rome. (Fo.7; 114; 113; 150 III(2) 6/8/40, 17/3/42; 12 f.184v; 74; 91).

LUCAS see Ayroli, John Baptist; Burke, Charles.

LUCAS, Anthony. Priest.

b. October 18th, 1633, County Durham. e. St Omers College c.1650. Place of studies and date of ordination not found. S.J. May, 1662. Liège 1663-4, 1667, 1669, 1672-9. Watten 1680-5 (Rector). Liège 1685-7 (Rector). E.C. Rome 1687-93 (Rector). Provincial 1693. d. October 3rd, 1693, Watten. (Fo.7; CRS.69; 114; DNB.; 113; Gil.4/336; 135 f.251; Nec).

LUCAS, John or Bernard *alias* Hall, Bernard. Priest.

b. May 5th, 1740. s. of Timothy. e. St Omers and Bruges Colleges 1756-63. S.J. September 7th, 1763. Watten (nov) 1764. Liège (theol) 1767, 1768. Ordained priest c.1767. London 1769. Liège 1770. London 1770. Maryland 1770-5, 1783-5, 1787, 1790, 1793. d. September 14th, 1794, Maryland. (Fo.7; 113; 117; CRS.69; Hu.Text 2/697; 151 ff.74-5, 77, 79, 82, 83, 85, 87, 90, 92, 94, 96, 101, 103, 112, 134, 216).

LUDD see Lodge, Thomas.

LUND, James. Scholastic.

?e. Stonyhurst 1812-? S.J. September 7th, 1816. Hodder (nov) 1816-8. Clongowes, Ireland 1820. Stonyhurst (theol) 1821. Left 1822, not ordained. (116. Stol; 113; 2).

LUTTRELL see Keynes, Alexander and Maximilian.

LYDIATE see Lidiate.

LYNCH see Price, William.

LYTHGOE, Francis. Priest.

b. February 14th, 1796, Warrington, Lancashire. Cousin of Randall. e. Stonyhurst 1809-16. S.J. September 7th, 1816. Hodder (nov) 1816-8. Stonyhurst (phil) 1818-24. Fribourg (theol) 1824-6. Ordained priest May 20th, 1826, Fribourg. Holywell 1826-42. Liverpool 1842-4. St Leonards-on-Sea 1844-6. Stonyhurst 1846. Mount St Mary's College 1846-7. New Hall 1847-66. Stonyhurst 1866-73. d. June 5th, 1873, Stonyhurst. bu. Stonyhurst. (Fo.7; 115; CRS.3/108, 131-4; CRS.17/95. For writings see Sut. and Som.).

LYTHGOE, Randall. Priest.

b. November 28th, 1793, Eccleston, Lancashire. s. of Thomas of Southworth Hall. Cousin of Francis. e. Stonyhurst 1808-12. S.J. September 7th, 1812. Hodder (nov) 1812-4. Stonyhurst (phil, etc.) 1814-23. Rome (theol) 1823-4. Paris and Dôle (theol) 1824-7. Ordained priest October 1st, 1826, Pignerol. Stonyhurst 1827. Preston 1827-32. Lincoln 1832. Stonyhurst 1832-3. London 1833-41. Lydiate 1841. Provincial 1841-8. London 1849-51. Yarmouth 1851-5 (Rector of the College of the Holy Apostles). d. January 25th, 1855, Yarmouth. bu. Yarmouth. (Fo.7; 115; Gib.1/293; 11 ff.196, 226, 230, 245, 257; Nec).

McCANN, Henry. Priest.

b. June 15th, 1801, Drogheda, Ireland. e. Stonyhurst 1813-c.19, 1821-3. S.J. September 6th, 1823. Rome (nov) 1823-5. Rome (phil) 1825-7. Stonyhurst 1827-33. St Mary's Hall (theol) 1833-7. Ordained priest September 24th, 1836, Stonyhurst. Stonyhurst 1837-8. Paris 1838-9. Stonyhurst 1839-44. Calcutta 1844-7. Stonyhurst 1847-51. St Beuno's College 1851 (Rector). Stonyhurst 1851-5. Malta 1855-8 (Rector). London 1859-71. Beaumont College 1871-2. Stonyhurst 1872-5. Mount St Mary's College 1875-7. Beaumont 1877-88. d. May 15th, 1888, Beaumont College. bu. Beaumont. (115. 52 f.24v; Nec).

McCANN, Matthew. Priest.

b. November 12th, 1810, Drogheda, Ireland. e. Stonyhurst 1820-8. S.J. September 7th, 1828. Hodder (nov) 1828-30. St Mary's Hall (phil) 1830-3. Stonyhurst 1833-8. St Mary's Hall (theol) 1838-40. Ordained priest September 19th, 1840, Stonyhurst. Clitheroe 1841-3. St Mary's Hall (tert) 1844. Portico 1844-9. St Helens 1849-52. Spetchley 1852-5. Hereford 1855-7. Tunbridge Wells 1857-8. Lincoln 1858-60. Wardour 1860-1. Exeter 1861-3. Bristol 1863-8. Yarmouth 1868-9. Portico 1869-73. Wardour 1873-4. d. June 1st, 1874, Wardour. (Fo.7; 115; Nec).

McINTOSH see Boult, Henry.

MACKENZIE, Alexander *alias* Clinton. Priest.

b. March 23rd, 1730, Scotland. s. of Kenneth and Catherine (Gordon). e. S.C. Douay 1740-9, St Omers College 1749. S.J. October 25th, 1749 in Rome. Liège (phil) 1753-5. Liège (theol) 1756-8. Ordained priest c.1758. London 1760-80. Wardour 1780. Lulworth 1781-95. Portico c. 1797. Ireland c.1797. d. June 5th, 1800, near Dublin. (Fo.7; CRS.69; 113. LR.1/81, 3/5-6; CRS.6/366; CRS.42/158; CRS.50/69n; CRS.59/40; 1 f.113; 7 f.130v; 8 I f.32; 21 v.2; 13 f.114; 65; Gil.4/388; 166 I p.55; CRS.12/73; 157; CRS.19 index; 181, 186; 173; 01.265; 103; RSC.83; Ley.135; Ber.182, 195-6. For writings see Som. and Sut.)

McCLUNE, John. Priest.

b. April 19th, 1809, Liverpool. e. Stonyhurst 1820-6. S.J. September 7th, 1826. Avignon (nov) 1826-7. Hodder (nov) 1827-8. Stonyhurst (phil) 1828-30, 1830-7. St Mary's Hall (theol) 1837-40. Ordained priest December 24th, 1839, Clongowes, Ireland. Worcester 1840-1. Stonyhurst 1841-2 (supplying at Chipping 1841). Portico 1842-4. Leigh 1844-5. Mount St Mary's College 1845-6. Stonyhurst 1846-8. d. December 16th, 1848, Stonyhurst. bu. Stonyhurst. (Fo.7; 115. CRS.36/4; Nec).

MADGEWORTH, Christopher *alias* Towneley and Sands. Priest.

b.1658 or 1659, Lancashire. s. of Hugh of Preston. e. St Omers College 1673-9. S.J. September 7th, 1679. Watten (nov) 1679, 1680. Liège (phil) 1681, 1682. Liège (theol) 1683, 1684. Ordained priest April 21st, 1685. Ghent (tert) 1685. Ghent 1686-7, 1689-90. College of St Aloysius 1691. d. March 7th, 1692, in England. (Fo.7; CRS.69; 114; 113; Chad.193; Nec).

MAGEE, David *alias* Johnson. Priest.

b. February 22nd, 1737, near Ennis, Ireland. S.J. September 7th, 1755. Liège (nov and phil) 1756-8. Liège (theol) 1761. Ordained priest c.1762. Residence of St Stanislaus 1763. Arlington 1764-8. d. November 8th, 1768, Arlington. (Fo.7; 114; 91; 113; 01.336; Nec).

MAHON, Henry. Priest.

b. September 25th, 1804, Dublin. e. Stonyhurst 1815-?, 1821-3. S.J. November 1st, 1823. Montrouge (nov) 1823-5. St Acheul (phil) 1825-7. London School 1827-31. St Mary's Hall (theol) 1831-5. Ordained priest December 20th, 1834, Stonyhurst. Wardour 1835-8. Preston 1838-40. Hodder (tert) 1840-2 (supplying at Lydiate 1841). Spetchley 1842-7. Shepton Mallet 1848-9. Bristol 1849-51. London 1851-8. Yarmouth 1858-60. Edinburgh 1860-1. St Beuno's College 1861-5. Yarmouth 1865. Worcester 1865-7. Yarmouth 1867-70. London 1870-1. Liverpool 1871-2. Stonyhurst 1872-9. d. May 4th, 1879, Stonyhurst. bu. Stonyhurst. (Fo.7; Gib.1/293; 115; Nec).

MAILLART, Levinius. Laybrother.

b. March 20th, 1727 or 1731, Ghent. S.J. December 31st, 1752. Watten (nov) 1753, 1754. Antwerp 1755-64. E.C. Rome 1768-9, 1771-8. d. November 1778, Rome. (Fo.7; 113; 117; 108; AHSJ.42/295).

MAIN-DE-FER or MAIN-DE-FERRE, Peter. Laybrother.

b. December 20th, 1708 or 1709, Picardy. S.J. September 7th, 1733. Watten (nov) 1734. St Omers College 1735-41. Boulogne School 1743-4, 1746-7. d. May 17th, 1748, Boulogne. (Fo.7; 113; 91; Nec).

MAINWARING, Joseph. Scholastic.

b.1654 or 1655, ?Malpas, Cheshire. e. Brasenose College, Oxford 1672-5, St Omers College 1675-6. S.J. September 7th, 1676. Watten (nov) 1676-8. d. September 24th, 1678, Liège, not ordained. (Fo.7; CRS.69; 113; 123 I f.96; Fos.III, 960; Nec).

MAIRE, Christopher. Priest.

b. March 6th, 1697. s. of Christopher and Frances (Ingleby) of Hartbushes, Durham. br. of James, Peter and Thomas. Uncle of Edward and George. e. St Omers College 1714 or earlier-15. S.J. September 7th, 1715. Watten (nov) 1715, 1716. Liège (phil) 1718, 1720. St Omers College 1723, 1724. Liège (theol) 1725-8. Ordained priest c.1727. Liège 1730. St Omers College 1733. Liège 1734-8. E.C. Rome 1739-55 (Rector 1744-50). St Omers College 1756-8. Ghent 1761, 1763-4. d. February 22nd, 1767, Ghent. (Fo.7; CRS.69; 114; 91; 113; RH.10/340; CRS.62 index; 12 ff.179 ff; DNB; Gil.4/393; 155 I 45; 156 I; 51 f.311; Nec. For writings see Som.).

MAIRE, Edward ?*alias* Burdett. Priest.

b. November 18th, 1726. so of George and Mary (Hussey) of Hartbushes, Durham. br. of George. Nephew of Christopher, James, Peter and Thomas. e. St Omers College c.1735-42. S.J. September 7th, 1742. Watten (nov) 1743. Liège (phil) 1744, 1746. Paderborn (theol) 1747. Büren (theol) 1748, 1749. Ordained priest c.1749. Liège 1750. Ghent (tert) 1752. Liège 1753-5. College of St Ignatius 1756-7.

Residence of St Michael 1758. College of St Hugh 1763-4 (?Irnham). Residence of St Michael 1767-8. Holderness 1769. Residence of St Michael 1771. Holderness 1772, 1773, c.1780, c.1783. ?London 1786. d. April 13th, 1797, London. (Fo.7; CRS.69; 114; 113; 91; CRS.50/239; RH.10/341; 155 II 127; 167 p.38; 111; 117; Nec).

MAIRE, George. Priest.

b. March 21st, 1738. s. of George and Mary (Hussey) of Hartbushes, Durham. br. of Edward. Nephew of Christopher, James, Peter and Thomas. e. St Omers College 1749-54. S.J. September 7th, 1754. Watten (nov) 1755. Liège (phil) 1756-8. ?Liège (theol) 1761. Ordained priest c.1762. Rome 1763, 1764. Residence of St Michael 1767. Swynnerton 1768, 1769. College of St Chad 1771. Swynnerton and Aston-by-Stone 1772, 1773, 1775, 1784, 1790, 1794. d. October 31st, 1796, Aston or Stafford. bu. Stone. (Fo.7; CRS.69; 114; 91; 113; RH.9/230, 10/341; CRS.62/20; SCH.3/12, 12/18, 22; 13 f.159; 54 f.26v; 68 pp.168, 213; 64 f.128; Ki.154-5; 111; Nec).

MAIRE, James. Priest.

b. March 26th, 1705. s. of Christopher and Frances (Ingleby) of Hartbushes, Durham. br. of Christopher, Peter and Thomas. Uncle of Edward and George. e. St Omers College 1715-25. S.J. September 7th, 1725. Watten (nov) 1726, 1727. Liège (phil) 1728, 1730. Liège (theol) 1733. Ordained priest 1733. St Omers College 1734-40. College of the Holy Apostles 1741, 1743-6 (?Oxburgh. Bury's Hall ?-1746). d. February 25th, 1746, Bury's Hall, Norfolk. (Fo.7; CRS.69; 114; 113; RH.10/341; 43 f.72v; 91; CRS.7/228; Nec; 120).

MAIRE, Peter. Priest.

b. July 28th, 1707. s. of Christopher and Frances (Ingleby) of Hartbushes, Durham. br. of Christopher, James and Thomas. Uncle of Edward and George. e. St Omers College ?-1726. S.J. September 7th, 1726. Watten (nov) 1727. Liège (phil) 1728, 1730. Douay (theol) 1733. Liège (theol) 1734. Ordained priest c.1734. St Omers College 1735. Residence of St John 1736-8. ?Barnborough 1739-41. York 1741-63. (Superior of the Residence of St Michael 1755-63). d. June 24th, 1763, York. bu. Holy Trinity churchyard. (Fo.7; CRS.69; 114; 91; 113; CRS.Mon.2/388-9; RH.10/341; 36 ff.208, 263; HMC. 10th Report App.4/192; Gil.5/95; 156 App.1; CRS.4/376; YA.72/198, 199, 77/195; Nec).

MAIRE, Thomas. Priest.

b. April 18th, 1703. s. of Christopher and Frances (Ingleby) of Hartbushes, Durham. br. of Christopher, James and Peter. Uncle of Edward and George. e. St Omers College 1714-20. S.J. September 7th, 1720. Liège (phil) 1723, 1724. Liège (theol) 1725-8. Ordained priest c.1729. In England 1730. Residence of St John 1733-8 (Gateshead c.1730-6). Residence of St Mary 1739. Culcheth c.1741-c.48. College of the Immaculate Conception 1748-50, 1752 (Husbands Bosworth 1752). d. December 3rd, 1752, Leicester. (Fo.7; CRS.69; CRS.62/20; 114; 91; 113; RH.10/341; 64 p.199; HMC. 10th Report App.4/187; 155 I 45, II

42; 156 App.1; CRS.13/371; Nec).

MANNERS see Pelcom or Percom, Peter; Sittensperger, Matthias.

MANNOCK, see Petre, John and Robert.

MANNOCK, Francis *alias* Arthur. Priest.

b. January 3rd, 1670, London. s. of Sir Francis, 2nd Bart. and Mary (Heneage) of Gifford's Hall, Suffolk. e. St Omers College ?-1686. S.J. September 7th, 1686. Watten (nov) 1687. Liège (phil) 1689-91. St Omers College 1692. Rome (theol) 1693, 1696-7. Ordained priest c.1696. College of the Holy Apostles 1699-1701. Chester c.1701-10. York 1710. Liverpool 1711, 1712. College of St Ignatius 1714-6, 1718, 1720. Residence of St John 1724, 1725. Ellingham 1726, 1727. York 1727. Ellingham 1729. York c.1734-48. d. December 21st, 1748, York. bu. Holy Trinity churchyard. (Fo.7; CRS.69; 91; 113; CRS.Mon.2/156, 162, 268, 388; SCH.3/13, 9/8; ER.12/112; 150 II(3)28/10/92, III(2) 16/1/40, 14/1/41, 21/6/41; 23 f.35; 74; NB.1/284, 2/4; E and P.254; 156 App.1; CRS.4/370, 376; CRS.9/181-2; CRS.25/115; CRS.35/3; Col.121, 153; Nec).

MANNOCK, Sir George. Priest.

b. July 1st, 1723 or 1724, Suffolk. s. of Sir Francis, 4th Bart. and Frances (Yates) of Gifford's Hall, Suffolk. e. St Omers College 1733-41. S.J. September 7th, 1741. Watten (nov) 1741. Liège (phil) 1743, 1744. Strasbourg (theol) 1746-9. Ordained priest c.1749. Rheims 1750. Liège 1752-8, 1761. College of the Holy Apostles 1763, 1764. Gifford's Hall 1766-9. College of the Holy Apostles 1771. Gifford's Hall 1772-4-?87. 9th Bart. 1781. d. May 6th, 1787, near Dartford, Kent. (Fo.7; CRS.69; 114; 91; 113; CRS.42/153; SCH.12/16; ER.4/117-8, 10/37, 41; 41 nn.27, 31, 35; HMC. 10th Report App.4/186; 54 f.126v; Ki.158; 111; Nec).

MANSELL, Thomas *alias* or *vere* Harding. Priest.

b. June 15th, 1668, Oxfordshire. ?br. of William. e. St Omers College ?-1686. S.J. September 7th, 1686. Watten (nov) 1686. Liège (phil) 1687, 1689-90. St Omers College 1691-5. Liège (theol) 1695-7. Ordained priest c.1695. Ghent (tert) 1699. Maryland 1701-24 (Superior 1713-24). d. March 18th, 1724, Maryland. (Fo.7; CRS.69; 114; 113; Hu.Text 2/684; 170 ff.150, 179; Nec).

MANSELL, William *alias* or *vere* Harding. Priest.

b. October 15th, 1669 or 1670, Oxfordshire. ?br. of Thomas. e. St Omers College ?-1686. S.J. September 7th, 1686. Watten (nov) 1686, 1687. Liège (phil) 1688-91. Liège (theol) 1692, 1693. Ordained priest c.1694. Ghent (tert) 1696. St Omers College 1697, 1699-1701. Loretto 1701-6. St Omers College 1706, 1708-16, 1718, 1720. d. August 28th, 1720, St Omers College. (Fo.7; CRS.69; 113; 114; 170 ff.245, 254v; Nec).

MANSELL see Talbot, John (1) and Thomas.

MANSFIELD or MANSFELD, Robert. Priest.

b. July 1st, 1652, Surrey or Buckinghamshire. s. of Count Mansfield or Mansfeld. e. St Omers College ?-1669. S.J. October or November

24th, 1669. Liège (phil) 1672, 1673. Rome (theol) 1674, 1678. Ordained priest c.1680. Liège 1683-7, 1689-92. Residence of St George 1693. Liège 1696. Paris 1696, 1698. E.C. Rome 1699-1704 (Rector). College of the Immaculate Conception 1705. College of the Holy Apostles 1706, 1708. d. September 21st, 1708, Nancy. (Fo.7; CRS.69; 113; 114; 150 II(2) 16/6/74, September 1678, II(3) 16/1/83, III(1) 16/7/98, 13/9/98; Ki.158; 135 f.179; 43 f.30; Nec. For writings see Som.).

MANSFIELD see Talbot, John (1) and Thomas.

MARIA, José. Laybrother.

b.1726. From London. S.J. July 6th, 1748, in Brazil. No further information found. (Lei.7/269).

MARIN or MARAINE or MARINE, James. Laybrother.

b. February 1659, Artois. S.J. October 1693. Watten (nov) 1696-7, 1699-1701, 1703-6, 1708-16, 1718, 1720, 1723-8, 1730, 1733-40. d. April 4th, 1740, Watten. (Fo.7; 91; 114; 113; Nec).

MARSH, John.

e. St Omers College ?-1652. E.C. Valladolid 1652-4. d. October 18th, 1654, E.C. Valladolid, not ordained. Adm. S.J. *in articulo mortis.* (CRS.69; CRS.30/166; 197).

MARSH, William, or John. Priest.

b.1637, Lancashire. e.St Omers College 1656-8. S.J. September 14th, 1658. Watten (nov) 1658, 1659. Liège (phil) 1660, 1661. Liège (theol) 1663-5. Ordained priest July 1666. Ghent (tert) 1667. Seville c.1669. Residence of St George 1672. College of St Aloysius 1672. College of St Hugh 1673-80. d.1681, in England. (Fo.7; CRS.69; 114; 113; Nec).

MARSHALL, Claudius. Scholastic or Laybrother.

d. date and place not recorded. (Fo.7; 114).

MARSHALL, Joseph. Priest.

b. October 18th, 1683, Gloucestershire. S.J. September 7th, 1708. Watten (nov) 1709, 1710. Liège (phil) 1711, 1712. Antwerp (phil) 1713. Louvain (theol) 1714-6. Ordained priest c.1715. Lierre (tert) 1716. Loretto 1719-23. Rome 1723. Watten 1724-6. Socius to the provincial 1727, 1728, 1733. Bristol c.1727-34. E.C. Rome 1734-9 (Rector 1734-8). d. June 26th, 1739, Rome. (Fo.7; 114; 113; 91; 150 III(2) 25/7/39; 9 nn.74, 78, 92, 103, 163; 74; CRS.3/181; 109; Nec).

MARTHE or MARTHES, James de. Laybrother.

b. May 31st, 1711, Blandecques, Artois. S.J. September 7th, 1736. Watten (nov) 1736, 1737, 1738. St Omers College 1739, 1740. E.C. Rome 1740-1, 1743-4, 1746-9. Ghent 1750, 1752-8, 1761, 1763-4, 1767-9. d. August 24th, 1770, Ghent. (Fo.7; 114; 91; 113; 12 f.183v; 111; Nec).

MARTIN, Henry. Priest.

b.1642, Norfolk. s. of Richard and Jane (Bedingfeld) of Long Melford, Suffolk. br. of John. e. St Omers College ?-1662. S.J. September 7th, 1662. Watten (nov) 1663. Liège (phil) 1664-7. Liège (theol) 1669, 1672. Ordained priest 1672. d. November 15th, 1672, in England. (Fo.7; CRS.69; 114; 113; Nec).

MARTIN, John. Priest.

b.1644 or 1645, Norfolk or Suffolk. s. of Richard and Jane (Bedingfeld) of Long Melford, Suffolk. br. of Henry. e. St Omers College ?-1667. S.J. April 10th, 1667. Watten (nov) 1667. Liège (phil) 1669. Liège (theol) 1672. Ordained priest August 14th, 1672. St Omers College 1672, 1673. College of the Holy Apostles 1674, 1675. Residence of St Stanislaus 1676, 1678-94, 1696-7 (Superior 1685-c.94). College of the Holy Apostles 1699-1701, 1703-6, 1708-16 (Rector 1709-11. ?Long Melford 1701-7, 1712-7). d. December 24th, 1717, in England. (Fo.7; CRS.69; 114; 113; LR.8/3-6; E and P.63; 150 III(1) 15/7/06; Nec).

MARTIN, Thomas.

'Formerly a Jesuit' (1684) (Fo.7; ?Ans.2/212; ?Che.12/80).

MARTINASH, John *alias* White. Priest.

b.1679, London. e. St Omers College c.1698. S.J. July 30th, 1699. Watten (nov) 1699-1701. Liège (phil) 1703. Liège (theol) 1704-6. Ordained priest c.1707. Ghent (tert) 1708. College of the Holy Apostles 1708-16 (Norwich c.1709). Residence of St George 1716. College of St Thomas of Canterbury 1718. College of the Holy Apostles 1720, 1723. Residence of St Michael 1724. d. November 12th, 1725, in England. (Fo.7; CRS.69; NA.37/165; 113; 43 ff.31, 35, 36).

MARTINDALE, John *alias* Holland. Priest.

b. June 9th, 1666, Lancashire. s. of John. e. St Omers College ?-1689. E.C. Rome 1689-90. S.J. July 30th, 1690. ?Rome (nov and phil) 1690-c.95. Liège (theol) 1696-8. Ordained priest 1698. College of St Hugh 1699-1701, 1703-6, 1708-16, 1718, 1720 (Rector 1710-c.16). Residence of St Winefrid 1723-5. In England 1726. Near Penybont 1727. In England 1728, 1730. Residence of St Winefrid 1733, 1734. d. November or December 9th, 1734, in England. (Fo.7; CRS.69; 114; 113; 91; Ki.122; CRS.40/107).

MASSEY see Stanley, Thomas.

MASSEY, Francis. Priest.

b.1782, Lancashire. s. of Edward and Mary (Clare). e. Stonyhurst 1798-1803. S.J. September 26th, 1803. Hodder (nov) 1803-5. Stonyhurst (theol) 1807-c.11. Ordained priest c.1810. South-hill 1812-22. d. August 15th, 1822, South-hill. (Fo.7; 113; 114; Stol; 8 II n.121; 13 ff.376, 430; 21 v.2; 55 ff.88v, 149; 93 pp.60, 69; CRS.4/435; 116; Nec).

MASSIE or MASIE, John *alias* or *vere* Hodges. Priest.

b. November 21st, 1698, London. e. St Omers College 1714 or earlier-15 or later. S.J. September 7th, 1717. Watten (nov) 1718. Liège (phil) 1720. Liège (theol) 1723-5. Ordained priest c.1725. Ghent (tert) 1726. West Grinstead 1727-33. College of St Aloysius 1733. College of St Francis Xavier 1734-41, 1743-4, 1746-50, 1752-8 (near Hereford, Lyde Arundel, 1751. Hereford 1758). d. January 10th, 1760, Hereford. bu. Hereford parish church. (Fo.7; CRS.69; 114; 113; 34 ff.24, 27; 64 p.88; 91; HMC. 10th Report App.4/190; 126; CRS.62/158; Nec).

MASSIE, Ralph. Laybrother.

b. March 24th, 1709, Cheshire. S.J. September 7th, 1752. Watten (nov) 1752-4. St Omers College 1755. d. September 23rd, 1756, Ghent. (Fo.7; 114; 113; 91; Nec).

MASHTER or MASTER, Francis *alias* Tichborne. Priest.
b. December 17th, 1678 or 1679, Lancashire. e. St Omers College 1698-1701. S.J. September 7th, 1701. Watten (nov) 1703. Liège (phil) 1704-6. Liège (theol) 1708-10. Ordained priest c.1711. Ghent (tert) 1711. Residence of St George 1712-6, 1720. d. September 24th, 1723, in England (?Grafton Manor, Worcestershire). (Fo.7; CRS.69; 114; 113; Nec).

MATHEWS, Edmund *alias* Poyntz or Poins.
b. c.1653, ?in Ireland. e. St Omers College c.1664-7. d. September 27th, 1667, St Omers College. Adm. S.J. *in articulo mortis.* (Fo.7; CRS.69; CRS.3/59ff; Chad.175).

MATTHEWS see Swindall, Stephen.

MATTHEWS, Ignatius. Priest.
b. January 25th, 1730, Maryland. e. St Omers College c.1754-6. E.C. Valladolid 1756-63. Ordained priest c.1763. S.J. October 31st, 1763. Watten (nov) 1763, 1764. Maryland 1766-9, 1771-3-?90. d. May 11th, 1790, Maryland. (Fo.7; CRS.69; 91; 114; 113; Hu.Text 2/696; Ans.4/188; CRS.30/190; 77; Nec).

MATTHEWS or MATTHEW, John. Priest.
b.1658, London. s. of Thomas and Mary (Robinson). e. S.C. Douay 1673-7. S.J. October 9th, 1677. Liège (nov and phil) 1679-81. Liège (theol) 1682-5. Ordained priest March 17th, 1685. Maryland 1686-94. d. December 8th, 1694, Maryland. (Fo.7; 114; 113; Hu.Text 2/683; RSC.52; Nec).

MATTHEWS or MATHEWS, Peter *alias* Neville. Priest.
b. September 2nd, 1692, London. S.J. September 7th, 1711. Watten (nov) 1712, 1713. Liège (phil) 1714, 1715. St Omers College 1716, 1718. Liège (theol) 1720. Ordained priest c.1722. Liège 1723-8. In England 1730. Residence of St Michael 1733. College of St Hugh 1734, 1735. Paris 1737-41. Travelling 1743-4. Boulogne School 1746. College of St Thomas of Canterbury 1747. Ince Blundell 1747. Brinn 1749-51. Garswood 1752. d. January 13th, 1752, in England (?Garswood). bu. Windleshaw cemetery. (Fo.7; 114; 113; 24 f.347; 64 pp.346, 486; 85; 86; 89; 91; 140 n.45; 156 App.1; Nec).

MATTINGLEY, John. Priest.
b. January 25th, 1745, St Mary's County, Maryland. s. of Clement. e. St Omers and Bruges Colleges c.1760-3. E.C. Valladolid 1763-6. S.J. September 7th, 1766. Liège (nov and theol) 1767-9, 1771. Ordained priest 1770. Rome 1772, 1773. Liège Academy 1782, 1784, 1785, 1788. Durham c.1793. Garswood 1795. Travelling 1801. Hooton 1802, 1803. Bath 1803, 1804. Dublin 1805. Crosby 1806. d. November 23rd, 1807, Causetown, Ireland. (Fo.7; CRS.69; 114; 113; 91; 6 ff.166, 186; 7 f.148v; 13 ff.117v, 328; 54 f.256v; 57 I f.34v, 72v, 205A, II f.60v; 94 f.41v; 157; Ki.160; CRS.30/190-1; 131; Nec).

MAUDSLEY see Turner, Robert.
MAURICE see Morris, James.
MAXWELL, Albert or Herbert. Priest.
      b.1653 or 1655 or 1659, Galloway, Scotland. s. of Baron of
Kirkonnell and Agnes (Laury). e. S.C. Douay 1668-? S.J. November
5th, 1675, Scottish mission. To English province c.1695. St Germain
1696-7, 1699-1701, 1703-6, 1708-16, 1720. Watten 1723-9. d. January
18th, 1729, Watten. (Fo.7; 114; RSC.47; 113; 91; Ki.89; Nec).
MAXWELL, George. Priest.
      b. October 13th, 1714. s. of William of Kirkonnell and Joanna. br. of
James. S.J. September 28th, 1732, Scottish mission. Liège Academy
1776. d. November 5th, 1805, Edinburgh. (Fo.7; 90 f.54; 122;
Chad.367; 97; RSC.74).
MAXWELL, James *alias* Stuart. Priest.
      b. March 30th, 1710 or 1711, in Scotland. s. of William of Kirkonnell
and Joanna. br. of George. e. S.C. Douay 1721-8. S.J. September 29th,
1728, Scottish mission. Liège 1756-8, 1761, 1763-4, 1767-9, 1771-3,
1776. d. March 18th, 1784, Liège Academy. (Fo.7; 114; 113; RSC.71;
90 f.54; CRS.12/39; CRS.17/173; Nec. For writings see Som.).
MAYNARD see Cuffaud, Joseph.
MEARA, George *alias* Brinkhurst. Priest.
      b. July 15th, 1675, Berkshire. s. of William and Mary. br. of
William. e. St Omers College ?-1694. S.J. September 7th, 1694. Watten
(nov) 1696. Liège (phil) 1697. St Omers College 1699, 1700. Liège
(theol) 1701, 1703-4. Ordained priest 1703. Residence of St John 1705.
Residence of St Michael 1706-8. Residence of St George 1708.
Residence of St John 1708, 1709. College of St Ignatius 1710. Residence
of St John 1711. College of St Thomas of Canterbury 1712, 1713.
Residence of St Mary 1714. College of the Immaculate Conception
1715, 1716. College of St Thomas of Canterbury 1718, 1720. Residence
of St Winefrid 1724, 1725. Pelham Furneux 1726-30. St Omers College
1730, 1733-8. d. October 15th, 1739, St Omers College. (Fo.7; 91;
CRS.69; 114; 113; ER.12/77; CRS.62/128, 132, 282; 40 ff.34, 192;
Nec).
MEARA, William *alias* Brinkhurst. Priest.
      b. August 17th, 1678, Berkshire. s. of William and Mary. br. of
George. e. St Omers College 1694 or earlier-98. S.J. September 7th,
1698. Watten (nov) 1699, 1700. Liège (phil) 1701, 1703. Liège (theol)
1704-6. Ordained priest c.1707. Ghent (tert) 1708. St Omers College
1709. Watten 1710. St Omers College 1711. College of St Thomas of
Canterbury 1712-6, 1718, 1720. Stonyhurst 1722. College of St
Aloysius 1723, 1724. Residence of St Michael 1725. York c.1727. d.
August 26th, 1728, St Omers College. (Fo.7; 114; CRS.69; 91; 113;
NB.3/76; Gil.4/326; Nec).
MELLING, Thomas *alias* More. Laybrother.
      b.1656, Lancashire. e. St Omers College ?-1675. S.J. September 7th,
1675. Watten (nov) 1676. Liège (nov) 1678. No further information

recorded. It is not clear that he completed the noviceship. (Fo.7; CRS.69; 113; 140 n.45).

MENDOZA, Christopher de *alias* Lane, Love or Lowe. Priest.
b.1641, London. S.J. June 13th, 1657-75, in Spain. To English province 1672. Madrid 1672-4. College of St Aloysius 1675. (Fo.7; 113; 150 (II) 6/7/75, 5/8/75, 28/10/75; 123 IIIA f.40).

MERCER, William. Priest.
b. August 21st, 1738 or 1739, Crosby, near Liverpool. e. St Omers College 1750-5. S.J. September 7th, 1755. Watten (nov) 1756. Liège (phil) 1757, 1758. Liège (theol) 1761, 1763. Ordained priest 1763, Cologne. Liège 1764, 1767-73, 1775-6. d. August 1st, 1777, Liège Academy. (Fo.7; CRS.69; 114; 91; 113; 13 f.60v; 54 f.37v; 90 f.54; NewH.65-6; Nec).

MERCIER, James. Laybrother.
b. January 14th, 1698, Liège. S.J. September 7th, 1724-47. St Omers College (nov) 1725. Watten 1726, 1727. Ghent 1728, 1729. St Omers College 1730. Liège 1733-7. Paris 1738-42. St Omers College 1743, 1744. (113; 91; 140 n.45).

MERCIER, Laurence. Laybrother.
b.1707, Liège. S.J. September 23rd, 1728. Watten (nov) 1730. St Omers College 1733-8. d. July 7th, 1740, St Omers College. (Fo.7; 91; 114; 113; 74; Nec).

MEREDITH, Amos *alias* Langford, Abraham. Scholastic.
b.1658 or 1659, Cornwall. s. of Edward and – (Langford). br. of Edward. S.J. April 22nd, 1679. Watten (nov) 1679. Liège (nov and phil) 1680-2. Liège (theol) 1683-6. d. May 12th, 1687, Ghent, not ordained. (Fo.7; 114; 113; Gil.4/563; 168 ff.76v, 84; Nec).

MEREDITH, Edward *alias* Langford. Scholastic.
b.1648, Cornwall. s. of Edward and – (Langford). br. of Amos. e. Westminster and Christ Church, Oxford. S.J. September 7th, 1684. Watten (nov) 1684, 1685. College of St Ignatius 1686, 1687. In England 1688. France 1689, 1690. St Germain 1691-3. Rome (theol) 1696, 1699-1701. Naples 1702-3, 1706-8, 1712, 1714-5. d. c.1715, ?Rome, ?not ordained. (Fo.7; 113; Gil.4/563; CRS.62 index; 190 ff.22, 28, 34-5, 40-3, 46-9, 57-8, 64-5; DNB; Nec; Woo.4 col.653; Fos.3 col.1001; Che.48/137-40; Dod.3/465. For writings see Che.48 and Gil.4/563).

MEREDITH, Richard *alias* Knight. Priest.
b. February 9th or August 24th, 1696, London. s. of – Meredith and – (Knight). e. St Omers College 1712 or earlier-16. S.J. September 7th, 1716. Watten (nov) 1716, 1718. Liège (phil) 1720. Liège (theol) 1723, 1724. Douay (theol) 1724, 1725. Ordained priest 1725. Residence of St Mary 1725. Ghent (tert) 1726. In England 1727-8, 1730 (Sherfield c.1727-?). Kelvedon 1731. Ongar 1731. Worcester 1732. College of St Hugh 1732-41, 1743-54 (Rector 1743-54. Little Paunton). d. October 26th, 1754, St Omers College. (Fo.7; 91; 113; CRS.62 index; 114; ER.9/109, 14/83; 150 III(2) 27/7/43; 9 nn.226-8, 230-2, 234; CRS.43/5; 50 f.28v; 43 f.52v; 64 pp.173, 245, 299, 300; Ki.48, 162;

CRS.69; 125; 111; 51 f.311; CRS.4/261; Nec).

MERESCHAL or MERSHAL, Nicholas. Scholastic.

b.1745. S.J. October 9th, 1761. To English province 1769. Liège (theol) 1769. No further information recorded. (91; 113).

MERO, Joseph. Laybrother.

b. June 26th, 1807, Manduria, Lecce, Italy. S.J. June 29th, 1827, Naples. To English province c.1844. Calcutta 1844-6. St Beuno's College 1852-4. Beaumont Lodge 1855-63. Roehampton 1864-76. St Beuno's College 1877-88. d. December 27th, 1888, St Beuno's College. bu. Pantasaph. (113; 52 f.23v; CDSJ.; Nec).

MESSENGER, John. Priest.

b.1688 or 1689, Yorkshire. s. of John and Margaret (Scroope) of Fountains Abbey, Yorkshire. S.J. September 7th, 1708. Watten (nov) 1709, 1710. Liège (phil) 1711-3. Liège (theol) 1714-6. Ordained priest c.1716. Liège 1718, 1720, 1723-4. Residence of St Michael 1725. In England 1726-8, 1730. Residence of St Michael 1733-41, 1743-4, 1746-50 (Burghwallis 1727, 1735, 1741, 1743). d. May 24th, 1752, Burghwallis. bu. St Helen's churchyard. (Fo.7; 114; 91; 113; E and P.307; 156 App.1; Nec; YA.71/64, 77/100; CRS.32/127; Ann.22).

METCALFE see Leigh, Philip.

METCALFE, Joseph *alias* Draper. Priest.

b. May 21st, 1670 or 1671, Worcestershire. ?s. of John. e. St Omers College ?-1692. S.J. September 7th, 1692. Watten (nov) 1693. Liège (phil) 1696. Liège (theol) 1697, 1700-1701. Ordained priest 1701, Liège. Ghent (tert) 1701. Lydiate 1701-3. d. April 7th, 1703, Lydiate. bu. St. Katherine's chapel, Lydiate. (Fo.7; CRS.69; 113; 114; 23 f.35v; 27 f.215v; Gib.1/285; Nec).

MEYNELL, James. Priest.

b. May 4th, 1689, Yorkshire. e. St Omers College ?-1708. S.J. September 7th, 1708. Watten (nov) 1709, 1710. Liège (phil) 1711, 1712. Liège (theol) 1713, 1714. Ordained priest 1713. St Omers College 1715-7. Ghent 1718. In England 1720. Residence of St Michael 1724-5. In England 1726-8, 1730. Residence of St Michael 1733-44, 1746 (Pontefract 1727-8, 1735, 1741, 1743). d. December 16th, 1746, Pontefract. (Fo.7; CRS.69; 113; 89; 91; 156 App.1; YA.71/127, 77/195-6, 212; 114; CRS.25/112; CRS.28/50; CRS.32/237, 296; Nec).

MEYNELL, Thomas. Priest.

b. September 29th, 1737, Yorkshire. s. of Roger and Barbara (Selby) of Kilvington. e. St Omers College c.1749-56. S.J. September 7th, 1756. Watten (nov) 1756-8. Liège (theol) 1761. Ordained priest c.1762. St Omers and Bruges Colleges 1762-3. Residence of St Michael 1763-4. College of St Aloysius 1767. Hooton c.1768. Carleton 1768-73. London 1775, 1780. Yarm 1783-7, 1792-3, 1796-7, 1803. d. February 1st or 4th, 1804, London. bu. Old St Pancras churchyard. (Fo.7; CRS.69; 91; 113; RH.8/162; 121; LR.3/7, 7/18; 7 f.149; 64; 114; 72; HMC. 10th Report App.4/183, 196; Pa.2/35; 94 f.38; Gil.4/548; 155 II 127; Ki.163; 166 II p.109; CRS.1/142; CRS.14/254; 167 p.38; 1 ff.35-6; 111; 8 I 90; Nec).

MEYNELL, William. Priest.
b. May 3rd, 1744, Yarm, Yorkshire. e. St Omers College 1753-6 or later. S.J. September 7th, 1761. Liège (phil) 1763, 1764. Bruges College 1766-9, 1771. Travelling 1771. Ordained priest c.1773. Eccleston or travelling 1776, 1778, 1780-1, 1783-5, 1787-90. Ellingham 1799-1803. Travelling 1803, 1807, 1810, 1815. Richmond, Surrey 1818, 1820, 1825. d. September 16th, 1826, Richmond, Surrey. (Fo.7; CRS.69; 113; 114; 150 (1750-1853) f.4; 7 f.371; 11 f.2Bv; 28 f.229; 56 f.243; 57 I ff.119v, 194v, 195v, 261v, II ff.10v, 68, 93v, 152, 161, 167; 77; 25 ff.57, 65, 80, 113; 80; 53 f.52; 89; 155 II 129; 167 p.29; 119 f.32; Nec).

MICO, Edward *alias* Baines and Harvey. Priest.
b.1628 or 1630, Essex. s. of Richard and Anne (Lambe) of London. e. St Omers College 1643 or earlier-47. E.C. Rome 1647-50. S.J. June 15th 1650. Watten (nov) 1651. Liège (phil) 1652, 1653. Liège (theol) 1654-6. Ordained priest March 31st, 1657. Ghent (tert) 1657. St Omers College 1658, 1659. College of St Ignatius 1660. College of St Thomas of Canterbury 1661, 1663-5, 1667, 1669. Socius to the provincial 1672-6. Antwerp 1676-7. Socius to the provincial 1678. d. under arrest, December 3rd, 1678, London. Declared Venerable. (Fo.7; CRS.69; 114; 113; CRS.47/46n; LR.3/8; 150 II(2) 6/2/72; Chad.190; Gil.5/7; CRS.40/39-40; HMC. 11th Report App.2/68; CRS.55/503; 135 f.183; FAB.99, 101, 183-4; BR.1-8; 108; Nec. For writings see Som.).

MIDDLEHURST, James *alias* Ashby. Priest.
b. October 18th, 1714, Lancashire. e. St Omers College 1732-3. E.C. Valladolid 1733-9. Ordained priest c.1738. S.J. June 13th, 1739. Watten (nov) 1739. St Omers College 1740. Maryland 1741 or 1742-61, 1762?, 1763-4-?-7. d. September 23rd, 1767, Newtown, Maryland. (Fo.7; 114; CRS.69; 113; Ans.4/189; CRS.30/188; 92; 91; 140 n.45; Hu.Text 2/691; Nec).

MIDDLEHURST, John. Priest.
b. February 8th, 1805, Wigan. e. Stonyhurst 1822-8. S.J. September 7th, 1828. Hodder (nov) 1828-30. St Mary's Hall (phil) 1830-2. St Mary's Hall (theol) 1832-5. Ordained priest December 20th, 1834, Stonyhurst. Norwich 1835-8. Broughton Hall 1838-41. Chipping 1841-3. Stonyhurst 1843-5. Leigh 1845-77. d. February 12th, 1877, Southport. bu. Leigh public cemetery. (Fo.7; 115; NA.37/162; CRS.36/5; Nec. For writings see Sut.).

MIDDLETON see Thornton, Robert.

MIDDLETON, Charles *alias* Wilson. Priest.
b. April 4th, 1660, Gloucestershire. In the Army ?-1685. e. St Omers College 1685. S.J. July 1686 or 1687. Watten (nov) 1687. Liège (phil) 1689. St Omers College 1690, 1691. Ordained priest c.1692. Residence of St George 1693. Liège 1695. Ghent 1696. College of St Ignatius 1697, 1699. Ghent 1700, 1701, 1703-6, 1708-16, 1718, 1720, 1723-8, 1730, 1733-41. d. May 29th, 1743, Ghent. (Fo.7; CRS.69; 114; 113; 150 II(3) 25/6/95; 91; Cam.1845, Perth Letters p.43; Nec).

MILDMAY see Bedingfeld, Matthew.

MILES see Mills.

MILLEGATE, William. Laybrother.
>   b. August 9th, 1640, Lancashire. S.J. March 30th, 1679 or 1680.
>   Watten (nov) 1680. St Omers College 1682. Ghent 1683-5. Liège
>   1685-7, 1689-91. Ghent 1692. St Omers College 1693. Ghent 1696-7. St
>   Omers College 1699-1702. d. November 9th, 1702, St Omers College.
>   (Fo.7; 114; 113; Nec).

MILLS or MILES, Francis. Priest.
>   b. July 13th, 1650 or 1651, London. S.J. September 7th, 1672.
>   Watten (nov) 1672-5. Liège (phil) 1676, 1678. Liège (theol) 1679-81.
>   Ordained priest March 28th, 1682. Ghent 1682. College of St Hugh
>   1683-6. College of St Francis Xavier 1687. In England 1688. Ghent
>   1689, 1690. Loretto 1690-3. d. December 16th, 1693, Loretto. (Fo.7;
>   114; 113; 150 II(3) 14/10/90; 139 f.295; Nec).

MINSHALL see Coniers or Conyers, John.

MOLE, Francis. Scholastic.
>   b. October 3rd, 1747. e. Bruges College 1766-c.68. S.J. September
>   7th, 1768. Ghent (nov) 1768, 1769. Liège (phil) 1771-3. Left 1773, not
>   ordained. (113; CRS.69; 91; 77).

MOLIEN, Everard or Edward. Priest.
>   b. January 23rd or 24th, 1701, Calais. br. of John Baptist. e. St
>   Omers College 1714 or earlier-15 or later. S.J. September 7th, 1720.
>   Liège (phil) 1723, 1724. Liège (theol) 1725-7. Louvain (theol) 1728.
>   Ordained priest c.1728. St Omers College 1730, 1733-44, 1746-50,
>   1752-58, 1761. d. September 14th, 1761, St Omers College. (Fo.7;
>   CRS.69; 114; 91; 113; 140 n.45; 111; 51 f.311; CRS.62/172, 228; Nec).

MOLIEN, John Baptist. Priest.
>   b. January 5th, 1703, Calais. br. of Everard or Edward. e. St Omers
>   College 1714-15 or later. S.J. September 7th, 1721. Watten (nov) 1723.
>   Liège (phil) 1724-6. Liège (theol) 1727, 1728. Louvain (theol) 1728,
>   1730. Ordained priest September 1729. Ghent (tert) 1730. Canford
>   1731, 1732. College of St Thomas of Canterbury 1733, 1734. Canford
>   1735. Ladyholt c.1735. College of St Ignatius 1735-7. Residence of St
>   John 1738. College of the Holy Apostles 1739. Residence of St George
>   1740. College of St Ignatius 1741, 1743-4, 1746. Ghent 1747. Watten
>   1748. St Omers College 1749, 1750. Ghent 1752. Watten 1753-5. Ghent
>   1756-8, 1761. Watten 1763-5, 1767 (Superior 1767). Calais 1771. Liège
>   1772-3. Ghent 1773. d. December 20th, 1775, Ghent or 1774, Lille.
>   (Fo.7; 117; 113; CRS.69; AHSJ.42/291; 150 III(2) 8/10/17, 4/12/28,
>   4/12/47; 16 ff.21, 35; 64 p.87; 66; 74; 91; 201 pp.795-8. Nec;
>   CRS.62/172).

MOLYNEUX see Wilkinson, Thomas.

MOLYNEUX, Henry. Priest.
>   b. September 10th, 1693, London. s. of Richard and Barbara
>   (Stephens). br. of Richard (1). e. St Omers College ?-1713. S.J.
>   September 7th, 1713. Watten (nov) 1714. Liège (phil) 1715, 1716, 1718.
>   La Flèche (theol) 1720. Ordained priest c.1722. St Omers College 1723.

College of the Holy Apostles 1724. College of St Thomas of
Canterbury 1725. In England 1726-8, 1730 (Bury St Edmunds 1727).
East Grinstead 1727, 1733, 1737. College of St Ignatius 1737. College of
St Thomas of Canterbury 1738-41, 1743-4, 1746-50, 1752-8, 1763-4
(Reigate 1752. Redhill 1760-1, supplying at Firle 1754-c.68). Redhill
1767-71. Reigate 1771. d. August 1st, 1771, Redhill. (Fo.7; CRS.69;
114; 91; 113; RH.13/117; 44 ff.118, 197, 215, 236, 269; 43 f.47; HMC.
10th Report App.4/191; 125; CRS.62/137-8; Nec).

MOLYNEUX, Joseph *alias* Tickle. Priest.
    b. February 25th, 1732. From Lancashire. s. of Richard and
Elizabeth (Tickle) of Alt Grange, Lancashire. e. St Omers College
c.1746-52. S.J. February 2nd, 1752. Watten (nov) 1752. Liège (phil)
1753-5. St Omers College 1756-8, 1761. Liège (theol) 1763, 1764.
Ordained priest September 1763, Cologne. Bodney 1765. Slindon
1765-9. College of St Thomas of Canterbury 1771. Slindon 1772-8. d.
September 3rd, 1778, Slindon. (Fo.7; CRS.69; 117; 113; 91;
RH.13/118; 13 f.60v; 44 ff.227v, 270; 65; 68 pp.75, 105; HMC. 10th
Report App.4/191; 94 f.250; CRS.7/355; CRS.22/309, 319; 111; 41
n.24; Nec).

MOLYNEUX, Richard (1). Priest.
    b. March 20th, 21st or 26th, 1696. s. of Richard and Barbara
(Stephens). br. of Henry. e. St Omers College 1714 or earlier-15. S.J.
September 7th, 1715. Watten (nov) 1715, 1716. Liège (phil) 1718, 1720.
Liège (theol) 1723, 1724. Ordained priest c.1723. Residence of St John
1725. In England 1726. Gateshead 1727, 1729, supplying at Morpeth.
Maryland 1730-49 (Superior 1735-42, 1747-9). Marnhull 1749-61.
Bonham 1761-6 (Rector of College of St Thomas of Canterbury
c.1759-65). d. May 17th or 18th, 1766, Bonham. (Fo.7; CRS.69; 91;
113; 114; Hu.Text 2/689; CRS.56/171; CRS.Mon.1/172, 247; 51
f.311; NCH.8/12, 9/14; 13 f.43; 44 ff.87, 267; 64 pp.242, 417, 552;
Gil.3/507; Ki.166n; CRS.25/115; 65; HMC. 10th Report App.4/184,
189, 190-1, 197; 92; 01.256; 111; CRS.62/137, 285n; Nec).

MOLYNEUX, Richard (2) *alias* Howe. Priest.
    b. May 3rd, 1700, Staffordshire or Shropshire. s. of Christopher and
Alice (Howe). e. St Omers College ?-1722. S.J. September 7th, 1722.
Watten (nov) 1723, 1724. Liège (phil) 1725, 1726. Liège (theol) 1727,
1728. Ordained priest c.1729. In England 1730. College of St Thomas
of Canterbury 1733-41, 1744, 1746-50, 1752-8, 1763-4 (Lulworth 1736.
Marnhull 1737, 1740. Canford 1754, 1757, 1759). Stapehill 1761-6.
Bonham 1767. Marnhull 1767-9. d. June 5th, 1769, Marnhull. (Fo.7;
CRS.69; 114; 91; 113; CRS.56/171; CRS.Mon.1/157; 44 ff.87, 249,
269-71, 273, 275; 65; 67; 77; HMC. 10th Report App.4/191; Gil.3/507;
126; 71; 74; 189 IV n.93; Ans.3/151-2; Nec).

MOLYNEUX. Robert. Priest.
    b. July 24th, 1738, at or near Formby, Lancashire. ?s of Robert. br.
of William (2). e. St Omers College c.1751-7. S.J. September 7th, 1757.
Watten (nov) 1757, 1758. Liège (phil) 1760, 1761-2. Bruges College

1763-5, 1767. Liège (theol) 1767-9. Ordained priest c.1767. Bruges College 1769. Ghent 1770. Maryland 1770-1808 (Superior 1805-8). Readm. S.J. 1805. d. December 9th, 1808, Georgetown, Maryland. (Fo.7; CRS.69; 114; 91; 113; Hu.Text 2/698; 4 f.106; 6 f.267v; 7 13v; 16 f.12; 54 ff.55v, 163v; 68 pp.125, 195; 77; 119 ff.11, 40; AHSJ.42/306; 150 (1750-1853) f.77; Nec. For writings see Som.).

MOLYNEUX, Viscount William (1). Priest.

b. January 20th, 1685, Sefton, Lancashire. s. of William, 4th Viscount and Bridget (Lucy). S.J. September 7th, 1704. Watten (nov) 1705, 1706. Liège (phil) 1708, 1709. Liège (theol) 1710-13. Ordained priest c.1713. Ghent 1714. College of St Aloysius 1715-6, 1718, 1720, 1724-5. In England 1726, 1727. College of St Aloysius 1728-44, 1746-59 (Rector 1728-34. Scholes 1727. Croxteth 1728. Scholes 1728, 1732-3, 1737, 1741-52, 1755-6). 7th Viscount 1745. d. March 3rd 1759, Scholes. bu. Sefton. (Fo.7; 114; 91; 113; GEC.; 6 f.279; 21 v.2; 23 f.274v; 24 f.347v; 27 f.320; 84; 86; NB.2/119n; HMC. 10th Report App.4/189, 191, 196; Gil.5/61; 158; 156 App.1; CRS.17/69; CRS.25/114; 120; 100; 111; 28 f.45 Nec).

MOLYNEUX, William (2). Priest.

b. February 1st, 1726, Lancashire. ?s. of Robert. br. of Robert. e. St Omers College c.1742-8. S.J. September 7th, 1748. Watten (nov) 1749. Liège (phil) 1750, 1752. Liège (theol) 1753-5. Ordained priest June 13th, 1756, Liège. Ghent (tert) 1756. Watten 1757. College of St Ignatius 1757. ?Stapehill 1757. College of St Aloysius 1758, 1763-4 (Ince Blundell 1758, 1759). Ince Blundell 1767-9. College of St Aloysius 1771. Ince Blundell 1772, 1773. Stonyhurst c.1774-83. Brinn 1783-9. d. April 30th, 1789, Brinn. bu. Brinn. (Fo.7; CRS.69; 114; 91; 113; CRS.43/127; 6 f.267v; 13 f.122; 21 v.2; 26 ff.94, 284v, 285; 28 f.227; 54 f.156; 152 n.10; 68 p.133; 155 II 129; 155 III 185c, 271c; 25 ff.80, 86, 90, 96; 105; 80; 86; Gil.4/327; CRS.16/518; 167 pp.24, 29; 01.356-7; 119 ff.7, 17, 40; CRS.OP.1/42; Nec).

MONA, William. Laybrother.

b. October 1st, 1705. From Liège. S.J. September 7th, 1735. Watten (nov) 1735. Ghent 1736-42. Watten 1744. Liège 1746-7. d. November 12th, 1747, Liège. (Fo.7; 114; 113; 91; Nec).

MONET, Christopher. Scholastic or Laybrother.

d. date and place unrecorded. (Fo.7; 114).

MONNIER, Ignatius. Laybrother.

b. January 9th, 1792, Serre, France. S.J. December 23rd, 1815, in France. To English province 1843. Calcutta 1844-6. St Mary's Hall 1847-57. d. October 23rd, 1857, Stonyhurst. bu. Stonyhurst. (Fo.7; 113; 52 f.23; CDSJ.; CG.; Nec).

MONNINGTON see Williams, John (3) and Peter (2).

MONTFORD see Mumford.

MONTFORD, Joseph see Armstrong, David.

MONTROY or MONROY, Maximilian. Laybrother.

b. November 2nd, 1660, Lille. S.J. May 7th, 1689. Watten (nov)

1689-91. Watten 1692, 1693. Liège 1693, 1696-7, 1699-1702. d. May 25th, 1702, Liège. (Fo.7; 114; 113; Nec).

MOORE see More, RICHARD.

MORE see Houghton, Henry; Melling, Thomas; Vaudry or Vaudrey, John.

MORE, Christopher. Priest.
> b. May 10th, 1729, Yorkshire. s. of Thomas and Catherine (Giffard) of Barnborough Hall, Yorkshire. br. of Thomas. e. St Omers College c.1739-46. S.J. September 7th, 1746. Watten (nov) 1747. Liège (phil) 1748-50. Liège (theol) 1752-4. Ordained priest c.1754. St Omers College 1755-8. College of St Aloysius 1759, 1763-4. Thurnham or York 1765-9. Bath or Thurnham 1769-74, 1776. d. November 27th, 1781, Bath. bu. Bath Abbey. (Fo.7; CRS.69; 114; 91; 113; CRS.65/73; CRS.66/46; CRS.Mon.2/278; 54 f.42v; 65; Gil.5/94; CRS.12/21; CRS.15/224; CRS.20/183; 111; BAT.73; Nec).

MORE, Francis. Priest.
> b. October 19th, 1698, Somerset. S.J. September 7th, 1718. Watten (nov) 1720. Liège (phil) 1722, 1723. Pont-à-Mousson (theol) 1725, 1726. Liège (theol) 1727. Ordained priest c.1727. d. September 19th, 1727, St Omers College. (Fo.7; 114; 113; 91; 9 n.138; Nec).

MORE, Henry or Francis *alias* Ford. Priest.
> b.1666, Brussels. e. St Omers College ?-1684. S.J. September 7th, 1684. Watten (nov) 1684, 1685. Liège (phil) 1686, 1687. Liège (theol) 1689-91. Ordained priest April 4th, 1691. Watten 1692. College of St Chad 1693. College of St Ignatius 1696-7, 1699. Ghent 1700-01, 1703-4. College of St Thomas of Canterbury 1705-6, 1708-9. College of St Ignatius 1710-16, 1718, 1720, 1723-5. In England 1726-8 (Hawkwell 1727). d. December 21st, 1729, Kent. (Fo.7; CRS.69; 91; 113; Nec).

MORÉ, Hippolite. Priest.
> b. March 23rd, 1800, in France. S.J. September 4th, 1823, in France. Calcutta 1834-43. d. October 29th, 1843, Calcutta. (Fo.7; 113; CDSJ; 52 ff.30, 69, 71; 45 f.97a; 46 ff.72-3; Nec; JICH.20 ff. For writings see Som.).

MORE or Moore, Richard. Priest.
> b. April 29th, 1672, Warwickshire. s. of Richard. e. St Omers College c.1687-93. S.J. September 7th, 1693. Liège (phil) 1696, 1697. Liège (theol) 1699-1701. Ordained priest 1702. In England 1703. College of St Aloysius 1705-6, 1708-16, 1718, 1720, 1723-5 (Highfield c.1701). In England 1726. Holywell 1727-31. Richmond, Surrey 1731, 1733, 1740, 1741. Holywell 1741-53. d. May 6th, 1753, ?Holywell. (Fo.7; CRS.69; 114; 113; 23 f.35; 74; 89; 91; HMC. 10th Report App.4/191, 198; CRS.3/107; CRS.7/297; Bur.1/174; Nec).

MORE, Thomas. Priest.
> b. September 19th, 1722. s. of Thomas and Catherine (Giffard) of Barnborough Hall, Yorkshire. br. of Christopher. e. St Omers College c.1736-41. S.C. Douay 1741-? S.J. July 19th, 1752. Watten (nov) 1752. Liège (phil) 1753-5. Liège (theol) 1756-8. Ordained priest c.1760. St Omers College 1761. Liège 1763. College of St Ignatius 1763-73

(Provincial 1769-73). London 1774, 1781-3, 1786, 1788, 1790. Bath
1793-5. d. June 20th or July 3rd, 1795, Bath. bu. St Joseph's chapel,
Bristol. (Fo.7; CRS.69; 114; 91; 117; 113; 90 f.36; CRS.65/73;
CRS.66/122; LR.3/9; 13 ff.56, 103; 15 f.6v; 41 nn.73, 110; 44 f.45; 47
f.25; 54 f.101v; 50 f.144v; 29 f.322; 152 n.52; 63 ff.235, 254, 266v;
HMC. 10th Report App.4/187, 189, 191, 194; Ki.169; CRS.19/227;
175; 176; 132; RSC.83; Nec).

MORGAN, George. Priest.
      b.1636, Worcestershire. e. St Omers College 1652 or earlier-57. S.J.
September 7th, 1657. Watten (nov) 1658. Liège (phil) 1659-61. St
Omers College 1663-5, 1667. Liège (theol) 1669, 1672. Ordained priest
c.1671. St Omers College 1672, 1673. College of St Thomas of
Canterbury 1674. d. December 16th, 1674, in England. (Fo.7; CRS.69;
114; 113; 140 n.45; Nec).

MORGAN, James. Scholastic.
      b. c.1648, Monmouthshire. S.J. September 7th, 1667. Watten (nov)
1669. Liège (phil) 1672. Left 1672, not ordained. (113).

MORGAN, Richard. Priest.
      b. February 26th, 1746, Colford, Gloucestershire. e. St Omers and
Bruges Colleges c. 1759-63. E.C. Valladolid 1763-6. S.J. September
7th, 1766. Ghent (nov) 1766. Liège (nov and theol) 1767-9. Ordained
priest 1770. Ghent (tert) 1771. Bruges College 1772, 1773. Liège
Academy 1774-6. Preston 1783-1814. d. March 9th, 1814, Preston.
(Fo.7; CRS.69; 114; 91; 113; 16 ff.97v, 100; 6 ff.96v, 120, 167v; 7
f.143v; 8 II 36; 13 f.231v; 21 v.2; 54 ff.223, 283; 30 f.7Av; 90 f.54;
Chad.363; 94 ff.3-4, 41, 42, 81, 82; Gil.5/121; Ki.169; CRS.12/127;
CRS.30/190-1; 155 II 129; 167 pp.21, 30; Nec. For writings see Sut. and
Som.).

MORGAN, Robert see Needham, Sebastian.

MORGAN, William (1). Priest.
      b.1623, Cilcen, Flintshire. s. of Henry and Winefrid (Gwynne). e.
Westminster School and Trinity College, Cambridge. E.C. Rome
1648-51. S.J. September 30th, 1651 in Rome. Rome 1651-60. Ordained
priest c.1657. Liège 1661, 1663-5, 1667, 1669. Residence of St Winefrid
1672-9 (Superior. Powis c.1675). Socius to the provincial 1679, 1680.
Liège 1681. In prison in England 1683. E.C. Rome 1683-6 (Rector).
Holland 1687. Provincial 1689. d. September 28th, 1689, St Omers
College. (Fo.7; 114; 113; Ven.III 212; CRS.40/42; CRS.55/510-11;
Nec; 168 f.5).

MORGAN, William (2) *alias* Winter. Priest.
      b. February 18th, 1648, Monmouthshire. e. St Omers College 1664
or earlier-69. S.J. September 7th, 1669. Liège (phil) 1672, 1673. Liège
(theol) 1674-8. Ordained priest April 9th, 1678. Ghent 1679. France
1680. In England 1688. Rouen 1689, 1690. Abbeville 1691-3. College of
St Ignatius 1695-7, 1699-1701, 1703-10 (Rector 1703-c.07). d. February
11th, 1710, London. (Fo.7; CRS.69; 114; 113; 150 II(3) 12/11/95;
Nec).

MORIN, Michael. Scholastic.
 b. August 17th, 1808, Liverpool. e. Stonyhurst 1823-? S.J.
 September 7th, 1828. Hodder (nov) 1828-30. St Mary's Hall (phil)
 1830-2. St Mary's Hall (theol) 1832-? Left 1836, not ordained. (115; 2).
MORPHY see Murphy.
MORRICE see Morris, James.
MORRIS, Francis (1). Scholastic.
 b. May 9th, 1710. From St Germain. S.J. September 7th, 1727. Liège
 (phil) 1729, 1730. Left 1730, not ordained. (91; 113; 150 III(2)
 12/8/30).
MORRIS, Francis (2). Scholastic.
 b. June 2nd, 1791, Norwich. e. Stonyhurst 1804-? S.J. September
 7th, 1810. Hodder (nov) 1810-12. Stonyhurst 1815, 1820. d. August
 14th or 18th, 1821, Preston, not ordained. bu. Stonyhurst. (Fo.7; 113;
 114; 116; CDSJ.; CRS.12/149; Stol; Nec).
MORRIS or MAURICE or MORRICE, James *alias* or *vere* Cross. Priest.
 b.1674, Kilkenny. S.J. September 7th, 1699. Watten (nov) 1699,
 1700, 1701. Liège (phil) 1703, 1704. Liège (theol) 1705, 1706, 1708.
 Ordained priest 1708. College of St Ignatius 1709-14. d. August 2nd,
 1715, in England. (Fo.7; 114; 113; CRS.62/index; Nec).
MORRIS, Peter. Priest.
 b. March 8th, 1743. e. St Omers College ?-1760. S.J. September 7th,
 1760. Watten (nov) 1761. Liège (phil) 1763, 1764. Liège (theol) 1767.
 Ordained priest 1767. Ghent 1768. Maryland 1768-73-?83. d.
 November or December 19th, 1783, Newtown, Maryland. (Fo.7;
 CRS.69; 91; 114; 113; 65; Hu.Text 2/697; CRS.9/39; Nec).
MORRON, Edward. Priest.
 b. January 1st, 1797, ?Dublin. e. Stonyhurst 1813-8. S.J. September
 7th, 1818. Hodder (nov) 1818-20. Stonyhurst (phil and theol) 1820-3.
 Ordained priest 1823, Wolverhampton. Courtfield 1823-4. Rotherwas
 1824-7. Leigh 1827-8. Chipping 1828-37. Hodder (tert) 1837. Chipping
 1837-8. Wigan 1838-44. Gillmoss 1844-62. Liverpool 1862. d.
 November 12th, 1862, Liverpool. bu. Gillmoss. (Fo.7; 115; Gil.5/61;
 CRS.4/428; CRS.36/4; Che.72/101ff; Nec).
MOSELEY, Joseph. Priest.
 b. November 16th, 1731, Lincolnshire. br. of Michael. e. St Omers
 College c.1741-c.46. S.J. September 7th, 1748. Watten (nov) 1748,
 1749. Liège (phil) 1750, 1752. Liège (theol) 1753-5. Ordained priest
 c.1755. Watten (tert) 1756. Maryland 1756-73-?87. d. June 3rd, 1787,
 St Joseph's, Talbot County, Maryland. (Fo.7; CRS.69; 114; 91; 113;
 92; Hu.Text 2/695; Nec).
MOSELEY, Michael *alias* Byers. Priest.
 b. August 17th, 1720, Lincolnshire. br. of Joseph. e. St Omers
 College 1732-9. S.J. September 7th, 1739. Watten (nov) 1739, 1740.
 Liège (phil) 1741. Munster (theol) 1744. Cologne (theol) 1746.
 Ordained priest c.1746. Ghent (tert) 1747. St Omers College 1748, 1749.
 E.C. Rome 1750-8. Bromley Hall 1759-62. Aldenham 1762. Residence

of St Winefrid 1762-7. Holywell 1767-9, 1771-3 (Superior of the Residence of St Winefrid 1763-73). ?Holywell 1773-7. d. November 29th or 30th, 1777, Holywell. (Fo.7; CRS.69; 114; 91; 113; 12 ff.188 ff; 21 v.2; 64 pp.59, 270; ER.4/117, 10/39; 65; 80; CRS.3/108; 117; 108; Nec).

MOSTYN, Andrew. Priest.

b. November 29th, 1663, Talacre, Flintshire. s. of Edward, 1st Bart. and Elizabeth (Downes). br. of John. Uncle of Piers. e. St Omers College c.1680. E.C. Douay ?-1687. St Gregory's Paris 1687-90. S.J. February 1st, 1691. Watten (nov) 1692. Ordained priest December 21st, 1692. St Omers College 1693, 1696. Watten 1697. Travelling 1699. Residence of St Winefrid 1700-01. Residence of St George 1701-3, 1704-6. College of St Ignatius 1709. d. April 14th, 1709, in England (?Worcester). (Fo.7; CRS.69; 114; 113; CRS.19/108-11; Nec).

MOSTYN, John. Priest.

b. June 22nd, 1657, Flintshire. s. of Sir Edward, 1st Bart. and Elizabeth (Downes). br. of Andrew. Uncle of Piers. e. St Omers College c.1675. Date and place of ordination to priesthood not found. S.J. October 18th, 1693. Liège (theol) 1696. Residence of St Mary 1697, 1699-1701, 1703. Lydiate 1704-21. d. November 3rd, 1721, Lydiate. bu. St Katherine's chapel. (Fo.7; CRS.69; 114; 113; 150 II(3) 28/7/93; 28 f.191; NB.1/135, 146, 287, 2/111, 217, 3/16; Gib.1/286; Nec).

MOSTYN, Sir Piers. Priest.

b. March 15th, 1687, Flintshire. s. of Sir Piers, 2nd Bart. and Frances (Selby) of Talacre, Flintshire. Nephew of Andrew and John. e. St Omers College ?-1707. S.J. January 5th, 1707. Watten (nov) 1708. Liège (phil) 1709-11. Liège (theol) 1712-4. Ordained priest c.1715. Ghent (tert) 1715. Residence of St Winefrid 1718, 1720. College of St Aloysius 1723-5. In England 1726-8, 1730 (Wigan 1727, 1728). College of St Aloysius 1733-4 (Wigan c.1734). 3rd Bart. 1720. d. August 29th, 1735, in England (?Wigan). (Fo.7; CRS.69; 91; 113; 85; CRS.25/114; Nec).

MOTET or MOTTET, Ferdinand. Priest.

b. April 3rd, 1658, Brussels. ?s. of Sir Giles, Bart. and Elizabeth (Langhorne). e. St Omers College ?-1677. E.C. Valladolid 1677-84. Ordained priest c.1684. S.J. August 14th, 1684. Watten (nov) 1684, 1685. St Omers College 1685-7, 1689-91. d. November 17th, 1691, St Omers College. (Fo.7; CRS.69; 114; 113; Ans.3/154; CRS.30/169, 172; Nec).

MOUCHLIN or MOUCLIN, John. Laybrother.

b. 1637, Artois. S.J. August 25th, 1659. Watten (nov) 1660, 1661. St Omers College 1664-5, 1667, 1669, 1672. Liège 1673, 1674. d. November 18th, 1674, Liège. (Fo.7; 114; 113; Nec).

MOUTARDIER or MONTARDIER, Benjamin Louis. Priest.

b. November 22nd, 1786, Laigle, France. s. of Peter and Elizabeth. e. in France and Stonyhurst 1807-1810. S.J. June 20th, 1810. Hodder (nov) 1810-12. Stonyhurst (phil and theol) 1812-7. Ordained priest

September 4th, 1813, Stonyhurst. Dunkenhalgh (supply) 1815-7. Lulworth 1817-55. Pontefract 1855. St Acheul, Amiens 1855-7. d. February 6th, 1857, St Acheul. bu. St Acheul. (Fo.7; 115; 113; 13 f.472v; 21 v.2; 55 f.150v; 93 p.81; CRS.6/368; Ber.216; Nec. For writings see Sut.).

MOYEN, John Baptist. Priest.
    S.J. in France. d. 1797 or 1798, in England. (CRS.12/67).

MOYLEN, William. ?Priest.
    b. December 26th, 1746 or 1747 or 1749, London. e. St Omers and Bruges Colleges 1761-c.67. S.J. September 7th, 1767. Ghent (nov) 1767-9. Liège (phil) 1771. Bruges College 1772, 1773. Liège Academy 1776, 1781, 1783. ?Ordained priest. d. c.1800 or later. (Fo.7; AHSJ.42/293; CRS.69; 113; 3 ff.37, 51; 16 f.98; 75 p.141v; 90 f.54; HMC. 10th Report App.4/192; 17 f.B).

MUMFORD or MONTFORD, Gervase. Priest.
    b.1635, Nottinghamshire. e. St Omers College 1653 or earlier-c.58. S.J. September 7th, 1658. Watten (nov) 1658, 1659. Liège (phil) 1660, 1661. Liège (theol) 1663. St Omers College 1664, 1665. Liège (theol) 1667, 1669. Ordained priest c.1669. St Omers College 1671, 1672. Liège 1672-7. Antwerp 1677-8. Liège 1679. Watten 1680. Liège 1682. Brussels 1682-4. d. March 22nd or 23rd, 1684, Brussels. (Fo.7; CRS.69; 114; 113; 150 II(2) 11/12/77, Feb.79; 140 n.45; 108; Nec).

MUMFORD or MONTFORD see Armstrong, Daniel.

MURPHY or MORPHY, Cornelius. Priest.
    b. October 24th, 1696, Flanders. S.J. September 7th, 1711. Watten (nov) 1712, 1713. Liège (phil) 1714, 1715. Liège (theol) 1716, 1718, 1720. Ordained priest c.1720. ?St Omers College 1721. College of St Aloysius 1724, 1725. In England 1726-8, 1730. College of St Aloysius 1733-47 (Rector 1741-c.47. Scarisbrick 1727, 1728, 1732. Wigan 1739. Scarisbrick 1741. Liverpool 1742, 1743. Croxteth 1747. Scarisbrick 1747). College of St Ignatius 1748-58, 1763-6 (Rector 1748-c.52. London 1750-2, 1754, 1763). d. October 31st, 1766, London. (Fo.7 and p.1405; 114; 91; 113; LR.3/9; 150 III(2) 28/3/39, 18/3/41; 9 n.104; 14 f.38v; 24 f.345; 27 f.229; 31 f.12; HMC. 10th Report App.4/183-4, 189; CRS.4/434; 63 ff.56, 66v, 100, 169; CRS.25/113; CRS.30/xl; 109; 156 App.1; Nec. For writings see Som.).

MURPHY or MORPHY, John. Priest.
    b.1657, Lille. e. St Omers College ?-1678. S.J. September 7th, 1678-89. Watten (nov) 1679. Liège (phil) 1680-2. Liège (theol) 1683-6. Ordained priest 1687. College of St Aloysius 1687. In England 1688. Bruges 1689. (Fo.7; CRS.69; 113; 150 (II(3) 8/10/89).

MURPHY, Melchior. Priest.
    b. October 6th, 1664 or 1665, Brussels. e. St Omers College ?-1684. S.J. September 7th, 1684. Liège (phil) 1686, 1687. Liège (theol) 1689-93. Ordained priest March 21st, 1693. Watten 1696-7, 1699-1701, 1703-6, 1708. Ghent 1709. Watten 1710-11. Ghent 1712-5. Watten 1715-6, 1718, 1720. Liège 1723. Ghent 1724. Liège 1725-8, 1730.

Watten 1733-6. d. February 14th, 1736, Liège. (Fo.7; CRS.69; 91; 113; CRS.62/70, 303; Nec).

MURPHY or MORPHY, Michael. Priest.

b. September 18th, 1725 or 1726, Montserrat, West Indies. e. St Omers College 1737-45. S.J. September 7th, 1745. Watten (nov) 1746. Liège (phil) 1747-9. Liège (theol) 1750, 1752. Ordained priest 1752. Ghent (tert) 1753. Maryland 1753-9. d. July 8th, 1759, near Newtown, Maryland. (Fo.7; CRS.69; 91; 114; 113; Hu.Text 2/695; 92; Nec).

MURPHY or MORPHY, Richard *alias* Turner. Priest.

b. July 23rd, 1716, London. e. St Omers College ?-1734. S.J. September 7th, 1734. Watten (nov) 1735. Liège (phil) 1736-38. Liège (theol) 1739-41. Ordained priest c.1741. Ghent 1743. Slatedelf 1743, 1745, 1747. College of the Immaculate Conception 1747, 1748. Swynnerton 1748. Stella 1748-75. Newcastle 1776. Salisbury 1776-94 (serving Odstock from 1781). d. May 14th or 15th, 1794, Salisbury. bu. Cathedral cloister. (Fo.7; CRS.69; 114; 91; 113; CRS.Mon.1/166-8; CRS.12/44; 21 v.2; 35 ff.137v, 198v, 203v; 64 pp.264-5; 85; Gil.4/106; Ki.73, 107, 238; 01.424; 36 ff.136v, 164, 182; 117; Nec; 156 IV, XXIV, App.1).

MURPHY, Thomas. Scholastic.

b. November 13th, 1732, America. e. St Omers College c.1750-51. S.J. September 7th, 1751. Watten (nov) 1752. Liège (phil) 1753-5. d. March 15th, 1757, Liège, not ordained. (Fo.7; CRS.69; 114; 91; 113; Hu.Text 2/704; Nec).

MUSKET or MUSQUET, Thomas. Laybrother.

b. 1652 or 1653, Chester or Chichester. S.J. November 20th, 1695. Watten (nov) 1696, 1697, 1699-1701, 1703-5. d. April 8th, 1706, St Omers College. (Fo.7; 114; 113; Nec).

MUSSON, Christopher. Scholastic.

b.1682, London. s. of John. br. of John ?and Samuel. e. St Omers College 1694-1700. S.J. September 7th, 1700. Watten (nov) 1701. Liège (phil) 1703-5. Liège (theol) 1706, 1708. Left 1708, not yet ordained. (CRS.69; 113; 150 III(1) 3/11/08).

MUSSON, John. Priest.

b. November 16th, 1680, London. s. of John. br. of Christopher ?and Samuel. e. St Omers College 1694-9. S.J. September 7th, 1699. Watten (nov) 1699-1701. Liège (phil) 1703, 1704. Liège (theol) 1705-6, 1708. Ordained priest 1708. Ghent (tert) 1709. Liège 1710-6, 1718, 1720. College of St Hugh 1724. College of the Immaculate Conception 1725. In England 1726-8, 1730 (Holt 1726. Bath 1727-?). College of the Holy Apostles 1733-7. Residence of St Mary 1738. College of St Thomas of Canterbury 1739-41, 1743-4, 1746-50, 1752-5 (?Winchester 1741, 1745, 1752, 1753). d. November 21st, 1755, Winchester. (Fo.7; CRS.69; 91; 113; CRS.42/7, 9; CRS.1/159; CRS.65/72; 9 n.247; 44 f.265; 126; Nec. For writings see Som).

MUSSON, Samuel *alias* Brown. Priest.

b. December 7th, 1686, London. ?s. of John. ?br. of Christopher and John. S.J. October 9th, 1705. Watten (nov) 1706. Liège (phil) 1708-10. Liège (theol) 1711-3. Ordained priest c.1713. Ghent 1714. St Omers College 1715-6, 1718. In England 1720. College of St Thomas of Canterbury 1723. College of St Hugh 1724. Residence of St Mary 1725. In England 1726. Blyborough c.1727 then Reasby and Dunston. In England 1730. College of the Holy Apostles 1731, 1732. Calehill 1732, 1733. College of St Ignatius 1734-41, 1743-4, 1746-50, 1752-8 (?St Stephen's, Canterbury 1753), 1763-4. St Stephen's, Canterbury 1766-9. d. September 28th, 1769, St Stephen's, Canterbury. (Fo.7; 114; 91; 113; 41 n.67; 68 p.132; 64 pp.162, 241; 74; HMC. 10th Report, App.4/192; Gil.5/132; 43 ff.52v, 54v, 55v; Nec).

MUTH, Francis. Priest.
    b. December 6th, 1782, Hainburg, Austria. s. of Francis and Anna Maria. e. Pressburg. Vienna (phil) 1798, 1799. Dillingen (phil) 1800. Entered Company of Fathers of the Faith June 21st, 1799. Dillingen and Rome (theol) 1800-06. To England 1806. Ordained priest May 23rd, 1807, Old Hall Green, Hertfordshire. London (German chapel) 1810-36. S.J. February 9th, 1815. St Mary's Hall 1836-41. d. May 5th, 1841, Preston. bu. St Ignatius' churchyard, Preston. (Fo.7; 114; 115; LR.3/7; 6 f.141; 106; LMAS, 1977, pp.323-5; Nec).

NANDYKE, Thomas. Priest.
    b. October or December 16th, 1726, Yorkshire. ?s. of John and Mary (Wilson). e. St Omers College c.1741-5. S.J. September 7th, 1745. Watten (nov) 1746, 1747. Liège (phil) 1748, 1749. Liège (theol) 1750, 1752. Ordained priest 1752, Liège. Ghent (tert) 1753. London 1753-61. York 1762-9. Yarm 1770-93. d. March 17th, 1793, Yarm. (Fo.7; CRS.69; 114; 113; 91; CRS.Mon.2/278, 390; RH.8/163; 68 p.253; 90 f.179v; HMC. 10th Report App.4/191-2; E and P.304; 155 II 127; 167 p.38; 173; 111; 117; 41 n.66; Nec).

NEALE, Benedict. Priest.
    b. August 3rd, 1709, Maryland. e. St Omers College c.1723-8. S.J. September 7th, 1728. Watten (nov) 1730. St Omers College 1733-8. Liège (theol) 1738-40. Ordained priest c.1741. Maryland 1742-4, 1746-50, 1752-8, 1763-4, 1767-9, 1771-3-?87. d. March 20th or June 9th, 1787, Newtown, Maryland. (Fo.7; CRS.69; 91; 114; 113; Hu.Text 2/692; 92; 140 n.45; Nec).

NEALE, Charles. Priest.
    b. October 10th, 1751. s. of William and Anne (Brooke) of Portobacco, Maryland. br. of Leonard and William. e. Bruges College 1764-71. S.J. September 7th, 1771. Ghent (nov) 1772, 1773. ?Maryland 1775. Liège Academy 1776. Ordained priest at Liège (date not recorded). Maryland 1785. Antwerp 1786, 1790. Maryland 1792, 1793, 1800-?23. Readm. S.J. 1805. Superior S.J. in U.S.A. 1808, 1811, 1821, 1823. d. April 27th or 28th, 1823, Georgetown, Maryland. (Fo.7;

CRS.69; 114; Hu.Docs.1/163A; Hu.Text 2/701; 113; AHSJ.42/307; 53 ff.51, 52; 150 (1750-1853) f.130v; 4 f.63v; 54 f.37v; 56 f.273; 67; 90 ff.54, 167; 94 ff.202-3; 131; Nec).

NEALE, Henry (1). Priest.

b. July 29th, 1702, Maryland. e. St Omers College ?-1724. S.J. September 7th, 1724. Watten (nov) 1725, 1726. Liège (phil) 1726-28. St Omers College 1730, 1733-5. Liège (theol) 1735-8. Ordained priest April 5th, 1738. Maryland 1740. Pennsylvania 1741-8. d. May 5th, 1748, Philadelphia. bu. St Joseph's, Philadelphia. (Fo.7; CRS.69; 114; 113; Hu.Text 2/690; 150 III(2) 20/12/38; 64 p.354; 91; 92; 140 n.45; Nec).

NEALE, Henry (2). Novice.

b. April 1st, 1733, Maryland. e. St Omers College c.1750-4. S.J. September 7th, 1754. d. October 8th, 1754, Watten. (Fo.7; CRS.69; 114; 91; Hu.Text 2/704; 111; Nec).

NEALE, Leonard. Archbishop.

b. October 15th, 1747, Maryland. s. of William and Anne (Brooke) of Portobacco. br. of Charles and William. e. St Omers and Bruges Colleges 1761-7. S.J. September 7th, 1767. Ghent (nov) 1767-9. Liège (phil) 1771. Bruges College 1772-3. Liège (theol) 1773. Ordained priest 1773. Maryland 1773. Hardwick c.1773-7. Guiana 1780-3. Maryland 1783. Consecrated bishop December 7th, 1800. Archbishop of Baltimore December 3rd, 1815. d. June 15th, 1817, Baltimore or Georgetown. bu. Georgetown. (Fo.7; CRS.69; 91; 114; 113; Hu.Text 2/576, 700; AHSJ.37/153; 51 ff.304, 307; 90 f.171; CRS.4/248; Nec. For writings see Som.).

NEALE, William. Priest.

b. August 14th, 1743, Maryland. s. of William and Anne (Brooke) of Portobacco. br. of Charles and Leonard. e. St Omers College 1753-60. S.J. September 7th, 1760. Watten (nov) 1761. Liège (phil) 1763, 1764. Liège (theol) 1767. Ordained priest c.1767. Ghent 1768. Bodney 1768-70. Rixton and Southworth 1770-3. ?Stonyhurst 1773. Rixton 1774-83 (supplying Leigh, Slatedelf, Dutton). Manchester 1784. d. December 11th, 1799, Manchester. (Fo.7; CRS.69; 114; 91; 113; SCH.12/16; 21 v.2; 23 f.245; 26 f.201; 80; 41 nn.25, 52, 80, 86, 101; 65. 76 ff.46, 53; 68 pp.78, 161; 25 ff.7, 11, 13, 22, 28, 34, 40, 45, 49, 56, 76, 113; 155 II 129; 155 III 185c; 54 f.15; Nec).

NEEDHAM, Daniel *alias* Platt. Priest.

b. June 24th, 1721, Lancashire. e. St Omers College 1738-41. S.J. September 7th, 1741. Liège (phil) 1743, 1744. Munster (theol) 1746-9. Ordained priest 1749. Lynn 1749. College of St Aloysius 1750. College of the Holy Apostles 1751-5 (?Thelton 1753). Lincoln 1755. Residence of St George 1756-8, 1763-7 (?Worcester 1756-66. Aldenham 1767. Superior of Residence of St George 1763-c.67). Ellingham 1767-9. Wealside c.1769-80. ?Worcester 1780-3. d. May 21st, 1783, Worcester. (Fo.7; CRS.69; 114; 91; 113; ER.5/37, 9/111; WR.11/18, 20/70; 6 ff.242, 276; 21 v.2; 38 f.197; 41 n.73; 50 f.138; 43 f.78v; 64 p.525; 65; 68

p.94; HMC. 10th Report App.4/192; 194; 188 n.97; Nec).

NEEDHAM, Sebastian *alias* Morgan, Robert. Priest.

b.1671, 1673 or 1674, Hilston, Monmouthshire. s. of Robert and Susan (Morgan) of Upper Hilston. e. St Omers College c.1691. S.J. September 7th, or October 2nd, 1691. Paris (nov) 1693. Liège (phil) 1696. Liège (theol) 1697, 1699-1701. Ordained priest 1700. In England 1701. Leigh c.1701. College of St Aloysius 1704-7 (?Ince 1705, 1707). Southworth 1708-c.16. College of St Aloysius 1718. College of St Ignatius 1720, 1723-5. In England 1726. College of St Ignatius 1727-9, 1733-43 (Rector 1736-?43). d. January 4th, 1743, London. (Fo.7; CRS.69; 114; 113; LR.2/21, 3/5, 3/8; 150 III(2) 7/1/36; 12 f.124; 23 f.35v; NB.1/91, 128; 91; HMC. 10th Report App.4/192; E and P.185-6, 339, 356; CRS.13/398; Nec).

NEIL see O'Neill, John and William.

NELSON see O'Neil, William: Newton, James.

NELSON, Francis. Priest.

b.1632 or 1633, Brussels. S.J. February 12th, 1650. Liège (phil) 1652-5. Liège (theol) 1656-9. Ordained priest March 27th, 1660. Watten 1660, 1661 (tert). Liège 1663-5. St Omers College 1667, 1669-70. Twickenham 1671. College of Ignatius 1672. Brussels 1673-5. d. August 28th, 1675, Brussels. (Fo.7; 114; 113; ER.13/44; 150 II(2) 20/12/59, 23/3/69, 5/7/70; 108; Nec).

NEVILLE see Matthews, Peter; Scarisbrick, Edward (1), (2) and (3), Francis (1) and (2), Henry (1) and (2), Joseph or Thomas Joseph and Thomas.

NEVILLE, Charles *alias* Dillon. Priest.

b. April 8th, 1746. s. of Cosmas Henry and Lady Mary (Lee) of Holt, Leicestershire. e. St Omers and Bruges Colleges 1758-63. S.J. September 7th, 1763. Watten (nov) 1763, 1764. Liège (theol) 1767-9, 1771. Ordained priest c.1771. Liège 1772-5. To England 1775. ?Liège 1782. d. April 4th, 1792, Bristol. bu. St Joseph's, Bristol. (Fo.7; CRS.69; 114; 113; 7 f.102v; 51 ff.155v, 304, 306v; 53 f.2; 23 f.270; Ki.173; CRS.8/393; 125; Nec. For writings see Som.).

NEWPORT see Keynes, Charles and Maximilian.

NEWSHAM, Joseph. Priest.

b. May 16th, 1781, Westby, Lancashire. S.J. September 7th, 1813. Hodder (nov) 1813-5. Stonyhurst (theol) 1815-9. Ordained priest July 3rd, 1819, Dublin. Wigan 1819-29. Portico 1829-32. Stonyhurst 1832-49. d. February 8th, 1849, Stonyhurst. bu. Stonyhurst. (Fo.7; 115; 13 f.502v; 28 f.196v; Nec).

NEWSHAM, Robert. Priest.

b. June 19th, 1783, Westby, Lancashire. s. of John and Elizabeth (Boothe). e. Stonyhurst 1798-1803. S.J. September 26th, 1803. Hodder (nov) 1803-5. Stonyhurst (phil, theol, etc.) 1805-18. Ordained priest February 16th, 1808, Wolverhampton. Oxford 1818-30. St Mary's Hall (tert) 1830. Left 1832. (2; 115; 150 (1750-1753) f.196; 6 f.223v; 8 II n.122; 55 ff.147, 198, 225; 93 p.74; Gil.5/176; CRS.7/392, 409-31).

NEWTON, Edward John Baptist. Priest.

b. March 9th, 1720 or 1721, Lincolnshire. s. of Baptist Braylsford and Elizabeth (Messenger) of Irnham. br. of William (2). e. St Omers College 1732-7. S.J. September 7th, 1737. Watten (nov) 1737, 1738. Liège (phil) 1739-41. Wurzburg (theol) 1743, 1744. Molsheim (theol) 1746. Ordained priest c.1746. Liège 1747-9. Travelling 1750, 1752, 1753. College of the Holy Apostles 1754, 1755. St Omers College 1756. Travelling 1757, 1758. Antwerp 1759-75. Liège Academy 1776. Coldham 1784-?8. d. April 29th, 1788, Bury St Edmunds. bu. St Mary's churchyard, Bury. (Fo.7; CRS.69; 91; 114; 113; SCH.12/23; LR.8/7; ER.19/107; 7 ff.131, 151v; 90 f.54; 15 f.16v; 54 ff.34v, 74, 90, 116; 51 f.145v; 56 f.334v; CRS.12/29; 97; 108; 111; OSBB.199; Nec. For writings see Som.).

NEWTON, James *alias* or *vere* Nelson. Priest.

b. June 10th or 16th, 1736, London. e. St Omers College c.1746-54. S.J. September 7th, 1754. Watten (nov) 1755. Liège (phil) 1756-8. ?Liège (theol) 1761. Ordained priest c.1763. Hoogstraet 1764. Richmond, Yorkshire 1765-c.7. Liverpool c.1767-70. College of St Aloysius 1771. Liverpool 1772, 1773-? London 1777-85. Antwerp 1785. Bristol 1800-03. d. April 2nd, 1803, Bristol. bu. St Joseph's churchyard, Bristol. (Fo.7; CRS.69; 91; 117; 113; LR.3/5; 4 f.106v; 48 f.35v; 64 p.318; 65; 68 pp.132, 153, 372; 69; 72; 73; 75 p.133v; 80; 90 f.186; Pa.2/63; 155 III 185c; CRS.3/322; 119 ff.30, 35, 38; Nec).

NEWTON, William (1) *alias* Braylsford. Priest.

b. November 14th, 1683 or 1684, Lincolnshire. s. of John and Elizabeth (Braylsford) of Irnham. e. St Omers College 1696-1702. S.J. September 7th, 1702. Watten (nov) 1703, 1704. Liège (phil) 1705, 1706. Liège (theol) 1708-11. Ordained priest c.1712. Ghent (tert) 1712, 1713. Watten 1714-6, 1718, 1720, 1723-8, 1730. Paris 1730, 1732-5. Travelling 1736, 1737. College of St Ignatius 1738-41, 1743-5. St Omers College 1745-50, 1752-6. d. February 5th, 1756, St Omers College. (Fo.7; CRS.69; 114; 91; 113; CRS.63/98; 64 p.82; 74; 81; 120; 111; Nec).

NEWTON, William (2). Priest.

b. October 30th, 1718, Lincolnshire. s. of Baptist Braylsford and Elizabeth (Messenger) of Irnham. br. of Edward John Baptist. e. St Omers College ?-1736. S.J. September 7th, 1736. Watten (nov) 1736, 1737. Liège (phil) 1738-40. Liège (theol) 1741. Cologne (theol) 1743, 1744. Ordained priest c.1744. In England 1746. ?Rixton 1747. Loretto 1747, 1748. College of St Thomas of Canterbury 1749. Travelling 1750. Rixton 1750, 1751. Biddleston 1751, 1752. Residence of St George 1752. Residence of St Mary 1753-5. d. October 16th or 19th, 1755, Tusmore. (Fo.7; CRS.69; 91; 114; 113; LR.1/118; 21 v.2; 23 f.69; 24 f.36; 35 f.41v; 64 pp. 57, 58, 428, 429; 68 p.185; 85; 36 f.137; CRS.7/396; CRS.14/251; 109; 156 Appl.1; Nec).

NICHOLS, James. Scholastic or Laybrother.

d. date and place unknown. (Fo.7; 114).

?NICOLAS, John. Priest.

b. c.1740. ?S.J. in France. Liège Academy 1781, 1783. Left in charge of the Liège property, 1794. d.1824. (Fo.7; 3 ff.37, 51; 15 f.45; SM.35/120ff, 190ff, 237ff; Nec).

NICOLSON, James. Scholastic.

b.1783. S.J. September 26th, 1755. Watten (nov) 1756, 1757. Liège (phil) 1758. No further information recorded. (Fo.7; 113; 91; 111).

NIHILL or NIHELL, Edward. Priest.

b. January 18th, 1752, Antigua, West Indies. br. of John. e. Bruges College 1763-c.9. S.J. September 7th, 1769. Ghent (nov) 1771. Liège (phil) 1772, 1773. Bruges College 1773. Liège (theol) 1773. Liège Academy 1774, 1776. Ordained priest 1776. London 1782, 1786, 1787. Wardour 1788-1802. Trinidad 1802-?6. d. November 4th, 1806, Trinidad. (Fo.7; CRS.69; 114; 91; 113; 90 ff.54, 167; CRS.43/125; CRS.Mon.1/162; LR.3/5; 13 ff.203, 280; 16 f.98; 21 v.2; 54 f.246v; 57 II f.74v; CRS.19/388; 173 (1782); 01.364; 6 f.7; 51 f.306; 3 f.149; 166 II p.93; 34 f.15v; Nec).

NIHILL or NIHELL, John. ?Priest.

b. June 24th, 1750, Antigua, West Indies. br. of Edward. e. Bruges College 1763-c.8. S.J. September 7th, 1768. Watten (nov) 1769. Liège (phil) 1771-3. Liège (theol) 1773. Liège Academy 1774, 1775. To West Indies 1775. ?Ordained priest. Date and place of death not recorded. (Fo.7; CRS.69; 91; AHSJ.42/293; Hu.Text 2/704; 54 f.37v; 113; 51 ff.304, 306; Chad.363).

NIXON, Edward or Edmund *alias* Poynz or Poyntz or Poins or Poines. Priest.

b. March 10th, 1675, London. e. St Omers College ?-1694. S.J. September 7th, 1694. Watten (nov) 1696. Liège (phil) 1697. Liège (theol) 1699-1701, 1703. Ordained priest 1703. Ghent 1704. ?Stapehill 1704-6. Residence of St Michael 1706. Crosby 1706-7. ?Ince 1707. College of St Aloysius 1708-10. Residence of St Michael 1711. Ghent 1712-6, 1718, 1720-22. Watten 1723-8. d. September 11th, 1728, Watten. (Fo.7; CRS.69; 114; 91; 113; CRS.43/126; 150 III(2) 7/6/21, 18/4/22; NB.1/123, 129, 144; Nec).

NIXON, Thomas. Priest.

b. October 6th, 1735, Lancashire. s. of Cuthbert and Helen (Baines). e. St Omers College ?-1750. E.C. Rome November 14th, 1750-August 18th, 1756. S.J. October 9th, 1756. Watten (nov) 1756-8. Liège (theol) 1759, 1761. Ordained priest c.1761. Ghent 1761. York c.1763-84. Haggerston 1785, 1786. ?Berrington 1787, 1788. Served Berwick 1787, 1788. Alnwick 1790-3. d. November 5th, 1793, Alnwick. bu. Alnwick. (Fo.7; CRS.69; 114; 91; 113; CRS.40/207-8; CRS.Mon.2/389; 21 v.2; 35 ff.65v, 235, 236, 247, 257, 259, 262; 41 n.66; 36 ff.86v, 261; 65; 117; 167 p.38; 25 ff.17, 22; 155 II 127; CRS.4/254; Ki.173; CRS.12/44; 119 f.6; Nec).

NOEL, Martin. Laybrother.

b. 1685. S.J. August 14th, 1717. Watten (nov) 1718. Liège 1720. d.

March 17th, 1720, Liège; (Fo.7; 114; 113; Nec).

NORRICE see Norris, Andrew and John.

NORRIS see Tucker, James.

NORRIS or NORRICE, Andrew *alias* Baines. Priest.

b.1654, Lancashire. s. of John and Eleanor (Beauvoyr) of Speke,
Lancashire. br. of Charles and Richard (1). e. St Omers College
1669-73. E.C. Rome October 3rd, 1673-76. S.J. July 30th, 1676, in
Rome or Naples. Rome 1683-5. Ordained priest c.1685. Residence of St
Michael 1686, 1687. College of St Hugh (?Lincoln) 1688. In prison
1689. College of St Hugh 1690-3, 1696-1711 (Rector 1697-1708).
Residence of St John 1712-4. Rome 1715, 1716. College of St Hugh
1716, 1718-22 (Rector 1718-22). d. January 26th, 1722 in England.
(Fo.7; CRS.69; 114; 113; NB.2/134; CRS.40/86-7; 123 II f.131;
CRS.62/295, 297; Nec).

NORRIS, Charles. Priest.

b. March 5th, 1646, Speke, Lancashire. s. of John and Eleanor
(Beauvoyr) of Speke. br. of Andrew and Richard (1). ?e St Omers
College ?-1663. E.C. Rome October 16th, 1663-5-? Ordained priest
June 15th, 1670, in Rome. S.J. May 13th, 1682. Watten (nov) 1682.
Liège 1683-5. Watten 1685. College of St Ignatius 1686, 1687. In
England 1688. Watten 1689. d. June 10th, 1690. Watten. (Fo.7;
CRS.69; 113; Ans.3/155; CRS.40/69; 168 f.42; 135 ff.175-6;
CRS.55/599; Nec).

NORRIS, John (1). Scholastic.

b.1656, Lancashire. e. St Omers College ?-1673. S.J. September 7th,
1673. Watten (nov) 1673-5. Liège 1676. d. June 15th, 1676, Liege, not
ordained. (Fo.7; CRS.69; 113; 114; Nec).

NORRIS or NORRICE, John (2). Priest.

b. February 10th, 1671 or April 4th, 1672, London. s. of Andrew and
Charity. E.C. Rome October 18th, 1691-April 5th, 1692. S.J. April
5th, 1692, in Rome. Rome (nov) 1693. Rome (phil, theol etc.) 1696-7,
1699-1701, 1703-6, 1708-9. Ordained priest c.1706. Liège 1710-2. St
Omers College 1713-5. Ghent 1715-9 (Rector). Travelling 1720. Burton
Park 1722-31 (Rector of the College of St Thomas of Canterbury
1725-c.28). E.C. Rome 1733-8. Gifford's Hall 1739, 1740. Slindon
1740-54. d. May 10th, 1754, in England (?Burton, ?Kelvedon,
?Slindon). (Fo.7; 114; 91; 113; CRS.40/111; CRS.62/300; RH.13/116;
150 III(1) 3/11/08, 9/3/15; 150 III(2) 6/2/34, 8/3/38; 43 f.62v; 89;
HMC. 10th Report App.4/192; Bur.1 facing p.148; Ki.173;
CRS.22/307, 312-5; 44 f.207; Nec).

NORRIS, John (3). Novice.

b. August 12th, 1726. e. St Omers College 1744-9. S.J. 1749. Watten
(nov) 1750. d. February 22nd, 1751, St Omers College. (Fo.7; CRS.69;
114; 91; 113; Nec).

NORRIS, Richard (1). Priest.

b. 1658, Lancashire. s. of John and Eleanor (Beauvoyr) of Speke,
Lancashire. br. of Andrew and Charles. e. St Omers College ?-1677.

E.C. Rome October 6th, 1677-November 9th, 1680. S.J. November 9th, 1680, in Naples. Naples (nov) 1682. Naples 1683, 1684. Milan 1685, 1686. Ordained priest c.1686. Residence of St Stanislaus 1687, 1689-1715 (Superior 1696-c.1708, 1714-5. ?Exeter c.1688-?). College of St Thomas of Canterbury 1715. Kelvedon 1716-7. d. June 21st, 1717 in England. (Fo.7; CRS.69; 114; 113; ER.5/95, 9/109; 43 f.35v; 89; CRS.40/93; 01.366; 123 IIIB ff.291-3; Nec).

NORRIS, Richard (2). Priest.
    b. April 13th, 1792, Martinscroft, near Warrington, Lancashire. e. Stonyhurst 1802-9. S.J. September 7th, 1809. Hodder (nov) 1809-11. Stonyhurst (phil and theol) 1811-6. Ordained priest December 2nd, 1816, Wolverhampton. Stockeld Park 1816-7. Stonyhurst 1817-9. Wigan 1819-22. Worcester 1822-4. Pylewell 1824. Worcester 1824-6. Stonyhurst 1826-32 (Rector 1829-32). Provincial 1832-8. St Mary's Hall 1838-42 (Superior). Stonyhurst 1842-3. Preston 1843-5 (Rector of the College of St Aloysius 1844-5). Stonyhurst 1845-6 (Rector). d. May 5th, 1846, Worcester. bu. Worcester chapel burial ground. (Fo.7; 115; WR.20/70; CRW.56ff; 94 ff.5-6; Nec. For writings see Som. and Sut.).

NUGENT see Bermingham, William.

OAKLEY, Francis *alias* Auckland. Priest.
    b. August 3rd, 1694, Worcestershire. ?s. of Thomas of Brailes, Warwickshire. e. St Omers College 1714 or earlier-15. S.J. September 7th, 1715. Watten (nov) 1716. Liège (phil) 1718, 1720. St Omers College 1723-6. La Flèche 1726. Liège (theol) 1727, 1728. Ordained priest c.1729. Ghent 1730. Watten 1732-40. Danby c.1741-55 (Superior of the Residence of St Michael 1746-55). d. July 12th, 1755, ?Danby. (Fo.7; CRS.69; 114; 91; 113; 9 n.259; 90 f.175v; HMC. 10th Report App.4/192; Pa.2/28; CRS.13/229, 236; 174; 140 n.45; CRS.62 index; 156 App.1; Nec).

O'BRIEN or BRIAN, John. Priest.
    b. February 29th, 1796, Enniscorthy, Wexford, Ireland. e. Stonyhurst 1821-7. S.J. September 30th, 1827. Montrouge, France (nov) 1827. Hodder (nov) 1828-30. St Mary's Hall (theol) 1830-2. Ordained priest September 22nd, 1832, Stonyhurst. Lincoln 1833-40. Spinkhill 1840-2. Portico 1842. St Mary's Hall 1842-3. Stonyhurst 1843-54. d. December 19th, 1854, Stonyhurst. bu. Stonyhurst. (Fo.7; 115; 50 f.27; Nec).

O'BRIEN or BRIAN or BRIANT, Peter. Priest.
    b. March 28th, 1735, Ireland. e. St Omers College ?-1754. S.J. September 7th, 1754. Watten (nov) 1755. (phil before entering S.J.) Liège (theol) 1756-8. Ordained priest c.1759. Ghent 1760. Liverpool 1760-4. Antigua 1766-?c.71. College of St Ignatius 1772. Antigua 1772-1800. Bristol 1800. New Hall 1800-07. Readm. S.J. 1803. d. February 28th or March 5th, 1807, New Hall. bu. New Hall. (Fo.7; 113;

CRS.69; LR.1/84, 3/5; ER.5/96; AHSJ.37/164; 3 f.149v; 13 ff.264, 278v, 284; 21 v.2; 65; 68 p.121; 86; CRS.9/186; CRS.17/91, 155; 173; 110; 91; NewH. p.126; 119 ff.11, 16, 21, 25; 150 (1750-1853) f.56v; Nec).

O'BRIEN, William. Priest.

b. August 15th, 1795 or 1796, Dublin. S.J. September 9th, 1814, in Ireland. Hodder (nov) 1814-6. To the English province c.1843. Boston 1844-5. Ackworth 1845-6. Pylewell 1846-51. d. October 1st, 1851, Pylewell. (Fo.7; 115; 113; CRS.14/298; 116; Nec).

O'CARROLL, Richard. Priest.

b. July 14th, 1807, Dublin. e. Stonyhurst 1821-5. S.J. September 18th, 1825. Chieri (nov) 1825-7. Dôle (phil) 1827-8. Aix (phil) 1828-9. Stonyhurst (theol) 1829. St Mary's Hall (theol) 1830-2. Stonyhurst 1832-4. Ordained priest December 20th, 1834, Stonyhurst. St Mary's Hall 1834-8 (supplied at Worcester 1835). Stonyhurst 1838-41. St Mary's Hall 1841-2. Holywell 1842-3. St Mary's Hall 1844-9. Liverpool 1849-58. d. February 14th, 1858, Liverpool. bu. Gillmoss. (Fo.7; 115; CRW.67. Nec).

OLDCROFT see Holcroft.

OLIVER, Charles. Priest.

d. January 4th, 1683, Urgel, Spain. The name is not found in the catalogues of the English province. (Fo.7; 95; Nec).

O'NEILL or O'NEALE, James *alias* Gore, William.

b. c. April, 1644, London. s. of Hugh. E.C. Rome January 18th, 1667. d. June 15th, 1667, Rome. Adm. S.J. *in articulo mortis.* (Fo.7; CRS.40/73-4; CRS.55/611-2; Nec).

O'NEILL or NEIL, John *alias* Gradell or Gradwell. Priest.

b. June 11th, 1716, St Germain. ?s. of John and Elizabeth (Gradell or Gradwell). ?br. of William. e. St Omers College 1726-33. E.C. Valladolid 1733-9. Ordained priest c.1739. S.J. September 9th, 1740. Watten (nov) 1741. Residence of St Stanislaus 1743-4, 1746-58 (Trevithick 1751). d. January 6th, 1760, in England. (Fo.7; 91; 113; CRS.30/188; CRS.19/158; HMC. 10th Report App.4/188; 01.315; 140 n.45; Nec).

O'NEILL, Stephen. Laybrother.

b. ?May, 1765, Ireland. S.J. September 26th, 1803. Hodder (nov) 1803-5. Stonyhurst 1807, 1810, 1815, 1820, 1825. d. July 18th, 1826, Stonyhurst. bu. Stonyhurst. (Fo.7; 113; CDSJ.; 94 f.36; 116; Nec).

O'NEILL or NEIL, William *alias* Nelson. Priest.

b. April 20th, 1714, St Germain. ?s. of John and Elizabeth (Gradell or Gradwell). ?br. of John. S.J. September 7th, 1732. Watten (nov) 1733, 1734. Liège (phil) 1734-6. Liège (theol) 1737-40. Ordained priest c.1739. Hoogstraet 1743. St Germain 1744. Residence of St Michael 1746-50, 1752-8, 1763-4 (Sutton 1749. ?Richmond. Pontefract 1753). Watten 1767. Ghent 1768. Waterperry 1768-70. d. July 10th or 11th, 1770, Waterperry. bu. Waterperry church. (Fo.7; 114; 91; 113; 48 f.416; 65; 68 p.191; 158; 156 App.1; CRS.7/397; Nec).

O'REILLY, Philip Joseph. Priest.
b. November or December 10th, 1719, Ardeath, County Meath, Ireland. s. of Patrick and Mary (O'Reilly). e. Lierre and Ghent. S.J. September 26th, 1741 in Belgium. West Indies and French Guyane 1751-c.65. Philadelphia 1767-9. Ireland 1769. d. February 24th, 1775, Dublin. (Fo.7 and Irish section; AHSJ.9/208 ff; 113; Hu. Text 2/600 n.6, 694; L and N.XI pp.289 ff. For writings see Som.).
ORMES, Christopher or Henry see Challoner, Henry.
OSBALDESTON or OSBASTON or OSBESTON or OSBOSTON, John. Priest.
b.1655, Lancashire. S.J. September 7th, 1674. Watten (nov) 1674, 1675. Liège (phil) 1676, 1678. Liège (theol) 1679-82. Ordained priest March 13th, 1683. Ghent (tert) 1683. College of St Aloysius 1684-7, 1689-90. d. December 22nd, 1690, in England. (Fo.7; 114; 113; Nec).
OSWALD, Anthony. Laybrother.
b. October 24th, 1723, Switzerland, S.J. December 20th, 1751. Watten (nov) 1752, 1753. St Omers College 1754, 1755. E.C. Rome 1756-8, 1761, 1763. Paris 1764. Antwerp 1767-9. Ghent 1769, 1771-4, 1797. d.1799, Hamburg. (Fo.7; 113; AHSJ 42/295; 91; 15 f.12; 16f. 22v; 108; OSBG.79; 117; Nec).
OWENS, John. Laybrother.
b. in Wales. S.J. in Rome. E.C. Rome 1711-6, 1720, 1724-8. d. March 1st, 1728, Rome. (Fo.7; 113; 91; Nec).

PADBURY, Thomas. Laybrother.
b. August 5th or 9th, 1714, Oxfordshire. S.J. July 18th, 1754. Watten (nov) 1755. Watten 1756-8. St Omers College 1761-4. Bruges College 1767-9, 1771-3. Bruges 1773-92. d. March 1792, Bruges. (Fo.7; 91; 113; AHSJ.42/295; 117; Chad.304; CRS.12/37; 23 f.270; Nec).
PAINE or PAYNE, John. Laybrother.
b. April 5th, 1661, Warwickshire. S.J. September 7th, 1698. Watten (nov) 1699. Watten 1700-01, 1703-6, 1708-12. St Omers College 1713. Antwerp 1713-c.26. Liège 1726-8, 1730, 1733-8. d. June 13th, 1738, Liège. (Fo.7; 114; 91; 113; 108; Nec).
PAINS or PAINE, James Philip. Priest.
b. April 30th, 1767, Noards, Normandy, France. s. of Peter and Mary (Feret). S.J. June 28th, 1808. Hodder (nov) 1808-9. Stonyhurst (theol) 1809-13. Ordained priest 1810, Stonyhurst. Served Clitheroe 1810-13. St Helens 1813-31. Hodder (tert) 1831. St Helens 1831-4. d. September 4th, 1834, St Helens. bu. Windleshaw. (Fo.7; 113; 115; 93 p.76; 116; Nec).
PALMER see Poulton, Giles, Henry, John and Thomas (1).
PALMER, George. Priest.
b. November 10th, 1692, London. S.J. September 7th, 1713. Watten (nov) 1714. Liège (phil) 1715, 1716, 1718. Liège (theol) 1720. Ordained

priest c.1722. St Omers College 1723, 1724. Ireland 1724. College of St
Aloysius 1725. In England 1726. Eccleston 1727-c.29. Slatedelf,
Brindle, Wheelton 1729-c.43. Eccleston 1743-56. d. January 13th,
1758, Eccleston. bu. Prescot church. (Fo.7; 114; 91; 113; 21v.2; 13
f.24v; 24 ff.5v, 347v; 27 ff.202-3; 29 f.93; 85; 86; HMC. 10th Report
App.4/192; CRS.4/434; CRS.23/6; CRS.25/114; 158; 119 f.16; 23
f.90; 28 ff.9, 14, 51, 148-9; 156 App.1; Nec).

PANTING, John. Priest.
b. November 26th, 1732, London. e. St Omers College c.1743-9. S.J.
September 7th, 1749. Watten (nov) 1750. Liège (phil) 1752-4. Liège
(theol) 1755-7. Ordained priest April 17th, 1757, Liège. Watten School
1758. Watten 1761, 1763-5. Bruges 1766. Bonham 1767-9, 1772-83. d.
May 30th, 1783, Bonham. bu. Stourton church. (Fo.7; CRS.69; 91;
113; CRS.Mon.1/148n, 173; 13 f.90; 34 f.145; 44 ff.46, 87, 229v, 246v;
65; HMC. 10th Report App.4/192; Chad.332-3; 125; 111; 126; 51
f.142; 201 pp. 795-8; CRS.14/168; Nec. For writings see Som. Gil.).

PARDOW, Gregory. Scholastic.
b. November 9th, 1804, near Alcester, Warwickshire. e. Stonyhurst
1817-? S.J. October 6th, 1823, in Rome. Rome (nov) 1823-5. Rome
(phil) 1825. Fribourg (phil) 1826. Hodder 1827. Stonyhurst (phil) 1827.
Left June 23rd, 1828, not ordained. (115; Stol; 113; 2).

PARKER see Buck, John; Culcheth, Charles, James, Thomas (1) and
William; Thompson, Charles.

PARKER, James (1). Scholastic or Laybrother.
d. in England, date and place unknown. No further information
found. (Fo.7; 114).

PARKER, James (2). Priest.
b. April 3rd, 1747, Liverpool. s. of John. e. St Omers and Bruges
Colleges c.1758-63. E.C. Valladolid 1763-6. S.J. September 7th, 1766.
Ghent (nov) 1767. Liège (theol) 1768-9, 1771. Ordained priest c.1771.
Ghent 1772, 1773. Spetchley 1777. ?Canford 1781. St Giles Camborne,
Dorset 1787, 1788, 1791, 1796, 1801. (?Worcester 1795, 1798-9,
1800-2). Bristol ?1803, 1807, 1809, 1810, 1812, 1814-6, 1820. Liverpool
1820-2. d. October 29th, 1822, Liverpool. bu. Sefton. (Fo.7; 114;
CRS.69; 113; CRS.42/138; 142; CRS.65/216; CRS.Mon.1/166n; 32
ff.161 ff; 34 f.109v;38 ff.35v, 43v, 81v, 108, 128v, 144v, 207; 54 ff.51v,
234; 39 ff.12v, 234A; 55 ff.69v, 255v, 257v; 61; 76 f.143; 69; 25 ff.16,
31; RH.15/297; 72; 80; 89; CRS.30/190, 192; 01.373; 107; 119 f.41;
Nec).

PARKER, Richard (1). Laybrother.
b. March 27th, 1691, Lancashire. S.J. September 7th, 1723. Watten
(nov) 1724. Liège 1724-8, 1730, 1733-42. d. April 15th, 1742, Liège.
(Fo.7; 114; 91; 113; Nec).

PARKER, Richard (2). Priest.
b. July 23rd. 1791, Preston. e. Sedgley Park 1802-4, Stonyhurst
1804-10. S.J. September 7th, 1810. Hodder (nov) 1810-12. Stonyhurst
(phil) 1812-7. Stonyhurst (theol) 1817-20. Ordained priest December

1819, Dublin. Wardour 1820-32. St Mary's Hall (tert) 1832. Wardour
1832. Stonyhurst 1832-6. d. September 3rd, 1836, Chorley, Lancashire.
bu. Stonyhurst. (Fo.7; 115; 7 f.413; SCH.3/23; Nec).
PARKER, Thomas *alias* or *vere* Burchard. Priest.
    b. November 19th, 1739, Lancashire. s. of Thomas and Betty of
Kirkby, Walton-on-the-Hill, Lancashire. e. St Omers College c.1755-6.
E.C. Valladolid October 24th, 1756-April 6th, 1763. Ordained priest
c.1763. S.J. June 6th, 1763. Bruges (nov) 1764. Waterperry 1765.
Residence of St Mary 1767. Kirkby 1767. Waterperry 1768, 1769.
Fowey 1769. Residence of St Stanislaus 1771. Fowey 1772, 1773.
?Puddington 1775. Weston 1778-c.83. Beoley and Heath Green
c.1783-1820. d. October 26th, 1820, Heath Green. (Fo.7; CRS.69; 91;
114; 113; Ans.4/202; SCH.15/28; WR.5/15, 7/13 ff,20/62, 23/40; 3
f.33v; 38 f.71; 65; 68 pp.75, 189; 69; 25 f.31; 72; CRS.30/190; 117;
CRS. OP.1/49; Nec).
PARKINSON, Richard. Priest.
    b. April 11th, 1681, Yorkshire. s. of William and Alicia. e. St Omers
College ?-1699. E.C. Rome August 23rd, 1699-January 24th, 1704. S.J.
January 24th, 1704, in Rome. In Rome till 1714 and ordained priest
there. Liège 1715-6, 1718. Liège (O.S.B. monastery of St Lawrence)
1720, 1723, 1724. College of St Ignatius 1725. In England 1726-8, 1730.
College of St Ignatius 1733-7. College of St Aloysius 1738-40 (Hopcar
1740). College of the Holy Apostles 1740-8 (Cranham Park 1742-8). d.
July 27th, 1748, Ghent. (Fo.7; CRS.69; 114; 113; CRS.40/125;
ER.4/120, 9/103; 150 III(1)7/10/1719; 85; 91; Bur.1/209; Ki.176-7; 43
ff.65, 69, 71, 75, 77; Nec. For writings see Som.).
PARRY see Conway, William (1); Rogè, Joseph.
PARRY, Edward. Scholastic.
    b. July 4th or 30th, 1684, Denbighshire or Shropshire. e. St Omers
College 1700-02 or later. S.J. October 31st, 1704. Watten (nov) 1705,
1706. Liège (phil) 1708, 1709. Liège (theol) 1710. Ghent 1711. d.
December 29th, 1711, in England, not ordained. (Fo.7; CRS.69; 114;
113; 150 III(1) 31/1/1711; 169/6; Nec).
PARRY, George. Scholastic or Laybrother.
    d. date and place not recorded. (Fo.7; 114; Nec).
PARRY, John. ?Scholastic.
    b. August 20th, 1718, Denbighshire. e. St Omers College 1732-7. S.J.
September 7th, 1737. Watten (nov) 1738, 1739. Left 1739; it is unlikely
that he completed the noviceship. (Fo.7; CRS.69; 91; 113; 150
III(2)29/8/39, 7/11/39).
PARSONS or PERSONS, Robert. Priest.
    b.1648, Suffolk or Norfolk. e. St Omers College 1659-65. S.J.
September 7th, 1665. Liège (phil) 1667, 1669. St Omers College 1672,
1673. Rome 1674. Ordained priest c.1678. St Omers College 1679-80. d.
August 8th, 1680, St Omers College. (Fo.7; CRS.69; 114; 113; 168 f.75;
Nec).
PATER, Joseph. Priest.

b. January 8th, 1798, Liverpool. e. Stonyhurst 1812-8. S.J.
September 7th, 1818. Hodder (nov) 1818-20. Stonyhurst (phil) 1820-22.
St Acheul (theol) 1822-3. Brig (theol) 1823-4. Ordained priest April
11th, 1824, Sion. Stonyhurst 1824-6. Enfield, Lancashire 1826-31. St
Mary's Hall 1835-7. Stonyhurst 1837-8. St Helens 1838-9. St Mary's
Hall or Stonyhurst 1839-61. d. May 11th, 1861, Stonyhurst. bu.
Stonyhurst. (Fo.7; 115; CRS.36/218, 273-9; Nec).

PATOUILLET, Nicholas. Priest.
S.J. in France. Portuguese chapel, London 1672-3. Returned to
France. (113; 150 II(2) 3/9/72, 3/6/73; 108).

PAUCHET or POECHET or POCHET, Francis. Laybrother.
b. October 9th or 10th, 1699, Flanders. S.J. October 9th or 30th,
1729. Watten (nov) 1730. Watten 1733-43. d. May 8th, 1743, Watten.
(Fo.7; 114; 113; 91; Nec).

PAUL, Peter. Laybrother.
b. February 15th, 1660, Antwerp. S.J. December 15th, 1688-9 and
February 2nd, 1691. Watten (nov) 1691. St Omers College 1693.
Watten 1696-7, 1699-1701. St Omers College 1703, 1704. Watten
1705-6, 1708. St Omers College 1709-16, 1718, 1720. d. February 21st,
1722, St Omers College. (113; 114; 140 n.45; CRS.62/237, 271, 288).

PAYNE, Henry, ?Laybrother.
At Antwerp 1689. No further information found. May be an *alias*.
(113).

PAYNE see Paine, John.

PEAKE, Robert *alias* Kendrick or Kenderick. Scholastic.
b. August 24th, 1673. e. St Omers College c.1693. S.J. September
7th, 1693. Liège (phil) 1696, 1697. Liège (theol) 1699-1701. Left 1701,
not ordained. (113; CRS.69; 150 III(1) 20/5/1701).

PEARCE, Francis *alias* or *vere* West. Scholastic.
b. 1722, Cornwall. e. St Omers College ?-1742. S.J. September 7th,
1742. Watten (nov) 1743. Liège (phil) 1744. d. August 2nd, 1746, Liège,
not ordained. (Fo.7; CRS.69; 140 n.45; 113; 114; Nec).

PEARCE, James *alias* Chamberlain. Priest.
b. January 25th, 1692, Somerset. e. St Omers College ?-1713. S.J.
September 7th, 1713-27. Watten (nov) 1714. Liège (phil) 1715, 1716.
Liège (theol) 1718, 1720. Ordained priest c.1720, Liège. Maryland
1722-4. Residence of St George 1725. In England 1726, 1727. (Fo.7;
CRS.69; 91; 113; 150 III(2) 5/8/24, 25/8/25, 15/3/27; Hu.Text 2/687).

PEARCE or PEARSE, John or Edward see Hayman, Richard.

PEARSON or PIERSON, Thomas. Priest.
b.1646, Yorkshire or County Durham. S.J. September 7th, 1667.
Watten (nov) 1669. Liège (theol) 1672-4. Ordained priest December
2nd, 1764. Residence of St John 1675, 1676, 1678. Liège (theol) 1679.
Watten (tert) 1680-4. Residence of St John 1684-93, 1696-8 (Superior
1685-90. Durham ?1685-98). Watten 1699-1701, 1703-6. Residence of
St John 1708-16, 1720, 1724-5. In England 1726-8, 1730 (Durham
?1708-32). d. February 4th, 1732, Durham. bu. St Oswald's, Durham.

(Fo.7; 113; CRS.62/17; NCH.4/11; 21 v.2; 36 f.261; 91; Sur.180/46; 123 II f.170; Nec).

PECKET, Robert. Laybrother.

b.1640, Lancashire. S.J. September 8th, 1675, in Rome. Rome 1683-7, 1689, 1691-3, 1696-7, 1699-1701, 1703-6. d. January 8th, 1706, Rome. (Fo.7;113; 114; Nec).

PELCOM or PELCON or PERCOM, Peter *alias* Manners, Barton? and Catwell. Priest.

b.1631, 1632 or 1633, London. s. of Daniel and Catherine (Peters). e. Amsterdam. E.C. Rome April 12th, 1654-May 23rd, 1656. S.J. 1656. Watten (nov) 1657. Liège (phil) 1658-60. Liège (theol) 1661, 1663. Ordained priest c.1663. Watten 1663, 1664. Ghent (tert) 1664, 1665. Maryland 1667, 1669. d. April 24th, 1669, Maryland. (Fo.7; 114; 113; Hu.Text 2/680-1; CRS.40/54; CRS.55/545; Nec).

PELHAM see Waldegrave, Francis; Warren, Henry.

PELLENTZ, James. Priest.

b. January 19th or 20th, 1727, Germany. S.J. October 19th, 1744. To English province c.1756. Ghent 1757. Maryland or Pennsylvania 1758, 1761, 1763-4, 1767-9, 1771-3-1800. d. February or March 13th, 1800, Conewago, Pennsylvania. (Fo.7; 113; Hu.Text 2/695; 1 f.116; 92).

?PELLETIER, John Peter. Priest.

?S.J. in France. Marnhull c.1798-1802. Returned to France. (01.374; CRS.56/173, 187).

PEMBER, George. Scholastic.

b.1634, Buckinghamshire. e. St Omers College 1648 or earlier – 53. S.J. 1653. Watten (nov) 1653-5. Liège (phil) 1656-8. Liège (theol) 1659, 1660. d. April 22nd, 1661, Ghent, not ordained. (Fo.7; CRS.69; 114; 113; Nec).

PEMBERTON, John William *alias* or *vere* Blundell. Priest.

b. June 1st, 1705 or 1707 or October 10th, 1708, Lancashire. e. St Omers College ?-1726. E.C. Valladolid November 26th, 1726-April 12th, 1733. Ordained priest c.1733. S.J. June 20th, 1733. Watten (nov) 1733, 1734. St Omers College 1734-40. Travelling 1741-5. ?Haggerston 1745. In England 1746. Residence of St John 1747-49. Ellingham 1749-63. Served Alnwick 1749-54. d. July 10th, 1763, Ellingham. bu. Ellingham church. (Fo.7; CRS.69; 114; 91; 113; Ans.4/206; NCH.5/15; 21 v.2; 36 ff.136, 139, 170, 261; RH.14/176; CRS.6/340; CRS.30/185; 35 ff.43-5, 87-8, 106v; 117; 156 App.1; 160; Nec).

PENDRIL see Howe, Joseph and William.

PENDRIL, Richard *alias* Fletcher. Priest.

b. August 4th, 1710, London or Staffordshire. e.?. St Omers College ?-1730. S.J. September 7th, 1730-40. Liège (phil) 1733. Antwerp (phil) 1733-5. Liège (theol) 1735-8. Ordained priest April 5th, 1738. Ghent (tert) 1739. (91; 113; 150 III(2) 20/8/40; 74; 108).

PENDRIL, William *alias* Birch. Priest.

b.1682, Shropshire. ?s. of Edmund and Anne (Starling). e. St Omers College ?-1701. E.C. Valladolid October 22nd, 1701-January 23rd,

1708. Ordained priest c.1707. S.J. May 31st, 1708. Watten (nov) 1709.
Liège (theol) 1710. St Omers College 1711. Residence of St John
1712-6, 1720, 1724-5 (Haggerston 1713-5). In England 1726.
Haggerston 1727. In England 1728. Residence of St John 1729-48
(Superior 1729-c.36. Callaly 1729. Berrington c.1741. Biddleston
?-1748). d. February 21st, 1748, in England (?Biddleston). bu.
Alwinton church. (Fo.7; CRS.69; 114; 113; CRS.62 index; Ans.3/163;
LR.1/117; 36 f.261; 91; CRS.25/115; CRS.30/181; 156 App.1; Nec).

PENISTON, James. Priest.

b. March 3rd, 1809, Salisbury. e. Stonyhurst 1820-5. S.J. September
18th, 1825. Chieri, Italy (nov) 1825-7. Dôle (phil) 1827-8. Aix (phil)
1828-9. Stonyhurst 1829-35. St Mary's Hall (theol) 1835-7. Rome
(theol) 1837. Ordained priest November 11th, 1838, ?Rome. St Mary's
Hall (theol) 1838-9. Stonyhurst 1839-40. Preston 1840-2. Stonyhurst
1842-3. St Acheul (tert) 1843-4. Calcutta 1844-7. Malta 1847-53.
Bombay 1853-6. d. June 30th, 1856, Bombay or Poona. (Fo.7; 115; 52
f.25; Nec).

PENKETH, John *alias* Rivers (1). Priest.

b.1627 or 1630, Lancashire. s. of Richard and - - - (Patrick) of
Penketh, Lancashire. e. St Omers College ?-1651. E.C. Rome October
20th, 1651-April 24th, 1658. Ordained priest December 17th, 1656.
Brussels 1659-1662. S.J. April 16th, 1663. St Omers College 1664, 1665.
To England 1666. College of St Aloysius 1667, 1669, 1672-6, 1678
(?Croxteth 1666. Scarisbrick 1673-?9, serving Brindle and Leigh). In
prison Lancaster and condemned to death 1679-c.84. College of St
Aloysius 1685-7, 1689-93, 1696-7, 1699-1701 (?Leigh and Culcheth
1689-1701 or 1702). d. August 1st, 1701 or 1702, in England (?Leigh or
Culcheth). (Fo.7; CRS.69; 114; 113; Ans.2/240; 26 ff.2v, 10;
CRS.4/432; CRS.13/370-1; CRS.23/4-5; CRS.55/530; Nec).

PENKETH, John *alias* Rivers (2).

?b.c.1681, Lancashire. ?s. of Richard and Alice (Charnley). ?e. St
Omers College 1697-1702. S.J. September 7th, 1702. Watten (nov)
1703, 1704. Left 1704. It is very unlikely that he completed the
noviceship. (113; CRS.40/134; Ans.3/164; CRS.69).

PENNINGTON, Francis. Priest.

b.1644, Worcestershire. S.J. January 13th, 1664. Liège (phil) 1667,
1669. St Omers College 1670-2. Liège (theol) 1672-5. Ordained priest
March 25th, 1674. Maryland 1675-6, 1678-93 (Superior 1684-c.93). To
England 1693. d. February 22nd, 1699 on his return journey to
Maryland. (Fo.7; 114; 113; Hu.Text 2/681; Nec).

PENNINGTON, John. Priest.

b.1647, London. S.J. September 7th, 1665. Liège (phil) 1669. Liège
(theol) 1672-5. Ordained priest March 25th, 1674. Ghent (tert) 1676.
College of the Immaculate Conception 1678. College of St Ignatius
1679. St Omers College 1680, 1681. Residence of St Michael 1682.
College of the Holy Apostles 1683. Maryland 1684-5. d. October 18th,
1685, Maryland. bu. Newtown. (Fo.7; 114; 113; Hu.Text 2/682; Nec).

PENNINGTON, Roger. Scholastic.
b.1659, Lancashire. s. of Richard and ?Catherine (Sherburne) of
Pennington Hall, Lancashire. br. of William. S.J. September 11th,
1681. Watten (nov) 1681, 1682. Liège (phil) 1683, 1684. d. July 17th,
1685, Liège, not ordained. (Fo.7; 114; 113; CRS.9/182; Nec).
PENNINGTON, William. Priest.
b.1661, Lancashire. s. of Richard and ?Catherine (Sherburne) of
Pennington Hall, Lancashire. br. of Roger. S.J. September 11th, 1681.
Watten (nov) 1681. Liège (phil) 1683, 1684. Liège (theol) 1685-7.
Ordained priest c.1689. Ghent (tert) 1689. Sawston 1689. College of St
Ignatius 1691-3. College of the Immaculate Conception 1696-7,
1699-1701, 1703-6, 1708-11 (Chaplain to Marshal Tallard at
Nottingham ?1704-?11). College of the Holy Apostles 1714-6, 1718,
1720, 1723-4. Liverpool c.1724-36. d. June 8th, 1736, ?Liverpool. bu.
Harkirke cemetery, Crosby. (Fo.7; 91; 113; 43 f.106; NB.3/141, 143,
210; CRS.9/182; Che. NS.12; Nec).
PERCOM see Pelcom
PERCY, Charles. Priest.
b. November 18th, 1665, Yorkshire. s. of Thomas and Cecily (Shawe
or Shaws) of Stubbs Walden, Yorkshire. br. of Philip and Robert. e. St
Omers College ?-1685. S.J. September 7th, 1685. Watten (nov) 1685,
1686. Liège (phil) 1687-90. Liège (theol) 1691-3. Ordained priest
c.1694. Residence of St George 1696-7, 1699-1708, 1710-16, 1720,
1723-5. In England 1726, 1728, 1730. Residence of St George 1733-5
(Superior 1701-c.07, 1734-5. Grafton c.1701, 1703, 1714-6, 1727,
1734). d. October 4th, 1735, in England (Grafton ?). (Fo.7; CRS.69;
91; 113; WR.4/41, 8/28, 10/15, 20/71; 39 f.107; Sur.36/7; 40 ff.46, 48;
E and P.315; Nec).
PERCY, Philip. Priest.
b.1660 or 1663, Yorkshire. s. of Thomas and Cecily (Shawe or
Shaws) of Stubbs Walden, Yorkshire. br. of Charles and Robert. e. St
Omers College ?-1683. S.J. September 7th, 1683. Watten (nov) 1684.
Liège (phil) 1685-7. In England 1688. Liège (theol) 1689-92. Ordained
priest c.1692. Bruges (military chaplain) 1693. Residence of St Michael
1696-7, 1699-1701, 1703-12 (Superior 1704-c.09). St Omers College
1713. Residence of St Michael 1714-8, 1720-4 (Superior 1720-c.23). d.
May 11th, 1724, in England (?Yorkshire). (Fo.7; CRS.69; 113;
Sur.36/7; 114; Nec).
PERCY, Robert alias Smith, Francis. Priest.
b.1652 or 1653, Yorkshire. s. of Thomas and Cecily (Shawe or
Shaws) of Stubbs Walden, Yorkshire. br. of Charles and Philip. e. St
Omers College ?-1674. S.J. September 7th, 1674. Watten (nov) 1674,
1675. Liège (phil) 1676, 1678. Liège (theol) 1679-82. Ordained priest
March 23rd, 1682. Ghent (tert) 1683. Residence of St Michael 1684.
College of the Immaculate Conception 1685-97, 1699-1701, 1703-6,
1708-14 (Rector 1686-c.95, 1708-c.11. Served Stannington. Spinkhill
?-c.1715). d. July 2nd, 1715, in England. (Fo.7; CRS.69; 114; 113;

Sur.36/7; 150 III(1) 24/7/1706; 156 XXX: Nec).

PERCY, Thomas. Priest.

b.1648, Shropshire. ?br. of Walter. S.J. September 7th, 1667. Watten (nov) 1669. Liège (phil) 1672. St Omers College 1672-5. Liège (theol) 1676, 1678. Ordained priest c.1677. Ghent (tert) 1679, 1680, 1681 (military chaplain). Lierre 1681. To England 1681. Maryland 1682-3. Ghent 1683-5. d. January 25th, 1685, Ghent. (Fo.7; 114; 113; Hu.Text 2/682; 150 II(3) 2/5/82, 19/10/82; 168 f.49; 108; Nec).

PERCY, Walter. Priest.

b.1651, Shropshire. ?br. of Thomas. S.J. August 14th, 1674. Watten (nov) 1674, 1675. Liège (phil) 1676, 1678. Liège (theol) 1679-81. Ordained priest March 23rd, 1682. Ghent 1682. College of St Hugh 1683. College of the Holy Apostles 1684. St Omers College 1685. Left 1685 to become a Carthusian. (Fo.7; 113; 150; II(3) 7/7/85).

PERKINS see Hawkins, Thomas.

PERKINS, Richard.

Watten (nov) 1664. Does not appear again under this name; no evidence to show that he completed the noviceship. (113)

PERNE, Nicholas de. Laybrother.

d. September 6th, 1681. Not in the English province catalogues under this name. (Fo.7; 95 p.817; Nec).

PERROT or PEROT see Plowden, Edmund and Francis.

PERSALL, John *alias* Harcourt. Priest.

b. January 23rd, 1633, Staffordshire. e. St Omers College 1648-53. S.J. September 7th, 1653. Watten (nov) 1653-5. Liège (phil) 1656-8. St Omers College 1659-61. Rome (?theol) 1663. Ordained priest c.1666. Liège 1669, 1672-6, 1678-82. College of St Thomas of Canterbury 1683, 1684. College of St Ignatius 1685-8 (London Savoy College and Royal preacher 1687). Watten 1689. Ghent 1689. Ireland 1691 (military chaplain). College of St Thomas of Canterbury 1692, 1693 (with Sir John Shelley 1692). Liège 1694-8 (Rector). College of St Ignatius 1699-1701. d. September 9th, 1701, in England. (Fo.7; CRS.69; 114; 113; DNB.; 150 III(1) 17/12/1701; 9 ff.1, 2, 4; 12. f.145; Gil.5/272; 123 II ff.154, 156; Che. 64/453. For writing see Som.).

PERSONS see Parsons, Robert.

PETERS see Lalart, John Baptist.

PETERSON see Hammerton, Peter.

PETIAN or PETHIAN, Peter, Scholastic or Laybrother.

d. date and place unknown. (Fo.7; 114; Nec).

PETIT, Cyriac or Charles *alias* Stanley, Charles.

b.1672, Kent. ?br of Roger. e. St Omers College 1693 or earlier -96. S.J. February 3rd, 1697. Watten (nov) 1697. Liège (phil) 1699, 1700, 1701. Liège (theol) 1703-5. Ordained priest c.1704. Ghent (tert) 1706. St Omers College 1708. Watten 1709. Residence of St Winefrid 1710. d. January 11th, 1710, in England. (Fo.7; CRS.69; 114; 113; Nec).

PETIT, Roger.

?br. of Cyriac. e. St Omers College ?-c.1708. d.c.1708, St Omers

College. Adm. S.J. *in articulo mortis*. (Fo.7; Chad.245; 123 II f.69).

PETRE, Charles *alias* Spencer. Priest.

b. November 4th, 1646, London. s. of Sir Francis, 1st Bart. and Elizabeth (Gage) of Cranham, Essex. br. of Edward and William. e. St Omers College 1662 or earlier -67. S.J. September 7th, 1667. Watten (nov) 1669. Liège (theol) 1672-5. Ordained priest April 4th, 1673. Ghent (tert) 1676. St Omers College 1678, 1679. Liège 1680. Residence of St Winefrid 1683-6. London (Fenchurch Street school, Superior) 1687. In prison in Dover 1688. Ghent 1689. Ireland 1690. Ghent 1691. College of St Ignatius 1692-3, 1695-1700. St Omers College 1701-6, 1708-12. d. January 18th, 1712, St Omers College. (Fo.7; CRS.69; 114; 113; 170 ff. 10, 18v, 59v, 139v, 142, 251; 123 II ff.160, 177; 95 p.801; Nec; DNB.s.v.Petre, Edward).

PETRE, Sir Edward *alias* Spencer, Bart. Priest.

b. ?March 4th 1633, London. s. of Sir Francis, 1st Bart. and Elizabeth (Gage) of Cranham, Essex. br. of Charles and William. e. St Omers College c.1644-52. S.J. March 1st, 1653. Watten (nov) 1653, 1654. Liège (phil) 1655-9. Liege (theol) 1660, 1661, 1664. Ordained priest October 22nd, 1662. College of St Thomas of Canterbury 1665. Ghent (tert) 1667. To England 1667. College of St Thomas of Canterbury 1669, 1672-6, 1678-9 (Rector c.1678-80). In prison in London 1679-80. College of St Ignatius 1680-8 (Rector 1680-2. In prison ?-1683). In France 1689. Abbeville 1691, 1692. St Omers College 1693-7 (Rector). Watten 1697. 3rd Bart. c.1679. d. May 15th, 1699, Watten. (Fo.7; CRS.69; Gil.5/290; 114; 113; 150 II(2) Nov.1667, 8/5/77, 14/2/93; 193 Anglia 35/85; 168 ff.29v, 54, 83; 135 ff.200, 203, 246; 140 pp.63-5; Mil.229 ff.; Chad.230 ff.; DNB; Hay pp.154 ff; KR.3/62; Nec. For writings see Som.).

PETRE, John (1) *alias* Rivers. Laybrother.

b. December 29th, 1640. s. of John and Elizabeth (Pordage) of Fithelers, Essex. e. St Omers College 1652 or earlier -53 or later. m. Mary Mannock (she died 1687). Father of John (2), Robert (2) and Thomas. S.J. May 1689. Paris 1691-3. St Omers College 1696-8. d. February 4th, 1698, St Omers College. (Fo.7; CRS.69; 114; 113; Nec).

PETRE, John (2) *alias* Mannock. Priest.

b. August 15th, 1661, Essex. s. of John and Mary (Mannock) of Fithelers, Essex. br. of Robert (2) and Thomas. e. St Omers College ?-1680. S.J. October 27th, 1680. Watten (nov) 1681. Liège (phil) 1682-4. Liège (theol) 1685-7. Ordained priest 1689. Watten (tert) 1689. Antwerp 1690-2. Residence of St George 1693, 1696-7, 1699-1700 (Superior 1700. Worcester 1693, 1699, 1700). E.C. Rome 1701, 1703-6. Residence of St George 1707-16, 1720, 1723-5. In England 1726-8, 1730. Residence of St George 1733-7 (Superior 1712-c.15. Weston c.1710-?38). d. August 9th, 1738, in England (?Weston). (Fo.7; CRS.69; 114; 91; 113; WR.5/13, 20/62, 20/67; 37 ff.180 ff.; 40 pp.10, 34, 192; 74; 170 ff.149v, 175, 245v; 123 IIIB f.360; 136 f.281; 102; 108; Nec).

PETRE, Richard *alias* Williams. Priest.

b. February 27th, 1634, Essex. ?s. of William and Lucy (Fermor) of Belhouse, Essex. br. of Robert (1). e. St Omers College 1649 or earlier -c.54. S.J. September 7th, 1654. Watten (nov) 1654, 1655. Liège (phil) 1656-8. Liège (theol) 1659, 1660. Ordained priest April 16th, 1661. Ghent (tert) 1661. Ghent 1663-5. College of the Holy Apostles 1667, 1669, 1672-5. St Omers College 1676. College of the Holy Apostles 1678, 1679. St Omers College 1680, 1681. Ghent 1682, 1683. St Omers College 1684-92. d. September 21st, 1692, Ghent. (Fo.7; CRS.69; 114; 113; 123 IIIB f.357; Nec).

PETRE, Robert (1) *alias* Williams and Spencer. Priest.

b. October 12th, 1632, Essex. ?s. of William and Lucy (Fermor) of Belhouse, Essex. br. of Richard. e. St Omers College 1648 or earlier -c.54. S.J. September 7th, 1654. Watten (nov) 1654, 1655. Liège (phil) 1656-8. Liège (theol) 1659-62. Ordained priest March or April 24th, 1663. College of the Holy Apostles 1663. Ghent (tert) 1663, 1664. College of St Chad 1669, 1672, 1678. In prison in Stafford 1678-82. London in prison 1683. College of St Francis Xavier 1684-6. Norwich 1687. In prison in Norwich 1688-9. College of the Holy Apostles 1690-3. Ghent 1693, 1696-7, 1699-1701, 1703-6, 1708-13. d. May 16th, 1713, Ghent. (Fo.7; CRS.69; 114; 113; CRS.47/148n, 307; 43 f.20; NA.37/157; 168 f.61v; 135 f.203).

PETRE, Robert (2) *alias* Mannock. Priest.

b.1667 or 1668. s. of John and Mary (Mannock) of Fithelers, Essex. br. of John (2) and Thomas. e. St Omers College ?-1686. S.J. September 7th, 1686. Watten (nov) 1686, 1687. Liège (phil) 1689-91. Liège (theol) 1692, 1693. Ordained priest c. 1695. Ghent (tert) 1696. Watten 1697. Liège 1699-1701. Watten 1703-5. E.C. Rome 1705, 1706. St Omers College 1707. College of St Thomas of Canterbury 1708. College of St Aloysius 1709-13. Watten 1714. College of St Ignatius 1715, 1716. St Omers College 1718, 1720, 1722. Liège 1722, 1723. Residence of St John 1724. Liège 1724-7. d. July 17th, 1727, Liège. (Fo.7; CRS.69; 91; 113; 150 III(1) 14/8/06, 26/3/07; 9 n.127; Nec).

PETRE, Robert (3). Priest.

b. May 3rd or 27th, 1700, Belhouse, Essex. s. of William and Penelope (Woolfe) of Belhouse. e. St Omers College 1714 or earlier -c.19. S.J. September 7th, 1719. Watten (nov) 1720. Liège (phil) 1723, 1724. Liège (theol) 1725-8. Ordained priest c.1727. Ghent (tert) 1728. In England 1730 (?Eccleston). Callaly 1732-3. College of St Aloysius 1733-8 (Hopcar, Southworth, Leigh 1733-?). College of St Hugh 1739, 1740. College of St Aloysius 1741-4, 1746-c.55 (Hopcar 1741. Preston 1747, 1750-2. Brinn 1752-4). Dunkenhalgh c.1755-66. d. April 27th, 1766, Dunkenhalgh. (Fo.7; CRS. 69; 114; 91; 113; CRS.62 index; 24 f.347v; 26 f.5v; 30 f.34; 64 p.182; 74; 85; 89; 158; HMC. 10th Report App.4/192; 94 ff.231, 232; CRS.7/319; CRS.36/218; 126; 111; CRS.6/340; 119 ff.1, 3, 4; 156 App.1; Nec).

PETRE, Thomas. Priest.

b.1662 or 1663, Essex. s. of John and Mary (Mannock) of Fithelers, Essex. br. of John (2) and Robert (2), e. St Omers College ?-1679. S.J. September 7th, 1679. Watten (nov) 1679, 1680. Liège (phil) 1681-3. Liège (theol) 1684-8. Ordained priest c.1688. Residence of St Michael 1689 (in prison ?in York). ?College of the Holy Apostles 1690. Residence of St Michael 1691-3, 1696-7, 1699-1701, 1703-6, 1708-16, 1718, 1720, 1723-5 (Superior 1709-c.12). In England 1726-9 (Walton Hall ?1690-1729). d. January 5th, 1729 in England (?Walton Hall). (Fo.7; CRS.69; 91; 113; Nec. For writings see Som.).

PETRE, William *alias* Gage. Priest.

b.1650, Suffolk or London. s. of Sir Francis, 1st Bart. and Elizabeth (Gage) of Cranham, Essex. br. of Charles and Edward. e. St Omers College ?-1670. S.J. September 7th, 1670. Watten (nov) 1672. Liège (phil) 1672-5. Liège (theol) 1676, 1679. Ordained priest April 1st, 1679. Ghent (tert) 1679. France 1680. Rouen 1681, 1682. College of the Holy Apostles 1683-8. College of St Ignatius 1689 (in prison), 1690. College of the Holy Apostles 1693, 1696. College of St Thomas of Canterbury 1697. College of the Holy Apostles 1699. College of St Thomas of Canterbury 1700-01, 1703-16 (Slindon 1707). College of St Ignatius 1718, 1720. d. February 22nd, 1722, Ghent. (Fo.7; CRS.69; 114; 113; NA.37/157; 43 ff.17, 20; 44 f.162; Nec).

PHILLIPS see Cotton, Richard; Stafford, Nathaniel.

PHILLIPS, Thomas. Priest.

b. July 5th, 1708, Ickford, Buckinghamshire. s. of Thomas and Elizabeth (Crosse) of Ickford. e. St Omers College ?-1726. S.J. September 7th, 1726. Watten (nov) 1727. Liège (phil) 1728, 1730. Liège (theol) 1732. Left 1733, not ordained. Ordained priest in Rome. ?Readm. S.J. June 16th, 1768. d. June 20th or 30th, 1774, Liège. (Fo.7; CRS.69; 91; Gil.5/305-8; 117; 113; DNB; RH.1/48; 150 III(2) 4/7/33; 74; Chad. 365; E and P.15; Nec. For writings see Gil.).

PHILLIPS, Vincent *alias* or *vere* Astley. Priest.

b. September 23rd, 1698, Worcestershire. e. St Omers College c.1715. S.J. September 7th, 1717. Watten (nov) 1718. Liège (phil) 1720. Liège (theol) 1723-6. Ordained priest c.1726. St Omers College 1726, 1727. Gifford's Hall 1728. Maryland 1728-52. ?Residence of St Winefrid 1753. Residence of St Mary 1753-8. Ghent 1759. d. February 22nd, 1760, Ghent. (Fo.7; CRS.69; 91; 114; 113; Hu.Text 2/689; 43 f.47v; 64 p.532; 65; CRS.62/316; Nec).

PHILMOT or PHILMOTT, Philip. Priest.

b.1652 or 1655, Staffordshire. e. St Omers College 1669 or earlier -c.74. S.J. September 7th, 1674. Watten (nov) 1674, 1675. Liège (phil) 1676, 1678. Liège (theol) 1679-83. Ordained priest March 3rd, 1683. Ghent (tert) 1683. College of St Chad 1684-7. In prison (Stafford and London) 1688-9. College of the Immaculate Conception 1689-92. College of St Chad 1693, 1696-1702 (Rector 1696-1702). College of St Ignatius 1703-6, 1708. College of St Francis Xavier 1709-10. College of St Ignatius 1711-6, 1718, 1720, 1723. Watten 1724-5. d. June 20th,

1725, Watten. (Fo.7; CRS.69; 114; 113; 123 IIIB ff.261-2; Nec).

PIATT or PYATT, John. Priest.

b. September 3rd, 1686 or 1687, Yorkshire. e. St Omers College 1700 or earlier -c.06. S.J. September 7th, 1706. Watten (nov) 1708. Liège (phil) 1709-11. Liège (theol) 1712-5. Ordained priest c. 1715. Ghent (tert) 1715. Residence of St Michael 1720, 1723. York c.1724-43. d. January 19th, 1743, York. (Fo.7; CRS.69; 114; 113; 156 App.1; ?E and P.306; CRS.Mon.2/268, 389; 91; CRS.4/370; CRS.32/341; YA.77/221; Nec).

PIERSON see Pearson.

PIGOT see Clorivière, Peter de.

PIGOT or PIGOTT, Adam *alias* Griffin. Priest.

b.1673 or 1675, London. s. of Adam. e. St Omers College 1693 or earlier -94. S.J. December 31st, 1694. Watten (nov) 1696. Liège (phil) 1697, 1699-1700. Liège (theol) 1701. Douay (?theol) 1703, 1704. Ordained priest c.1702. Ghent 1705, 1706. College of St Ignatius 1708-16, 1718, 1720, 1724, 1725. In England 1726. Calehill 1727. In England 1728, 1730. College of St Ignatius 1733-40, 1742-7 (Twickenham 1741). College of the Holy Apostles 1748-51 (?Crondon Park). d. April 19th, 1751, Crondon Park. (Fo.7; CRS.69; 114; 91; 113; LR.1/73; ER.4/119; Bur.1/175; HMC. 10th Report App.4/192; CRS.6/329; Pa.17; Nec).

PILE, Henry. Priest.

b. May 24th, 1743, Maryland. e. St Omers College 1754-61. S.J. September 7th, 1761. Liège (phil) 1763, 1764. Liège (theol) 1766-8. Ordained priest c.1768. Ghent 1768. Stubbs Walden 1768 or 1769. Residence of St Michael 1771. Stubbs Walden 1772, 1773. Burghwallis 1774. Stubbs Walden ?-1784. Maryland 1784. d. February 18th, 1813, St Thomas's, Maryland. (Fo.7; 91; 113; CRS.69; Hu.Text 2/700; 4 f.63v; 7 f.149v; 65; 68 pp.78, 375; Pa.2/26; 155 II 127; 48 ff.389-90; CRS.1/138; 167 p.38; 117; AHSJ.42/308).

PILLE, James Joseph. Laybrother novice.

b. July 29th, 1721. S.J. November 26th, 1750. d. December 12th, 1750, Watten. (Fo.7; 113; 114; Nec).

PINNINGTON see Aspinall, Edward.

PINTLET or PINTLETT or PINTELET, Peter. Laybrother.

b. February 1st, 1655, Liège. S.J. 1683 or 1684. Ghent (nov) 1684, 1685-7, 1689-91. Liège 1692-3, 1696-7, 1699-1701, 1703-5. d. August 5th, 1705, Liège. (Fo.7; 114; 113; Nec).

PIPPARD see Brown, George.

PIPPARD, Luke *alias* Stanfield. Priest.

b. September 29th, 1716, London. e. St Omers College 1724-33. S.J. September 7th, 1733. Watten (nov) 1734. Liège (phil) 1735-7. Liège (theol) 1738-40. Ordained priest c.1742. Ghent (tert) 1742. College of St Aloysius 1743-4, 1746 (Ince Blundell c.1742-?) Residence of St George 1747. Crondon Park c.1748-c.51. College of the Holy Apostles 1752-5 (?Cranham 1754). Residence of St Mary 1756-8. d. January 5th, 1761,

Crondon Park. (Fo.7; CRS.69; 114; 91; 113; ER.4/119, 5/94, 9/103; 150 III(2) 6/9/38; 43 ff.67, 77, 79, 81-2; 64 p.472; 40 p.114; HMC. 10th Report App.4/194; CRS.6/329; 188 n.117; 156 App.1; Nec).

PITTS, Henry, Priest.

b.1638 or 1639, Warwickshire. e. St Omers College 1654 or earlier -59. S.J. November 14th, 1659. Watten (nov) 1660. Liège (phil) 1661, 1663. Liège (theol) 1664-8. Ordained priest March 31st, 1668. St Omers College 1669, 1670. Residence of St George 1672-6, 1678-87, 1689-90. d. November 19th or December 9th, 1690, in England. (Fo.7; CRS.69; 114; 113; 140 n.45; Nec).

PLACE see Constable, Ignatius.

PLATT see Needham, Daniel.

PLEASINGTON, Joseph *alias* Walmesley *vere* Catesby, Richard, Priest.

b. June 16th, 1715, near Blackburn. ?s. of John and Margaret (Pleasington). e. St Omers College ?-1733. E.C. Valladolid 1733-7. S.J. October 12th, 1737. Watten (nov) 1738. Liège (theol) 1739-42. Ordained priest c.1742. Ghent 1742. St Omers College 1743, 1744. Oxburgh Hall 1745-?49. Courtfield 1750. St Omers College 1750-2. Callaly 1752-74 (serving Alnwick 1755-6). Alnwick 1774-81. d. March 29th, 1781, Alnwick. bu. Alnwick parish church. (Fo.7; CRS.69; 114; 91; 113; CRS.30/187-8; CRS.7/320; NCH.1/21; ER.9/103; 150 III(2) January 1740; 21 v.2; 34 f.60; 36 ff.166, 205; 43 ff.71v, 72v, 73-4, 78-9; 64 pp.57, 396; 85; 90 f.174; CRS.12/20; 35 f.39, 40, 42, 44, 47, 49, 51, 57, 84-5, 91, 100, 105, 146-7, 199, 203-4, 206-7, 215-6, 218; 164; 167 p.19; 120; 117; Nec).

PLOTHO, Delphin. Priest.

b. May 25th or 28th, 1668 or 1669, Ghent. S.J. September 7th, 1687. Watten (nov) 1687. Liège (phil) 1689-91. Liège (theol) 1692, 1693. Ordained priest March 21st, 1693. Watten 1696, 1697. Liège 1699-1701, 1703-5. Ghent 1706. Liège 1708-13. Watten 1714-6, 1718, 1720, 1723-4. Ghent 1724-8, 1730, 1733-40, 1742-4, 1746-7. d. November 12th, 1747, Ghent. (Fo.7; 114; 113; 91; Nec).

PLOWDEN see Bryon, Francis; Dean, Thomas.

PLOWDEN, Charles *alias* Simons or Simeon. Priest.

b. May 1st, 1743, Plowden Hall, Shropshire. s. of William Ignatius and Frances (Dormer) of Plowden Hall. br. of Francis Peter and Robert. e. St Omers College 1754-9. S.J. September 7th, 1759. Watten (nov) 1761. Bruges College 1763-4, 1767-9. Rome (?theol) 1769, 1770. Bologna (theol) 1770, 1771. Ordained priest ?September 30th, 1770, Rome. Travelling 1772. Bruges College 1772, 1773. Liège Academy 1774-6. Travelling 1776. Rome 1780. Ellingham 1781-4. Lulworth 1784-94. Stonyhurst 1794-1803. Hodder 1803-16. Stonyhurst 1817-21 (Rector 1817-9. Provincial 1817-21). d. June 13th, 1821, Jougne, France. bu. Jougne. (Fo.7; CRS.69; 114; 113; CRS.Mon.2/388; DNHA.99/33 ff.; 16 ff.12, 97v; 150 (1750-1853) ff.192 ff.; 4 ff.57-60, 73v; 6 ff.22v, 33v; 7 *passim*; 8 I/31, 87v, 120, 124, 126, 129, 158, 164, 168, 172, 176, 8 II/2av, 25, 35, 47, 61, 76, 92, 102, 111, 127, 140; 10

ff.52v, 76v; 57 I/15v, 25v, 70v, 137v, 172, 197, 268; 57 II/1, 57v, 114v,
173v, 204, 250; 22 ff.22, 45; 90 f.54; Chad.336 ff.; 94 ff.21-4, 65;
Gil.5/523; 157; CRS.4/385; CRS.6/367; Ki.185; 106; 17 pp.82, 97;
Nec. For writings see Som. Sut.).

PLOWDEN, Edmund *alias* Simons and Simeon, Gage and Perrot. Priest.
    b. April 7th, 1665, Oxfordshire or London. s. of Edmund and
Penelope (Drummond) of Plowden Hall, Shropshire. br. of Francis,
Richard and Thomas Percy. e. St Omers College ?-1682. S.J. December
2nd, 1682. Watten (nov) 1683. Liège (nov) 1684. Liège (phil) 1685,
1686. St Omers College 1687, 1689-92. Liège (theol) 1692, 1693, 1696.
Ordained priest c.1694. Liège 1697, 1699-1701. St Omers College 1703.
College of St Chad 1704, 1705. College of the Holy Apostles 1706, 1708
(?Belhouse 1707). Liège 1709. College of the Holy Apostles 1710.
College of St Aloysius 1711-6. College of St Ignatius 1718, 1720,
1723-31 (Rector 1728-c.31. London 1721-7). Liège 1731-6 (Rector
1731-4). College of St Ignatius 1737. Ghent 1738-40. d. September 3rd,
1740, Ghent. (Fo.7; CRS.69; 114; 91; 113; ER.4/120-1; 150 III(2)
9/8/27, 24/2/31, 28/8/34; 9 nn.81, 130, 236, 294; 12 ff.106, 111, 112,
116, 118, 120; 43 f.31; 193 Anglia 35/352; 170 f.177; Nec).

PLOWDEN, Francis *alias* Simons, Simeon and Perrot. Priest.
    b. May 3rd, 1661 or November 20th, 1662, Oxfordshire. s. of
Edmund and Penelope (Drummond) of Plowden Hall, Shropshire. br.
of Edmund, Richard and Thomas Percy. e. St Omers College ?-1682.
S.J. December 2nd, 1682. Watten (nov) 1683, 1684. Liège (theol)
1685-9. Ordained priest 1689. Watten (tert) 1690. Liège 1691, 1692.
Watten 1693, 1696. Travelling 1697, 1699. Liège 1700. Paris 1700.
Watten 1701. Paris 1701-12. College of St Ignatius 1713-6, 1718, 1720,
1724-5 (arrested 1716, 1720). In England 1726. Paris 1727-8, 1730.
Watten 1733-6. d. June 22nd, 1736, Watten. (Fo.7; CRS.69; 114; 91;
113; 9 nn.3, 4; CRS.56/141n; 150 III(2) 25/11/30; 12 ff.100, 107;
CRS.3/91; CRS.62 index; 170 ff.139v, 140v, 172; 123 II f.141; 184
n.96; Nec).

PLOWDEN, Francis Peter *alias* Simeon. Scholastic.
    b. July 10th, 1749, Plowden Hall, Shropshire. s. of William Ignatius
and Frances (Dormer) of Plowden Hall. br. of Charles and Robert. e.
St Omers and Bruges Colleges 1760-66. S.J. September 9th, 1766.
Ghent (nov) 1766, 1767. Liège (phil) 1768, 1769. Bruges College 1771-3.
Left 1773, not ordained. (Fo.7; CRS.69; 91; 113; AHSJ.42/292; 16
f.98; Gil.5/328).

?PLOWDEN, George. Priest.
    b.1651, Shiplake, Oxfordshire. s. of Edmund and Elizabeth (Cotton)
of Shiplake and Plowden Hall, Shropshire. br. of Joseph. e. St Omers
College ?-1670. E.C. Rome October 14th, 1670-May 4th, 1677.
Ordained priest April 14th, 1676. Oxford 1688. ?S.J. He does not
appear in the records of the English province. d. March 13th, 1694,
Pontoise. (Fo.4, 5 and 7; CRS. 69; Ans.3/171; CRS.40/82;
CRS.8/400).

PLOWDEN, Joseph. Priest.
 b.1655, Oxfordshire. s. of Edmund and Elizabeth (Cotton) of
Plowden Hall, Shropshire. br. of George. e. St Omers College ?-1676.
S.J. September 7th, 1676. Watten (nov) 1676. Liège (phil) 1679, 1680.
Liège (theol) 1681-4. Ordained priest March 17th, 1685. St Omers
College 1685-7, 1689. Ireland 1690, 1691 (Military chaplain). France
1692 (Military chaplain). d. February 6th, 1692, in camp in France
(?Brittany). (Fo.7; CRS.69; 114; 113; Nec).

PLOWDEN, Percy (or Peter or Joseph or Thomas). Priest.
 b. March 20th, 1672, Oxfordshire or London. s. of Edmund and
Penelope (Drummond) of Plowden Hall, Shropshire. br. of Edmund,
Francis and Richard. e. St Omers College ?-1693. S.J. June 7th, 1693
(phil before entering). Watten (nov) 1693. St Omers College 1695-7,
1699-1700. Rome (theol) 1701-4. Ordained priest c.1703. Florence
1705. E.C. Rome 1706. Liège 1708-12. St Omers College 1713-6.
College of St Chad 1718. Antwerp 1719-27. E.C. Rome 1728-34 (Rector
1731-4). Ghent 1735-9 (Rector). St Omers College 1739-42 (Rector).
Watten 1743-5. d. September 21st, 1745, Watten. (Fo.7; CRS.69; 114;
113; 150 III(1) 27/3/1700, 24/6/02, 4/9/06, III(2) 28/8/34, 31/3/42; 9
nn.14-7, 109, 240, 243, 249, 280, 294, 298, 303; 91; 193 Anglia 35/350;
170 f.22v; 123 IIIB f.357; 108; Nec. For writings see Som.).

PLOWDEN, Richard *alias* Saville, Simeon and Richards, Joseph. Priest.
 b. July 9th, 1663, Oxfordshire or London. s. of Edmund and
Penelope (Drummond) of Plowden Hall, Shropshire. br. of Edmund,
Francis and Percy. e. St Omers College ?-1679. S.J. September 7th,
1679. Watten (nov) 1679, 1680. Liège (phil) 1681-3. St Omers College
1684-6. Liège (theol) 1687. London (Savoy College) 1687-8. Liège
(theol) 1689-92. Ordained priest March 23rd, 1690. Liège 1693, 1696-7,
1699-1701, 1703-8 (Rector 1704-8). St Omers College 1709-12 (Rector).
E.C. Rome 1712-6 (Rector). Provincial 1716-9 (arrested in London
1719). College of St Ignatius 1720. Liège 1720-4 (Rector). St Omers
College 1725-8 (Rector). Watten 1728-9. d. September 15th, 1729,
Watten. (Fo.7; CRS.69; 114; 113; 150 III(2) 9/3/20; 12 ff.80, 105-6,
106v; Chad.259-65, 268; CRS.30/xxxvi-xxxvii, 185-6; 193 Anglia
35/280; 123 II f.157; 91; 118; CRS.62 index; 9 *passim*; Nec. For
writings see Som.).

PLOWDEN, Robert. Priest.
 b. January 27th, 1740, Plowden Hall, Shropshire. s. of William
Ignatius and Frances (Dormer). br. of Charles and Francis Peter. e. St
Omers College 1751-6. S.J. September 7th, 1756. Watten (nov) 1756-8.
Liège (theol) 1761, 1763, 1764. Ordained priest c.1764. Hoogstraet
1764, 1767-9, 1771-5. Liège Academy 1775-6. Arlington 1777-87.
Bristol 1787-1815. Swynnerton 1815-20. Wappenbury 1820-3. Readm.
S.J. 1807. d. June 17th, 1823, Wappenbury. bu. St Anne's churchyard,
Wappenbury. (Fo.7; 91; CRS.69; 114; 113; SCH.3/14; WR.20/60-1;
150 (1750-1853) f.91; 7 ff.2v, 5v, 9v, 26v, 65v, 71v, 77v, 87v, 114v,
122v, 126v, 128v, 132v, 136v, 151v; 15 ff.25, 28v; 8 II nn.21, 37, 84,

104, 118, 144; 10 f.64v; 13 ff.82v, 94v, 115v; 19 pp. 169, 172; 32 ff.152, 170, 172; 51 ff.151v, 196; 53 ff.5v, 7v; 55 f.283v; 90 f.54; 94 ff.298-9; AHSJ 42/307; CRS.3/181, 209, 287; 01.383; 61; Nec. For writings see Som. and Sut.).

PLOWDEN, Thomas Percy see Plowden, Percy.

PLUNKETT, Arthur. Scholastic.

    b. August 10th, 1730, in Ireland. ?s. of Robert, 6th Earl of Fingall and Mary (Magenis). e. St Omers College 1741-7. S.J. September 7th, 1747. Watten (nov) 1747-9. Liège (phil) 1750. Liège (theol) 1752, 1753. Left 1754, not ordained. (Fo.7; CRS.69; 91; 113).

PLUNKETT, Robert. Priest.

    b. April 23rd, 1752, London. s. of Thomas and Mary (Underhill). e. Bruges College c.1763-c.68. E.C. Douay 1768-9. S.J. October 9th, 1769. Ghent (nov) 1771. Liège (?phil) 1772, 1773. Left 1773. E.C. Douay July 31st, 1776-80. Ordained priest December 18th, 1779, Arras. Brussels 1780. To U.S.A. between 1791 and 1795. ?Readm. S.J. d. January 15th, 1815, Georgetown, U.S.A. bu. Georgetown Visitation convent cemetery. (Fo.7; 113; 91; CRS.69; Hu.Text 2/703; CRS.63/418; Ans 4/216; Nec).

POECHET, Francis see Pauchet.

POINS or POINES see Poyntz.

POLDING, John. Priest.

    b. March 20th, 1807, Croxteth, near Liverpool. e. Stonyhurst 1823-9. S.J. March 23rd, 1829. Hodder (nov) 1829-32. St Mary's Hall (phil) 1832-4. Stonyhurst 1834-8. St Mary's Hall (theol) 1838-40. Louvain (theol) 1840-2. Ordained priest c.1841. Stonyhurst 1842-3. Mount St Mary's College 1843-4 (Rector), 1844-5. Stonyhurst 1845-7. Mount St Mary's 1847-c.52. Norwich c.1852-8. d. April 25th, 1858, Norwich. bu. Yarmouth Catholic cemetery. (Fo.7; 113; 115; NA.37/166; Nec).

POLE or POOLE see Birkbeck, Edward and Gervase; Foxe, James.

POLE or POOLE, Anthony. Priest.

    b.1627 or 1629, Spinkhill, Derbyshire, s. of George and Ursula (Thwaites) of Spinkhill. ?br. of Francis (1), George and John. e. St Omers College c.1641-6. E.C. Rome October 19th, 1646-November 8th, 1648. S.J. (already ordained priest) October 8th, 1658. St Omers College 1659-61, 1663-5, 1667-9. Liège 1672. St Omers College 1673-6, 1678. Liège 1679-87, 1689-92. d. July 13th, 1692, Liège. (Fo.7; CRS.69; 114; 113; CRS.40/38; CRS.55/500; CRS.14/165n; Ans.2/248; Nec).

POLE or POOLE, Charles de la. Priest.

    b. October 3rd, 1669, French Flanders. ?br. of Toussaint. S.J. September 8th, 1688. Watten (nov) 1689, 1690. Liège (phil) 1691-3. Liège (theol) 1696, 1697. Ordained priest 1697. Ghent (tert) 1697. Bar-le-Duc 1699-1701. Lorraine 1703. Liège 1704-6, 1708-11. College of St Ignatius 1712-6, 1718, 1720, 1723-5. In England 1726-8, 1730. College of St Ignatius 1733-8 (Sutton Place 1714, 1727 -?40). d. June 21st, 1740, in England (?Sutton Place). (Fo.7; 114; 91; 113; CRS.62/129, 135; Nec).

POLE or POOLE, Felix. Priest.

b. April 19th, 1809, Pontefract. e. Stonyhurst 1817-28. S.J. January 24th, 1828. Hodder (nov) 1828-30. St Mary's Hall 1830-2. London (Marylebone school) 1832 or 1834-6. St Mary's Hall (theol) 1836-8. Ordained priest September 22nd, 1838, Stonyhurst. Preston 1828-39. St Helens 1839-40. Chipping 1840-41. Leigh 1841-3. Mount St Mary's College (serving Wingerworth) 1843-7. Brough 1847-9. Portico 1849-52. Norwich 1852-5. Mount St Mary's 1855-61. Blackpool 1861-3. Pontefract 1863-4. Prescot 1864-8. d. October 20th, 1868, Rhyl. (Fo.7; 115; LR.3/65; NA.37/166; CRS.36/4; Nec).

POLE or POOLE, Francis (1). Priest.

b.1624, Derbyshire. ?s. of George and Ursula (Thwaites) of Spinkhill, br. of George and John ?and Anthony. E.C. Valladolid 1644-51. Ordained priest 1649. S.J. October 3rd. 1653. Watten (nov) 1653, 1654. St Omers College 1655. Liège 1655. St Omers College 1657-9. College of the Immaculate Conception 1660-1, 1663-5, 1667-76, 1678-84. (Rector 1667-73). d. November 4th, 1684, in England. (Fo.7; 114; 113; CRS.30/162; Ans.2/248; 150 II(2) 5/6/67; Nec).

POLE or POOLE, Francis (2). Scholastic.

b.1681, Staffordshire. s. of Sir James, 1st Bart. and Anne (Eyre) of Poole, Cheshire. e. St Omers College 1694-9. S.J. September 7th, 1699. Watten (nov) 1699-1701. Liège (phil) 1703, 1704. Liège (theol) 1705, 1706. College of St Aloysius 1708-11. Left 1711, not ordained. (Fo.7; CRS.69; 113; 150 III(1) 30/5/1711).

POLE or POOLE, Francis (3). Priest.

b. December 15th, 1711, Lancashire. e. St Omers College ?-1728. S.J. September 7th, 1728. Liège (theol) 1733-6. Ordained priest 1736. Ghent (tert) 1737. St Omers College 1738-40, 1742-4. Ghent 1746. Residence of St George 1747. Residence of St Mary 1748-50, 1752-8, 1763-4 (Waterperry 1752, 1755, 1763, 1764). ?Bath 1765. Sarnesfield 1765. d. December 23rd, 1767, Sarnesfield. (Fo.7; CRS.69; 91; 113; 38 f.191; 64 p.206; 68 p.85; HMC. 10th Report App.4/192; CRS.7/395, 397, 400; 111; Nec).

POLE or POOLE, George. Priest.

b.1628, Derbyshire. ?s. of George and Ursula (Thwaites) of Spinkhill. br. of John and Francis (1) ?and Anthony. E.C. Valladolid 1649-56. Ordained priest June 7th, 1653. S.J. 1656. Liège 1657. Residence of St Michael 1658-60. Residence of St John 1661, 1663-5. College of the Holy Apostles 1667. Maryland 1668, 1669. d. October 31st, 1669, Maryland. (Fo.7; CRS.30/164; 113; 114; Hu.Text 2/681; Ans. 2/248; Nec).

POLE or POOLE, Gervase. Scholastic.

Date of birth not recorded. S.J. in another province. Ingolstadt (?phil) 1682-4. Liège (theol) 1685-7. Ghent 1689. d. April 26th or 28th, 1690, Bruges, not ordained. (Fo.7; 114; 113; Nec).

POLE or POOLE, John. Priest.

b.1621, Derbyshire. ?s. of George and Ursula (Thwaites) of Spinkhill. br. of Francis (1) and George ?and Anthony. e. St Omers College ?-1642. E.C. Valladolid September 27th, 1642-March 25th, 1649. Ordained priest March 17th, 1647, Astorga. To England 1649. S.J. March 24th, 1660. Watten (nov) 1660. Residence of St Michael 1661, 1663-5. d. September 3rd, 1666, in England. (Fo.7; CRS.30/159; CRS.69; 113; 114; Ans.2/249; Nec).

POLE or POOLE, Michael (1) *alias* Killingbeck. Scholastic.

b.1661, Derbyshire. e. St Omers College ?-1678 or later. S.J. September 7th, 1681. Watten (nov) 1681, 1682. Liège (phil) 1683-5. Liège (theol) 1686. d. April 7th, 1687, in England, not ordained. (Fo.7; CRS.69; 114; 113; Nec).

POLE or POOLE, Michael (2). Priest.

b. August 20th, 1687, Yorkshire. S.J. September 7th, 1707. Watten (nov) 1707-9. Liège (phil) 1710-12. Liège (theol) 1713-5. Ordained priest c.1716. Ghent (tert) 1716. St Omers College 1718. In Ireland 1720. ?Residence of St Stanislaus 1723. St Omers College 1724-8. In England 1730. College of St Thomas of Canterbury 1733-40, 1742-4, 1746-7 (Stapehill 1730, 1732. Wardour 1735, 1738, ?c.1740). d. April or May 23rd, 1748, in England (?Odstock or Canford). (Fo.7; 114; 113; CRS.Mon.1/153, 155, 164, 244; 64 p.220; 44 ff.249, 250, 259; 74; 91; HMC. 10th Report App.4/184; Nec).

POLE or POOLE, Peter. Priest.

b. November 12th, 1728. S.J. October 1st, 1748 ?in another province. In Paraguay. Liège 1768. College of St Ignatius 1769-71. London 1772-5, 1785, 1791. d. January 9th, 1793, London. (Fo.7; 114; 113; LR.3/5; 45 ff.16 ff;67; 173; 103; Nec).

POLE or POOLE, Toussaint de la. Priest.

b. February 9th, 1673, French Flanders. ?br. of Charles. e. St Omers College ?-1694. S.J. September 7th, 1694. Watten (nov) 1696. Liège (phil) 1697. Liège (theol) 1699-1701, 1703. Ordained priest 1703. Ghent (tert) 1704. St Omers College 1705-6, 1708-9. Going to Maryland 1710. d. May 22nd, 1710, in England. (Fo.7; CRS.69; 114; 113; Hu.Text 2/685; Nec).

POLE or POOLE, William. Priest.

b. December 16th, 1752. e. Bruges College 1765-7 or later. S.J. September 7th, 1771. Ghent (nov) 1772, 1773. Liège Academy 1773-4, 1776, 1781. Ordained priest c.1778, Liège. Derbyshire ?-1790. Exeter 1790-1807. Stonyhurst 1807. Leigh 1808-28. Readm. S.J. 1804. d. February 27th, 1828, Leigh. bu. Leigh Catholic chapel. (Fo.7; CRS.69; 114; 113; 115; 3 f.37; 15 f.12; 21 v.2; 26 f. 6v; 47 ff.26, 45, 110, 113; 51 ff.304, 307; 53 f.51; 90 f.54; 01. 346, 384; AHSJ. 42/306; Nec).

PONCELET, Henry. Laybrother.

b. July 21st, 1731, Liège. S.J. July 1st, 1752. Watten (nov) 1752, 1753. Boulogne School 1754, 1755. Watten School 1755-8, 1761, 1763-4. Bruges School 1767-9. Liège 1771-3. Liège Academy 1776, 1781. d. September 17th, 1783, Liège. (Fo.7; 114; 91; 113; 3 f.41; 16

f.12v; 90 f.54; AHSJ.42/294; Nec).

PORDAGE, William *alias* Collins. Priest.

b. June 23rd, 1651 or 1652, Kent. s. of Thomas and – (Ive) of Rodmersham, Kent. e. St Omers College ?-1670. E.C. Rome October 14th, 1670 or 1671-November 11th, 1670 or 1671. S.J. January 21st, 1671 or 1672. Watten (nov) 1672. Liège (phil) 1673, 1674. Liège (theol) 1676, 1679-80. Ordained priest April 20th, 1680. Watten (tert) 1680. College of St Thomas of Canterbury 1681-3. College of the Holy Apostles 1684-6. College of St Ignatius 1687. In England 1688. St Omers College 1689, 1690. Dunkirk 1691. Watten 1693. College of the Holy Apostles 1694-7, 1699. Oxburgh Hall 1699 or earlier-1736 (Rector of the College of the Holy Apostles 1701-8, 1711-c.13, 1720-c.25). d. August 30th, 1736, Oxburgh Hall. bu. Bedingfeld chantry in parish church. (Fo.7; CRS.69; 91; 113; ER.4/120; 150 III(1) 15/8/99, 28/1/19; KR.1/10; CRS.7/46, 226, 329; CRS.40/83; E and P.88-9; 43 ff.16-8, 21, 25, 30, 33, 38-9, 53, 55, 60-1; Nec).

PORTER see Corbusier, John.

PORTER, James. Priest.

b. November 9th, 1733, Brussels. e. St Omers College 1746-52. S.J. September 7th, 1752. Watten (nov) 1752-4. Liège (phil) 1755-7. Lyons (theol) 1757, 1758. Ordained priest c.1759. College of the Immaculate Conception 1761, 1763. Holt 1764. Sizergh (serving Furness) 1764-6. Beckford 1766-7. Salisbury 1767-9. Stapehill 1770-1800. Portico 1802-5, 1807. d. March 28th, 1810, Portico. (Fo.7; CRS.69; 114; 91; 113; CRS.43/127; CRS.Mon.1/167; 1 ff.13, 39v; 6 f.179; 7 f.131v; 13 ff.165, 247; AHSJ.42/308; 34 f.36v; 44 ff.273, 276, 277, 278; 54 ff.73, 101; 55 f.4; 65; 68 pp.38-9; HMC. 10th Report App.4/193; Gil.4/106; 119 ff.27, 32; Nec).

PORTER, Nicholas. Priest.

b. September 10th, 1724 or 1725, Porto S. Maria, near Cadiz. e. St Omers College ?-1741. S.J. September 7th, 1741. Watten (nov) 1742. Liège (phil) 1743, 1744. Trèves (theol) 1746. Cologne (theol) 1747-9. Ordained priest c.1748. College of the Holy Apostles 1750-4 (Oxburgh Hall 1750, 1751). Ghent 1754, 1755. E.C. Rome 1756-8, 1761. E.C. Valladolid 1764-6. Ghent 1767. E.C. Rome 1767-9, 1771-3. Rome 1775, 1782-5. Naples 1786-9. Rome 1789-90. Naples 1790-2-?4. Rome 1796, 1799-1802. d. August 25th, 1802, Rome. (Fo.7; CRS.69; 114; 91; 113; CRS.30/xxxix, 173, 191; AHSJ.42/291; 11 f.57; 43 f.79v; 56 f.330; 57 I ff.49, 126v, 185v, 220v; 57 II ff.20v, 61v, 117v, 153, 167v, 194, 222v, 261v; 65; 72; HMC. 10th Report App.4/192; 17 pp.1-2; 111; Nec).

POSTGATE, Ralph. Priest.

b. January 30th or June 23rd, 1648, Oxfordshire. s. of William and Jane (Mylot). e. E.C. Douay 1661-71. E.C. Rome October 26th, 1671-74. Ordained priest March 24th, 1674, Rome. S.J. November 4th, 1674, Rome. Residence of St Michael 1678. Liège (theol) 1679-81. Watten 1681, 1682. Residence of St George 1683-5. Rome 1686, 1687. Loretto 1688-90. Rome 1691-3. E.C. Rome 1693-9 (Rector). Rome

1699-1701, 1703. E.C. Rome 1704-7 (Rector), 1708-16. d. January
25th, 1718, Rome. (Fo.7; 114; 113; Ans.3/173; CRS.40/85;
CRS.55/617; CRS.63/20; 150 II(3) January 1686, III(1) 15/3/04; 139
f.295; 140 n.45; Ki.188; 9 nn.5-18, 20, 24-32, 34-6, 45, 50, 56, 59, 60-1,
63, 65-6, 68-9; Nec).

POSTLEWHITE or POSTLETHWAITE, Joseph. Priest.
      b. April 7th, 1784, Westby, Lancashire. s. of William and Elizabeth
(Hodgson) of Westby. e. Stonyhurst 1797-1803. S.J. September 26th,
1803. Hodder (nov) 1803-5. Stonyhurst (phil and theol) 1805-17.
Ordained priest September 15th, 1817, Wolverhampton. Wardour
1817-20. Hodder (tert) 1820-21. Courtfield 1821-3. Wigan 1823-7.
Stonyhurst 1827-8. London 1828-9. Boston 1829-37. Worcester 1837-9
(Superior of the Residence of St George). Irnham 1839-40. Left 1840.
At Westby and Ulverston. Readm. S.J. March 1st, 1845. St Acheul
1845-6. Stonyhurst 1846-70. d. March 30th, 1870, Stonyhurst. bu.
Stonyhurst. (Fo.7; 115; 39 f.13; 90 f.147; 93 p.41; CRS.4/424;
CRS.20/12; CRS.15/6-7; Nec. For writings see Sut. and Som.).

POTTER see Stafford, Ignatius and Nathaniel.

POULTON or PULTON, Andrew. Priest.
      b. January 20th, 1654, Northamptonshire. s. of Ferdinand and Mary
(Giffard) of Desborough, Northamptonshire. br. of Thomas (1). e. St
Omers College 1669-74. S.J. October 31st, 1674. Watten (nov) 1674,
1675. Liège (phil) 1676, 1678. Liège (theol) 1679. St Omers College
1680-3. Liège (theol) 1684-6. Ordained priest May 3rd, 1685. London
(Savoy College) 1687, 1688. In prison at Canterbury 1688. St Omers
College 1689. Ireland 1690. St Germain 1691-3, 1696-7, 1699-1701,
1703-10. d. August 5th, 1710, St Germain. (Fo.7; CRS.69; 114; 113;
Gil.5/351; 123 II f.156; Che.48/136-40, 64/321; Dod.3/493; DNB;
Woo.4 col.440; Nec. For writings see Som.).

POULTON, George. Priest.
      b. October 24th, 1689, Northamptonshire. s. of Ferdinand and
Juliana (Garter) of Desborough, Northamptonshire. br. of Giles,
Henry and Thomas (2). e. St Omers College ?-1707. S.J. September
7th, 1707. Watten (nov) 1708-9. Liège (phil) 1710-12. Liège (theol)
1713. Ghent 1714. Liège (theol) 1715, 1716. Ghent 1718, 1720, 1723-8,
1730. Ordained priest c.1732. Watten 1733-9. d. January 1st, 1739,
Watten. (Fo.7; CRS.69; 91; 113; E and P.199; CRS.62/4, 71; Nec).

POULTON, Giles *alias* Palmer. Priest.
      b. September 7th, 1694, Northamptonshire. s. of Ferdinand and
Juliana (Garter) of Desborough, Northamptonshire. br. of George,
Henry and Thomas (2). e. St Omers College 1708-14. E.C. Rome
October 16th, 1714-September 24th, 1721. Ordained priest April 8th,
1719. S.J. December 12th, 1721. Watten (nov) 1723. St Omers College
1724. College of the Immaculate Conception 1725. In England 1726-8,
1730 (Dunkenhalgh 1728). College of the Immaculate Conception 1733
(Belgrave. Queeniborough). Residence of St Winefrid 1734-40, 1742
(Plowden Hall). Watten 1743-4, 1746-8. Brussels 1749. College of St

Ignatius 1750. d. January 3rd, 1752, London. (Fo.7; 91; CRS.69;
CRS.62 index; 114; 113; Ans.4/221; CRS.40/153; 89; E and P.199; Ki.
192; CRS.25/113; CRS.36/217; Nec).

POULTON, Henry *alias* Palmer. Priest.

b.1679, Northamptonshire or London. s. of Ferdinand and Juliana
(Garter) of Desborough, Northamptonshire. br. of George, Giles and
Thomas (2). e. St Omers College ?-1700. S.J. September 7th, 1700.
Watten (nov) 1701. Liège (phil) 1703-5. Liège (theol) 1706-9. Maryland
1709-12. d. September 27th, 1712, Newtown, Maryland. (Fo.7;
CRS.69; 114; 113; E and P.199, Hu.Text 2/685; Nec).

POULTON, John *alias* Palmer and Coniers. Priest.

b. September 16th, 1610, Desborough, Northamptonshire. s. of
John and Francis (Walliston or Wollaston) of Desborough. e. St Omers
College 1626-30. E.C. Rome October 22nd, 1631-September 21st,
1638. Ordained priest October 12th, 1636. To England. S.J. 1650.
Watten (nov) 1651. To England 1652. College of St Ignatius 1654.
College of the Holy Apostles 1655. d. August 7th, 1656, in England.
(Fo.7; CRS.69; 114; 113; Ans.2/251; CRS.40/1; CRS.55/416; Nec).

POULTON, Thomas (1) *alias* Palmer. Priest.

b. June 21st, 1668, Northamptonshire. s. of Ferdinand and Mary
(Giffard) of Desborough, Northamptonshire. br. of Andrew. e. St
Omers College ?-1685. S.J. September 7th, 1685. Watten (nov) 1685,
1686. Liège (phil) 1687, 1689, 1690. Liège (theol) 1691-3. Ordained
priest c.1694. College of St Thomas of Canterbury 1696-7, 1699-1701.
Residence of St Mary 1703-6, 1708-16, 1720, 1724. d. July 1st, 1725,
Ghent. (Fo.7; CRS.69; 113; 114).

POULTON, Thomas (2). Priest.

b. May, June or July, 1697, Northamptonshire. s. of Ferdinand and
Juliana (Garter) of Desborough, Northamptonshire. br. of George,
Giles and Henry. e. St Omers College ?-1716. S.J. September or
December 7th, 1716. Watten (nov) 1716, 1718. Liège (phil) 1720. Liège
(theol) 1723, 1724. Ordained priest c.1724. St Omers College 1725-8,
1730. E.C. Rome 1733, 1734. College of the Holy Apostles 1735-8.
Maryland 1738-40, 1742-9 (Superior 1742-c.46). d. January 13th, 1749,
Maryland. (Fo.7; CRS.69; 91; 114; 113; Hu.Text 2/690; 92; 43 ff.58-9;
CRS.62/89n; Nec).

POWELL, Charles. Priest.

b. March 6th, 1660, Staffordshire or Oxfordshire. S.J. September
7th, 1679. Watten (nov) 1680. Liège (phil) 1681-3. Liège (theol) 1684-7.
Ordained priest c.1687. Watten 1689. Liège 1690-2. Cadiz 1693,
1696-9. Liège 1700-01, 1703-6, 1708. College of St Ignatius 1709.
Spetchley 1709-10. Residence of St Winefrid 1710. College of St
Aloysius 1711-6, 1718, 1720, 1723-5. (Arrested 1717. Dunkenhalgh
c.1724). In England 1726-8, 1730 (Richmond, Surrey). Ghent 1733-8.
d. January 15th, 1738, Ghent. (Fo.7; 91; 113; 150 II(3)24/1/93,
21/6/98, III(1) 22/8/99; 12 f.103; 23 f.210v; 40 pp.38, 192; 89;
CRS.36/217; 170; 174; Nec).

POWELL, Francis *alias* Ashton. Priest.

b. September 13th, 1658, Essex. e. St Omers College ?-1677. S.J.
September 7th, 1677. Watten (nov) 1678. Liège (phil) 1679-81. St
Omers College 1682-6. Liège (theol) 1687, 1689-91. Ordained priest
1689. St Omers College 1692, 1693. Liège 1696, 1697. E.C. Rome
1699-1701, 1703-12 (Rector 1707-12). Liège 1712-5 (Rector). St Omers
College 1715-20 (Rector). Socius to the Provincial 1722-6. Idsworth
1727-?30. Liège 1730. d. January 23rd, 1733, Liège. (Fo.7; CRS.69;
CRS.62 index; 114; 91; 113; CRS.44/12; RH.8/184; 150 III(2) 25/7/22;
74; 193 Anglia 35/308; 135 f.245; Nec).

POWELL, Laurence. Scholastic.

b.1665, Monmouthshire. e. St Omers College ?-1684. S.J. September
7th, 1684. Watten (nov) 1684, 1685. Liège (phil) 1686. d. June 25th,
1687, in England, not ordained. (Fo.7; CRS.69; 114; 113; Nec).

POWELL, William. Scholastic.

b.1658. e. St Omers College ?-1678. S.J. 1678. Watten (nov) 1679.
Liège (phil) 1680. d. July 8th, 1681, St Omers College, not ordained.
(Fo.7; CRS.69; 114; 113; Nec).

POWER, Edmund. Priest.

b. April or May 3rd, 1736, Clonmel, Ireland. s. of Thomas of
Clonmel. ?br. of James. S.J. September 7th, 1754. Watten (nov) 1755.
Liège (phil) 1756-8. Liège (theol) 1761. Ordained priest c.1761. Ghent
1762. Weston 1763-78. d. August 30th, 1778 or March 1779, in France.
(Fo.7; Fo.7 Irish section; 113; 91; SCH.3/17; WR.20/62; 65; 111; 117).

POWER, James. Priest.

b. March 27th, 1725, Ireland. ?s. of Thomas of Clonmel. ?br. of
Edmund. S.J. January 13th, 1741 or 1742, in France. To English
province. College of St Ignatius 1763, 1764. St Stephen's Green,
Canterbury 1766-9. College of St Ignatius 1771. St Stephen's Green,
Canterbury 1772, 1773. Liège Academy 1781, 1783, 1785. d. March
11th, 1788, Liège. (Fo.7; Fo.7 Irish section; 114; 113; 3 ff.37, 51; 45
n.27; 77; CRS.12/29; CRS.17/91; Nec. For writings see Som.).

POWER see Reeve, John.

POYNTZ or POYNZ see Nixon, Edward or Edmund; Mathews, Edmund.

?POYNTZ, Augustine Newdigate. Priest.

b. March 19th, 1679 or 1680, London. s. of Thomas and Sarah
(Lane). E.C. Douay April 12th, 1697-October 23rd, 1703. Arras
October 23rd, 1703-January 1704. E.C. Douay January
1704-November 25th, 1704. E.C. Rome July 11th, 1705-April 30th,
1707. Ordained priest April 3rd, 1706. Bruges 1707-23. ?S.J. *in articulo
mortis*. d. August 15th, 1723, Ghent. (Ans.3/174; RH.6/72;
Chad.252-4; Ki.191; CRS.28/16, 21; CRS.62 index; Gil.3/176;
CRS.40/137).

POYNTZ, John *alias* Beaumont and Price. Priest.

b. June 23rd, 1709, Devonshire. s. of Giles and Ann of Yarnscombe,
Devonshire. e. E.C. Lisbon 1723-6; St Omers College 1728-32. S.J.
September 7th, 1732. Watten (nov) 1733. Liège (nov and phil) 1734,

1735. Liège (theol) 1736, 1737, 1738. Ordained priest c.1739. Ghent
(tert) 1739, 1740. Residence of St Stanislaus 1740, 1742 (Trevithick).
College of St Ignatius 1743-4, 1746-58, 1760-5. Switzerland 1766. Liège
1769, 1771-3. Liège Academy 1776, 1781, 1783, 1788. d. May 21st,
1789, Liège. (Fo.7; CRS.69; 114; 113; RH.6/72-4; 91; LR.3/5;
Cro.242/3 ff.37, 51; 13 f.125; 45 nn.63, 77; 74; 66; E and P.230-1; 90
ff.54, 186v; HMC. 10th Report App.4/185-7, 193-4, 197; 92; 173; 126;
51 f.311v; Nec).

PRACID, Jeremiah or John *alias* Cornwallis or Brent or Brand. Priest.
   b. c.March 23rd, 1639, Yorkshire. s. of Jeremiah (or Samuel) and
Ruth. E.C. Rome November 4th, 1661-May 2nd, 1669. Ordained priest
April 4th, 1665. Brussels 1669-75. S.J. March 18th, 1675. College of St
Ignatius (nov) 1676-8 (Hammersmith ?-1678). York, in prison,
1678-c.85. York 1685-6. d. April 1st, 1686, York. bu. St Michael le
Bow, York. (Fo.7; 114; 113; CRS.40/64; CRS.55/582;
CRS.Mon.2/102, 104; Ans.3/174; 150 II(2) 19/9/76, 9/1/77;
CRS.4/375; LR.8/31; 168 ff.34, 77, 83; Col.74-6; Sur.40/232 ff.272;
193 Anglia 35/79).

PRATER, Richard.
   S.J. 1662, *in articulo mortis*. (Fo.7).

PRESTON, Hon. Edmund. Scholastic.
   b. February 14th, 1808. s. of Jenico, 12th Viscount Gormanston and
Margaret (Arthur) of Gormanston Castle, Ireland. e. Stonyhurst
1819-?26. S.J. *in articulo mortis*. d. September 24th, 1826, West
Teignmouth. bu. Parish churchyard. (Fo.7; 114; Stol; 117; CDSJ).

PRESTON, Sir Thomas, Bart. *alias* Saville. Scholastic.
   b.1639 or 1641 or 1643, Lancashire. s. of Sir John, 1st Bart. and Jane
(Morgan) of the Manor of Furness. e. St Omers College 1657 or
earlier-60 or later. 3rd Bart. 1663. m.(1) Elizabeth de Planzye (2) Mary
Molyneux who d.1673. S.J. June 28th, 1674. Watten (nov) 1674, 1675.
Liège (phil) 1676. Liège (theol) 1678-80. St Omers College 1681-6.
Watten 1687, 1689-93, 1696-7, 1699-1701, 1703-9. Did not accept
ordination. d. May 25th, 1709, Watten (Fo.7; CRS.69; 114;
RH.13/212; 113; 150 II(2) 19/9/76; 135 ff.181, 234; CWAA.79/133;
NWCH.5/20; CRS.20/2; Nec).

PRESTON, William *alias* Vincent and Baines. Priest.
   b.1637, Northamptonshire. s. of William and Elizabeth (Realton) of
Slipton, Northamptonshire. e. St Omers College 1651 or earlier -55.
E.C. Rome September 24th, 1655-May 22nd, 1662. Ordained priest
April 9th, 1661. S.J. August 9th, 1662. College of the Holy Apostles
1663-5. Liège 1667, 1669, 1672. College of the Holy Apostles 1673-5.
Liège 1676, 1678-83. College of St Ignatius 1684, 1685. College of St
Thomas of Canterbury 1685-7, 1689-1702 (Rector 1696-1702). d.
December 14th, 1702, in England. (Fo.7; CRS.69; 114; 113;
Ans.3/176; CRS.40/56; CRS.55/552; Nec).

PRICE see Poyntz, John; Scudamore, John.
PRICE, James. Laybrother.

b. July 20th, 1731. S.J. January 5th, 1750. Watten (nov) 1750.
Boulogne School 1752, 1753. d. January 12th, 1754, St Omers College.
(Fo.7; 114; 113; 91; Nec).

PRICE, John. Priest.

b. August 3rd, 1739, near Lanherne, Cornwall. e. St Omers College
1753-8. S.J. February 14th, 1758. Watten (nov) 1758. Liège (phil) 1761.
Liège (theol) 1763, 1764. Ordained priest 1765. Bruges 1766. Linstead
Lodge 1767. Husbands Bosworth 1767, 1768. Bruges 1768, 1769.
?Liège 1769. Liverpool 1769. College of St Aloysius 1771. Liverpool
1772. Worcester 1772-6. Liverpool 1776, 1782-3, 1785, 1789, 1792,
1803-4, 1807, 1810. Readm. S.J. 1804. d. February 5th, 1813,
Liverpool. bu. St James cemetery. (Fo.7; CRS.69; 114; 113;
WR.20/70; 21 v.2; 38 ff.35v, 109; 51 f.207; 30 f.31; 57 I f.34; 65; 76
ff.53v, 142; 68 pp.41-2; 77; AHSJ.42/306; 72; 80; 94 ff.3-4;
CRS.9/187; 155 II 129; 155 III 211c; 157; Nec).

PRICE, William *alias* Lynch. Laybrother.

b. London. S.J. 1734, in Brazil. d. April 25th, 1774, in prison in
Portugal. (Lei.7/267-8).

PRICHARD, Charles. Priest.

b.1637, Monmouthshire. ?s. of James and Elizabeth (Lewis) of
Monmouthshire. S.J. November 16th, 1662. Ordained before S.J.
College of St Francis Xavier 1663-5, 1667, 1669, 1672-6, 1678-9. d.
March 14th, 1680, in England. (Fo.7 and 5; 114; 113; CRS.27/211;
Nec).

PRINCE, Richard *alias* Lacey and Ellis. Priest.

b.1648, Oxford. e. St Omers College ?-1668. E.C. Rome 1668. S.J.
December 14th, 1668. Watten (nov) 1669. Liège (phil) 1672. Liège
(theol) 1673-6. Ordained priest c.1677. To England 1678. College of the
Holy Apostles 1679. London, in prison in Newgate, 1680. d. March
10th, 1680, Newgate prison. (Fo.7; CRS.69; 114; 113; CRS.47/258; 150
II(2) 13/10/68; CRS.34/288; 168 f.80v; 135 f.200; FAB.168-9;
BR.81-4; 43 f.11; Cha.566; Dav.53n; Nec).

PULTON see Poulton.

PURCELL see Persall.

PYATT see Piatt.

QUIN, Charles.

d. date not recorded, in London. (Fo.7; 114; Nec).

QUIN, James. Priest.

b. September 23rd, 1698, London. S.J. September 7th, 1717. Watten
(nov) 1718. Liège (phil) 1720. Liège (theol) 1723-5. Ordained priest
c.1725. Ghent (tert) 1726. Maryland 1727-8, 1730, 1733-40, 1742-5. d.
November 27th, 1745, Choptank River, Maryland. (Fo.7; 114; 113;
Hu.Text 2/689; 91; HMC. 10th Report App.4/197; Nec).

RABBETT see Rappet.

RABY, Richard. Priest.

  b. May 20th, 1797, York. e. Stonyhurst 1815-20. S.J. September 7th, 1820-50. Hodder (nov) 1820, 1821. Rome (nov) 1821-2. Ferrara (phil) 1822-4. Rome (phil and theol) 1824-8. Ordained priest April 5th, 1828. Stonyhurst 1828-31. Enfield 1831-3. Stonyhurst 1833-9. Hodder (tert) 1839-40. Stonyhurst 1840-41. Belgium 1841-3. Calcutta 1843-5. St Mary's Hall 1845. Chipping 1845-6. Clitheroe 1846-7. Wigan 1847-50. (115; 19 p.212; 2; 21 v.2; 52 f.24; CRS.36/279, 285).

RADFORD, Joseph. Priest.

  b.c.1646, London. S.J. September 7th, 1677-86. Liège (phil) 1679-81. Liège (theol) 1682-4. Ordained priest April 21st, 1685. College of St Hugh 1685. (113; 150 II(3) 2/3/86).

RAM, Clement. Scholastic or Laybrother.

  d. date and place not recorded. (Fo.7; 114).

RAPPET or RAPPITT or RABBETT, Edward. Laybrother.

  b.1638, Northamptonshire. S.J. September 7th or November 10th, 1663. Watten (nov) 1663, 1664. Liège 1667, 1669, 1672. Ghent 1673. Watten 1675. d. December 9th, 1675, Watten. (Fo.7; 113; 114; Nec).

RAYMOND or RAYMENT, Charles. Priest.

  b.1665, Seville, Spain. e. St Omers College ?-1686. S.J. September 7th, 1686. Watten (nov) 1686, 1687. Liège (phil) 1689-91. Liège (theol) 1692. E.C. Valladolid (theol) 1692-5. Ordained priest c.1694. E.C. Valladolid 1695-8. St Omers College 1699-1701. To England 1701. Residence of St Winefrid 1703. Residence of St George 1704-6, 1708-16, 1720, 1723-4 (Superior 1708-c.11). d. July 19th, 1725, in England. (Fo.7; CRS.69; 113; CRS.30/xxxiv, 178; CRS. 29/331; 150 II(3) 21/6/98, III(1) 14/2/99; 170 f.245v; Nec).

REDFORD, Sebastian *alias* or *vere* Exton. Priest.

  b. April 27th, 1701, Paris or London. e. St Omers College 1715 or earlier -19. S.J. September 7th, 1719. Watten (nov) 1720. Liège (phil) 1723, 1724. St Omers College 1724, 1725. Watten 1725, 1726. Liège (theol) 1727, 1728. Ordained priest c.1729. Ghent (tert) 1730. Ladyholt 1730-31. Kelvedon 1731-2. Residence of St Winefrid 1732-40, 1742-4, 1746-8 (Superior 1743-c.48. Powis 1732-c.48). College of St Thomas of Canterbury 1748-50, ?1752. Croxteth c.1750-6. Residence of St Michael 1756-8. ?Crondon Park 1758. Norwich 1758-60. Wealside 1761. d. January 2nd, 1763, Wealside. (Fo.7; CRS.69; 114; 113; ER.5/35, 95, 9/10, 14/83; NA.37/165; 14 ff.36, 39, 48, 49, 54v, 56, 63, 66, 76; 43 f.54v; 64 pp.86, 87, 254, 377, 384, 404, 434, 475; 65; 74; 85; 91; HMC. 10th Report App.4/193; Gil.5/61, 400; Ki.34, 176; 156 App.1; 158; 169/155/18; 119 f.11; CRS.62/237; Nec. For writings see Som).

REDING, Henry. Priest.

  d. February 10th, 1682, Fribourg. Not found in the English province catalogues under this name. (Fo.7; 95 p.817).

REEVE, John *alias* Power. Priest.

b.1781 or 1782, Whitechurch, Herefordshire. s. of John and Alice (Green). Nephew of Joseph, Richard and Thomas. e. Stonyhurst 1796-1803. S.J. September 26th, 1803-33. Hodder (nov) 1803-5. Stonyhurst (theol) 1805-7. Ordained priest December 19th, 1807, Wolverhampton. Clitheroe 1807-11. Bristol 1811-2. Lulworth 1812-6. Pontefract 1816-20. Stapleton Park 1820-33. (115; 113; 2; 21 v.2; 90 ff.145v. 146v; 93 pp.73, 75; CRS.6/367; CRS.3/182; 01.401).

REEVE, Joseph *alias* Haskey. Priest.

b. May 11th, 1733, Warwickshire. s. of Richard and Anne (Haskey) of Island Hill, Studley, Warwickshire. br. of Richard and Thomas. Uncle of John. e. St Omers College 1746-52. S.J. September 7th, 1752. Watten (nov) 1752-4. Liège (phil) 1755, 1756. St Omers College 1757-8, 1761-2. Bruges College 1762, 1763 (theol), 1764, 1765. Ordained priest c.1765. Liège 1767. Ghent 1767. Ugbrooke 1767-9. Residence of St Stanislaus 1771. Ugbrooke 1772-1820. Readm. S.J. 1803. d. May 2nd or 11th, 1820, Ugbrooke. (Fo.7; 114; CRS.69; 91; 113; 13 ff.70, 494; 15 f.195v; 46 f.2; 47 f.32; 54 ff.154, 297, 318; 65; 67; 01.395; 117; 166 I p.71; Chad.293, 312 ff.394; Gil.5/402; Ki.196; AHSJ.42/305; Nec. For writings see Sut. Som.).

REEVE, Richard *alias* Haskey. Priest.

b. February 25th, 1740. s. of Richard and Anne (Haskey) of Island Hill, Studley, Warwickshire. br. of Joseph and Thomas. Uncle of John. e. St Omers College 1749-57. S.J. September 7th, 1757. Watten (nov) 1757, 1758. Liège (phil) 1761. Liège (theol) 1763, 1764. Ordained priest c.1765. Hammersmith 1765. College of St Aloysius 1767. Puddington 1768, 1769. College of St Aloysius 1771. Puddington 1772, 1773. Lulworth 1777. Salford Hall 1778. Slindon 1780-2. Liège 1788. Southworth 1795-1800. Stonyhurst 1803. St Petersburg 1804-7. Stonyhurst 1807, 1810, 1813, 1815-6. Readm. S.J. 1807. d. May 31st, 1816, Stonyhurst. bu. Stonyhurst. (Fo.7; CRS.69; 114; 113; 91; LR.1/32; AHSJ.37/164; 150 (1750-1853) f.101; 6 ff.22v, 63; 13 f.120v; 26 ff.201bv, 201d; 47 f.71; 65; 77; 25 ff.56, 75; 80; 155 III 185c; 157; CRS.6/365; 109; CRS.7/355, 360-1; CRS.13/400-02; 01.323; CRS.OP.1/178; AHSJ.42/306; Nec).

REEVE, Thomas *alias* Haskey. Priest.

b. September 7th, 1752. s. of Richard and Anne (Haskey) of Island Hill, Studley, Warwickshire. br. of Joseph and Richard. Uncle of John. e. Bruges College 1764-70. S.J. September 7th, 1770. Ghent (nov) 1771, 1772. Liège (phil) 1773. Liège Academy 1776, 1779, 1781-3, 1785-6, 1788, 1792-4. Ordained priest at Liège, date not recorded. Stonyhurst 1795, 1798, 1800-01, 1803, 1805, 1807, 1808, 1810. New Hall 1812-26. Readm. S.J. 1803 or 1804. d. September 7th, 1826, London. bu. Old St Pancras churchyard. (Fo.7; CRS.69; 114; 113; 90 ff.54, 145v, 146v, 167; ER.5/97; AHSJ.42/306; 93 pp.27, 33, 41, 69; Chad.394; 94 f.324; 157; CRS.17/98; 6 f.22v; 7 f.401v; 21 v.2; 47 ff.53, 59v; 51 ff.306, 307; 3 ff.37, 51; 56 f.337; 132; Nec).

RELEIGH see Riley.

RENOULT, Romanus. Priest.
b. July 19th, 1703, Rouen. S.J. August 17th, 1722, Paris province.
To English province 1768. Liège 1768-9, 1771-3. Liège Academy 1774.
d. February 28th, 1776, Liège. (Fo.7; 91, 113; 114; 90 f.33v; 7 f.108; 51
f.307; Nec).
REVELL, John. Scholastic.
b.1677, Yorkshire. e. St Omers College 1693 or earlier -97. S.J.
September 7th, 1697. Watten (nov) 1697. d. February or April 25th,
1699 or 1700, in England. (Fo.7; 113; 114; CRS.69; Nec).
REYNOLDS, Richard. Laybrother.
b. February 1st, 1687, Lancashire. S.J. December 2nd, 1719. Watten
(nov) 1720. Liège 1723-4. Maryland 1725-36. d. September 1st or 6th,
1736, Maryland. (Fo.7; 91; 114; 113; Hu.Text 2/689; Nec).
REYNOLDSON, John. Priest.
b.1655, London. e. St Omers College 1666-70 or later. S.J.
September 7th, 1673. Watten (nov) 1673-5. Liège (phil) 1676, 1678.
Liège (theol) 1679, 1680. France (?theol) 1681. Ordained priest c.1681.
College of St Ignatius 1682, 1683. College of St Aloysius 1684, 1685. d.
April 1st, 1686, in England. (Fo.7; CRS.69; 114; 113; Nec).
RICH, Bernard see Diderich, John Baptist.
RICHARD, Aloysius. Priest.
b. July 16th, 1681, Leitmeritz, Bohemia. He is not in the English
province catalogues under this name. (Fo.7; 95 p.817).
RICHARD or RICHART, John. Priest.
S.J. in another province. To the English province 1768. Ordained
priest c.1768. Liège (theol) 1768, 1769. Nothing further is recorded.
(91; 113).
RICHARDS, Andrew Wyndham. Scholastic.
?e. Stonyhurst 1810-? S.J. September 7th, 1812. Hodder (nov) 1812.
Stonyhurst (phil) 1815. Stonyhurst 1816. Stonyhurst (theol) 1818. Left
1818, not ordained. (116; 2; 113; 93 p.83).
RICHARDS, Joseph see Plowden, Richard.
RICHARDSON see Shuttleworth, John.
RICHARDSON, James. Priest.
b.1650, Durham or Northumberland. S.J. September 7th, 1669.
Liège (phil) 1672, 1673. Liège (theol) 1674-6, 1678. Ordained priest
April 9th, 1678. Madrid 1679. St Omers College 1680-3. College of St
Francis Xavier 1684-97, 1699-1701, 1703-6, 1708-16, 1718, 1720,
1723-5. In England 1726. d. 1726 ?in England. (Fo.7; 113; 9 n.246; 89;
112 p.84; CRS.2/299-300; 168 ff.62, 76, 86; 123 IIIB ff.262-4; 140 n.45;
Nec).
RICHARDSON, John (1) ?*alias* Holcroft or Oldcroft. Priest.
b.1662, Lancashire. ?e. St Omers College ?-1684. S.J. September
7th, 1684. Watten (nov) 1684, 1685. Liège (phil) ?1686, 1687. Liège
(theol) 1689, 1691. Ordained priest April 14th, 1691. Watten 1692.
College of St Chad 1693. College of St Aloysius 1696, 1697, 1699-1701,
1703-6, 1708-16, 1718, 1720, 1723-5 (Brindle, Slatedelf ?1698-1728). In

England 1726-8. d. September 27th, 1728, in England (?Brindle).
(Fo.7; CRS.69; 91; 114; 113; 23 f.35v; CRS.4/434; CRS.23/6; Nec).

RICHARDSON, John (2). Priest.

b. May 12th, 1734. e. St Omers College c.1752-5. S.J. September 7th,
1755. Liège (nov and phil) 1756-8. Liège (theol) 1761, 1762. Ordained
priest c.1762. Biddleston 1762-3. Brindle 1763-71. College of St
Ignatius 1771. Hammersmith 1772, 1773. Ellingham 1773-9. Retired to
Sunderland 1779. d. March 27th, 1782, at or near Wigan. (Fo.7;
CRS.69; 114; 113; LR.1/33; 21 v.2; 35 ff.106, 153-4; 36 ff.177-9; 76
ff.48, 78-9; 68 p.125; 25 ff.1, 7, 10, 13, 19; 80; 86; Gil.2/467;
CRS.4/434; CRS.23/139; 119 ff.16. 21, 24, 30, 35, 38, 42; 28 ff.45, 51;
Nec).

RICHARDSON, Richard. Priest.

b. December, 1669 or 1670 or February 12th, 1671, Lancashire. S.J.
September 11th, 1690. Paris (nov) 1690-2. Liège (phil) 1693. Liège
(theol) 1696, 1697. Ordained priest 1699. Residence of St George 1699.
Ghent (tert) 1699, 1700. Dutton Lodge 1701. St Omers College 1701.
To England 1702. College of St Aloysius 1703-6, 1709. College of St
Ignatius 1710-14. Ghent 1715, 1716. College of St Ignatius 1718, 1720,
1723-4. Rome 1724-5. Ghent 1728. Rome 1729. Socius to the provincial
1730. Provincial 1731-3. College of St Ignatius 1734-7. d. April 6th,
1738, St Omers College. (Fo.7; 114; 91; 113; 9 nn.211, 279; 150 III(2)
11/12/24, 12/8/29; 23 f.35; 40 f.8; 170 f.245v; CRS.62/31, 65, 135,
140; Nec).

RICHARDSON, Robert alias Garbot. Priest.

b. February 11th, 1671, London. e. St Omers College ?-1688. S.J.
September 7th, 1688. Watten (nov) 1689, 1690. Liège (phil) 1691-3. St
Omers College 1696. Liège (theol) 1697, 1699. Ordained priest c.1698.
Louvain 1700, 1701. St Omers College 1703, 1704. Gravelines 1705.
Rome (penitentiary at St Peter's) 1706-12. Watten 1713. College of St
Francis Xavier 1714-25 (Rector 1715-c.24). In England 1726-8, 1730
(Monmouth 1727). College of St Thomas of Canterbury 1733-7 (Rector
1734-?37. Lulworth 1733, 1737). d. January 17th, 1737, in England
(?Lulworth). (Fo.7; CRS.69; 91; 113; 150 III(1) 15/7/06; 44 f.175;
CRS.6/365; Nec).

RICHARDSON, William alias Bulmer. Priest.

b.1652, County Durham. e. St Omers College ?-1674. S.J.
September 7th, 1674. Watten (nov) 1674, 1675. Liège (phil) 1675, 1676.
Liège (theol) 1678. Ordained priest April 1st, 1679. Ghent (tert) 1679.
St Omers College 1680. Residence of St John 1681, 1682. Residence of
St Michael 1683-7, 1689. d. October 21st, 1689, in England. (Fo.7;
CRS.69; 114; 113; Nec).

RICHART see Richard. John.

RIDDELL, Peter. Priest.

b.1636, Northumberland. ?s. of Sir William and Catherine
(Widdrington) of Gateshead. ?Uncle of William. e. St Omers College
1652 or earlier -56. S.J. September 7th, 1656. Watten (nov) 1656. Liège

(phil) 1657-9. Liège (theol) 1660, 1661, 1663. Ordained priest April
12th, 1664. Ghent (tert) 1664. ?To Maryland. d. ?Maryland, date not
recorded. (Fo.7; CRS.69; 114; NCH.3/11; 113; 36 f.270; Nec).

RIDDELL, William. Priest.

b. October 7th, 1669 or 1670, Northumberland. ?s. of William and
Margaret. ?Nephew of Peter. e. St Omers College ?-1687. S.J. January
20th or September 7th, 1687. Watten (nov) 1687. Liège (phil) 1689-91.
Liège (theol) 1692, 1693. Ordained priest c.1695. Residence of St John
1696-7, 1699-1701, 1703-11 (Gateshead ?1696-1711). d. March 29th,
1711, in England (?Gateshead). (Fo.7; CRS.69; NCH.3/11, 13; 114;
113; CRS.35/200n; Hu.Text 2/683; 36 f.264; E and P.47; Nec).

RIGBY see Barrard, Richard.

RIGBY, John (1). Priest.

b. June 8th, 1712, Lancashire. s. of John and Anne (Spencer) of
Billinge, near Wigan. e. St Omers College c.1727-32. S.J. September
7th, 1732. Watten (nov) 1733. Liège (phil) 1734-6. Liège (theol)
1737-41. Ordained priest c.1738. St Omers College 1742. Ghent 1743.
Brussels 1744, 1746. Hardwick 1746. Ghent 1747. Hardwick 1747-9.
Liverpool 1749-58. d. September 26th, 1758, Hooton. bu. Eastham
church. (Fo.7; CRS.69; 114; 91; 113; 21 v.2; 24 f.41v; 35 f.49; 64 p.121;
85; 86; 119 ff.2, 17; HMC. 10th Report App.4/193; Gil.5/421;
CRS.9/186; 108; 158; 156 App.1; Nec. For writings see Gil.5/421).

RIGBY, John (2). Priest.

b. October 8th, 1737 or 1738, Lancashire. e. St Omers College
c.1753-8. S.J. September 7th, 1758. Liège (theol) 1763-4, 1766.
Ordained priest 1765. d. January 1st, 1767, Dinant. (Fo.7; CRS.69;
114; 91; 113; 90 f.99v; 119 ff.22, 32; Nec).

RIGBY, John (3). Priest.

b. June 8th, 1809, Wigan. e. Stonyhurst 1816-27. S.J. September
20th, 1827. Hodder (nov) 1827-9. Hodder (phil) 1830. St Mary's Hall
(phil and theol) 1830-4. Ordained priest December 20th, 1834,
Stonyhurst. Worcester 1834-8. Hodder (tert) 1838. St Mary's Hall
1838-41. Brough 1841-7. St Mary's Hall 1847 (Superior). St Helens
1847-9. Brough 1849-51. Liverpool 1851-2. Lymington 1852. St
Beuno's College 1853. Boston 1854-8. Pontefract 1858-65. Worcester
1865. New Hall 1865-79. Wigan 1879. Roehampton 1879. St Beuno's
College 1879-81. Skipton 1881-2. Stonyhurst 1882-9. d. February 25th,
1889, Stonyhurst. bu. Stonyhurst. (115; CRS.17/91; Nec).

RIGMEADON, John *alias* Rothwell. Priest.

b. September 8th, 1710, Lancashire. e. St Omers College c.1727-32.
S.J. September 7th, 1732. Watten (nov) 1733. Liège (phil) 1734, 1735.
Liège (theol) 1736-8. Ordained priest 1739. St Omers College 1739.
Watten 1740. Ghent (tert) 1741. Haggerston 1741. Berrington c.1741-5.
Preston 1746. Kilvington c.1746-82. d. September 29th, 1782,
Kilvington. bu. Thornton-le-Street. (Fo.7; CRS.69; 114; 113; 91; 90
f.173; Gil.5/5; 158; 155 II 127; 156 App.1; CRS.6/243; CRS.12/22;
111; 202. Nec).

RILEY or RYLEY or RELEIGH, Thomas. Laybrother.
	b. December 21st, 1642 or 1641, Lancashire. S.J. December 21st,
1669. Liège 1672-6, 1678-82. Watten 1683-7. Liège 1689-93, 1696-7,
1701, 1703-6, 1708. d. August 17th, 1708, Liège. (Fo.7; 114; 113; Nec).
RISDON, Thomas *alias* Bluett. Priest.
	b. January 21st, 1662 or 1663, Devonshire. e. St Omers College
?-1685. S.J. September 7th, 1685. Watten (nov) 1685, 1686. Liège (phil)
1687-90. Liège (theol) 1691-3. Ordained priest c.1694. College of the
Immaculate Conception 1696. Residence of St Stanislaus 1697,
1699-1701, 1703-6, 1708-33 (Superior 1709-c.12, 1715-c.33. Ugbrooke
1727, 1729, 1733). College of St Ignatius 1734-6. College of the Holy
Apostles 1737-40. College of St Ignatius 1740-1. Watten 1743. d.
February 12th, 1744, Watten. (Fo.7; CRS. 69; 114; 113; 89; 91;
01.403-4; 43 ff.61v, 62, 63v; CRS.8/404; Nec).
RITTER, John Baptist de. Priest.
	From Germany or Belgium. To the English province (already
ordained) c.1763. Watten 1764. Maryland 1765-87. d. February 3rd,
1787 (or 1786), Maryland or Pennsylvania. (Fo.7; 114; 113; Hu.Text
2/696; 92; CRS.12/26; Nec).
RIVERS see Clorivière, Peter de; Penketh, John (1) and (2); Petre, John (1).
RIVES, Thomas. Scholastic or Laybrother.
	d. date and place unknown. (Fo.7; 114).
ROBECK see Lefevre, George.
ROBERTS see Busby, Thomas; Swindall, Stephen.
ROBERTS, Joseph see Dicconson, Thomas.
ROBERTS, Roderick or Thomas. Priest.
	b.1642, 1644 or 1645, Carnarvonshire. S.J. September 26th, 1665 or
1666. Watten (nov) 1667. Liège (phil) 1669. Ordained priest July 5th,
1670. Residence of St Winefrid 1672-6, 1678-96 (Superior 1687-96.
Welshpool. Holywell ?1687-96). College of St Francis Xavier
1696-1716, 1718, 1720 (Rector 1696-c.1707). d. June 26th, 1721, in
England. (Fo.7; 114; 113; CRS.3/107; 112 p.83; Nec).
ROBERTS, Thomas. Priest.
	b.1673, Anglesey. e. St Omers College 1693 or earlier -96. S.J.
September 7th, 1696. Watten (nov) 1697. Liège (phil) 1699-1701. Liège
(theol) 1703-5. Ordained priest c.1705. Ghent (tert) 1706. Residence of
St Winefrid 1708-10. College of St Francis Xavier 1711-13. College of
St Thomas of Canterbury 1714. College of St Francis Xavier 1715.
Residence of St Winefrid 1716, 1718, 1720, 1724-5. In England 1726.
Holywell ?-1727. d. May 2nd, 1727, Holywell. bu. Holywell parish
church. (Fo.7; 91; 113; CRS.69; CRS.3/107; Nec).
ROBINSON see Robson, Christopher; Vezzozi, Joseph.
ROBINSON, Andrew. Priest.
	b. August 1st, 1741, Yorkshire. e. St Omers and Bruges Colleges
c.1756-c.63. S.J. January 27th, 1763. Watten (nov) 1763, 1764. Liège
(theol) 1767-9. Ordained priest c.1769. ?Stratford 1770. Ghent 1771.
Residence of St Mary 1771 (?Swynnerton). Spetchley 1772-1773.

?Swynnerton ?1773-?80. ?Spetchley ?1780-?96. Grafton 1796.
Worcester 1797-1826. d. February 28th or March 1st, 1826, Worcester.
(Fo.7; CRS.69; 114; 91; 113; AHSJ.42/310; RH.1/48; SCH.9/23n, 48,
12/20; ER.5/34-5; WR.7/3, 8/28, 15/9, 14, 19/16, 20/70, 30/12;
CRW.42 ff.8 II n.162; 13 f.262v; 21 v.2; 34 f.211v; 38 ff.124, 128, 143,
197v; 39 f.210; 68 p.195; 72; Ki.200; CRS.12/169; 117; Nec).

ROBINSON, John *alias* or *vere* Gazain or Gazin. Priest.
 b. December 23rd, 1699, London. ?s. of John and Elizabeth. e. St
Omers College 1714 or earlier -18. S.J. September 7th, 1718. Watten
(nov) 1720. Liège (phil) 1723. Liège (theol) 1724. Pont-à-Mousson
(theol) 1725-6. Liège (theol) 1727. Ordained priest c.1727. Liège 1728,
1730-31. Burton Park 1731-2. College of St Aloysius 1733-39. Preston
1739-42. d. March 6th, 1742, Preston. (Fo.7; CRS.69; 114; 91; 113; 24
f.396; RH.13/116; 64 pp.86-7; 74; CRS. 22/307, 314-5; 120;
CRS.62/120; 156 App.1; Nec).

ROBINSON, William. Novice.
 b.1655. S.J. September 7th, 1674. Watten (nov) 1674. d. May 17th,
1675, Watten. (Fo.7; 113; 114; Nec).

ROBSON, Christopher *alias* Robinson and Fines. Priest.
 b. June 23rd, 1619, County Kilkenny, s. of Thomas and Mary
(Fines). e. St Omers College 1645-6. E.C. Rome October 16th,
1646-June 21st, 1647. S.J. 1647. Nov and phil in another province.
Liège (theol) 1656. Ordained priest 1657. Ghent (tert) 1657. St Omers
College 1658. Residence of St Michael 1659. Left S.J. 1661. Readm.
S.J. June 19th, 1669. College of the Holy Apostles 1672-6, 1678-82.
College of St Thomas of Canterbury 1683, 1684. d. June 3rd, 1685, in
England. (Fo.7; CRS.40/37; CRS.55/497; 113; CRS.69; Nec).

ROCKLEY, Francis *alias* Ireland. Priest.
 b.1656, Yorkshire. ?s. of Francis. e. St Omers College ?-1675. S.J.
September 7th, 1675. Watten (nov) 1676. Liège (phil) 1678, 1679. Liège
(theol) 1680-3. Ordained priest June 12th, 1683. Ghent (tert) 1684.
College of the Holy Apostles 1684-7. Bury St Edmunds 1687. Ipswich
1687. Ipswich gaol 1688. College of the Holy Apostles 1689-93. College
of St Ignatius 1696-7, 1699-01, 1703-5. Residence of St Mary 1706.
College of St Ignatius 1708-10. Residence of St Mary 1711-16, 1720.
College of St Ignatius 1724. d.1724 or 1725, in England. (Fo.7; CRS.69;
113; 43 ff.17-20; Hun.50; Nec).

ROCKLIFFE, Robert. Scholastic.
 b.1797. e. Stonyhurst 1809-?14. S.J. September 7th, 1814. Hodder
(nov) 1814-16. Stonyhurst (phil) 1817. Stonyhurst (theol) 1818. Left
1818, not ordained. (116; 113; 2; Stol).

ROELS see Rousse, Charles and Louis.

ROELS, Norbert. Laybrother.
 b.1649, Belgium. S.J. December 31st, 1668. Watten (nov) 1669,
1672-4. Liège 1675-6, 1678-82. d. April 8th, 1682, Liège. (Fo.7; 114;
113; Nec).

ROGÈ, Joseph *alias* St George and Parry. Priest.

b. January 17th, 1681, London. S.J. November 1704. Liège (phil)
1708, 1709. Liège (theol) 1710-12. Ordained priest 1712. Ghent (tert)
1713. Liège 1714-6, 1718, 1720, 1724. College of St Ignatius 1724.
Ghent 1725-7. In England 1728. Liège 1730, 1733-41, 1743-4, 1746-50,
1752-8, 1761. d. January 17th, 1763, Liège. (Fo.7; 114; 91; 113; 74; 150
III(2) 8/4/41; 51 f.311; Nec).

ROGERS, Edward. Laybrother.
b. April or August 17th, 1662, Hampshire. S.J. December 12th,
1692. Watten (nov) 1693, 1696. Rome 1697, 1699-1701, 1703-6,
1708-16, 1720, 1723-4. d.c.1724, ?Rome. (Fo.7; 113; 150 II(3)
15/11/92; Nec).

ROGERS, Henry. Laybrother.
b. October 9th, 1625, Sussex. S.J. September or October 1655.
Watten (nov) 1656, 1657. St Omers College 1658-61, 1663-5, 1667,
1669, 1672-6, 1678-87, 1689-93. d. December 21st, 1695, St Omers
College. (Fo.7; 114; 113; Nec).

ROGERS, Philip *alias* Anselm. Priest.
b. November 2nd, 1691, Denbighshire. e. St Omers College 1714 or
earlier -17. S.J. September 7th, 1717. Watten (nov) 1718. Liège (phil)
1720. St Omers College 1723. Liège (theol) 1724-7. Ordained priest
c.1727. E.C. Rome 1728, 1730. Courtfield 1731. Clytha 1733.
Residence of St George 1734-8 (Superior 1735). E.C. Rome 1739-41.
Spetchley 1742. Residence of St George 1743-4, 1746-7, 1749-50, 1752.
Residence of St Michael 1753-8 (Bransby 1753-?). d. February 3rd,
1761, in England. (Fo.7; CRS.69; 114; 91; 113; 150 III(2) 15/7/41; 12
f.183v; 74; HMC. 10th Report App.4/184; 158; 156 App.1;
YA.77/200; 140 n.45; CRS.62 index; Nec).

ROGERSON, George. Priest.
b. May 10th, 1800, Garstang, Lancashire. e. Stonyhurst 1812-18.
S.J. September 7th, 1818. Hodder (nov) 1818-20. ?Stonyhurst (phil)
1820-22. St Acheul (?phil) 1822. Stonyhurst (theol etc.) 1822-32.
Ordained priest November 13th, 1830, Stonyhurst. Preston 1832-5.
Pylewell 1835-6. St Mary's Hall (tert) 1836-8. Worcester 1838-40. d.
January 27th, 1840, Worcester. bu. Chapel graveyard, Worcester.
(Fo.7; 115; CRW.68; Nec).

ROKEBY or ROOKESBY, Ralph or John. Laybrother.
b.1628, Northumberland, S.J. August 25th, 1659. Watten (nov)
1659, 1660. St Omers College 1661, 1663-5, 1667, 1669. Socius to the
provincial 1672. Watten 1673. Paris 1674-6, 1678-83. St Omers College
1684, 1685. Antwerp 1686-9. d. February 8th, 1690, Watten. (Fo.7;
114; 113; 123 II f.112; 108; Nec).

ROOKWOOD, Henry. Priest.
b. November 8th, 1658 or 1659, Suffolk. s. of Ambrose and
Elizabeth (Caldwell or Cadwell) of Stanningfield, Suffolk. e. St Omers
College ?-1681. S.J. September 7th, 1681. Watten (nov) 1681, 1682.
Liège (phil) 1683-5. Liège (theol) 1686-7, 1689. Ordained priest c.1690.
Watten (tert) 1690. Bruges 1691. College of the Holy Apostles 1693,

1696-7, 1699-1701, 1703-6, 1708-16, 1718, 1720, 1723-5. In England
1726-8 (Coldham Hall ?1691-1727-?). d. April 20th or 21st, 1730,
Norfolk. bu. Stanningfield church. (Fo.7; CRS.69; 91; 113; 60 f.6; 43
ff.21 ff; Nec).
ROPER, Thomas. Priest.
b. January 24th, 1654, Kent. ?s. of Christopher, 4th Lord Teynham
and Philadelphia (Mill *née* Knollys). e. St Omers College ?-1673. S.J.
August 14th, 1673. Watten (nov) 1673. Liège (phil) 1674-6. St Omers
College 1678-82. Liège (theol) 1682-5. Ordained priest September 19th,
1683. Watten (tert) 1686. Residence of St George 1687, 1689-93
(Superior 1689-c.92), 1696-1700 (Superior 1696-c.1700. ?Evesham
c.1693-c.1700). Antwerp 1700-10. Ghent 1711-6. d. May 12th, 1716,
Ghent. (Fo.7; CRS.69; 114; 113; 150 III(1) 2/8/98; 140 n.45; 108;
CRS.62/134, 191, 285-6; 40 pp.8, 188; Nec).
ROSE, Christopher. Priest.
b. September 1st, 1741. e. St Omers and Bruges Colleges c.1758-63.
S.J. September 7th, 1763. Watten (nov) 1763, 1764. Liège (theol)
1767-9. Ordained priest c.1769. Ghent 1770. Yarm 1770. Hardwick
1770. Residence of St John 1771. Hardwick 1772-1825. Durham 1825.
?Readm. S.J. d. July 8th, 1826, Durham. bu. St Oswald's, Durham.
(Fo.7; CRS.69; 114; 91; 113; NCH.4/16; 21 v.2; 36 ff.173, 262; 51
f.206; 68 p.195; 90 f.171; CRS.4/248; 163; 167; 125; 117;
AHSJ.42/310; Nec).
ROTHWELL see Rigmeadon, John.
ROUSSE, Charles *alias* Roels. Priest.
b. April 17th, 1690, Watten. ?Uncle of Louis. e. St Omers College
?-1710. S.J. February 1st, 1710. Watten (nov) 1711. Liège (phil) 1712-4.
Liège (theol) 1715-6, 1718. Ordained priest c.1718. Liège 1720-64
(Rector 1743-52, 1752-9). d. March 22nd, 1764, Liège. (Fo.7; CRS.69;
114; 91; 113; 90 f.21; 150 III(2) 29/6/43, 27/7/43, CRS.17/92; 109;
Nec).
ROUSSE, Louis *alias* Roels. Priest.
b. November 12th, 1732, Watten. ?Nephew of Charles. e. St Omers
College 1748-c.53. S.J. September 7th, 1753. Watten (nov) 1753-5.
Liège (phil) 1756-8. Ordained priest c.1761. Maryland 1761, 1763,
1767-9, 1771-94. d. February 24th or 27th, 1794, St Thomas's,
Maryland. (Fo.7; CRS.69; 91; 114; 113; Hu.Text 2/695; 68 p.269;
CRS.12/44; 92; Nec).
ROWE, William. Priest.
b. July 6th, 1803, Blackburn. e. Ushaw College. S.J. June 6th, 1822.
Montrouge (nov) 1822-4. St Acheul (phil) 1824. Paris (theol) 1824-6.
Dôle (theol) 1826-8. Ordained priest October 7th, 1827, Fribourg.
Stonyhurst 1828. Bristol 1828-30. St Mary's Hall 1830-1. Stonyhurst
1831-2. Norwich 1832-5. St Mary's Hall (tert) 1835. Stonyhurst 1836-8.
Wigan 1838-9. Spinkhill 1839-40. Tunbridge Wells 1840-1. Stonyhurst
1841. St Mary's Hall 1842-4. Stonyhurst 1844-5. Tunbridge Wells
1845-6-? Westminster 1852-5. Tunbridge Wells 1855-9. London

1859-60. Stonyhurst 1860-1. Liverpool 1861-7. Beaumont College 1867-8. Mount St Mary's College 1869. d. June 23rd, 1869, Rhyl. bu. St Beuno's College. (Fo.7; 115; NA.27/162; 113; Nec).

ROWLAND see Crosby, John.

ROYALL, John. Priest.

    b. February 22nd, 1729, Pennsylvania. e. St Omers College c.1740-7. S.J. September 7th, 1747. Watten (nov) 1747-9. Liège (phil) 1750. Liège (theol) 1752-5. Ordained priest c.1755. Plowden Hall 1756-62. Great Canford 1762-6. Swynnerton 1766, 1767. Culcheth, Southworth, Croft 1767, 1768. Husbands Bosworth 1768, 1769. d. April 17th, 1770, Husbands Bosworth. (Fo.7; CRS.69; 114; 91; 113; SCH.3/14, 9/10, 12/17; RH.10/165 ff;21 v.2; 41 n.94; 44 ff.223v, 227v, 270-1; 12 f.129; 64 pp.270, 514; 119 f.37; CRS.OP.1/67; 65; 68 p.42; 80; HMC. 10th Report App.1/194; 169/155/8; Nec).

ROYCROFT or RYCROFT, Thomas. Laybrother.

    b.1641, Lancashire. S.J. May 31st, 1670. Watten (nov) 1672. Rome (nov) 1672. Rome 1683-7, 1689, 1691-3, 1696-7, 1699-1701, 1703-4. d.c.1704, ?Rome. (Fo.7; 113; Nec).

ROZIER see Boucher, William.

RUGA, Bartholomew *alias* Bartholomew, John. Priest.

    b. April 1st, 1634, Milan. S.J. c.1650. To the English province c.1687. College of St Ignatius (chaplain to the Queen) 1687, 1688. In France 1689. St Germain 1691-3, 1696-7, 1699-1701, 1703-6, 1708-14. d. April 10th, 1715, Paris. (Fo.7; 114; 113; 123 IIIB f.250; CRS.62/162, 174, 252, 253, 257; Nec).

RUSSELL, Alexander. Priest.

    b. February 13th or April 17th, 1669, Edinburgh. s. of William and Catherine (Leslie). S.C. Douay 1688. S.J. August 15th or 19th, 1691 in the Scottish mission. In England 1729. Paris 1730. Liège 1733-40, 1742. d. September 14th, 1742, Liège. (Fo.7; 113; 114; RSC.60).

RUSSELL, John. Laybrother.

    b. April 1666 or 1668 or 1669, Flanders. S.J. October 31st, 1689. Watten (nov) 1690, 1691, 1692-3, 1696, 1699-1701. Liège 1703. St Omers College 1704-6, 1708-12. Watten 1713-6, 1718, 1720. d. February 15th, 1721, St Omers College. (Fo.7; 114; 113; Nec).

RUSSELL, Thomas. Priest.

    b.1655, Worcestershire. s. of Thomas and ?Jane (Smith) of Little Malvern, Worcestershire. e. St Omers College ?-1676. S.J. September 7th, 1676. Watten (nov) 1676-8. Liège (phil) 1679, 1680. Liège (theol) 1681-4. Ordained priest March 17th, 1685. Ghent (tert) 1685. Residence of St George 1686-7, 1689-94 (?Worcester 1693). College of St Thomas of Canterbury 1696-7. Residence of St George 1699. College of St Francis Xavier 1700-01. Residence of St George 1701, 1703-6, 1708-16, 1720, 1723-4 (Little Malvern c.1703, 1711, 1715, 1724). d.?1724, ?in England. (Fo.7; CRS.69; 113; WR.3/26, 4/31, 20/71; E and P.271, 276; Nec).

RYCROFT see Roycroft.

RYLEY see Riley.

RYTHER, Thomas. Priest.
b.1663, Yorkshire. e. St Omers College ?-1683. S.J. September 7th,
1683. Watten (nov) 1684, 1685. Liège (phil) 1685-7. Liège (theol)
1689-92. Ordained priest December 27th, 1691. Ghent 1693. College of
St Thomas of Canterbury 1696-7, 1699-1700. Residence of St
Stanislaus 1701. College of St Thomas of Canterbury 1703-6, 1708-16,
1718, 1720, 1724-5 (Little Crabbets ?-1707-?). In England 1726.
London 1727. Watten 1727. St Omers College 1728, 1730-1, 1733. d.
December 21st, 1733, St Omers College. (Fo.7; CRS.69; 91; 114; 113;
44 f.162; 64 pp.86-7; Nec).

ST GEORGE see Rogè, Joseph.

ST GERMAIN, Peter de. Priest.
From France. London 1673-5 (Preacher to the Duchess of York).
(113; Phi.104).

ST LEGER see Chapman, James and John.

ST LEGER, John. Priest.
b. June 26th, 1798, Waterford, Ireland. br. of Robert. S.J.
September 7th, 1818, Irish province. Calcutta mission 1834-9. (Fo.7: 52
f.23; CDSJ; JICH.7/18 ff).

ST LEGER, Robert. Priest.
b. February 7th, 1788, Waterford, Ireland. br. of John. e.
Stonyhurst 1805-? S.J. September 7th, 1807, Irish province. Calcutta
mission 1834-9. (Fo.7; Stol; 52 f.23; JICH.7/18 ff; CDSJ. For writings
see Som.).

SABRAN, Louis de *alias* Whitmore or Witmore, James. Priest.
b. March 1st, 1652, Paris or London. s. of Marquis de Sabran. e. St
Omers College 1663-70. S.J. September 7th, 1670. Watten (nov) 1672.
Liège (phil) 1673-5. St Omers College 1678, 1679. Liège (theol) 1679-81.
Ordained priest August 28th, 1679. Ghent (military chaplain) 1682,
1683. Brussels 1684. College of St Ignatius 1685-8. France 1689, 1690.
(chaplain to the Prince of Wales). St Germain 1691, 1692. Socius to the
provincial 1693. Liège 1696, 1697. Liège Episcopal Seminary
(President) 1699-1701, 1703-4. St Omers College 1705, 1706. St
Germain 1708. Vice-provincial 1709-12. St Omers College 1712-6
(Rector 1712-5). E.C. Rome c.1717, 1719-21, 1723-8, 1730. d. January
22nd, 1732, Rome. (Fo.5 and 7; CRS.69; 114; CRS.62; 113; Gil.5/460;
150 II(2) 8/7/79, III(1) 29/10/07, 13/11/17, 3/2/18, 9/4/18; 9 nn.73,
82 ff; 191 n.6; 90 f.187; 91; 171; CRS.63/104; Chad.249-59, Ki.203; 168
f.66; 123 IIIB ff.237, 253-6; 140 n.45; 108; Che.48 pp.146 ff, 64 pp.408
ff,450; DNB. Nec. For writings see Som.).

SACHMORTER, Philip *alias* Jameson. Priest.
b. November 8th, 1720, Dunkirk. S.J. September 7th, 1738. Watten
(nov) 1738, 1739. Liège (phil) 1740, 1742. Louvain (theol) 1743-6.

Ordained priest c.1745. Dunkirk 1746. Ghent (tert) 1747, 1748. Watten 1749-50, 1752-8. St Omers College 1761. Watten 1763-4, 1767. Liège 1768. Hammersmith 1769. Hammersmith 1771, 1772-?95. d. September 6th, 1795, Hammersmith. bu. St Paul's churchyard, Hammersmith. (Fo.7; 114; 91; 113; CRS.59/47; 108; LR.1/33; Nec).

SADLER or SADLEIR, Benjamin. Scholastic.

b.1667, London. ?br. of Edward and John. e. St Omers College ?-1686. S.J. 1686. Watten (nov) 1686, 1687. Liège (phil) 1689, 1690. d. August or October 14th, 1690, Liège, not ordained. (Fo.7; CRS.69; 114; 113; Nec).

SADLER or SADLEIR, Edward. Priest.

b.1663 or 1668 or 1673, London. ?br. of Benjamin and John. e. St Omers College ?-1690. S.J. September 7th, 1690. Watten (nov) 1690, 1692. Liège (phil) 1693. Liège (theol) 1696, 1697. Ordained priest 1699. Ghent (tert) 1699, 1700-01. College of St Ignatius 1703-6. Residence of St Michael 1708-16, 1720 (York c.1710). College of the Holy Apostles 1724-6. Ingatestone 1727. College of the Holy Apostles 1728-38. Residence of St Mary 1739, 1740. College of the Holy Apostles 1743-4, 1746-50. d. May 8th, 1751, Wealside, Essex. (Fo.7; CRS.69; 114; 91; 113; ER.5/36, 9/105-6, 112; CRS.4/376; Ki.122; 108; 43 ff.44-52, 54-62, 79).

SADLER or SADLEIR, John. Priest.

b.1664 or 1665, London. ?br. of Benjamin and Edward. e. St Omers College ?-1683. S.J. September 7th, 1683. Watten (nov) 1684, 1685. Liège (phil) 1685-7. Liège (theol) 1689-92. Ordained priest April 14th, 1691. Liège 1693, 1694. College of the Holy Apostles 1695, 1696. Bury St Edmunds 1697, 1698. d. February 22nd, 1699, in England. (Fo.7; CRS.69; 114; 113; 43 ff.21, 26-8; Nec).

SALE, John. Priest.

b. October 20th, 1722, Hopcar, Lancashire. s. of William and Anne (Tristram) of Hopcar. e. St Omers College 1738-41. S.J. September 7th, 1741. Watten (nov) 1742. Liège (phil) 1743, 1744. Munster (theol) 1746-9. Ordained priest 1748. St Omers College 1750-52. Residence of St Mary 1752. Biddleston 1752-6. Soberton 1757-9. Crosby 1759-63. ?Holywell 1763. Crosby 1763-72. Walton Hall 1773. Manchester 1773. Leigh 1775-7. Ulverston 1780-91. d. October 23rd, 1791, Ulverston. (Fo.7; CRS.69, 91; 114; 113; 3/28; 21 v.2; LF.27; 23 f.245; 44 ff.167, 218, 268; 36 f.167; 55 f.39v; 64 pp.57, 375, 466; 25 ff.2, 9, 13, 17, 21, 69, 78, 103, 111, 117; 80; L and C.117/84; 155 II 129; Ki.270; CRS.6/117; CRS.3/107; CRS.12/37; CRS.20/10; 167 p.31; 109; 24 ff.29, 75; 119 ff.7, 9, 13, 16, 22, 25, 35, 39, 42; CRS.OP.1/43; Nec).

SALKELD, Thomas.

Watten (nov) 1686, 1687. Does not appear again under this name; no evidence to show that he completed the noviceship. (113).

SALTMARSH, Edward *alias* Lewis. Priest.

b. September 16th, 1656, Yorkshire. s. of Edward and Geraldine (Meynell *née* Ireland) of Saltmarsh, Yorkshire. e. St Omers College

?-1678. S.J. September 7th, 1678. Watten (nov) 1679. Liège (phil) 1680-2. Liège (theol) 1683-6. Ordained priest 1687. Watten 1687. Residence of St Michael 1689-93. Residence of St John 1696-7, 1699-1701, 1703-6. Residence of St Winefrid 1708-11. Liège 1712-6, 1718, 1720. Ghent 1722-5 (Rector). Liège 1725-7. York c.1728, 1729. Great Warningfield 1729-?33. College of St Aloysius 1733-6. d. May 21st, 1737, Watten. (Fo.7; CRS.69; 91; 114; 113; E and P.332; 74; CRS.Mon.2/388; 43 ff.48v, 51v, 54v, 56v; CRS.4/376; CRS.25/112; Nec).

SAMFORD see Sandford.

SANDERS, Francis *alias* Baines. Priest.

b.1648, Worcestershire. s. of John. e. St Omers College 1663 or earlier -67. E.C. Rome November 6th, 1667-74. Ordained priest April 16th, 1672. S.J. June or July 4th, 1674. Watten (nov) 1674, 1675. St Omers College 1676. College of the Immaculate Conception 1676. Liège 1678-87. College of St Ignatius 1689. Socius to the provincial 1691, 1692. St Germain 1693-4, 1696-7, 1699-1701, 1703-6, 1708-10. d. February 19th, 1710, St Germain. (Fo.7; CRS.69; 114; 131; 113; CRS.40/75; 150 II(2) 14/7/74, 5/9/76, III(1) 20/11/06; Gil.5/475; Ki.204; DNB; 137 ff.212-3; 190 ff.5-8, 31-3; Ans.3/195; Nec. For writings see Som.).

SANDERS, or SAUNDERS, Thomas. Priest.

b. October 1st, 1724, Warwickshire. ?s. of Richard and Mary. e. St Omers College c.1738-c.44. S.J. September 7th, 1744. Watten (nov) 1746. Liège (phil) 1747. Germany (theol) 1748. Molsheim (theol) 1749. Liège (theol) 1750. Ordained priest c.1751. St Omers College 1752-4. Burton Park 1755-7. Spinkhill 1757. Burton Park 1757-72. Reigate 1772-7. Worcester 1777-90. d. November 12th, 1790, Worcester. bu. Worcester. (Fo.7; CRS.69; 91; 114; 113; RH.13/117; SCH.12/20; WR.7/3, 20/70; CRW.28 ff; 21 v.2; 6 f.242; 44 ff.267, 269, 273, 275-6; 54 f.73; 64 pp.518, 545; 39 f.15; 76 f.32; 68 p.35; HMC. 10th Report App.4/191; CRS.22/308, 316-8; Nec).

SANDERS, William. Priest.

b.1638, Yorkshire. e. St Omers College ?-1657. S.J. September 7th, 1657. Watten (nov) 1658. Liège (phil) 1659. Liège (theol) 1660, 1661. Ordained priest c.1662. St Omers College 1663. Ghent (tert) 1664, 1665. Residence of St Michael 1665-76. d. April 17th, 1676, in England. (Fo.7; CRS.69; 114; 113; 118; Nec).

SANDERSON, Nicholas (1). Laybrother.

b. October 20th or 29th, 1693, Lancashire. S.J. September 7th, 1725. Watten (nov) 1725-7. St Omers College 1727-8, 1730, 1733-40, 1742-4, 1746-50, 1752-8. d. September 22nd, 1761, St Omers College. (Fo.7; 114; 113; 91; Nec).

SANDERSON, Nicholas (2) *alias* Thompson. Priest.

b. January 22nd, 1731, Lancashire. s. of John. S.J. September 7th, 1750. Watten (nov) 1750. Liège (phil) 1752, 1754-5. Ordained priest July 11th, 1756. E.C. Valladolid 1756-63. Swinburn Castle 1763-77.

Haggerston c.1779. Berrington (serving Berwick) 1780-4. Alnwick 1784-90. d. December 30th, 1790, Alnwick. bu. Alnwick parish church. (Fo.7; CRS.69; 117; 113; 91; 57 I f.128; 1 ff.6-7; 7 ff.128, 133; 13 f.116; 21 v.2; 35 ff.108, 141-2, 206v. ff.217, 225, 228, 230-1, 262; 36 ff.4a, 65v, 186, 262; 65; 164; CRS.4/254; CRS.30/xxxix, 174, 189; 167 p.34; 125; 119 ff.12-3; Nec).

SANDERSON, Robert. Priest.

b. September 7th, 1715, Lancashire. e. St Omers College ?-1737. S.J. September 7th or 15th, 1738. Watten (nov) 1738-40. Liège (phil) 1740-2. Munster (theol) 1743-6. Ordained priest c.1747. Ghent (tert) 1747, 1748. College of St Thomas of Canterbury 1749-50, 1752. Residence of St Michael 1753-8, 1763-4 (Frickley 1753, 1759). Burghwallis ?1767-9. Residence of St Michael 1771. Burghwallis 1772-?81. d. December 2nd or 4th, 1781, Burghwallis. bu. St Helen's church. (Fo.7; CRS.69; 114; 117; 113; 91; 65; HMC. 10th Report App.4/187; CRS.12/21; 158; 155 II 127; 167; Ann.26; Nec).

SANDFORD or SAMFORD see Jenison, Augustine.

SANDS see Madgeworth.

SANDYS see Wignall, Francis.

SAUNDERS see Sanders, Thomas.

SAVAGE see Swinburn or Swinborne, John.

SAVILLE see Plowden, Richard; Preston, Sir Thomas; Smith, Richard.

SCARISBRICK, Edward (1) *alias* Neville. Priest.

b.1639, Lancashire. s. of Edward and Frances (Bradshaigh) of Scarisbrick Hall, Lancashire. br. of Francis (1), Henry (1) and Thomas. e. St Omers College 1653-9. S.J. September 7th, 1659. Watten (nov) 1660. Liège (phil) 1661, 1663. St Omers College 1664-5, 1667, 1669. Liège (theol) 1672, 1673. Ordained priest April 6th, 1672. Ghent (tert) 1674. St Omers College 1675-6, 1678-9. College of St Aloysius 1680-2, 1684-5. College of St Ignatius (royal preacher) 1686, 1687. In England 1688. In France 1689, 1690. St Omers College 1691. Watten 1692. College of St Aloysius 1693, 1696-7, 1699-1701, 1703-6, 1708-9 (Culcheth Hall ?1693-1709). d. February 19th, 1709, Culcheth Hall, Lancashire. bu. Winwick. (Fo.7; CRS.69; 114; 113; 23 f.35v; Gil.5/482; CRS.6/216; CRS.13/371; Che.64/454; Nec. For writings see Som.).

SCARISBRICK, Edward (2) *alias* Neville. Priest.

b. January 26th, 1664, Lancashire. s. of James and Frances (Blundell) of Scarisbrick Hall, Lancashire. br. of Joseph. e. St Omers College 1678 or earlier -82. S.J. September 7th, 1682. Watten (nov) 1682, 1683. Liège (phil) 1684-6. Liège (theol) 1687, 1689-91. Ordained priest c.1690. Watten 1692. St Omers College 1693, 1696-7, 1699. College of the Immaculate Conception 1700-01, 1703. College of St Aloysius 1704, 1706. College of the Immaculate Conception 1708-27 (Rector 1715-c.27. Clifton ?-1727-c.1731). In England 1728, 1730. College of St Ignatius 1734, 1735 (Bushey c.1731-c.1734). d. November 15th, 1735, Bushey or London. (Fo.7; CRS.69; 91; 113; ER.12/81, 84;

CRS.6/216; 170 f.245v; E and P.108; Nec).
SCARISBRICK, Edward (3) *alias* Neville. Priest.
b. March 23rd or 25th, 1698, Lancashire. s. of Robert and Anne
(Messenger) of Scarisbrick Hall, Lancashire. br. of Francis (2) and
Henry (2). e. St Omers College 1710-c.16. S.J. September 7th, 1716.
Watten (nov) 1716, 1718. Liège (phil) 1720. Liège (theol) 1723, 1724.
Ordained priest c.1725. College of St Ignatius 1725. In England 1727-8,
1730. Residence of St George 1733-44, 1746-50, 1752-5 (Wappenbury
?1726-39, 1752). College of the Immaculate Conception 1756-8,
1763-7. Holt 1767-9 (Rector of the College of the Immaculate
Conception 1763-c.70). Scarisbrick Hall 1771-8. d. July 7th, 1778,
Scarisbrick Hall. bu. Ormskirk. (Fo.7; CRS.69; CRS.6/216; 90 f.34;
113; SCH.3/17; 54 f.3; WR.20/61; 91; HMC. 10th Report App.4/187;
111; 51 f.311; 155 III 185c; CRS.62 index. Nec).
SCARISBRICK, Francis (1) *alias* Neville. Priest.
b.1643, Lancashire. s. of Edward and Frances (Bradshaigh) of
Scarisbrick Hall, Lancashire. br. of Edward (1), Henry (1) and
Thomas. e. St Omers College 1659 or earlier-63. S.J. September 7th,
1663. Watten (nov) 1663, 1664. Liège (phil) 1667. St Omers College
1669, 1672-3. Liège (theol) 1673-6, 1678. Ordained priest 1676. Liège
1679-82. Watten 1683-5. Liège 1686-7. College of St Aloysius 1689-93,
1696-7, 1699-1701, 1703-6, 1708-10 (Poole Hall 1692, c.1701. Crosby
1703). College of the Holy Apostles 1711-3. d. September 20th, 1713, in
England. (Fo.7; CRS.69; 114; CRS.6/216; 113; 150 II(2) 9/10/73; 43
ff.33, 35v; 9 n.4; 23 f.35; NB.1/39; Nec).
SCARISBRICK, Francis (2) *alias* Neville. Priest.
b. April 5th, 1703, Scarisbrick Hall, Lancashire. s. of Robert and
Anne (Messenger) of Scarisbrick Hall. br. of Edward (3) and Henry (2).
e. St Omers College c.1714-c.22. S.J. September 7th, 1722. Watten
(nov) 1723, 1724. Liège (phil) 1725-7. St Omers College 1728, 1730.
Liège (theol) 1733-5. Ordained priest 1735. E.C. Valladolid 1736-9.
Watten 1739, 1740. College of St Francis Xavier 1740, 1742. E.C.
Rome 1742-50. College of St Francis Xavier 1750. Ghent 1752.
Antwerp 1753-8. St Omers College 1759, 1761-2 (Rector 1761-2).
Bruges College 1762-4. Liège 1764-c.67 (Rector). Brussels 1768, 1769.
Bruges College 1771-3. Liège Academy 1776. d. July 16th, 1789, Liège.
bu. In church of the English Canonesses of the Holy Sepulchre, Liège.
(Fo.7; CRS.69; 114; 113; 12 f.184; 16 ff.97v, 100; 66; 68 p.99; 74; 90
f.54; 91; Chad.318; CRS.17/97, 173; CRS.30/xxxviii, 189; 121; 108;
111; CRS.6/216; Nec).
SCARISBRICK, Henry (1) *alias* Neville. Priest.
b.1641, Lancashire. s. of Edward and Frances (Bradshaigh) of
Scarisbrick Hall. br. of Edward (1), Francis (1) and Thomas. e. St
Omers College 1655-61. S.J. September 7th, 1661. Watten (nov) 1661.
Liège (phil) 1663-5. Liège (theol) 1667, 1669. Ordained priest c.1670.
Liège 1672. College of St Aloysius 1672-6, 1678-81, 1683-7, 1689-93,
1696-7, 1699-1701 (Scarisbrick Hall 1679-88). d. December 24th, 1701,

in England. (Fo.7; CRS.69; 114; 113; 121; CRS.4/433; CRS.6/216; Nec).

SCARISBRICK, Henry (2) *alias* Neville. Scholastic.
b. August 5th, 1711 or 1712, Lancashire. s. of Robert and Anne (Messenger) of Scarisbrick Hall. br. of Edward (3) and Francis (2). e. St Omers College c.1725-9. S.J. September 7th, 1729. In England 1733-7. St Omers College 1738. Liège (phil) 1739, 1740. Liège (theol) 1741. Lyons (theol) 1743. d. March 13th, 1744, Lyons, not ordained. (Fo.7; CRS.69; 114; 113; CRS.6/216; Nec).

SCARISBRICK, Joseph or Thomas Joseph *alias* Neville. Priest.
b. July 11th, 1673, Lancashire. s. of James and Frances (Blundell) of Scarisbrick Hall. br. of Edward (2). e. St Omers College ?-1692. S.J. September 7th, 1692. Watten (nov) 1693. Liège (phil) 1696. Liège (theol) 1697, 1699-1701. Ordained priest c.1701. Ghent (tert) 1701. St Omers College 1703, 1704. College of St Ignatius 1705. Residence of St George 1706, 1708-13. Residence of St Stanislaus 1714. College of the Holy Apostles 1715-6, 1718, 1720. College of St Aloysius 1723-5. In England 1726-8 (Dutton ?-1725-7, ?1728). d. January 20th, 1729, in England. (Fo.7; CRS.69; 91; 43 ff.35, 39; 113; 95/781; 23 f.62v; 40 f.46; 79 p.6; 89; CRS.6/216; CRS.25/114; Nec).

SCARISBRICK, Thomas *alias* Neville. Priest.
b.1642 or 1643, Lancashire. s. of Edward and Frances (Bradshaigh) of Scarisbrick Hall. br. of Edward (1), Francis (1) and Henry (1). e. St Omers College 1657-63. S.J. September 7th, 1663. Watten (nov) 1663. Rome 1664. Liège (phil) 1667. Liège (theol) 1669, 1672. Ordained priest c.1672. College of St Aloysius 1672 (?Lytham). d. May 4th, 1673, in England (?Scarisbrick Hall). (Fo.7; CRS.69; 114; 113; CRS.6/216; Nec).

SCHEPENS, Gerard. Priest.
S.J. in another province. Watten 1689. Nothing further found in English province records.

SCHILDERS, Abraham. Laybrother.
b. February 16th, 1680, Ghent. S.J. December 7th, 1705. Watten (nov) 1706. St Omers College 1708-16, 1718, 1720, 1723-4. Watten 1725-8, 1730. St Omers College 1733. d. October 29th, 1733, St Omers College. (Fo.7; 91; 114; 113; Nec).

SCHNEIDER, Theodore. Priest.
b. April 7th, 1703, Heidelberg, Germany. S.J. September 29th, 1721. To the English province c.1740. Pennsylvania 1741-4, 1746-50, 1752-8, 1763-4. d. July 10th, 1764, Pennsylvania. (Fo.7; 114; 113; Hu.Text 2/691; 150 III(2) 16/7/40, 29/9/40; 140 n.45; Nec).

SCHRYNWEERKER, Peter. Laybrother.
b. July 29th, 1678. S.J. February 14th, 1710, in another province. E.C. Rome 1738-40, 1746-50, 1752. d. August 2nd, 1753, Rome. (Fo.7; 113).

?SCHWARTZ, – . ?Priest.
Liège Academy 1776. Nothing further recorded. (90 f.54).

SCOLES, Erasmus. Priest.

d. October 2nd, 1684, Loretto. Not found in English province catalogues under this name. (Fo.7; 95 p.819).

SCOREY or SCORAY, Thomas. Priest.

b. December 30th or 31st, 1681, Yorkshire. e. St Omers College 1699-1703. S.J. September 7th, 1703. Watten (nov) 1704. Liège (phil) 1705, 1706. Liège (theol) 1708-11. Ordained priest 1710. Ghent (tert) 1712, 1713. Residence of St Michael 1714. College of the Immaculate Conception 1715, 1716. Residence of St Michael 1720. d. October 2nd, 1720, in Yorkshire. bu. Dewsbury church. (Fo.7; 202; CRS.69; 113; Nec).

SCOTT, Edward. Priest.

b. April 8th, 1776, Reigate, Surrey. s. of Adam and Mary (Bowyer). S.J. September 7th, 1811. Hodder (nov) 1811-2. Stonyhurst (theol) 1812-7. Ordained priest September 15th, 1816, Wolverhampton. London 1817-32. Hodder (tert) 1832. London 1832-3. Norwich 1833-5. Stonyhurst 1835-6. d. May 20th, 1836, Stonyhurst. bu. Stonyhurst. (Fo.7; 115; LR.3/7, 64; NA.37/165; 150 (1750-1853) ff.244, 260; 4 ff.143 ff; 6 f.238v; 7 ff.407, 413v, 417v, 420v, 422v, 427v, 429v; 8 II nn.172, 175A; 11 f.290v; 36 f.227v; 47 f.165v; 93 p.83; CRS.4/418; Nec. For writings see Sut.).

SCOTT, John. Priest.

b. February 25th, 1793, Shevington, near Wigan. e. Stonyhurst 1809-15. S.J. September 7th, 1815. Hodder (nov) 1815-7. Stonyhurst (phil) 1817-9. Clongowes (theol) 1819-23. Ordained priest September 1822, Dublin. Durham 1823-7. Preston 1827-33. Hodder (tert) 1833. St Mary's Hall 1834. Bury St Edmunds 1834-6. Norwich 1836-8. Boston 1838-54. d. December 17th, 1854, Boston. bu. Boston. (Fo.7; 115; NCH.4/13; NA.37/165; 21 v.2; Nec).

SCROOP or SCROPE, Robert. Scholastic.

b.1650 or 1652, Lincolnshire. S.J. September 7th, 1671. Watten (nov) 1672. Liège (phil) 1673-5. Liège (theol) 1676, 1678-80. Left 1681, not ordained. (Fo.7; 113; 150 II(2) 14/8/77, 10/5/81; 168 f.32v).

SCROPE or SCROOP see Hart, William.

SCUDAMORE see Jones, John (2).

SCUDAMORE, John *alias* Price. Priest.

b. March, 1696, Monmouthshire. ?s. of Henry and Mary of Pembridge, Herefordshire. e. St Omers College 1714-5 or later. S.J. September 7th, 1718. Watten (nov) 1720. Liège (phil) 1723. Liège (theol) 1724-7. Ordained priest c.1727. In England 1728, 1730 (Pyle, Glamorgan c.1728). College of St Francis Xavier 1733-40. Bristol c.1740-78. d. April 8th, 1778, Bristol. bu. Bristol. (Fo.7; CRS.69; 90 f.34; 113; 117; 21 v.2; CRS.62/170, 247; 51 ff.127, 311; 71; 91; HMC. 10th Report App.4/189, 194; Pa.21; E and P.184; CRS.3/181; 125; Nec).

SECHLY or SECHLI, Francis *alias* Soli. Laybrother.

b. April 5th, 1675. From Switzerland. S.J. February 10th, 1710 in

Rome. E.C. Rome 1716, 1723-8, 1730, 1733-9, 1746-50, 1752-7. d.
March 12th, 1758, Rome. (Fo.7; 113; 114; 91; 111; Nec).

SEED, Thomas. Priest.

b. February 12th, 1807, Preston. e. Stonyhurst 1819-25. S.J. August
28th, 1825. Montrouge (nov) 1825-7. Dôle (phil) 1827-8. Aix (phil)
1828-9. Stonyhurst 1829-36. St Mary's Hall (theol) 1836-40. Ordained
priest September 21st, 1839, Stonyhurst. Stonyhurst 1840-2.
Stonyhurst (tert) 1843. Stonyhurst 1843-5. Bury St Edmunds 1845-6.
Mount St Mary's College 1846-7 (Superior). Stonyhurst 1847-50.
Clitheroe 1850-1. Wigan 1851-60. Provincial 1860-4. St Beuno's
College 1864-71 (Rector). Beaumont College 1871-2. London 1872-3.
St Beuno's College 1873-4. d. January 28th, 1874, Rhyl. bu. St Beuno's
College. (Fo.7; 115; Nec. For writings see Sut. and Som.).

SEFTON or SEPHTON, John. Scholastic.

b. March 20th, 1742. ?From Lancashire. e. St Omers and Bruges
Colleges c.1757-62. S.J. September 7th, 1762. Watten (nov) 1763, 1764.
Liège (phil) 1765. d. April 24th, 1766, Ghent, not ordained. (Fo.7;
CRS.69; 114; 91; 113; 68 p.129; Nec).

SEFTON or SEPHTON, Thomas ?alias Worthington. Priest.

b. July 1st, 1719, Lancashire. e. St Omers College c.1732-8. S.J.
September 7th, 1738. Watten (nov) 1738, 1739. Liège (phil) 1740, 1741.
Paderborn (theol) 1743, 1744. Ordained priest c.1745. Liège 1746.
Ghent 1747, 1748. d. February 6th, 1748, Ghent. (Fo.7; CRS.69; 114;
113; Nec).

SEGRAVE, Henry. Priest.

b. October 22nd, 1806, Dublin. e. Stonyhurst 1815-23, Trinity
College, Dublin 1823-8. S.J. March 24th, 1828. Hodder (nov) 1828-30.
Stonyhurst (theol etc.) 1830-6. St Mary's Hall (theol) 1836, 1837.
Ordained priest September 24th, 1836, Stonyhurst. Wigan 1837-8. St
Mary's Hall 1838-41. Preston 1841-3. Stonyhurst 1844-9. Malta
1849-55 (Rector). London 1855-7. Barbados 1857-62. London 1862-4.
Wardour 1864-5. Beaumont College 1866. Stonyhurst 1867. d.
February 13th, 1869, Stonyhurst. bu. Stonyhurst. (Fo.7; 115; Nec).

SELBY see Blundell, Joseph; Janion, George; Smith, William.

SELBY, Thomas. Laybrother.

b. March 10th, 1707, Northumberland. s. of Thomas. e. St Omers
College c.1725-c.28. S.J. September 7th, 1731. Watten (nov) 1733,
1734. Liège 1735. Ghent 1736-41, 1743-50, 1752-9. d. January 7th,
1759, Ghent. (Fo.7; CRS.69; 114; 91; 113; 70 f.76; 111; ?E and P.205.
Nec).

SELBY, William alias Banister. Scholastic.

b.1636, Northumberland. s. of Sir William and Ellen (Haggerston)
of Biddleston. e. St Omers College 1651 or earlier -56. S.J. September
7th, 1656. Watten (nov) 1657. Liège (phil) 1658-60. St Omers College
1661, 1663-5. d. December 6th, 1666, Watten, not ordained. (Fo.7;
CRS.69; 113; 114; Nec).

SELOSSE or CELOSSE, Anthony (1). Priest.

b.1621, Artois. ?Uncle of Anthony (2). S.J. October 8th, 1658
(already ordained). Watten (nov) 1658. St Omers College 1659-61,
1663-5, 1667, 1669, 1671-6, 1678-87. d. March 23rd, 1687, St Omers
College. (Fo.7; 114; 113; 150 II(2) 26/12/71; Nec).

SELOSSE, Anthony (2). Priest.

b. April 25th, 1653, French Flanders. ?Nephew of Anthony (1). e. St
Omers College ?-1671. S.J. October 5th, 1671. Watten (nov) 1672.
Liège (phil) 1673-5. Liège (theol) 1676, 1678-80. Ordained priest April
20th, 1680. Watten (tert) 1680. College of St Ignatius 1681, 1682.
Burton Park c.1682-8 (serving Chichester). Horsham gaol 1688-90.
College of St Thomas of Canterbury 1690-2 (?Burton Park). St Omers
College 1693. d. May 11th, 1696, St Omers College. (Fo.5 and 7;
CRS.69; 114; 113; RH.13/115; CRS.22/305-6; 171; Nec).

SELOSSE, Peter see Coloss or Coloos.

SEMMES, Joseph. Priest.

b. December 1st, 1743, Maryland. s. of Joseph Milburn and Rachel
(Prater or Prather). e. St Omers College 1754-c.61. S.J. September 7th,
1761. Liège (phil) 1763, 1764. Liège (theol) 1767-9. Ordained priest
c.1767. Liège 1771-3. Liège Academy 1775, 1776. Dusseldorf 1779.
Munich 1780-2. Liège Academy 1783-4, 1788, 1792-4. Stonyhurst
1794-5, 1798, 1800-01, 1803, 1807-9. Readm. S.J. 1803 or 1804. d.
September 26th, 1809, Stonyhurst. bu. Stonyhurst. (Fo.7; CRS.69;
114; 91; 113; AHSJ.42/306; 6 ff.22v, 187v; 13 f.158; 21 v.2; 22 f.44; 54
ff.37v, 60v, 64; 57 I f.102v; 90 ff.54, 145v, 146v; 93 pp.19, 27, 35, 38,
43, 69; 127; 157; 55 f.147v; Nec. For writings see Som.).

SEMPLE or SEMPILL, Hugh. Priest.

b.1701, Scotland. s. of Robert and Elizabeth (Abercromby) of
Glasford, Scotland. S.J. 1717, ?Scottish mission. Ordained priest. To
English province c.1728. Watten 1730. ?Ghent 1732. Watten 1733-4.
Left 1734. (Fo.7; 113; 91; RSC.69; 150 III(2) 1/5/28, 12/4/32,
13/9/32, 22/5/34).

SEPHTON see Sefton; Worthington, John and Thomas.

SERRELL, James. Laybrother.

b. March 9th or 10th, 1664, Bruges. S.J. October 30th, 1687. Watten
(nov) 1689, 1690-3, 1696-7. St Omers College 1699-1701, 1703-6,
1708-15. d. August 9th, 1716, Dunkirk. (Fo.7; 114; 113; CRS.62 index;
Nec).

SEWALL, Charles. Priest.

b. July 4th, 1744, St Mary's County, Maryland. s. of N. L. Sewall.
br. of Nicholas. e. St Omers and Bruges Colleges 1758-64. S.J.
September 7th, 1764. Liège (phil) 1766, 1767. Liège (theol) 1769, 1771.
Ordained priest c.1771. Ghent 1772. Liège 1773. Maryland 1774-1806.
d. November 10th or 18th, 1806, Maryland. (Fo.7; CRS.69; 114; 91;
113; Hu.Text 2/700; 117; 4 f.63v; 16 f.33v; 54 f.163v; 51 ff.304, 307;
Nec).

SEWALL, Nicholas. Priest.

b. December 9th, 1745, St Mary's County, Maryland. s. of N. L.

Sewall. br. of Charles. e. St Omers and Bruges Colleges 1758-64. S.J.
October 31st, 1766. Ghent (nov) 1767. Liège (phil) 1768, 1769. Liège
(theol) 1771-3. Ordained priest April 2nd, 1772. Bruges School 1773.
Liège Academy 1774. Preston 1774-83. Eccleston 1783-7. Scholes
1787-90. Portico and Prescot 1790, 1793, 1796, 1799, 1801, 1803,
1805-8. Stonyhurst 1808-13 (Rector). Preston, Gillmoss, Stockeld Park
1814-6. Stonyhurst 1816-7 (Rector). Hodder 1817-21. Provincial
1821-6. Hodder 1826. Worcester 1827-34. Readm. S.J. 1803. d. March
14th, 1834, Worcester. bu. Worcester Catholic churchyard. (Fo.7; 114;
CRS.69; 113; 115; WR.20/70; CRW.59 ff; 150 (1750-1853) f.192; 4
ff.79, 88v; 1 f.68; 6 ff.135, 159, 164, 166, 169v, 175, 185, 187, 199, 211,
275v; 11 ff.127v, 154v, 212v, 254v, 258v; 16 f.78; 21 v.2; 23 ff.259v,
266, 269; 27 f.320; 152 n.33; 76 f.50; 25 ff.24, 120; 80; 93 pp.61, 76, 77,
78; 94 ff.37-8, 233-4; Gil.5/61; 155 II 129; CRS.7/417; CRS.20/11, 16,
17; 167 pp.23, 31; 105; 17; AHSJ.42/306; Nec. For writings see Sut.
Som.).

SHARPE see Stuart, William.

SHAW see Woodcock, William.

SHAW, John. Priest.

b. March 26th, 1739. ?From Lancashire. e. St Omers College
c.1751-c.58. S.J. September 7th, 1759. Watten (nov) 1761. Liège (phil)
1762. Liège (theol) 1763-4, 1766. Ordained priest c.1765. Ghent 1766.
Stubbs Walden 1767-9. Hooton 1769, 1772-3. Leigh c.1773, 1778-80,
1783-4, 1789, 1792, 1794-6, 1798, 1803-4, 1807-8. Hodder 1808.
Readm. S.J. 1803 or 1804. d. September 1st, 1808, Hodder. bu.
Stonyhurst. (Fo.7; CRS.69; 114; 91; 113; AHSJ.42/306; 7 f.197v; 21
v.2; 26 ff.4, 201c; 55 f.168v; 62 n.58; 65; 68 pp.75, 125; 25 ff.48, 51,
130, 141, 145, 150, 161; 97; 80; 155 II 129; 155 III 185c; 167 pp.23, 29;
119 ff.15, 31; Nec).

SHEFFIELD, Ignatius see Anderson, William.

SHELDON see Elliott, Nathaniel.

SHELDON, Edward. Priest.

b. March 29th, 1716, Warwickshire. s. of Edward and Elizabeth
(Shelley) of Weston and Beoley. e. St Omers College c.1729-33. S.J.
September 9th, 1733-50. Watten (nov) 1734. Liège (phil) 1735-7.
Ingolstadt (theol) 1738-41. Liège (theol) 1742. Ordained priest c.1741.
Watten 1743-4, 1746. Liège 1748-9. (Fo.7; CRS.69; 91; 113; 150 III(2)
13/3/42).

SHELDON, Henry (1). Priest.

b.1652, Oxfordshire, s. of Edward and Catherine (Constable) of
Steeple Barton, Oxfordshire. Uncle of Henry (2) and Ralph. e. St
Omers College ?-1670. S.J. September 7th, 1670. Watten (nov) 1672.
Liège (phil) 1672-5. Liège (theol) 1676, 1678-9. Ordained priest April
1st, 1679. Ghent (tert) 1679, 1680. Liège 1680-5. Loretto 1686, 1687.
Rome 1688, 1689. Loretto 1690. E.C. Rome 1690, 1691. Watten 1692.
Liège 1693. E.C. Rome 1696. Liège 1697. Residence of St Winefrid
1699, 1700. Liège 1701, 1703. Ghent 1703-7 (Rector). St Omers College

1708, 1709. Liège 1710, 1711. Watten 1712-4. d. October 20th, 1714, St Omers College. (Fo.7; CRS.69; 114; 113; 150 II(3) 26/7/86, 14/10/90; 168 f.86v; 139 f.295; CRS.62/94, 164, 168, 175, 179, 183-4, 195; Nec).

SHELDON, Henry (2) or Joseph. Priest.

b. March 3rd, 1686, Worcestershire. s. of Ralph and Mary Anne (Elliot) of Weston and Beoley. br. of Ralph. Nephew of Henry (1). e. St Omers College 1699 or earlier – 1702 or later. S.J. September 7th, 1705. Watten (nov) 1706. Liège (phil) 1708-10. St Omers College 1711-14. Liège (theol) 1715-6, 1718. Ordained priest c.1718. St Omers College 1720, 1723-4. Travelling (Italy, France etc.) 1725-8, 1730, 1733-5. Residence of St George 1736, 1737. E.C. Rome 1738-44 (Rector). Provincial 1744-51. E.C. Rome 1750-6 (Rector). d. January 1st, 1756, Rome. (Fo.7; CRS.69; 114; 113; 150 III(2) 18/7/44; 9 n.72; 12 f.183 ff; HMC. 10th Report App.4/194; Ki.206; 91; Nec).

SHELDON, Henry (3). Scholastic.

b. March 19th, 1670. S.J. September 8th, 1691. Paris (nov) 1693. Liège (phil) 1696. Liège (theol) 1697. Nothing further recorded under this name. (113).

SHELDON, Ralph *alias* Elliot. Priest.

b. August 13th, 1681, Oxfordshire. s. of Ralph and Mary Anne (Elliot) of Weston and Beoley. br. of Henry (2). Nephew of Henry (1), e. St Omers College c.1694-1700. S.J. September 7th, 1700. Watten (nov) 1701. Liège (phil) 1703-5. Liège (theol) 1706, 1708-9. Ordained priest c.1709. Ghent (tert) 1710, 1711. Liège 1712-6, 1718. College of St Chad 1720, 1723-4. St Omers College 1725. In England 1726. Watten 1727. Antwerp 1728. London 1730-1, ?1732. Ghent 1733, 1734. Liège 1735-41. d. March 8th, 1741, Liège. (Fo.7; CRS.69; 114; 91; 113; 43 ff.52-5; 150 III(2) 7/4/31; 9 nn.72, 240 and *passim*; CRS.62/110, 230; Nec).

SHELLEY, Francis see Lewis, Theodore.

SHELLEY, Henry. Scholastic.

b.1662. e. St Omers College ?-1682. S.J. September 7th, 1682. Watten (nov) 1682, 1683. Liège (phil) 1684. d. April 20th, 1684, Liège, not ordained. (Fo.7; CRS.69; 114; Nec).

SHELLEY, John. Scholastic.

b. January 22nd, 1728. From Ireland. S.J. September 7th, 1747. Watten (nov) 1747, 1749. Liège (phil) 1752, 1753. Left 1754, not ordained. (113; 91).

SHELLEY, Walter. Priest.

b. February 13th, 1701, London. ?s. of Sir John, 3rd Bart. and Mary (Gage) of Michelgrove, Sussex. e. St Omers College ?-1717. S.J. September 27th, 1717. Watten (nov) 1718. Liège (phil) 1720. Liège (theol) 1723-5. Ordained priest c.1725. Ghent (tert) 1726, 1727. Liège 1728, 1730, 1733-41, 1743. Antwerp 1743-50. d. February 21st, 1750, Antwerp. (Fo.7; CRS.69; 114; 91; 113; 74; 108; CRS.62/23, 72, 278; Nec. For writings see Som.).

SHEPHERD, Peter. Scholastic.

b. May 18th, 1703 or 1704. ?From Blackrod, Lancashire. ?s. of John
and Ellen. S.J. 1725. Watten (nov) 1725-7. Liège (phil) 1728, 1730. d.
March 21st, 1733, Büren, Germany. (Fo.7; 114; 91; 113; 81; E and
P.152; Nec).

SHIREBURN or SHERBURN, Charles. Priest.

b.1684, Lancashire. e. St Omers College 1697-1702. S.J. September
7th, 1702. Watten (nov) 1703, 1704. Liège (phil) 1705, 1706. St Omers
College 1708-12. La Flèche (theol) 1713, 1714. Liège (theol) 1715.
Ordained priest 1715. Ghent (tert) 1716. St Omers College 1718,
1723-4. College of the Holy Apostles 1724, 1725. In England 1726,
1727. College of the Holy Apostles 1728-40 (Bury's Hall ?-1727,
1728-?). Provincial 1740-44. College of St Ignatius 1744. d. January
17th, 1745, London. (Fo.7; CRS.69; 114; 113; CRS.62/96, 102, 112,
114, 215, 256, 295, 310; LR.3/8; 150 III(2) 16/7/40; 89; 91; HMC. 10th
Report App.4/185, 194; 43 ff.44, 45, 51-5, 57-8, 64, 66; CRS.7/171;
Pa.47; SCR.79; Nec).

SHIREBURNE or SHERBURN, Thomas. Laybrother.

b.1627, Lancashire. S.J. 1651 or 1652. Watten (nov) 1652. Ghent
1653-5. St Omers College 1656-8. Rome 1659-68. St Omers College
1669. Maryland 1669-70. d. July 23rd, 1670, Maryland. (Fo.7; 114;
113; 150 II(2) October 1668; Hu.Text 2/681; Nec).

SHIRLEY see Huddleston, John.

SHORT, Francis *alias* Curtis, Maximilian. Priest.

b. September 23rd, 1718, Suffolk or Worcestershire. s. of
Maximilian. e. St Omers College 1732-7. S.J. September 7th, 1737.
Watten (nov) 1738. Liège (phil) 1739-41. Wurzburg (theol) 1743-4,
1746. Ordained priest c.1746. Watten 1747. St Omers College 1748,
1749. Burghwallis or Frickley 1750. West Grinstead 1750-4. Slindon
1754. Soberton 1754-5. d. November 9th, 1755, Soberton. (Fo.7;
CRS.69; 114; 91; 113; CRS.44/11; 44 f.167; HMC. 10th Report
App.4/194; 156 App.I; 118; WGC.345, 349, 352; Nec).

SHUTTLEWORTH, John *alias* Richardson. Priest.

b. May 18th, 1708, Lancashire. e. St Omers College c.1725-30. S.J.
September 7th, 1730. Liège (phil) 1733, 1734. St Omers College
1735-40. Clermont (theol) 1740, 1741. St Omers College 1742-4.
Ordained priest c.1743. Liège 1744. E.C. Rome 1747-50. College of St
Aloysius 1750. Rudge 1751. College of St Aloysius 1751. Residence of
St Mary 1751-65 (Superior 1755-64. Britwell 1751-2, 1758). d. June
25th, 1765, Britwell. bu. Britwell churchyard. (Fo.7; CRS.69; 114; 91;
113; 150 III(2) 27/10/42; 12 ff.186-8; 64 p.466; 74; HMC. 10th Report
App.4/193; CRS.7/389, 391, 394; CRS.13/292-3; 140 n.45; Nec).

SIDDLE, Charles or John see Hodgkinson, Charles.

SIMEON see Plowden, Charles, Edmund, Francis, Francis Peter and
Richard.

SIMEON, Edward *alias* Simon or Simons and Smith. Priest.

b.1632, London. s. of Sir George and Margaret (Molyneux) of
Britwell, Oxfordshire. e. St Omers College 1644-9. E.C. Rome

November 13th, 1649-52. S.J. June or July 1st, 1656. Watten (nov) 1656. Liège (theol) 1657-61. Ordained priest April 16th, 1661. Ghent (tert) 1661. College of St Thomas of Canterbury 1663, 1664. College of St Aloysius 1667. Pontoise 1668-71. College of the Holy Apostles 1672. Residence of St George 1672, 1673. College of St Thomas of Canterbury 1674-6, 1678. Ghent 1679. Brussels 1679-82. College of St Aloysius 1683-7, 1689-93, 1696-7, 1699-1701 (Rector 1689-c.92). d. January 6th, 1701, Garswood. bu. Winwick. (Fo.7; CRS.69; CRS.40/93; CRS.55/515; 113; 114; 150 II(2) 3/5/70, II(3) 19/6/88; CRS.8/411; 168 ff.19v, 86; 108; 121; Nec).

SIMEON, Francis. Scholastic.

b.1654, London or Staffordshire. S.J. September 7th, 1673. Watten (nov) 1673. Liège (phil) 1674-6. d. June 1st, 1678, Liège, not ordained. (Fo.7; 113; 114).

SIMEON, James. Scholastic.

b. February 27th, 1692, Staffordshire. s. of Sir James, 1st Bart. and Bridget (Heveningham) of Chilworth, Oxfordshire. e. St Omers College ?-1709. S.J. September 7th, 1709. Watten (nov) 1710, 1711. Liège (phil) 1712, 1713. d. May 21st, 1714, Liège, not ordained. (Fo.7; CRS.69; 114; 113; CRS.62 index; Nec).

SIMEON, Joseph. Laybrother.

b. March 22nd, 1691, Warwickshire. S.J. June 28th, 1713. Liège (nov) 1714-6, 1718, 1720, 1723-4. Ghent 1725-8. d. July 9th, 1728, Ghent. (Fo.7; 113; 91; Nec).

SIMEON or SIMON, Walter. Priest.

d. July 18th, 1691, Liège. Not in English province catalogues under this name. (Fo.7; 95 p.825).

SIMEON or SIMON, William. Priest.

d. July 28th, 1698, Louvain. Not in English province catalogues under this name. (Fo.7; 95 p.829).

SIMNER, George. Laybrother.

b. August 10th, 1725, Lancashire. S.J. September 7th, 1747. Watten (nov) 1747-9. Boulogne School 1750. E.C. Rome 1725-8, 1761, 1763, 1767-9, 1771-83. d. November, 1783, Rome. (Fo.7; 91; 113; 12 f.189; 20 pp.13, 166; 57 I ff.126v, 128-44v, 225, 241, 248, 319; AHSJ.42/294-5; Nec).

SIMON see Simeon, Edward, Walter and William.

SIMONS see Plowden, Charles, Edmund and Francis; Simeon, Edward.

SIMPSON see Anderson, John.

SIMPSON, Anthony Aloysius *vere* Sionest. Priest.

b. June 1741 or 1742, Nevers, France. S.J. October 11th, 1756, in France. Ordained priest in France. Liège Academy 1787, 1788. Twyford 1790. Standon Hall 1792. Stonyhurst 1801, 1803, 1805, 1807, 1809, 1810, 1815. Readm. S.J. 1803 or 1804. To France 1817, d. June 25th, 1820, St Acheul, France. (Fo.7; 113; CDSJ.; CG.; AHSJ.42/307; 150 (1750-1853) f.179; 3 f.151; 1 f.220; 6 f.22v; 13 f.126v; 57 II f.169v; 72; 90 f.146v; 93 p.76; 157; Nec).

SIMPSON, Joseph. Priest.

b.1629, Durham. e. St Omers College c.1650. S.J. 1656. Watten
(nov) 1657. Liège (phil) 1658-60. Liège (theol) 1661-5. Ordained priest
c.1665. d. October 11th, 1667, Ypres. (Fo.7; CRS.69; 114; 113;
FAB.63-4; Nec).

SIMS see Booth, Ralph.

SIONEST see Simpson, Anthony Aloysius.

SITTENSPERGER, Matthias *alias* Manners. Priest.

b. September 20th, 1719, in Germany. S.J. September 14th, 1737, in
Germany. To English province 1751. Maryland 1752-8, 1763-4, 1767-9,
1771-3. d. June 16th, 1775, Bohemia, Maryland. (Fo.7; 91; 113;
Hu.Text 2/694; Nec).

SKINNER, John. Priest.

b.1662, Derbyshire. S.J. September 7th, 1679. Watten (nov) 1679,
1680. Liège (phil) 1681-3. Liège (theol) 1684, 1685. Left 1686. Readm.
S.J. January or September 7th, 1687. Liège (theol) 1689-91. Ordained
priest c.1690. Watten 1692. College of St Francis Xavier 1693. College
of St Aloysius 1696-7, 1699-1701, 1703-6, 1708 (Brinn c.1701). d.
October 16th, 1708, Brinn. bu. Winwick. (Fo.7; 114; 113; 23 f.35;
CRS.8/413; Nec).

SLATER see Hothersall, Thomas.

SLAUGHTER or SLATER, Edward. Priest.

b. January 5th, 1655, Herefordshire. S.J. September 7th, 1673.
Watten (nov) 1673-5. Liège (phil) 1676, 1678. Liège (theol) 1679-82.
Ordained priest March 28th, 1682. Ghent (tert) 1683. Liège 1684-7,
1689-93, 1696-7, 1699-1701, 1703-4 (Rector 1701-4). St Omers College
1705-9 (Rector). Liège 1709-16, 1718. Ghent 1719-22 (Rector). Liège
1722-9. d. January 20th, 1729, Liège. (Fo.7; 91; 113; 150 II(3)
15/11/92; 9 n.131; Chad.245; DNB; Nec. For writings see Som.).

SLUYPER, Peter. Laybrother.

b. February or July 1666, Flanders. S.J. February 5th or September
7th, 1690. Watten (nov) 1691. Ghent 1692-3, 1696. Watten 1697,
1699-1701, 1703-6. Ghent 1708-16, 1718, 1720, 1723-5. Liège 1726-8,
1730. d. February 21st, 1733, Liège. (Fo.7; 91; 114; 113; Nec).

SMALLWOOD, Joseph. Laybrother.

b. March 19th, 1666 or 1667, Staffordshire. S.J. March, 1694.
Watten 1696-7, 1699. Ghent 1700-01, 1703-4. Maryland 1705-6,
1708-10. Watten 1711-3. Ghent 1714-6. d. April 9th, 1716, Ghent.
(Fo.7; 114; 113; Hu.Text 2/685; Nec).

SMITH see Blackiston, Francis; Simeon, Edward; Thornton, Robert;
Turville, Charles.

SMITH, Clement. Priest.

b.1657, Warwickshire. ?br of Edmund. e. St Omers College 1672-8.
S.J. September 7th, 1678. Watten (nov) 1679. Liège (phil) 1680-2. Liège
(theol) 1683-6. Ordained priest 1687. College of St Aloysius 1687,
1689-93 (Bardsea c.1688-?). d. September 8th, 1696, Bardsea Hall, near
Ulverston. bu. Urswick. (Fo.7; CRS.69; 114; 113; Chad.228;

CRS.20/8; 123 IIIB f.275; LF.17; Nec).

SMITH, Edmund ?*alias* or *vere* Kitchen or Kitchin. Priest.

b. April 18th, 1666, Warwickshire. ?br. of Clement. e. St Omers College ?-1690. S.J. September 7th, 1690. Watten (nov) 1691. Liège (phil) 1692, 1693. Liège (theol) 1696, 1697. Ordained priest 1698. Watten 1699. College of St Aloysius 1700-01, 1703-6, 1708-16, 1718, 1720, 1723-5. In England 1726-7 (Croston ?-1700, 1710, c.1716, 1719. Bank Hall c.1716. Wigan or Blackrod c.1725). d. August 11th, 1727, ?Wigan. (Fo.7; CRS.69; 91; 113; 23 ff.35, 66; NB.1/263, 2/249; Pa.84; E and P.350, 354; 123 IIIB f.358; 140 n.45; Nec).

SMITH, Francis see Percy, Robert.

SMITH, George ?*alias* or *vere* Graves. Scholastic.

b. November 24th, 1682, Staffordshire. e. St Omers College c.1699-1702 or later. S.J. September 7th, 1703. Watten (nov) 1704, 1705. Liège (phil) 1706, 1708. Liège (theol) 1709-12. d. March 15th, 1712, Liège, not ordained. (Fo.7; CRS.69; 114; 113; Nec).

SMITH, Henry. Priest.

b. November 11th, 1699, Berwick. e. St Omers College 1714-8. E.C. Valladolid October 30th, 1718-June 17th, 1724. Ordained priest c.1724. S.J. September 7th, 1724. St Omers College (nov) 1725. Liège (theol) 1726, 1727. In England 1728. Horsley 1729-c.31. Dutton 1731. College of St Aloysius 1733. Dutton 1734-41. College of St Aloysius 1742, 1743. Dutton 1744. College of St Aloysius 1746. Culcheth 1747. College of St Aloysius 1748, 1749. Rixton 1750, 1751. Culcheth 1751. College of St Aloysius 1752-5. d. May 1st, 1756, Culcheth. bu. Winwick. (Fo.7; CRS.69; 114; 91; 113; Ans.4/248; 24 ff.36, 343, 347v; 64 p.48; 81; 83; 84; 85; 86; 89; HMC. 10th Report App.4/194; CRS.13/371-2; CRS.25/115; CRS.30/183; CRS.62 index; 158; 156 App.I; Nec).

SMITH, John (1) *alias* Durham. Priest.

b.1616. From Dumfries, Scotland. S.C. Douay 1632-? Ordained priest. To England or Scotland. S.J. October 27th, 1659. Residence of St John (nov) 1660, 1661, 1663-5, 1667, 1669, 1672-3. d. March 29th, 1674, in England. (Fo.7; 113; 114; RSC.26).

SMITH, John (2) *alias* Dormer and Carrington. Priest.

b.1632 or c.1635. From Sussex. s. of Charles, 1st Lord Carrington and Anne (Caryll). e. St Omers College c.1647-53. E.C. Rome November 4th, 1653-September 13th, 1654. S.J. September 7th, 1663. Watten (nov) 1664. Liège (phil) 1667. Liège (theol) 1669. Ordained priest September 29th, 1671. College of the Holy Apostles 1672, 1673. St Omers College 1674, 1675. College of the Holy Apostles 1676, 1678-84. College of St Ignatius (military chaplain) 1685. Residence of St George 1686, 1687. Court preacher 1687. d. March 18th, 1689, St Omers College or Ghent. (Fo.7; CRS.69; 114; 113; WR.24/4; CRS.40/53; CRS.55/543; Nec).

SMITH, John (3). Priest.

b. October 7th, 1669, Warwickshire. e. St Omers College ?-1688.

S.J. September 7th, 1688. Watten (nov) 1689, 1690. Liège (phil) 1691-3. Cologne (theol) 1696. Ordained priest c.1695. Ghent (tert) 1697. Residence of St John 1699-1701. Scarisbrick c.1702, 1703. College of St Aloysius 1704, 1705. College of St Ignatius 1706, 1708-16, 1718, 1720, 1723-5. In England 1726-8, 1730 (?Horsley 1729). College of St Ignatius 1733-40, 1743-50, 1752-4 (Rector c.1743-8. London 1712, 1722-4, 1727, 1731, 1746, 1753). d. August 4th, 1754, London. (Fo.7; CRS.69; 114; 91; 113; LR.3/5-8; 150 III(2) 27/7/43; 23 f.35; NB.1/17, 46, 221n; HMC. 10th Report App.4/189; Pa.75; CRS.19/367; CRS.38/71; CRS.25/115; 170 n.26; 111; 51 f.311; CRS.62 index; Nec).

SMITH, John (4). Laybrother.

b. September 9th, 1788, Bristol. S.J. September 7th, 1807-28. Hodder (nov) 1807-9. Bristol 1809-17. Stonyhurst 1817-28. (115; 113; 7 f.221; 55 f.253v; 2).

SMITH, Joseph. Priest.

b. December 10th, 1725, Leicestershire. e. St Omers College c.1739-46. S.J. September 7th, 1746. Watten (nov) 1747. Liège (phil) 1748-50. St Omers College 1752-6. Pont-à-Mousson (theol) 1757. France (theol) 1758. Ordained priest c.1760. ?Ghent (tert) 1761. Preston 1762-8. d. May 1st, 1768, Preston. (Fo.7; CRS.69; 114; 91; 113; 21 v.2; 30 ff.7av, 34, 38-9; 64 f.167; CRS.OP1/139; Nec).

SMITH, Joseph see Gerard, Philip.

SMITH, Michael. Laybrother.

b. November 14th, 1798, near Blackburn, Lancashire. S.J. September 20th, 1827. Hodder (nov) 1827-32. St Mary's Hall 1832-6. d. October 9th, 1836, St Mary's Hall. bu. Stonyhurst. (Fo.7; 115; 113; Nec).

SMITH, Richard *alias* Saville. Priest.

b.c.1660, Sussex. s. of John. e. St Omers College 1673-9. E.C. Rome October 7th, 1679-May 15th, 1680. S.J. July 21st, 1680. Watten (nov) 1680. Liège (phil) 1681-3. Liège (theol) 1684-7. Ordained priest c.1687. College of St Chad 1689, 1690. College of St Aloysius 1691. College of St Chad 1692. College of St Aloysius 1693, 1696-7. College of St Thomas of Canterbury 1699 (Lulworth c.1697). College of St Ignatius 1700. College of St Thomas of Canterbury 1701, 1703-5. College of the Holy Apostles 1706. College of St Thomas of Canterbury 1708, 1709 (Lulworth c.1707). College of St Ignatius 1710, 1711. College of St Aloysius 1712-6, 1718, 1720, 1723-8 (Rector 1724-c.28. Culcheth 1718, 1724, 1727). In England 1730. Culcheth 1733-5. d. September 22nd, 1735, Culcheth. (Fo.7; CRS.69; 91; 113; 150 III(2) 22/4/24; 23 ff.54, 66-7; 44 f.158v; 82; 83; 84; NB.2/220; CRS.6/365; CRS.13/371; CRS.40/95; Ber.90; Nec).

SMITH, Thomas (1). Priest.

b.c.1631, Lancashire. E.C. Valladolid October 1657-November 1st, 1661. Ordained priest April 1659. To England 1661. S.J. May 27th, 1662. College of St Aloysius 1663-5, 1669, 1672-6, 1678-9. d. January 31st, 1681, in England. (Fo.7; 114; 113; 150 II(2) January 1663;

CRS.30/167; Ans.2/301; CRS.29/157; Nec).

SMITH or SMYTHE, Thomas (2) *alias* or *vere* Lewis. Priest.
b. October 18th, 1674, County Durham. e. St Omers College ?-1691.
Watten (nov) 1692, 1693. Liège (phil) 1696. Liège (theol) 1697,
1699-1700. Ordained priest c.1700. Ghent (tert) 1701. St Omers College
1703-6. College of St Thomas of Canterbury 1708, 1709. Residence of
St John 1710 (?Berwick c.1709). College of St Ignatius 1711-3. Liège
1714-6, 1718, 1720. Burton Park 1720-1. d. April 9th, 1721, in England.
(Fo.7; CRS.69; 114; 113; RH.13/116; CRS.22/306, 312; 162;
CRS.62/110, 132, 137; Nec).

SMITH, Thomas (3). Laybrother.
b.1675, Surrey. S.J. September 7th, 1698. Watten (nov) 1699. Liège
1700-01. Paris 1703-6, 1708-16, 1720, 1722-3. St Omers College 1724.
Liège 1725, 1726. Antwerp 1726-32. Liège 1733-40, 1742-4. d. August
2nd, 1745, Liège. (Fo.7; 114; 91; 113; 9 n.120; Chad.257; 108; CRS.62
index; Nec).

SMITH, William *alias* Selby. Scholastic.
b. February 18th, 1728, Northumberland. e. St Omers College
1739-45. S.J. September 7th, 1745. Watten (nov) 1746. He may have
completed the noviceship. ?d. or left c.1748. (Fo.7; CRS.69; 113; Nec).

SMITHERS, William. Priest.
b.1656, Paris. e. St Omers College 1669-75. S.J. September 7th,
1675. Liège (phil) 1676, 1678. Liège (theol) 1679-82. Ordained priest
1682. Ghent (tert) 1683. Watten 1684. St Omers College 1685. d. June
13th or 14th, 1685, St Omers College. (Fo.7; CRS.69; 114; 113;
Chad.218; Nec).

SMITHSON, John. Laybrother.
b. July 1677, ?Sussex. S.J. December 2nd, 1719. Watten (nov) 1720,
1723-8, 1730, 1733-8, 1740, 1742-4, 1746-8. d. February 16th, 1748,
Watten. (Fo.7; 114; 113; Nec).

SMYTHE see Smith, Thomas (2).

SOLI see Sechly.

SOMERS or SOMMERS or SOMER or SOMMER, Charles. Laybrother.
b. December 23rd, 1686, Flanders. S.J. July 1st, 1708. Watten (nov)
1709-12. Maryland 1712-6. d. February 12th, 1716, Maryland. (Fo.7;
114; 113; Hu.Text 2/686; Nec).

SOMERSET see Anderson, James.

SOMERVILLE, William. Scholastic.
b. February 21st, 1709, Scotland. S.J. May 23rd, 1733, ?Scottish
mission. Watten (nov) 1733. Liège (phil) 1734. Left 1735, not ordained.
(91; 113; 150 III(2) 7/2/33).

SOMMER or SOMMERS see Somers.

SOPHIA see Wise or Wyse, George.

SOUTHCOTE, Edward. Priest.
b. June 24th, 1697, Essex or Suffolk. s. of Sir Edward and Juliana
(Tyrwhitt) of Witham Place, Essex. S.J. March 18th, 1719. Watten
(nov) 1720. Liège (phil) 1723. Liège (theol) 1724-7. Ordained priest

c.1727. Ghent (tert) 1728. Ingatestone 1729-30. France 1730. Travelling
1733. College of St Ignatius 1734-40, 1742-4, 1746-7. College of the
Holy Apostles 1748-50. ?Woburn Farm 1751. College of the Holy
Apostles 1752. College of St Ignatius 1753-8. Woburn Farm 1762-80. d.
February 25th, 1780, Woburn Farm. (Fo.7; 114; 113; LR.3/6;
ER.5/72-3, 11/29, 12/110; E and P.58; 74; 91; HMC. 10th Report
App.4/194; CRS.38/74-5; 118; CRS.8/414; Nec).

SOUTHERN or SOUTHEREN, Francis or Thomas. Laybrother.
        b. ?September 13th, 1686, diocese of Durham. S.J. August 9th,
1720. St Omers College 1723-7. E.C. Rome 1727-8, 1730. Ghent
1733-4. Antwerp 1735-6. St Omers College 1737-40, 1742-4, 1746-50,
1752-4. d. July 25th, 1754, St Omers College. (Fo.7; 114; 113; 91; 150
III(2) 19/4/27; 108; 51 f.311v; Nec).

SPEAKMAN, Thomas. Priest.
        b. January 18th, 1811, Ashton-le-Willows, Lancashire. e.
Stonyhurst 1820-9. S.J. March 26th, 1829. Hodder (nov) 1829-32. St
Mary's Hall (phil) 1832-4. Stonyhurst (theol etc.) 1834-42. Ordained
priest September 19th, 1840, Stonyhurst. The Grange near Pontefract
1842. Gillmoss 1842. Hodder (tert) 1844. Croft 1844. Stonyhurst
1845-7. Bristol 1847-8. Lydiate 1848-60. Lincoln 1860-9. Skipton
1869-71. Accrington 1871-3. Wigan 1873-9. Stonyhurst 1879. Clitheroe
1879-89. Stonyhurst 1889. d. October 10th, 1889, Stonyhurst. bu.
Clitheroe Catholic church. (115; Nec).

SPENCER see Adams, James; Charnock, John; Petre, Charles, Edward
        and Robert (1).

SPENCER or SPENSER, Joseph. Scholastic.
        b. October 17th, 1798, Lancashire. e. Stonyhurst 1812-?17. S.J.
September 7th, 1817. Hodder (nov) 1817-9. Stonyhurst (phil) 1820-1.
d. June 8th, 1823, Fano, Italy, not ordained. (Fo.7; 114; Stol; 116; 113;
CDSJ; 11 f.210v; Nec).

STAFFORD see Kelly, John Joseph.

STAFFORD, Bernard *alias* Cassidy. Priest.
        b. December, 1713 or January, 1714, Ireland. e. St Omers College
?-1735. S.J. September 7th, 1735. Watten (nov) 1735. Liège (phil)
1736-8. Liège (theol) 1739-41. ?Antwerp (theol) 1741. Louvain (theol)
1742. Ordained priest c.1741. Geist 1743. In England 1744. College of
St Ignatius 1746, 1748-58 (London 1746-?. Hammersmith 1750-2).
Oxburgh 1758, 1760. Warkworth 1761-c.71 (Superior of Residence of
St Mary c.1765-c.71). Dorchester, Oxfordshire 1772, 1773-? Thame
Park ?-1788. d. June or July 11th, 1788, Thame Park. bu. Thame Park.
(Fo.7; CRS.69; CRS.12/30; CRS.13/300; 113; 91; LR.1/32, 3/5; 150
III(2) 8/9/36; 8 II nn.140, 168; 204 n.36; 57 II f.87; HMC. 10th Report
App.4/184; Gil.3/360; CRS.7/209, 390; 173; 109; 108; 111; 117; Nec).

STAFFORD, Charles *alias* Hill or Hills. Priest.
        b. March 2nd, 1653, Suffolk. S.J. September 7th, 1676. Watten
(nov) 1676-8. Liège (phil) 1679, 1680. Liège (theol) 1681-4. Ordained
priest 1684. Ghent (tert) 1685. College of St Ignatius 1686, 1687. In

England 1688. Liège 1689. St Omers College 1690. Watten 1691.
College of St Ignatius 1692-3, 1696-7, 1699-1701, 1703-5 (London
1694-5, 1698). College of St Thomas of Canterbury 1706, 1708-12
(Rector c.1708-11). Watten 1712. College of St Thomas of Canterbury
1714-6, 1718, 1720, 1723-5. In England 1726. Canford c.1727. In
England 1728, 1730. ?College of the Holy Apostles 1731. d. February
29th, 1732, Ghent. (Fo.7; 114; 113; CRS.43/123; 44 f.15; 43 f.52; 91; E
and P.59; 170 ff.58v, 92v, 134v; 123 IIIB f.355; Nec).

STAFFORD, Ignatius *alias* Thorpe, Xavier and Potter. Priest.
    b.1652, Staffordshire, Suffolk or Cambridgeshire. e. St Omers
College ?-1670. E.C. Valladolid 1670-2. S.J. October 15th, 1672, in
Spain. Spain (nov and phil). Liège (theol) 1680-3. Ordained priest
March 8th, 1682. Ghent (tert) 1684. Monmouth 1685, 1687. In prison
1689. College of St Francis Xavier 1690-3. ?Linstead Lodge 1694.
College of St Ignatius 1696. Desborough 1697. Writtle Park 1698. Bury
St Edmunds 1698. Holywell 1698-9. Kingerby 1699-1701. St Omers
College 1701-4. College of St Francis Xavier 1705. College of St
Ignatius 1706. Boscobel 1706-9. College of St Francis Xavier 1709.
West Grinstead 1710-11. College of St Chad c.1712. Canford c.1712-8.
Monmouth c.1718. d. June 17th, 1720, Worcester. (Fo.7; CRS.69; 114;
113; 43 ff.26-7; CRS.30/170; ER.4/119, 9/112-3; WR.30/6; CRW.2-6;
E and P.347; CRS.2/299; CRS.3/107, 109-10; 170 f.254v; 123 IIIB
f.360; Nec).

STAFFORD, Nathaniel *alias* Potter and Phillips. Priest.
    b.1634, 1635 or 1637, Suffolk. e. St Omers College 1652 or
earlier – 53 or later. S.J. September 7th, 1656. Watten (nov) 1657.
Liège (phil) 1658-60. Liège (theol) 1661-5. Ordained priest c.1665.
Ghent (tert) 1667. College of the Holy Apostles 1669, 1672-c.95 (Rector
1689-c.95. Norwich 1670s). St Omers College c.1695-7. d. October 10th
or 11th, 1697, St Omers College. (Fo.7; CRS.69; 114; 113; NA.37/156;
150 II(3) 21/2/88, 4/7/88; 43 ff.10-19, 21v, 24-5; 170 f.2; Nec).

STAMFORD see Dalas.

STANFIELD see Pippard, Luke.

STANFIELD, Gervase. Scholastic.
    b.1674, Yorkshire. e. St Omers College 1693 or earlier -97. S.J.
September 7th, 1697. Watten (nov) 1697. Liège (phil) 1699-1701. Liège
(theol) 1703-5. d. May 7th, 1705, Liège, not ordained. (Fo.7; CRS.69;
114; 113; Nec).

STANFIELD, Robert. Priest.
    b. August 24th, 1668, Yorkshire. S.J. January 20th, 1687. Watten
(nov) 1687. Liège (phil) 1689-91. Liège (theol) 1692, 1693. Ordained
priest c.1695. Ghent (tert) 1696. Residence of St Michael 1697. Ghent
1699. Liège 1700-01, 1703. Travelling 1704. College of the Immaculate
Conception 1705. Residence of St Michael 1706. College of the
Immaculate Conception 1708-11. Residence of St Michael 1712-6,
1720. St Omers College 1723-7. In England 1728, 1730. Residence of St
Michael 1733-40, 1742-4, 1746-7 (Kilvington c.1731-41. York 1741-?).

Watten 1748-51. d. September 17th, 1751, Watten. (Fo.7; 114; 91; 113;
CRS.Mon.2/389; Gil.5/5; 156 App.1; YA.77/221-2; CRS.32/245;
Nec).

STANFORD see Dalas.

STANFORD, William. Scholastic.
> b.1652, Staffordshire. ?e. St Omers College. S.J. September 6th,
1671. Watten (nov) 1672. Liège (phil) 1673-5. d. February or March
5th, 1675, Liège, not ordained. (Fo.7; 114; 113; 193 Anglia 34/388;
Nec).

STANLEY see Bodenham, John; Fortescue, Francis; Petit, Cyriac
or Charles.

STANLEY, Henry (1) *alias* Culcheth. Priest.
> b. September 11th, 1688, Lancashire. s. of Richard and Anne
(Culcheth) of Eccleston-in-the-Fylde, Lancashire. e. St Omers College
c.1701. S.J. September 7th, 1706. Watten (nov) 1708. Liège (phil)
1709-11. Liège (theol) 1712-4. Ordained priest c.1714. Ghent (tert)
1715. Liège 1716, 1718. Residence of St John 1720, 1723-4. Residence
of St Mary 1725. In England 1726. Residence of St Mary 1727-44,
1746-7 (Superior 1727-43. Waterperry 1727, 1731-2, 1742). College of
St Aloysius 1747-53 (Culcheth 1747, 1751, 1753). d. November 27th,
1753, Culcheth. bu. Winwick. (Fo.7; CRS.69; 91; 114; 113; 24 f.347v;
74; 85; HMC. 10th Report App.4/194; 119 f.3; CRS.7/391;
CRS.13/371, 399; Nec).

STANLEY, Henry (2). Priest.
> b. March 12th or June 4th or 5th, 1713, Cheshire. s. of Sir William,
3rd Bart. and Catherine (Eyre) of Hooton, Cheshire. br. of Thomas.
S.J. September 7th, 1732. Watten (nov) 1733. Liège (phil) 1734-6. Liège
(theol) 1737-41. Ordained priest 1739. Watten 1741. Liverpool
c.1741-9. Leigh and Southworth 1749-63. Moor Hall near Ormskirk
1763-69. College of St Aloysius 1771. Moor Hall 1772-86. d. November
30th, 1786, Moor Hall. (Fo.7; 114; 91; 113; 85; 86; E and P.21; 158; 156
App.1; 155 III 185c; CRS.13/399; 167 p.30; 111; 51 f.311v; 119 ff.3, 5,
6, 7, 10, 11, 13, 16, 18; 54 f.207; Nec).

STANLEY-MASSEY, Thomas *alias* Massey. Priest.
> b. January 1716, Hooton, Cheshire. s. of Sir William Stanley, 3rd
Bart. and Catherine (Eyre) of Hooton. br. of Henry (2). S.J.
September 7th, 1732. Watten (nov) 1733. Liège (phil) 1734-6. Liège
(theol) 1737, 1738. St Omers College 1739-42. Lyons (theol) 1743-6.
Ordained priest c.1746. E.C. Rome 1747-54. College of the Holy
Apostles 1755-8 (Oxburgh 1755, 1756). ?Bury St Edmunds c.1760.
College of St Ignatius 1763, 1764. College of St Thomas of Canterbury
1765. Rookley near Winchester 1766-9. ?Stapehill 1769. (Rector of the
College of St Thomas of Canterbury 1765-9). Bruges College 1769-73
(Rector). Britwell 1773-? Lulworth ?-1778-1805. Readm. S.J. 1803.
Assumed the name Massey. d. June 2nd, 1805, Lulworth. bu.
Lulworth. (Fo.7; 91; 113; 114; 150 III(2) 14/12/37; 7 f.130v; 8 I p.7; 10
ff.111, 158; 12 f.187; 13 f.248v; CRS.1/142; 31 f.16; 44 f.41v; 01.415;

54 f.87v; 42 f.165; 126; 76 f.83; 68 p.109; 89; HMC. 10th Report
App.4/186, 194; AHSJ.42/305; NWCH (1979) 15; 188 n.108;
CRS.6/366; Gib.1/313; E and P.21; 57 I f.54; Nec).

STAPLETON, Thomas. Priest.
b.1632, Lincoln. e. St Omers College 1646 or earlier – 48 or later.
S.J. September 7th, 1651. Watten (nov) 1651, 1652. Liège (phil) 1653-5.
St Omers College 1656-60. Liège (theol) 1661-5. Ordained priest April
12th, 1664. Ghent (tert) 1667. Liège 1669. St Omers College 1672. Liège
1672, 1673. St Omers College 1674, 1675. Brussels 1675-7. St Omers
College 1678-83 (Rector 1679-83). Liège 1683-5 (Rector). d. November
21st, 1685, Rome. (Fo.7; CRS.69; 114; 113; 150 II(2) 16/3/69, 11/9/77,
October 1678; 135 f.192; 108; Chad.209-10; Nec).

STARKEY, Francis ?or Brian or Briant. Scholastic.
b. May 7th, 1729, London. ?e. St Omers College c.1741-6. S.J.
September 7th 1746. Watten (nov) 1747. Liège (phil) 1748, 1749.
Nothing further recorded under this name. (Fo.7; 113; CRS.69).

STAVELEY see Cary, Charles.

STEFFENS see Stephens, John.

STEPHANI see Stephens, Henry Robert.

STEPHENS or STEVENS, Adrian. Laybrother.
b. March 8th or October 19th, 1700, Gravelines. S.J. April 17th,
1725. Watten (nov) 1725-8, 1730, 1733. St Omers College 1734-41,
1743-4, 1746-50, 1752-8, 1761-4. d. January or February 5th, 1764, St
Omers College. (Fo.7; 114; 113; 91; Chad.304; 117; CRS.6/340; Nec).

STEPHENS or STEPHANI, Henry Robert. Priest.
b. August 5th, 1665, Liège. e. St Omers College ?-1683. Phil before
S.J. S.J. September 7th, 1683. Watten (nov) 1684, 1685. Liège (theol)
1685-7. Ordained priest c.1688. Liège 1690-2. College of St Ignatius
1693. College of the Immaculate Conception 1693. Liège 1696-7. Liège
Episcopal Seminary 1699-1723 (President 1705-23). d. June 15th, 1723,
Liège. (Fo.7; CRS.69; CRS.62 index; 114; 113; 150 II(3) 19/7/92, III(1)
22/8/22; 9 nn.154-5; Nec. For writings see Som.).

STEPHENS or STEVENS or STEFFENS, John. Laybrother.
b. August 15th, 1693, Gravelines. S.J. August 14th, 1717. Watten
(nov) 1718, 1720, 1723-8. Liège 1730, 1733. Maryland 1733-8. Watten
1740-1, 1743-4, 1746. d. August 9th, 1747, St Omers College. (Fo.7;
114; 113; Hu.Text 2/690; 91; 92; Nec).

STEPHENS or STEVENS, Joseph. Laybrother.
b. March 15th, 1684, Buckinghamshire. S.J. October 9th, 1711.
Watten (nov) 1712. St Omers College 1713-6, 1718, 1720. Watten
1723-4. E.C. Rome 1725-8, 1730, 1733-40, 1743-4, 1746-50, 1752-6. d.
January 27th, 1756, Rome. (Fo.7; 114; 113; 91; Nec).

STEPHENS or STEVENS, Thomas. Laybrother.
b. February 3rd, 1698, Berkshire or London. S.J. August 10th, 1720.
Ghent 1723, 1724. Liège 1725-7. Watten 1727. Paris 1728, 1730. E.C.
Rome 1733-9. d. May 23rd or 24th, 1740, Paris. (Fo.7; 114; 91; 113; 150
III(2) 30/4/40; 12 f.178v; Nec).

STEPHENSON, John. Priest.

b.1641, Derbyshire. S.J. September 7th, 1663. Watten (nov) 1663, 1664. Liège (phil) 1667. Liège (theol) 1669, 1672. Ordained priest April 6th, 1672. Liège 1673. Watten 1674, 1675. Lytham 1676-92 (Rector of the College of St Aloysius 1684-8). d. January 13th, 1692, in England. (Fo.7; 114; 113; CRS.16/423; Nec).

STEVENS see Stephens.

STEYNMEYER, Ferdinand *alias* Farmer. Priest.

b. October 13th, 1720, in Germany. Phil before S.J. S.J. September 1743. To English province 1751. Maryland, Pennsylvania, New York and New Jersey 1752-86. d. August 17th, 1786, Philadelphia. (Fo.7; Hu.Text 2/694; 114; 197; 91; 113; 11 f.50; 64 p.498; Nec).

STOCKWOOD see Harrison, James.

STOKES see Englefield, John.

STONE, Francis. Laybrother.

b. February 28th, 1691 or 1694, Buckinghamshire or Hampshire. S.J. June 28th, 1713. Watten (nov) 1714. Liège 1715-6, 1718, 1720, 1723-7. St Omers College 1728, 1730, 1733-41, 1743-4, 1746-51. d. December 18th, 1751, St Omers College. (Fo.7; 91; 114; 113; Nec).

STONE, Marmaduke. Priest.

b. November 28th, 1748, Draycott, Staffordshire. s. of Benjamin and Sarah (Perrins) of Draycott. e. St Omers and Bruges Colleges 1761-7. S.J. September 7th, 1767. Ghent (nov) 1767-9. Liège (phil) 1771-3. Ordained priest December 26th, 1775. Liège Academy 1774-1794. (President 1790-4). Stonyhurst 1794-1817 (President and Rector 1794-1808. Provincial 1803-17). Hodder 1817. Stonyhurst 1818-28. St Helens 1829-34. Readm. S.J. 1803. d. August 21st, 1834, St Helens. bu. Windleshaw cemetery. (Fo.7; CRS.69; 114; 91; 113; 115; 94 ff.319-20; 3 ff. 37, 51; 1 f.257; 6 ff.3v, 117 ff; 51 f.307; 56 ff.276 ff; 90 ff.54, 145v, 146v; Ans.4/259; HMC. 10th Report App.4/186, 188; 93 *passim*; AHSJ.42/305; Chad.376 ff; Nec. For writings see Sut. Som.).

STRACHAN, Sir Alexander, Bart. Priest.

b. October 21st, 1727, in Scotland. s. of Sir Alexander, Bart. and Jane (Bremner). e. S.C. Douay 1741-? S.J. September 19th, 1746, in Paris for the Scottish mission or a French province. Assumed baronetcy c.1760. Hammersmith 1767-9. Liège Academy 1788-93. d. January 3rd, 1793, Liège. (Fo.7; 114; 117; RSC.84; 113; LR.1/32; 13 ff.121v, 125; 67; RH.14/283; Nec).

STRECKLEY, William. Scholastic or Laybrother.

d. St Omers College, date not recorded. No further details found. (Fo.7; 114).

STRICKLAND, William. Priest.

b. October 28th, 1731, Sizergh, Westmorland. s. of Thomas and Mary (Scrope). e. St Omers College 1741-8. S.J. September 7th, 1748. Watten (nov) 1748, 1749. Liège (phil) 1750, 1752. Liège (theol) 1753-5. Ordained priest 1756. Ghent (tert) 1756. Liège 1757, 1758. Sizergh 1759-61, serving Furness. ?Stonyhurst c.1762. Croft, Leigh,

Southworth, Rixton 1764-7. Ugbrooke 1767. Rixton etc. 1768-70.
Alnwick 1770-84 (Superior of the Residence of St John 1773). Liège
1784-90 (President). London 1790-1819. Readm. S.J. 1803. d. April
23rd, 1819, London. bu. Old St Pancras churchyard. (Fo.7; CRS.69;
91; 114; 113; LR.3/7, 7/21; 150(1750-1853) ff.12, 14, 48, 67, 87, 102v,
112, 121, 139, 167; 3 f.165v; 4 ff.61-2; Chad.369 ff; 1 ff.29v, 39, 63, 74,
148, 151; 6 ff.3v, 5v; 7 ff.128, 153v; 10 f.73v; 21 vv.1 and 2; 35 ff.113 ff.
156; 56 ff. 179-256; 57 I f.23; 152 n.18; 65; 68 pp.125, 132; 25 f.12; 80;
HMC. 10th Report App.4/188, 196, 198; Pa.2/29; Gil.4/327; 155 II
127; CRS.13/239; 36 f.65v; 167 p.19; 109; 117; 01.416; 119 ff.13, 22,
25, 27, 30, 35, 39, 43; AHSJ.42/305; Nec).

STROTHER or STRUTHER, William. Scholastic.
    b. October 17th, 1682, Northumberland. ?s. of Edward of Alnwick.
S.J. September 7th, 1701. Watten (nov) 1703. Liège (phil) 1704-6. Liège
(theol) 1708. Left 1708, not ordained. (CRS.69; 113; 150 III(1)
22/10/06; 193 Anglia 35/280).

STUART, William or John *alias* Sharpe. Priest.
    b. London. S.J. 1640, in Rome. ?Scottish mission. Holme-on-
Spalding-Moor 1673-7. d. May 25th, 1677 ?in England. (Fo.7; RSC.24.
110; 113; CRS.4/272; Nec. For writings see Som.).

STUART see Maxwell, James.

SUMNER, Richard. Priest.
    b. October 15th, 1801, Birmingham. e. Stonyhurst 1814-20. S.J. May
7th, 1820. Hodder (nov) 1820-1, 1823-4. Stonyhurst (phil and theol)
1824-31. Hodder (tert) 1831. Ordained priest September 22nd, 1832,
Stonyhurst. Stonyhurst 1832-4. Calcutta mission etc. 1834-44. St
Mary's Hall 1845-6 (Superior). Stonyhurst 1847-8. London 1848-51,
Liverpool 1851-66. Exeter 1867-8. Norwich 1868-73. Great Yarmouth
1873-5. Bury St Edmunds 1875-7. d. September 30th, 1877, Bury St
Edmunds. bu. Bury St Edmunds cemetery. (Fo.7; 115; NA.37/166;
Gil.5/536; Nec. For writings see Som. and Sut.).

SURMONT, James. Priest.
    d. May 15th, 1700, Ghent. Not found under this name in the English
province catalogues. (Fo.7; 95 p.829).

SWAN, John. Laybrother.
    b. December 12th, 1706, Norwich. S.J. September 7th, 1728-35.
Liège 1733-5. (113; 91; 150 III(2) 10/9/35, 29/10/35).

SWARBRICK see Edisford, John (3).

SWINBURN or SWINBORNE, John *alias* Savage. Priest.
    b. March 21st, 1660, Derbyshire. e. St Omers College ?-1680. S.J.
September 7th, 1680. Watten (nov) 1680, 1681. Liège (phil) 1682-4.
Liège (theol) 1685-7. Ordained priest c.1688. Ghent (tert) 1689. Watten
1690, 1691. St Omers College 1692, 1693. Antwerp 1693-9. College of
St Aloysius 1699-1701, 1703-5 (Eccleston c.1701). College of St Chad
1706, 1708. Watten 1709-11. St Omers College 1712. College of St
Aloysius 1714, 1715 (Eccleston 1714). d. September 11th, 1716, in
England. (Fo.7; CRS.69; 114; 113; CRS.62 index; 23 f.35v; NB.2/95;

135 f.244; 108; Nec).

SWINDALL, Stephen *alias* Roberts and Matthews. Priest.
 b. August 6th, 1677, London. e. St Omers College 1693 or earlier-95.
 S.J. September 7th, 1695. Watten (nov) 1696. Liège (phil) 1697,
 1699-1700. Liège (theol) 1701, 1703-4. Ordained priest c.1703. College
 of St Thomas of Canterbury 1705, 1706. Linstead 1708-9. Liège 1710.
 Ghent 1711. College of St Thomas of Canterbury 1712, 1713. College
 of St Francis Xavier 1714-6, 1718, 1720, 1723-4. Residence of St George
 1725. In England 1726-8, 1730 (Barton-on-the-Heath 1727). Residence
 of St George 1733-9. College of St Chad 1740-1. Ghent 1742-6 (Rector).
 College of St Ignatius 1747-50. London 1752. Ghent 1752-8 (Rector
 1752-3). d. December 5th, 1758, Ghent. (Fo.7; CRS.69; 114; 91; 113;
 LR.3/9; WR.20/71; 150 III(2) 9/6/42; 40 p.97; HMC. 10th Report
 App.4/193; 153/70/5; Nec).

SYDALL see Hodgkinson, Charles.

TALBOT see Hesketh, Roger.

TALBOT, Gilbert *alias* Grey, Earl of Shrewsbury. Priest.
 b. January 4th or 11th, 1672 or 1673, Staffordshire. s. of Gilbert (s.
 of John, 10th Earl of Shrewsbury) and Jane (Flatsbury). e. St Omers
 College ?-c.1694. S.J. April 10th or 12th, 1694. Liège (phil) 1696. Liège
 (theol) 1697, 1699-1701. Ordained priest 1700. York c.1701. College of
 St Aloysius 1703-6, 1708-12 (Rector 1711-2. Dunkenhalgh, Preston,
 Billington ?-?1711). Ingatestone 1711-c.27. In England 1726-8, 1730.
 College of St Aloysius 1733-8. (Rector. Dunkenhalgh c.1727-?).
 College of St Ignatius 1738. College of St Aloysius 1739. College of St
 Ignatius 1740, 1741. 13th Earl of Shrewsbury 1718. d. July 22nd, 1743,
 in England. bu. Old St Pancras. (Fo.7; CRS.69; 114; 113; LR.3/9;
 ER.5/70, 12/109, 113; 26 ff.57-8; 21 v.2; 89; 91; CRS.4/376; Ki.225-7;
 CRS.14/118; CRS.36/217; 43 ff.39, 40v; 170 f.245v; 23 f.35v; Nec).

TALBOT, Gilbert. Priest.
 d. August 28th, 1682, Rome. Not found under this name in the
 records of the English province. (Fo.7; 95 p.817).

TALBOT, John (1) *alias* Mansell and Mansfield. Priest.
 b. December 27th, 1708, Lancashire. s. of John of Wheelton. br. of
 Thomas. Uncle of John (2). e. St Omers College c.1726-8. S.J.
 September 7th, 1728. Liège (phil) 1730, 1731. St Omers College 1733-7.
 Liège (theol) 1738. Ordained priest c.1739. Paris (?theol) 1739.
 Clermont (theol) 1740, 1741. St Omers College 1742. ?Liverpool,
 Preston 1743. Lytham 1743-?95 (Rector of the College of St Aloysius
 1758-c.68). d. June 9th, 1799, Walton near Preston. (Fo.7; CRS.69;
 114; 91; 113; 13 ff.29, 66v; 23 f.195v; 24 f.347v; 27 ff.230v, 239; 28
 ff.21v, 24v, 26, 28, 31; 29 f.231; 25 ff.42, 47, 50, 56, 63, 72, 76, 79, 85,
 90; 74; 89; 90 f.173; HMC. 10th Report App.4/196; 155 III 185c;
 CRS.OP.1/130; CRS.4/249; 158; 167 p.21; 155 II 129; 156 App.1;
 Ki.158; CRS.9/183; CRS.16/424-5; 140 n.45; 152 II n.20; 111; 119

f.40; Nec).

TALBOT, John (2). Priest.

b. August 22nd or 28th, 1737. s. of James and Mary (Parke) of Walton, Lancashire. Nephew of John (1) and Thomas. e. St Omers College c.1752-7. S.J. September 7th, 1757. Watten (nov) 1758. Liège (phil) 1759, 1761. Liège (theol) 1763, 1764. Ordained priest c.1764. Ghent 1764. Odstock 1765-9. Walthamstow 1769-73-?74. Canford ?1779, 1793, 1795. London 1795-7. Rixton 1797, 1798, 1800, 1801. d. May 19th, 1801, Rixton. (Fo.7; CRS.69; 114; 91; 117; 113; CRS.Mon.1/165; ER.19/105 ff; 44 ff.225v, 273; 65; 68 pp.123, 129; 77; 25 f.121; 87; HMC. 10th Report App.4/196; 157; CRS.23/87; 119 ff.8, 14; Nec).

TALBOT, Thomas *alias* Mansell and Mansfield. Priest.

b. July 21st, 1717, Lancashire. s. of John of Wheelton. br. of John (1). Uncle of John (2). e. St Omers College c.1732-5. S.J. September 7th, 1735. Watten (nov) 1735-7. Liège (phil) 1738, 1739. St Omers College 1740-1, 1743-4, 1746. Strasbourg (theol) 1746-9. Ordained priest c.1750. St Omers College 1750. ?Crosby 1750-1. College of St Aloysius 1752-4. Canford and Odstock 1754. Alnwick 1755. York 1755-7. Ongar Hill 1758-60, 1764. Croxdale 1764. Watten 1765. London 1766-9, 1771-3, 1781-?99. d. October 12th, 1799, London. bu. St Giles-in-the-Fields churchyard. (Fo.7; 91; 114; CRS.69; 113; LR.3/9; 21 v.2; 35 f.91v; 41 n.62; 51 ff.81, 110-11; 56 f.335; 57 I f.251; 01.419; 64 p.316; 65; 68 pp.127, 331; 86; 156 App.1; 125; 24 f.343; 107; 109; 119 ff.6, 10, 11, 21; CRS.43/123; CRS.Mon.1/165; CRS.Mon.2/388; CRS.4/376; Nec).

TARTER, Dominic. Laybrother.

b. May 12th, 1728. From Blandecques, France. br. of William. S.J. April 13th, 1750. Watten (nov) 1752, 1753-8, 1761, 1763-4. Ghent 1765-73. Bonham ?-1783. Wardour 1783-1800. d. August 16th, 1800, Wardour. (Fo.7; 114; 91; 113; AHSJ.42/294; 117; CRS. Mon.1/181; 16 ff.22v, 31; Nec).

TARTER, William. Laybrother.

b. April 2nd, 1732. From Blandecques, France. br. of Dominic. S.J. May 14th, 1760. Watten (nov) 1760, 1764-5. Bruges School 1767-9, 1771-3. d. September 12th, 1792, Blandecques. (Fo.7; 91; 113; 117; AHSJ.42/295; 16 f.12v; Nec).

TASBURGH, Francis. Scholastic.

b. February 7th, 1686, Norfolk. s. of John Beaumont and Elizabeth (Blount) of Bodney, Norfolk. e. St Omers College 1696-1702. S.J. September 7th, 1702. Watten (nov) 1703, 1704. Liège (phil) 1705, 1706. Left 1707, not ordained. (Fo.7; CRS.69; 113; E. and P.193).

TASBURGH, Henry *alias* Tichborne. Priest.

b.1641 or 1642, Suffolk. e. St Omers College 1659 or earlier-64. S.J. September 7th, 1664. Liège (phil) 1667, 1669. Ordained priest September 21st, 1671. St Omers College 1672. College of St Ignatius 1672. Watten (tert) 1673. College of St Aloysius 1674-87, 1689-93,

1696-7, 1699-1706, 1708-18 (Ince 1701, 1702, c.1706, serving Formby. New House, Ince c.1709-18). d. January 27th, 1718, New House. bu. Harkirke cemetery, Little Crosby. (Fo.7; CRS.69; 114; 113; NB.1/16-296 *passim*, 2/106, 221; NWCH(1969) 85; 23 f.35; Gil.2/309; E and P.340; 140 n.45; Che.12/82; Nec).

TASBURGH, Richard. Priest.
 b. December 29th, 1693, Hampshire. s. of Richard and Mary (Heneage) of Flixton, Suffolk. e. St Omers College ?-1710. S.J. September 7th, 1710. Watten (nov) 1711, 1712. Liège (phil) 1713, 1714. St Omers College 1715-6, 1718, 1720. Liège (theol) 1723, 1724. Ordained priest c.1723. College of the Holy Apostles 1725. In England 1726. Flixton 1727. Norwich 1728, 1729. College of the Holy Apostles 1733-5. d. January 11th, 1735, Watten or in England. (Fo.7; CRS.69; 114; 91; 113; 43 ff.45, 58; NA.37/165; E and P.257; CRS.62/285, 290, 298; Nec).

TASBURGH, Thomas *alias* Darell. Priest.
 b. September 29th, 1672 or 1673, Norfolk. s. of John and Elizabeth (Darell) of Bodney, Norfolk. e. St Omers College ?-1691. S.J. September 7th, 1691. Watten and Mechlin (nov) 1691-3. Liège (phil) 1696. Liège (theol) 1697-1700. Ordained priest 1700. Ghent (tert) 1701. College of the Holy Apostles 1701. College of St Ignatius 1703-6, 1708-16, 1718, 1720, 1723-5. In England 1726. London 1727. d. July 5th, 1727, Dublin. bu. St Michan's. (Fo.7; CRS.69; 114; 113; 91; CRS.62/46, 79, 83; 150 II(3) 14/6/98; 108; Nec).

TATE, Joseph. Priest.
 b. December 3rd, 1771, Appleton, Yorkshire. s. of Joseph and Elizabeth (Flintoff). br. of Thomas. e. Liège Academy. Stonyhurst 1794, 1800-01, 1803. Ordained priest c.1803. Preston 1803-?8. Wigan 1808-10. S.J. September 18th, 1810 (briefly). Wigan 1810-11. Stonyhurst 1811-2. ?Ince 1812. Bristol 1812-22. ?Pontefract 1822. S.J. February 12th, 1823, in Rome. Rome (nov) 1823-4. Great Yarmouth 1824-35. Bury St Edmunds 1835-8. Norwich 1838-c.40. (Superior of the College of the Holy Apostles 1836-c.40). St Mary's Hall 1841. d. July 16th, 1842, St Mary's Hall. bu. Stonyhurst. (Fo.7; 115; 113; CRS.65/205; NA.37/165; 6 ff.23, 96v, 202, 204; 8 II n.184; 13 f.492v; 15 f.201v; 19 f.173; 21 v.2; 28 f.196v; 42 ff.38v, 101v, 124v, 212v, 245v, 248v, 295v; 55 ff.180, 253; 90 ff.145v, 146v; 93 p.38; 94 ff.130-1; CRS.3/182; Nec. For writings see Sut.).

TATE, Thomas. Priest.
 b.1780, Appleton, Yorkshire. s. of Joseph and Elizabeth (Flintoff). br. of Joseph. e. Stonyhurst 1795-?. S.J. September 26th, 1803. Hodder (nov) 1803-5. Stonyhurst (phil) 1807. Stonyhurst (theol) 1810, 1811. Ordained priest c.1811. Wigan 1811-9. d. March 29th, 1819, Wigan. (Fo.7; 114; Stol; 113; 6 f.202; 13 f.492v; 21 v.2; 93 p.61; 94 f.60; Nec).

TATLOCK, Henry *alias* Forster. Priest.
 b. February 4th or 10th, 1709, Kirkby, Lancashire. s. of Thomas and

Helen (Fazakerley). e. St Omers College c.1724-9. S.J. September 7th, 1729. Liège (theol) 1733-6. Ordained priest 1736. Ghent (tert) 1737. Fazakerley, serving Lydiate c.1737-71. d. August 17th, 1771, Warbrick Moor. (Fo.7; CRS.69; 91; 114; 113; 6 f.275v; 13 f.85v; 23 ff.191; 24 f.347v; 27 ff.216, 228v, 236, 255; 25 f.3; 80; 85; HMC. 10th Report App.4/196; Gib.1/290; E and P.120; 156 App.1; CRS.6/132; CRS.9/179, 203; 111; 119 ff.7, 11, 13, 14, 38, 43; CRS.OP.1/45; Gil.2/155; Nec).

TATLOCK, John *alias* Ward. Priest.

b. May 8th, 1709, Staffordshire. S.J. September 7th, 1729. Liège (phil) 1733. Liège (theol) 1734, 1735. Ordained priest c.1736. St Omers College 1736. Ghent (tert) 1737. Residence of St Mary 1738-41, 1743-4, 1746-8. College of the Holy Apostles 1750, 1752. Residence of St Mary 1753-5 (East Hendred 1752-?56). d. April 4th, 1756, East Hendred. (Fo.7; 114; 91; 113; HMC. 10th Report App.4/197; CRS.7/396; Nec).

TAYLOR see Gardiner, William.

TAYLOR, Edward. Laybrother.

b.1665, Lancashire. S.J. October 9th, 1697. Watten (nov) 1697, 1699-1701. Ghent 1703-5. Liège 1706, 1708-12. d. March 21st, 1712, Liège. (Fo.7; 114; 113; Nec).

TAYLOR, Ralph *alias* Candish. Priest.

b. October 23rd, 1678, London. s. of Ralph and Catherine (Marchant). e. St Omers College ?-1699. E.C. Rome October 12th, 1699-April 26th, 1706. Ordained priest March 22nd, 1704. S.J. July 7th, 1706. St Omers College 1708. Liège 1709. St Omers College 1710-12. Liège 1713. Residence of St Michael 1714-6, 1720, 1723-7 (Superior 1725. York-?1727). d. January 26th, 1727, York. (Fo.7; CRS.69; 91; 113; CRS.40/128-9; CRS. Mon.2/388; Ans.3/222; CRS.4/376; CRS.62/62, 92, 95, 99; Nec).

TAYLOR, Thomas. Priest.

b.1670, 1673 or 1674, Lancashire. s. of Ralph and Margaret. e. St Omers College 1693 or earlier-95. E.C. Rome October 18th, 1695-May 17th, 1702. Ordained priest March 26th, 1701. S.J. July 29th, 1702. Watten (nov) 1703, 1704. Ypres 1705. Ghent 1706. E.C. Rome c.1706-15. St Omers College 1715. College of St Thomas of Canterbury 1716, 1718, 1720, 1723-5 (?Idsworth c.1715-?). In England 1726. d.1726, in England. (Fo.7; CRS.69; 113; CRS.40/118; CRS.62/292, 297, 300; Ans.3/222; 150 III(1) 14/8/06; 123 II 127; Nec).

TEMPEST, Charles. Priest.

b. April 30th, 1699, Broughton Hall, Yorkshire. s. of Stephen and Elizabeth (Fermor) of Broughton. br. of John. e. St Omers College 1714 or earlier-18. E.C. Valladolid January 30th, 1718-June 17th, 1724. Ordained priest c.1723. S.J. September 7th, 1724. St Omers College (nov) 1725. Liège (theol) 1726, 1727. St Omers College 1728. In England 1730. College of St Francis Xavier 1733-41, 1743-4, 1746-50, 1752-8 (Clytha. Hereford ?1746-?61). College of St Ignatius 1763, 1764. Chiswick 1767-8. d. July 28th, 1768, Chiswick. (Fo.7; CRS.69;

114; 91; 113; Ans.4/276; LR.1/30; 111; HMC. 10th Report
App.4/196-7; E. and P.311; 34 ff.17-21,57; CRS.30/183; CRS.62/92,
152, 153; Nec).

TEMPEST, Henry *alias* or *vere* Thornton. Scholastic.
b.1664, Northumberland. s. of William of Netherwitton. e. St Omers
College 1673-80. S.J. September 7th, 1680. Watten (nov) 1680, 1681.
Liège (phil) 1682-4. St Omers College 1685, 1686. Residence of St John
1687. Left 1687, not ordained. (Fo.7; CRS.69; 113; 150 III(2) 10/8/86,
11/10/87).

TEMPEST, John. Priest.
b. June 6th, 1694, Yorkshire. s. of Stephen and Elizabeth (Fermor)
of Broughton. br. of Charles. e. St Omers College ?-1712. S.J.
September 7th, 1712. Watten (nov) 1713, 1714. Liège (phil) 1715, 1716.
St Omers College 1718, 1720, 1723. La Flèche (theol) 1724. Rome
(theol) 1725-7. Ordained priest c.1727. In England 1728. Travelling
(Constantinople etc.) 1730, 1731. Ingatestone and Thorndon 1732-7. d.
February 22nd, 1737, Thorndon. bu. St Nicholas' church, Ingrave.
(Fo.5 and 7; CRS.69; 91; 113; ER.4/37/, 5/73, 9/106, 12/111; E. and
P.311; Ki.231; 43 ff.47-8, 56; Nec. For writings see Som.).

TEMPEST, Nicholas. Priest.
b.1631 or 1633, Lancashire. e. St Omers College 1649 or earlier-52.
S.J. September 7th, 1652. Watten (nov) 1652, 1653. Liège (phil) 1654-6.
Liège (theol) 1657-60. Ordained priest April 16th, 1661. Ghent (tert)
1661. College of St Aloysius 1665, 1667, 1669, 1672-9. d. February
26th, 1679, in prison (?Lancaster). (Fo.7; CRS.69; 114; 113; BR.26;
Nec).

TEMPEST, Thomas. Scholastic.
b. March 11th, 1808, Broughton Hall, Yorkshire. s. of Stephen and
Elizabeth (Blundell). e. Stonyhurst 1815-?. S.J. September 7th, 1826.
Montrouge (nov) 1826. Hodder (nov) 1827. Stonyhurst (phil) 1828.
Left 1829, not ordained. (115; 2).

TEMPEST see Hardesty, John.

TERRETT see Tyrwhitt.

THELWELL, Joseph. Laybrother novice.
b.1731. br. of Walter. S.J. November 26th, 1750. d. August 3rd,
1752, Watten. (Fo.7; 113; 114; Nec).

THELWELL, Walter. Laybrother.
b. August 15th, 1722, Crosby, Lancashire. br. of Joseph. S.J.
August 27th, 1747. Watten (nov) 1747-9, 1750, 1752-7. St Omers
College 1758, 1761. Bruges College 1763-4, 1767-9, 1771-3. Wardour
Castle ?1774-1808. d. April 23rd, 1808, Wardour. (Fo.7; 91; 114; 113;
AHSJ.42/294; CRS. Mon.1/181; 13 f.380; 16 f.98; L and C.117/91).

THIERRY, Nicholas. Laybrother.
b. March 24th or 25th, 1677 or 1673 or 1675, Liège. S.J. October 21st
or 22nd, 1707. Watten (nov) 1708-9, 1710-12. Liège 1713-6, 1718, 1720,
1723-8, 1730, 1733-41, 1743-4, 1746-50, 1752-8, 1761. d. August 28th,
1763, Liège. (Fo.7; 114; 91; 113; 90 f.20v; CRS.6/340; 51 f.311; 117).

THOMAS, Richard *alias* Webster. Priest.
 b. January 16th, 1685, London. S.J. September 7th, 1704. Watten
(nov) 1705, 1706. Liège (phil) 1708, 1709. Liège (theol) 1710-3.
Ordained priest c.1713. Maryland 1713 or 1714-6, 1720, 1723-8. In
England 1730. College of St Aloysius 1733, 1734. d. January 5th, 1735,
in England or at Watten. (Fo.7; 114; 91; 113; Hu. Text 2/686; Nec).
THOMPSON see Butler, John and Thomas (2); Hawker, John; Jenison,
 John; Sanderson, Nicholas (1).
THOMPSON, Charles *alias* Parker. Priest.
 b. September 5th, 7th or 11th, 1746, Maryland. e. St Omers and
Bruges Colleges 1760-66. S.J. September 7th, 1766. Ghent (nov) 1767.
Liège (phil) 1768, 1769. Liège (theol) 1771. Ordained priest 1771.
Bruges College 1772, 1773. Witham 1774-83. Gifford's Hall 1787-90.
Bury St Edmunds 1790, 1793. Bath 1795. d. April 6th, 1795, Bristol or
Bath. bu. St Joseph's churchyard, Bristol. (Fo.7; CRS.69; 114; 91; 113;
Hu. Text 2/704; ER.3/43, 112, 6/24, 9/112, 10/40; 16 f.100; 21 v.2; 54
ff.52, 147v, 150; CRS.22/278; 42 ff.176, 179v, 182, 209; 43 ff.320v,
321v, 323v, 325v; HMC. 10th Report App.4/187, 197; Ki.231; O1.420;
CRS.3/218; Nec).
THOMPSON, Richard. Priest.
 d. date and place not recorded. (Fo.7; 114).
THORN, Thomas. Laybrother.
 b.1645 or 1646, Suffolk. S.J. November 12th, 1682. Watten (nov)
1682-7. Liège 1689. Ghent 1690. Watten 1691. d. September 2nd or
December 26th, 1691, Watten. (Fo.7; 114; 113; Nec).
THORNTON see Le Hunt, John; Tempest, Henry.
THORNTON, James *alias* Ireland. Priest.
 b. April 14th, 1680 or 1678 or 1682, Lancashire. e. St Omers College
1695-1700. S.J. September 7th, 1700. Watten (nov) 1701. Liège (phil)
1703-5. St Omers College 1706. Liège (theol) 1708-11. Ordained priest
c.1711. Ghent (tert) 1712-6, 1718, 1720. College of St Thomas of
Canterbury 1723. Residence of St George 1724, 1725. Watten 1726-8,
1730. Ghent 1733-41, 1743-4, 1746-50, 1752. d. December 2nd or 3rd,
1752, Ghent. (Fo.7; CRS.69; 114; 91; 113; Nec).
THORNTON, Robert *alias* Smith and Middleton. Priest,
 b. September 17th, 1658, Yorkshire. S.J. September 7th or 11th,
1678. Watten (nov) 1679. Liège (phil) 1680-2. Ordained priest May
20th, 1683. Residence of St Mary 1683. College of St Chad 1684-7,
1689-93, 1696-7, 1699-1701, 1703. College of St Thomas of Canterbury
1704. d. February 14th, 1704, in England. (Fo.7; 114; 113; Nec).
THOROLD see Knight, Richard.
THOROLD, Alexander. Priest.
 b.1631, Lincolnshire. S.J. September 7th, 1655. Watten (nov) 1656.
Liège (phil) 1656, 1657. Liège (theol) 1659-61. Ordained priest 1663.
Military chaplain 1663. Ghent (tert) 1664, 1665. Residence of St
Dominic 1667, 1669, 1672-6 (now College of St Hugh) 1678-80. d. May
21st, 1681, in England. (Fo.7; 114; 113; Nec).

THOROLD, Edmund (1). Priest.

b.1657, Berkshire. ?s. of William and Mary. ?br. of George. e. St Omers College ?-1677. S.J. September 7th, 1677. Watten (nov) 1678. Liège (phil) 1679-81. Liège (theol) 1682-6. Ordained priest 1686. St Omers College 1686. Watten (tert) 1687. Welshpool 1687. In prison 1689. Residence of St Winefrid 1689-93, 1696-1707, 1709-14 (Superior c.1696-c.1706. Powis Castle c.1689, 1692). Holywell 1715. d. November 7th, 1715, ?Holywell. (Fo.7; CRS.69; 114; 113; 21 v.2; 112; Ki.231; CRS.3/107; CRS.8/422; CRS.9/107; 193 Anglia 35/125; Nec).

THOROLD, Edmund (2) Epiphanius *alias* Turner. Priest.

b. January 16th, 1670 or 1669, Lincolnshire. S.J. January 20th, 1686. Watten (nov) 1687. Liège (phil) 1689-91. Liège (theol) 1692, 1693. Ordained priest c.1695. Ghent (tert) 1696. St Omers College 1697, 1699. Liège 1700. College of St Hugh 1701, 1703-6, 1708-16, 1718, 1720, 1723-5. In England 1726-8. College of St Hugh 1730 (Rector. Kirmond ?-1727-?). d. December 16th 1732, in England (?Market Rasen). (Fo.7; 91; 113; 50 f.28v; 109; Nec).

THOROLD, George. Priest.

b. February 11th, 1670, 1671 or 1672, Buckinghamshire. ?s. of William and Mary. ?br. of Edmund (1). e. St Omers College ?-c.1691. S.J. February 2nd, 1691. Watten (nov) 1691, 1692. Liège (phil) 1693. Liège (theol) 1696, 1697. Ordained priest 1698. Ghent (tert) 1699. York 1700. Maryland 1700-42 (Superior 1725-34). d. November 15th, 1742, Portobacco, Maryland. (Fo.7; CRS.69; 114; 113; Hu. Text 2/684; CRS.62/315; 91; HMC. 10th Report App.4/197; 12 f.105; CRS.4/376; Nec).

THOROLD, William. Scholastic.

b.1660, Northumberland. e. St Omers College ?-1680. S.J. September 7th, 1680. Watten (nov) 1680, 1681. Liège (phil) 1682, 1683. Left 1684, not ordained. (Fo.7; CRS.69; 113; 150 II(3) 8/7/84).

THORPE see Stafford, Ignatius.

THORPE, Andrew. Priest.

b. March 7th, 1741, ?London. e. St Omers College 1752-6 or later. S.J. September 7th, 1758. Liège (phil) 1761. Liège (theol) 1763, 1764. Ordained priest c.1765. ?Antwerp 1766. Dunkenhalgh 1767-9. College of St Aloysius 1771. Dunkenhalgh 1772, 1773. d. January 1st, 1779, Dunkenhalgh. (Fo.7; CRS.69; 114; 117; 113; 21 v.2; 65; 68 p.132; 155 III 185c; CRS.36/218, 229, 239, 248; CRS.OP.1/101; Nec).

THORPE, John. Priest.

b. October 21st, 1726, Halifax, Yorkshire. e. St Omers College c.1741-7. S.J. September 7th, 1747. Watten (nov) 1747-9. Liège (phil) 1750. St Omers College 1752-5. Rome (theol) 1756-c.1760. Ordained priest c.1759. Rome 1760-92. d. April 12th, 1792, Rome. (Fo.7; CRS.69; 114; 113; 91; 13 f.36v; 56 *passim*; 57 I and II *passim*; Nec. For writings see Sut. and Som.).

THROCKMORTON, John.

Watten (nov) 1689. Not found again under this name; no evidence to show that he completed the noviceship. (113).

THUILLER or THUILLIER, Joseph. Laybrother.

b. September 26th or 28th, 1717, Artois. S.J. April 24th, 1748.
Watten (nov) 1749, 1750, 1752-8, 1761, 1763-4. d. March 25th, 1768,
Liège. (Fo.7; 91; 114; 113; 111; Nec).

THWINGE see Vavasour, William.

TICHBORNE see Master or Mashter, Francis; Tasburgh, Henry.

TICHBORNE, Sir John (1) Hermenegild *alias* Cotton. Priest.

b. April 29th, 1679, Hampshire. s. of Sir Henry, 3rd, Bart. and Mary
(Arundell). e. St Omers College c.1694-8 or later. Phil. before S.J. S.J.
October 21st, 1700. Watten (nov) 1701. Liège (phil) 1703. St Omers
College 1704-6, 1708. Rome (theol) 1709-13. Ordained priest 1711.
Liège 1713, 1714. To England 1714. College of St Thomas of
Canterbury 1716, 1718, 1720. Ghent 1723-8, 1730, 1733-41, 1743-4,
1746-8. 5th Bart. 1743. d. May 5th, 1748, Ghent. (Fo.7; CRS.69; 114;
113; CRS.62/5, 28-9, 92, 154, 156, 175; CRS. 43/5; 91; Nec).

TICHBORNE, John (2). Priest.

b. March 26th, 1694, Hampshire. ?s. of William of Sherfield
English, Hampshire. ?br. of Michael. e. St Omers College ?-1712. S.J.
September 7th, 1712. Watten (nov) 1713, 1714. Liège (phil) 1715, 1716.
St Omers College 1718, 1720, 1723. Clermont (theol) 1725. Ordained
priest c.1725. St Omers College 1725, 1726. Liège (theol) 1726. St
Omers College 1727-8, 1730, 1733-7. ?Travelling 1738. Boulogne 1739.
Watten 1740-5 (Rector 1741-5). Residence of St Michael 1746.
Southend 1747. College of St Thomas of Canterbury 1748. College of
St Aloysius 1749. College of St Thomas of Canterbury 1750, 1752-4
(Padwell 1752). College of the Holy Apostles 1755-7 (Crondon Park
?-1757). College of St Ignatius 1757, 1758. London 1758, 1763, 1764,
1765, 1767, 1771-2 (Socius to the provincial). d. April 20th, 1772,
London. (Fo.7; CRS.69; 114; 91; 113; CRS.43/5; CRS.44/11; LR.3/9;
ER.5/94; 150 III(2) 28/10/41; 9 n.262; 13 f.43v; 41 nn.8, 36; 44 f. 167;
63 ff.251v, 254v; 64 pp.314, 516; HMC. 10th Report App.4/190; 151
K.13, EE.10; Nec).

TICHBORNE, Michael. Priest.

b. January 26th, 27th or 29th, 1692, Hampshire. ?s. of William of
Sherfield English, Hampshire. ?br. of John (2). e. St Omers College
?-1712. S.J. September 7th, 1712. Watten (nov) 1712, 1713. Antwerp
(phil) 1714. Liège (phil) 1715. Liège (theol) 1716, 1718, 1720. Ordained
priest 1720. St Omers College 1723-7. Hooton 1728-?41. College of St
Aloysius 1743-4. Liverpool c.1746-9. Rixton 1749-51. Brinn 1751. d.
June 23rd, 1751, Brinn. bu. Ashton chapel. (Fo.7; CRS.69; 114; 91;
113; 9 nn.262, 264, 272; CRS.62/116; 21 v.2; 24 f.347v; 28 ff.9, 10, 14,
20; 85; 156 App.1; CRS.9/184-5; CRS.25/114; Nec).

TICKLE see Molyneux, Joseph.

TICKLE, William. Laybrother.

b. July 25th, 1717, Lancashire. S.J. July 15th, 1748. Watten (nov)
1748. Ghent (nov) 1749. Liège 1750, 1752-8, 1761, 1763-4, 1767-9,

1771-3. Liège Academy 1776, 1781, 1783. d. September 3rd, 1787, Liège. (Fo.7; 91; 117; AHSJ.42/294; 113; 3 ff.41, 55; 90 f.54; CRS.12/28; Nec).

TIDDER or TYDDER, Edward *alias* Ingleby. Priest.
  b.1630, Suffolk. e. St Omers College 1648 or earlier-52. S.J. September 7th, 1652. Watten (nov) 1652, 1653. Liège (phil) 1654-6. Liège (theol) 1657-60. Ordained priest April 16th, 1661. Ghent (tert) 1661. Maryland 1662-7. College of the Holy Apostles 1669, 1672-6, 1678. College of St Ignatius 1679-87, 1689-97 (London 1685. Savoy College 1687). d. January 2nd, 1699, in England. (Fo.7; CRS.69; 114; 113; Hu. Text 2/680; 123 II f.156; 174; CRS. 62/238; 43 ff.11-2, 16-7, 24; Nec).

TOCKETS, Alexius *alias* Condestable and Young. Priest.
  b. April 4th, 1665, County Durham. ?s. of Joseph and Katherine (Draper *née* Eden). E.C. Valladolid 1685-June 8th, 1689. Ordained priest April 24th, 1689. S.J. October 1st, 1689. Watten (nov) 1690. Liège (phil) 1691-3. Liège (theol) 1696. St Omers College 1697, 1698. Ghent 1698. Residence of St John 1699-1701, 1703-6, 1708-16, 1720, 1723-5. In England 1726-8, 1730 (Durham ?-1727, 1729). d. January 20th, 1731, in England (?Durham). bu. St Oswald's, Durham. (Fo.7; 114; 91; 113; Ans.3/227; CRS.30/175; NCH.4/11; 150 III(1) 19/7/98; 36 f.262; CRS.25/114; 95 p.793; CRS.62/133, 135, 202; Nec).

TODD, Henry. Priest.
  b.1666 or 1667, Kent. S.J. September 7th, 1687. Watten (nov) 1687. Liège (phil) 1689-92. Ingolstadt (theol) 1693, 1696. Ordained priest c.1696. St Omers College 1697. College of the Holy Apostles 1699. Residence of St Winefrid 1700-01, 1703-6, 1708-12 (Superior c.1708-12. Aston 1703. Pepperhill 1708, 1711). d. February 25th, 1712, Holywell. (Fo.7; 114; 113; 89; 170 f.245v; 169/155/2, 3; Nec).

TOENS, James. Laybrother.
  b.1638, Flanders. S.J. April 13th or 20th, 1672. Watten (nov) 1672-5. d. December 2nd, 1675, Watten. (Fo.7; 114; 113; Nec).

TONA, Arnold. Laybrother.
  b. ?February 15th, 1621, Liège. S.J. May 1671 or 1670. Watten (nov) 1672, Liège 1673-6, 1678-87, 1689-93, 1696-7, 1699. d. November 21st, 1699, St Omers College or Liège. (Fo.7; 114; 113; Nec).

TOUCHET see Audley, James.

TOULOTT, Matthew. Priest.
  b.1639, Flanders. e. St Omers College 1658 or earlier-60. S.J. September 9th, 1660. Watten (nov) 1660, 1661. Liège (phil) 1663-5. Ordained priest c.1666. St Omers College 1667. Watten 1669, 1672. Ghent 1672, 1673. St Omers College 1674, 1675. College of St Ignatius 1676. d. July 27th, 1677, in England. (Fo.7; CRS.69; 114; 113; Nec).

TOWNELEY see Madgeworth, Christopher.

TRAVAGAN see Blackiston, William.

TRAVANNIAN see Trevannian.

TRESSAM or TRESHAM, Thomas. Priest.

b.1637, Dorset. S.J. 1662 or 1663. Liège (phil) 1663-5. St Omers
College 1667. Liège (theol) 1669. Ordained priest c.1670. d. October
18th, 1671, in England. (Fo.7; 114; 113).

TREVANNIAN or TREVANNION or TRAVANNIAN or
TRAVAGNAN, Charles *alias* Drummond. Priest.
b.1667 or 1669, London. s. of Charles and – (Drummond) of
Carhayes, Cornwall. S.J. September 7th, 1685. Watten (nov) 1685,
1686. Liège (phil) 1687, 1689-90. Liège (theol) 1691, 1692. La Flèche
(theol) 1693. Ordained priest c.1694. Fithelers 1695-6. College of St
Hugh 1697, 1699. London 1700. Ghent 1700, 1701. College of St
Thomas of Canterbury 1703. College of St Ignatius 1704-6, 1708-11.
Residence of St Stanislaus 1712, 1713. College of St Ignatius 1714.
Residence of St Stanislaus 1725. In England 1726. Richmond, Surrey
1727-37. d. March 17th, 1737, Richmond. (Fo.7; 114; 91; 113;
ER.9/105; 150 III(1) 22/5/1700; 43 f.24; CRS.7/297; 01.424; Nec).

TRISTRAM, Joseph *alias* or *vere* Cross. Priest.
b. June 2nd, 1766, Ince Blundell. Nephew of Thomas Cross. e. Liège
Academy 1781-7. Liège (phil) 1785. Liège (theol) 1787. Ordained priest
April 4th, 1791. Spinkhill 1791-1812. S.J. October 10th, 1803. London
1812-17. Lulworth 1817. Stonyhurst 1818-27 (Rector 1819-27).
Worcester 1827-37 (Superior 1832-?7). New Hall 1837-43. d. April
14th, 1843, New Hall. bu. New Hall convent cemetery. (Fo.7; 113; 115;
LR.3/7; WR.20/70; CRW.58ff.; 150 (1750-1853) ff.182, 192; 4
ff.137ff, 153ff.; 63 ff.288ff.; 7 ff.260v, 270v, 280v, 285v, 320v; 8 II
nn.99, 106, 114; 13 ff.291, 436, 501; 21 v.2; 93 p.15; 94 ff.56-61, 66-7,
69-70; CRS.6/368; CRS.17/93; 92; 202; CRS.13/211; Nec).

TRYOEN, James. Laybrother.
b.1706 or 1707, Dunkirk. S.J. September 7th, 1728. Watten (nov)
1730. d. November 30th, 1731, St Omers College. (Fo.7; 114; 91; 113;
Nec).

TUCHET or TOUCHET see Audley, James.

TUCKER, James *alias* Norris. Priest.
b. February 5th, 1710, Somerset. e. St Omers College c.1723-8. S.J.
September 7th, 1728-42. Watten (nov) 1730. Liège (theol) 1733-5.
Ordained priest c.1735. College of the Immaculate Conception 1736,
1737. College of St Chad 1738, 1739. College of the Holy Apostles
1740, 1741. (CRS.69; 113; 91; 150 III(2) 27/7/43; 74).

TUCKER, Robert. Laybrother.
b. January 28th, 1710, Dorset. S.J. ?September 7th, 1752. Watten
(nov) 1753, 1754. St Omers College 1755-8, 1761. Bruges College
1763-4, 1767-9, 1771-3. Liège Academy 1776, 1781, 1783. d. December,
1790, Liège. (Fo.7; 114; 117; 91; 113; AHSJ.42/294; 3 ff.41, 55; 16
f.98; 68 p.332; 90 f.54; CRS.12/35; Nec).

TUNSTALL, Thomas. Priest.
b.1635, Yorkshire. e. St Omers College 1653 or earlier-55. S.J. 1655.
Watten (nov) 1656. Liège (phil) 1657-9. Liège (theol) 1660-4. Ordained
priest April 12th, 1664. Ghent (tert) 1664. d. February 6th, 1665,

Ghent. (Fo.7; CRS.69; 114; 113; Nec).

TURBERVILLE, John *alias* Fermor. Priest.

b.1663, Berkshire. ?s. of John and Anne (Anderton) e. St Omers College ?-1683. S.J. September 7th, 1683. Watten (nov) 1683, 1684. Liège (phil) 1685-7. In England 1688. Liège (theol) 1689-92. Ordained priest December 27th, 1691. College of St Aloysius 1693, 1696-7, 1699-1701, 1703-6, 1708 (Lostock c.1701). College of St Ignatius 1709. Residence of St Michael 1710, 1711. College of St Aloysius 1712-4 (Ince 1711, 1714). Travelling 1715. College of St Aloysius 1716. Formby 1718. Lostock ?-1720. London 1720. St Omers College 1721 (Rector). College of St Ignatius 1724. Provincial 1725-31. College of St Ignatius 1731-5 (Rector. London 1729, 1734). d. October 31st, 1735, London. (Fo.7; CRS.69; 114; 91; 113; LR.3/8; 150 III(2) 12/4/21; 23 f.35; NB.1/293, 2/99, 163-4, 3/194; Chad.259; Gib.1/64, 73-6, 79, 168-9; 126; Nec).

TURBERVILLE, Thomas. Laybrother.

b. ?October 2nd, 1678, London. S.J. December 24th or 25th, 1702. Watten (nov) 1703-5. Liège 1706, 1708-14. St Omers College 1715-6, 1718, 1720, 1723-8, 1730. Ghent 1733-4. d. September 7th, 1734, Ghent. (Fo.7; 114; 91; 113; Nec).

TURNER see Aldred, Robert; Murphy or Morphy, Richard; Thorold, Edmund (2) Epiphanius.

TURNER, Anthony *alias* Ashby and Baines. Priest.

b.1628, near Melton Mowbray, Leicestershire. s. of Toby and Elizabeth (Cheseldine) of Little Dalby, Leicestershire. br. of Edward. e. Uppingham and Peterhouse and St John's College, Cambridge. E.C. Rome October 27th, 1650-April 18th, 1653. S.J. June 21st, 1653. Watten (nov) 1653-5. Liège (theol) 1656-9. Ordained priest April 12th, 1659. St Omers College 1659. Watten (tert) 1660. Residence of St George 1661, 1663-5, 1667, 1669, 1672-8 (Superior 1670-c.78). Executed at Tyburn, June 20th, 1679. bu. St Giles-in-the-Fields churchyard. Beatified. (Fo.7; 114; 113; CRS.47/266; CRS.40/45; WR.4/18 ff.16/6; 37 *passim*; 135 ff.193-4; Ven.I 4/273; FAB.119, 156 ff.173-5; BR.48-53; Nec. For writings see Som.).

TURNER, Edward *alias* Ashby, John. Priest.

b.1625, Leicestershire. s. of Toby and Elizabeth (Cheseldine) of Little Dalby, Leicestershire. br. of Anthony. e. Uppingham and St John's College and Corpus Christi, Cambridge and St Omers College 1647 or earlier-1648 or later. E.C. Rome October 27th, 1650-April 18th, 1653. S.J. January, 1658. Watten (nov) 1658. Ordained priest c.1658. Liège 1659-61, 1663-4. College of the Immaculate Conception 1665, 1667, 1669, 1672-6, 1678 (Holbeck ?-1677, 1678). In prison in London 1679-81. d. March 19th, 1681, the Gatehouse, Westminster. (Fo.7; CRS.69; 114; 113; CRS.40/45; 154 f.15; 135 f.203; 138 n.94; Ven.I 4/274; 141 f.44; BR.48-50; Nec).

TURNER, John *alias* Herbert and Weedon, Thomas. ?Priest.

b.c.1640, Monmouthshire. e. St Omers College 1654-9. E.C. Rome

October 17th, 1659-1662 or 1663. S.J. 1662 or 1663. Perhaps he is the John Herbert who left the novitiate in 1663 or perhaps he has been confused with another John Turner, S.J. 1623. (Fo.7; CRS.69; 114; CRS.40/61; CRS.55/572; 113; Nec).

TURNER, Robert *alias* Maudsley. Priest.

b. January 12th, 1677, Lancashire. e. St Omers College 1698-1701. S.J. October 8th or 9th, 1701. Watten (nov) 1703, 1704. Liège (phil) 1705, 1706. St Omers College 1708-11. Liège (theol) 1712-4. Ordained priest 1712. E.C. Rome 1715, 1716. College of St Aloysius 1720, 1723-5. In England 1726-7 (Hooton, ?-1725-7). Liège 1728. Watten 1728. In England 1730. Callaly ?-1733. Burton Park 1733-4. d. November 29th, 1734, Burton Park. bu. Burton church. (Fo.7; CRS.69; 91; 114; 113; CRS.62/292; RH.13/116; 64 p.49; 74; 89; NB.3/162, 216; 156 xi; CRS.7/319; 120; 95 f.787; Nec).

TURNER, William. Scholastic.

b. November 11th, 1681, 1682 or 1683, Monmouthshire. e. St Omers College c.1698-1703. S.J. September 7th, 1703. Watten (nov) 1704, 1705. Liège (phil) 1706, 1708. St Omers College 1709-12. Paris (theol) 1712. d. August 26th, 1712, Paris. (Fo.7; CRS.69; 114; 113; Nec).

TURVILLE, Charles ?*alias* Smith. Priest.

b. March 10th, 1681, Leicestershire. s. of William and Isabella (Cokayne) of Aston Flamville. br. of Henry. e. St Omers College ?-1700. S.J. September 7th, 1700. Watten (nov) 1701. Liège (phil) 1703-5. Liège (theol) 1706. Ordained priest c.1708. Douay (theol) 1708, 1709. St Omers College 1710. Ghent (tert) 1711. College of St Aloysius 1712-6, 1718, 1720, 1723-4 (Ince 1711, 1718, 1720, 1722). College of St Ignatius 1725. In England 1726-8, 1730. Louvain 1732. Antwerp 1733-6. College of St Thomas of Canterbury 1736, 1737. Travelling 1738. Ghent 1739-42 (Rector). Louvain 1743-6. Liège 1747. Brussels 1748-50. College of St Ignatius 1752. London 1753. Watten 1753-5. d. January 11th, 1757, Watten. (Fo.7; CRS.69; 91; 114; 113; LR.3/8; 9 n.300; NB.1/297, 300, 2/220, 3/15, 69, 85; HMC. 10th Report App.4/197; 108; 111; 51 f.311; Nec).

TURVILLE, Henry. Priest.

b. November 10th, 1674, Leicestershire. s. of William and Isabella (Cokayne) of Aston Flamville. br. of Charles. S.J. April 1693. Watten (nov) 1693. Liège (phil) 1696, 1697. Liège (theol) 1699-1701. Ordained priest 1701. Liège 1703-6, 1708-9. Liège Episcopal Seminary 1709-13. d. March 25th, 1714, Ghent. (Fo.7; 114; 113; CRS.62/50, 74, 77, 82, 84, 86; Nec. For writings see Som.).

TWISDEN, Bartholomew see Chetwin, Ralph.

TYDDER see Tidder.

TYRER, Joseph. Priest.

b. May 12th, 1734, Lancashire. e. St Omers College c.1752-3. S.J. September 7th, 1753. Watten (nov) 1754, 1755. Liège (phil) 1756-8. Liège (theol) 1760-2. Ordained priest c.1762. Ghent 1762. Plowden Hall 1762-77. Holywell 1777-98. d. December 22nd, 1798, Holywell.

bu. Holywell churchyard. (Fo.7; CRS.69; 91; 114; 117; RH.10/165 ff;
WR.25/36; 3 f.29; 21 v.2; 64 p.270; 68 p.215; 69; CRS.3/118-21; 113;
169/155/9, 18; 119 ff.11, 16; Nec).

TYRER, Robert. Scholastic.
b. October 11th, 1798, Preston. e. Stonyhurst 1810-?. S.J.
September 7th, 1816. Hodder (nov) 1816-8. Stonyhurst 1820-1. Paris
(theol) 1824-6. d. November 23rd, 1826, Dôle. (Fo.7; 113; Stol; 117; 11
f.234, 247; 13 f.499; CRS.12/174; CDSJ; CG. For writings see Som.).

TYRWHITT or TYRWHIT or TERRETT or TYRRET, Henry *alias*
Guillim. Priest.
b. May or June 15th, 1672, London. e. St Omers College 1689 or
earlier-91. E.C. Rome October 18th, 1691-April 26th, 1692. S.J. April
30th, 1692, Naples. Naples (nov) 1693. Naples (phil) 1696, 1697. Naples
(theol) 1699-1701. Ordained priest c.1702. Ghent (tert) 1703-5. St
Omers College 1706. Ghent 1708. E.C. Valladolid 1708-11. St Omers
College 1711-6, 1718, 1720. Ghent 1723-8, 1730, 1733-40. d. January
11th, 1742, Ghent. (Fo.7; CRS.69; 114; 91; 113; CRS.30/xxxiv, 181;
150 III(2) 4/12/23; Ki.108; Nec).

?VALLAS or VALLES, Joseph. ?Priest,
Liège Academy 1776. Nothing further recorded. (90 f.54).

VAN BREDA see Breda.

VAN DAME, Louis see Le Fevre, Peter.

VAN DEN ABEEL, Baldwin. Laybrother.
b.1638, Flanders. ?br. of James. S.J. September 7th, 1662. Watten
(nov) 1663-5. Liège 1667. Ghent 1669. St Omers College 1672-9. d.
October 13th, 1679, St Omers College. (Fo.7; 113; 114; Nec).

VAN DEN ABEEL, James. Laybrother.
b. March 9th, 1643, Bruges. ?br. of Baldwin. S.J. September 7th,
1671. Watten (nov) 1672. Ghent 1672-6, 1678-9. Madrid 1680-3. St
Omers College 1684-7, 1689-93, 1696-8. d. February 10th, 1698, St
Omers College. (Fo.7; 113; 114; 168 f.86v; Nec).

VAN DEN BUSCHE, Francis. Laybrother.
b. November 26th, 1662, Ostend. S.J. November 11th, 1688. Watten
(nov) 1689, 1690. Liège 1691. Watten 1692. St Omers College 1693,
1696-8. d. February 17th, 1698, St Omers College. (Fo.7; 113; 114;
Nec).

VAN DEN CRUYS or CRUISE, Martin. Laybrother.
b.1644 or 1646, Liège. ?br. of Toussaint. S.J. September 7th, 1670 or
1671. Watten (nov) 1672. St Omers College 1673-6, 1678-87, 1689-92.
d. August 23rd, 1692, St Omers College. (Fo.7; 113; 114; Nec).

VAN DEN CRUYS or CRUISE, Toussaint. Laybrother.
b. May 8th, 1652, Liège. ?br. of Martin. S.J. October 3rd, 1677.
Watten (nov) 1678-87, 1689-91. Liège 1692, 1693. d. September 9th,
1694, Ghent. (Fo.7; 113; 114; Nec).

VAN DEN DORP, Everard. Laybrother,
> b. November 20th, 1675, 1676, 1678 or 1679, Bruges. S.J. October 9th, 1704. Watten (nov) 1705, 1706, 1708-16, 1718. St Omers College 1720. d. September 4th, 1721, Ghent. (Fo.7; 113; 114).

VAN DER HAEGHE, Philip. Laybrother novice.
> b.1662, Flanders. S.J. c.1686. Watten (nov) 1687. d. February 17th, 1688, Watten. (Fo.7; 114; 113; Nec).

VAN EUPEN, Andrew. Laybrother.
> b. March 15th, 1705, Brabant. S.J. March 3rd, 1736. Watten (nov) 1736-8. E.C. Rome 1739-41, 1743-4, 1748-50, 1752-8, 1761, 1763-4, 1767-9. d. July 16th, 1770, Rome. (Fo.7; 113; 91; 114; 111; Nec).

VAN PARYS, John *alias* Brent. Laybrother,
> b. September 26th, 1710. S.J. September 7th, 1732, in Belgium. To the English province 1763. Watten 1764. Ghent 1767-9. Nothing further recorded. (113).

VAN RODE or Van de Roode, Peter. Laybrother.
> b. October or December 10th, 1668, Dunkirk. S.J. March 18th, 1694. St Omers College 1696-7, 1699-1701. d. August 10th, 1702, St Omers College. (Fo.7; 114; 113; Nec).

VAN WAMBEKE or Van Wambeeke, Adrian. Priest.
> b.1630, Bruges. S.J. March 25th, 1666 (already ordained priest). Watten (nov) 1666-7, 1669, 1672-6. Liège 1678-81. Ghent 1682-7. d. January 20th, 1687, Ghent. (Fo.7; 114; 113; Nec).

VAST, Andrew. Laybrother.
> b.1670 or 1674, Saint-Omer. S.J. October 9th, 1698 or 1699. Watten (nov) 1700-01, 1703-6, 1708-9. Liège 1710-2. d. February 2nd, 1712, Liège. (Fo.7; 114; 113; Nec).

VAUDREY or VAUDEREY or VAUDRY, John *alias* More, *alias* or *vere* Worsley. Priest.
> b.1658, ?Chichester (or Chester). S.J. October or November 9th, 1677. Watten (nov) 1678. Liège (phil) 1679-81. Liège (theol) 1682. St Omers College 1683. La Flèche (theol) 1684-6. Ordained priest c.1686. Residence of St John 1688-90 (in Berwick prison), 1691-3. College of St Thomas of Canterbury 1696-7, 1699-1701, 1703-6, 1708-16, 1718, 1720, 1724 (Rector 1711-5. ?Sherfield English c.1707). d. October 19th, 1725, in England. (Fo.7; 113; 123 IIIB f.290; 135 f.240; Nec).

VAUGHAN, Richard. Priest.
> b. January 14th, 1675, Monmouthshire. s. of Richard and Agatha (Berington) of Welsh Bicknor. e. St Omers College ?-1690. S.J. September 7th, 1690. Watten (nov) 1692. Liège (phil) 1693. Liège (theol) 1696-7. Ordained priest 1699. Liège 1699-1700. Ghent (tert) 1701. Liège 1703-6, 1708-16, 1720-4. Ghent 1725-7 (Rector). d. October 13th, 1727, Ghent. (Fo.7; CRS.69; 91; 113; 9 nn.79, 85, 87, 107, 109, 121; Nec).

VAUGHAN, William. Priest.
> b.1644, in Wales. s. of William of Brecon. e. St Omers College ?-1668. E.C. Rome October 18th, 1668-c.1671. S.J. January 2nd or

20th, 1672. Watten (nov) 1672. Liège (theol) 1673-6. Ordained priest
April 17th, 1677. College of St Francis Xavier 1678-87 (Rector 1683-7).
d. January 9th, 1687, in England or Wales. (Fo.7; CRS.69; CRS.40/77;
114; 113; Nec).

VAVASOUR, Sir Walter. Priest.
      b.1662, Yorkshire. s. of Peter and Elizabeth (Langdale) of York. e.
St Omers College ?-1681. S.J. September 7th, 1681. Watten (nov) 1681,
1682. Liège (phil) 1683-5. Liège (theol) 1686-9. Ordained priest 1689.
Residence of St Michael 1693, 1696-7. ?Norwich c.1699. College of St
Ignatius 1699. College of St Aloysius 1700-01, 1703-6, 1708-16, 1718,
1720, 1723-5 (Bailey Hall c.1700, 1701. Alston and Hothersall 1705,
1714-6, 1718. ?Preston). In England 1726-8, 1730 (Preston c.1727).
College of St Aloysius 1733-40. 4th Bart. 1713. d. April 10th, 1740,
Preston or Stydd. bu. Stydd. (Fo.7; CRS.69; 114; 91; 113; E and P.316,
340; NA.37/165; 21 v.2; 43 f.28; 23 f.35; 30 ff.34, 38; CRS.6/147;
Ki.241; CRS.15/316; CRS.31/260-1; CRS.36/112, 117; Tyl.171;
Gil.HP.63; Nec).

VAVASOUR, William *alias* Thwinge and Giffard. Priest.
      b.1618, Yorkshire. ?s. of Sir Thomas, 1st Bart. and Ursula (Giffard).
e. St Omers College c.1635. S.J. March 24th, 1665. Watten (nov) 1666.
Liège (theol) 1667, 1669. Ordained priest c.1668. College of the Holy
Apostles 1672-8. Boscobel 1678. Ghent 1679-82. d. April 22nd or 23rd,
1683, Nieuport. (Fo.7; CRS.69; 114; 113; CRS. 47/66n; 168 f.49; 140
n.45; Nec).

VERBELEN, James Leonard. Laybrother.
      b. August 5th, 1745, Belgium. S.J. July 23rd, 1771. Ghent (nov)
1771-3. Left, date not recorded; it is possible that he completed his
novitiate. (Fo.7; 113).

VERDCHEVAL or VERDECHEVAL, Leonard. Laybrother.
      b.1683, Liège. S.J. July 30th, 1706. Watten (nov) 1708, 1709-10. St
Omers College 1711-3. Watten 1714-6, 1718, 1720, 1723-5. Ghent
1725-30. d. November 15th, 1730, Ghent. (Fo.7; 91; 113; Nec).

VEZZOZI, Joseph *alias* Robinson. Priest.
      b. August 5th, 1720, Rome. s. of Michele and Ann (Robertson). E.C.
Rome October 19th, 1731-September 17th, 1743. Ordained priest
September 8th, 1743. S.J. December 26th, 1743. Watten (nov) 1744-6.
Residence of St George 1747-50, 1752-5 (Weston ?-1756). Spinkhill
1756. Residence of St George 1757. College of the Immaculate
Conception 1758, 1763-4. York 1766-70. Bruges College 1771, 1772. d.
December 18th, 1772, Bruges. (Fo.7; 114; 91; 113; CRS. Mon.2/388;
Ans.4/285-6; WR.20/62, 72; 64 p.420; 68 p.37; 77; CRS.4/377;
CRS.40/184; 111; Ki.200; Nec).

VILLIERS see Fitzwilliam, John.

VINCENT see Preston, William.

VISCONTI, Hermes Mary. Priest.
      b. March 9th or 13th, 1650, Milan. S.J. September 4th, 1665. To the
English province c.1676. Liège (theol) 1678, 1679. Ordained priest

April 19th, 1678. Watten (tert) 1680. Liège 1681-3. Antwerp 1684-90.
Ghent 1690-3 (Rector). St Omers College 1693, 1696. Travelling 1697.
To Rome 1698. Nothing further found in English province records.
(Fo.7; 113; 150 II(2) 14/3/76, II(3) 30/7/89, 28/1/90, 3/7/94, 15/3/98;
170 f.172; 135 f.243; 140 n.45; 108).

VISSCHER see de Visscher.

VRANKEN or VRANCKEN, John Joseph. Laybrother.
    b. May 8th, 1718, Liège. S.J. September 7th, 1740. Watten (nov)
1741-2, 1743-4, 1746-7. Ghent 1748-50, 1752. Liège 1753-8, 1761,
1763-4, ?1765. Nothing further recorded. (Fo.7; 113; 140 n.45; 91).

WADSWORTH, Thomas. Scholastic.
    b. December, 1692, Lancashire. s. of Nicholas and Judith of
Haighton Hall. S.J. September 7th, 1712. Watten (nov) 1713, 1714.
Liège (phil) 1715, 1716. Liège (theol) 1718. d. July 16th, 1719, Liège,
not ordained. (Fo.7; 114; 113; Nec).

WAINWRIGHT, Arthur. Priest,
    b. October 19th, 1797, near Liverpool. e. Stonyhurst 1810-6. S.J.
September 7th, 1816-30. Hodder (nov) 1816-8. Stonyhurst (phil etc.)
1818-23. Brig (theol) 1823. Fribourg (theol) 1824-6. Ordained priest
May 20th, 1826, Fribourg. Southend 1826-30. (115;2).

WAKEMAN see Jeffery, Thomas.

WAKEMAN, Joseph. Priest.
    b.1647, Beckford, Gloucestershire. s. of Edward and Mary (Cotton)
of Beckford. e. St Omers College 1660-5. S.J. September 7th, 1665.
Liège (phil) 1667, 1669. St Omers College 1672. Liège (theol) 1673-5.
Ordained priest April 15th, 1675. Ghent (tert) 1676. Liège 1678-85.
College of St Ignatius 1685. Residence of St Mary 1686. Residence of St
George 1687. Residence of St Mary 1689-93. Socius to the provincial
1695-7, 1699-1701, 1703-6, 1708. College of St Ignatius 1709-20.
(Rector 1712-7). d. December 8th, 1720, Watten. (Fo.7; CRS.69; 113;
114; 150 II(3) 23/4/95, III(1) 25/10/19; E and P.70; CRS.62/249; Nec.
For writings see Som.).

WALDEGRAVE, Francis *alias* Pelham. Priest.
    b.1625, Wiltshire. s. of Nicholas and Lucy (Mervin). e. St Omers
College 1640-5. E.C. Rome May 27th, 1645-52. Ordained priest March
25th, 1651. To England 1652. S.J. September 30th, 1655. Watten (nov)
1656. Liège 1657. College of St Aloysius 1658-61, 1663-5, 1667, 1669,
1672-87, 1689-93, 1696-7, 1699-1701 (Rector c.1678-83. Crosby 1672,
1673, 1678. Garswood 1680, 1681. Lydiate 1681, 1696, 1697). d.
November 28th, 1701, Lydiate. bu. St Katherine's chantry chapel
Lydiate. (Fo.7; CRS.69; 114; 113; Ans.2/332; 150 II(2) 8/5/77;
CRS.40/42-3; CRS.55/456; Gib.1/277-284; Gib.2/64-5; 27 f.215;
WB.137, 149, 190-3; Nec).

WALKEDEN, John. Priest.

b. December 26th, 1663, London. e. St Omers College ?-1682. S.J.
September 7th, 1682. Watten (nov) 1682, 1683. Liège (phil) 1684-6. St
Omers College 1687, 1689-91. Rome (theol) 1692-5. Ordained priest
c.1694. Ghent (tert) 1696. St Omers College 1699-1701, 1703-6,
1708-16, 1718. d. November 8th, 1718, St Omers College. (Fo.7; 114;
CRS.69; 113; 150 II(3) 16/4/95; 170 f.62; CRS.62/79, 83, 92, 128, 200,
248, 299-300; Nec).

WALKER see Westby, Peter.

WALKER, George. Laybrother.

b.1640, Lancashire. S.J. July 31st, 1665. St Omers College 1667,
1669, 1672-6, 1678-9. Liège 1679. d. October 16th, 1680, Liège. (Fo.7;
114; 113; 168 f.82; Nec).

WALLACE, William. Priest.

d. May 31st, 1682, Sandomierz. Not found under this name in the
English province catalogues. (Fo.7; 95 p.817).

WALLIS see Harrison, John.

WALMESLEY see Pleasington, Joseph.

WALMESLEY, Christopher *alias* Harris. Priest.

b. August 10th, 1684, Westwood, Wigan, Lancashire. e. St Omers
College 1700 or earlier-1701. E.C. Valladolid October 20th, 1701-April
24th, 1708. Ordained priest 1707. S.J. July 21st, 1708. Watten (nov)
1709. Liège (theol) 1710. Liège 1711-16, 1718, 1720, 1723-8, 1730-4. d.
October 22nd, 1734, Liège. (Fo.7; CRS.69; 114; 91; 113; CRS.30/180;
Ans.3/242; NewH.79; Nec. For writings see Som.).

WALMESLEY, Henry Worthington. Priest.

b. January 5th, 1811, Westwood, Wigan, Lancashire. e. Stonyhurst
1819-27. S.J. October 26th, 1827. Hodder (nov) 1827-9. Hodder (phil)
1829-30. St Mary's Hall (phil) 1830-2. Stonyhurst 1832-9. St Mary's
Hall (theol) 1839-40. Louvain (theol) 1840-3. Ordained priest
September 8th, 1842, Liège. Preston 1843-4. Hodder and St Mary's
Hall 1844-5. Stonyhurst 1845-7. Worcester 1847-9. Preston 1849-55.
(Rector 1852-5). Wardour 1855-60. London 1860-1. Socius to the
provincial 1861-4. Edinburgh 1864-73. Lulworth 1873-4. Wigan
1874-8. Holywell 1878. d. November 20th, 1878, Holywell. bu.
Pantasaph cemetery. (Fo.7; 115; 113; Nec).

WALMESLEY, John. Scholastic.

s. of Richard and Jane (Hoghton or Houghton) of Sholley,
Lancashire. e. St Omers College c.1693-c.1700. S.J. September 7th,
1706. Watten (nov) 1708. Liège (phil) 1709. Left 1709, not ordained.
(113; CRS.69; 150 III(1) 10/8/09, III(2) 14/9/09; E and P.100;
CRS.23/112).

WALMESLEY, Thomas. Priest.

b. July 19th, 1716, Lancashire. e. St Omers College c.1728-c.37. S.J.
September 7th, 1737. Watten (nov) 1738. Liège (phil) 1739-41. Büren
(theol) 1743. Ordained priest c.1744. Geist (tert) 1744. Watten 1746.
College of St Thomas of Canterbury 1747. Ince 1747. Kelvedon
c.1747-52. St Omers College 1753. College of St Ignatius 1754.

?Wardour 1754. Ince 1755-?8. ?Hereford 1759. College of St Aloysius 1763-4. Stockeld Park c.1767-9. Culcheth 1769-?85. Rixton ?1785-92. d. January 5th, 1792, Rixton. (Fo.7; 114; CRS.69; 91; 113; 117; ER.9/114n, 14/83; 64 pp.274, 541; 76 f.46; 25 ff.66, 87-8, 92, 103, 105, 113, 118, 139; 80; 86; 111; HMC. 10th Report App.4/194, 196; 158; 155 II 129; 156 App.1; 155 III 185c; CRS.13/372; 204 n.36; 43 ff.75, 77, 81; 167; 120; 119 f.42; Nec).

WALMESLEY, William. Priest.

b. May 27th or June 1st, 1712, Lancashire. e. St Omers College c.1725-32. S.J. September 7th, 1732. Watten (nov) 1733. Liège (phil) 1734-6. Liège (theol) 1737-40. Ordained priest c.1740. St Omers College 1741. Residence of St George 1743-4, 1746-50, 1752-8, 1763-4 (Spetchley 1748. Wappenbury 1752). Wappenbury 1767-9. d. July 22nd 1769, Worcester. (Fo.7; CRS.69; 114; 91; 113; WR.20/61; 41 n.60; 40 p.108; 65; HMC. 10th Report App.4/187, 197; Nec).

WALSH or WALSHE, Edward. Priest.

b. January 24th, 1739, in France. e. St Omers College 1755 or earlier-56. S.J. September 7th, 1756. Watten (nov) 1756-8. St Omers College 1761, 1762. Bruges College 1762-4. Pont-à-Mousson 1767. Ordained priest c.1767. Colmar 1768. Rome 1769, 1771. Durham 1772-1822. d. October 22nd, 1822, Durham. bu. St Oswald's, Durham. (Fo.7; CRS.69; 91; 114; 113; NCH.4/13ff; 150(1750-1853) f.188; 6 ff.87, 93, 124; 7 ff.2, 61, 177v; 14 f.243; 19 p.37; 21 v.2; 35 f.118; 36 f.262; 55 ff.296-9; CRS.12/152; 163; 56 ff.327, 329; 62 nn.302,314; 94 ff.251-2, 306-7; Chad.314; 167 pp.35, 45; 125; 121; Nec. For writings see Sut. and Som.).

WALSH or WALSHE, John. Priest.

b. January or June 10th or August 24th, 1700, Tipperary, Ireland. S.J. September 7th, 1720. Liège (phil) 1723, 1724. Liège (theol) 1725-8. Ordained priest c.1728. St Omers College 1730, 1733-5. Travelling 1736-40. Residence of St John 1740. Ellingham 1741. Gateshead ?-1745-6. Newcastle c.1747-73. (Superior of the Residence of St John c.1751-73). d. May 26th, 1773, Newcastle. bu. St Nicholas churchyard, Newcastle. (Fo.7; 113; NCH.5/16; AHSJ.38/468; 21 v.2; 35 ff.65v ff., 156; 36 ff.138, 159, 181, 262, 269; 66; 91; 156 App.1; Ki.244; 160; CRS.35/200; 164; 111; 117; 90 f.23v; 51 f.311; Nec).

WALTON, James. Priest.

b. June 10th, 1736. From Lancashire. s. of James and Ann of Broughton. br. of Thomas. e. St Omers College 1753-7. S.J. September 7th, 1757. Watten (nov) 1757, 1758. Liège (phil) 1761. Liège (theol) 1763, 1764. Ordained priest c.1765. Maryland 1766-1803. d. February 19th, 1803, St Ignatius', Maryland. (Fo.7; CRS.69; 91; 113; 117; Hu. Text 2/696; 68 p.75).

WALTON, Roger. Scholastic.

b.1660, Lancashire. e. St Omers College ?-1681. S.J. September 7th, 1681. Watten (nov) 1681, 1682. d. September 24th, 1683, Watten, not ordained. (Fo.7; CRS.69; 114; 113; Nec).

WALTON, Thomas. Priest.

b. August 5th, 1740. s. of James and Ann of Broughton. br. of James. e. St Omers College 1753-7. S.J. September 7th, 1757. Watten (nov) 1757, 1758. Liège (phil) 1761. Liège (theol) 1763, 1764. Ordained priest c.1765. Bruges 1766. Irnham 1767-9, 1771-97. d. May 1797, Irnham. (Fo.7; 91; 117; 113; 21 v.2; 50 ff.15v, 79, 136-7, 201; 65; 68 p.151; CRS.69; CRS.12/57; CRS.OP.1/146; Nec).

WALTON, William. Priest.

b.1651, Lancashire. S.J. September 7th, 1671. Watten (nov) 1672. Liège (phil) 1673-5. St Omers College 1676, 1678-80. In France (?theol) 1681. La Flèche (?theol) 1682. Liège (theol) 1683, 1684. Ordained priest c.1684. Ghent (tert) 1685. Liège 1686, 1687. Paris 1689-93. Socius to the provincial 1694-5. College of St Thomas of Canterbury 1696. St Omers College 1697-1701 (Rector). To England 1701. College of St Thomas of Canterbury 1703-6. d. September 11th, 1706, in England. (Fo.7; 114; 113; 150 II(3) 20/1/93, 14/2/93, 29/8/94, 7/9/97, III(1) 15/7/06; 170 ff.30v, 245v; Nec).

WAPPELER, William. Priest.

b. January 22nd or August 4th, 1711, Westphalia. Uncle of Herman Kemper. S.J. October 10th or 18th, 1728, in Germany. Ordained priest 1739. To the English province 1741. Pennsylvania 1741, 1743-4, 1746-8. In Germany 1749. St Omers College 1750, 1752-6. Liverpool 1757. Danby 1758-64. Liverpool 1764-6. Bruges College 1767-9. Ghent 1769-73. Bruges ?-1781. d. September, 1781 or October 11th, 1781, Bruges. (Fo.7; 113; Hu. Text 2/691; AHSJ.42/291; 15 f.21v; 16 ff.12, 21, 35v; 21 v.2; 65; 111; 64 pp.318, 539; 68 pp.126, 130; 90 f.178v; Pa.2/28; 140 n.45; 119 ff.14, 16, 24; CRS.9/186; CRS.12/21; CRS.13/230. For writings see Som.).

WARD see Tatlock, John.

WARD, Joseph. Scholastic.

b. March 28th, 1719. From County Durham. e. St Omers College c.1735-9. S.J. September 7th, 1739. Watten (nov) 1739, 1740. Liège (phil) 1741. Paderborn (phil) 1743. Left 1744, not ordained. (91; CRS.69; 113; 150 III(2) 9/5/44).

WARD, William. Priest.

b. March 14th, 1708, Staffordshire. S.J. September 7th, 1727-37. Watten (nov) 1728. Liège (phil) 1730. Liège (theol) 1733-5. Ordained priest 1735. College of St Chad 1736. (91; 113; Bur.2/13, 24-6; 150 III(2) 3/10/33, 16/3/37, 29/6/37).

WARE, George. Scholastic or Laybrother.

d. Prague, date unrecorded. (Fo.7; 114).

WARNER, John (1). Priest.

b.1682, Warwickshire. s. of Robert of Ratley, Warwickshire. e. ?in Spain. E.C. Douay. Ordained priest 1653. E.C. Douay c.1657-1661 or 1662. S.J. December 31st, 1662. Watten (nov) 1663, 1664. Liège 1665, 1667, 1669. Paris 1671-6. Liège 1678 (Rector). Provincial 1679-83. St Omers College 1683-7 (Rector). College of St Ignatius 1687 (Royal

chaplain). London 1688. Maidstone prison 1688. St Germain 1688.
Ireland 1689. St Germain 1690-2. d. November 2nd, 1692, St Germain.
(Fo.7; 114; 113; Ans.2/338; 150 II(3) 17/4/88; Chad 211, 230; 37 f.152;
WB.249; CRS.11/539; CRS.63/19; CRS.47/v, 243-4, 276, 284;
CRS.48/537 ff.; 168 *passim*; CRS.8/21, 431; 123 II f.177; DNB.; Nec.
For writings see Som. and CRS.48 pp.537 ff.).

WARNER, Sir John (2) *alias* Clare. Priest.

b. 1640, Parham, near Framlingham, Suffolk. s. of Francis and
Elizabeth (Rous). m. Trevor Hanmer. Created Bart. 1660. He and his
wife agreed to separate and enter religious orders. S.J. January or
March 1665. Liège (phil) 1666, 1667, 1669. Liège (theol) 1672.
Ordained priest April 5th, 1670. Watten (tert) 1673-8. Paris 1678-84.
Watten 1684-9 (Rector 1685-9). Provincial 1689-93. Watten 1696-7,
1699-1701, 1703-5. d. May 30th or 31st, 1705, Watten. (Fo.7; 114; 113;
150 II(2) 27/11/77, 29/12/78, 13/5/79, 9/3/83, 4/3/84; 123 II f.107;
DNB.; 140 n.45; Nec. For writings see Som.).

WARREN, Henry *alias* Pelham. Priest.

b.1635, Kent. s. of William and Anne (Downes). e. St Omers College
1647 or earlier-52. S.J. September 7th, 1652. Watten (nov) 1652, 1653.
Liège (phil) 1654-6. Liège (theol) 1657-60. Ordained priest April 16th,
1661. Maryland 1661-76 (Superior 1663-c.75). Residence of St Mary
1676, 1678-97, 1699-1702 (Superior 1683-c.95. Oxford 1692). d. June
7th, 1702, in England (?Waterperry). (Fo.7; CRS.69; 114; 113;
Hu.Text 2/680; 150 II(3) 5/4/92; CRS.7/395; Nec).

WARRILOW, William. Priest.

b. July 13th, 1738. From London. e. E.C. Douay 1751-7. E.C.
Douay (phil) 1757, 1758. E.C. Douay (theol) 1759. To England
October 16th, 1759. S.J. September 7th, 1760. Watten (nov) 1761.
Liège (theol) 1763, 1764. Ordained priest c. 1766. Liège 1767-9.
Ellingham 1769-73. Newcastle 1773-1807. d. November 13th, 1807,
Newcastle. bu. St John's churchyard, Newcastle. (Fo.7; 114; 91; 113;
CRS.63 index; 1 ff.167v, 195v; 7 ff.128v, 190; 13 ff.252, 301, 368, 371;
21 v.2; 35 f.124; 36 ff.196, 262, 269; 67; 68 p.93; HMC.10th Report
App.4/188; Ki.244; CRS.35/206; 117; 163; 167 pp.29, 34; 125;
CRS.28/279, 281, 290, 296; 6 f.81a; Nec).

WASSEIGE, John. Laybrother.

b. November, 1685, Liège. S.J. September 7th, 1713. Watten (nov)
1714-6. Ghent 1718, 1720. Watten 1723, 1724. d. February 21st, 1726,
Watten (Fo.7; 113; Nec).

WATERS, Ignatius. Laybrother.

b. June 7th, 1659, Kent. S.J. November 29th, 1680. Watten (nov)
1681. Liège 1682-6. College of St Ignatius 1687, 1689-91. St Omers
College 1692-3, 1696-7, 1699-1700. Watten 1701, 1703-6, 1708-9. Liège
1710-6, 1718, 1720. d. January 13th, 1721, Liège. (Fo.7; 114; 113; Nec).

WATERS, John. Laybrother.

b. April 11th, 1663, Kent. S.J. March 14th or May 11th, 1690.
Watten (nov) 1690-3. d. December 28th, 1694, St Omers College or

December 29th, 1694, in England. (Fo.7; 113; 95 f.825; 114; Nec).

WATERTON, Charles. Priest.

b. November 11th, 1744, Walton Hall, Yorkshire. s. of Charles and Mary (More). br. of Christopher. e. St Omers College 1756-62. S.J. September 7th, 1762. Watten (nov) 1763, 1764. Bruges School 1767-9, 1771-3. Ordained priest c.1771. d. August 5th, 1773, Blackenburg, Bruges. (Fo.7; CRS.69; 114; 113; Nec).

WATERTON, Christopher. Scholastic.

b. October 14th, 1746. s. of Charles and Mary (More). br. of Charles. e. St Omers and Bruges Colleges 1759-65. S.J. September 7th, 1765. Liège (phil) 1767-9. Bruges School 1771-3. Left 1773, not ordained. (Fo.7; 91; 6 f.234; AHSJ.42/292; 113; CRS.69).

WATERTON, Francis. Scholastic.

b. July, 1726, Yorkshire. s. of Charles and Anne (Poole). Half-br. of Thomas. e. St Omers College 1738-44. S.J. September 7th, 1744. Watten (nov) 1744, 1746. Liège (phil) 1747. Left 1748, not ordained. (Fo.7; CRS.69; 113; E and P.317; 150 III(2) 22/4/48).

WATERTON, Thomas. Priest.

b. June 4th, 1701, Yorkshire. s. of Charles and Anne (Gerard) of Walton Hall. Half-br. of Francis. e. St Omers College ?-1721. S.J. September 7th, 1721. Watten (nov) 1723. Liège (phil) 1724-6. Liège (theol) 1727, 1728. Ordained priest c.1729. ?Ghent (tert) 1730. Residence of St John 1730. Durham c.1730-66, serving Bishop Auckland. d. August 16th, 1766, ?Durham. bu. St Oswald's, Durham. (Fo.7; CRS.69; 114; 91; NCH.4/11 ff.; 113; 21 v.2; 36 ff.136, 184, 262; 64 p.48; 74; E. and P.317; 35 ff.21 ff.; 156 App.1; CRS.14/136-7; Nec).

WATERTON, William. Priest.

b. December 9th, 1794, Walton Hall, Yorkshire. s. of Thomas and Anne (Bedingfeld). e. Stonyhurst 1806-15. S.J. September 7th, 1815. Hodder (nov) 1815-7. Hodder (phil) 1817-9. Clongowes, Ireland (theol) 1819-23. Ordained priest 1823. Stonyhurst 1823-4. Pontefract 1824-6. Pylewell 1826-35. Hodder (tert) 1835-6. Pylewell 1836-41. Tunbridge Wells 1841-5. Wardour 1845-8. Croft 1848-9. Leigh 1849-? Stonyhurst ?-1852. d. January 18th, 1852, Stonyhurst. bu. Stonyhurst. (Fo.7; 115; 113; CRS.13/400; CRS.14/297; Ol.433; Nec).

WATERWORTH, William. Priest.

b. June 22nd, 1811, St Helens, Lancashire. e. Stonyhurst 1823-9. S.J. March 26th, 1829. Hodder (nov) 1829-31. St Mary's Hall (phil) 1831-3. London School 1833. St Mary's Hall (theol) 1833-7. Ordained priest September 24th, 1836, Stonyhurst. Rome (theol) 1837-8. St Mary's Hall 1838-41. Hereford 1841-54. London 1854-7 (Rector). Worcester 1857-78. Wigan 1878-9. Norwich 1879. London 1879-80. Bournemouth 1880-2. d. March 17th, 1882, Bournemouth. bu. Stapehill cemetery. (115; DNB.; WR.34/27: Nec. For writings see Som. and Sut.).

WATSON see Daniel, Thomas; ?Widdrington, Robert.

WEBB, George. Priest.

b. September 18th, 1653, London. S.J. September 7th or October

9th, 1672. Watten (nov) 1673. Liège (phil) 1674-6. Liège (theol) 1678-81. Ordained priest April 5th, 1681. Residence of St Michael 1681-2. College of St Chad 1683-7, 1689-94 (Rector 1690-c.94). Ghent 1696. College of St Ignatius 1697. La Flèche c.1698-1701. College of St Ignatius 1703. Residence of St Winifred 1704, 1705. College of St Ignatius 1706, 1708-12 (Rector 1708-12). College of St Thomas of Canterbury 1713, 1714. Orleans 1715. College of St Thomas of Canterbury 1716, 1718, 1720, 1723-4 (?Wardour c.1712-c.24). d.?1724. (Fo.7; 113; CRS.Mon.1/153, 243; 150 III(1) 15/7/06; 121; Nec).

WEBSTER see Thomas, Richard.

WEEDON, Thomas see Turner, John.

WELD, John. Priest.

b. June 15th, 1780, Lulworth Castle. s. of Thomas and Mary (Stanley) of Lulworth. e. Stonyhurst 1794-? Stonyhurst (theol) 1800. S.J. September 26th, 1803. Hodder (nov) 1803-5. Ordained priest 1807. Stonyhurst 1807, 1809-11, 1813-6 (Rector 1813-6). d. April 7th, 1816, Stonyhurst. bu. Stonyhurst. (Fo.7; Stol; SCR.137n; 113; 114; 116; 7 f.238; 55 ff.84, 88; 90 ff.146, 146v; 93 pp. 45, 60; Ber.192, 206-7, 238; Nec).

WELDON or WELTON, James or Charles *alias* Hunter, James Charles. Priest.

b. June 14th, 1716, Northumberland. br. of Thomas (1). e. St Omers College ?-1733. E.C. Valladolid October 8th, 1733-March 4th, 1739. Ordained priest c.1738. S.J. June 13th or September 7th, 1739. Watten (nov) 1739, 1740. Residence of St George 1741, 1743-4, 1746-50, 1752-8 (Grafton 1743, 1748, ?1750. Wootton Wawen 1751. Grafton 1755). Southend 1759-? College of St Thomas of Canterbury 1763, 1764. Salisbury 1765, 1766. Beckford 1766-8. Sizergh 1768-73-?. Swinburn Castle 1776. ?Felton, Morpeth c.1778-c.86. Waterperry 1788. Britwell 1788, 1792-?95. London 1800-2 or 1803. d. December 10th, 1802 or 1803. (Fo.7; CRS.69; 114; 91; 113; CRS.30/187-8; 21 v.2; CRS.Mon.1/167; Ans.4/294; WR.8/28, 10/15, 15/4, 20/65, 72; 65; 34 f.37v, n.206; 54 f.222; 39 f.107; CRS.12/85; 44 ff.218, 268, 273; 64 p.426; 40 pp.124; 134; 65; 69; 73 n.100; 75 p.132v; 80; HMC. 10th Report App.4/184, 197, 198; CRS.7/389; 155 III 185c; CRS.32/46; 35 ff.219 ff.; 167; 119 f.40; 117; 152 I nn.46, 60, II nn.19, 34; 6 f.137v; Nec).

WELDON or WELTON, Thomas (1) or Fenwick *alias* Hunter. Priest.

b. July 17th, 1705, Northumberland. br. of James. S.J. September 7th, 1723. Watten (nov) 1724. Liège (phil) 1725-7. Liège (theol) 1728, 1730. Ordained priest c.1731. St Omers College 1733, 1734. College of St Aloysius 1735-8. Residence of St Michael 1739-41, 1743-4, 1746-7 (Richmond c.1741). Residence of St George 1748-50, 1752-5 (Badgecote ?-1755. Grafton 1755). College of St Aloysius 1755-8, 1763-4 (Scholes 1758-9, 1763). Scholes 1767-9. College of St Aloysius 1771. Scholes 1772-86. d. April 26th, 1786, Scholes. bu. Windleshaw cemetery. (Fo.7; 113; CRS.63/373; WR.8/28, 15/4; 21 v.2; 39 f.107; 64

pp.380, 382, 538; 40 pp.124, 201; 25 ff.40, 46, 50, 56, 76, 86; 80; 91;
HMC. 10th Report App.4/183, 184; 156 App.1; 155 II 129; 155 III
185c; 167 pp.23, 30; 99; 119 ff.5, 20, 34; Nec. For writings see Sut.).

WELDON, Thomas (2). Priest.

b. March 18th, 1714, Ireland. S.J. in France, March 8th, 1731. To
English province c.1750. Garswood c.1750, 1751. College of St
Aloysius 1752. Brinn 1753, 1756-76. d. February 15th, 1776, Brinn.
(Fo.7; 91; 113; 117; 21 v.2; 28 f.280; 65; 77; 25 ff.4, 12, 17, 22, 28; 80;
158; 156 App.1; 119 ff.5 ff.; CRS.OP.1/70; Nec).

WELDON or WELTON, William *alias* Hunter. Priest.

b. December 12th or July 2nd, 1711, Northumberland. S.J.
September 7th, 1732. Watten (nov) 1733. Liège (phil) 1734-6. Liège
(theol) 1737-40. Ordained priest c.1739. Ince c.1740-1-?. Westby
c.1742-61. d. December 3rd, 1761, in England (?Westby). (Fo.7; 91;
114; 113; 24 f.347v; 68 p.121; 85; 86; HMC. 10th Report App.4/189;
158; 156 App.1; Ki.271; CRS.15/3; 126; Gil.HP.236; 117; 119 ff.6, 8,
10, 13-4, 16; Nec).

WELLS, Charles. Priest.

b. March 14th, 1702, Hampshire. s. of Henry and Lady Mary of
Brambridge. br. of Gilbert. e. St Omers College 1714-20. S.J.
September 7th, 1720. Liège (phil) 1723, 1724. St Omers College 1725-8,
1730. Liège (theol) 1733. Ordained priest 1733. St Omers College 1734.
Ghent (tert) 1735. St Omers College 1736. College of St Ignatius 1737.
St Omers College 1738-40. Watten 1747. Socius to the provincial 1743.
College of St Ignatius 1744. St Omers College 1746-8 (Rector). Ghent
1749. Liège 1750. Antwerp 1752. Ghent 1753-7 (Rector). d. April 1st,
1757, Ghent. (Fo.7; CRS.69; 91; 113; 114; HMC. 10th Report
App.4/194, 197; CRS.27/42-3; 140 n.45; CRS.8/432; 108; Nec).

WELLS, Gilbert *alias* Williams. Priest.

b. November 22nd, 1713 or 1714, Hampshire. s. of Henry and Lady
Mary of Brambridge. br. of Charles. e. St Omers College 1728 or
earlier-31. S.J. October 18th, 1731. Liège (phil) 1733-5. Liège (theol)
1736-9. Ordained priest 1739. Ghent (tert) 1740, 1741. Residence of St
Mary 1741, 1743-4, 1746-50, 1752-8 (Dorchester 1752, 1758.
Waterperry 1758). College of St Thomas of Canterbury 1763, 1764.
Winchester 1767-9. College of St Thomas of Canterbury 1771.
Winchester 1772, 1773. d. October 17th, 1777, in England. (Fo.7;
CRS.69; 91; 113; 117; 90 f.34; 150 III(2) 29/4/41; HMC. 10th Report
App.4/193, 197; CRS.7/390-1, 394; CRS.27/42-3; 01.434; Nec).

WELTON see Weldon.

WESLEY see Wisely.

WESLEY or WESTLEY, John. Laybrother.

b. 1686, Staffordshire or Northamptonshire. S.J. July or October
30th, 1706. Watten (nov) 1708. Ghent 1709-13. Maryland 1713-6, 1720,
1723-8, 1730, 1734-41. Nothing further recorded; probably died in
Maryland 1741-3. (Fo.7; Hu. Text 2/686; 113; 91; Nec).

WEST see Daniel, Thomas; Pearce, Francis.

WEST, Francis. Priest.

b. October 29th, 1782, St Helens, Lancashire. s. of Thomas and Frances (Green). e. Stonyhurst 1796-1801. Stonyhurst (phil) 1801-3. S.J. September 26th, 1803. Hodder (nov) 1803-5. Stonyhurst (theol etc.) 1805-11. Ordained priest May 27th, 1809, Wolverhampton. Preston 1811-2. Stonyhurst 1812-32. Socius to the provincial 1832. St Mary's Hall 1832-4. Preston 1834-42. St Helens 1842-5. Liverpool 1845-52 (Superior). d. December 21st, 1852, Liverpool. bu. Gillmoss. (Fo.7; 115; 21 v.2; 90 f.147; 93 pp.65, 75, 77, 83; Gil.3/39; CRS.6/172; Nec).

WESTBY, Peter *alias* or *vere* Walker. Priest.

b. May 20th or 22nd, 1727, Preston. s. of John and Mary (Hawett) of Rawcliffe. e. St Omers College 1745-9. S.J. September 7th, 1749. Watten (nov) 1750. Liège (phil) 1752-4. St Omers College 1755, 1756. Liège (theol) 1757. Ordained priest 1757. Ghent (tert) 1758. St Omers College 1759. Moseley 1759-? Bodney 1765-1769. Courtfield 1769-73. Ghent 1773. Waterperry 1785. Scholes 1786, 1788. d. November 13th or 15th, 1788, Scholes. bu. Windleshaw. (Fo.7; CRS.69; 114; 91; 113; 6 f.163; 16 ff.21v, 35v; 21 v.2; 34 ff.38v, 52v; 41 n.28; 64 p.257; 65; 68 pp.27, 162; CRS.7/391, 401; CRS.12/30; 99; 57 II f.108; 111; Nec).

WESTBY, Thomas *alias* Green. Priest.

b. August 1st, 1703, Lancashire. S.J. September 7th, 1724. Watten (nov) 1725, 1726. Liège (phil) 1727, 1728. Liège (theol) 1730. Ordained priest c.1733. Ghent (tert) 1733. College of St Thomas of Canterbury 1734, 1735. d. February 18th, 1736, in England. (Fo.7, 91; 113).

WESTLEY see Wesley.

WESTON, Francis. Scholastic.

S.J.1685. Watten (nov) 1685, 1686. d. September 16th, 1687, Watten. (Fo.7; 114; 113; 150 II(3) 11/10/87; Nec).

WESTON, John. Priest.

b. August 1st, 1793, Chudleigh, Devon. s. of John. Half-br. of Thomas. e. Stonyhurst 1807-12. S.J. September 7th, 1812. Hodder (nov) 1812-4. Stonyhurst (phil) 1814-6. Stonyhurst (theol) 1816-8. Clongowes, Ireland (theol) 1818-21. Ordained priest September 23rd, 1820. South-hill 1821-8. Stockeld Park 1828-32. Hodder (tert) 1832. St Helens 1833-7. d. January 3rd, 1837, St Helens. bu. Windleshaw cemetery. (Fo.7; 115; 113; 21 v.2; 48 f.412v; CRS.4/435; 01.434-5; 114; Nec).

WESTON, Thomas. Priest.

b. December 22nd, 1804, Chudleigh, Devon. s. of John and Jane (Heptonstall). Half-br. of John. e. Stonyhurst 1813-?24. S.J. September 7th, 1824. Montrouge (nov) 1824-6. Montrouge (phil) 1826, 1827. St Acheul (phil) 1827-8. Stonyhurst (theol etc.) 1828-33. St Mary's Hall (theol) 1833-5. Ordained priest December 20th, 1834, Stonyhurst. Allerton Park 1835-41 (Superior of the Residence of St Michael). Hodder (tert) 1841-2. Preston 1842-63. Blackpool 1863-7. Rhyl 1867. d. November 14th, 1867, Rhyl. bu. Pantasaph. (Fo.7; 115;

113; Stol; 01.435; Nec).

WHARTON, Charles. Priest.

b. July 25th, 1748, Maryland. e. St Omers and Bruges Colleges 1760-66. S.J. September 7th, 1766. Ghent (nov) 1767. Liège (phil) 1768, 1769. Liège (theol) 1771-3. Ordained priest c.1773. Liège Academy 1773-5. To England 1775. Worcester 1779-81. To America c.1783. (CRS.69; 113; AHSJ.42/291; 91; RH.10/200; WR.20/70; CRW.29 ff; 7 f.103; 54 f.34; 51 ff.304, 307; 57 I f.294; 94 ff.251-2; CRS.17/368; Mel.89 ff).

WHARTON, Francis. Scholastic.

b. November 9th, 1729. e. St Omers College c.1741-9. S.J.1749. Watten (nov) 1750. Liège (phil) 1752. d. March 31st, 1753, Liège, not ordained. (Fo.7; CRS.69; 114; 113; 91; Nec).

WHEBLE or WHEEBLE, James *alias* Giffard or Gifford. Priest.

b. December 4th, 1725, Tisbury, Wiltshire. s. of James. e. St Omers College 1736-43. S.J. September 7th, 1743. Watten (nov) 1744. Liège (phil) 1746. Paderborn (theol) 1748, 1749. Liège (theol) 1750. Ordained priest c.1750. London 1752-64. Wardour 1764-88 (Rector of the College of St Thomas of Canterbury c.1770-?73). d. January 29th, 1788, Wardour. bu. Wardour. (Fo.7; CRS.69; 91; 114; 113; CRS.42/136; CRS.Mon.1/148n, 156, 244; LR.3/5-6; 21 v.2; 54 ff.10-11,65; 47 f.21v; 65; 20 f.173; 68 p.253; HMC. 10th Report App.4/183-4, 187, 192-3; 186; 126; 173; 01.435; 111; 57 II f.67; Nec).

WHETENHALL, Henry. Priest.

b. August 31st, 1694, Kent. s. of Henry and Lettice (Tichborne) of East Peckham, Kent. e. St Omers College ?-1713. S.J. September 7th, 1713. Watten (nov) 1714. Liège (phil) 1715-6, 1718. Liège (theol) 1720. Ordained priest c.1722. London 1723. Maryland 1724-35. College of St Ignatius 1736. Lulworth 1737. Burton Park 1738-44. d. May 17th, 1745, in London. (Fo.7; CRS.69; 114; 113; Hu.Text 2/687; RH.13/116-7; 44 f.250; 64 f.81; 74; 91; Bur.1/148 plate; E and P.85; CRS.6/365; CRS.8/433; CRS.22/308; CRS.62/155, 234, 242, 247, 269, 272, 316; Nec).

WHITE see Martinash, John; Wright, Stephen.

WHITE or WHYTE, Henry *alias* or *vere* Brunchard. Priest.

b. December 15th, 1662, London. e. St Omers College ?-1680. S.J. September 7th, 1680. Watten (nov) 1680, 1681. Liège (phil) 1682-4. Liège (theol) 1685, 1687. Ordained priest 1689. Watten (tert) 1689. College of St Ignatius 1691. Liège 1692, 1693. d. November 13th, 1693, Liège. (Fo.7; CRS.69; 114; 113; Nec).

WHITE, John. Priest.

b. February, 1744. ?s. of John of Great Eccleston, Lancashire. e. Fernyhalgh, St Omers College 1756-c.60. S.J. January 20th, 1763. Watten (nov) 1763, 1764. Liège (theol) 1767-9. Ordained priest c.1769. To England 1770 or 1771. Hammersmith 1771. d. September 27th, 1771, Hammersmith. (Fo.7; CRS.69; 91; 114; 113; LR.1/33; 76 f.78; 77; CRS.23/130; Nec).

WHITE, William ?*alias* Gwynn. Priest.
    b. 1631 or 1632, Carnavonshire. s. of John and Mary (Edwards) of Neigwl, Llandegwning, Carnavonshire. e. Ghent. E.C. Rome October 16th, 1651-April 25th, 1658. Ordained priest May 21st, 1657. S.J. December 4th, 1658. Watten (nov) 1659, 1660. College of St Aloysius 1661. College of St Francis Xavier 1663-5. Residence of St Winefrid 1667, 1669, 1672-6, 1679-87. d. February 26th, 1688, in England or Wales. (Fo.7; 114; 113; Ans.2/354; CRS.40/48; Nec).

WHITELY see Wright, Stephen.

WHITFIELD, Cuthbert see Lawson, Henry.

WHITGREAVE or WHITGRAVE, James. Priest.
    b. March 14th, 1689 or 1699, Staffordshire. s. of Thomas and Isabella (Turville) of Moseley, Staffordshire. br. of Thomas. e. St Omers College 1714 or earlier-15. S.J. October 9th, 1715. Watten (nov) 1715, 1716. Liège (phil) 1718, 1720. Liège (theol) 1723, 1724. Ordained priest c.1724. Maryland 1725-38. Moseley 1738-50. (Rector of the College of St Chad 1743-?50). d. July 26th, 1750, Moseley. bu. Bushbury parish church. (Fo.7; CRS.69; 91; 114; 113; Hu.Text 2/688; RH.9/222; SCH.3/17, 19/3, 10; 150 III(2) 27/7/43; E. and P.173, 246; Ki.248; CRS.62/285n, 306; Nec).

WHITGREAVE or WHITGRAVE, Thomas. Priest.
    b. February 8th, 1696 or 1697, Moseley, Staffordshire. s. of Thomas and Isabella (Turville) of Moseley. br. of James. e. St Omers College 1714 or earlier-17. E.C. Douay (phil) 1717-8. S.J. September 7th, 1718. Watten (nov) 1720. Liège (phil) 1723. Liège (theol) 1724-7. Ordained priest c.1726. In England 1728, 1730. Residence of St Mary 1733-41, 1743-4, 1746-50, 1752 (Salden ?-1741-?). Moseley c.1752-7 (Rector of the College of St Chad 1756-7). d. November 30th, 1757, in England (?Moseley). bu. Bushbury parish church. (Fo.7; CRS.69; 114; 91; 113; CRS.28/51; SCH.3/17, 19/3, 10; E and P.173, 246; Nec).

WHITLEY see Wright, Stephen.

WHITMORE, James see Sabran, Louis.

WHYTE, Henry see White, Henry.

WIBORN, Edward. Scholastic.
    b.1635, London. S.J. 1651. Liège (theol) 1664-6. Left 1666, not ordained. (Fo.7; 113; 150 II(2) January 1666, 13/2/66. For writings see Som.).

WIDDRINGTON, ?Hon. Anthony. Priest.
    b.1664, Durham or Lincolnshire. ?s. of William, 1st Baron Widdrington and Mary (Thorold). S.J. September 2nd, 1665. Liège (phil) 1667, 1669. Ordained priest c.1670. Loretto 1674-? Residence of St John 1676, 1678. (?Felton 1678). Paris 1678, 1679. Ghent 1681. d. May 5th, 1682, Ghent. (Fo.7; 113; 150 II(2) May 1669, 1/9/74; 168 f.5v; 123 II f.105; 203; 135 f.182; Nec).

WIDDRINGTON, Hon. Henry. Priest.
    b. May 19th, 1667, Northumberland. s. of William, 2nd Lord Widdrington and Elizabeth (Bertie). ?br. of Robert. S.J. September

7th, 1687. Watten (nov) 1687. Liège (phil) 1689-92. Rome (theol) 1693. Liège (theol) 1695, 1696. Ordained priest April 21st, 1696. College of St Hugh 1697, 1699-1700. Residence of St John 1701, 1703-6, 1708-16, 1720, 1724-5 (Superior 1712-c.16. Gateshead 1714. Callaly ?-1727, 1729, serving Alnwick). d. November 16th, 1729, in England (?Callaly). (Fo.7; 91; 113; 36 ff.264-5; 150 II(3) 28/10/92, 30/7/95; E and P.165, 205; 156 xi; Ki.249; 161; CRS.7/319; Nec).

WIDDRINGTON, ?Hon. Robert ?*alias* Watson. Priest.
    b.1660, Northumberland. ?s. of William, 2nd Lord Widdrington and Elizabeth (Bertie). ?br. of Henry. e. St Omers College ?-1679. S.J. October 7th, 1679. Milan (nov) 1679. ?Genoa 1682. Milan 1683. Liège (phil) 1683. Liège (theol) 1684-7. Ordained priest c.1688. St Omers College 1689. In England 1690. Residence of St John 1693, 1696. In England 1700. Residence of St John 1703, 1704. Residence of St George 1705. Residence of St John 1706, 1708-16, 1720-5. In England 1726-8, 1730. Residence of St John 1733-42 (Superior c.1720-5-?9. Widdrington ?-c.1716, serving Alnwick. Biddleston 1727-c.36). d. January 26th, 1742, Durham. bu. St Oswald's churchyard. (Fo.7; CRS.69; 114; 91; 113; LR.1/117; 21 v.2; 36 ff.36, 262; 89; ?E and P.208; 156 xi, App.1; Ki.249; CRS.14/251; CRS.25/115; 168 ff.44v, 75v, 94v; 123 II f.127; Nec).

WIGNAL, Francis *alias* Sandys. Priest.
    b. October 25th, 1678 or 1680, London. e. St Omers College 1693 or earlier-97. S.J. September 7th, 1697. Watten (nov) 1697. Liège (phil) 1699-1701. Liège (theol) 1703-6. Ordained priest 1706. Liège 1708-11. College of St Hugh 1712-6, 1718. Residence of St Mary 1720. ?Berrington 1721. College of St Aloysius 1723, 1724. College of St Hugh 1725. In England 1726. Dunston near Lincoln 1727. d. December 19th, 1728, in England (?Dunston). (Fo.7; CRS.69; 91; 113; 58 n.1; Nec).

WILKINS, James. Laybrother.
    b.1685, Lancashire. S.J. September 7th, 1704. Watten (nov) 1704-6. St Omers College 1708, 1709. Socius to the provincial 1710, 1711. Antwerp 1712-4. d. January 19th, 1714, Antwerp. (Fo.7; 114; 113; 108; CRS.62/37-9, 42-3, 47-50, 54, 59; Nec).

WILKINSON, Thomas *alias* Molyneux. Priest.
    b. 1638, Lancashire. E.C. Valladolid November 18th, 1660-c.66. Ordained priest March 25th, 1662, Segovia. S.J. September 20th, 1667. Watten (nov) 1669. E.C. Valladolid 1670-77. ?Long Horsley 1678. Morpeth gaol 1679-81. d. January 12th, 1681, Morpeth gaol or Newcastle. (Fo.7; 114; 113; CRS.30/xxxii, 168, 175-6; Ans.3/248; 168 f.31; CRS.6/202n).

WILLIAMS see Beaumont, Francis; Gittins, Joseph; Petre, Richard and Robert (1); Wells, Gilbert.

WILLIAMS, Charles see Hacon, Hubert.

WILLIAMS, Francis *alias* Crimmes. Priest.
    b.c.1622, Cheshire. ?e. Cambridge. S.J. April 9th, 1659. Watten

(nov) 1659. Liège (theol) 1660-4. Ordained priest April 12th, 1664.
Ghent (tert) 1664. Liège 1665, 1667, 1669, 1672. Watten 1672-80
(Rector). Liège 1680. d. February 13th, 1681, Liège. (Fo.7; 114; 113;
174; Nec).

WILLIAMS, John (1). Priest.
b. 1656 or 1658, Carnavonshire. e. St Omers College ?-1678. S.J.
September 7th, 1678-97. Watten (nov) 1679. Liège (phil) 1680-2. St
Omers College 1683-7. La Flèche (theol) 1689-91. Liège (theol) 1693.
Ordained priest March 21st, 1693. Residence of St Winefrid 1696.
(Fo.7; CRS.69; 113; 140 n.45; 150 II(3) 12/10/97).

WILLIAMS, John (2). Priest.
b. September 16th or 18th, 1691 or 1692, Monmouthshire. ?br. of
Peter (1). S.J. September 7th, 1712. Watten (nov) 1713. College of St
Francis Xavier (nov) 1714. Watten (nov) 1715. Liège (phil) 1716, 1718.
St Omers College 1720. Liège (theol) 1723, 1724. Ordained priest
c.1723. E.C. Rome 1725-7. Liège 1728, 1729. In England 1730.
Residence of St Winefrid 1733-41, 1743-4, 1746-50, 1752-8 (Superior
1748-?61. Holywell 1732, 1733, 1747-61). d. September 23rd, 1761,
Holywell. (Fo.7; 114; 91; 113; 21 v.2; 9 nn.197, 214; 14 ff.36v, 39v, 48v,
52v, 57v, 63v, 66v, 76v, 91; 64 p.288; 74; 85; 111; HMC. 10th Report
App.4/193; CRS.3/107; 169 nn.2, 3, 7, 18; 51 f.311; Nec).

WILLIAMS, John (3) *alias* Monnington. Priest.
b. November 27th, 1730, Flintshire. s. of Thomas and Elizabeth
(Monnington) of Nerquis, Flintshire. br. of Peter (2). e. St Omers
College c.1744-c.50. S.J. September 7th, 1750. Liège (phil) 1752-5.
Ordained priest c.1755. St Omers College 1756, 1757. Maryland
1758-68. Arlington 1769. London 1769-81. Little Malvern 1782-1801.
d. February 14th, 1801, Little Malvern. (Fo.7; CRS.69; 91; 113; 114;
Hu.Text 2/695; LR.3/5; WR.3/26, 21/8, 17, 23/25n; 13 f.234; 38 f.29;
65; CRS.12/78; CRS.19/339-43; 92; 173; 125; 117; 17 f.78; Nec).

WILLIAMS, Peter (1). Priest.
b. August 4th, 1689, Flintshire. ?br. of John (2). S.J. September 7th,
1710. Watten (nov) 1711, 1712. Liège (phil) 1714. Liège (theol) 1715-6,
1718. Ordained priest c.1719. Liège 1720, 1723-4. College of St Ignatius
1725. London 1726, 1727. College of St Ignatius 1728, 1730. London
1731. Ingatestone 1732-?. Thorndon ?-1739. Residence of St George
1739, 1740 (Superior). College of the Holy Apostles 1741. London
1743-8. Dagnams c.1749. Paris 1750, 1752. College of St Ignatius 1753.
Ingatestone 1754-5. d. March 22nd, 1755, Ingatestone. (Fo.7; 114; 91;
113; LR.3/8; E.5/74, 9/106, 12/113, 116n; 9 n.242; 40 p.99; 66; HMC.
10th Report App.4/198; E and P.170; 43 ff.59-62, 65, 67, 75v; 120
7/8/32; Nec).

WILLIAMS, Peter (2) *alias* Monnington. Priest.
b. January 12th, 1717, Flintshire. s. of Thomas and Elizabeth
(Monnington) of Nerquis, Flintshire. br. of John (3). e. St Omers
College 1729-c.36. S.J. September 7th, 1736. Watten (nov) 1736, 1737.
Liège (phil) 1738-41. Liège (theol) 1742. Wurzburg (theol) 1743. Liège

(theol) 1744. Ordained priest c.1744. St Omers College 1746. Residence of St George 1747. Bromley, Staffordshire 1747-?. Ince 1749-50, 1752-3. d. November 26th, 1753, Ince Blundell. bu. Harkirke cemetery. (Fo.7; CRS.69; 114; 91; 113; WR.21/17; 64 p.264; HMC. 10th Report App.4/198; Che.12/84; 156 App.1; Nec).

WILLIAMS, William. ?Scholastic.

S.J.1690, in Rome. Rome 1693. Naples (phil) 1696-7, 1699. Rome (theol) 1700, 1701. Nothing further recorded under this name in the English province catalogues. (Fo.7; 113).

WILLIAMSON, George. Priest.

b. July 31st, 1695, Yorkshire. e. St Omers College 1714-c.18. S.J. September 7th, 1718. Watten (nov) 1720. Liège (phil) 1723. Liège (theol) 1724-7. Ordained priest c.1725. St Omers College 1728. Antwerp 1730-3. In England 1733. College of St Ignatius 1734-5. London 1736. College of St Ignatius 1737-8. College of the Holy Apostles 1739-40. London 1740. d. ?January 3rd, 1741, in England (?London).(Fo.7; 91; CRS.69; 113; 114; LR.1/73, 3/8; 74; 85; 43 ff. 57-8, 63; HMC. 10th Report App.4/192; 108; 111; 125; CRS.62/141-2).

WILLIAERT or WILLIART, Nicholas. Laybrother.

b.1648, Flanders. S.J. June 20th, 1676. Watten (nov) 1676, 1678-9. St Omers College 1680-2. Ghent 1683. Maryland 1684-98. d. 1698, Maryland. (Fo.7; 114; 113; Hu.Text 2/682; Nec).

WILSON see Middleton, Charles.

WILSON, Charles. Priest.

b. August 7th, 1660 or 1662, London. S.J. September 7th, 1680. Watten (nov) 1680, 1681. Liège (phil) 1682-4. Liège (theol) 1685-9. Ordained priest 1689. Watten (tert) 1689. St Omers College 1690-2. Residence of St Mary 1693. ?College of the Holy Apostles c.1694. Residence of St George 1696-7, 1699 (Ravenshill or Spetchley c.1695-?). Ghent 1700-01, 1703-6, 1708. Watten 1709-11. St Omers College 1712. Ghent 1713. St Omers College 1714-6. Watten 1718, 1720, 1723-8, 1730. d. August 20th, 1730, Watten. (Fo.7; 91; 113; RH.1/46; 39 f.1; WR.20/66; 43 f.21; Nec).

WILSON, John (1). Priest.

b.1637, Yorkshire. e. St Omers College 1654 or earlier-58. S.J. September 14th, 1658. Watten (nov) 1658. Liège (phil) 1659, 1660. St Omers College 1661, 1663-6. Ordained priest c.1663. d. November 11th, 1666, St Omers College. (Fo.7; CRS.69; 114; 113; Nec).

WILSON, John (2). Laybrother.

b.c.1696. From Yorkshire. S.J. May 17th, 1726-36. Watten (nov) 1726-8. Ghent 1730, 1733-6. (113; 91; 150 III(2) 5/5/31, 26/5/36, 14/5/36).

WILSON, Joseph. Laybrother.

b.1665, Lincolnshire. S.J. July 30th, 1697. Watten (nov) 1697, 1699. Maryland 1700-02. d.1702, Maryland. (Fo.7; 114; 113; Hu.Text 2/684; Nec).

WILSON, Ralph. Priest.

    b. September 10th, 1743, Yorkshire. e. St Omers and Bruges Colleges c.1757-63. S.J. September 7th, 1763. Watten (nov) 1763, 1764. Bruges College 1767-9. Liège (theol) 1769. Ordained priest 1770. d. February 3rd, 1770, Lincoln. (Fo.7; CRS.69; 114; 91; 113; 16 f.12; 67; 77; 41 n.82; Nec).

WILSON, Simon. Priest.

    b. March 16th, 1623 or 1624 or 1625, Staffordshire. e. St Omers College 1637-44. E.C. Rome September 20th, 1644-April 10th, 1651. Ordained priest March 20th, 1649. To England 1651. In London 1686. S.J. July 13th, 1692. Watten (nov) 1693-5. d. March 7th or 9th, 1695, Watten. (Fo.5; Ans.2/359; CRS.69; 113; 114; 150 II(3) 28/6/92; CRS.40/29; CRS.55/480; 135 f.252; Nec).

WINTER see Bedingfeld or Mildmay, Matthew; Morgan, William.

WINTER or WINTERE, Charles. Laybrother.

    b. October 7th, 1699, Artois. S.J. June 20th, 1723. Watten (nov) 1723-6. St Omers College 1726, 1727. Watten 1728, 1730. Ghent 1730. d. October 25th, 1730, Ghent. (Fo.7; 91; 113).

WINTERFIELD, Christopher. Priest.

    d. date and place unrecorded. (Fo.7).

WISE or WYSE, George *alias* Sophia. Priest.

    b.1643, Mechlin. e. St Omers College 1657-63. E.C. Valladolid September 1663-April 1670. Ordained priest c.1669. S.J. July 21st, 1670. Liège 1672. Ghent (military chaplain) 1673-5. Ghent 1676. College of St Thomas of Canterbury 1678-9. College of the Holy Apostles 1680-1681. College of St Ignatius 1682-1683. College of St Thomas of Canterbury 1684-7. College of St Ignatius 1689-93. Arrested but soon released on bail 1694. College of St Ignatius 1696-7, 1699-1700. Watten 1701, 1703-4. d. October 31st, 1704, Watten. (Fo.7; 114; CRS.69; 113; CRS.30/169; Ans.3/250; Nec).

WISELY or WESLEY, John. Priest.

    b.1660 or 1662, Leinster, Ireland. ?e. St Omers College ?-1682 or 1683. S.J. September 7th, 1682 or 1683. Watten (nov) 1683, 1684. Liège (phil) 1685-7. To Irish mission. (Fo.7-Irish section; 113; CRS.69).

WISEMAN, John. Laybrother.

    b.1705, 1708 or 1709, Yorkshire. S.J. February 1st or 2nd, 1734. Watten (nov) 1734. St Omers College 1735-41, 1743-4, 1746-8. Boulogne School 1749, 1750. Liège 1752-8, 1761. d. May 20th or 28th, 1763, Liège. (Fo.7; 114; 91; 113; 111; 117; Nec).

WITHY or WYTHY or WYTHIE, Edward. Priest.

    b. April 14th or June 10th, 1689, ?Sawston, Cambridgeshire. e. St Omers College 1701-2 or later. S.J. September 7th, 1707. Watten (nov) 1708, 1709. Liège (phil) 1710-2. St Omers College 1713-6. Liège (theol) 1718, 1720. Ordained priest c.1721. College of St Thomas of Canterbury 1723-5 (?Wardour c.1724. Burton Park 1725). Wardour c.1727. Paris 1728, 1730. Travelling 1733. Paris 1734. Travelling 1735-7. College of St Thomas of Canterbury 1738. Travelling 1739.

College of St Thomas of Canterbury 1740-1, 1743-4, 1746-8 (?Wardour). College of St Ignatius 1749-50, 1752-9 (Rector 1752-9). Liège 1759-64 (Rector). Ghent 1767-9. d. November 22nd, 1769, Liège. (Fo.7; 113; 91; CRS.69; 114; CRS.Mon.1/153-4; RH;13/116; ?E and P.16; CRS.22/307, 313; 01.440; 51 f.311; CRS.62/17, 42, 65, 74; 41 n.75; Nec).

WITMORE, James see Sabran, Lewis.

WOEDTS, Peter. Laybrother.
    b. September 3rd, 1699, Flanders. S.J. September 7th, 1732. Watten (nov) 1733-8, 1740-1, 1743-4, 1746-50, 1752-8, 1761, 1763-4, 1767. Liège 1768-9, 1771-3. d. March 12th, 1773, Liège. (Fo.7; 114; 113; Nec).

WOLFALL, John *alias* Cary. Priest.
    b. April 1682, Lancashire. s. of William and Mary (Carus) of Wolfall Hall, Aughton, Lancashire. e. St Omers College 1697-1702. S.J. September 7th, 1702. Watten (nov) 1703, 1704. Liège (phil) 1705, 1706. Liège (theol) 1708-11. Ordained priest 1711. Ghent (tert) 1712. St Omers College 1713. Watten 1714-6, 1718, 1720, 1723-7. Paris 1728, 1730. Watten 1730. Liège 1733. Ghent 1734-42. d. July 9th, 1742, Ghent. (Fo.7; CRS.69; 114; 91; 113; 150 III(2) 29/4/41; Ans.3/255; 9 nn.282-307; 74; E and P.112; CRS.62/252n; 286; Nec).

WOLFE, Francis. Priest.
    b.1647, Buckinghamshire, Staffordshire or Shropshire. S.J. November 13th, 1668. Watten (nov) 1669. Liège (phil) 1672. Liège (theol) 1673-7. Ordained priest April 17th, 1677. St Omers College 1678. Liège 1679. College of St Thomas of Canterbury 1680-2. Residence of St Mary 1683-7, 1689-93 (Oxford c.1685). College of St Francis Xavier 1696-7. Residence of St Winefrid 1699-1701, 1703. Residence of St George 1704-5. College of St Ignatius 1706, 1708-11. Residence of St Mary 1712-3. Residence of St Winefrid 1714-6, 1718, 1720. d. March 2nd, 1720, in England or Wales. (Fo.7; 114; 113; 112; Nec);

WOOD or WOODS, Edward. Priest.
    b. September or November 16th or 17th, 1663, Staffordshire. e. St Omers College ?-1683. S.J. September 7th, 1683. Watten (nov) 1683-5. Liège (phil) 1685-7. St Omers College 1689-93. Liège (theol) 1696. Ordained priest 1695. Ghent (tert) 1697. College of St Thomas of Canterbury 1699-1701, 1703-6, 1708-9. St Omers College 1710. Antwerp 1710-6. Residence of St Winefrid 1718-25 (Superior c.1718-25. Bromley 1721, 1725. Holywell 1726). d.?1726, ?in England or Wales. (Fo.7; CRS.69; 113; 150 II(3) 17/2/95; 9 n.269; 108; 169 155/3; Hun.267; CRS.62 index; Nec).

WOOD, William *alias* Guillick, Kellick or Killick. Priest.
    b. February 16th, 1671, Surrey. e. St Omers College ?-1689. S.J. September 1689. Watten (nov) 1689-91. Liège (phil) 1692, 1693. Liège (theol) 1696, 1697. Ordained priest 1698. Watten 1699. Maryland 1700-20. d. August, 1720, Maryland. (Fo.7; 114; CRS.69; 113; Hu.Text 2/684; Nec).

WOODCOCK, William *alias* Shaw. Priest.
  b.1659 or 1661, Lancashire. S.J. September 7th, 1682. Watten (nov) 1682, 1683. Liège (phil) 1684-6. Liège (theol) 1687-91. Ordained priest c.1690. Watten 1692. College of St Francis Xavier 1693. College of St Aloysius 1696. Kelvedon 1696-7. Left 1697. Readm. October 10th, 1709. St Omers College (nov) 1710. Worcester 1710, 1711. College of St Thomas of Canterbury 1713. College of St Ignatius 1714. Residence of St Winefrid 1715, 1716. d. October 11th, 1717, in England or Wales. (Fo.7; 114; 113; ER.5/95, 9/108; 150 II(3) 20/8/97, III(1) 5/9/05, 28/11/05; 43 f.25; 48 pp.38, 194; Nec).

WOODS see Wood, Edward.

WORSLEY see Vaudrey or Vauderey or Vaudry, John.

WORTHINGTON see Sefton or Sephton, Thomas.

WORTHINGTON, John *alias* Sephton. Priest.
  b. April 24th, 1713, Lancashire. e. St Omers College 1733-5. S.J. September 7th, 1735. Watten (nov) 1735. Liège (phil) 1736-8. Liège (theol) 1739-42. Ordained priest c.1742. College of St Chad 1743-4, 1746. College of St Thomas of Canterbury 1747-50, 1752-3. College of St Chad 1754-8 (Rudge 1754-5). Blackrod and Wigan 1759-77. d. June 2nd, 1777, Wigan. (Fo.7; CRS.69; 113; 117; 21 v.2; 23 f.242; 28 f.280; 54 f.48; 64 p.512; 25 ff. 12, 21, 31,; 80; 155 III 185c; 119 ff.9, 13, 16, 18, 21, 24, 26-7, 30, 32, 36, 39, 42-3; CRS.OP.1/54; Nec).

WORTHINGTON, Thomas *alias* Sephton. Scholastic.
  b.1675, Lancashire. e. St Omers College 1693 or earlier-97. S.J. October 9th, 1697. Watten (nov) 1697. Liège (phil) 1699-1701. In England 1703. College of St Aloysius 1704-6. Left 1706, not ordained. (Fo.7; CRS.69; 113).

WRIGHT see Conway, William (2); Gerard, Thomas (3).

WRIGHT, Charles. Priest.
  b. October 27th, 1752. s. of Anthony and Anne (Biddulph) of Wealside, Essex. e. Bruges College 1763-9. S.J. September 7th, 1769. Ghent (nov) 1771. Liège 1772, 1773. Nancy (theol) 1773. ?Liège 1775. Ordained priest c.1775, Liège. ?Wealside ?-1783. Liège Academy 1784-94. Stonyhurst 1794-1827. d. October 13th, 1827, Wigglesworth, Whalley, Lancashire. bu. Stonyhurst. (Fo.7; CRS.69; 114; 98; 113; ER.9/114n; 16 ff.132-3; 6 f.22v; 7 ff.128v, 131; 146; 13 f.104; 21 v.2; 22 f.44; 51 f.307; 54 f.36; 56 f.301; 67; 91 ff.145, 146v; HMC. 10th Report App.4/192; 93 pp.7, 37; Chad.377, 392; 94 ff.69-70; 157; CRS.8/439; 131; SCR.91ff,98; Nec).

WRIGHT, Edward. Priest.
  b. March 4th, 1752, Chertsey, Surrey. e. Bruges College 1763-c.65. S.J. September 7th, 1768. Ghent (nov) 1768, 1769. Liège (phil) 1771-3. Bruges College 1773. Liège Academy 1776. Ordained priest c. 1776. Winsley (Hereford) 1779-99. Holywell 1799-1826. Readm.S.J.c.1825. d. April 9th, 1826, Holywell. bu. Holywell. (Fo.7; CRS.69; 91; 114; 113; CRS.3/106, 108, 118-30; 6 f.253; 13 f.279; 16 ff.7, 98; 21 v.2; 34 f.62v; 54 f.248; 55 f.91; 69; 72; 91 f.54; 109; AHSJ.42/310; Nec).

WRIGHT, Henry. Priest.

b. January 27th, 1797, Middleton-Tyas, Yorkshire. s. of John and Elizabeth (Lawson) of Kelvedon, Essex. e. Stonyhurst 1808-?16. S.J. September 7th, 1816. Hodder (nov) 1816-8. Hodder (phil) 1818-20. Rome (theol) 1820-4. Ordained priest July 11th, 1824, Rome. Stonyhurst 1824-5. Holywell 1825-6. Bury St Edmunds 1826-32. Worcester 1832-5. d. April 15th, 1835, Worcester. bu. Worcester Catholic churchyard. (Fo.7; 115; Stol; CRW.71; 6 f.282; 21 v.2; 42 f.208; 94 ff.328-9; CRS.3/108, 130-1; Nec).

WRIGHT, Joseph. Priest.

b. December 31st, 1699 or March 30th, 1698, Portugal. s. of Edmund. e. St Omers College 1713 or earlier-15 or later. S.J. March 31st, 1720. Liège (phil) 1723, 1724. Liège (theol) 1725-7. Ordained priest c.1727. Ghent (tert) 1728. ?Wardour c.1729. Calehill 1731-2. Travelling 1733. College of St Hugh 1734. Residence of St George 1735-8. College of St Aloysius 1739, 1740. Watten 1741. Kilvington 1741-3. Cheeseburn Grange 1743-4. Watten 1746-8. Ghent 1749. Watten 1750-1. College of the Holy Apostles 1752-4 (Norwich 1753). College of St Thomas of Canterbury 1754-8 (Soberton 1755-7). d. March 14th, 1760, Ghent. (Fo.7; 91; CRS.69; 114; 113; CRS.Mon.1/153; NA.37/165; 44 ff.167, 264; 64 pp.162-3, 316, 515, 518, 527; 74; 85; HMC. 10th Report App.4/199; Gil.5/5; 01.442; 140 n.45; 51 f.311; YA.77/208; CRS.62 index; 156 App.1; Nec).

WRIGHT, Matthew *alias* Giffard. Priest.

b. September 20th, 1647, Madrid. s. of Sir Benjamin and Jane (Williams) of Cranham Hall, Essex. e. St Omers College 1662 or earlier-67. S.J. February 18th, 1668. Watten (nov) 1669. Liège (phil) 1672. St Omers College 1673-6. Ordained priest April 9th, 1678. College of the Immaculate Conception 1678. France 1679. Rome 1680. Ghent 1682. Kelvedon c.1684. St Omers College 1684-7, 1689. Ireland 1690. Ghent 1691-2. Antwerp 1692-3. Watten 1694-9 (Rector). St Omers College 1699-1701. Travelling 1703. St Omers College 1704-6. Ghent 1707-11 (Rector). d. August 22nd, 1711, Dunkirk. (Fo.7; CRS.69; 114; 113; ER.5/95, 9/108; 150 III(1) 4/4/99; 193 Anglia 35/269; 168 ff.75v, 90; 108; 43 f.17; ?Hun.107; Nec).

WRIGHT, Philip. Priest.

b. June 17th, 1665, Essex. S.J. September 7th, 1684. Watten (nov) 1684, 1685. Liège (phil) 1687. Liège (theol) 1689-93. Ordained priest March 21st, 1693. Loretto 1694-5. College of St Aloysius 1696-7, 1699-1701. Residence of St George 1701. Residence of St Winefrid 1704-6, 1708-11. College of St Chad 1712. Residence of St Winefrid 1713-6, 1718, 1720 (Superior c.1713-4). Ghent 1723-8, 1730, 1733-7. d. November 5th, 1737, Ghent or Watten. (Fo.7; 91; 113; 150 II(3) 16/4/95; 40 p.188; 139 f.295; Nec).

WRIGHT, Richard. Priest.

d. date and place not recorded. (Fo.7; 114).

WRIGHT, Robert. Priest.

S.J.1683, already ordained. Watten (nov) 1683. Liège (nov and theol) 1684. To Scotland 1685. (Fo.7; 113; 150 II(3) 12/8/84).

WRIGHT, Stephen *alias* White, Whitley and Whitely. Priest.

b.c.1620, Kelvedon, Essex. s. of Sir John and Anne (Sulyard) of Kelvedon. e. St Omers College 1636 or earlier-41. E.C. Rome November 5th, 1641-April 18th, 1648. Ordained priest July 2nd, 1645. To England 1648. S.J. January 24th, 1653. College of the Holy Apostles 1653-61, 1663-5, 1667, 1669, 1672-6, 1678-80. d. August 30th, 1680, Kelvedon. bu. Kelvedon. (Fo.7; CRS.69; 114; 113; CRS.40/25; Ans.2/368; ER.5/95, 9/108, 20/60; CRS.55/471; 43 ff.7-12; Nec).

WRIGHT, Thomas see Green, Edward or Thomas.

WYSE see Wise.

WYTHY or WYTHIE see Withy.

XAVIER see Stafford, Ignatius.

YEATMAN see Bray or Bracey, James.

YOUNG see Hammerton, Peter; Le Jeune, Joseph; Tockets, Alexius.

INDEX

1. More than one entry on a page is not noted in the index.
2. Attention is drawn to point 10 among the points to be noted in regard to the period before the suppression of the Society in 1773, listed in the Introduction.
3. Places of birth and education (excluding ecclesiastical education) are not entered in the index.
4. The counties in the index are the old counties.

284

Maryland, U.S.A., 21, 23, 28, 31, 36, 37, 39, 42, 43, 48, 53, 54, 55, 56, 59,
73, 77, 78, 80, 82, 83, 84, 91, 93, 94, 95, 99, 101, 102, 104, 105, 107, 109,
111, 112, 113, 114, 119, 122, 125, 126, 129, 131, 135, 138, 139, 140, 141,
145, 148, 149, 151, 154, 158, 161, 165, 167, 168, 171, 174, 175, 176, 186,
187, 188, 190, 193, 194, 199, 200, 203, 206, 209, 211, 212, 215, 225, 228,
230, 233, 237, 238, 245, 246, 248, 257, 259, 262, 264, 265, 267, 268, 270
and see under individual places.
Maynes Hall, Lancashire, 31
Maynooth, Ireland, 42, 59
Mechlin, 147
Milan, 23, 24, 44, 181, 266
Military chaplains, 35, 43, 58, 91, 125, 129, 131, 190, 197, 217, 231, 245, 269
Milton, Berkshire, 47
Modena, 145
Molsheim, 73, 152, 178, 219
Monmouth, 20, 82, 140, 210, 235
Montargis, France, 94
Monte Porzio, Italy, 40, 77
Montgomeryshire, 140 and see Powis and Welshpool.
Montpellier, France, 125
Montreuil, France, 124
Montrouge, France, 27, 39, 59, 62, 70, 75, 121, 153, 156, 181, 215, 224, 244,
263
Montserrat, West Indies, 73, 148
Moor Hall, Lancashire, 236
Morpeth, Northumberland, 123, 167, 261, 266
Moseley, Staffordshire, 22, 27, 32, 120, 263, 265
Mount St Mary's College, Derbyshire, 17, 25, 59, 62, 68, 87, 154, 155, 198,
216, 224
Munich, 84, 225
Munster, Germany, 53, 138, 145, 176, 218

Nancy, 159, 271
Naples, 163, 181, 201, 252, 268
Netherwitton, Northumberland, 108
Newcastle-upon-Tyne, 19, 60, 147, 174, 257, 259, 266
Newgate prison, London, 110, 131, 139, 206
New Hall, Essex, 20, 27, 30, 41, 45, 62, 91, 94, 119, 133, 134, 136, 154, 181,
208, 211
New House, Lancashire, 23, 61, 95, 146, 153, 242
New Jersey, U.S.A., 238
Newtown, Maryland, U.S.A., 23, 36, 37, 53, 165, 171, 174, 175, 188, 203
New York, U.S.A., 97, 112, 113, 238
Nieuport, Flanders, 254
North Ockendon, Essex, 101